JAPANESE CINEMA: TEXT CONTEXTS

Japanese Cinema: Texts and Contexts includes twenty-four chapters on key films of Japanese cinema, from the silent era to the present day, providing a comprehensive introduction to Japanese cinema history and Japanese culture and society.

Studying a range of important films, from *Late Spring*, *Seven Samurai* and *In the Realm of the Senses* to *Godzilla*, *Hana-Bi* and *Ring*, the collection includes discussion of all the major directors of Japanese cinema including Ozu, Mizoguchi, Kurosawa, Oshima, Suzuki, Kitano and Miyazaki.

Each chapter discusses the film in relation to aesthetic, industrial or critical issues and ends with a complete filmography for each director. The book also includes a full glossary of terms and a comprehensive bibliography of readings on Japanese cinema.

Bringing together leading international scholars and showcasing pioneering new research, this book is essential reading for all students and general readers interested in one of the world's most important film industries.

Contributors: Carole Cavanaugh, Darrell William Davis, Rayna Denison, David Desser, Linda Ehrlich, Freda Freiberg, Aaron Gerow, Alexander Jacoby, D. P. Martinez, Keiko I. McDonald, Joan Mellen, Daisuke Miyao, Mori Toshie, Abé Mark Nornes, Alastair Phillips, Michael Raine, Donald Richie, Catherine Russell, Isolde Standish, Julian Stringer, Mitsuyo Wada-Marciano, Yomota Inuhiko, Mitsuhiro Yoshimoto.

Alastair Phillips is Associate Professor in Film Studies at the University of Warwick.

Julian Stringer is Associate Professor in Film Studies at the University of Nottingham.

JAPANESE CINEMA: TEXTS AND CONTEXTS

*Edited by Alastair Phillips
and Julian Stringer*

Routledge
Taylor & Francis Group

LONDON AND NEW YORK

First published 2007
by Routledge
2 Park Square, Milton Park, Abingdon, Oxon OX14 4RN

Simultaneously published in the USA and Canada
by Routledge
711 Third Ave, New York, NY 10017

Routledge is an imprint of the Taylor & Francis Group, an informa business

British Library Cataloguing in Publication Data
A catalogue record for this book is available from the British Library

Library of Congress Cataloging-in-Publication Data
Japanese cinema : texts and contexts / edited by Alastair Phillips and
Julian Stringer
p. cm
Includes bibliographical references.
1. Motion pictures—Japan.   I. Phillips, Alastair, 1963–
II. Stringer, Julian, 1966–
PN1993.5.J3J27 2007
791.430952—dc22
2007019975

ISBN10: 0–415–32847–0 (hbk)
ISBN10: 0–415–32848–9 (pbk)

ISBN13: 978–0–415–32847–0 (hbk)
ISBN13: 978–0–415–32848–7 (pbk)

Typeset in Garamond
by RefineCatch Limited, Bungay, Suffolk

CONTENTS

CONTENTS

CONTENTS

LIST OF FIGURES

Unless stated otherwise, illustrations are courtesy of BFI (British Film Institute) Stills, Posters and Designs.

NOTES ON CONTRIBUTORS

The Editors

Alastair Phillips is Associate Professor in the Department of Film and Television Studies at the University of Warwick, UK. He is the author of *City of Darkness. City of Light: Emigré Filmmakers in Paris 1929–1939* (Amsterdam University Press, 2004) and the co-editor (with Ginette Vincendeau) of *Journeys of Desire: European Actors in Hollywood* (British Film Institute, 2006). His articles have appeared in a number of journals and edited collections including *Screen, Iris, Positif, The French Cinema Book* (British Film Institute, 2004) and *Film Analysis: A Norton Reader* (W. W. Norton, 2005). He is currently completing a book on Jules Dassin's *Du rififi chez les hommes* (I.B. Tauris).

Julian Stringer is Associate Professor of Film Studies at the University of Nottingham, UK. He is author of *Blazing Passions: Contemporary Hong Kong Cinema* (Wallflower Press, forthcoming), editor of *Movie Blockbusters* (Routledge, 2003), co-editor (with Mark Jancovich, Antonio Lázaro Reboll, and Andy Willis) of *Defining Cult Movies* (Manchester University Press, 2003), and co-editor (with Chi-Yun Shin) of *New Korean Cinema* (Edinburgh University Press/New York University Press, 2005). He is also co-ordinating editor of *Scope: An Online Journal of Film Studies* (www.scope.nottingham.ac.uk) and a member of the editorial advisory boards of *New Cinemas* and *Screen*.

The Contributors

Carole Cavanaugh is Professor of Japanese Studies at Middlebury College. Her publications include *Sansho Dayu* (with Dudley Andrew, British Film Institute, 2000) and *Word and Image in Japanese Cinema* (co-editor, Cambridge University Press, 2000).

Darrell William Davis teaches film studies at the University of New South Wales, Sydney. His books include *Picturing Japaneseness: Monumental Style, National Identity, Japanese Film* (Columbia University Press, 1996), *Taiwan New Directors: A Treasure Island* (co-author, Columbia University Press, 2005),

East Asian Screen Industries (co-author, British Film Institute, 2007), and *Cinema Taiwan: Politics, Popularity and State of the Arts* (co-editor, Routledge, 2007). His current book project is a study of ethnicity, technology and evangelism.

Rayna Denison is Lecturer in Film and Television Studies at the University of East Anglia. She wrote her PhD thesis on Miyazaki Hayao's *Princess Mononoke* in the Institute of Film and Television Studies at the University of Nottingham.

David Desser is Professor of Cinema Studies at the University of Illinois, Urbana-Champaign. His many books include *The Samurai Films of Akira Kurosawa* (UMI Research Press, 1983), *Eros Plus Massacre: An Introduction to the Japanese New Wave Cinema* (Indiana University Press, 1988), *Reframing Japanese Cinema: Authorship, Genre, History* (co-editor, Indiana University Press, 1992), *Cinematic Landscapes: Observations on the Visual Arts and Cinema of China and Japan* (co-editor, University of Texas Press, 1994), and *Ozu's Tokyo Story* (editor, Cambridge University Press, 1997). He also provided the commentary for the DVD of the Criterion edition of *Tokyo Story*.

Linda Ehrlich is Associate Professor in Japanese at Case Western Reserve University, and has published articles on world cinema in *Film Quarterly*, *Cinema Journal*, *Literature/Film Quarterly*, *Film Criticism* and *Cinemaya*, among others. She is the co-editor (with David Desser) of *Cinematic Landscapes: Observations on the Visual Arts and Cinema of China and Japan* (second edition, University of Texas Press, 2000). Her second book, *An Open Window: The Cinema of Víctor Erice* (Scarecrow Press) was published in 2000.

Freda Freiberg has spent the past 30 years researching Japanese film history. In addition to a monograph on Mizoguchi, she has published numerous articles on silent, classic, wartime, post-war and more recent Japanese cinema, including *anime*, in academic journals, film magazines, textbooks and website film journals. She has taught Asian Cinema at Monash University and Contemporary Japanese Cinema and Society at the University of Melbourne. Most recently she has contributed commentaries for DVD releases of *Tokyo Story* (for Madman) and three Naruse Mikio movies (for the British Film Institute).

Aaron Gerow is an Assistant Professor in Film Studies and East Asian Languages and Literatures at Yale University. He has published numerous articles in English, Japanese, and other languages on early, wartime, and contemporary Japanese film and culture. He is the author of *Kitano Takeshi* (British Film Institute, 2007) and has several books forthcoming, including *Page of Madness* (Center for Japanese Studies, University of Michigan) and a book on 1990s Japanese cinema.

Alexander Jacoby is a PhD student researching the representation of Kyōto in post-war Japanese cinema. His articles on film have appeared in *Cine-Action* and *Senses of Cinema* and he is on the editorial board of the web-based journal *Film Intelligence*. He writes regularly on film and other subjects for

The Japan Times and *The Japan Times Weekly*. His first book, *A Critical Handbook of Japanese Film Directors* (Stone Bridge Press) is due to be published in 2007.

D. P. Martinez is Senior Lecturer in Anthropology with Reference to Japan at the School of Oriental and African Studies, University of London. She is the editor (with Jan van Bremen) of *Ceremony and Ritual in Japan* (Routledge, 1995), editor of *The Worlds of Japanese Popular Culture* (Cambridge University Press, 1998) and author of *Identity and Ritual in a Japanese Diving Village* (University of Hawai'i Press, 2004). She is currently writing a book on remakes of Kurosawa films.

Keiko I. McDonald is a Professor of Japanese Cinema and Literature at the University of Pittsburgh. Her major books include *Cinema East: A Critical Study of Major Japanese Films* (Fairleigh Dickinson University Press, 1983), *Mizoguchi* (Twayne, 1984), *Japanese Classical Theatre in Films* (Associated University Presses, 1994), *From Book to Screen: Modern Japanese Literature in Films* (M.E. Sharpe, 1999) and *Reading a Japanese Film: Cinema in Context* (University of Hawai'i Press, 2006). She is currently working on two books: one on filmmaker Shimizu Hiroshi and the other on Japanese women directors.

Joan Mellen is Professor of English and Creative Writing at Temple University in Philadelphia. She is the author of 18 books. In the field of Japanese film her works include *Voices from the Japanese Cinema* (Liveright, 1975), *The Waves at Genji's Door: Japan through its Cinema* (Pantheon, 1976), *Seven Samurai* (British Film Institute, 2002), and *In the Realm of the Senses* (British Film Institute, 2004). Her two most recent books are *Modern Times* (British Film Institute, 2005) and *A Farewell to Justice: Jim Garrison, JFK's Assassination and the Case That Should Have Changed History* (Potomac Books Inc., 2005).

Daisuke Miyao is Assistant Professor in Japanese Film at the University of Oregon. He is the author of *Sessue Hayakawa: Silent Cinema and Transnational Stardom* (Duke University Press, 2007). He is currently writing a book on the transnational history of cinematography and cinematographers.

Mori Toshie has an MA in Film Studies from the University of Reading, UK. She has conducted research on modernity and femininity in Shochiku's films of the 1930s and the representation of women in Mizoguchi's Occupation films.

Abé Mark Nornes is an Associate Professor in the University of Michigan's Department of Asian Languages and Cultures and Program in Film and Video Studies. His specialisation is in Japanese cinema. He is author of *Japanese Documentary Film: The Meiji Era through Hiroshima* (University of Minnesota Press, 2003) and *Forest of Pressure: Ogawa Shinsuke and Postwar Japanese Documentary* (University of Minnesota Press, 2007).

Michael Raine received a PhD in Film Studies from the University of Iowa and has taught at the University of Michigan, Yale University, and Bard College. He has published articles on Ishihara Yujiro in *Word and Image in Japanese Cinema* (Cambridge University Press, 2000) and on *Punishment Room* in *Ichikawa Kon* (Toronto, 2001). He is currently Assistant Professor in Japanese Cinema at the University of Chicago, where he is finishing a manuscript on Japanese New Wave Cinema and embarking on a project on Japanese wartime cinema as visual culture.

Donald Richie went to Japan 60 years ago where he first worked as a staff writer for the *Pacific Stars and Stripes*. He has been interpreting Japanese film and society to international audiences ever since and, as the author of several groundbreaking books such as *The Japanese Film: Art and Industry* (with Joseph Anderson) (second edition, Princeton University Press, 1982) and *Ozu: His Life and Films* (University of California Press, 1984), he remains the foremost authority in English on Japanese cinema. Recent publications include *A Hundred Years of Japanese Films: A Concise History* (second edition, Kodansha, 2005) and *The Donald Richie Reader* (ed. Arturo Silva) (Stone Bridge Press, 2001).

Catherine Russell is Professor of Film Studies at Concordia University in Montreal. She is the author of *Narrative Mortality: Death, Closure and New Wave Cinemas* (University of Minnesota Press, 1985) and *Experimental Ethnography: The Work of Film in the Age of Video* (Duke University Press, 1999). Her book *Naruse Mikio: Women and Japanese Modernity* is forthcoming from Duke University Press. See http://cinema.concordia.ca/index.php/russell

Isolde Standish is Senior Lecturer in Film and Media at the University of London, School of Oriental and African Studies. She is author of *Myth and Masculinity in the Japanese Cinema: Towards a Political Reading of the Tragic Hero* (RoutledgeCurzon, 2000) and *A New History of Japanese Cinema: A Century of Narrative Film* (Continuum, 2005). She has also published various articles on Japanese and Korean cinema.

Mitsuyo Wada-Marciano is Assistant Professor of Film Studies in the School for Studies in Art and Culture at Carleton University. She is the author of *Nippon Modern: Cinema and Modernity in 1920s and 1930s Japan* (University of Hawai'i Press, forthcoming). Her articles have appeared in a number of journals including *Asian Cinema*, *Camera Obscura*, and *Iconics*. She is also the co-editor of *Asian Extreme: Changing Borders of Nation and Culture in Asian Horror Cinema* (Hong Kong University Press, 2007).

Yomota Inuhiko is a Professor of Film Studies and Comparative Literature at Meiji Gakuin University in Tokyo. He has published more than forty books in Japanese, Korean and Italian. He is the editor of *Eiga kantoku Mizoguchi Kenji* [*Mizoguchi Kenji Film Director*], Shin'yō-sha, 1999, and the author of *Nihon Eiga shi 100 nen* [*100 Years of Japanese Film History*], Shuei-sha, 2000. He is also known as Pasolini's Japanese translator.

Mitsuhiro Yoshimoto is Associate Professor and Director of Graduate Studies in the Department of East Asian Studies at New York University. He is author of *Kurosawa: Film Studies and Japanese Cinema* (Duke University Press, 2000), co-author (with Masao Miyoshi) of *Site of Resistance* (Rakuhoku Shuppan, 2007), and co-editor (with Jung-Bong Choi and Eva Tsai) of *Television, Japan, and Globalization* (Center for Japanese Studies/The University of Michigan, forthcoming).

ACKNOWLEDGEMENTS

We would first like to thank all the contributors to *Japanese Cinema: Texts and Contexts* for their enthusiastic and resourceful efforts in contributing to the project. We are grateful to everyone for their hard work and patience in seeing through what has necessarily been a very complicated and sometimes time-consuming process. It has been a pleasure to work with everyone concerned.

We are enormously grateful to Routledge for taking up the idea of this book with such commitment and enterprise. Thank you to Rebecca Barden in the first instance and then to the supportive team of Helen Faulkner, Natalie Foster, Aileen Storry and Charlie Wood who have so ably guided the book to publication.

Japanese Cinema: Texts and Contexts has numerous intellectual debts. While we hope that its breadth of material and concerns will display the dynamic nature of Japanese film studies today, we also want it to serve as a guide to some of the formative influences within the field. As editors, we would especially like to thank the following for various kinds of assistance and guidance: Dudley Andrew, Mark Cousins, David Desser, Dimitris Eleftheriotis, Freda Freiberg, Aaron Gerow, Kyoko Hirano, Keiko McDonald, Gary Needham, V. F. Perkins, Douglas Pye, Michael Raine, Donald Richie, Isolde Standish, Ginette Vincendeau and Nick Wrigley.

Librarians at the following institutions have also provided valuable assistance: the Bodleian Japanese Library at the Nissan Institute, University of Oxford; the National Film Library at the British Film Institute; and the libraries of the Universities of Nottingham, Reading and Warwick.

This book would literally not have seen the light of day without the enormous professional contribution made by Yuna de Lannoy who has so expertly checked all the transliterated Japanese language material and much else besides. Our thanks also go to Sachiko Shikoda for her work on translation and to Rayna Denison, Alex Jacoby and Mori Toshie for their sterling contributions to the Bibliography.

Japanese Cinema: Texts and Contexts has partly been designed to come alive in the classroom and we would like to thank all our students who have engaged so enthusiastically and responsively in our Japanese cinema classes over the years. Alastair would especially like to remember the hours of pleasurable conversation and exchange with his students at the University of Reading. He remembers you all.

Finally, some personal notes. Alastair might not have ended up editing this book at all without the encouragement of the late John Gillet at the British Film Institute who once suggested a few Naruse titles to see at the National Film Theatre in the 1980s. Jim Hickey of the Edinburgh Film Festival shared his love of Japan at a crucial turning point: the year that Suzuki Seijun came to town. Finally, Mark Kurzemnieks, whom he subsequently met in Tokyo on the night the Emperor Hirohito died, has shared more talk about Japanese film (and food) than anyone else over the years and he continues to provide inspiration today.

Julian would like to acknowledge the help and support of Kimijima Megumi, Maeshima Shiho, Jeeyoung Shin and other friends at Indiana University-Bloomington in the 1990s; Mark Gallagher, Gianluca Sergi and other colleagues at the University of Nottingham; and especially fellow Japanese cinema *aficionado* Nikki J. Y. Lee for ongoing conversation and encouragement.

INTRODUCTION

Alastair Phillips and Julian Stringer

Japanese cinema is historically one of the world's most important national cinemas and its films and directors continue to appeal to a wide range of domestic and international audiences. *Japanese Cinema: Texts and Contexts* examines twenty-four major Japanese films from the silent period to the present day. Each chapter discusses the aesthetic specificities of a single film in relation to a range of issues which move from questions of industrial, cultural and critical practice to the historical formations of stardom and genre. In addition to giving an introduction to single works by major Japanese directors such as Kurosawa Akira, Ozu Yasujirō, Mizoguchi Kenji, Ichikawa Kon and Kitano Takeshi, each chapter includes a list of references and a complete filmography. The book also contains an extended bibliography, a full glossary of key terms and a guide to resources for the study of Japanese film.

This volume has been assembled in the belief that even with the valuable contribution of anthologies such as *Reframing Japanese Cinema* (Nolletti and Desser 1992) and *Word and Image in Japanese Cinema* (Washburn and Cavanaugh 2001), as well as recent books by Bowyer (2004) and McDonald (2006), there has been to date no single volume on the subject which offers such a wide-ranging set of critical perspectives suitable for the undergraduate student and advanced reader alike. This new collection of critical essays draws upon the expertise of established and emerging scholars from Asia, Europe, and North America both to re-examine the established field of canonical texts and also to explore previously undervalued areas of interest. The book thus considers famous films such as *Seven Samurai* (*Shichinin no samurai*, Kurosawa Akira, 1954) and *Godzilla* (*Gojira*, Honda Ishirō, 1954) while also investigating lesser-explored texts across the chronological range of Japanese film such as *Ornamental Hairpin* (*Kanzashi*, Shimizu Hiroshi, 1941), *Giants and Toys* (*Kyojin to gangu*, Masumura Yasuzō, 1958) and *Fire Festival* (*Himatsuri*, Yanagimachi Mitsuo, 1985). The result is a comprehensive volume of original scholarship that presents an accessible and multi-faceted overview of the enduring significance of Japanese film.

In terms of method and approach, *Japanese Cinema: Texts and Contexts* models itself upon Susan Hayward and Ginette Vincendeau's *French Film: Texts and Contexts* (2000 [1990]). The family resemblance between the two books is entirely fitting. While other national cinemas certainly deserve similar in-depth

1

critical treatment, France and Japan are linked historically as two of the most formidable of Hollywood's rivals. Both countries have long maintained vibrant film cultures and surprisingly strong industries. They have produced an array of outstanding filmmakers many of whose films are absolutely central to existing conceptions of film art. Like French cinema, Japanese cinema will always matter to Film Studies because of the size of the Japanese corpus (between 300 and 550 films a year since 1920), because of the great many masterpieces known throughout the world (Japan has taken home more than its share of international film festival prizes), and because of the powerful debates about film theory and history that have grown out of attention to Japan (particularly in the late 1970s).

Japanese Cinema: Texts and Contexts discusses a single film per chapter, out of the conviction that film students should pursue topics through the analysis of strong films and that critical discussion should lead out of the films themselves towards matters of aesthetics, culture, history and society. In both cases, the cumulative effect of such an arrangement is that it allows for the presentation of a simultaneously synchronic and diachronic approach to the study of a national cinema. While individual chapters provide in-depth analysis of particular moments and key texts, the chapters as a whole cohere into a detailed and multi-dimensional presentation of Japanese cinema's cumulative history and wider significance. Like its predecessor, the present volume also considers a cross-section of different conceptions of film, from popular genre cinema to 'art cinema' to cult cinema. In line with this multi-dimensional approach, readers will encounter a diverse range of critical tools and methodologies adopted by contributors drawn from the various disciplines where Japanese cinema studies is customarily located, including Film Studies, Japan Studies, Asian Studies, Art History and Cultural Studies.

Considering the range of perspectives and arguments to be found in *Japanese Cinema: Texts and Contexts*, it is important to observe that the field of Japanese cinema studies is currently in a state of transition. At the dawn of cinema's second century, and given in particular the changing concerns of Film Studies in what may be termed its 'internationalising' moment, the terms of critical analysis are shifting. New issues need to be addressed. In what follows, we shall attempt to map out the contours of these changes, explaining in the process how and why Japanese cinema studies currently finds itself at such an important and exciting moment in its history.

It is helpful in this regard to present first a brief narrative of Japanese film history, as well as its English-language academic study, before moving on to a more detailed explication of the specific contents of this book. Behind this archaeology of past and present concerns lies a forward-thinking motivation. While providing an in-depth study of the history of this extraordinary national cinema, *Japanese Cinema: Texts and Contexts* also suggests – through the inclusion of much innovative new research – something of how much we still do *not* know, how much there remains to be done in Japanese cinema studies. To give one example, an immediate question is the extent to which it is imperative to see Japanese cinema within its own terms of reference and in its own specificity, as against the necessity of seeing it in its relational dimensions or against other cinemas and in international contexts. We explore this key consideration in more detail below.

An outline of Japanese film history

Japanese Cinema: Texts and Contexts surveys key aspects of Japanese film production from the early 1930s onwards. Before looking at the way the book's contents inter-relate with Japan's film history in the sound era, we shall briefly sketch in some of the formative aspects of Japan's national cinema beginning with the introduction of the moving image at the end of the nineteenth century.

The Lumière's Cinématographe and Edison's Kinetoscope were both exhibited in Japan during the latter half of 1896, and by the spring of 1897 Lumière's East Asian representative, Constant Girel, had shot the first films in Japan. Girel was soon to be followed by the likes of Shibata Tsunekichi whose early films comprised either shots of local *geisha* and other views of urban life or scenes taken from *kabuki* such as *Maple Viewing* (*Momijigari*, 1898). By the turn of the century, the Japanese market was dominated by the French, Americans and British. Film exhibition took place in theatres and variety venues and the figure of the *benshi* (film narrator or lecturer) became a prominent aspect of the filmgoer's experience of the moving image. The *benshi*, who continued well into the sound period, served varying interpretative tasks such as explaining crucial foreign objects or concepts for the domestic audience, recounting the lines of the actors and relaying important narrative information before, and then as plots and scripts became more elaborate, during the actual screening.

In 1903, the first cinema auditorium appeared in Asakusa in Tokyo and by 1908 the first Japanese studio in Meguro, Tokyo, was opened to produce films by the Yoshizawa company. Japanese audiences tended to perceive film 'as a new form of theatre' (Richie 2001: 22) during these years to the extent that film companies began to divide their releases between films which drew upon the older conventions of *kabuki* and those which followed the contemporary melodramatic principles of *shinpa* ('new school' drama). The latter, based in the nation's capital, often drew upon sentimental contemporary subject matter while the former, often shot in Kyōto and referred to as *kyūha* ('old school' drama), consisted of *samurai* characters and prolific action-based swordfighting scenes. This tendency had evolved by the 1920s into the crucial distinction between *jidai-geki* (period drama) and *gendai-geki* (contemporary drama). The significance of early Japanese cinema's links with theatre may also be signalled by the presence of the *oyama* (female impersonator) and the popularity of *rensageki* ('chain drama') which combined live performance with filmed scenes.

The 1910s saw a considerable expansion in the operations of the Japanese film industry. By 1914, companies such as Nikkatsu and its rival, Tenkatsu, were averaging fourteen films a month (Komatsu 1996a: 178). The following year, they were producing films of about forty minutes comprising fifteen to thirty set-ups (in the case of Nikkatsu) and fifty to seventy set-ups (in the case of Tenkatsu) (Richie 2001: 32). By this stage, many practitioners were well acquainted with the methods of their American competitors through visits to the US and audiences too had developed a taste for foreign films.[1] A Japanese star system had begun to proliferate, with actors such as Onoe Matsunosuke, and as the length and narrative complexity of domestic films evolved, the profitability of Japanese films increased substantially.

Although changes such as a greater concentration on scriptwriting had been well under way in the years beforehand, the devastating Kantō earthquake of 1923 proved a turning point in terms of industrial organisation and film output. Companies such as Nikkatsu moved their operations to the ancient capital of Kyotō and, given the abundance of historical locations, naturally specialised in *jidai-geki*. The *chanbara* or *kengeki eiga* (swordfighting film) began to innovate during these years with an increased emphasis on a more dynamic visual style in films such as Itō Daisuke's *A Diary of Chuji's Travels* (*Chūji tabi nikki*, 1927). Meanwhile in Tokyo, in places such as the Kamata studios of the recently founded Shōchiku studios, new filmmakers such as Shimizu Hiroshi, Shimazu Yasujirō and Ozu Yasujirō (see Chapter 1) began to explore the textures of everyday life in the late Taishō (1912–1926) and early Shōwa (1926–1989) eras. These films, often featuring new female stars such as Tanaka Kinuyo, were made for predominantly female audiences.

The 1920s was marked by greater debate about exploring the cinematic potential of the moving image – evidenced by Kinugasa Teinosuke's remarkable *A Page of Madness* (*Kurutta ippeiji*, 1926) and *Crossroads* (*Jūjiro*, 1928) – and attention was paid to developments in European and US filmmaking with the

Figure 1 Exploring the textures of everyday life: *I Was Born, But . . .* (1932). BFI Stills, Posters and Designs.

Figure 2 The cinematic potential of the moving image: *A Page of Madness* (1926). Kinugasa Productions/The Kobal Collection.

work of filmmakers such as F.W. Murnau and Sergei Eisenstein and the comedy and action films of the likes of Harold Lloyd and Douglas Fairbanks fascinating both critics and audiences. The possibility of a *jun'eiga undo* (pure film movement) continued to be discussed, and important companies such as Kokkatsu recruited people such as Inoue Masao to advise on virtuoso cinematic realism and the director Murata Minoru advocated the 'Westernisation' of storytelling practices.[2] The decade also saw the proliferation of the independently produced *keikō eiga* ('tendency film'). Films such as Suzuki Shigekichi's *What Made Her Do It?* (*Nani ga kanojo o sō sasetaka*, 1930), which was Japan's most profitable film to date (Richie 2001: 91), examined the ways in which deeply rooted social and political trends impacted on people ordinarily untouched by the glamour and spectacle of the cinema. In 1924, Japan produced a phenomenal 875 films ('Lights from the East'). Four years later, it was making more films than any other country in the world, a situation that was to endure for a further ten years (Richie 2001: 44).[3]

Perhaps for reasons outlined earlier, but also because of the generally precarious capital base of the Japanese film industry, the full-scale introduction of sound was delayed in Japan until the mid-1930s despite early attempts at sound film production from 1927 onwards. Gosho Heinosuke's *The Neighbour's Wife and Mine* (*Madamu to nyōbō*, 1931), a typical *shomin-geki* (home drama of everyday folk) of the period, is generally acknowledged to have been a major breakthrough in terms of the implementation of recorded sound and dialogue. This was also the time that Japanese films began to be distributed on the international market with films like Naruse Mikio's *Wife, Be Like a Rose* (*Tsuma yo bara no yō ni*, 1935) being shown, for example, to American audiences (Ōkubo 2007).

Historians have argued that the introduction of sound technology enhanced the potential of a 'behavouralist' style of cinematic narration in Japanese cinema whose more 'expressive style' linked to more 'social realist narrative themes' formed a kind of 'backlash against the *shinpa*-derived, *benshi*-driven, melodramatic traditions of filmmaking' (Standish 2005: 64). This is certainly visible in films such as Mizoguchi Kenji's *Osaka Elegy* (*Naniwa erejī*, 1936) and Yamanaka Sadao's *Humanity and Paper Balloons* (*Ninjō kamifūsen*, 1937) (see Chapters 2 and 3).

The 1930s were also marked by a rise in nationalism and the turn to militarism on behalf of the Japanese government with the eventually disastrous onset of the Fifteen Years' War after the invasion of Manchuria in 1931. On 1 October 1939, the Film Law was passed (amended August 1941) which brought Japan's film industry under the control of the Cabinet Propaganda Office (*Naikaku Jōhōkyoku*). Fiction film production was placed under the aegis of three main conglomerates (Nikkatsu, Shinkō and Daitō) with features being increasingly designed to enhance the apparently virtuous ideology of the national Family System (the *ie* system). *Kokusaku eiga* ('national policy film') such as *The Story of Tank Commander Nishizumi* (*Nishizumi senshachō-den*, Yoshimura Kōzaburō, 1940) and *Navy* (*Kaigun*, Tasaka Tomotaka, 1943) emphasised patriarchal male self-sacrifice while other films such as Shimizu's *Ornamental Hairpin* were marked by the direct absence of battle and imperial conflict (see Chapter 4).

By 1945, following the extensive firebombing of Tokyo, 40 per cent of all Japan's cinemas (Komatsu 1996b: 421) and much of its existing cinematic heritage had been destroyed. One of the first acts of the American Occupation, which lasted until 1952, was to burn a further 225 films perceived to be dangerous relics of the military era (Ibid.). Several major personnel in the industry were permanently or temporarily removed from office. With the formation of the Civil Information and Education Section (CIE) on 22 September 1945, the Japanese film industry fell under new legislative strictures with an emphasis placed on the representation of the virtues of democratic opinion and the rehabilitation of the positive virtues of female identity (strikingly presented in *No Regrets for Our Youth* [*Waga seishun ni kui nashi*, Kurosawa Akira], 1946).

One of the early outcomes of the Occupation, nonetheless, was a greater politicisation of those involved in domestic film production. Important strikes in 1946 and 1948 swept the Tōhō studios and this turn to left-wing activism underlined the presence of the term *hyūmanisumu* (humanism) within critical discourse, and to some extent in filmmaking with the resurgence of the *gendai-geki* in *shomin-geki* dramas such as *Late Spring* (*Banshun*, Ozu Yasujirō, 1949) and *Late Chrysanthemums* (*Bangiku*, Naruse Mikio, 1954) (see Chapters 5 and 9 respectively). Under this rubric, writers have identified two major postwar themes: a secular humanism which typically represents the 'individual's capacity for self-cultivation and improvement' (e.g. much of the work of

Figure 3 A 'national policy film': *The Story of Tank Commander Nishizumi* (1940). The Kobal Collection.

Kurosawa) and a type of 'victimisation' (*higaisha ishiki*) where the 'individual is often depicted as a powerless pawn, caught in the machinations of a geo-political trajectory' (e.g. *A Japanese Tragedy* [*Nihon no higeki*], Kinoshita Kei-suke, 1953) (Standish 2000: 220).

The post-war period was also marked by a rapid resurgence in old and new popular Japanese film genres such as the comedy (exemplified by Japan's first colour feature *Carmen Comes Home* [*Karumen kokyō ni kaeru*, Kinoshita Keisuke], 1951); the musical drama such as the phenomenally successful *The Sad Whistle* (*Kanashiki kuchibue*, Ieki Miyoji, 1949), starring Misora Hibari; and the science-fiction monster film such as *Godzilla* (see Chapter 7). *Kaidan* (ghost story) were commonly released in the summer period and versions of the *Chūshingura* (Tale of the Forty Seven *rōnin*) were often part of the *oshōgatsu* (New Year) festivities. By the middle of the 1950s, 19 million cinema tickets per week were being sold in Japan (Thompson and Bordwell 1994: 462) with the industry reaching a financial peak of over one billion admissions in

Figure 4 Democracy and female identity: *No Regrets for Our Youth* (1946). BFI Stills, Posters and Designs.

1958 (Richie 2001: 177). This is also the time when, aided by the Japanese government's economic policies, prestigious *jidai-geki* such as *The Life of O-Haru* (*Saikaku ichidai onna*, Mizoguchi Kenji, 1952), *Seven Samurai*, and *Conflagration* (*Enjō*, Ichikawa Kon, 1958) were exported with great acclaim to the international film circuit (see Chapters 6, 8 and 10 respectively). For many Western audiences today, these films remain lasting symbols of the virtues of a certain kind of 'quality' Japanese filmmaking.

The 1950s saw Japanese cinema engage with social and cultural change in a number of ways. As part of the explosion in youth culture, the *taiyōzoku eiga* ('sun tribe' film) became a media phenomenon caused by the success of Ishihara Shintarō's male star persona. Films such as *Giants and Toys* responded in satirical fashion to the sensory impact of an increasingly media-saturated and technologically advanced economy (see Chapter 11). New directors such as Ōshima Nagisa and Imamura Shōhei (see Chapter 17) emerged from the now ageing studio system and appealed for a greater degree of artistic licence in order to break with the conventions of generic representation (see Chapters 12 and 17). Through his critical writings as well as his films, Ōshima became a leading figure in the publicity-driven phenomenon of the Japanese *nūberu bāgu* ('New Wave'). Other important filmmakers nominally associated with the Japanese 'New Wave' included Hani Susumu, Yoshida Yoshishige, Teshigahara Hiroshi (see Chapter 13) and Suzuki Seijun (see Chapter 14).

The 'New Wave', like its counterpart in France (*nouvelle vague*), coincided with the ascendancy of television and the rise of a metropolitan cine-literate audience in the large cities of Japan. This fuelled the growth of the alternative distribution (and later production network) provided by the Art Theatre Guild (ATG) who circulated, for example, *Funeral Parade of Roses* (*Bara no sōretsu*, Matsumoto Toshio, 1969) and *Double Suicide* (*Shinjū ten no amijima*, Shinoda Masahiro, 1969) (see Chapter 15). Despite technological innovations in colour and widescreen (introduced by Tōei in 1957) and investment in spectacular star-driven genres such as the *ninkyō yakuza eiga* ('chivalrous gangster film') and *chanbara* over the course of the 1960s, the Japanese box-office began to fall into decline. In 1963, the year before the Tokyo Olympic Games and its symbolic status as a turning point in terms of Japan's self-identity as a modern nation, cinema admissions had fallen by 50 per cent compared with the figure five years previously (Thompson and Bordwell 1994: 549). *Pinku eiga* ('pink film' or soft-core pornography) accounted for 40 per cent of domestic production by 1965 (Satō, quoted by Standish 2000: 268). By the beginning of the 1970s, a number of leading studios such as Daiei and Shin-Tōhō had either collapsed or, in the case of Nikkatsu, turned to specialise in *roman poruno* (romantic soft-core porn) (see Chapter 16).

Popular domestic genre cinema continued to flourish throughout the 1970s, especially in terms of the profitability and popular reception of ongoing series such as the *Scarlet Peony Rose Gambler* (*Hibotan bakuto*) series of *jidai-geki* films (1968–72) and the *War Without Morality* (*Jingi naki tatakai*) series (1973–6) which exemplified the shift in the *yakuza* (gangster) genre towards a tougher and more realistic style of filmmaking. Critics have often argued that such work achieved success for its ability to refract the pressures and social conflicts in contemporary Japanese society in a way that would have been impossible through more direct means. The reception of Japanese cinema *outside* Japan has to some extent always been determined by the vagaries of international festival and distribution networks, and it was in this way that new independent filmmakers such as Morita Yoshimitsu (see Chapter 18), Yanagimachi Mitsuo (see Chapter 19) and Itami Jūzō (see Chapter 20) came to international attention in the following decade.

Throughout the 1990s and into the twenty-first century, it has increasingly been possible to view Japanese cinema in a fuller range of international and transnational contexts. Films such as *Maborosi* (Kore-eda Hirokazu, 1995) (see Chapter 21) and, especially, *Hana-Bi* (Kitano Takeshi, 1997) (see Chapter 22), demonstrate the popularity of a certain kind of psychologically acute, formally self-aware filmmaking that has been well received across the world. Meanwhile, the phenomenal appeal of horror and *anime* (animated film and television), in export terms perhaps the two most profitable elements of Japanese cinema to date, can be illustrated by Nakata Hideo's now canonical *Ring* (*Ringu*,

1998) (see Chapter 23) and Miyazaki Hayao's Studio Ghibli production *Spirited Away* (*Sen to Chihiro no kamikakushi*, 2001) (see Chapter 24). As Japanese film companies increasingly work on co-productions across Asia, and the relationship between Japanese and other East Asian popular cultural forms continues to intensify, a film such as *Swallowtail Butterfly* (*Suwarouteiru*, Iwai Shunji, 1996), in which the characters speak a hybrid language derived from Japanese, Chinese and English, seems especially to belong to its time (Hitchcock 2003). In 2005, the consequences of a more interventionist model of engagement with the country's film industry on the part of the Japanese government resulted in an enhanced 41.3 per cent share of the Japanese film market (Gerow 2006). This figure, along with its continued presence on international screens of all kinds, demonstrates that Japanese cinema continues to be a vital force.

Japanese film studies: A brief overview

Japanese film studies is a hybrid concern occupying a central role in the serious study of film history and theory as well as Japanese culture and society. This has always been the case from the time in the 1950s and 1960s when English-language Japanese film critics and historians posited what now appears to be a contradiction between a form of essentialised cultural specificity and a transcendental set of universally recognisable human characteristics in relation to their object of attention. This impulse both to locate the 'Japanese-ness' of Japanese cinema and then simultaneously to argue for its international application as a form of humanist cultural expression can be found, for example, in several of the early writings of Donald Richie (1961; 1972).

In conjunction with the dissemination of Japanese films at international film festivals and in metropolitan *cinémathèques* and art-house cinemas across the Western world, Richie's important work helped to promulgate a sense of the ways in which Japanese cinema could convey 'national character'. 'National character' mattered in a dual sense: it could be allied to the ways in which Japan needed to be defined in the post-war context as a 'good neighbour' to the West and it also aided in the institutionalisation of cinema studies as a subject of serious scholarly concern. It is almost forgotten today that some of the founding English-language texts in the study of national cinemas, especially in relation to authorship, related to Japanese 'masters' such as Kurosawa and Ozu. Indeed, as Mitsuhiro Yoshimoto has argued, 'the position of Japanese cinema is inseparable from the question of how film studies has constituted itself, legitimated its existence, and maintained its institutional territoriality through a double process of inclusion and exclusion' (Yoshimoto 2000: 8).

Another important facet of Richie's work may be related to the notion of seeing its author as a kind of watchful 'distant observer'. Unlike Noël Burch (1979) – from whose influential and remarkable book, *To the Distant Observer*, the term springs – Richie has adopted this stance from the vantage point of locating himself *within* the culture he seeks to describe. This question of perspective has continually dogged English-language Japanese film studies. During the 1970s, Burch, Schrader (1972), and others, problematically chose to define their engagement from *without*, more or less by reproducing a supreme sense of the 'otherness' of the field. Burch, especially, sought to demonstrate the ways in which Japanese cinematic conventions apparently repudiated what was then seen as the dominant Western bourgeois mode of filmmaking to the extent that his work generated a slew of articles taking issue with his politically motivated, but ultimately erroneous views regarding Japanese cinema and modernist film practice (Cohen 1981; Malcomson 1985; Lehman 1987; Nygren 1989). (For more on Burch and Schrader, especially in relation to Ozu criticism, see also Abé Mark Nornes' overview in Chapter 5.)

Of course, no national cinema is ever intrinsically static and it is always wrong to seek to define any non-Western cinema in terms of its supposed relation to a set of different, equally mutable, mainstream norms. As David Bordwell suggested in an important intervention, 'a historical examination of the Japanese cinema must confront the fact that it is not wholly other, not a blank drastic alternative' (Bordwell 1979: 46). Japanese cinema's history, as already mentioned, has been remarkably porous and it has been continually marked by a productive engagement with other film cultures; most noticeably perhaps the international practices of Hollywood, but also other parts of the world including Europe and certainly of course the Asian region itself. Today, it is widely recognised by scholars and critics that there is no such thing as 'the Japanese' or indeed a single 'Japanese cinema'.

One of the particular ways in which other critical voices from the 1970s began to consider this fact was to relate Japanese cinema to the debates within second-wave feminism. In an undervalued body of work, writers such as Joan Mellen (1975; 1976) and Audie Bock (1978) began to combine work on authorship with an engagement with gender representation. Though at times their arguments were simplified by a tendency to depend on reflectionist descriptions of how Japanese cinema apparently 'mirrored' Japanese society, their work opened up significant avenues of interpretation which are today forming part of a dual strategy of linking gender to wider questions of culture and social change.[4] Recent scholarship by writers such as Catherine Russell (1995; 1998; 2005) and Mitsuyo Wada-Marciano (1998; 2005) is exemplary in terms of the way in which it offers a new horizon for the consideration of gender representation within a broader, more dynamic conception of Japanese mass culture.[5]

Another way in which Japanese film studies has sought to propose links between cinema and society beyond the prevalent notion of a seamless linearity is to concentrate on matters of genre and industry (especially in relation to film style); something called for in Bordwell's original essay, but with the notable exception of Anderson and Richie's pioneering work (1982 [1959]), notably absent in many earlier accounts. In order to move beyond a limited asocial and monolithic concept of Japanese film culture, scholars have had to provide a sense of the various ways in which the cultural form of Japanese cinema has been produced, appropriated and consumed historically. Donald Kirihara (1992), for instance, echoing Bordwell's call for more scrupulous attention to be paid to local, temporally specific case studies, published a finely tuned investigation of the norms of film style in relationship to Mizoguchi's films of the 1930s which also divulged important information about the social and industrial contexts of the films' production. David Desser (1988) produced an important study of aspects of the Japanese New Wave which was alert to many of the ways in which 1960s Japanese film culture may be understood though a contextual approach.

Bordwell himself has sought to continue to refine his style-based analysis of major Japanese filmmakers through work which argues beyond a singular inter-pretation of Japanese film culture. His study of Ozu explored the ways in which, for example, traditional aspects of Japanese culture were selectively used and appropriated by the director in order to establish a formal system which, although far from being 'typically Japanese', nonetheless conveyed a certain 'poeticization of everyday life' (Bordwell 1988: 50). His recent work on Mizoguchi (Bordwell 2005) continues this trend in, for example, its analysis of the eclectic ways in which the director's 'pictorial intelligence affected his story-telling and his conception of performance' especially in relation to an under-standing of the continuity system and 'other editing trends . . . at play in world cinema of the 1920s' (Bordwell n.d.). In contradistinction to this vein of more formalist work, it is important also to note Isolde Standish's recent turn to a cultural history grounded in a more sustained concern with the ideological trends within the social formation of the Japanese film industry. Her ground-breaking case studies of 'the relationship between filmmaking practice, the con-text of the economic and sociopolitical, and their connections to narrative themes in cinema' (2005: 338), like the recent work of writers such as Michael Raine (2001), has opened up the archive of non-canonical popular generic forms such as the musical, *yakuza* film and 'youth film' for serious scholarly investigation.

Standish's work is not just distinguished by its attempt to move away from the 'authorship model'; it also returns to the question of periodisation and the benefits of more contemporary, revised notions of film historiography which challenge a singular teleological account of the 'development' of Japanese film. In a chapter which refers to the neglected aspect of wartime film production, for example, Standish, like Eric Cazdyn (2002) in his recent meta-criticism of Japanese film studies, argues less for a 'consideration of history as organised around moments of foundational break and reconfiguration' (Nygren 2004: 539) than for an approach which in fact fails to see the war in terms of any kind of 'ideological or an institutional caesura' (Cazdyn 2002: 162). Instead, Standish argues, perhaps controversially, that post-war Japanese cinema should 'be analyzed from an historical perspective of an institutional and political dis-course of continuity' (Standish 2005: 162). Having said this, however, Standish is equally keen to locate the sphere of wartime cinema in terms of its multiple temporalities and locations. One of the great challenges for future English-language scholarship in the field is to take further into account this complex relationship between Japan, its former colonial territories such as Korea and Taiwan, and the adjoining regions of Asia.

This points to the ways in which Japanese cinema history is now beginning to be configured in terms of series of tensions which are heightened by the particularities of Japan's engagement with modernity. As a cultural form that came into being during the years of Japan's most fundamental engagement with the modern world, Japanese cinema has clearly always been bound up with national and international notions of tradition and change. This is no less important in the contemporary era of intensified transnational film production and consumption. The most interesting work that is being done today in the field of English-language Japanese film studies has therefore moved beyond the need to pin down the particularities of what apparently makes 'the Japanese' and 'their cinema' different from 'us'. It now acknowledges the need to refute seeing 'the identity of the West [and Japan] as something transparent, natural and self-evident' (Yoshimoto 2000: 27) and instead recognises a model of inter-active flow and exchange which is useful in relation to the study of Japanese film only if it is historically and theoretically nuanced by circumstances and evidence germane to the particular subject under discussion.

Japanese cinema studies in transition

As we now turn to consider the contents and rationale of the present book in further detail, we find Japanese film studies at a moment of transition. Critical approaches to the concept of national cinema have changed somewhat since Hayward and Vincendeau published *French Film: Texts and Contexts*. To better understand the nature and source of these developments, it is necessary to con-sider the shift in perspective on the twin set of key terms presented in this book's title: 'Japanese Cinema' and 'Texts and Contexts'.

Taking the latter of these key terms first, the relation of 'texts' to their various 'contexts' has always been of central and ongoing concern to Film Studies, and the question of how these two variables should be conceptualised in relation to each other continues to provoke discussion and disagreement. At the furthest extreme, some balk at the very thought of single film analysis altogether, considering it to be both a highly limited and a highly limiting approach. Certainly, the case against text-centred criticism may appear compel-ling. Just how much can scholars really learn from one individual film? How is it possible to make judgements concerning which film to analyse from among the many thousands produced by a developed nation over decades? In light of all the invaluable new knowledge gained through sophisticated research methods in film historiography and issues of cultural reception, why advance such a wilfully 'old-fashioned' text-oriented perspective?

Some of these objections have already been addressed by Chris Berry (2003: 1–7) in his powerful defence of the usefulness of approaching Chinese cinema 'one film at a time'. Berry argues that in order to comprehend the historical complexity of any national cinema, it is necessary to discuss a diversity of films in both depth and detail. Furthermore, in response to critics who urge scholars to downplay textual analysis so as to focus on more 'empirical' and 'material' considerations, Berry makes the additional point that circuits of film produc-tion, exhibition and reception are all inter-connected, and that the film 'text' itself – a material commodity if ever there was one – plays a centrally important role in the workings of each. As he puts it, rather than setting up 'an opposition between empirical institutional study and textual interpretation, I would argue

13

that Cinema Studies requires a range of approaches to the cinema that understands the singularity of the film and the importance of the cinema as an
institution without trying to divide them or set them in opposition to each
other' (3). We concur with this particular argument, and would add that the
advancing of critical methods such as these is all the more important in the case
of Japanese cinema, After all, while it is true that Japan's cinema is of great
historical importance internationally, it is also true that, to date, only a relatively very small number of its films have circulated globally and received much
in-depth scholarly attention in English.

As many of the chapters in *Japanese Cinema: Texts and Contexts* therefore
demonstrate, the choice of an ostensibly textual method and approach does not
rule out the analysis of supposedly 'non-textual' factors such as distribution,
exhibition and critical reception. Indeed, the example of a single film case study
may vividly illuminate larger issues within film culture. For instance, Daisuke
Miyao discusses issues of film production and cultural policy in his analysis of
Branded to Kill, Isolde Standish tackles complex questions of censorship while
discussing *In the Realm of the Senses*, Mitsuyo Wada-Marciano considers issues of
distribution and exhibition in her analysis of *Woman in the Dunes*, and Rayna
Denison looks into the specific nature of domestic and overseas film marketing
in her discussion of *Spirited Away*.

Having said all this, however, it must also be admitted that there is one
important area of analysis not developed in the following pages (just as it is all
but absent in both the Hayward and Vincendeau and the Chris Berry anthologies) – audience response. Historical audience reaction to Japanese cinema is
one area of investigation bracketed out of this volume's contents, as we believe
it requires separate treatment as a vital if roundly under-explored critical issue.[6]

The text–context relation is also relevant to the concept of 'Japanese Cinema'
itself. The primary consideration here is the vexed question of the presentation
of issues of authorship in *Japanese Cinema: Texts and Contexts*. Simply put, a
potential objection to the book's method and approach may be that it privileges
a narrow view of authorship based on a conception that it is the director who
matters most in the creative filmmaking process. This is a powerful argument,
albeit far from a simple one to resolve. For whether film scholars like it or not,
Japanese cinema continues to circulate globally as what Mitsuhiro Yoshimoto
(2000: 267) terms 'cultural capital on an international scale', and it does so
largely on the basis of the specific values that have accrued across time around
the reputations of a few key '*auteurs*' such as Kurosawa, Mizoguchi, Ozu and
Kitano.[7] Indeed, such a viewpoint has been reproduced by Japanese and international journalists and scholars so often that the compulsion to adopt an
auteurist lens may be thought of as *the* dominant paradigm at work historically
in Japanese cinema studies.

There is clearly much to be learned from critical approaches which
thoroughly research the collective production contexts of individual films and
filmmakers (Lovell and Sergi 2005), and the reconsideration of authorship in
Japanese cinema studies may, in part, be pursued by following up some of the
concerns signalled in this book. For example, some contributors pay specific

historical attention to the actual production circumstances of filmmaking as a collective enterprise in Japan, and in particular to the role of screenwriters, cinematographers and producers as well as directors and performers. Freda Freiberg's study of *Humanity and Paper Balloons*' collaborative theatrical influences and Donald Richie's elucidation of the commercial 'interference' that characterised the making of *Fire Festival* may be thought of as exemplary in this respect. Equally, Film Studies as a whole knows very little about how 'artists' relate to 'technicians', and indeed about how and why such distinct categories are constructed and maintained in the first place (Lovell and Sergi 2005; Stringer and Yu 2007). Future empirical research into Japanese cinema may profitably pursue these lines of enquiry through methods of oral history, as illustrated in the case of Chinese cinema, for example, through numerous recent valuable archaeologies painstakingly unearthed in East Asia by the pioneering efforts of researchers affiliated with the Hong Kong Film Archive.

In addition, the continuing vitality and importance of notions of authorship in Japanese cinema may be re-engaged in terms of the text–context relation through deeper analysis of the diverse factors underpinning what Michel Foucault (1979: 153) influentially termed the 'author function'. How do authorial names function as brands within both local and global media economies, and in the case of Japanese cinema why are only a very limited number of brands on display at present? Another way of saying this is to state that in the current critical context, the simple act of valorising the work of a previously neglected Japanese filmmaker carries a polemical edge. At a time when Film Studies is frequently dismissing notions of authorship altogether, the promotion of relatively 'unknown' Japanese directors holds strategic importance, especially within diverse reception environments where only a limited number of the nation's numerous and highly talented filmmakers currently possess substantial cultural capital. As Alexander Jacoby therefore points out in his discussion of Shimizu Hiroshi in Chapter 4 of this volume, it is hard enough merely to 'add' the name of another important *auteur* to the list of internationally famous Japanese directors. Moreover, while perusing the various directors' filmographies included at the end of each chapter of this book, readers may be surprised to learn precisely how many films some of Japan's most famous filmmakers have actually directed over the years as very frequently the majority of these still remain unavailable outside their country of origin.

Certainly, the brand name of the *auteur* continues to provide the terms of reference through which cultural institutions both inside and outside Japan present and promote Japanese cinema. For example, the influential Japan Foundation has in recent years funded and organised large-scale retrospectives of filmmakers such as Masumura, Suzuki and Wakamatsu Kōji, and the trickle-down effect of such activities has been that critics and international film festival programmers alike now pay increased attention to titles by these directors whom the Japan Foundation has recently endorsed. Similarly, the film industry in Japan, as well as distribution companies overseas, often position their theatrical and DVD releases of Japanese films in terms of who the director is and what s/he has produced to date.

15

The notion of personal authorship therefore remains an important ideology that cannot simply be ignored and probably should not be too hastily discarded. After all, questions of authorship encompass interesting complexities and ironies particularly where questions of cross-cultural reception are concerned. The formation of critical canons around the reputations of celebrated Japanese directors is a variedly situated and ongoing process that does not necessarily signify the same thing in Japan as it does elsewhere.

In order to illustrate this particular point, it is worth briefly comparing data from two separate surveys designed to answer the question of who the 'great Japanese directors' are. The first of these polls was conducted at a major Japanese film festival and encompasses the perspectives of various visiting foreign dignitaries. The second was conducted for a Japanese film magazine as part of its efforts to assemble responses from Japanese celebrities as well as 'ordinary' readers.

In 1995, the Committee for the Centenary of Cinema at the 1995 Tokyo International Film Festival asked '100 of the World's Film Authorities' to vote for 'My Favorite Work of Japanese Cinema'. The 131 non-Japanese luminaries eventually polled encompassed directors, producers, festival directors and programmers, writers, and critics from countries such as France, Taiwan and the US. The list included such eminent names as King Hu, Jean Douchet, Paul Verhoeven, Eric Rohmer, Peggy Chiao, Hou Hsiao-hsien, Raymond Bellour, Claire Denis, Richard Pena, Spike Lee, Agnès Varda, Edward Yang and Wong Kar-Wai. Out of the 131 available votes, the directors listed in Table 1 polled more than one vote each.[8]

Table 1 represents what may be termed a cine-literate 'outsider' view of Japanese cinema. It is usefully supplemented by Table 2, listing the 'Favourite Works of Japanese Cinema' as chosen by the same collection of eminent personalities from the international film industry. Once again, all titles which polled more than one vote each (out of 131 available) have been included.

Table 1 Favourite Japanese directors of the 'World's Film Authorities'

Name	Number of votes
Ozu Yasujirō	36
Kurosawa Akira	25
Mizoguchi Kenji	22
Naruse Mikio	11
Ōshima Nagisa	10
Gosho Heinosuke	4
Ichikawa Kon	4
Imamura Shōhei	3
Suzuki Seijun	3
Yamanaka Sadao	3
Kitano Takeshi	2
Shindō Kaneto	2
Takita Yōjirō	2
Tezuka Osamu	2

Source: Hasumi and Yamane (1995)

Table 2 Favourite Japanese films of the 'World's Film Authorities'

Position	Film/Director/Year	Number of votes
1	*Tokyo Story* (*Tōkyō monogatari*, Ozu Yasujirō, 1953)	14
2	*Rashomon* (*Rashōmon*, Kurosawa Akira, 1950)	13
3	*Ugetsu* (*Ugetsu monogatari*, Mizoguchi Kenji, 1953)	10
4	*Late Spring* (*Banshun*, Ozu Yasujirō, 1949)	6
5	*I Was Born, But . . .* (*Umarete wa mita keredo*, Ozu Yasujirō, 1932)	5
6	*Floating Clouds* (*Ukigumo*, Naruse Mikio, 1955)	4
6	*Seven Samurai* (*Shichinin no samurai*, Kurosawa Akira, 1954)	4
6	*Ikiru* (Kurosawa Akira, 1952)	4
9	*Humanity and Paper Balloons* (*Ninjō kamifūsen*, Yamanaka Sadao, 1936)	3
10	*An Autumn Afternoon* (*Samma no aji*, Ozu Yasujirō, 1962)	2
10	*Broken Down Film* (*Onboro firumu*, Tezuka Osamu, 1985)	2
10	*The Burmese Harp* (*Biruma no tategoto*, Ichikawa Kon, 1956)	2
10	*The Ceremony* (*Gishiki*, Ōshima Nagisa, 1971)	2
10	*Good Morning* (*Ohayō*, Ozu Yasujirō, 1959)	2
10	*The Man Who Left His Will on Film* (*Tōkyō sensō sengo hiwa*, Ōshima Nagisa, 1970)	2
10	*In the Realm of the Senses* (*Ai no korīda*, Ōshima Nagisa, 1976)	2
10	*The Naked Island* (*Hadaka no shima*, Shindō Kaneto, 1960)	2
10	*Princess Yang Kwei-fei* (*Yōkihi*, Mizoguchi Kenji, 1955)	2
10	*Sansho the Baliff* (*Sanshō dayū*, Mizoguchi Kenji, 1954)	2
10	*Sisters of Gion* (*Gion no kyōdai*, Mizoguchi Kenji, 1936)	2
10	*Sonatine* (Kitano Takeshi, 1993)	2
10	*Sound of the Mountain* (*Yama no oto*, Naruse Mikio, 1954)	2
10	*Tokyo Drifter* (*Tōkyō nagare-mono*, Suzuki Seijun, 1966)	2
10	*When a Woman Ascends the Stairs* (*Onna ga kaidan o agaru toki*, Naruse Mikio, 1960)	2

Source: Hasumi and Yamane (1995)

Table 2 presents a canon of Japanese films largely available in international distribution markets and directed by many of the same filmmakers whose names appear in Table 1. However, against these two pieces of evidence may be placed a second source also originating from within Japan, but which has this time been compiled by 'insider' Japanese themselves. The November 2000 issue of *Kinema Junpō* (no. 1320) included two separate lists of favourite Japanese film directors, the first (represented in column *a* of Table 3) compiled from the views of 104 public celebrities and the second (in column *b* Table 3) from the views of 1502 'ordinary' readers.

What do we learn by looking at these figures? Comparing Table 3 with Tables 1 and 2, one can only conclude that much of what the Japanese public and critics see as their national film heritage is unrelated to what is actually available to view outside Japan. This discrepancy begins to highlight the complexities of the cultural politics of canon formations as these circulate around the reputations of Japanese film directors in both the domestic and the international sphere.

Perceptions regarding which Japanese films are most 'noteworthy' outlined

Table 3 Favourite Japanese directors as reported by *Kinema Junpō*

Favourite director	a: Reported by public celebrities in Japan	b: Reported by 'ordinary' film magazine readers in Japan
1	Kurosawa Akira	Kurosawa Akira
2	Ozu Yasujirō	Ozu Yasujirō
3	Mizoguchi Kenji	Kinoshita Keisuke
4	Kinoshita Keisuke	Yamada Isuzu
5	Naruse Mikio	Mizoguchi Kenji
6	Yamada Isuzu	Ichikawa Kon
7	Ichikawa Kon	Naruse Mikio
8	Uchida Tomu	Kitano Takeshi
9	Ōshima Nagisa	Imai Tadashi
10	Fukasaku Kinji	Imamura Shōhei
11	Kawashima Yūzō	Ōbayashi Nobuhiko
12	Shindō Kaneto	Miyazaki Hayao
13	Makino Shōzō	Uchida Tomu
14	Imamura Shōhei	Ōshima Nagisa
15	Okamoto Kihachi	Fukasaku Kinji
16	Kitano Takeshi	Yamanaka Sadao
17	Suzuki Seijun	Kawashima Yūzō
18	Masumura Yasuzo	Masumura Yasuzo
19	Miyazaki Hayao	Kumashiro Tatsumi
20	Morita Yoshimitsu	Kobayashi Masaki

Source: *Kinema Junpō* 1320 (November 2000)

in the tables above demonstrate that the narrative feature film remains the most compelling and the most commercially important example of Japanese national cinema – *Japanese Cinema: Texts and Contexts* therefore attends specifically to this particular form of filmmaking. Since this book looks *only* at Japan's astonishingly rich traditions of feature film production, however, we can do no more than gesture towards the conspicuous lack of existing critical work on other important kinds of filmmaking activities, such as the Japanese documentary (Nornes 2003; 2007), the made-for-television movie and indeed television production more generally, non-theatrical features, government newsreels, student films, amateur movies, shorts, web films, digital cinema, and so on. The establishment in recent years of a plethora of general and specialised film festivals both inside Japan (e.g. Fukuoka, Yamagata) and across East Asia (e.g. Hong Kong, Pusan) has by now created vital possibilities for new historiographies of all kinds of Japanese movies to be researched and written.

In seeking to relate various Japanese narrative feature films to a diverse range of historically specific contexts, the book's contributors confirm the importance of 'intertextuality' in numerous ways. However, on this point *Japanese Cinema: Texts and Contexts* departs in a significant way from its predecessor, *French Film: Texts and Contexts*. In their introduction, Hayward and Vincendeau state that '[I]f the definition of the film "text" is relatively unambiguous, that of "context" is more problematic' ([1990] 2000: 3). We would argue that as a result of recent developments in Film Studies, notions of 'context' *and* 'text' require similar levels of interrogation. While synchronic and diachronic contexts are certainly multifarious as well as shifting, recent scholarship has questioned what 'the text' may actually be. For example, notions of intertextuality can be constructively deployed in the tracking not only of aesthetic influences between texts, but also of the network of commercial intertexts, such as trailers, posters and DVD releases, that interact with, and also in part constitute, the very meaning of the so-called 'film itself' (Klinger 1986; Schatz 2003 [1993]).

These differing approaches to the intertextual relationships among Japanese cinema texts and contexts may be identified within many of the chapters in this book. For example, while Alastair Phillips in his discussion of *I Was Born, But . . .* and Linda Ehrlich in her discussion of *Tampopo* both place their respective films in relation to the presence of Hollywood's influence, other contributors focus on inter-media relationships, as in the case of Freiberg's and Cavanaugh's discussion of theatre and *manga* (comic books) respectively, and McDonald's and Russell's analyses of literary adaptations. Moreover, the book closes with two chapters that explicitly question the status of the 'text' in Japanese cinema studies by foregrounding questions of intertextuality as an overarching concern. Julian Stringer discusses perceptions of what the 'original' *Ring* text actually is, and Rayna Denison considers *Spirited Away*'s unstable identity across different international marketplaces, thus exhibiting the same kind of concern for notions of cultural translation and translatability also highlighted by Dolores Martinez, Mitsuyo Wada-Marciano and Donald Richie in their chapters on *Seven Samurai*, *Woman in the Dunes*, and *Fire Festival* respectively.

The chapters on *Ring* and *Spirited Away* are also the ones which most explicitly raise the question of how Japanese cinema may be thought of in relation to transnational contexts. Indeed, this important focus on issues of transnationalism may be taken as emblematic of Japanese cinema studies' broader shifting identity and status. Is Japanese cinema studies' emerging 'transnational turn' anything more than a passing fad as Film Studies passes through its current 'internationalising' moment?

Two points need to be emphasised in response to this question. First, it is worth reiterating how vital it is that the 'internal' history of Japanese cinema continue to be brought to light through the invaluable work of Japanese scholars as well as those non-Japanese equipped with enough linguistic capability to conduct primary research.[9] Equally, however, it is also important to perceive Japanese cinema in terms of its 'external' and relational dimensions. Similar to any 'imagined' national community (Anderson 1991 [1983]), Japan is not so much a bounded entity as an 'idea' dependent upon its imagined links to other outside communities for its very definition and meaning. In this sense, the recent focus on transnationalism opens up a series of compelling new ways of revisiting and de-centering existing paradigms concerning Japanese cinema and its varied Others.

Two specific examples may be cited as representative of the challenges posed by this new kind of innovative work. On the other hand, Japanese cinema studies is currently being re-positioned as a vital component of a regional Asian cultural identity, one part of what Koichi Iwabuchi (2002: 6) describes as 'a source for the articulation of a new notion of Asian cultural commonality, difference and asymmetry'. In the light of Japan's colonialist adventures in the early twentieth century, as well as its key strategic position as an Asian bulwark for the United States in the Cold War, and after decades of participating in what some have characterised as a mutual policy in the East Asian region of 'hate your neighbour', many are now welcoming new-found opportunities to 'love your neighbour' in Asia, at a time when Japan and other Asian countries, such as South Korea and Taiwan, renegotiate the historical perspectives they adopt towards one another. This 'East Asian' discourse may over time supply much-needed paradigms of knowledge that will help 'internationalise' and 'De-Westernise' ('Easternise'?) Film Studies and its cognate disciplines.[10]

Such developments signal a new focus upon scholarship produced from within East Asia itself that is likely to have a highly significant and beneficial effect upon English-language Japanese cinema studies. They also, of course, follow on from the global traffic in Japanese popular culture that provides our second example of why issues of transnationalism now constitute a vital area of scholarly endeavour. The emergence of globalisation and transnationalism clearly challenges existing paradigms of the Japanese nation and 'the text'. One obvious mark of this is the development of thorny questions concerning the role of so-called 'minorities' in the nation's cinema. For example, recent movies such as *Go* (*GO*, Yukisada Isao, 2001) and *Blood and Bones* (*Chi to hone*, Sai Yoichi, 2004) investigate the topic of *zainichi* Korean (Japanese–Korean) identity.

Moreover, the time has also surely come to revisit and re-evaluate the question of Japanese cinema's relationship to 'Hollywood', and in turn the latter's status as the central focus of so much English-language Film Studies. As has already been noted, a common criticism of much previous scholarship in this area is that it has worked to establish Japan's feature film industry in a primary relationship to US commercial cinema – by such means has the 'dominant fiction' (Silverman 1992) of 'Hollywood' been constructed so as to provide the 'norm' against which Japanese cinema must be measured. In a timely contribution, Mitsuhiro Yoshimoto (2003) has recently criticised the tendency in Film Studies to 'centre' Hollywood through the deployment of such critical terms as 'classical Hollywood film style', 'post-classical-Hollywood', and so on. Such concepts do indeed position the US film industry at the centre of the global film map, reinforcing in the process the sense that 'Hollywood' – *wherever* and indeed *whatever* that is these days – is not just a dominant but also a rather monolithic entity. It is our hope that the chapters in this book avoid falling into that particular trap, just as we would resist having *Japanese Cinema: Texts and Contexts* subsumed under the currently fashionable but overly loose label of 'world cinema studies'.

The above arguments have been advanced with the aim of providing some key coordinates for readers to engage with as they follow the book's chapters. We hope that they provide some indication of the way in which the work represented herein marks a moment of transition in the critical discussion of Japanese cinema. To conclude, *Japanese Cinema: Texts and Contexts* reiterates the importance of single film analysis and foregrounds the significance of film interpretation (especially in light of Western readings of non-Western cinemas).

It simultaneously takes on board a further range of complicated issues that include the nature and status of 'film texts', the question of how these should be researched and analysed, and the range of various contexts within which notions of Japanese cinema may be placed. As well as providing a diachronic overview of Japan's impressive cinema history, the book also adopts a range of scholarly viewpoints and so stresses the importance of approaching Japanese cinema from a variety of critical methodologies. Japanese cinema studies may currently be in a state of flux, but it is an exciting moment nevertheless, and one which may fruitfully accommodate both 'insider' and 'outsider' perspectives.

A note to the reader

In view of its usefulness as a course book for studying Japanese cinema, the selection of films in *Japanese Cinema: Texts and Contexts* has primarily been driven by the availability of films on DVD and VHS with English subtitles. (This is the reason why Japanese silent cinema is unfortunately relatively under-represented within these pages.) Rapid advances are currently being made in this area with the emergence of multi-region DVD players making it possible for international cinephiles to access more of Japan's cinematic heritage than ever before. With a few exceptions that have been deliberately chosen in order to extend the English-language Japanese cinema 'canon', we have resisted the temptation to commission chapters on films that are not readily available to UK and North American-based researchers. We have also omitted films for which a more thorough critical text is already readily available, as in the case of the three films which topped the 1995 Tokyo International Film Festival poll discussed above: *Tokyo Story* (Desser 1997), *Rashomon* (Richie 1987) and *Ugetsu* (McDonald 1993).

All Japanese names and titles in this book have been romanised according to the simplified Hepburn system – the only exception is the word 'Tokyo' (Tōkyō) which (given its recurrence across the following pages) has been preserved in its English variant for the reader's convenience. In those cases where the name of a film already has currency in English (e.g. *Ugetsu*), these particular usages have been retained. Japanese names are presented in Japanese style, i.e. surname first, given name last (e.g. Kurosawa Akira), except in cases where individuals have chosen to transliterate their name in Western form, i.e. given name first, surname last (e.g. Sachiko Shikoda). This general rule of thumb encompasses the presentation of Chinese and Korean names as well.

Notes

1 Universal set up a distribution branch in Tokyo around 1915 and other American studios followed suit in the 1920s (Bordwell 1979: 47).
2 For more on the *juneiga undo*, see Bernardi (2001) and Gerow (2006).
3 Japanese film production averaged between 400 and 500 films a year in the 1920s and 1930s (Kirihara 1996: 503). 'The number of film theatres in Japan increased steadily from 470 in 1921 to 1,057 in 1926, and 1,538 in 1934. Attendances likewise rose steadily from 153,735,449 (first recorded attendance figures) in 1926 to 244,389,636 in 1934' (Yamada in Freiberg 2000).
4 For another important feminist intervention, see Freiberg (1981).

5 See also Phillips (2006).
6 On the other hand, it is significant that film reviews – a particular kind of audience response – are discussed and treated as evidence by a number of different contributors to this book.
7 See also Stringer (2002).
8 In the course of an interesting and useful article on the overseas reception of Ozu Yasujirō, H. C. Li (2003) also discusses the significance of this particular example of canon formation.
9 For an indication of the extent and scope of such work, see the Bibliography of Works on Japanese Cinema included at the end of this book.
10 In this regard consider the formation of important journals such as *Inter-Asia Cultural Studies*, the publication of wide-ranging anthologies such as *Asian Media Studies* (Ernie and Chua 2005) and *Rogue Flows* (Iwabuchi, Muecke and Thomas 2004), and the establishment of organisations such as the Trans-Asia Screen Cultures Institute at the Korean National University of Arts, Seoul.

References

Anderson, Benedict (1991 [1983]) *Imagined Communities: Reflections on the Origins and Spread of Nationalism*, London: Verso.
Anderson, Joseph L. and Richie, Donald (1982 [1959]) *The Japanese Film: Art and Industry*, Princeton: Princeton University Press. Revised edition.
Bernardi, Joanne (2001) *Writing in Light: The Silent Scenario and the Japanese Pure Film Movement*, Detroit: Wayne State University Press.
Berry, Chris (2003) 'Introduction: One Film at a Time', in Chris Berry (ed.), *Chinese Films in Focus: 25 New Takes*, London: British Film Institute: 1–7.
Bock, Audie (1978) *Japanese Film Directors*, Tokyo: Kōdansha International.
Bordwell, David (1979) 'Our Dream Cinema: Western Historiography and the Japanese Film', *Film Reader*, 4: 45–62.
—— (1988) *Ozu and the Poetics of Cinema*, Princeton: Princeton University Press.
—— (2005) *Figures Traced in Light: On Cinematic Staging*, Berkeley: University of California Press.
—— (n.d.) 'David Bordwell website'. Online. http://www.davidbordwell.net/
Bowyer, Justin (ed.) (2004) *The Cinema of Japan and Korea*, London: Wallflower Press.
Burch, Noël (1979) *To the Distant Observer: Form and Meaning in the Japanese Cinema*, London: Scolar Press.
Cazdyn, Eric (2002) *The Flash of Capital: Film and Geopolitics in Japan*, Durham, NC, and London: Duke University Press.
Cohen, Robert (1981) 'Toward a Theory of Japanese Narrative', *Quarterly Review of Film Studies*, 6 (2): 181–200.
Desser, David (1988) *Eros Plus Massacre: An Introduction to the Japanese New Wave Cinema*, Bloomington: Indiana University Press.
—— (ed.) (1997) *Ozu's Tokyo Story*, Cambridge: Cambridge University Press.
Ernie, John Nguyet, and Chua, Siew Keng (eds.) (2005) *Asian Media Studies: Politics of Subjectivities*, Oxford: Blackwell.
Foucault, Michel (1979) 'What is an Author?', in Harari, Josué V., *Textual Strategies*, Ithaca, NY: Cornell University Press: 141–60.
Freiberg, Freda (1981) *Women in Mizoguchi Films*, Melbourne: Japanese Studies Centre.
—— (2000) 'Comprehensive Connections: The Film Industry, the Theatre and the State in the Early Japanese Cinema'. *Screening the Past*. Online. http://www.latrobe.edu.au/screeningthepast/firstrelease/fr1100/fffr11c.htm (accessed 18 August 2006).

Gerow, Aaron (2006) 'Recent Film Policy and the Fate of Film Criticism in Japan'. *Midnight Eye*. Online. http://www.midnighteye.com/features/recent-film-policy.shtml (accessed 12 August 2006).

Hasumi, Shigehiko, and Yamane, Sadao (eds.) (1995) *1995 Tokyo International Film Festival Nippon Cinema Classics: 'My Favourite Works of Japanese Cinema as Chosen by 100 of the World's Film Authorities'*. Tokyo International Film Festival booklet.

Hayward, Susan, and Vincendeau, Ginette (eds.) (2000 [1990]) *French Film: Texts and Contexts*, London: Routledge. Second edition.

Hitchcock, Lori (2003) 'Third Culture Kids: A Bakhtinian Analysis of Language and Multiculturalism in *Swallowtail Butterfly*', *Scope: An Online Journal of Film Studies*. February. Online. www.nottingham.ac.uk/film/scopearchive/articles/third-culture-kids.htm

Iwabuchi, Koichi (2002) *Recentering Globalization: Popular Culture and Japanese Transnationalism*, Durham, NC: Duke University Press.

Iwabuchi, Koichi, Muecke, Stephen, and Thomas, Mandy (eds.) (2004) *Rogue Flows: Trans-Asian Cultural Traffic*, Hong Kong: Hong Kong University Press.

Kirihara, Donald (1992) *Patterns of Time: Mizoguchi and the 1930s*, Madison: University of Wisconsin Press.

—— (1996) 'Reconstructing Japanese Film', in Bordwell, David and Carroll, Noel (eds.) *Post-Theory: Reconstructing Film Studies*, Madison: University of Wisconsin Press: 501–19.

Klinger, Barbara (1986) 'Digressions at the Cinema: Reception and Mass Culture', *Cinema Journal*, 28 (4): 3–19.

Komatsu, Hiroshi (1996a) 'Japan: Before the Great Kanto Earthquake', in Nowell-Smith 1996: 177–82.

—— (1996b) 'The Classical Cinema in Japan', in Nowell-Smith 1996: 413–21.

Lehman, Peter (1987) 'The Mysterious Orient, The Crystal Clear Orient, the Non-Existent Orient: Dilemmas of Western Scholars of Japanese Film', *Journal of Film and Video*, 39: 5–15.

Li, H. C. (2003) '*Tokyo Story* through Western Eyes: The Occidental Appreciation of Ozu's Art', in Li, Cheuk-to, and Li, H.C. (eds.), *Ozu Yasujiro: 100th Anniversary*, Hong Kong Arts Development Council: 27th Hong Kong International Film Festival Programme: 49–54.

'Lights from the East: Japanese Silent Cinema 1898–1935'. Pordenone Film Festival programme notes. Online. http://www.cinetecadelfriuli.org/gcm/previous_editions/edizione2001/japanese_silent.html (accessed 12 August 2006).

Lovell, Alan, and Sergi, Gianluca (2005) *Making Films in Contemporary Hollywood*, London: Hodder Arnold.

Malcomson, Scott (1985) 'The Pure Land beyond the Seas: Barthes, Burch and the Uses of Japan', *Screen* 26 (3–4): 23–33.

McDonald, Keiko I. (ed.) (1993) *Ugetsu*, New Brunswick, NJ: Rutgers University Press.

—— (2006) *Reading a Japanese Film: Cinema in Context*, Honolulu: University of Hawai'i Press.

Mellen, Joan (1975) *Voices from the Japanese Cinema*, New York: Limelight.

—— (1976) *The Waves at Genji's Door: Japan through Its Cinema*, New York: Pantheon.

Nolletti, Arthur Jr., and Desser, David (eds.) (1992) *Reframing Japanese Cinema: Authorship, Genre, History*, Bloomington: Indiana University Press.

Nornes, Abé Mark (2003) *Japanese Documentary Film: The Meiji Era Through Hiroshima*, Minneapolis: University of Minnesota Press.

—— (2007) *Forest of Pressure: Ogawa Shinsuke and Postwar Japanese Documentary*, Minneapolis: University of Minnesota Press.

Nowell-Smith, Geoffrey (ed.) (1996) *The Oxford History of World Cinema*, Oxford: Oxford University Press.

Nygren, Scott (1989) 'Reconsidering Modernism: Japanese Film and the Postmodern Context', *Wide Angle*, 11 (3): 6–15.

—— (2004) '*The Flash of Capital: Film and Geopolitics in Japan* (review)', *The Journal of Japanese Studies* 30 (2): 538–42.

Ōkubo, Kiyoaki (2007) 'Kimiko in New York'. *Rouge* 10. Online. http://www.rouge.com.au/10/kimiko.html (accessed 3 March 2007).

Phillips, Alastair (2006) 'Pictures of the Past in the Present: Modernity, Femininity and Stardom in the Post-War Films of Ozu Yasujiro', in Grant, Catherine and Kuhn, Annette (eds.), *Screening World Cinema*, London and New York: Routledge: 86–99.

Raine, Michael (2001) 'Ishihara Yujiro: Youth, Celebrity, and the Male Body in Late 1950s Japanese Culture', in Washburn and Cavanaugh 2001: 202–25.

Richie, Donald (1961) *Japanese Movies*, Tokyo: Japan Travel Bureau.

—— (1972) *Japanese Cinema: Film Style and National Character*, London: Secker and Warburg.

—— (ed.) (1987) *Rashomon: Akira Kurosawa, Director*, New Brunswick, NJ: Rutgers University Press.

—— (2001) *A Hundred Years of Japanese Film*, Tokyo: Kōdansha.

Russell, Catherine (1995) 'Overcoming Modernity: Gender and the Pathos of History in Japanese Film Melodrama', *Camera Obscura*, 35: 130–57.

—— (1998) 'Mikio Naruse and the Japanese Women's Film', *Asian Cinema*, 10 (1): 120–5.

—— (2005) 'Naruse Mikio's Silent Films: Gender and the Discourse of Everyday Life in Interwar Japan', *Camera Obscura*, 60: 57–89.

Schatz, Thomas (2003 [1993]) 'The New Hollywood', in Stringer, Julian (ed.), *Movie Blockbusters*, London and New York: Routledge: 15–44.

Schrader, Paul (1972) *Transcendental Style in Film: Ozu, Bresson, Dreyer*, Berkeley: University of California Press.

Silverman, Kaja (1992) *Masculinity at the Margins*, New York: Routledge.

Standish, Isolde (2000) *Myth and Masculinity in the Japanese Cinema: Towards a Political Reading of the 'Tragic Hero'*, Richmond: RoutledgeCurzon.

—— (2005) *A New History of Japanese Cinema*, London and New York: Continuum.

Stringer, Julian (2002) 'Japan 1951–1970: National Cinema as Cultural Currency', *Tamkang Review*, 33 (2): 31–53.

Stringer, Julian and Yu, Qiong (2007) '*Hero*: How Chinese Is It?', in Paul Cooke (ed.), *World Cinemas' Dialogues with Hollywood*, London: Palgrave: 238–54.

Thompson, Kristin and Bordwell, David (1994) *Film History. An Introduction*, New York: McGraw-Hill.

Wada-Marciano, Mitsuyo (1998) 'The Production of Modernity in Japanese National Cinema: Shochiku Kamata Style in the 1920s and 1930s', *Asian Cinema*, 9 (2): 69–93.

—— (2005) 'Imaging Modern Girls in the Japanese Woman's Film', *Camera Obscura*, 60: 15–55.

Washburn, Dennis, and Cavanaugh, Carole (eds.) (2001) *Word and Image in Japanese Cinema*, Cambridge: Cambridge University Press.

Yoshimoto, Mitsuhiro (2000) *Kurosawa: Film Studies and Japanese Cinema*, Durham, NC: Duke University Press.

—— (2003) 'Hollywood, Americanism and the Imperial Screen: Geopolitics of Image and Discourse after the End of the Cold War', *Inter-Asia Cultural Studies*, 4 (3): 451–9.

1

THE SALARYMAN'S PANIC TIME

Ozu Yasujirō's *I Was Born, But . . .* (1932)

Alastair Phillips

By the time that Ozu Yasujirō directed *I Was Born, But . . .* (*Umarete wa mita keredo*) in 1932, he had been working for Shochiku studios for almost a decade. His film went on to win a number of awards that year, including the prestigious *Kinema Junpō* First Prize, and it is remembered today as a moving, but also splendidly comic, film about the relationship between a Japanese white-collar office worker or 'salaryman' and his two young sons who on moving with their parents to a new house in the Tokyo suburbs have to learn about the disappointing social rules their father abides by. Ozu's film remains an outstanding example of the director's inflection of the 'Kamata style' which had evolved under the managerial guidance of the Kamata studio boss, Kido Shirō, in order to depict the experiences and concerns of Japan's ordinary urban citizens as the nation underwent the convulsions and changes of modern life in the late Taishō (1912–1926) and early Shōwa (1926–1989) eras.

I Was Born, But . . . is an understated, but revealing, investigation of masculine identity, failure and what David Bordwell has usefully termed 'the social use of power' (Bordwell 1988: 224). It is also, as the film itself tells us, 'A Picture Book for Adults'. If we take this latter formulation, we may identify a number of ways in which the film may be related to a discussion of the wider issues of gender, belonging and modernity identified two years previously in *Sararīman kyōfu jidai* [*The Salalaryman's Panic Time*] – Aono Suekichi's seminal contemporary analysis of the Japanese white-collar businessman's malaise. Ozu's film works in many ways as a fascinating compendium of images about modern life, especially in its treatment of the representation of class and social space. One can also see how the film's picturing of the ordinary Japanese salaryman's anxieties around industrialisation and social identity intersects with the development of the early Shōwa era's *Shinkō Shashin* (New Photography) which attempted, in a similar fashion, to interpret the new cultures of city life and society from dynamic and innovative visual perspectives. These images (often collected in their own picture books) were attempts to record faithfully social change and then interpret this upheaval in terms of a newly mechanised mass culture. By looking at these developments in photography in relation to the film's own visual and discursive strategies, particularly those concerning the construction of spectatorial knowledge specifically *about* questions of seeing, we may understand how *I Was Born, But* . . .'s careful narrative social concern works within a pictorial regime ideally suited to delineating the unease felt by the salaryman seen here, and elsewhere in contemporary Japanese culture of the time.

It is hard not to think of Ozu himself as a 'salaryman' who was to be employed by the same filmmaking corporation for most of his working life. Certainly, the nature of Shōchiku's managerial and organisational structures confirms the notion that it was one of the pre-eminent sites from which Japanese mass culture engaged with changes in contemporary society. The company had originally become known for its involvement in popular theatre and had established filmmaking operations in 1920 with the appointment of the American-born son of Japanese immigrants, Henry Kotani. Ozu joined after an introduction by his uncle, and a year later, in 1924, the same year that the influential figure of Kido Shirō took over as head of Shōchiku's Kamata studios, he was appointed to the rank of assistant cinematographer. By 1926, he had become an assistant director under the guidance of Ōkubo Tadamoto. Shōchiku, under the paternalistic guidance of Kido, who made several visits to the West Coast of the US during the decade, soon established a hierarchical set of production methods akin in part to the Hollywood studio system involving teams of trained cinematographers, scriptwriters, editors and publicists. A house journal, *Kamata*, evoked the evolving ethos of the warm-hearted, but also potentially socially acute, '*Kamata* flavoured' *shōshimin eiga* (home drama of lower-middle-class people) and *shomin eiga* (home drama of everyday folk) which featured, like other Shōchiku genre productions, a rota of new and established stars and actors.

Despite the coincidence of this relationship between Tokyo and Los Angeles and the pervasive popularity of American cinema for mainstream domestic audiences, it is important to note that Ozu's salaried existence within Shōchiku did not entail a wholesale replication of modern American production methods and ideologies. For one thing, as Hasumi Shigehiko has pointed out, in contrast to a competing company such as Tōhō who based their mode of production around the central figure of the producer, the studio actually favoured a more formalised 'director system'. This allowed figures such as Ozu the means 'to assemble a team of people for different, specialised fields of production and to cultivate them so they could continue to work together' (Hasumi n.d.). Hence we see, throughout the director's long career, the profound significance in terms of collaborative working partnerships of key figures such as the cinematographers Mohara Hideo and Atsuta Yūharu, the scriptwriter Noda Kōgo and the production designer Hamada Tatsuo.

Like Ozu himself, these fellow practitioners should not be seen as professionals keen simply to emulate the methods and forms of a dominant Western model of influence. The Japanese film industry needs to be observed within the historical context of its own contested and evolving relationship with the nation's modernity and all its associated economic upheaval and dynamic social and industrial transformation. One way of thinking about this in more concrete terms would be to see *I Was Born, But . . .* as a text which, in terms of its production background and methods, is symptomatic of the very culture it seeks to represent on screen. Hence, as we shall see later, the nods the film makes towards its self-reflexive status as a distinctively modern text cunningly concerned with the fallibilities of the modern world and the means by which visual culture can transmit knowledge about the societies that inhabit it.

As Bordwell has convincingly argued, *I Was Born, But . . .* is a hybrid genre production which combines the sentimental appeal of the *shōshimin eiga* with the social commentary of the 'salaryman film' and the physical humour of the *nansensu* (nonsense) idiom so prevalent in Japanese mass culture of the period (1988: 14). Co-scripted by Ozu and Fushimi Akira, the film revolves around the decision of Mr Yoshii (Saitō Tatsuo) and his family to move to a new Tokyo suburb where the two Yoshii sons (Aoki Tomio and Sugawara Hideo) struggle to find acceptance within a group of neighbourhood boys who include the son of Mr Yoshii's boss, Mr Iwasaki (Sakamoto Takeshi). The Yoshii children hold their father in high esteem, unaware of his vulnerability at work. After the screening of a home movie shot by Iwasaki, and projected in his wealthy residence to his employees and neighbours, the boys are forced to realise how fallible their father is when they see him ingratiating himself in public at the behest of his patron. Stunned, they react angrily towards their parents before learning to realise that subordination and duty are necessary within capitalist social relations and that their predicaments within the school and in play are only a prelude to the necessary compromises of modern adult life.

Ozu had already begun to delineate the milieu of the Japanese salaryman in films such as *The Life of an Office Worker* (*Kaishain seikatsu*, 1929), *The Luck Which Touched the Leg* (*Ashi ni sawatta kōun*, 1930), *The Lady and the Beard* (*Shukujo to hige*, 1931), and *Tokyo Chorus* (*Tōkyō no kōrasu*, 1932), and he continued to portray the various affective crises and entanglements of Japan's white-collar classes in subsequent features such as *Where Now are the Dreams of Youth?* (*Seishun no yume ima izuko*, 1932) and the post-war successes *Early Spring* (*Sōshun*, 1956), *Good Morning* (*Ohayō*, 1959) and *An Autumn Afternoon* (*Sanma no aji*, 1962). What marks *I Was Born, But . . .* is its subtle, but nonetheless emphatic, questioning of the whole ethos of the system that supported the nation's white-collar culture. This may well be due to the thesis advanced by Mitsuyo Wada-Marciano who claims that by the beginning of the decade in Japan 'aspects of modernization such as capitalization, centralized political power, industrialization, propagation of rationalism and urbanism had reached their limits, and the conflict between classes, the widening of the local communities and their ethos, signalled the unfulfilled hopes of the modernization project. The films of *Shochiku Kamata* studios belong to this period and parallel the vicissitudes of Japanese modernity in crisis' (Wada-Marciano 1998: 73). In other words, *I Was Born, But . . .*, despite its many humorous episodes, is marked by a sense of controlled despair about the price of social change. In constructing such a close analogy between the worlds of the children and the adults it may also be seen to be positing an argument about the future direction of Japan's modernity.

To examine these issues in further detail, we should first look at the film in terms of its iconography and particular representation of class and space. Ozu's film is marked by a distinctive sense of social stratification despite the fact that the generational gap between the children and the adults in the film is actually bridged by a comparative strategy which analyses the ways in which the social world of the children provides an echo and precursor of the ways in which the adult characters then lead their lives. There are three groupings which underline this point. At the core of the film are the tentatively mobile petit-bourgeois Yoshii family within which the sons first look up to their father's lot in life, then reject it, then learn to consider its virtues despite the father's forlorn admission to the mother that he hopes that neither of their sons will 'become an employee like me'. Above them we see the casual professional and leisured affluence of the Iwasaki family which includes the smartly dressed son Tarō, a prominent member of the gang which taunts the Yoshii sons. Below them are the young *sake* seller and another blue-collar worker or tradesman and his son who is reduced to tears by the gang at one point.

To think of the subtleties of the dynamics of class relations in Ozu's film, we need to consider the social and economic situation Japan was facing at this point in its history. By the early 1930s, the country, like many other industrialised economies, was well into a protracted period of economic depression which had been precipitated by a national financial crisis in 1927 only three years after a temporary post-earthquake reconstruction boom. The beginning of the Shōwa era in 1926 was thus marked by a growing sense of the fragility behind the dynamic, if uneven, process of modernisation which had characterised the preceding Taishō era. If in 1930 'one out of five non-agricultural male workers was a clerical employee in a firm or government bureau' (Bordwell 1998: 34), in 1932, the year *I Was Born, But* . . . was made, one in five of all unemployed workers was a middle-class white-collar male (Schwartz 1999). The film thus portrays all the insecurities of a world in which its central male salaryman character is striving to construct a tentative domestic security for his family while simultaneously being beholden to an enterprise seemingly marked by inertia and deference. Aono Suekichi's commentary in his publication *The Salaryman's Panic Time*, published in 1930, the same year that Siegfried Kracauer's analysis of the malaise of the German office worker, *Die Angestellten*, also appeared, thus seems particularly prescient. As Harry Harootunian argues, Aono's work sought to analyse 'the social structure of the salaryman's class . . . within the larger context of capitalist social relations in order to explain how and why they were fated to a life of continued unhappiness and psychological depression caused by the growing disparity between their consumerist aspirations and their incapacity to satisfy them' (Harootunian 2000: 202). The 'panic' that Aono's text referred to was the abiding sense of 'both a diminution of [the salarymen's] social position and the disappearance of the culture they had once known' (208).

This sense of being locked into an inevitable and potentially regressive working adulthood is vividly portrayed in *I Was Born, But* . . . in the famous sequence in which Ozu's formal command of geometrical spatial organisation is harnessed to provide an explicit commentary on the fate that might befall the schoolboys. The Yoshii children have bunked off school and are pictured enjoying an early lunch on the wasteland that is the neighbourhood playground. Their anarchical freedom is contrasted with the subsequent sight of the school sports teacher organising a class of schoolboys into line. One figure stands out of turn and moves into the prescribed pattern but facing in the incorrect direction. Eventually, he succeeds in joining the others and the boys start marching leftwards in pairs. At this point, Ozu reconstructs a sense of dissonance by tracking in the opposite direction as if to reject any sense of editorial complicity between the on-screen figures and the camera. We cut to a further tracking shot in the same direction which now reveals a line of salarymen at work. This is the seemingly predictable future that the schoolboys are marching towards. As the camera tracks down the line of adult men each yawns in turn, as if on cue, until we pause and then track back and stop in front of a man hunched over his desk who has failed to signal his boredom and fatigue. He then duly yawns and the camera can begin to move again before the shot concludes with the sight of a black-suited supervisor's body filling the frame. On one level, this is a witty moment of filmic self-referentiality, typical of a young filmmaker exploring the boundaries of a new expressive medium, but on another, it nicely anticipates the thematically significant construction of a film within a film which ensues when we subsequently watch Yoshii called to his boss's office. Here, we see Yoshii's employer in a director's hat and covered in reels of celluloid. Before much more information may be deduced, however, a secretary leaves the room and at the moment she closes the door behind her, Ozu provides a match-cut to the other side of the door, thus aligning the spectator with the chorus of fellow office workers speculating about the proceedings inside.

As with all of Ozu's cinema, I Was Born, But . . . is acutely sensitive towards the representation of social space. As we have already observed, the film is marked by both a sense of class stratification and the transition between the world of adulthood and the world of childhood. But what is equally of significance in the film in terms of its portrayal of the modernity of the milieu of the Japanese salaryman is its awareness of the implications of change within the material fabric of the nation. It is no accident that the film is located on the outskirts of central Tokyo in one of the growing suburban landscapes that were becoming a feature of the peripheries of the capital as it expanded in population size due to the rise in labour-intensive heavy industries, factories and offices after the First World War. We thus see a form of intermediary location which is signalled by a sense of constant flux provided by the flow of trains in the compositional background of the images. The buildings are, for the most part, relatively recent, suggesting formative networks of social organisation which, as we now know from hindsight, will soon become denser and more heavily marked by the introduction of further light industry and housing. The Yoshii family's new suburban home appears in the film as a kind of frontier space in this terrain against which natural ground is linked to the spontaneity and freedom of childhood and the built-up environment is associated with the pressures and constraints of adult life. The white picket fence is the primary indicator of this, suggesting both a securing of suburban identity and a residual uncertainty about a loss of intrinsic naturalness.

This sense of loss was a fundamental aspect of Aono's examination of the Japanese salaryman's plight for it fed into an underlying insecurity about both the promise of modernisation and its ancilliary consumer benefits and the danger of letting go completely of what made Japanese national life so distinctive. As he wrote, 'within the content of the salaryman's consciousness . . . there was the nature of the fields and gardens, the true circumstances of the parents' home, the obligations of relatives, and the relations of friends' (quoted in Harootunian 2000: 204). This sense of the natural order is present within the landscape that the boys inhabit as they play on the, as yet undeveloped, ground near their home and discover the alleged potency of the sparrow's egg. It is also ideologically transcribed in the figure of the wife and mother (Yoshikawa Mitsuko) who, like many such characters in Ozu's films and among the *shomin geki* and *shōshimin geki* in general, becomes a conciliatory condensation of both tradition and modernity. Mrs Yoshii represents a sense of continuity as she maintains the house through her domestic activities of laundry, sewing and cooking and her concern for the affective well-being of her husband and children. Her organisational control over the domestic space of the household indicates an alternative, more nurturing social order than the dutiful company family that Yoshii also has to subscribe to in order to preserve his material well-being. Crucially, she is the one who voices concern at the cost of the hardship and progress she and her husband have endured. When talking of her sons she asks her husband, 'will they lead the same kind of sorry life that we have?'

What is also interesting about Mrs Yoshii is how she avoids being seen as merely an indicative emblem of the new urban *bunka seikatsu* (cultural living) which posited a subjectivity supposedly enthralled to the phenomenon of modern life announced in the new mass media of popular magazines, newspapers, advertisements, radio and movies. As Harootunian has suggested, this contemporary identity 'pointed to the ceaseless changes in material life introduced by new consumer products and a conception of life vastly different from the rhythms of received, routine practices' (2000: 13). Thus, while Mrs Yoshii may well importantly enjoy the benefits of new technologies such as the electric iron, she also appears to refute the more overt consumerist temptations of the advertising placards in the neighbourhood apparently announcing fashionable beauty products for the leisured female. In this sense, the Yoshii home becomes the commonsensical repository of governmental values increasingly being urged upon ordinary Japanese citizens in the early years of the 1930s. In response to the perceived excesses of the early Taishō period, and a corresponding despair about the need to preserve an indigenous and harmonious sense of spiritual well-being and collective co-operation, we see the emergence of the *seikatsu kaizen undō* (daily life reform movement) and *shinpuru raifu undō* (simple life movement). These discourses served to implement a programme that 'would emphasise efficiency and economies yet encourage people to avoid excess and immersing themselves too deeply in the new commodity culture' (Harootunian 2000: 15). *I Was Born, But* . . .'s representation of domestic space serves to underline this tendency in the way that it strives to incorporate real social change yet retain a disciplined sense of the virtues of tradition commensurate with the logic of Japan's *ryōsai kenbo* (good wife, wise mother) ideology that dated back to the Meiji era (1867–1912). (See Sakai 1989; Silverberg 1993; and Uno 1993 for further discussion of these issues.)

A key way in which the film constructs this meshing of convention and modernity is in its sense of iconography. Ozu's ordering of composition, so frequently seen by critics as just a pictorially minded formal element, actually works to suggest a dimension of material continuity. Hence we are frequently called upon to observe the ordinary and also reassuring presence of a kettle, a pile of *futon* and a set of rice bowls at regular intervals throughout the narration. It can, in fact, be argued that the film as a whole is especially sensitive about regimes of seeing and looking and this can be examined more closely by turning to how the visual style of the film, through its analogies to contemporary photography and to the very nature of cinematic storytelling, also provides a commentary on the social experience contained within the film and, in turn, implicitly contained within the audience the film wished to address.

Hasumi Shigehiko has suggested that Shōchiku differed from a number of other leading Japanese film studios of the 1920s and 1930s in that in terms of its cinematographic practices it was more beholden to the influence of Holly-wood shooting styles. 'Most other cinematographers at the time', he argues, 'were from the industrial retail side of image making, whose hands-on know-ledge of cinematography came from working on photography and development in regular photo shops' (Hasumi n.d.). This may be true, on one level, but on another, that of the pattern of representation, there is evidence of a greater degree of cross-fertilisation. It can be argued that along with film, photography was at the core of the new regime of visual culture that crossed into all spheres of social and cultural life in Japan. This was the era of the establishment of photojournalism, important advances in photo printing techniques, and especially the appearance and spread of influential amateur and professional photographic groups, such as the *Shinkō Shashin Kenkyūkai* (New Photography Association), and publications such as *Asahi Camera* (1926–). In a key essay which appeared in the second issue of the journal *Kōga* (1932–), Ina Nobuo discerned three main categories in contemporary photographic expression of 'events and objects' (quoted in Okatsuka 1995: 12). Rather than dwelling on the first which referred to 'those who attempt to [simply] express the distinctive beauty of the subject', we may consider the similarities between the second and third and Ozu and Mohara Hideo's visual style: 'those who see the photograph as sculpture in light' and 'those who see the art of photography as recording one's age and reporting on how people live' (12). We have already noticed, for example, the proliferation of the carefully lit and positioned everyday object within the film which now also recalls an attention to detail and composition comparable with the efforts of contemporary still photographers such as Shimamura Hōkō. But it is in likening Ozu's film to the practice of new docu-mentary photographers such as Kimura Ihei and Kuwabara Kineo that the similarities emerge most fully. Several of Kimura's humanistic observations of

Tokyo children playing against the backdrop of a modernising cityscape instantly convey the same emotional timbre and interest in ordinary gesture and social realities. Kuwabara's interest in densely woven visual compositions detailing the layers of Japan's modernity recalls several shots within the film as well as the overall social milieu of petit-bourgeois suburban space in transition. This is a cinema and photography that has not forgotten it has been constructed by 'social beings' (Ina quoted in Okatsuka 1995: 173).

The key to understanding the complexities behind the film's visual style is in the significance of the film within the film that is alluded to in the sequence previously discussed early on in the film when we see Yoshii invited into the boss's office. It is obvious at this point that the boss is an amateur filmmaker, but it is only much later in the narrative that the results of his endeavours are displayed for both the diegetic audience and the cinematic spectator. Among other images in the home movie of a Sunday in the zoo and park at Ueno in the centre of Tokyo, we also see Yoshii forced to comply with the boss's demands and make a fool of himself by making ridiculous faces and gestures for the camera. This withdrawal of the film's alignment with the subjectivity of Yoshii is crucial for it signals that the conceptual idea of visual doubling is fundamental to the means by which the film works to create meaning about the world it depicts. By deciding to reinsert the boss's film in narrative terms only within the wider public sphere of a screening that also includes the two Yoshii sons, Ozu creates a distillation of the entire film's method which twins the emotions and dilemmas of the boys with the circumstances of their father. Crucially, the point on screen when the reels of film unspool in front of its audience becomes both the very moment when both sons become aware of the true nature of their father's subordination and that when the spectator simultaneously becomes aware of the humiliation that has taken place in the room previously hidden from view. From now on in the film, there is a sense of perceptual and affective division between the boys and the father that is shared by the spectator as we see the full plight of parental despair that the illusions of childhood about the stature of the father have vanished.

The idea of doubling regarding visual knowledge is reinforced by the boys' fascination with the nature of the zebra in the zoo images featured in the home movie. The pair are unable to agree whether the animal has white stripes on a black background or the other way around. This fundamental perceptual problem relates back to the issue of seeing signalled in the displacement of 'real time' and the diegetic insertion of 'cinematic time' regarding the construction and display of the boss's home movie, but it also signals the conflicting means by which the world of the film may be seen and understood by adults and children alike. The 'lesson' of the film within the film for the boys is that they must learn to become aware that the distinctive power relations enacted in their play are no mere distraction from the conventions of adulthood. Rather, more darkly, they are a means of simply practising for a future already set out before them. As the mother says when the family return home, 'It is a problem they'll have to live with for the rest of their lives'.

There is a further dimension to the notion of doubling that relates to

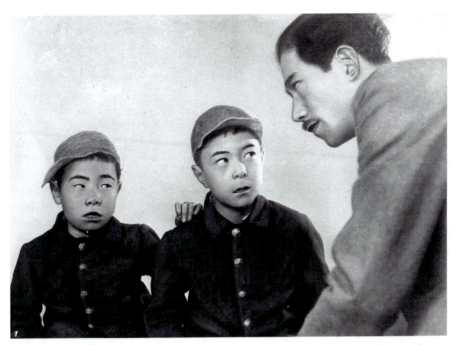

Figure 5 I Was Born, But . . . (1932) twins the emotions and dilemmas of the two boys with the circumstances of their father. BFI Stills, Posters and Designs.

the manner in which contemporary critics repeatedly turned to the phrase in written discourse to describe the material and affective experience of Japan's modernity. Harootunian has observed that many Japanese writers and thinkers of the time understood the social experience of people such as Yoshii in terms of 'a *doubling* that imprinted a difference between the new demands of capitalism and the market and the face of received forms of historical and cultural patterns' (2000: xvii). This suggests a level of awkward unevenness – even a lack of solidity – which is conveyed in the film's very fabric when the inauthentic diegetic film is interwoven with presumably more authentic social realities of office, family and school life. It is interesting that other images contained within the boss's film serve to create a sense of difference between their own somewhat playful and idealised images of everyday modern life and the more demanding, constraining and even impoverishing reality that we observe elsewhere in the film. Here, the artifice of Ozu's self-reflexivity actually serves as a form of commentary on the presumed counterfeit artifice of the social order his film contends with. Yoshii's boss's film thus appears concerned far more with an aspirational and leisured view of the modern world that encapsulates privileged views of public parks, tram systems, shopping streets and office life to evoke a sense of the optimistic promise that modern life has delivered on. It is only on another perceptual level that this regime may be called into question.

When Ozu later recollected the making of *I Was Born, But* . . . he said, 'I started to make a film about children and ended up with a film about grown ups; while I had originally planned to make a fairly bright little story, it changed while I was working on it, and came out very dark' (quoted in Richie 1974: 215). Richie recalls that Shōchiku were so uncertain about the film that they delayed its release by two months until June 1932. In its vivid treatment of the social and political disappointments of everyday life, the film may be said to occupy a turning point in Ozu's career – his next film was the even more plaintively titled *Where Now are the Dreams of Youth?* (1932). It was the last of the films which conveyed the rhetorical but also wistful hanging participle 'but'; the others being *I Graduated, But . . .* (*Daigaku wa deta keredo*, 1929) and *I Flunked, But . . .* (*Rakudai wa shita keredo*, 1930). What did this 'but' signify? In one sense, it suggests the disappointments of life, some of which have been suggested in this chapter. However, to conclude, we may also summise another register of feeling, one that was indicated by the critic Sato Haruo around the time of the film's original reception. 'My favourite among the symbols of modernity is the motion pictures', he wrote. 'When I reflect on them, I feel duty bound to live in the present' (quoted in Harootunian 2000: 23). Perhaps the 'but' contained within the title may also evoke the way that all human life after birth is mediated and conditioned by social experience and that, as Ozu's complex but deeply felt film attests, even in the very moment of the here and now it is beholden on that most immediate of all forms, cinema, to produce a vivid and real sense of how this happens.

Acknowledgements

The author would like to thank Kyoko Hirano for her kind permission to reproduce her Ozu Yasujirō English-language filmography published in Yoshida Yoshishige [Yoshida Kijū] (2003) *Ozu's Anti-Cinema*, Ann Arbor: Center for Japanese Studies, University of Michigan.

References

Bordwell, David (1988) *Ozu and the Poetics of Cinema*, London: British Film Institute.

Gordon, Andrew (ed.) (1993) *Postwar Japan as History*, Berkeley: University of California Press.

Harootunian, Harry (2000) *Overcome by Modernity: History, Culture and Community in Interwar Japan*, Princeton: Princeton University Press.

Hasumi, Shigehiko (n.d.) 'On the Everydayness of a "Miracle"'. Online. http://www.um.u-tokyo.ac.jp/dm2k-umdb/publish_db/books/ozu/english/02.html

Miyoshi, Masao and Harootunian, H.D. (eds) (1989) *Japan in the World*, Durham, NC: Duke University Press.

Okatsuka, Akiko (1995) *The Founding and Development of Modern Photography in Japan: Consciousness and Expression of the Modern*, Tokyo: Tokyo Metropolitan Museum of Photography.

Richie, Donald (1974) *Ozu*, Berkeley: University of California Press.

Sakai, Naoki (1989) 'Modernity and Its Critique: The Problem of Universalism and Particularism', in Miyoshi and Harootunian 1989: 93–122.

Schwartz, Dennis (1999) '*I Was Born, But* . . .' 5 November. Online. http://www.sover.net/~ozus/iwasbornbut.htm

Silverberg, Miriam (1993) 'Constructing a New Cultural History of Prewar Japan', in Miyoshi and Harootunian 1989: 115–43.

Uno, Kathleen (1993) 'The Death of "Good Wife, Wise Mother"?', in Gordon 1993: 293–322.

Wada-Marciano, Mitsuyo (1998) 'The Production of Modernity in Japanese National Cinema: Shochiku Kamata Style in the 1920s and 1930s', *Asian Cinema* 9 (2): 69–93.

Yoshida, Yoshishige [Yoshida Kijū] (2003) *Ozu's Anti-Cinema*, Ann Arbor: Center for Japanese Studies, University of Michigan.

Ozu Yasujirō Filmography

Sword of Penitence (*Zange no yaiba*, 1927)
Dreams of Youth (*Wakōdo no yume*, 1928)
Wife Lost (*Nyōbō funshitsu*, 1928)
Pumpkin (*Kabocha*, 1928)
A Couple on the Move (*Hikkoshi fūfū*, 1928)
Body Beautiful (*Nikutaibi*, 1928)
Treasure Mountain (*Takara no yama*, 1929)
Days of Youth (*Wakaki hi*, 1929)
Fighting Friends–Japanese Style (*Wasei kenka tomodachi*, 1929)
I Graduated, But . . . (*Daigaku wa deta keredo*, 1929)
The Life of an Office Worker (*Kaishain seikatsu*, 1929)
A Straightforward Boy (*Tokkan kozō*, 1929)
An Introduction to Marriage (*Kekkongaku nyūmon*, 1930)
Walk Cheerfully (*Hogaraka ni ayume*, 1930)
I Flunked, But . . . (*Rakudai wa shita keredo*, 1930)
That Night's Wife (*Sono yo no tsuma*, 1930)
The Revengeful Spirit of Eros (*Erogami no onnen*, 1930)
The Luck Which Touched the Leg (*Ashi ni sawatta kōun*, 1930)
Young Miss (*Ojōsan*, 1930)
The Lady and the Beard (*Shukujo to hige*, 1931)
Beauty's Sorrows (*Bijin aishū*, 1931)
Tokyo Chorus (*Tōkyō no kōrasu*, 1931)
Spring Comes from the Ladies (*Haru wa gofujin kara*, 1932)
I Was Born, But . . . (*Umarete wa mita keredo*, 1932)
Where Now Are the Dreams of Youth? (*Seishun no yume ima izuko*, 1932)
Until the Day We Meet Again (*Mata au hi made*, 1932)
A Woman in Tokyo (*Tōkyō no onna*, 1933)
Dragnet Girl (*Hijōsen no onna*, 1933)
Passing Fancy (*Dekigokoro*, 1933)
A Mother Should Be Loved (*Haha o kowazuya*, 1934)
A Story of Floating Weeds (*Ukikusa monogatari*, 1934)
An Innocent Maid (*Hakoiri musume*, 1935)
Kikugoro's Kagami-jishi (*Kikugorō no Kagami-jishi*, 1935)
An Inn in Tokyo (*Tōkyō no yado*, 1935)
College is a Nice Place (*Daigaku yoitoko*, 1936)
The Only Son (*Hitori musuko*, 1936)
What Did the Lady Forget? (*Shukujo wa nani o wasuretaka*, 1937)

Brothers and Sisters of the Toda Family (Toda-ke no kyōdai, 1941)
There Was a Father (Chichi ariki, 1942)
Record of a Tenement Gentleman (Nagaya shinshiroku, 1947)
Late Spring (Banshun, 1949)
The Munekata Sisters (Munekata kyōdai, 1950)
Early Summer (Bakushū, 1951)
The Flavor of Green Tea over Rice (Ochazuke no aji, 1952)
Tokyo Story (Tōkyō monogatari, 1953)
Early Spring (Sōshun, 1956)
Tokyo Twilight (Tōkyō boshoku, 1957)
Good Morning (Ohayō, 1959)
Floating Weeds (Ukigusa, 1959)
Late Autumn (Akibiyori, 1960)
The End of Summer (Kohayagawa-ke no aki, 1961)
An Autumn Afternoon (Sanma no aji, 1962)

2

ALL FOR MONEY

Mizoguchi Kenji's *Osaka Elegy* (1936)

Mori Toshie

The year 1936 was a seminal one for Mizoguchi Kenji, just as it was a key moment in the history of Japanese film in general. In that year, Mizoguchi made his sixtieth film, *Osaka Elegy* (*Naniwa erejī*), which is now widely regarded as his first successful sound film.[1] The critical consensus is that the film not only opened up a new chapter in the director's career, but with his subsequent film *The Sisters of Gion* (*Gion no kyōdai*, 1936) often being invoked in association, it was also the first true Japanese 'realist film' (Shindō 1976: 45–6).

Osaka Elegy's realism centres on its combination of a portrait of an ordinary young woman's life in a modern city with a detailed depiction of Ōsaka around 1936 – a historic moment in that it was the year of the 2.26 (February 26) Incident, the military revolt in Tokyo by extremists which symbolised the transition towards out-and-out state militarism. The phase of Japan's 'modernism', which had been ushered in towards the late 1920s and which should be perceived differently from the Western sense of the term (Minami 1983: 5), was about to end. The serendipitous coming together of this shifting socio-political background with Mizoguchi's maturity as a film director therefore renders the film an invaluable document of Japanese urban life in a highly significant year.

After giving a brief outline of the director's career prior to *Osaka Elegy*, this chapter will shed light on the context of the film in terms of its representation of the life of a young working girl, Ayako (Yamada Isuzu), during the time of the Depression in Japan. The heroine, a telephone operator who is burdened with the financial penury of her family, becomes the mistress of her company's boss, Asai (Shiganoya Benkei), but she then decides to marry her fiancé, Nishimura (Hara Kensaku), in order to remake her life. Her recurring family problems lead Ayako to the final and more risky decision to cheat Asai's friend, Fujino (Shindō Eitarō), out of his money. Mizoguchi's representation of Ayako's choices in the process of controversially becoming a *moga* (modern girl) is served by an elaborate mise-en-scène which can arguably be seen as the embryonic manifestation of the director's later universal insights into the place of female exploitation in society.

In 1922, Mizoguchi started his career as a director at Nikkatsu Mukōjima

Studio in Tokyo. The studio at this time specialised in the production of *shinpa* (new school) films based on the contemporary urban theatrical melodramas popular during the Meiji period (1868–1912) – particularly the 1890s – which often focused on the sacrifice of women for the sake of the family (Komatsu 1996: 418). Mizoguchi's first film, *Resurrection of Love* (*Ai ni yomigaeru hi*, 1923), released in February the following year, belonged to this influential genre.

Though Mizoguchi started his career with a few *shinpa* style films and had the reputation for being a director who was adept at portraying female characters and themes, he also became known for his versatility in producing films in a variety of genres. His work varied from a detective film, *813* (1923), to an experimental film influenced by German Expressionism, *Blood and Spirit* (*Chi to rei*, 1923), to a comedy film, *Money* (*Kane*, 1926), and even an experimental operetta, *The Man of the Right Moment* (*Toki no ujigami*, 1932). This variety is indicative of his penchant for adapting to his own cinematic orientation what was in stylistic currency at any given moment. He was also prone to influence from government policy and made a propaganda film, *Song of Home* (*Furusato no uta*, 1925), his earliest existing film, as well as nationalist films such as *The Imperial Grace* (*Kō-on*, 1927).

Though Mizoguchi was a director hard to characterise in terms of genre, he seems to have contributed to two particular genres throughout his career (Yamada 1976: 90–5). The *shinpa* films characterised by a deep sympathy for a victimised woman constitute the first important strand in his filmography. *The*

Figure 6 Elaborate mise-en-scène in *Osaka Elegy* (1936) serves as an insight into the place of female exploitation in Japanese society. BFI Stills, Posters and Designs.

White Threads of the Waterfall (*Taki no shiraito*, 1933), which can still be screened as his oldest intact film, belongs to this genre. The influence of *keikō eiga* ('tendency films') was also important. During the short boom in Japanese film, Mizoguchi also had his leftist period which resulted in productions such as *Metropolitan Symphony* (*Tōkai kōkyōgaku*, 1929) and *And Yet They Go On* (*Shikamo karera wa yuku*, 1931). Like other proletarian filmmakers, Mizoguchi suffered from severe censorship and he eventually gave up directing films of this sort, but the ethos of criticising an oppressive society and having sympathy for the victim were enduring characteristics and would reappear in different contexts throughout Mizoguchi's career.

Before filming *Osaka Elegy*, Mizoguchi's spirit of thematic and technical innovation had already made him a well-known director. As will be seen, however, *Osaka Elegy* became the first occasion on which Mizoguchi was able to harness his own filmic style in order to create a more realistic level of representation on screen. Mizoguchi himself once wrote, with regard to his intentions in making *Osaka Elegy*, that he had taken pains to represent 'the smell of earth'. He was not content with previous Japanese films in that none of them:

> stuck to the ground and gave out the smell of earth. Their dramas could happen in any place, and were flavourless in their artificial imaginary quality, as if they were not the story of this life.
>
> (Mizoguchi 1991: 10)

As can be seen from this quotation, one of Mizoguchi's main concerns in making a film was to represent the reality of the locality or the characteristics of the place in which it was shot. The use of Ōsaka dialect (*Kansaiben*) in *Osaka Elegy* was an important aspect of this. Mizoguchi's accidental encounter with his life-long collaborator, the scriptwriter Yoda Yoshikata, contributed much to the realisation of the first fiction film to be narrated only in Ōsaka dialect. 'The smell of earth' of the regional tongue, its up-tempo rhythm and famed humorous undertones, helped to make the film almost a tragi-comedy despite the seriousness of its themes (Sasō 1997: 102).

Following the credit sequence and its accompanying non-diegetic jazz music – a symbol of modernity and contemporaneity – a night scene appears of Ōsaka's most popular entertainment district, Dōtonbori, which was famed at the time for its cafés and cabarets with jazz bands. The distinctive rotating cross of Ōsaka's largest café shines above the canal as if to symbolise the modernisation process that Ōsaka had been engaged in since the 1920s. During the course of this period, Ōsaka had grown exponentially as a manufacturing, commercial and shipping centre (Kirihara 1992: 36), and had introduced the twentieth century's first fully-fledged form of modern urban life in Japan (Hashimoto 2001: 128). Meanwhile, capitalist ideology and business practices flourished, altering people's lifestyle and engendering a more money-oriented philosophy. Cafés were a symbol of this climate and created a less expensive form of sexual pleasure for their customers than the traditional *geisha* by introducing a modern form of female exploitation or commercialised sexuality (Fujime 1990).

In contrast to the preceding nocturnal image, when dawn comes, the camera looks down the street of Doshō where its Edo-period pharmaceutical merchants' houses and large storehouses stand in a row. The scene dissolves into an *engawa* (long corridor) situated in the exterior of the traditional Japanese house of the Asai family, the owners of the Asai Pharmaceutical Company. There, young housemaids are seen scurrying to prepare their irritable master's breakfast while Asai, according to tradition, prays to the sun for the good fortune of his business. However, this sense of tradition does not flow seamlessly. His wife Sumiko (Umemura Yōko), a spoiled upper-class woman, has over-indulged the night before and is in the privileged position of choosing not to accompany her husband. Unlike Asai, who is seen eating a traditional Japanese breakfast, she partakes of a Western-style meal of a piece of bread and a cup of coffee.

As will already be apparent from these opening shots, *Osaka Elegy* sets out to show the same mixture of the modern and the traditional that existed in the time and place in which the film was set. The film's realism then mirrors the stage that the modernisation process had reached at this point, and offers a considerable amount of detail on what people in a large city like Ōsaka were actually experiencing.

The term applied to these emerging new cultural phenomena was *modanisumu*. The Japanese word *modanisumu* (the apparent translation of 'modernism') must, however, be interpreted differently from the Western sense of the term which refers instead to the modern thought and ideology that aimed to revolutionise and overturn traditional Western value systems. Though there is an argument which stresses the reverse influence of modernism on Japanese culture in order to contrast it with its Western counterpart (Nygren 1998), modernism in a general sense, suggesting both the dark and light side of social change, should, in fact, be translated as *kindaishugi* (Iwamoto 1991: 6–7). *Modanisumu*, on the other hand, referring to people's manners and customs, conveyed the lightness and the frivolity of the new. As a social phenomenon it initially represented women's advancement in society, with professional women such as Ayako, the film's heroine, being a typical example.

We next see Ayako being introduced in her position as a telephone operator in the offices of the Asai Company. This was a popular female occupation which had newly emerged during the course of communications technology modernisation. Various other new jobs for young women such as the café waitress, office clerk and shop assistant had also begun to appear in larger urban areas, especially Tokyo and Ōsaka, from the 1920s onwards (Kawamoto 2003: 32). These employment opportunities for women would have been viewed as part of the benefits of capitalism and they gave rise to the term *shokugyō fujin* (professional woman), although café waitresses were not socially accepted as such (Fujime 1990: 124).

Ayako, however, also experiences the demerits of capitalism in the form of the financial burden caused by the misfortunes of her father, who has lost all of his money on the stock market and has embezzled funds from his company. As if to prefigure her impecunious situation, Ayako's image in the telephone booth secluded by the glass partition thus shows her immobility and inability to speak out with her own voice (Cavanaugh 1998: 64). Watching Sumiko's seduction of her colleague and fiancé, Nishimura, from a short distance away, she cannot complain directly to him about his indecisive attitude. In the last shot of this sequence, the camera focuses on a woman's magazine article that Ayako is reading in her booth. The title proclaims: '*Kane yue ni daraku shita onna*' [Woman ruined, all for money] as if to suggest that her destiny may overlap with that of the *moga* who often featured in the pages of such contemporary periodicals.

Moga was the translated term for the Japanese 'modern girl' who dressed in Western fashion with distinctively bobbed hairstyles and clothes which imitated the style of contemporary European and Hollywood actresses. Once *moga* came to be seen as a particular icon of *modanisumu*, they were, more often than not, mentioned derogatorily and perceived as being sexually and morally decadent. For the 1936 audience, the *moga* article, as well as the jazz café in the opening shot, would have instantly brought connotations of a decadent mass culture already becoming associated with that period and generically called *ero guro nansensu* ('erotic, grotesque, nonsense') (Minami 1983).

After a series of successive gloomy sequences in which Nishimura refuses to lend Ayako money at Ōsaka Bay and Ayako discovers her father's company men collecting money at home, we surprisingly see her listening to tango music in a highly modernised apartment. Ayako is pictured seated in a long shot in the centre foreground and leaning against a *hibachi* (charcoal brazier) in a traditional Japanese room complete with *tatami* (straw matting). In the background to the left, we see a Western-style living room with table and chairs. Ayako moves across to the living room and sits on a chair and the camera pans slightly in order to keep her in the centre of the frame without approaching her. This nearly static long take shows the way in which Ayako can easily transgress the border between the traditional and the modern as if to demonstrate that she exists in both worlds. There is no visible partition between the two rooms in this novel bespoke apartment.

The connotations of this mixture of designs within the same apartment are rather complex as they reveal that the process of Japanese modernisation was far from being a unilateral movement towards Westernisation (Silverberg 1992). In the confines of a traditional space set within a modern environment, Ayako plays the role of a *kakoware-mono* (mistress). Isolated in the room from the outside world, she awaits her paramour. Ayako has now become Asai's mistress on the condition that he offers the money to pay off her father's debt, and that her father is also offered a job in Asai's company. By locating the setting in Ōsaka, where the urge to make money is paramount, Mizoguchi deliberately shows the ironic articulation of female sexuality through money within the schema of capitalism. Ayako's relationship with her paramour is thus formed and sustained 'all for money'.

Mizoguchi also extends the historical context of female victimisation to the pre-modern period in the next sequence, where the couple are seen at a *bunraku* (puppet drama) theatre. The play, *Shinjū ten no amijima*, written by Chikamatsu Monzaemon (1653–1724) in 1720, is based on the real-life story of the double suicide of a married Ōsaka man and his *oiran* (high-ranking courtesan).[2] The image of Ayako, sitting beside Asai with her traditional *marumage* hairstyle, appropriate only for married or *kakoware-mono* women, conveys the message that though Ayako is living in the modern world, she is also living within the eternal structure of female confinement (Cavanaugh 1998: 64).

Depicting the contrast as well as the conflict between the modern and the traditional, the figure of Ayako, so far, does not deviate fundamentally from the realm of traditional Japanese drama which foregrounds 'the role of suffering woman as an object to be admired with great outpouring of sympathy' (Nygren 1998: 73). In this respect, *Osaka Elegy* can be seen as following the pattern of *shinpa* tragedy, the genre that Mizoguchi had often used as a kind of 'filmic template'.

From this sequence onwards, Ayako gradually tries to escape from her confinement. When Asai's wife finally uncovers Ayako's liaison, the story fails to develop into the familiar melodramatic love triangle between the wife, the husband and the mistress. Instead, Ayako never shows her emotional attachment to the paramour and her 'rationality' underlines the new context of liaisons based on economics rather than affect.

Having lost her job and patron, Ayako imagines that only marriage to Nishimura can give her a fresh start in life. In order to see him, Ayako takes the underground train which was, at that time, a new form of transport and one of the most symbolic characteristics of life in the modern city (Kirihara 1992: 37). In a medium shot on the train, we see her brightly lit smiling face. She is a picture of excited anticipation at the prospect of realising her dreams. This brief, but exceptionally hopeful, sequence is the only time in the film that she is treated sympathetically by modern life.

When Ayako happens to see her sister, Sachiko (Ōkura Chiyoko), on the platform, the optimistic atmosphere gradually begins to dissipate. Ayako learns that their brother is in such a financial predicament that it has put his continued university education in jeopardy. Ayako bitterly refuses her sister's request to provide financial support in the place of their father. Halfway up the steps of the underground, Ayako pauses in a long shot which is held for a long time. We wonder what she is pondering.

After climbing the stairs, Ayako is next pictured in an extreme long shot, standing still at the entrance of a broad street on which cars are passing at terrific speed just in front of her. Mizoguchi cuts to an extreme low angle long shot from the staircase, which obscures our vision of the protagonist since she is blocked by a pole and a building in the background. This highly unusual image conveys Ayako's sense of powerlessness and her feeling of isolation within the big city. The iconography, while suggesting that the modern social environment has become relentlessly monotonous and cruel to Ayako, also indicates her growing inner agony which will eventually result in her becoming a 'delinquent', a form of being subject to overwhelming social oppression.

In the next scene, in a surprising turn of events, Ayako appears dressed up in the typical *moga* style of fashionable Western dress and hat. She meets Fujino, Asai's friend, in a *geisha* bar in order to obtain money from him by pretending to become his mistress. This is her decision to preserve her father's good name without selling her body any more. After leaving an embarassed Fujino, Ayako makes a desperate telephone call to Nishimura.

Mizoguchi seems to have delicately avoided identifying his heroine too specifically with the image of the *moga* that then prevailed in society. For the *shokugyō fujin*, sometimes used synonymously with the *moga* (Sakurai 1927: 169), freedom seemed to have been created in order to work and play alongside men (Silverberg 1991: 246). *Moga* thus also provoked an anxiety in society about female consumption due to newly disposable incomes (Sakurai 1927), a fact which might overlap with the figure of Ayako that we see earlier in the department store sequence. A more accurate assessment of the situation, however, indicates that the *moga* was not so much a term that referred to an identifiable group of women as an ideologically generated social construct, which 'begins to emerge as a means of displacing the very real militancy of Japanese woman' (Silverberg 1991: 260). The figure of the *moga*, therefore, is subject to contradictory connotations – on the one hand, women's desire to be seen as independent individuals and, on the other, the oppressive power of the dominant male society.

Mizoguchi's unique employment of the figure of the *moga* is interesting precisely because it seems to show the gradual process of the heroine obtaining her 'militancy' through her experiences in despair. Ayako's Westernised *moga* style would suggest that she has made a final decision to cast off the old persona symbolised by the *kimono*, but at the same time she refuses to be 'consumed' in the modern world by not indulging in the pleasures of modern urban life.

The next shot in which Ayako meets Nishimura in her flat, filmed in an extremely long take, constitutes in many ways the crystallisation of Mizoguchi's filmic style. The complex configuration of elements pictured in an indoor sequence in a long take with refined camera movements was something which he developed further in seminal films such as *The Story of Late Chrysanthemums* (*Zangiku monogatari*, 1939). At the start of the sequence, from the corridor outside her room, the camera peers through the window with closed curtains, thus involving the spectator almost voyeuristically in watching Ayako act out the role of a genuine *moga* in high spirits along with coffee pot and cigarette. She moves around to light the cigarette and sits down again, restlessly waiting for Nishimura. Finally, she approaches the window and looks down through it to see him in the hall on the ground floor. The camera pans diagonally to the lower left until it shows the hallway where he is standing. As he walks upstairs to the first floor, the camera follows him along the complicated and rather long maze-like route in a crane shot until finally he meets her at the doorway and they go into the room together. The camera follows the couple to the chairs on which she was sitting at the beginning of the shot.

Mizoguchi succeeds in creating plural connotations concerning the protagonist's possible emotions about her future condition. The long take set within the glass apartment gives us an impression of spacious openness with a sense of freedom (Sasō 1997: 102). Even the way that Mizoguchi pictures the arrival of Nishimura synchronises well with Ayako's growing expectations of a romantic ending for the couple, although the route may also seem too complicated to indicate simple closure. After the initial joy of seeing each other again, Ayako starts regretfully to confess her past as Asai's mistress. She moves from the bright stylish living room into the much darker Japanese room. The darkness recalls the fact that Ayako used to be a *kakoware-mono* confined within this flat. At this point, Nishimura's figure in the foreground is silhouetted and silent, which simultaneously underlies his ineffectuality and casts a pall over their relationship. The entire apartment seems to embody the paradoxical complexity of a society that is rooted in traditional moral values while practising modern patterns of behaviour.

While Ayako is earnestly pleading for marriage, Fujino storms into the flat and accuses her of having deceived him. In return, Ayako explodes in anger at Fujino. Her anger is so fierce that it appears to be targeting not only this lecherous man, but also something more fundamental: the oppressive nature of a society that has reduced a woman to something resembling a mere plaything.

The next sequence finds Ayako at the police station with journalists. On a superficial level, she is being viewed according to the terms of the article in the earlier sequence: *moga* ruins her life for money. In the interrogation room, beyond a thin partition, Ayako hears Nishimura's statement, which is aimed solely at protecting his own interests. In a medium close-up shot, we see Ayako's distressed profile through the darkness. Since this is the first close-up, it has the dramatic effect of inviting our sympathy for her psychological pain and anger. Though Ayako is released into her father's custody, his self-defence will not allow him to admit the damning truth, and thus Ayako is subjected to merciless recriminations from the rest of the family. Her brother labels her a juvenile delinquent. Ayako realises that there is no longer a place for her in this cold family and runs away.

In the final sequence, the camera is positioned on Ebisu Bridge – built in 1925 over Dōtonbori – at night. This was the first reinforced concrete bridge in Ōsaka and was celebrated as a symbol of urban modernisation. The café's neon sign is reflected in the river, just as in the opening scene, but this time the camera shows only the reflection. The bridge and the reflected sign hint at both the light and the dark sides of the modernisation process of the previous decade, as if to suggest that the hope and expectations of modernity were only an illusion, just like the shimmering image on the river.

We see Ayako in a high-angle long shot looking out over the bridge. Passers-by occupy the foreground. Mizoguchi cuts a couple of times between a low-angle medium profile shot of Ayako gazing blankly off-screen-right and a point-of-view shot of various debris floating on the river below. An off-screen male voice asks 'What's happened?' and Ayako looks up to the right. We then see Ayako in a medium long shot in the centre of the image. Her acquaintance, Asai's home doctor (Tamura Kunio), enters the frame from the right to ask what she is doing at a place like this. She replies that she's a 'stray dog' and doesn't know what to do. He asks if she is ill. Ayako answers ironically that she is suffering from 'a disease called juvenile delinquency' and asks how the doctor might go about curing such a person. 'That I can't give an answer to', he replies, and then exits screen left, literally giving the cold shoulder to this now abandoned woman. Throughout, Mizoguchi holds the camera in a static position to the extent that other people walking by sometimes blur the picture of the couple.

The objectivity of this composition conveys Ayako's solitude and anonymity within Ōsaka's night-time bustle. It also contrasts well with the subsequent camera movement in order to create a final dramatic effect. When Ayako starts to walk off towards the right, the camera accompanies her and gradually moves in closer until we see her features in profile. Then, in the very last shot of the film, we cut suddenly to a frontal medium shot. Steadily and confidently, Ayako now walks towards the camera until this shot becomes the only close-up image of her in the entire film. It is almost as if the camera itself is now standing in for Ayako's unyielding spirit of determination and heroism.

The strength of the contrast of this final shot with Mizoguchi's customary style throughout the film affords it great power, and its particular meaning has been the subject of much critical dispute. Even at a roundtable discussion with the director after the film's release, certain critics of the day argued that the final sequence should have been filmed in long shot. This was a view that the director did not take issue with (Mizoguchi et al. 1991 [1937]: 22–3). Satō Tadao (1982: 85), on the other hand, has claimed that it shows 'the shining beauty of facial expression' of a new type of woman who has the ability to stand on her own two feet in the face of adversity. However, Catherine Russell has interpreted this image as 'an ironic resignation to her [Ayako's] fated emancipation from sacrificial roles' (Russell 1995: 143). In her view, Mizoguchi's representation of Ayako's transformation is too abrupt and 'only serves as a sign of the historical limitation of his [Mizoguchi's] melodramatic mode' (146).

Nonetheless, when the final shot is seen within the context both of the narrative as a whole and of Mizoguchi's filmography in general, it can clearly be interpreted as an important element in the emergence of one of the director's enduring preoccupations. In the previous sequences, Ayako has realised that her penury was not brought about by one individual, but through the mechanisms of the male-dominant society to which her fiancé also belongs. In the conversation with the doctor, Ayako identifies her disease as delinquency. She also realises that this disorder cannot be cured by a practitioner whose medical ideology only allows the patient to be treated simply as an individual. Her delinquency stems in fact from society and it is the inevitable reaction of a woman who refuses to accept her subordinate position automatically. This realisation and its visual representation may be seen as the probable sub-text of the film's final close-up.

The full significance of this aspect of Ayako's realisation becomes clearer when it is seen intertextually in juxtaposition with the concluding scene of Mizoguchi's next film, *Sisters of Gion*. Here, Mizoguchi represents the plight of the protagonist Omocha by having her lament society's role in creating and exploiting the misery of *geisha* like herself. In his discussion of Mizoguchi's feminism, Satō (1995: 360) highlights Ayako's and Omocha's protests and contrasts them with protagonists of previous *shōshimin eiga* where individual people's lives were presented realistically, but with no critical perspective.

The pattern of both films, that of a woman's struggle to survive in a male-dominant society and her final realisation of the way in which the structure of this society results inevitably in women being victims, was to become a key leitmotif of the concluding scenes of Mizoguchi's later 'feminist' films. These include such titles as *My Love Has Been Burning* (*Waga koi wa moenu*, 1949), *Gion Festival Music* (*Gion bayashi*, 1953) and *The Woman of Rumor* (*Uwasa no onna*, 1954), though a focus on female bonding becomes more dominant in the later films.

The final shot in *Osaka Elegy* should therefore be interpreted in the context of the development of Mizoguchi's beliefs and insights as a whole. As mentioned previously, he had already been exposed to the depiction of female victimisation in the *shinpa* films as well as the representation of social oppression in the *keikō eiga*. *Osaka Elegy* was the first occasion on which a film director had portrayed the reality of contemporary society on screen in a realist style of presentation which represented female victimisation and social oppression in a manner that was neither as sentimental as *shinpa* drama nor as overtly ideological as the *keikō eiga*.

The value of these integrated insights, as Katō Mikirō (1998: 121) has pointed out, enabled Mizoguchi to shoot 'a feminist melodrama' as early as the 1930s and provided *Osaka Elegy* and *Sisters of Gion* with some of film history's earliest insights that still have the capacity to surprise Western and even Japanese audiences. Though Mizoguchi, as well as Ayako, was to endure the harsher realities of the late 1930s, when the modernisation process of the 1920s symbolised by the *moga* came to be displaced by the onset of total militarism, the integrated voice that emerged in the course of his film was to remain a constant until the end of his career. *Osaka Elegy* was to become, and will remain, a masterpiece in Japanese film history.

Notes

1 Mizoguchi had previously shot six films with sound, but the first, *Home Town* (*Furusato*, 1930), was only partly shot with sound, and the second, *The Man of the Right Moment* (*Toki no ujigami*, 1932), was an experimental operetta. The third and the fourth films contained only music. Mizoguchi's filmography of true sound films begins with *O'Yuki, The Virgin* (*Maria no Oyuki*, 1935). For his complete filmography with detailed data, see Sasō and Nishida 1997.

2 For more on this text, see Chapter 15 (by Carole Cavanaugh) of the present volume.

References

Cavanaugh, Carole (1998) 'Unwriting the Female Persona in *Osaka Elegy* and *The Life of Oharu*', in O'Grady 1998: 64–5.

Fujime, Yuki (1990) 'Senkan Ōsaka ni okeru "sekkyakufu" to sono undō' [Women Engaged in Sexual Services and Their Labor Movements in Ōsaka Between the Wars], *Shirin* 73 (2): 121–41.

Hashimoto, Osamu (2001) *Nijusseiki* [*The Twentieth Century*], Tokyo: Mainichi Shinbun-sha.

Iwamoto Kenji (1991) 'Modanisumu to Nihon eiga' [Modernism and Japanese Films], in Iwamoto Kenji (ed.), *Nihon eiga to modanisumu 1920–1930* [*Japanese Films and Modernism 1920–1930*], Tokyo: Riburopōto: 6–11.

Katō, Mikirō (1998) 'Shikaku to jōdō' [The Dead Angle and Emotion], *Taiyō* 97: 118–21.

Kawamoto, Saburō (2003) *Hayashi Fumiko no Shōwa* [*Hayashi Fumiko's Shōwa*], Tokyo: Shinshokan.

Kirihara, Donald (1992) *Patterns of Time: Mizoguchi and the 1930s*, Wisconsin: University of Wisconsin Press.

Komatsu, Hiroshi (1996) 'Kenji Mizoguchi', in Geoffrey Nowell-Smith (ed.), *The Oxford History of World Cinema*, New York and Oxford: Oxford University Press: 418–19.

Minami, Hiroshi (1983) 'Gaisetsu: Nihon modanizumu ni tsuite' [An Outline of Japan's Modernism], *Gendai no Esupuri* 188: 5–7.

Mizoguchi, Kenji (1991) 'Tsuchi no nioi: *Gion no kyōdai* o tsukuru maeni' [The Smell of Earth: Before Making *Sisters of the Gion*], in Nishida 1991: 10–13.

Mizoguchi, Kenji et al. (1991 [1937]) 'Mizoguchi Kenji zadankai' [Round Table Discussion with Mizoguchi Kenji], in Nishida 1991: 14–30.

Nishida, Nobuyoshi (ed.) (1991) *Mizoguchi Kenji shūsei* [*Compilation of Works on Mizoguchi Kenji*], Tokyo: Kinema Junpō-sha.

Nygren, Scott (1998) 'Reconsidering Modernism: Japanese Film and the Postmodern Context', in O'Grady 1998: 71–3.

O'Grady, Gerald (ed.) (1998) *Mizoguchi the Master*, Tokyo: The Japan Foundation.

Russell, Catherine (1995) ' "Overcoming Modernity": Gender and the Pathos of History in Japanese Film Melodrama', *Camera Obscura* 35: 131–57.

Sakurai, Heigorō (1927) 'Modan gāru to shokugyō fujin' [Modern Girls and Working Women], *Josei*, August: 169–74.

Sasō, Tsutomu (1997) 'Mizoguchi Kenji zen eiga' [The Complete Films of Mizoguchi Kenji], in Sasō and Nishida 1997: 56–131.

Sasō, Tsutomu and Nishida, Nobuyoshi (eds) (1997) *Eiga tokuhon Mizoguchi Kenji* [*Mizoguchi Kenji: A Film Reader*], Tokyo: Firumu Āto-sha.

Satō, Tadao (1982) *Sekai eiga zenshū, Nihon-hen* [*The Great Films of the World: Japan*], Tokyo: Kinema Junpō-sha.

—— (1995) *Nihon eiga-shi 1: 1896–1940* [*Japanese Film History Vol.1: 1896–1940*], Tokyo: Iwanami Shoten.

Shindō, Kaneto (1976) *Aru eiga-kantoku: Mizoguchi Kenji to Nihon eiga* [*A Film Director: Mizoguchi Kenji and Japanese Cinema*], Tokyo: Iwanami Shoten.

Silverberg, Miriam (1991) 'The Modern Girl as Militant', in Gail Lee Bernstein (ed.), *Recreating Japanese Women, 1600–1945*, Berkeley: University of California Press: 239–66.

—— (1992) 'Constructing the Japanese Ethnography of Modernity', *The Journal of Asian Studies* 51 (1): 30–54.

Yamada, Kazuo (1976) *Nihon eiga no 80 nen* [*Eighty Years of Japanese Cinema*], Tokyo: Issei-sha.

Mizoguchi Kenji Filmography

The Resurrection of Love (*Ai ni yomigaeru hi*, 1923)
Hometown (*Furusato*, 1923)
Dream of Youth (*Seishun no yumeji*, 1923)
Harbor of Desire (*Jōen no chimata*, 1923)

The Song of Failure (Haizan no uta wa kanashi, 1923)
813, The Adventures of Arsène Lupin (813, 1923)
Blood and Soul (Chi to rei, 1923)
Harbor in the Fog (Kiri no Minato, 1923)
The Night (Yoru, 1923)
In the Ruins (Haikyo no naka, 1923)
The Song of the Mountain Pass (Tōge no uta, 1923)
The Sad Idiot (Kanashiki hakuchi, 1924)
Death at Dawn (Akatsuki no shi, 1924)
The Queen of Modern Times (Gendai no jo-ō, 1924)
Strong is the Female (Josei wa tsuyoshi, 1924)
This Dusty World (Jinkyō, 1924)
The Trace of a Turkey (Shichimenchō no yukue, 1924)
Chronicle of the May Rain (Samidare zōshi, 1924)
The Death of Policeman Ito (Itō junsa no shi, 1924) (co-director)
An Axe to Cut Love (Koi o tatsu ono, 1924) (co-director)
Woman of Pleasure (Kanraku no onna, 1924)
Queen of the Circus (Kyokubadan no jo-ō, 1924)
No Money, No Fight (Uchen puchan, 1925)
Ah, The Special Service War Vessel, Kanto (Aa Tokumukan Kantō, 1925) (co-director)
Out of College (Gakusō o idete, 1925)
The Earth Smiles (Daichi wa hohoemu, 1925)
The White Lily Laments (Shirayuri wa nageku, 1925)
Under the Crimson Sunset (Akai yūhi ni terasarete, 1925) (co-director)
The Song of Hometown (Furusato no uta, 1925)
A Sketch on the Road (Gaijyo no suketchi, 1925)
The Human Being (Ningen, 1925)
General Nogi and Kuma-san (Nogi taishō to Kuma-san, 1925)
The Copper Coin King (Dōka-ō, 1926)
A Paper Doll's Whisper of Spring (Kami ningyō haru no sasayaki, 1926)
It's My Fault – New Version (Shinsetsu ono ga tsumi, 1926)
The Passion of a Woman Teacher (Kyōren no onna shishō, 1926)
The Boy from the Sea (Kaikoku danji, 1926)
Money (Kane, 1926)
The Imperial Grace (Kō-on, 1927)
The Cuckoo (Jihi shinchō, 1927)
A Man's Life Part 1: Money is All For Men (Hito no isshō-ningen banji kane no maki, 1928)
A Man's Life Part 2: How Hard Life Is (Hito no isshō-ukiyo wa tsuraine no maki, 1928)
A Man's Life Part 3: The Reunion of Kuma and Tora (Hito no isshō-Kuma to Tora saikai no maki, 1928)
My Loving Daughter (Musume kawaiya, 1928)
The Nihon Bridge (Nihonbashi, 1929)
The Morning Sun Shines (Asahi wa kagayaku, 1929)
Tokyo March (Tōkyō kōshinkyokyu, 1929)
Metropolitan Symphony (Tōkai kōkyōgaku, 1929)
Hometown (Furusato, 1930)
Okichi, Mistress of a Foreigner (Tōjin Okichi, 1930)
And Yet They Go on (Shikamo karera wa yuku, 1931)
The Man of the Right Moment (Toki no ujigami, 1932)
Dawn in Manchuria (Manmō kenkoku no reimei, 1932)

The White Threads of the Waterfall (*Taki no shiraito*, 1933)
Gion Festival (*Gion matsuri*, 1933)
The Shinpu Group (*Shinpū ren*, 1934)
The Mountain Pass of Love and Hate (*Aizō tōge*, 1934)
The Downfall of Osen (*Orizuru Osen*, 1935)
Oyuki, the Virgin (*Maria no Oyuki*, 1935)
Okichi (*Ojō Okichi*, 1935) (co-director)
The Poppy (*Gubigin sō*, 1935)
Osaka Elegy (*Naniwa erejī*, 1936)
The Sisters of Gion (*Gion no kyōdai*, 1936)
The Straits of Love and Hate (*Aien-kyō*, 1937)
The Song of the Camp (*Roei no uta*, 1938)
Ah, My Hometown (*Aa furusato*, 1938)
The Story of Late Chrysanthemums (*Zangiku monogatari*, 1939)
The Woman of Osaka (*Naniwa onna*, 1940)
The Life of an Actor (*Geidō ichidai otoko*, 1941)
The Loyal 47 Ronin (*Genroku chūshingura*, 1941–2) (two parts)
Three Generations of Danjuro (*Danjūrō sandai*, 1944)
Miyamoto Musashi (1944)
The Famous Sword, Bijomaru (*Meitō Bijomaru*, 1945)
Victory Song (*Hisshōka*, 1945) (segment only – rest of the film directed by Makino Masa-
    hiro, Shimizu Hiroshi and Tasaka Tomotaka)
The Victory of Women (*Josei no shōri*, 1946)
Utamaro and His Five Women (*Utamaro o meguru gonin no onna*, 1946)
The Loves of Sumako, the Actress (*Joyū Sumako no koi*, 1947)
Women of the Night (*Yoru no onna tachi*, 1948)
My Love Has Been Burning (*Waga koi wa moenu*, 1949)
A Picture of Madame Yuki (*Yuki fujin ezu*, 1950)
Miss Oyu (*Oyū-sama*, 1951)
Lady Musashino (*Musashino fujin*, 1951)
The Life of O-Haru (*Saikaku ichidai onna*, 1952)
The Tales of the Pale and Silvery Moon after the Rain (*Ugetsu monogatari*, 1953)
Gion Festival Music (*Gion bayashi*, 1953)
Sansho, the Bailiff (*Sanshō dayū*, 1954)
The Woman of Rumor (*Uwasa no onna*, 1954)
A Story from Chikamatsu (*Chikamatsu monogatari*, 1954)
The Empress Yang Kwei-Fei (*Yōkihi*, 1955)
New Tales of the Taira Clan (*Shin Heike monogatari*, 1955)
Red Light District (*Akasen chitai*, 1956)

3

TURNING SERIOUS

Yamanaka Sadao's *Humanity and Paper Balloons* (1937)

Freda Freiberg

Humanity and Paper Balloons (*Ninjō kamifūsen*, 1937) has a special place in the hearts of Japanese film scholars. The sorrow it arouses is due not only to the film's intrinsic qualities, but also to events extrinsic to the film. It is hard to separate one's response to *Humanity and Paper Balloons* from a deep sense of loss at the untimely demise of its talented young director, Yamanaka Sadao, on the battlefront in China, soon after its release.

In the celebrated final image of the film, a paper balloon, which has drifted out of the empty room formerly inhabited by the now dead *samurai* couple, eludes the grasp of a neighbourhood boy, lands in a gutter, and floats off into the background. This sublime scene has evoked much discussion because it is so powerful and because it evokes various levels of metaphorical interpretation. As Hasumi Shigehiko aptly describes it, it transforms the heavy materiality of existence into lightness (Chiba 1999a: 1031). Paper balloons are indeed the lightest of objects and they float in the lightest of breezes, leading Hasumi to read the scene as a metaphor for death. As it follows the untimely deaths of two of the main characters, Shinza, the good-natured larrikin and Unno, the refined but cowardly *rōnin* (unemployed/leaderless *samurai*), the balloon's movement and destiny can certainly be associated with their dashed hopes and their fate.

Some have also read the scene as symbolic of the traditional Buddhist notion of the fragility and brevity of life. Although this is usually associated with natural phenomena of brief duration such as cherry blossoms, autumn leaves and fireflies, it is associated here with a man-made object carried along by the natural phenomenon of the wind. Others, yet again, have read the scene as Yamanaka's premonition of his own demise, and the film as a whole as an expression of his own fears of mortality. Takizawa Hajime claims that Yamanaka's last two films were made under the shadow of his conscription (Chiba 1999a: 1056). A friend reported that when he said farewell to his friends at Kyōto station, he looked pale and wan and made no attempt to express patriotic sentiments. Instead, he pronounced the dismal words, 'It's all over' (Chiba 1999b: 371–2).

Figure 7 Humanity and Paper Balloons (1937): a bitter critique of traditional values focusing on the fragile existence of its *samurai* couple. BFI Stills, Posters and Designs.

In the light of this knowledge, it is easy to read the doomed destiny of both the cheeky Shinza and the cowardly *samurai* as a synecdoche of Yamanaka's own situation. The glint of the knife in the hand of the *samurai*'s traditional wife as she looms menacingly over the pathetic non-heroic *samurai*, the ominous sounds of the unsheathing of swords and the stamping of feet, as well as the glint of the sword in the hand of the *oyabun* (*yakuza* boss) presaging the end of Shinza, can all be linked to Yamanaka's personal fears and premonitions at the time. The overall darkness of the film and the prevalence of dismal weather in it can be read as objective correlatives of his gloomy and depressed mood. The final image of the floating balloon, wafting in the breeze and finally coming to a halt in the gutter, could represent his fragile existence, buffeted by the winds of time, briefly borne aloft by benign breezes, but finally deposited ignominiously in a dirty ditch.

Like Barthes responding to the last photograph of the doomed prisoner, Lewis Payne, we are overcome with the heart-rending realisation that 'he is dead and he is going to die' (Barthes 1981: 95). In succumbing to these thoughts and feelings, we are, however, reading the film as the expression of the thoughts and feelings of its 'author'. In so doing, we are overlooking the collaborative nature of film production, the importance of the industrial and social context, the formal construction of the film, and the fact that it is a *jidai-geki* (period film). Despite its power, the last scene is in many ways a postscript or epilogue to the dramatic action of the film, which is adapted from a *kabuki* stage play and performed by a troupe of radical *kabuki* actors. By examining the film's narrative and formal construction, as well as its performance style and place within various relevant industrial, critical and ideological contexts, we may also find other fruitful ways of assessing its significance.

Although he was barely 28 when he made *Humanity and Paper Balloons*, Yamanaka had already directed more than 20 films over the previous five years. Unfortunately only three of them have survived, so we have to rely on published responses by his contemporaries for accounts of the rest.[1] He was widely celebrated by the critics of his time as one of the great artists of Japanese cinema, and the loss of all but three of his films has therefore undoubtedly impoverished the study of Japanese film. Yamanaka was acclaimed from his directorial debut onwards and he was showered with awards in later years. In the first of a series of newspaper profiles of noteworthy new Japanese film directors published in 1933, Mori Iwao rated him superior to all other Japanese film directors in editing and camera skills (Chiba 1999a: 191–2). Just two years later, the critic Togata Sachio observed that Yamanaka was more widely discussed by Japanese critics than any other Japanese film director and that all his films had become talking points (Chiba 1999a: 303).

Critics writing in the leading Japanese film journals *Kinema Junpō* and *Eiga Hyōron*, such as Kishi Matsuo and Aikawa Kusuhiko, were initially impressed by Yamanaka's sophisticated use of the film medium and by the directorial control he exercised. They were excited by the unexpected discovery of such a talented film artist in an area of the industry which normally churned out cheap *chanbara* (swordplay films) that were little more than vehicles for the flamboyant performances of their stars. They also noted Yamanaka's striking use of framing and editing, his telling use of prop details, and his use of long shots and vertical lines to create depth of perspective and emotional effect (Chiba 1999a: 23–5 and 27–37). Yamanaka's film *The Life of Bangaku* (*Bangaku no isshō*, 1933) was widely hailed as a masterpiece and as the first serious *jidai-geki*. Yamanaka was also praised for highlighting social issues and exposing social injustice as well as being the first Japanese director properly to unite form with content (Chiba 1999a: 169–91).

By 1935, the critics were encouraging him to be more serious and realist. Though recognising his skill in balancing humour and pathos, in restraining the excesses of his star performers in order to obtain more subtle performances, and in introducing social criticism into commercial entertainment, people such as Ōtsuka Kyōichi expressed the view that he should pursue his true artistic bent – to describe the truth (Chiba 1999a: 315–21). Accordingly, they heaped praise on *The Village Tattooed Man* (*Machi no irezumi-mono*, 1935), his first collaboration with the Zenshinza theatre company and the first of his films without a star performer in the lead, for its naturalistic speech and performances as well as its seriousness and truthfulness (Chiba 1999a: 362–5, 381–3 and 385–7).

Post-war Yamanaka criticism has necessarily suffered from the small number of surviving film prints. Nevertheless, his work has received some attention. In their pioneering history of Japanese cinema, Anderson and Richie acknowledged his importance in the development of the *jidai-geki* towards greater realism (Anderson and Richie 1982: 92–5). Recent Western scholarship has acknowledged Yamanaka as a precursor of Kurosawa, as a practitioner of comedy akin to Ozu, and as a formal stylist (Barrett 1992: 218; Goodwin 1994: 109–12). By performing close analysis on *Humanity and Paper Balloons*, both Noël Burch and Donald Richie have demonstrated a quasi-geometric artistry in Yamanaka's framing and editing. Both also stress the 'Japaneseness' of his work, albeit on different grounds. Burch finds that his surviving comedy, *A Pot Worth a Million Ryo (Tange Sazen: hyakuman ryō no tsubo*, 1935), exemplifies the formal difference of pre-war and wartime Japanese cinema from dominant international modes of production in its extensive use of the long shot, avoidance of shot-reverse-shot editing, and use of 'empty' shots, i.e. shots devoid of human figures and apparently unrelated to the narrative (Burch 1979: 193). Richie finds Yamanaka's use of the inside/outside dichotomy a reversal of the usual American model and very 'Japanese' in locating safety and security at home, and danger and oppression in the outside world (Richie 1988: 55, 62).

Recent Japanese critics, on the other hand, have stressed Yamanaka's cosmopolitanism, his use of quotations from European and American films, as well as his genre-bending borrowings from contemporary filmmakers in Japan (Hasumi 1988; Satō 1988: 52–3; Yoshimoto 2000: 237). They assert that, along with other young innovators, he enriched the *jidai-geki* by importing the humour and humanism of the Shōchiku home drama into his Nikkatsu *jidai-geki* films.[2] In an extended essay originally published in 1985, Satō Tadao stressed Yamanaka's love of Hollywood cinema and his borrowings from it; but also noted his 'risky' move away from rather cheerful popular cinema (in which legendary heroes are portrayed by popular screen stars) to a more sombre and realist form of art cinema towards the end of his career (Chiba 1999a: 986–1009).

Early Japanese criticism of Yamanaka films no longer extant already noted his distinctiveness as a formal innovator and film stylist, and this aspect of his work has received further attention from Burch (1979: 192–7) and Richie (1988). While acknowledging the value of this writing, I now wish to stress Yamanaka's collaboration with the progressive theatre and debt to the left-leaning artistic culture of his time. I want to argue that, despite the growth of jingoistic, militaristic and imperialistic rhetoric at the upper levels of Japanese political and military culture, and despite the vigilance of the censors, a leftist fraternity of writers, critics, theatre performers and filmmakers remained active and productive in cultural production right through to the end of the 1930s. This grouping was cosmopolitan, critical of traditional Japanese institutions, concerned with the inequalities in Japanese society and sympathetic to the marginal battlers and losers in its midst. Its members were familiar with the theories and practices of Marxist and modernist literature, theatre and film, and were fans of European as well as of Hollywood cinema. The critics who promoted Yamanaka's career, the head of film production at Nikkatsu in 1935–38, and the theatrical troupe that performed in his later films all belonged to this progressive and socially critical sub-culture. The politicians and bureaucrats may have fostered the development of a monumental style of nationalistic film-making, but they were only partially successful. There was still strong support for works of social realism and incisive social criticism within Japanese film culture.

Yamanaka served an apprenticeship in screenwriting and direction at a Kyōto studio that specialised in *jidai-geki* and, at the tender age of 22, in his first year as a fully fledged director, he directed five silent movies in quick succession. They were apparently star vehicles for the *jidai-geki* star performer, Arashi Kanjurō, who had his own independent production company. In 1933, Yamanaka moved to one of the major film companies, Nikkatsu, where he made popular films featuring two other macho *jidai-geki* star performers, Ōkouchi Denjirō and Kataoka Chiezō, as well as two films with the Zenshinza theatre collective. He did not make his first sound film until July 1934, as Nikkatsu was late in converting to sound. In 1937, he left Nikkatsu while the company was in dire critical straits and being restructured under Shōchiku management. Yamanaka preferred to work instead for the dynamic new Tōhō company, which had now replaced Nikkatsu as Shōchiku's main rival. It was at the Kyōto sound studio of JO, which was incorporated into the Tōhō bloc of companies in 1936, that he made *Humanity and Paper Balloons* with Zenshinza, his first and last film for Tōhō.

All of Yamanaka's films were made in Kyōto and all were *jidai-geki*. The three surviving movies suggest that Yamanaka was moving away from cheerful light entertainment towards darker art cinema. I would argue that it was not just his conscription that influenced this shift, but also his collaboration with Zenshinza and the influence of left-liberal colleagues in the industry. Of the surviving films, *A Pot Worth a Million Ryo*, made for Nikkatsu, appears to exemplify the more cheerful, popular and commercial strain in his oeuvre and a comparison with *Humanity and Paper Balloons* is therefore instructive.

A Pot Worth a Million Ryo was a light entertainment starring Ōkouchi Denjirō as the popular *jidai-geki* hero, Tange Sazen.[3] A wild and rebellious outsider, Tange Sazen is one-eyed and one-armed as a result of injuries incurred during his notorious career as a swordsman. Itō Daisuke's earlier film version of his career, shot in 1933, had portrayed him as a tragic hero, a loyal retainer who is betrayed by his lord and exacts a terrible revenge (Barrett 1989: 213).[4] In Yamanaka's film, the character has become a lazy loafer kept as a bouncer by his mistress who runs an archery parlour staffed by pretty girls. They adopt an orphaned boy who keeps goldfish in a bowl that is, unknown to them all, a valuable heirloom of the feudal lord – the pot worth a million *ryō*. The pot, believed worthless, had been given to the lord's younger brother as a wedding present and then discarded as rubbish, ending up in the boy's hands. The pursuit of the pot, once its value is recognised, is delayed by the laziness and dalliance of Genzaburō, the young lord, and the jealousy of Hagino, his wife, but finally rendered fruitless by the connivance of Tange and Genzaburō, thus enabling the boy to retain his treasured goldfish bowl and the henpecked young lord to continue his affair with a pretty girl in the archery parlour.

The film's light comic tone is maintained by a plethora of visual and verbal gags and the recurrent use of jaunty mood music. The major action sequence, the fencing duel between Tange and Genzaburō, is rendered farcical, with both participants swinging their arms about, grunting and grimacing, and generally making a mockery of the event. Ōkouchi Denjirō indulges jokingly in his characteristic grimaces and gestures, and exhibits ridiculous extremes of behaviour – alternating between excessive inertia and excessive movement – in a probable parody of his performance style in Itō Daisuke's earlier film versions of the Tange Sazen legend. Nevertheless, the absence of swordplay and heroics suggests that Yamanaka's movie is not just a parody, but also a critique of the conventional *jidai-geki* macho lead. Tange Sazen is portrayed as a reluctant hero, more interested in wine and women than in action. He is motivated to engage in a duel only when he is desperately in need of money, and promptly agrees not to display his prowess against his hopelessly inferior competitor in return for a substantial reward. The young lord too is ridiculed as ineffectual and decadent. Both men, unlike the conventional self-sufficient and determined hero of *jidai-geki*, are dependent on women, lazy and demoralised. However, they do reveal a more humane side to their characters in their attitude to the orphaned boy. In forgoing a fortune so that he can keep his treasured goldfish bowl, they show that even if they are fond of their comforts and prone to deceit, they are not excessively mercenary. *Ninjō* (humanity and compassion), in other words, wins out over greed.

It was not this delightful 1935 comedy but two other Yamanaka movies that garnered critical awards that year. *Chuji Kunisada* (*Kunisada Chūji*), a film also starring Ōkouchi Denjirō and based on the career of another popular 'nihilistic' *jidai-geki* hero, came fifth in the Ten Best Japanese films of the year, and *The Tattooed Townsman* (*Machi no irezumi-mono*), his first collaboration with Zenshinza, came second.[5] It is interesting to note that the more highly rated film did not star Ōkouchi Denjirō or any other *jidai-geki* star performer, but the Zenshinza ensemble of actors who, as well as appearing in *Humanity and Paper Balloons*, went on to feature in Mizoguchi's wartime masterpiece, *The Loyal 47 Ronin* (*Genroku chūshingura*, 1941–2).

The Tattooed Townsman was adapted from the play of the same name by Hasegawa Shin that featured in Zenshinza's stage repertoire. It was the tragic story of a *yakuza* (gangster) who comes out of prison and finds it hard to find a place in society. Hasegawa Shin was a prolific popular playwright and novelist who specialised in affecting tales about wandering outlaws whose violent behaviour and aggressive demeanour masked a lonely personality yearning for love and affection. Yamanaka had already adapted one of his stories for his previous film, *Yatappe from Seki* (*Seki no Yatappe*, 1935).

Both *Shunso Kochiyama* (*Kōchiyama Shunso*, 1936) and *Humanity and Paper Balloons* were free adaptations of late *kabuki* plays by Mokuami Kawatake as well as collaborations with Zenshinza. (The former also featured a very young Hara Setsuko as the sweet young heroine who has to be saved from a fate worse than death.) The Zenshinza theatre troupe specialised in modernised perform-ances of *kabuki* plays, after finding that they could not attract audiences to avant-garde productions and were forbidden to stage contemporary left-wing plays. The founders of the company had been trained in the traditional *kabuki* theatre, but had abandoned it and founded their own independent company under the influence of modernism and Marxism. In doing so, they rejected the rigid hierarchy and star system of traditional *kabuki*, as well as its conservatism in repertoire and stagecraft. They modernised the use of spoken language so that it would be intelligible to the audience and closer to everyday contemporary speech. They also tried to make their settings, props and costumes historically accurate and abandoned the stylised gestures of traditional *kabuki* in favour of more naturalistic performances. In short, they tried to introduce realism into *kabuki*. They also lived in a collective and worked as an ensemble. In 1947 they joined the Japanese Communist Party (Powell 1979).

The Mokuami plays were a far cry from the more conservative *kabuki* repertoire. Rather than celebrating the feudal loyalty of retainers as traditional plays such as *The Treasury of Loyal Retainers* (*Kanadehon chūshingura*) and *The Subscription List* (*Kanjinchō*) did,[6] they focused on the more lower-class, disreputable residents of Edo (pre-modern Tokyo). Driven by lust for money and/or women, Mokuami's heroes – shrewd businessmen, dissolute monks, unscrupulous *rōnin* and *yakuza* – were lovable rogues who resorted to extortion, abduction and robbery (Miyake 1971: 130–6). They lived among the common people in town, in crowded tenements, and shared with them economic privation, harassment by the authorities and resentment of the privileged upper classes. Mokuami's plays belonged to the *kizewa-mono* genre and were entertaining, spiced with visual and verbal comedy, romantic songs and colourful characters (Halford and Halford 1956: 431; Miyake 1971: 49–50). Written in the hiatus between the fall of the Tokugawa and the consolidation of the Meiji regime, they reflected a time of the breakdown of traditional authority and morality when a certain anarchic spirit came to the fore.

The 1873 Mokuami play on which *Humanity and Paper Balloons* was based was known as *Kamiyui Shinza* (*Shinza the Barber*), although its formal title was *Tsuyu kosode mukashi hachijō* (*The Old Story of the Wet Silk Coat*). The two central characters are Shinza, a rascally barber and Chōbei, a shrewd landlord. Shinza is in love with Okuma, a merchant's daughter who is secretly in love with her father's clerk, Shushichi. Shinza tricks the lovers, pretending to help them elope, but disposes of Shushichi and abducts Okuma. The girl's father sends Chōbei, the landlord, to retrieve her with the ransom money for Shinza, but the cunning Chōbei manages to talk Shinza into returning the girl for half the ransom money, secretly pocketing the other half himself (Miyake 1971: 133–4; Halford and Halford 1956: 344–5).

Shinza and Chōbei remain major characters in the film, but they share the limelight with many other characters in a densely populated and intricately plotted narrative and their devious behaviour is detailed somewhat differently. Shinza is given more complex motivations for the abduction – including class resentment. He is also shown to be a likable lad with a generous nature, making him a popular local hero. He runs an illicit local gambling den and is harassed by the henchmen of the local *oyabun* (*yakuza* boss) who resents Shinza's private initiative because it threatens his monopoly of the gambling business. The 'respectable' people in town have good relations with the *yakuza* and use them to dispose of unwelcome visitors such as Shinza who has already been beaten up by the gang. It was Okuma's father and lover who called them in. Okuma's father, a timber merchant in the play, has become a moneylender with upwardly mobile aspirations in the film. He is busy arranging a match for his daughter with a *samurai*, Mori. This *samurai* also profits from the help of the *yakuza*. He is being pestered by a *rōnin* for help in gaining employment, apparently justified by a prior debt incurred by him to the *rōnin*'s father, but the *samurai* ignores both the debt and the pleas, displaying neither *giri* (a debt, duty of obligation) nor *ninjō* (human compassion). Instead, he asks his hosts to rid him of his unwanted visitor, and they promptly send for the gangsters.

Although the film retains the play's central dramatic scene of the landlord cheating Shinza of half his reward, Chōbei's deviousness is modified (he openly proposes splitting the ransom money with Shinza) and the episode is generally not weighted as the crucial dramatic scene of the film. The scenes in which Chōbei appears with Shinza provide some comic respite in a film which is otherwise much darker (literally and emotionally) than *A Pot Worth a Million Ryo*. The opening and closing of the film are gloomy, involving the ignominious death of a *rōnin* who cannot even end his life properly. The old *samurai* whose suicide marks the opening had sold his sword so that he could feed himself and so, unable to perform ritual *seppuku*, he has hanged himself. The other *samurai* does not have the courage or honesty to face his degradation and it is left to his wife to stage a double suicide by killing him and then herself with a humble knife. The scene in which the wife takes out the knife in readiness for these actions is preceded by a scene at the bridge, where Shinza keeps his appointment with the *yakuza* and is also apparently killed, by the sword of the *oyabun*, as punishment for his insubordination and misdemeanours.

But all these major actions are elided and are pre-figured and/or post-figured instead. The old *samurai*'s suicide is a *fait accompli* at the start; we see and hear the neighbours discussing it, the authorities coming to investigate it, and the wake following it, but the hanging is not shown. Shinza's abduction of Okuma is pre-figured by him downing his umbrella and moving stealthily towards her, but it is also not pictured. The film then turns its attention to the *rōnin* further along the street in the rain, waiting for another chance to importune Mori, the *samurai*, as he leaves the pawnbroker's home. Later Shushichi races around searching for Okuma and we see her tied up in Shinza's room. Shinza's death is pre-figured by an ominous stamping of feet and unsheathing of swords, but the film then cuts back to the interior of the *rōnin*'s room. We see the wife take out the knife and move towards her prone sleeping husband in the darkness, but the scene fades to the next morning. Again, as in the beginning, the neighbours announce what has happened: *shinjū* (double suicide).

There are very few gags. Shinza tricks the mean landlord into providing more alcohol at the wake; the blind masseur steals back his pipe from the man who has stolen it; a tenement resident expresses hope for fine weather for the imminent festival, and the next scene shows it pouring with rain; Chōbei wheedles half the ransom money out of Shinza. But these incidents seem more like sardonic comments than real jokes, and the mood on the whole is bleak. The wet weather mars the tenement festival celebration, soaks the *rōnin* and enables Okuma to become Shinza's prey when her lover leaves her alone to fetch an umbrella. There is a predominance of dark nocturnal shots with a series of night-time images of rain dripping on the pavements and leaking into the rooms in the latter half of the film. Mood music is used very sparingly – briefly only at the very beginning and end of the film – and it is far from jaunty. Not only are the deaths, the abduction and the fights elided, but Yamanaka denies viewers the exhilarating heroics of *chanbara* action. Instead, both Shinza and the *rōnin* are brutally beaten by the *yakuza* and Shinza is also slapped and kicked by the *oyabun*.

The main characters are even less heroic than those of *A Pot Worth a Million Ryo*. According to genre conventions, the *samurai* (or *rōnin*) hero disposes of his numerous opponents effortlessly, with speed and grace, especially when those opponents are presumptuous riff-raff (as the *yakuza* henchmen are here). The *rōnin* in *Humanity and Paper Balloons*, however, is no hero, but a weakling who is incompetent even as a fighter. The petty gangster Shinza is more of a hero – at least he has a cheeky spirit and spark of defiance that motivates him to take action and face the consequences when his pride is offended. The *samurai* cannot even kill himself; his wife has to do it.

Having said this, the issue of *ninjō* does recur and it is weighted this time by its presence in the title. Although the title is usually translated as 'Humanity and Paper Balloons', there is no connective between *ninjō* and *kamifūsen*, the humanity and the paper balloons. Normally there would be a *'no'* (possessive connective) or a *'to'* (and). Their absence instead suggests an equation: that *ninjō* has the value and weight of paper balloons. As noted already, the final shot of the film accrues a metaphorical density which partly seems to symbolise the fragile and ephemeral existence of the *samurai* couple. The wife made these paper balloons as a temporary livelihood, to maintain them while her husband was unemployed, so it also suggests that their hopes have been an unrealistic pipe dream and therefore, by extension, there is also no hope for the whole pitiful neighbourhood. But the image also incurs associations with the Buddhist notion of material life as a fragile, ephemeral and unstable 'floating world'. The association of the balloons with *ninjō* in the title brings the airy, unreal and fragile connotations of the balloon to bear on the traditional value of *ninjō*. We have already seen that Mori fails to practise either *giri* or *ninjō*, the prized values of the *samurai* class, in his behaviour towards the *rōnin*. We have seen too that the 'respectable' townspeople display no compassion for Shinza. On the other hand, the *rōnin* inspires *ninjō* in Shinza, the lowly gangster, who displays spontaneous compassion for his neighbour on several occasions, offering him material assistance and, on one occasion, even risking his own safety. In other words, the film suggests that although *ninjō* may appear to be a fictional construct for the privileged who certainly do not practise it, its vestiges survive among the under-privileged lower classes.[7]

The differences between the two Yamanaka films I have focused on here demonstrate a shift from the parodic and comic to the weighty and serious that

Davis has noted was characteristic of the *jidai-geki* in the later 1930s (Davis 1996: 81). While Davis associates this shift with the rise of a state-endorsed, nationalistic, monumental style of filmmaking, I would argue that serious filmmaking was equally encouraged by the Left and that its critical stance on Japanese culture and society continued to permeate Japanese cinema until the end of the 1930s. The extraordinary realism of the early war movies – which also astonished Washington intelligence analysts (Freiberg 1996: 33–4) – and the emphasis on the suffering and oppression of socially marginal characters even in some of the films that Davis labels monumental, suggest a lingering debt to leftist aesthetics and politics.

Unlike in the case of monumental cinema, *Humanity and Paper Balloons* does not seek to reify Japanese artistic or spiritual traditions. On the contrary, it provides a disillusioned and somewhat bitter critique of traditional values by exposing the selfishness and greed of the privileged classes, and focusing on the trials and tribulations of the marginal and the underprivileged. The camera repeatedly returns to the narrow street between the tenements which is pictured teeming with street-sellers, petty tradesmen and harassed housewives, whose movements into and out of frame are orchestrated and edited in ways that stress the overcrowded and congested living space of the poor. The film lacks the spectacular long takes and spectacular set design of Mizoguchi's *The Loyal 47 Ronin* that endowed traditional Japanese architecture and culture with monumental weight and grandeur – in fact, spectacle is altogether avoided. Furthermore, the making of paper balloons in itself was not a particularly Japanese artistic tradition. The motif was apparently borrowed from French cinema, inspired by a scene in Jacques Feyder's *Pension Mimosas* (1935) (Thornton 1995: 53; Hasumi 1988: 48).[8]

The pursuit of realism was advocated and supported by the leftist critics who had a strong influence on film culture, especially on the awards. Kishi Matsuo, the critic who first discovered Yamanaka and promoted his career, was an original member of the Friends of Prokino.[9] Critics at both *Kinema Junpō* and *Eiga Hyōron* urged Yamanaka to be less playful and more serious and to concentrate on a realist art cinema that truthfully reflected social realities while maintaining his formally innovative style. They endorsed and praised his collaborations with Zenshinza in preference to the films featuring popular stars such as Kataoka Chiezō and Ōkouchi Denjirō. Even after his death, and as late as 1939, they continued to support films that demonstrated a commitment to social realism and to leftist themes such as Naruse Mikio's *The Whole Family Works* (*Hataraku ikka*, 1939) and Uchida Tomu's remarkable neo-realist *Earth* (*Tsuchi*, 1939).[10]

Kawarazaki Chōjūrō, who played the *rōnin* in *Humanity and Paper Balloons*, toured the Soviet Union in 1928 where he performed with Ichikawa Sadanji's *kabuki* company and was impressed by what he observed. He later viewed productions of Marxist and modernist theatre in Berlin and Paris. In 1931, not long after his return to Japan, Kawarazaki had founded Zenshinza, together with another radicalised *kabuki* actor, Nakamura Kan'emon (who plays Shinza). It was Kawarazaki, rather than Yamanaka, who rehearsed the actors on the set

59

of *Shunso Kochiyama* (Thornton 1995: 53) – and also, one assumes, on the set of *Humanity and Paper Balloons*. *Kabuki* theatre is an actors' theatre; it does not employ a director. But while traditional *kabuki* theatre was hierarchical and dominated by the big star actor dynasties, Zenshinza prided itself on its collective, collaborative mode of operation. Yamanaka admired their modesty, their team spirit and their serious approach to artistic work. In 1935, he even promised to devote all his energies to the film adaptation of *Machi no irezumi-mono* 'for the sake of Zenshinsha' (Chiba 1999a: 1005).

By collaborating with this 'modest troupe', Yamanaka therefore felt that he could make a 'true film' free of the exaggerated mannerisms of the *jidai-geki* star system (Chiba 1999a: 1005). He continued to remain dependent on theatrically trained actors and base his scripts on theatrical sources. Some contemporary critical responses to *Humanity and Paper Balloons* expressed disappointment in the film on the grounds that it merely reproduced the same narrow world of his earlier work, and that it was not sufficiently realist (Chiba 1999a: 480–1 and 483–6). Perhaps these critics were insufficiently appreciative of the modest virtue of revisiting, re-interpreting and re-articulating a familiar terrain – always the strength of the best genre directors.

In conclusion, rather than being seen as the creation of a single author, *Humanity and Paper Balloons* should be read as the collaborative product of a dissident and socially critical sub-culture then working within the Japanese film industry. At the same time, as outlined at the opening of this chapter, it remains undoubtedly true that the film was endowed with a special depth of feeling and a particular poignancy as a result of the fact that the shadow of conscription was hanging over the head of its actual director. The combination of these socio-political, industrial, historical and personal factors in the conditions of the film's production generated a particularly bitter critique of the status quo in Japan – as well as a very moving elegy for its many victims. '*La commedia e finita!*'[11]

Acknowledgements

With thanks to my friends Yoko Pinkerton, Eiichi Tosaki and Kawamura Nozomu for their invaluable assistance with research and translation.

Notes

1 Along with *Humanity and Paper Balloons*, the surviving films are *A Pot Worth a Million Ryo* (*Tange Sazen: hyakuman ryō no tsubo*, 1935) and *Shunso Kochiyama* (*Kōchiyama Shunso*, 1936).
2 Okadaira Hideo, in his review of *The Life of Bangaku* in *Eiga Hyōron* (August 1933), had already noted that Yamanaka was reinvigorating the *jidai-geki* by employing the same methods as *gendai-geki* (contemporary films): '*Gendai mono* [*gendai-geki*] have combined the nonsense film with the tendency film to make social satire. The humour seduces the audience but also touches them. *Bangaku no isshō* has the same effect' (Chiba 1999a: 183).
3 The feats and adventures of Tange Sazen featured in 15 pre-war and 11 post-war Japanese films, according to a survey of popular *jidai-geki* made between 1926 and

1966 conducted by *Kinema Junpō* for its 1967 New Year's Day edition (Spalding 1992: 143).

4 This film has not survived, but Itō's script was used in the remake, *Tange Sazen* (Makino Masahiro, 1953).

5 The latter was actually rated the best period film of the year, as first place went to Naruse Mikio's *gendai-geki, Wife, Be Like a Rose* (*Tsuma yo bara no yō ni*).

6 Both of these plays formed the basis of later wartime productions. Mizoguchi Kenji directed a screen adaptation of *Genroku chūshingura*, the modernised version of the *chūshingura* story written by the playwright Mayama Seika in the 1930s, in his monumental *The Loyal 47 Ronin*. Kurosawa adapted *The Subscription List* (*Kanjinchō*) in *The Men Who Tread on the Tiger's Tail* (*Tora no o o fumu otokotachi*, 1945).

7 A similar conclusion is drawn in Mizoguchi Kenji's *The Sisters of Gion* (*Gion no shimai* 1936), which likewise exposes the moral precepts of *giri* and *ninjō* as more common in their breach than their observance in modern Kyōto. The film came first in the critics' poll of the ten best Japanese films of 1936 and must have been familiar to Yamanaka.

8 Feyder's film also featured a petty gangster who resorts to extortion.

9 Prokino was the abbreviated name of the Proletarian Film League, a Marxist association of filmmakers and critics which arose in the late 1920s and was suppressed in the early 1930s because of its communist ideology. Kishi disavowed his support for Prokino in 1937, claiming to be against its 'openly left-wing criticism' (Nornes 2003: 28) but, as Nornes argues, 'Prokino's radicalisation of the cinema between 1929 and 1934 found a continuing existence in the hidden discursive field of the later 1930s and early 40s' (47).

10 *Earth* came first in the critics' annual awards, despite the fact that it had been made without official blessing by committed Nikkatsu staff in their spare time. Both Yamanaka and Uchida had worked with Negishi Kan'ichi, head of production at Nikkatsu in Kyōto from 1935 to 1938, who was a renowned leftist with a commitment to realist cinema and adaptations of serious literature (Tanaka 1976: 275–7).

11 Final words of Leoncavallo's opera, *I Pagliacci*, first performed in Milan, 1892.

References

Anderson, Joseph and Richie, Donald (1982) *The Japanese Film: Art and Industry*, Princeton: Princeton University Press. Expanded edition.

Barrett, Gregory (1989) *Archetypes in Japanese Film*, London and Toronto: Susquehanna University Press.

—— (1992) 'Comic Targets and Comic Styles: An Introduction to Japanese Film Comedy', in Nolletti and Desser 1992: 210–26.

Barthes, Roland (1981) *Camera Lucida*, translated by Richard Howard, New York: Hill and Wang.

Burch, Noël (1979) *To the Distant Observer: Form and Meaning in the Japanese Cinema*, Berkeley: University of California Press.

Chambers, John Whiteclay and Culbert, David (eds) (1996) *World War II: Film and History*, New York and Oxford: Oxford University Press.

Chiba Nobuo (ed.) (1999a) *Kantoku Yamanaka Sadao* [*Yamanaka Sadao Film Director*], Tokyo: Jitsugyō no Nihon-sha.

—— (1999b) *Hyōden Yamanaka Sadao* [*Critical Biography of Yamanaka Sadao*], Tokyo: Heibon-sha.

Davis, Darrell William (1996) *Picturing Japaneseness: Monumental Style, National Identity, Japanese Film*, New York: Columbia University Press.

Freiberg, Freda (1996) '*China Nights* (Japan, 1940): The Sustaining Romance of Japan at War', in Chambers and Culbert 1996: 31–46.

Goodwin, James (1994) *Akira Kurosawa and Intertextual Cinema*, Baltimore: Johns Hopkins University Press.

Halford, Aubrey S., and Halford, Giovanna M. (1956) *The Kabuki Handbook*, Vermont and Tokyo: Charles Tuttle Company.

Hasumi Shigehiko (1988) 'Sadao Yamanaka or the New Wave in the 1930s in Kyoto', *Cinemaya* 2: 46–9.

Miyake Shūtarō (1971) *Kabuki Drama*, Tokyo: Japan Travel Bureau.

Nolletti, Arthur and Desser, David (eds) (1992) *Reframing Japanese Cinema: Authorship, Genre, History*, Bloomington: Indiana University Press.

Nornes, Abé Mark (2003) *Japanese Documentary Film*, Minneapolis: University of Minnesota Press.

Powell, Brian (1979) 'Communist *Kabuki*: a Contradiction in Terms?', in James Redmon (ed.), *Themes in Drama*, vol. 1, Cambridge: Cambridge University Press: 147–67.

Richie, Donald (1988) '*Humanity and Paper Balloons*: Some Remarks on Structure', *Cinemaya* 2: 54–62.

Satō, Tadao (1988) 'The Films of Sadao Yamanaka', *Cinemaya* 2: 50–53.

Spalding, Lisa (1992) 'Period Films in the Prewar Era', in Nolletti and Desser 1992: 131–44.

Tanaka Jun'ichirō (1976) *Nihon eiga hattatsushi* [*History of the Development of Japanese Film*], vol. 2, Tokyo: Chuei Koron Co.

Thornton, S. A. (1995) 'The Shinkokugeki and the Zenshinza: Western Representational Realism and the Japanese Period Film', *Asian Cinema* 7 (2): 46–57.

Yoshimoto Mitsuhiro (2000) *Kurosawa: Film Studies and Japanese Cinema*, Durham, NC: Duke University Press, 2000.

Yamanaka Sadao Filmography

The Genta Coast: Sleeping with a Dagger (*Iso no Genta: dakine no nagadosu*, 1932)
Koban Shigure (1932)
Ogasawara: The Governor of Iki (*Ogasawara ikinokami*, 1932)
The Whistling Samurai (*Kuchibue o fuku bushi*, 1932)
Umon's 30 Tales: Sexual Salvation (*Umon sanjuban tegara obitoke buppō*, 1932)
The Satsuma Courier: The Passionate Sword (*Satsuma bikyaku: kenkō aiyoku hen*, 1933)
The Life of Bangaku (*Bangaku no isshō*, 1933)
Jirokichi the Rat-Kid: Edo Reel (*Nezumikozō Jirokichi: Edo no maki*, 1933)
Jirokichi the Rat-Kid: The Journey (*Nezumikozō Jirokichi: dōchū no maki*, 1933)
The Elegant Swordsman (*Fūryū katsujinken*, 1934)
A Footman's Success Story (*Ashigaru shussetan*, 1934)
Gantaro's Travels (*Gantarō kaidō*, 1934)
Chuji Kunisada (*Kunisada Chūji*, 1935)
A Pot Worth a Million Ryo (*Tange Sazen: hyakuman ryō no tsubo*, 1935)
Yatappe from Seki (*Seki no Yatappe*, 1935)
The Village Tattooed Man (*Machi no irezumi-mono*, 1935)
Daibosatsu Pass: Kogen Ittoryu School (*Daibosatsu tōge: kōgen ittōryū no maki*, 1935)
The Burglar's White Mask: Part 1 (*Kaitō shirozukin: zenpen*, 1935)
Shunso Kochiyama (*Kōchiyama Shunso*, 1936)
Seacoast Highway (*Uminari kaidō*, 1936)
Ishimatsu from Mori (*Mori no Ishimatsu*, 1937)
Humanity and Paper Balloons (*Ninjō kamifūsen*, 1937)

4

COUNTRY RETREAT

Shimizu Hiroshi's *Ornamental Hairpin* (1941)

Alexander Jacoby

To describe *Ornamental Hairpin* (*Kanzashi*, 1941) as a neglected film is a solecism, since, occasional *cinémathèque* and film festival screenings aside, the entire output of Shimizu Hiroshi remains undistributed outside Japan. *Ornamental Hairpin* is one of its director's richest and most complex achievements: it both encapsulates and significantly develops his characteristic methods and concerns. Its importance, moreover, is not limited to the *auteur*ist level. Made in the year of Pearl Harbor, it is also noteworthy as a subversive film produced in the context of an industry increasingly geared to propaganda. As such, it throws light on the strategies available to dissenting filmmakers in the darkest period of modern Japanese history.

Ornamental Hairpin opens as a group of pilgrims, including the heroine, Emi (Tanaka Kinuyo) and her friend, Okiku (Kawasaki Hiroko), arrive for a brief stay at a country hot spring resort. Also at the inn are a number of more long-term guests: an old man and his two grandsons; a married couple, Mr and Mrs Hiroyasu; a scholar (Saitō Tatsuo) in search of quiet to continue his work; and Nanmura (Ryū Chishū), a soldier recuperating from a leg wound sustained in China. While bathing one day, Nanmura stands on a hairpin dropped into the pool by Emi, who has now left the resort. She returns to collect it and to apologise to the soldier. Rather than going back to Tokyo, Emi remains at the inn, and hints of a romance begin to develop between her and Nanmura. Later, Okiku returns to the resort to try to persuade Emi to go back to Tokyo, but she is now resolved to stay at the inn. Gradually, the other guests depart, and even the soldier, once he has recuperated, goes back to Tokyo, leaving Emi alone.

This slim plotline is derived from *Yottsu no yubune* ('The Four Bathtubs'), a story by Ibuse Masuji (later author of *Black Rain* [*Kuroi ame*, 1969], the pre-eminent novel about the effects of the Hiroshima bombing, which was adapted into a film of the same name by Imamura Shōhei [1989].) I have not been able to read this story, and so cannot attempt a comparison of the film with its source. In any case, according to Kimata et al. (2000: 148), 'the end product is a complete transposition of the original material to Shimizu's world' (translated in Yau and Li 2004: 80). Given the general lack of familiarity with either the film or its director, I will begin this chapter by mapping Shimizu's world, and situating *Ornamental Hairpin* in the context of his thematic and stylistic concerns.

Picaresque narrative

Many of Shimizu's more famous films appear rather loosely plotted, even plotless. One of his favourite genres was the road movie: films such as *Mr Thankyou* (*Arigatō-san*, 1936), *A Star Athlete* (*Hanagata senshu*, 1937) and *Children of the Beehive* (*Hachi no su no kodomo-tachi*, 1948) consist of journeys punctuated by a sequence of encounters, with characters woven in and out of the drama. The last two of these, in fact, do not really have a main character at all. *Ornamental Hairpin* is given a certain classical coherence by its unity of place and the central role of Emi, but it is still interrupted by diversionary moments – games, jokes, scenes of local life – designed more to develop character and atmosphere than to further a narrative. Shimizu's concern, here as elsewhere, was to portray not only individuals, but also a plausible environment, community and society. This is of crucial importance in *Ornamental Hairpin*, because Shimizu is attempting to outline a plausible alternative to the social and political structures dominant in wartime Japan.

Understated style

Noël Burch (1979: 247–56) regards Shimizu as carrying to an extreme a certain tendency in Japanese cinema, essentially towards filming scenes in long shot and eschewing rhetorical close-ups. This is acceptable enough as a generalisation applied to Shimizu's sound films: his silent films are rather more Westernised in technique and often quite baroque. In fact, even some of his later films (including *Ornamental Hairpin*) contain occasional expressive close-ups, but medium to long shots are overwhelmingly prevalent in Shimizu's work after 1935. It is often assumed that this sort of camera distance equates to a detached, non-judgemental approach. In fact, Shimizu is adept at using camera placement, the position of actors, and the environment around them, to comment obliquely on his characters, but it is nevertheless true that his approach allows the viewer an unusual freedom of response. As Shimizu tended to improvise on set, his actors, too, benefited from a certain freedom to shape their own roles and create their own performances. In *Ornamental Hairpin*, these techniques have a philosophical implication: they relate to the social organisation within the resort, characterised by liberties unavailable to the majority of Japanese in a time of political repression.

Children

Shimizu's interest in children was not limited to the screen: the most famous biographical fact about the director is that he founded an orphanage from private funds after the war. His reputation still rests on his films about children, and he directed them with outstanding sympathy and sensitivity. Critics such as Yamane Sadao (2003: 34–5) have tended to sentimentalise Shimizu's achievement, pigeonholing him as the maker of charming but shallow films. In fact, Shimizu was a social critic, and his children are usually socially marginalised: they include war orphans (*Children of the Beehive*), delinquents (*The Inspection Tower* [*Mikaeri no tō*], 1941), the ill or disabled (*The Shiinomi School* [*Shiinomi gakuen*], 1955), children who do not love (*The Tale of Jiro* [*Jirō monogatari*], 1955) or who are not loved (*A Mother's Love* [*Bojō*], 1950) by their parents, and children who are rejected by their fellows (*Forget Love for Now* [*Koi mo wasurete*], 1937). *Ornamental Hairpin* is atypical, though not unique, in that children play only a supporting role; it is also unusual in that they are happy. The contrast is telling. In many of Shimizu's films, children are made miserable by the pressures of conventional society; in *Ornamental Hairpin*, they flourish in an alternative one.

Vagrancy

Just as Shimizu's children tend to be outsiders, so he is more generally concerned with people who have no settled place in society. His favourite settings are those where people are in transit: harbours (*Forget Love for Now*, *Japanese Girls at the Harbour* [*Minato no Nihon musume*], 1933); vehicles, especially buses (*Mr Thankyou*, *A Mother's Love*); hotels, inns and resorts (*The Masseurs and the Woman* [*Anma to onna*], 1938; *Ornamental Hairpin*). Journeys on foot, too, are a recurrent motif, as in the case of the migrant workers in *Children of the Beehive*, the itinerant masseurs of *The Masseurs and the Woman* and the pilgrims in *Ornamental Hairpin*. Shimizu's heroines, particularly, tend to be persons of no fixed abode, with few ties or none; often, their wanderings are a means of escaping an unhappy past. The figure of the 'fleeing woman' (Hayashi 2004: 30) is as typical a Shimizu character as the alienated child; *Ornamental Hairpin* contains perhaps the most interesting such figure in his *oeuvre*.

Rural location

Most of Shimizu's later films are set mainly or wholly in the countryside. He filmed on location whenever possible, especially in the mountainous and inaccessible Izu Peninsula, or (as in *Ornamental Hairpin*) in rural hot spring resorts. Shimizu clearly loved, and liked to portray, the local colour of such areas: the details of life and work in small communities, their traditions (e.g. the strolling players in *A Mother's Love*) and their landscapes. Though Shimizu does not simply idealise the countryside, it tends to function as a site for rest and recuperation, and a repository of humane values. It is in rural milieux that the sick (*The Shiinomi School*), the injured (*Ornamental Hairpin*) and the delinquent (*The Inspection Tower*) can be rehabilitated. By contrast, Shimizu's city films – *Seven Seas* ([*Nanatsu no umi*], 1931–2), *Japanese Girls at the Harbour* and *Forget Love for Now* – present an environment rife with corruption, treachery, exploitative capitalism and prostitution. This urban/rural opposition is relevant to *Ornamental Hairpin*, with the city woman finding, in the country resort, a refuge from the urban lifestyle that she rejects.

Ornamental Hairpin is the most sophisticated example of this restorative motif in Shimizu's output, since the physical recovery of the soldier complements the emotional and moral regeneration of the heroine – herself the most fascinating of Shimizu's vagrants. Emi is introduced as a traveller; in the opening scene, she is making a pilgrimage. Like the unnamed heroine of *The Masseurs and the Woman*, she is also a woman in flight from her past. In the first scene, her friend and fellow pilgrim Okiku complains that the sun is making her sweat; Emi wryly comments that she doesn't mind, since perspiration will wash the makeup, alcohol and tobacco from her skin. The comment initiates the recuperative theme. The urban lifestyle is described in terms of its more decadent elements (Shimizu, it seems, was personally rather abstemious, and neither drank nor smoked); in contrast, the countryside is presented as a locale where rejuvenation can occur through natural means. The setting at a hot spring resort brings to the fore the theme of cleansing, physical and emotional: characters are always taking baths, while the heroine is shaking off the accumulated dirt of her past. It is, of course, an accident in a bath – Emi's loss of the hairpin – that causes the soldier's injury and, in turn, impels Emi to return to the inn and begin the process of taking stock of her life.

Though the details of Emi's past are kept somewhat ambiguous, her basic situation is made fairly clear through telegrams, telephone calls and conversations with Okiku. She is escaping from an unhappy relationship with a man who, it appears, supports her materially, but not emotionally (the implication of an unsuccessful romance is given a certain piquancy by the casting of Shimizu's ex-wife Tanaka). Emi's decision to renounce her past also involves a renunciation of material wealth; speaking by telephone to her servant, Ume, she instructs her to 'let him take all my things'. Later, in response to a question from one of the children as to whether they can come and stay with her in Tokyo, she casually remarks that she may no longer have a house in Tokyo. The rejection of the past entails an acceptance of the status of vagrant – though, ironically, it is Emi who, of all the characters, finally fails to move on from the resort, as if hoping to find a new home there.

Emi's dissatisfaction is, however, more general. She tells Okiku that she won't go back to Tokyo, explaining that she doesn't like what she was, and wants more meaning in her life. Their conversation is filmed with exquisite delicacy against the backdrop of the river that runs by the inn. In an earlier sequence, we had seen Emi washing dirty sheets in this river; now, as they speak, the women take the clean linen down from the poles on which it had been hung up to dry. The sense of renewal is carried visually by the brilliant whiteness of the sheets; as in many of Ozu's films, laundry is used to represent 'notions of cleansing and starting afresh' (Wood 2004: 57). As the scene reaches its emotional climax, with Okiku's offer to sort everything out for Emi in Tokyo, the heroine breaks down. The theme of regeneration, carried throughout the film by such cleansing liquids as perspiration, bath water and river water, reaches its catharsis with tears.

This account of one woman's emotional transition is, however, unsatisfactory if it implies that *Ornamental Hairpin* is straightforwardly a film 'about' Emi; in fact, this is only half true. Emi is certainly given a privileged status in the narrative, a status underlined by the fact that she is the only character to be played by a real star, Tanaka Kinuyo. (Ryū Chishū, who plays Nanmura, was not yet very well known – his appearance in Ozu's *There Was a Father* [*Chichi ariki*] the next year was to make his reputation.) Emi is the only character who talks openly about her feelings, she is given more screen time than anyone else, and she is also privileged by the structure of the film, which starts and ends with scenes in which she features, in the first as part of a group, in the last alone. For all these reasons, she is the most likely figure of audience identification; ultimately, after the departure of the other guests, she becomes the only one. Nevertheless, *Ornamental Hairpin* is a genuine group portrait. Though introduced in the first scene, the presumed heroine actually then disappears from the narrative for nearly 15 minutes, or a fifth of the film's total running time; in her absence, she remains a subject of discussion, but Shimizu uses this section primarily to develop the other characters, and to sketch out the dynamics of the group. Even when Emi returns, Shimizu continues to stage scenes in which she does not appear, or in which she is not the most important character. She is presented as a member of a community; moreover, her personal development is mediated through her relationships with the other members of that community.

The nature of the community is worth considering. As elsewhere in Shimizu's work, it is a temporary entity; it is not founded on any form of social obligation, nor, in this case, is its formation precipitated by a crisis, as with the war orphans of *Children of the Beehive* and *Children of the Great Buddha* (*Daibutsu-sama to kodomo-tachi*, 1952). Rather, like the community of fellow travellers on the bus in *Mr Thankyou*, it consists merely of people who happen to be in the same place at the same time. They are, consequently, a diverse group; the main thing uniting them is that they are people with leisure time and independent means, able to take an extended holiday. As anyone who has lived in Japan will be aware, this is not a common circumstance, and one may surmise that it was even rarer in a period of national emergency. In consequence, the film might appear, superficially, more escapist than others by Shimizu. Certainly, none of the characters are seen to worry about their material or financial well-being, in striking contrast to the threat of poverty and unemployment which looms large in *Mr Thankyou* and *Forget Love for Now*. Yet in the context of its time, the very bourgeois milieu of *Ornamental Hairpin* itself has subversive potential.

Ornamental Hairpin was made in the year of Pearl Harbor, at a time when national film production was increasingly harnessed to the goals of the military regime. Peter B. High has detailed the strictures laid with growing rigour on filmmakers in the late 1930s and early 1940s. As early as 1938, the Home Ministry Censorship Division had created a list of guidelines for scriptwriters, encouraging, among other things: 'celebrations of the "Japanese spirit" as seen in the family system and of the national spirit of self-sacrifice; use of film to re-educate the masses, especially young people and women, whose Westernisation has caused them to reject traditional values; [. . . and] suppression of the tendency toward individualism inspired by European or American films' (High 2003: 292). In 1939, the Diet had passed the Film Law, aiming 'to implement the development of cinema . . . in order to serve the progress of national culture'.

(73) This instituted pre-production censorship of scripts, and specifically discouraged 'slice-of-life' films, films about personal fulfilment, and films about the wealthy. By May 1941, the Information Bureau had devised the concept of *kokumin eiga*, or People's Cinema, defined as film that 'will loyally serve national policy as the organ of enlightenment and propaganda' (339). Although the directive was not very precise in explaining how films were to fulfil this function, it was clear that the industry was now expected to serve as an arm of the war effort.

The evolution of Shimizu's own films during this period is indicative of the growing force of official expectations. In the years before the Film Law, he was able to make films in which social criticism was fairly explicit: both *Forget Love for Now* (which was trimmed by the censors) and *Mr Thankyou* are scathing portraits of the iniquities of Japanese society, particularly as regards the situation of women. Both films also, through their presentation of Chinese and Korean characters, express a subtle but definite opposition to the imperialist policies of the time. *A Star Athlete*, which depicts a student military training exercise, satirises, while superficially upholding, militarist values. Although the film's ostensible project is the incorporation of dissident elements into the group, the dissidents themselves are the most interesting and sympathetic characters, and the slapstick humour of the climactic chase reduces the whole training exercise to farce.

Shimizu's films of 1938–9 – *The Masseurs and the Woman* and *Four Seasons of Childhood* – are more distanced from social and political realities. With their largely personal concerns (romantic and familial, respectively), they conform more closely to the Shōchiku tradition of the 'Ōfuna flavour': a tradition of low-key domestic drama, usually without overt political content. This style, despite its realism, was considered escapist and irresponsible by the authorities: in 1941, Shōchiku was threatened with dissolution after its contribution to the war effort was judged insufficient (High 2003: 147). The films that Shimizu made in that year, on the cusp of the Pacific War, are necessarily circumspect and ambiguous. *The Inspection Tower*, an ostensibly liberal work set in a home for delinquent children, nevertheless conforms to the ideals of the military regime in its stress on physical hardship and endurance in a greater cause. The sequence in which the children accept a regime of hard physical labour in order to build a canal would not be out of place in a combat movie. *Notes of a Female Singer (Utajo oboegaki*, 1941) carries over the feminism of *Forget Love for Now*, though the tone is rather less impassioned and the film distanced from contemporary experience by the Meiji era (1868–1912) setting. It is an impeccably liberal film, but its parameters are essentially personal: this was, we may assume, one of the apolitical dramas which convinced the authorities that Shōchiku was not doing its bit for the war effort. Shimizu's namesake, critic Shimizu Akira, put *Ornamental Hairpin* in the same class, complaining that 'film stock is so precious in these times, and yet Shimizu Hiroshi still comes up with such la-di-da stuff' (in Yau and Li 2004: 80). That the film got the go-ahead to be made at all may well be because of the inclusion of the 'patriotic' plot strand involving the recuperation of the wounded soldier, an element which Shimizu gracefully subverts.

Ornamental Hairpin, as a 'slice-of-life' film about characters seeking personal happiness and integrity, certainly falls into a category discouraged by the Film Law. The government favoured films about the working class – farmers and factory workers – since these could show the production of necessary materials; in 1941, to make an apparently apolitical, escapist film about the middle class at leisure was itself subversive. But *Ornamental Hairpin* is more than an escapist film; it is a film about the need to escape. Another link uniting the disparate group is that none of the characters (the recuperating soldier apart) are particularly keen to return to their homes in Tokyo. Emi is positively reluctant. Moreover, the community which they establish within the confines of the resort is crucially different from the conventional organisation of Japanese society. The nuclear family plays no role at all: the only blood relatives are the grandfather and his young grandsons, while the only married couple is childless. In place of conventional family bonds, the whole group becomes a kind of unorthodox extended family. Emi volunteers to do the laundry for the other guests, and begins to act vaguely as a surrogate mother to the two brothers, at one stage inviting them to sleep in her room. The fluidity of the sleeping arrangements in fact adds to the effect: as circumstances require, for instance with the arrival of a new character or tour group, the characters move from room to room, agreeing to share with one or more of their fellow guests. Initially, the only people sharing rooms are those for whom conventional proprieties dictate this: the married couple and the old man with his grandchildren. When the inn is at its fullest, all four adult male characters are packed into one room, the women and children into another.

Vital to the effect is the expertise with which Shimizu exploits the specific properties of traditional Japanese architecture. In an old-fashioned Japanese house, and particularly in an inn, where groups of varying sizes may need to be accommodated, the rooms are usually divided not by solid walls, but by *shōji*: thin wood-and-paper screens which can be slid back and forth at will. The boundaries of interior spaces are therefore not fixed but fluid. In *Ornamental Hairpin*, Shimizu uses this quality to strengthen the sense of community: no one has his own exclusive space, and every space is potentially communal. A remarkable example is the scene after Emi has returned to the inn to apologise to the injured Nanmura. In order to make room for her to stay, the scholar volunteers to share a room with the old man and his grandsons. The camera is placed so that the scholar's old room can be seen in the background of the image, through the open *shōji*; as we watch, his desk and books are carried through into the new, shared room in the foreground. The scholar moves to the *shōji* and draws it shut, saying 'We'll close it here'; thus the visual field is suddenly restricted to the foreground of the image, decisively dividing the two rooms. Yet, in a subsequent scene, the screen is open again, connecting them once more; and, due to the boys' complaints about the scholar's snoring, the sleeping arrangements have changed again, the brothers now sharing one room with Emi, the two old men occupying the other. Through the open *shōji*, the boys watch the old men snoring, and cheer on their grandfather to snore louder than the scholar: thus, the two rooms are connected both visually and aurally. Shimizu's staging actively stresses the fluidity of spatial boundaries within the inn, a quality that reflects the fluidity of the social relationships between the characters.

A key element of the social organisation at the resort is that the usual hierarchies are absent; the community contains no credible authority figure. Mr and Mrs
Hiroyasu are presented as a comic inversion of the traditional male-dominated
couple: the husband defers repeatedly to his wife's opinions, preceding every
other remark with 'My wife thinks that . . '. The proprietor of the inn, theoretically in charge, is obliged to serve his customers. The closest the film comes to an
authority figure is the irascible scholar, but only the diffident Mr Hiroyasu
appears intimidated by his dictatorial behaviour. His anger is taken seriously by
scarcely anyone else, and his pretensions are consistently deflated. A recurrent
joke revolves around the arrival at the inn of large groups, whom the scholar
condemns as 'noisy' (*urusai*); his fellow guests further anger him by preferring
such words as 'lively' (*nigiyaka*) and 'colourful' (*hade*). Despite his book learning,
his verbal authority is undermined from the start. He soon acquires a somewhat
ridiculous sheen, especially when the boys irreverently make him part of their
'snoring contest', and his surface authoritarianism is ultimately revealed as
mere bluster. In the latter half of the film, he is most often seen playing *go* with
the grandfather. Though he is soon evidently weary of the pastime, he appears
powerless to refuse the old man's demands for further games.

For André Bazin, the technique of staging in depth allows the spectator a
greater freedom than does montage-based cinema; in montage the director
'choose[s] what he should see', whereas staging in depth invites the viewer 'to
exercise at least a minimum of personal choice' (Bazin 1971: 36). Certainly, the
way in which Shimizu stages the bulk of the action, with characters at a fair
distance from the camera, and with little resort to rhetorical close-ups or expressive camera angles, allows the viewer an unusual amount of freedom to form his
or her own judgement of the characters (the exceptions are the close-ups that
privilege Emi's feelings). In this, moreover, the style of the film reflects the
democratic social organisation among the film's characters, who themselves
enjoy a degree of freedom remarkable in 1940s Japan. With the film's one
apparent authority figure actually impotent, decisions are made through amic-
able consensus. In one key scene, a meeting is held to discuss matters of concern
to the group, such as the monotony of the food at the inn; issues are raised,
verbally debated, and resolved. In the context of the time, the image of decision
by consensus, coupled with the absence of traditional family structures, has
subversive force. The inn is a space in which the hierarchical principles deriving
from Shintoist and Confucian thought, and central to the militarist doctrines of
the period, are replaced by democratic principles which, in the nation at large,
had virtually been eradicated. The resort becomes, in fact, a kind of egalitarian
utopia, providing a refuge from both political and social conservatism, from
the restrictive traditions and repressive policies of the mainstream in 1940s
Japanese society.

The film's only direct acknowledgement of the political situation of the time
is the presence at the inn of the wounded soldier. Even if it was this element
that earned the film permission to be made at all, Nanmura hardly personifies
the militarist ethos. Within the film, the sole evidence of his soldierly prowess
is a brief scene where he fires a rifle at a fairground booth. In fact, his wound

makes him seem a victim of war, a status which is admittedly evasive – Japan had, after all, been the aggressor in her campaigns during the 1930s – but which Shimizu develops intriguingly. Once the soldier is rehabilitated, he will go back to Tokyo and the war effort, if not to active service. Only at the inn can he escape such obligations. Moreover, the unspoken romance that develops between him and Emi does not present the man as a dominant partner, despite his ultra-masculine profession. In this light, we can read the soldier's leg wound as a symbolic emasculation, repeated early in the film when he again injures his foot by treading on Emi's hairpin. Within the resort's confines, the warrior can become a civilian, and the macho professional a 'New Man'. If Nanmura is eager to return to Tokyo, Shimizu never endorses that aim.

The sequences in which Nanmura performs his walking exercises are a key structuring element in the film. They take place in three different locations, and each exercise, as the soldier grows stronger, is more challenging than the last: first, a walk over a flat meadow to a tree; next, a journey across a river via stepping stones; finally, a climb up a flight of stone steps. After completing this last test, Nanmura considers himself fit enough to return to Tokyo. Formally, these sequences are set apart from the rest by their atypically rhetorical camera technique: shots from unusual angles, quick cuts between the soldier and his onlookers, extreme long shots interspersed with close-ups, and dramatic background music. This stylistic discrepancy can be partly explained by the fact that these are the film's only instances of dramatic physical action, but it also serves to emphasise the importance of these sequences in marking the progress, not only of Nanmura's bodily recuperation, but also of Emi's growing emotional attachment to him.

It is a tribute to the subtlety of Shimizu's direction that Emi is almost never seen alone with Nanmura, yet nor is the viewer in any doubt that she is falling in love with him. This awareness is mediated through subtleties of dialogue, staging, gesture and expression, and through the comments of others. The only sequence in which man and woman are actually alone together is in their first meeting, where their conversation consists of awkward banalities ('It's hot, isn't it?'); nevertheless, the scene initiates the manner in which Nanmura's disability cements a bond between them, Emi taking the soldier's arm as she helps him to the bath. By the time of their next encounter in the meadow, Shimizu's staging hints at a developing affection: the feeling is conveyed by the idyllic pastoral setting, by the physical proximity of the actors, and by the delicacy of Tanaka Kinuyo's performance, but equally by what is unsaid and unshown. The scene's first line of dialogue is Emi's 'I suppose I shouldn't have asked; I won't again'; this, we assume, is a response to Nanmura's reluctance to talk about the circumstances of his injury, and serves as evidence of her growing sensitivity to his feelings. As she speaks, Emi sits down close beside him on the grass, creating a new sense of physical intimacy. But Shimizu almost immediately cuts away, revealing that they are not, as we have assumed, alone, but are being observed by the two boys, who complain that Nanmura is always talking to Emi, and remind him that he should exercise. The sequence that follows, as Nanmura tries (this time unsuccessfully) to walk to the tree, strongly emphasises Emi's reactions as she watches him. In what for Shimizu is an unusually dramatic shot, she is seen advancing tensely towards the camera into full close-up, her hands clutching anxiously at the handle of her parasol. When he falls, she runs forward immediately to help him to his feet – the second example of physical contact between them. As he leans against a tree, Emi asks him if he comes to this meadow every day; his reply is 'You too?', to which she in turn responds, 'Yes, for sure'. This display of affection prompts the boys to react enviously: asked by Nanmura to fetch his crutches, they tell Emi to do it herself, since 'he's always talking to you'.

The sense of unstated sexual feeling is intensified in the sequence where Nanmura tries to cross the river. This, the most visually dramatic of all the exercise scenes, is the occasion for the most extensive physical contact between him and Emi. Again, the contact is functional: Nanmura falls, and Emi volunteers to carry him the rest of the way. The gesture is beautifully ambiguous – while Emi's willingness to touch the soldier hints at sexual feeling, the piggyback ride also has maternal connotations. Nanmura's helplessness makes him seem childlike, and this is one moment in which customary gender roles are inverted in their relationship, the weak, dependent man reliant on the physical strength of the woman.

Nanmura's successful crossing of the river is not shown, but merely reported; the next exercise sequence we see is his climactic attempt to climb the steps, the completion of which will allow him to return to Tokyo. In this last sequence, the dramatic musical accompaniment that has characterised the earlier exercise scenes is absent; we hear only the voices of the boys, counting Nanmura's steps as he climbs. The silence here not only has the effect of heightening the tension; it also transforms the mood. Whereas the earlier exercises were presented as action sequences, the suspense being of a physical order (will he, or won't he, make it?), the last one becomes a scene of profound emotional tension (will the heroine be separated from the man she loves?). The camera again cuts between shots of Nanmura's journey and close-ups of the tensely watching Emi; this time, however, she is evidently willing him to fail. When he reaches the top, she turns aside in despair, murmuring, 'He's going back'. If, in the eyes of the censors, the script of *Ornamental Hairpin* could be accepted as celebrating the recuperation of an injured soldier, the feeling of this last scene radically subverts any such intention. Nanmura's triumph becomes a melancholic, even tragic, occasion. The tone of the sequence is encapsulated in its last words: as Emi mounts the steps to congratulate the soldier, she turns to the boys, and remarks, 'You're all leaving me. Now I'm going to be alone'.

The film's last scene is perhaps the most touching coda in Shimizu's *oeuvre*. The group has dispersed; only Emi remains. She has just received a letter hinting that Nanmura has met another woman. Alone in the grounds of the resort, she retraces the scenes of his walking exercises, crossing the meadow and the river; finally, she slowly climbs the steps that he had conquered, heralding his return to Tokyo. Shimizu's camera tracks alongside her as she climbs; her face is an expressionless mask. The film fades out before she reaches the top of the stairs, so that she seems never to reach her destination. *Ornamental Hairpin* ends

Figure 8 In *Ornamental Hairpin* (1941), camera placement, the position of actors, and the environment around them comment obliquely on the characters. BFI Stills, Posters and Designs.

in suspension, with its heroine's future uncertain. Her only decision is a negative one: not to return.

We may compare this with the endings of two of Shimizu's silent films, both made less than ten years earlier. Both *Seven Seas* and *Japanese Girls at the Harbour* conclude with unhappy women actually leaving Japan to find a new life. Emi, by contrast, can only withdraw from society. The contrast speaks for the growing retrenchment and isolationism of Japanese society over that unhappy decade, and the increasing impotence of Japanese liberalism, an impotence strongly felt by those in the film industry personally opposed to the political trajectory of their country. Unlike in Nazi Germany, there was no mass exodus of film-making talent from Japan. The defection to Russia of actress Okada Yoshiko, already a communist sympathiser, was a unique instance. In general, the cultural gulfs between Japan and other major film-producing nations meant that exile was not a viable option. Dissidents within the industry were faced with only two choices: to capitulate, or to retire.

Shimizu's own career during the years of the Pacific War represents, in fact, a compromise between these two options. *Ornamental Hairpin* was the fifth film he had made in 1941 alone; he was to make only two features in 1942, one in 1943, none in 1944, and one short segment of a portmanteau film in 1945. Even then, however, he was not able to avoid making a contribution to the war effort. *Sayon's Bell* (*Sayon no kane*, 1943) was conceived as propaganda for the Japanese occupation of Taiwan, while Shimizu's contribution to the morale-boosting *Victory Song* (*Hisshōka*, 1945) revolves around a child who plays *kamikaze* games with model aeroplanes. In this light, the ending of *Ornamental Hairpin* can be read as a last, muted protest. In the context of the drama, Emi's plight is humanly moving. In the context of the political realities of the time, it signifies the passivity and weakness of Japanese liberalism – conditions that would contribute to the triumph of militarism, with dire consequences for Japan herself, and for other nations.

Acknowledgements

The filmography for this chapter is based on the filmography printed in Japanese in *Kinema Junpō* no. 698 (24 December, 1976 – *Nippon eiga kantoku zenshū*). I have also consulted Kimata et al. (2000). I would like to thank Hiroshi Komatsu for his help in romanising the Japanese script, and Etsuko Takagi for hers in devising appropriate English equivalents.

References

Bazin, André (1971) *What is Cinema?, vol. 1*, Berkeley: University of California Press.
Burch, Noël (1979) *To the Distant Observer: Form and Meaning in the Japanese Cinema*, Berkeley, University of California Press.
Hayashi, Sharon (2004) 'Women on the Run: Travel and Utopia in the Films of Shimizu Hiroshi', in Yau and Li 2004: 29–31.
High, Peter B. (2003) *The Imperial Screen: Japanese Film Culture in the Fifteen Years' War, 1931–1945*, Madison: University of Wisconsin Press.
Kimata Kimihiko, Satō Chihiro, Satō Takeshi, and Tanaka Masazumi (eds) (2000) *Shimizu Hiroshi eiga tokuhon*, Tokyo, Firumu Āto-sha.
Wood, Robin (2004) 'Notes Toward a Reading of *Tokyo Twilight*', *CineAction* 63: 57–8.
Yamane, Sadao (2003) 'Narrative Spectacle: Rediscovering the Work of Hiroshi Shimizu', in Morimune Atsuko (ed.), *Tokyo FILMeX 2003 Official Catalog*, Tokyo: Tokyo FILMeX Organizing Committee: 34–5.
Yau, Kinnia and Li Cheuk-to (eds) (2004) *Hiroshi Shimizu: 101st Anniversary*, Hong Kong: Hong Kong International Film Festival Society.

Shimizu hiroshi filmography

Beyond the Pass (*Tōge no kanata*, 1924)
The Love of a Mountain Man (*Yamaotoko no koi*, 1924)
Rather than Love, to the Theatre (*Koi yori butai*, 1924)
Song of the White Chrysanthemum (*Shiragiku no uta*, 1924)
Love-Crazed Blade (*Koi ni kuruu yaeba*, 1924)
Bonfire Night (*Kagaribi no yoru*, 1925)
The Little Itinerant (*Chiisaki tabi geinin*, 1925)
The Peach-Coloured Thorn (*Momoiro no toge*, 1925)
Roar of a Torrent (*Gekiryū no sakebi*, 1925)
Blade of a Righteous Man (*Gijin no yaeba*, 1925)
The Old-Fashioned Man (*Sutare-mono*, 1925)

The Killing of a Hundred Men at Isshin Temple (Isshinji no hyakunin giri, 1925)
Sharpness of the Blade (Kotetsu no kireaji, 1925)
Snare of Love (Koi no honawa,1925)
The Fleeing Warrior (Ochimusha, 1925)
Time of Worries (Nayamashiki koro, 1926)
The Beauty and the Ronin (Bijin to rōnin, 1926)
Song of a Double Suicide in Satsuma (Shinjū Satsuma uta, 1926)
True-Blood Passion (Shinku no netsujo, 1926)
Kyoko and Fumiko of Yamato (Kyōko to Yamato Fumiko, 1926)
The Betrayed Man (Uragirare-mono, 1926)
The Amorous Blade (Yōtō, 1926)
Feelings in Turmoil (Kyōdo ranshin, 1926)
Roses of Grief (Nageki no bara, 1926)
Three Daughters (Sannin no musume, 1927)
Oteru and Oyuki (Oteru to Oyuki, 1927)
The Man and the Widow (Kare to mibōjin, 1927)
Love-Crazed Madonna (Kyōren no maria, 1927)
Spring Rain (Haru no ame, 1927)
Idol of Love (Renbo yasha, 1927)
Love is Tricky (Koi wa kusemono, 1927)
Flaming Sky (Hono-o no sora, 1927)
Tears of Life (Jinsei no namida, 1927)
Victory over the Depression (Fukeiki seibatsu, 1927)
Shortcut to Success (Shusse no chikamichi, 1927)
A Country Gentleman (Inaka no dateotoko, 1927)
A Portrait of Changing Love (Aiyoku hensōzu, 1928)
The Woman Who Calls to the Sea (Umi ni sakebu onna, 1928)
A Couple's Pilgrimage of Love (Renai futari angya, 1928)
A Modern Woman (Shōwa no onna, 1928)
Childhood Friends (Osana najimi, 1928)
A Picked-up Bride (Hirotta hanayome, 1928)
Mountain Echo (Yamabiko, 1928)
Beautiful Best Friends (Utsukushiki hōbai-tachi, 1928)
The Village Blacksmith (Mori no kajiya, 1929)
Duck Woman (Ahiru onna, 1929)
Magic of Tokyo (Tōkyō no majutsu, 1929)
Smart Girl (Sutekki gāru, 1929)
Travel Manners of a Vagrant Girl (Ukikusa musume tabi fūzoku, 1929)
The Village Champion (Mori no ōja, 1929)
Cheerful Song (Yōki na uta, 1929)
Parent (Oya, 1929)
Proud of my Son (Jiman no segare, 1929)
Eternal Love (Fue no shiratama, 1929)
Father's Desire (Chichi no negai, 1929)
Little Song of Love (Renbo kouta, 1929)
Love, Part One (Renai dai ikka, 1929)
Crime on Red Lips (Kōshin tsumi ari, 1930)
True Love (Shinjitsu no ai, 1930)
Standing at a Crossroads (Kiro ni tachite, 1930)
Embrace (Hōyō, 1930)

March of the Sea (*Umi no kōshinkyoku*, 1930)
Flirtation is Another Thing (*Uwaki bakari wa betsumono da*, 1930)
Youthful Blood Dances (*Seishun no chi wa odoru*, 1930)
Face in the Fog (*Kiri no naka no akebono*, 1930)
Living in a New Time (*Shinjidai ni ikiru*, 1930)
Bully (*Gaki daishō*, 1931)
The Milky Way (*Ginga*, 1931)
Crossed Line Between Husband and Wife (*Konsen nita fūfu*, 1931)
Flower of Grief (*Ureibana*, 1931)
Shining Love (*Kagayaku ai*, 1931)
This Mother Has Sinned (*Kono haha ni tsumi ari ya*, 1931)
Windmill of Life (*Jinsei no fūsha*, 1931)
An Illustrated Guide to Youth (*Seishun zue*, 1931)
Seven Seas, Part One: Virginity Chapter (*Nanatsu no umi, zenpen shojo-hen*, 1931–2)
Passion (*Jōnetsu*, 1932)
Seven Seas, Part Two: Frigidity Chapter (*Nanatsu no umi, kōhen teisō-hen*, 1932)
Manchurian Marching Song (*Manshū kōshinkyoku*, 1932)
Army's Big March (*Rikugun daikōshin*, 1932)
King of the Sea (*Umi no ōja*, 1932)
Love's Windbreak (*Ai no bōfūrin*, 1932)
Dawn after the Midnight Sun (*Byakuya wa akuru*, 1932)
The Star of the Hall of Residence (*Gakuseigai no hanagata*, 1932)
Stormy Region (*Bōfūtai*, 1932)
Sleep, at Mother's Breast (*Nemure, haha no mune ni*, 1933)
A Lady Crying in Spring (*Nakinureta haru no onna yo*, 1933)
Japanese Girls at the Harbour (*Minato no Nihon musume*, 1933)
Dexterity in Love (*Renai ittō ryū*, 1933)
A Travellers' Dream (*Tabine no yume*, 1933)
The Boss's Son at College (*Daigaku no wakadanna*, 1933)
Oriental Mother (*Tōyō no haha*, 1934)
I Want to Know about Love (*Koi o shirisome mashisōrō*, 1934)
The Boss's Son at College: Record of Valour (*Daigaku no wakadanna: buyūden*, 1934)
Gion Festival Music (*Gion bayashi*, 1934)
The Boss's Son at College is Bossy (*Daigaku no wakadanna: taiheiraku*, 1934)
Eclipse (*Kinkanshoku*, 1934)
Love on a School Excursion (*Renai shūgaku ryokō*, 1934)
The Boss' Son: Fine Weather (*Daigaku no wakadana nihonbare*, 1934)
A Hero of Tokyo (*Tōkyō no eiyū*, 1935)
The Boss's Son's Youthful Innocence (*Wakadanna haru ranman*, 1935)
The Man and the Woman and the Boys (*Kare to kanojo to shōnen-tachi*, 1935)
Double Heart (*Sōshinzō*, 1935)
Love in Luxury (*Renai gōka ban*, 1935)
The Boss's Son is a Millionaire (*Wagadanna hyakumangoku*, 1936)
Mountain Range of Emotion (*Kanjō sanmyaku*, 1936)
Mr Thankyou (*Arigatō-san*, 1936)
Law of Love (*Ai no hōsoku*, 1936)
Heaven and Earth are Free (*Jiyū no tenchi*, 1936)
Sing in a Loud Voice! (*Kimi yo takaraka ni utae*, 1936)
Youth's Display (*Seishun mankanshoku*, 1936)
Loves of the Invincible Fleet (*Renai muteki kantai*, 1937)

The Golden Idol (*Konjiki yasha*, 1937)
Forget Love for Now (*Koi mo wasurete*, 1937)
The Star Athlete (*Hanagata senshu*, 1937)
Children in the Wind (*Kaze no naka no kodomo*, 1937)
Goodbye to the Front (*Saraba sensen e*, 1937)
New Domestic History (*Shin katei reki*, 1938)
Departure (*Shuppatsu*, 1938)
Cheerleaders' Song (*Ōenka*, 1938)
The Masseurs and the Woman (*Anma to onna*, 1938)
Domestic Diary (*Katei nikki*, 1938)
A Freeloader's Big Snore (*Isōrō wa takaibiki*, 1939)
Four Seasons of Childhood (*Kodomo no shiki*, 1939)
A Woman's Manners, Part One: Young Girl's Diary (*Onna no fūzoku, dai ichi-wa ojōsan no
    nikki*, 1939)
Flowering Weed (*Hana no aru zassō*, 1939)
Mulberries Are Red (*Kuwa no mi wa akai*, 1939)
I Have a Husband (*Watashi ni wa otto ga aru*, 1940)
Nobuko (1940)
Friends (*Tomodachi*, 1940)
Woman's Fickle Heart (*Nyonin tenshin*, 1940)
The Inspection Tower (*Mikaeri no tō*, 1941)
Notes of a Female Singer (*Utajo oboegaki*, 1941)
Acorns (*Donguri to shiinomi*, 1941)
Dawn Chorus (*Akatsuki no gasshō*, 1941)
Ornamental Hairpin (*Kanzashi*, 1941)
Record of a Woman Doctor (*Joi no kiroku*, 1942)
Meeting of a Brother and Sister (*Kyōdai kaigi*, 1942)
Sayon's Bell (*Sayon no kane*, 1943)
Victory Song (*Hisshōka*, 1945). (Co-directed with Mizoguchi Kenji, Tasaka Tomotaka and
    Makino Masahiro)
Children of the Beehive (*Hachi no su no kodomo-tachi*, 1948)
Tomorrow Japan Will Have Fine Weather (*Asu wa Nihonbare*, 1948)
At Eighteen a Girl Tells Lies (*Musume jūhachi usotsuki jidai*, 1949)
Mr Shosuke Ohara (*Ohara Shōsuke-san*, 1949)
A Mother's Love (*Bojō*, 1950)
Children of the Beehive: What Happened Next (*Sono go no hachi no su no kodomo-tachi*, 1951)
Under the Blossoming Peach (*Momo no hana no saku shita de*, 1951)
Children of the Great Buddha (*Daibutsu-sama to kodomo-tachi*, 1952)
Mole Alley (*Mogura yokochō*, 1953)
Profile of a City (*Tokai no yokogao*, 1953)
The Second Kiss (*Daini no seppun*, 1954)
The Shiinomi School (*Shiinomi gakuen*, 1955)
The Tale of Jiro (*Jirō monogatari*, 1955)
Why Did They Become Like This? (*Naze kanojora wa sō natta ka*, 1956)
Stupid with Kindness (*Ninjō baka*, 1956)
Children Seeking a Mother (*Haha o motomeru kora*, 1956)
Sound in the Mist (*Kiri no oto*, 1956)
Dancing Girl (*Odoriko*, 1957)
A Mother's Journey (*Haha no tabiji*, 1958)
Image of a Mother (*Haha no omokage*, 1959)

5

THE RIDDLE OF THE VASE

Ozu Yasujirō's *Late Spring* (1949)

Abé Mark Nornes

During the 1990s, a re-evaluation of Ozu Yasujirō in Japan stimulated a publishing spree that resulted in a veritable stack of books about the director. Among the most curious of these efforts was a biography of the director which was serialized in *Big Spirits Comics Special* between 1998 and 1999 and entitled *Ozu Yasujirō no nazo* [*The Riddle of Ozu Yasujirō*] (Sonomura and Nakamura 1999). The opening installment of the *manga* shows an American director named Stan on a visit to Japan. The first request he makes of his young handlers is a pilgrimage to Ozu's grave in Kamakura, the setting of *Late Spring* (*Banshun*, 1949). At the graveyard he finds a modest, black gravestone carved with a single Chinese character: *mu*. 'What does it mean?' he asks. 'It means "Nothing" ', his young escorts translate. The director responds, 'Nothing . . . Why . . . WHY? This giant of world cinema, why "Nothing?" ' He is rendered speechless, and the remaining 12 installments follow the foreign director as he attempts to uncover the meaning hidden in this obscure message from the dead.

Ozu's grave is indeed marked by this intriguing character, a favorite of Ozu's since he encountered a Chinese monk painting it during his military stint in World War Two (Tsuzuki 1993: 414–20). However, this rather mundane explanation leaves many dissatisfied. The inscription's lack of context – a simple marker amid a field of graves – invites its readers to imagine other, more profound meanings. They treat it as a puzzle, just as Stan did. This Hollywood director is typical of various publications in the 1990s, which inflated Ozu's reputation through homages provided by various Western fans and filmmakers such as Wim Wenders, Jim Jarmusch and Peter Greenaway. Wenders dedicated his *Wings of Desire* (*Der Himmel über Berlin*, West Germany/ France, 1987) to Ozu, calling him 'an angel of the cinema', and his own visit to Ozu's grave in *Tokyo-ga* (USA/West Germany, 1985) was probably the actual model for the *manga*. However, Stan is ultimately a stand-in for all of Ozu's admirers, because Ozu certainly did leave us with a collection of per-plexing films. Most of them are delightful comedies or powerful melodramas, but what ultimately sets Ozu far apart from other colleagues working in these genres is his unique approach to film style. This is the real puzzle '*mu*' is meant to symbolize.[1]

We often speak of a given director's style in individual, personalized terms; however, in actuality these filmmakers are almost invariably reproducing the codes of cinema they inherited, especially when they work in a popular mainstream industry. By contrast, Ozu developed, over the course of his career, his own particular and peculiar approach to film-making. This was a method that was largely in place by the production of *I Was Born, But . . .* (*Umarete wa mita keredo*, 1932) and it reached a certain kind of hermetic cohesiveness by the time of *Late Spring*. That we can refer to this as a kind of 'emplacement' of style indicates the degree to which Ozu consciously regularized and systematized its various component parts. Always playful, but rarely wavering from his self-imposed rules and strictures, Ozu refined his cinematic narration into an approach of remarkable elegance, precision, and intricacy.

On the surface, however, its mind-boggling complexity is not readily apparent and the casual viewer is probably oblivious to Ozu's astonishing departure from the rules of form that filmmakers around the world have adopted. If viewers do notice, they usually refer only to a few of the more obvious features to describe a certain 'aestheticism', much like the Japanese press throughout most of Ozu's career. Foreign filmmakers, critics, and scholars scarcely knew of his existence until major retrospectives were staged in the US and Europe starting in 1963, the year of his death. As word spread of these extraordinary films, Donald Richie devoted his second auteurist study to Ozu (1974). It helped spark a lively critical debate which has never been substantially resolved to this day.

In the course of this discussion, a significant literature has developed around Ozu's oeuvre. Its importance extends far beyond the hagiography of a master filmmaker. The key terms of the debate essentially start with the question raised by that cartoon director from Hollywood and move into some of the most central issues of film studies: What are we to make of Ozu's perplexing style, and how are we to position this exceptional cinema in relation to the cultures, ideologies, and cinemas of Japan and the world?

This chapter will examine the foreign debate over Ozu's cinema which, curiously enough, coincides with the institutionalization of film studies in the Euro-American academy. It will scrutinize the foreign reception of Ozu in relation to a single scene from *Late Spring*, where the director inserts two cutaways of a beautiful vase. The shots are excessively long. Nothing in all of Ozu's films has sparked such conflicting explanations; everyone seems compelled to weigh in on this scene, invoking it as a key example in their arguments. We will look at some of the analyses to see how the engagement with Ozu's work, which arguably constitutes the richest body of scholarship on the Japanese cinema, has gone hand in hand with the development of film studies. I am not interested in answering Stan's question – 'What does it all mean?' – as my approach is in line with a critical shift in film studies during the 1980s which turned toward historical audiences and argued for a multiplicity of readings for a given text. But at the same time, I point to the way Ozu's intriguing design actually targets a variety of readily identifiable spectatorial stances and their pleasures,

Figure 9 Father and Noriko travel to Kyōto for one last trip before she gets married in *Late Spring* (1949). Shōchiku/The Kobal Collection.

from the engagement in melodrama enjoyed by historical audiences to the particular desires of scholarly spectators. This is precisely what draws me to Ozu and *Late Spring*: my ability to identify with and circulate between these different audience positions.

The vase scene comes late in the film when the father, played by Ryū Chishū, and his daughter, Noriko (Hara Setsuko), travel to Kyōto for one last trip before she gets married. After a long day visiting temples with the father's friend, they lay in their *futon* at an inn. They chat about what a nice day they had, and after a beat Noriko begins what would certainly become a serious conversation. The father does not respond. A shot shows him sleeping, followed by another shot of Noriko looking at him. Ozu cuts to the vase, perfectly placed in an alcove with moonlit shadows of bamboo gracing the walls. Another shot of Noriko shows her staring at the ceiling, thinking. Ozu returns to the vase, holding the view for a long ten seconds. When he cuts back to Noriko she is flush with emotion and seems to be on the verge of tears. This is where the scene quietly ends.

The reason this scene has attracted the attention of so many writers is to do with its emotional power and its unusual construction. The vase is clearly essential to the scene. The director not only shows it twice, but he lets both shots run for what would be an inordinate amount of time by the measure of most filmmakers. At the same time, the vase is too obscure an object to hold symbolic or metaphoric meaning, which would constitute a conventional strategy. Ozu rarely ever deploys imagery in such a direct and transparent manner. Meaning, in Ozu's cinema, has a slipperiness that makes a wide range of interpretations possible. Ultimately, it is this undecipherable quality that the vase best represents, and which makes Ozu criticism so vibrant a tradition.

When Ozu came to the attention of the West, serious film study had yet to establish a disciplinary identity. The first extended treatment of the director came from an unlikely place, a critic under the tutelage of Pauline Kael named Paul Schrader (who would later become one of the great post-war American directors). Schrader came from a strict Calvinist background in Michigan, and his family was anti-icon, anti-image. While he obviously rejected the austere logocentrism of Calvinism, Schrader remained deeply indebted to its sense of spirituality. He was profoundly attracted to films shot in what he called a 'transcendental style'. In his *Transcendental Style in Film: Ozu, Bresson, Dreyer* (1972), the key stylistic features Schrader identified were an austerity of means, a privileging of decisive narrative moments, a gap between setting and action, and an unusual use of stasis. For Schrader, these constituted a spiritual cinema brought to perfection in the work of Carl-Theodor Dreyer, Robert Bresson, and Ozu Yasujirō.

'Perhaps the finest image of stasis in Ozu's films is the lengthy shot of the vase in a darkened room near the end of *Late Spring*', notes Schrader (1972: 49), after arguing that stasis – frozen motion – is a hallmark of religious art around the world and represents an image of another reality that stands beside ordinary reality:

> The vase is stasis, a form which can accept deep contradictory emotion and transform it into an expression of something unified, permanent, transcendent . . . The transcendental style, like the vase, is a form which expresses something deeper than itself, the inner unity of all things.
>
> (149–51)

What Schrader is essentially attempting to describe is the remarkable power that self-restricting cinema can achieve. This is the complex and contradictory quality that attracts him to Ozu – an approach to cinema in bold opposition to the narrative-driven, over-the-top affect of most popular cinemas. And, as Schrader points out today with dry irony, it is also a style in opposition to his own cinema, which invariably uses psychological realism to chase excessive pleasurable affect.[2]

Schrader continues to use the term transcendental style to discuss Ozu, although no one else has. At the same time, the more general terms of his approach were extremely influential at this early stage of Ozu criticism. At its heart, the premise of Schrader's methodology asserts that even though filmmakers may emphasize the particularity of their own cultures, they also express the universal. This notion dovetailed powerfully with two new approaches in the nascent field of film studies, auteurism and national character studies, and

Japanese cinema thus became a kind of Petri dish for working through issues central to the new discipline. The writings of Donald Richie made this positioning possible. The book Richie wrote with Joseph L. Anderson, *The Japanese Film: Art and Industry* ([1982] 1959), remains one of the finest studies of an entire national cinema. Likewise, examples plucked from Japanese cinema were important when auteurism, which credited the source of a film's meaning to the genius of the director, found a foothold in American criticism in an apolitical form. Among the first auteurist studies were Richie's books on Kurosawa (1999 [first published in 1965]) and Ozu (1974).

Richie's *Ozu* was the first monograph on the director in English. It is a critical biography filled with incisive discussions of Ozu's extant films and laced with fascinating anecdotes. Richie's approach at the time, best evidenced in his 1971 *Japanese Cinema: Film Style and National Character*, emphasized the cultural particularity of a given film. In discussing Ozu, so often called the 'most Japanese' of all directors, Richie sprinkled his analyses with references to religion (*mu*, the 'nothing' carved on Ozu's tombstone) and pre-modern aesthetic categories such as *mono-no-aware* and *wabi-sabi*. The Kyōto inn scene in *Late Spring* was a privileged moment, where he describes the vase as a 'container' for the emotions of the spectators. Note how he opens with a move reminiscent of Schrader's articulation of the particular and the universal:

> Primary to the experience is that in these scenes empty of all but *mu*, we suddenly apprehend what the film has been about, i.e. we suddenly apprehend life. This happens because such scenes occur when at least one important pattern in the picture has become clear. In *Late Spring* the daughter has seen what will happen to her: she will leave her father, she will marry. She comes to understand this precisely during the time that both we and she have been shown the vase. The vase itself means nothing, but its presence is also a space and into it pours our emotion.
>
> (Richie 1974: 174)

Richie never explains the apparent contradiction between these aesthetic categories of high art and the essentially popular nature of Ozu's films. (How many ordinary Japanese filmgoers entered theaters with a refined sense of *mono-no-aware*, or could even define it in the first place?) However, while the book is replete with such references, the quotation above suggests that Richie was ultimately a humanist. He concludes his book with this forceful example of his humanism: 'Having spent a few hours with [his characters], we find that we do not want to leave them. We have come to understand and consequently to love them. And with this understanding we come to know more about ourselves, and, with that, more about life' (Ibid.: 191). Other, far less compelling, writers such as Zeman (1972) and Vasey (1988) conformed more closely to Schrader's spiritualism, with its roots in 1960s popular appropriations of Zen. They too often generalize from narrowly defined categories of 'tradition' and 'aesthetics' into a simplified and impoverished vision of Japanese culture.

These approaches came under vigorous critique in the 1970s when the disciplinary qualities of film study began to coalesce under the influence of post-structuralism. A major thrust of this theory, which is most closely associated with the influential British journal *Screen*, brought the global hegemony of Hollywood under close scrutiny. The new scholarship theorized the ideological underpinnings of the continuity style, calling attention to the way film form is imbricated with political economy. By inviting spectators to immerse themselves in the narrative machinations of the film, films shot in the continuity style allegedly interpolated people into ideological positions determined by (especially American) capital and patriarchy. In a globalized industry where American film style claimed the norm, the search was on for alternatives.

It was in this context that the Ozu retrospectives staged by Richie and others provided grist for the theoretical mill. Here was a filmmaker whose own precision in style matched the rigor aspired to by new scholars such as David Bordwell and Noël Burch, many of whom were now based at major universities. The first articles were primarily taxonomies of the director's style. They celebrated Ozu's difference as a radical alternative to the Hollywood continuity system; however, at this early point, their attempts to explicate the political implications of Ozu's alternative were weak. In a kind of reaction to the traditionalism previous criticism had attributed to the director, some called Ozu a modernist.[3] This was quickly dropped when debate turned to the popular nature of his film-making and its industrial context. After a number of articles established the basic contours of Ozu's mystifying approach to film form, Burch's *To the Distant Observer* (1979) closed the decade's Ozu-related criticism with controversy, simultaneously marking a transition in our understanding of Japanese cinema.

Burch was a major film theorist in this early phase of film studies, and *To the Distant Observer* represents a brilliant, if flawed, attempt to rethink the whole of film history through a single national cinema. Although he is a Marxist theorist, Burch's basic argument holds striking similarities to the culturalist readings of Richie and Schrader. Japanese aesthetics, Burch argued, were fundamentally set in the Heian period (794–1185) and have thus continued, essentially unchanged, to inform every aspect of Japanese culture and artistic production into the modern era. Noting that most filmmakers displayed a remarkable ambivalence to Hollywood continuity style until the so-called 'Golden Age' of the 1950s, Burch argued that the timing of this shift was decisive. Filmmakers continued to use the codes of early cinema because Japan was one of the few cultures in the world to enter the nation-state system without being colonized by European or American empires. Previous critics who celebrated cinematic production in the 1950s did so because this was precisely when, thanks to the American Occupation (1945–52), Japanese filmmakers adopted Hollywood codes and 'their' cinema started looking like 'ours'. In this way, Burch uncovered the dominant values underlying the historiography of Japanese film, thus radically politicizing Japanese film scholarship while bringing the riches of the pre-war era to everyone's attention.

Burch's argument places Ozu in a central position, although he has nothing to say about *Late Spring* since it is an Occupation era production. Like a number of the 1970s critics before him, Burch felt that Ozu's techniques interfered with the smooth transparency of the narration (which is why some initially called Ozu a modernist). The director's work thus constituted a radical alternative which was informed by a thousand years of aesthetics unsullied by Western influence.

While those in film studies were sympathetic to – and indeed influenced by – Burch's larger project, *To the Distant Observer* sparked a storm of controversy that centered on what to do with Japanese cultural difference. Edward Said's influential book *Orientalism* (1978) had just been published and despite Burch's best intentions, he had provided an archetypal example of a discourse built on an 'othering' of a non-Western culture and a radical bifurcation of East and West. Scholars in both Japan area studies and film studies latched on to the Burch book in order to critique their respective disciplines with the new intellectual tools provided by Said. Burch was apparently stung by the criticism and basically disowned the book, but many of the provocative issues he raised in *To the Distant Observer* have yet to be addressed adequately and the role of Japanese culture in the historical transformations of Japanese cinema has hardly been put to rest.

The next major collection of work on Ozu de-emphasized the importance of politics and culture to focus on the transmutations of film form in the director's career. David Bordwell and Kristin Thompson had already written the best descriptions of Ozu's style during the debates of the 1970s. When Ozu began attracting the attention of filmmakers and scholars, solving the interlocking puzzles they found in the films must have been exciting and intimidating in equal measure. While many critics were offering culturalist explanations, Thompson and Bordwell countered with detailed formal descriptions that were challenging for their rigor. These two scholars helped establish what exactly we were looking at. At the same time, they were also laying out larger theoretical critiques within film studies through their engagement with Ozu's work. By the 1980s, Thompson and Bordwell were central figures in a faction within film studies that had rejected post-structuralist scholarship for what they called a 'historical poetics'. Essentially, they argued that Ozu's stylistic quirks constituted a set of parameters within which he worked. They suggested that the way in which he consciously manipulated these features with such undeniable sophistication gave them a prominence in the film that exceeded their contribution to the narrative or whatever meaning might have been invested in them. He playfully made 'unreasonable choices' that exploited our assumptions about cinematic narration, and Bordwell and Thompson were particularly attracted to Ozu for the amazing degree to which these choices were determined by a system intrinsic to the director's own particular cinema.

Contra Burch, Thompson and Bordwell convincingly argued that at the heart of the apparent difference of Japanese cinema in the 1930s, the continuity system still served a normative function. Thus, Ozu, in fact, took Hollywood style as a starting point, and elaborated upon it with those 'unreasonable choices' and according to his own idiosyncratic predilections. For example, rejecting Richie's metaphor of the vase as a container for emotions, Thompson wrote:

> If the vase . . . is really there to help release our emotions in some way, why does Ozu put it in too soon? Given the film's consistent use of cutaways in a non-narrative way, it seems more reasonable to see it as a non-narrative element wedged into the action. The choice of a vase for such a purpose is arbitrary; the shots could have shown a lantern in the garden, a tree branch, or whatever . . . They have never even glanced at the vase. The very arbitrariness of the choice should warn us against such simplistic readings.
>
> (Thompson 1988: 339–40)

In addition to her demand for precision, Thompson suggests that *Late Spring's* virtual cataloging of traditional Japanese iconography should not be exploited by culturalist or quasi-religious readings. She emphasizes the way these invocations of tradition serve to reconcile conservatism with the liberalism of the Occupation, particularly in terms of changing definitions of the structure of the family.

In the same year as Thompson's *Late Spring* chapter, David Bordwell released his massive *Ozu and the Poetics of Cinema* (1988), which contained perhaps the definitive description of the formal properties of Ozu's cinema. Bordwell's remarkable close analyses of Ozu's extant films demonstrated the degree to which Ozu *orchestrated* his often minute manipulations of film form. Not surprisingly, Bordwell invokes the *Late Spring* vase to describe Ozu's peculiar elaboration of the cutaway and point-of-view [POV] shot. He suggests that it exemplifies the fundamental instability of point of view in Ozu's cinema and refers to a 'fraying of POV cues' (1988: 117) that is emblematic of the director's overall approach to cinematic narration. The shot of the vase therefore becomes an image at odds with the singular spectatorial position envisioned by previous ideological criticism. It in effect loosens up the representation of character subjectivity and allows Ozu to depart from the strict demand to motivate everything through causality and the normative rules of the continuity style.

Bordwell and Thompson's seminal work did not, in the end, displace mainstream film theory, but instead became one possibility among many critical approaches to Ozu. One of the recent alternatives is represented by *The Flash of Capital: Film and Geopolitics in Japan* (2002), in which Eric Cazdyn places Ozu's treatment of time within the context of the reverse course policies of the American Occupation. He notes that late 1940s polls showed that a majority of Japanese recognized the American Occupation's betrayal of its own lofty rhetoric as Cold War politics over-ran policy. Apparently picking up on what Bordwell referred to as the 'fraying of POV' in the shots of the vase, Cazdyn turns this indeterminacy toward a reading of Ozu's film as an allegory for the socio-political moment in history:

> The time images of the vase and the clocks are read here as a way of coming to terms with a world in which various needs and desires were interpreted as symptoms of something larger, as something that, in however distorted or unknowable a form, exceeded immediate

demands. To be attentive, weary, and respectful of this 'something larger' . . . this is how a cutaway to a clock quietly implores us not to recoil into an exclusive and hazardous particularism. This is also how a seemingly apolitical film quietly implores us to read it allegorically.

(Cazdyn 2002: 235)

Similarly, Mitsuhiro Yoshimoto places *Late Spring* in the post-war moment of the Occupation, but he is ultimately more interested in a historiography of Ozu criticism and the way the previous generation of scholars were trapped in a 'simplistic understanding of cultural exchange, permeation, and traffic, so that regardless of whether it is accepted, appropriated, or rejected by the Japanese, Hollywood film – particularly its mode of narration – is said to play the role of norm for Japanese cinema' (Yoshimoto 1993: 125). Yoshimoto suggests that people use 'tradition' to describe Ozu because for them it helps to explain the general feeling or atmosphere created by the director's films. He writes:

What is at stake here is something which is much too amorphous to be articulated by the explicitly discursive language of the tradition/ modern dichotomy. This amorphous something is not an illusion but a concrete presence in people's social experiences. But as an emergent form of thinking, it does not have its own language or the articulate form of a discourse. Therefore, it can be expressed only in some already existing discursive form, or to be precise, it becomes apparent only as the difference introduced into the obvious use of language. It is this difference eluding any hegemonic use of language that Raymond Williams calls 'structure of feeling'.

(Ibid.: 124)

Yoshimoto does not follow this up with any satisfying suggestions for getting at this 'structure of feeling' in Ozu's cinema. However, it is precisely this that Bordwell and Thompson's approach veers away from in its formalism. When they correct Richie's and Schrader's loose descriptions of point-of-view in the Kyōto inn scene, they fail to engage with the two writers' central question, which asks why that vase is so oddly powerful. This power has something to do with style, but it cannot be reduced to Ozu's playful orchestration of cinematic tools.

A fascinating cinematic homage to Ozu by Suō Masayuki points to the crux of the problem. *Abnormal Family: My Brother's Wife* (*Aniki no yomesan*, 1983) is one of the most interesting examples of the soft-core *pinku* (pink) genre, and perhaps the only film that ever replicated Ozu's style down to the most minute detail.[4] The story, style, characters, and settings constantly invoke Ozu's iconography, and especially *Late Spring*. Suō's homage to Ozu's narrative ellipses delegates the wedding to somewhere off-screen while making the audience privy to the conjugal bed. A Ryū Chishū look-alike frequents his favorite bar, whose hostess just happens to be a dominatrix. Apparently, the audiences for this film were roughly split into two camps, both of which were laughing at different parts of the movie.

Actually, this is a rather revealing anecdote. As Thompson writes, 'The very fact that we so often must define Ozu's style by what he does *not* use indicates its sparseness ... Ozu's differences from other filmmakers suggest that a distinct set of perceptual skills may be appropriate to his work' (Thompson 1988: 341). I believe Ozu was also making his films with two audiences in mind. One segment can watch *Late Spring* and be moved to tears while being completely oblivious to its strange narrative machinations. The other – a segment of the audience with as sophisticated a sense of film aesthetics as Ozu himself – is called out to play by the director.

There is finally, however, another possibility. It could be that all of Ozu's elaborations of cinematic narration were merely a personal thing primarily meant for his own pleasure – a private obsession that went largely disregarded until the 1970s. Yamada Sakae (2002) has pointed out that Ozu was a great admirer of fine textiles and pottery, *kabuki* and *noh* theater. In fact, among the carefully arranged props on his stage are his own favorite pieces. Ozu was a collector, and his own art displays all the prototypical hallmarks of a collector's activity: the totalizing obsession with tiny detail, the fetishistic arrangements of favorite objects such as props and actors in space, the unending quest for refinement and the perfect collection, and a love of display combined with an obstinate indifference to the significance others might find in the collection's arrangement and composition. If anything makes the collector and the film director allies, it is their love of organizing all the elements of their collections and bringing every constituent part of that world under total control – spinning their comfortably individualized world within the historical world. That is to say, Ozu's 'unreasonable choices' may in fact have been those of a collector *par excellence*, which helps explain why the director refused to explain them away until his dying day.

Although film scholars have traditionally been sophisticated viewers able to recognize that Ozu was up to something extraordinary, his other more mainstream audience may have been all but oblivious to his 'unreasonable' narrative sleights of hand. Even when they noticed the difference, their main concern was naturally to immerse themselves in the proliferation of more melodramatic meanings exemplified by the image of the vase. They were too engrossed to care how bizarre Ozu's world actually was. Several film scholars have tried to bridge these two positions, although we could say that – like Suō's audience – Bordwell and Schrader were laughing at different parts.

Now that we know what we're looking at in an Ozu film, and recognize the traps of reducing the director to an emblem of an essentialized national idiom, the way lies enticingly open to a proliferation of approaches to Ozu's filmography. Richie was writing at the formative moment for film studies, when cinema was seen as the expression of national character and/or the genius of exceptional artists. Burch, Bordwell and Thompson's work was part of a dialogue over film study, and the manner in which they all cleave close to each other's arguments indicates the cohesiveness of the discipline before the 1990s.

At the turn of the century, however, a sense of crisis over disciplinary identity has become widespread. Books on the state of the field have proliferated and film studies departments have started contemplating name changes along with the integration of digital technologies into their pedagogies. A wrenching debate within the English language's main scholarly organization provoked a name change from the Society of Cinema Studies to the Society for Cinema and Media Studies. There are signs that film studies, which began as a thoroughly interdisciplinary discipline that coalesced into a solid identity around specific technological and textual concerns, has now begun reinvigorating its inter-disciplinary roots.

Japanese film studies (television is slowly coming into the sights of scholars) has capitalized on the fluidity of this situation with the embrace of area studies, especially concerning history and literature. Younger scholars are bringing a diverse set of disciplinary and methodological assumptions to the study of Japanese film, in addition to an ability to exploit richly the Japanese language archive. There may never be the kind of coherent dialogue evidenced in the Ozu criticism of old. This produced a small mountain of writings whose significance for us today is their authors' attention to the specificities of film texts in historical contexts, and their commitment to discovering the pleasures, powers, and politics of the moving image. Disciplinary questions haunt the background of most Ozu criticism of the past, and institutionalized film studies was as restricting as it was enabling. It will be interesting to see where the next sustained engagement with Ozu takes us. However, it would perhaps signify the end of the discipline itself if someone, sometime in the future, ever imagined a way definitively to explain that vase in *Late Spring*.

Notes

1 It would behoove us to describe Ozu's style in detail: however, to accomplish this adequately is far beyond the scope of this chapter as Ozu's style and its articulation in any given film is exceedingly complex. For the best introduction to this topic, I would direct the reader to Thompson (1988) and Bordwell (1988). Neither is without controversy, as I discuss, but they are by far the most careful analyses of Ozu's approach to cinematic narration in any language. Ozu has inspired such analysis and debate because he systematically rejected many of the core rules and regulations constituting the continuity style of filmmaking. Because his self-imposed rules were followed comprehensively, we can presumably find them in any part of *Late Spring*. Indeed, after seeing several works by the director, you will instantly know an Ozu film when you see it. The look and feel of the films is that distinctive. For further reading on *Late Spring*, see Ozu and Noda (1984), Desser (1985) and Yoshida (2003).
2 Paul Schrader in conversation with the author, January 2004.
3 The most important article here is Thompson and Bordwell (1976), although they quickly repudiated this position. Richie (1964) had already compared Ozu to Antonioni as early as 1964.
4 One could also say the film is an homage to the vastly influential Japanese language Ozu criticism of Hasumi Shigehiko. See, in particular, Hasumi 1983; Hasumi 1997.

References

Bordwell, David (1988) *Ozu and the Poetics of Cinema*, Princeton: Princeton University Press.

Burch, Noël (1979) *To the Distant Observer: Form and Meaning in the Japanese Cinema*, Berkeley: University of California Press. [Reprinted electronically by the Center for Japanese Studies, University of Michigan. Online. http://name.umdl.umich.edu/ aaq5060)]

Cazdyn, Eric (2002) *The Flash of Capital: Film and Geopolitics in Japan*, Durham, NC: Duke University Press.

Desser, David (1985) 'Late Spring', in Frank N. Magill (ed.) *Magill's Survey of Cinema: Foreign Language Films*, Englewood Cliffs, NJ: Salem Press: 1745–50.

Hasumi, Shigehiko (1983) *Kantoku Ozu Yasujirō [Ozu Yasujiro: Film Director]*, Tokyo: Chikuma Shobō.

—— (1997) 'Sunny Skies', in David Desser (ed.) *Tokyo Story*, Cambridge: Cambridge University Press: 118–29.

Ozu, Yasujirō, and Noda, Kōgo (1984) 'Late Spring', in Inoue Kazuo (ed.) *Ozu Yasujirō sakuhinshū III [Collected Works of Ozu Yasujiro III]*, Tokyo: Rippū Shobō: 201–44.

Richie, Donald (1964) 'Yasujiro: The Syntax of His Films', *Film Quarterly* 17 (2): 11–16.

—— (1971) *Japanese Cinema: Film Style and National Character*, New York: Doubleday. [Reprinted electronically by the Center for Japanese Studies, University of Michigan. Online. http://name.umdl.umich.edu/agc9004]

—— (1974) *Ozu: His Life and Films*, Berkeley: University of California Press.

—— (1999 [1965]) *The Films of Akira Kurosawa*, Berkeley: University of California Press. Third edition.

Richie, Donald, and Anderson, Joseph L. (1982 [1959]) *The Japanese Film: Art and Industry*, Princeton: Princeton University Press.

Said, Edward (1978) *Orientalism*, New York: Pantheon.

Schrader, Paul (1972) *Transcendental Style in Film: Ozu, Bresson, Dreyer*, Berkeley: University of California Press.

Sonomura, Masahiro, and Nakamura, Mariko (1999) *Ozu Yasujirō no nazo [The Riddle of Ozu Yasujiro]*, Tokyo: Shōgakukan.

Thompson, Kristin (1988) *Breaking the Glass Armor: Neoformalist Film Analysis*, Princeton: Princeton University Press.

Thompson, Kristin, and Bordwell, David (1976) 'Space and Narrative in the Films of Ozu', *Screen* 17 (2): 41–73.

Tsuzuki Masaaki (1993) *Ozu Yasujirō nikki [Ozu Yasujiro's Diary]*, Tokyo: Kōdansha.

Vasey, Ruth (1988) 'Ozu and the No', *Australian Journal of Screen Theory* 7 (80): 88–102.

Yamada Sakae (2002) 'Ozu eiga no kimono to kodōgu' [Props and Kimono in the Films of Ozu], *Cinema Dong Dong* 1: 16–8.

Yoshida, Kijū (2003) *Ozu's Anti-Cinema*, translated by Daisuke Miyao and Kyoko Hirano, Ann Arbor: Center for Japanese Studies Press.

Yoshimoto, Mitsuhiro (1993) 'Logic of Sentiment: The Postwar Japanese Cinema and Questions of Modernity', University of California, San Diego (unpublished Ph.D. dissertation).

Zeman, Marvin (1972) 'The Serene Poet of Japanese Cinema: The Zen Artistry of Yasujiro Ozu', *Film Journal* 1 (3–4): 62–71.

Ozu Yasujirō Filmography

See Chapter 1, on *I Was Born, But . . .*, for a full filmography.

6

HISTORY THROUGH CINEMA

Mizoguchi Kenji's *The Life of O-Haru* (1952)

Joan Mellen

From the early 1920s when he began to direct silent films, Mizoguchi Kenji was a revolutionary filmmaker whose every shot embodied his belief that injustice exposed was vulnerable to challenge. 'The films of Mizoguchi are meditations on man, posed in terms of mise-en-scène', French critic Philippe Sablon observed in *Cahiers du Cinéma* in May 1959. Human nature could be understood best by being observed in a particular historical and social context. The methodology most appropriate to studying Mizoguchi's films is one of analyzing the intersection between his characters and the moment in history in which the film is set. His period films, in turn, reverberate upon the historical moment in which Mizoguchi made the film.

Traditionally, Japanese directors made period films as a means of offering strong criticisms of Japanese society of the present – this is the reason why the most felicitous entrance into Japanese cinema in general is through its representation of Japanese history. Shortly after *The Life of O-Haru* (*Saikaku ichidai onna*, 1952) won the International Prize at the 1952 Venice Film Festival, Mizoguchi told Kishi Matsuo (1952), interviewing him for the Japanese film magazine *Kinema Junpō* in April of that year, that 'the present social system isn't so different from three hundred years ago. Comparing today with the Nara [710–784] and Genroku [1688–1704] periods, I don't find much difference: women have always been treated like slaves'. O-Haru's travail expresses only 'part of the long history of women' (Ibid.). In *The Life of O-Haru*, he attacks the brutalization of women in feudal Japan, even as he disavows the political, religious, and social institutions of feudalism.

For Mizoguchi, history is not immutable. O-Haru (Tanaka Kinuyo) and Katsunosuke (Mifune Toshirō), her suitor, may not triumph. Yet even the possibility of their freely choosing each other suggests transcendence. He portrayed, Mizoguchi remarked, 'what should not be possible in the world as if it should be possible' (quoted in Shinoda 1969a: 154).

Mizoguchi's sense of the mutability of history – that change is always possible – is reflected in the many small rebellions of O-Haru. These express not only one character's struggle against a system which denies her personal

Figure 10 The brutalization of women in feudal Japan: *The Life of O-Haru* (1952).
BFI Stills, Posters and Designs.

happiness. They amount, as Japanese critic Satō Tadao (n.d.) has said, to 'an inquisition of the whole male-dominated social structure'.

The method of exploring Japanese film through its response to Japanese history best facilitates an understanding of Mizoguchi's particular style. His one-time assistant who was later an important director in his own right, Shindō Kaneto, pointed out that his preference for the long take allowed Mizoguchi to cram 'all the struggles of life in one-cut, violently trying to capture reality in a single take' (Shindō n.d.). Attention to the minute particularities of the shot, at times for as long as a 15-minute take, allowed Mizoguchi, as he explained to Hazumi Tsuneo in an interview for NHK radio in 1950, to portray 'the lifestyle of a particular place'.

Portraying the historical moment in its specificity, through a realism bordering on naturalism, is thematically revealing. As Donald Richie (1973) has suggested, for Mizoguchi, history, leavened by a 'rigorous realism', never meant 'romanticism', but, as the director himself termed it, 'authenticity' (quoted in

Kishi 1952). Japanese critic Iwasaki Akira (1961) called *The Life of O-Haru* Mizoguchi's 'best film' precisely because 'the unique vitality of his naturalistic realism was preserved and . . . vividly saturates every moment'. Kurosawa Akira (1972) agreed: *The Life of O-Haru* was 'the fullest and ultimate expression of his artistry'.

Another of Mizoguchi's disciples was the Japanese New Wave director Shinoda Masahiro. Shinoda termed Mizoguchi's 'a film style of authentic realism', liberating even the theme of evil 'from the Buddhistic outlook of ballad-drama and Kabuki' (Shinoda 1969b). 'For the first time the camera saw the soot on the roof beam, the soiled fingerprints on the doorknob, the grimy hair-tonic on the geisha's comb, the tear stains on the tatami mat' (Ibid.). Mizoguchi's long takes, combined with the camera travelling at a leisurely pace, with its 'unhurried gaze', Shinoda said, 'allowed life to speak for itself'. Shinoda also judges *The Life of O-Haru* to be Mizoguchi's 'best film' and 'the fullest and ultimate expression of Mizoguchi's realism': his 'fluid camera follows O-Haru everywhere . . . unobtrusively but relentlessly' so that 'his accumulation of authentic details and the accumulation of passionate dialogue' culminates in a transcendence of realism. Mizoguchi 'soars into a realm of his own' (Ibid.).

To immerse the viewer in history, Mizoguchi eschewed montage. Only through the single set-up would the truth of human life reveal itself. 'Cinema with short cuts is too cinematic', Mizoguchi told Shinoda (1969a: 154). 'If you use cross-cuts', Mizoguchi said, 'there are inevitably a few cuts that shouldn't be included . . . the hypnotic power has been impaired' (quoted in Kishi 1952).

His purpose, Mizoguchi said, 'of never changing a set-up through a sequence, leaving the camera always at a certain distance from the action' was to 'portray humanity lucidly' (quoted in Morris 1967: 10). If the best means of understanding the individual was to place him in history, this meant a multi-layered deep focus shot, extended in time through the long take. This technique embodied Mizoguchi's perception that people live within circumstance, and that only with social change and the inevitable progress of history will their lives be altered.

Historical context defines personal identity. Because his characters had not yet broken free of the feudal environment, Mizoguchi allowed himself few close-ups. Meanwhile the mise-en-scène was to be authentic, recreating the historical moment in which his characters were trapped. In search of what Mizoguchi (in an interview with Hazumi Tsuneo for NHK radio in 1950) termed the 'moral atmosphere' of an era, he demanded extensive research, and historically authentic props, insisting that 'viewers today immediately spot fakery' (quoted in Takizawa 1952). In *The Life of O-Haru* he demanded that Katsunosuke's language be archaic Japanese, befitting the Genroku period in which the film is set.

History had not yielded a social order hospitable to the ordinary person, and did not appear likely to do so in the 1950s. Mizoguchi admitted to Hazumi Tsuneo that he both retained 'a strong attachment to the past', and entertained 'little hope for the future'. He would not make films offering the spectator an easy palliative. 'I want to make films which represent the way of life of a particular society', he declared, acknowledging that these might well drive the spectator to 'despair' (quoted in Morris 1967: 3). The transcendence Shinoda addresses came, as Satō (1982: 185) put it, in Mizoguchi's depiction of characters who 'assert themselves in the face of oppression, be it social or sexual'.

Feminism was Mizoguchi's persistent theme. It reached its culmination in *The Life of O-Haru*, but began with concentrated intensity in *Osaka Elegy* (*Naniwa erejī*, 1936) and *The Sisters of Gion* (*Gion no kyōdai*, 1936). At the close of *The Sisters of Gion*, Omocha (Yamada Isuzu), a *geisha* whose name means 'a toy', is lying in her hospital bed. Helpless and defeated, she issues an impassioned protest against the degraded condition of women, clearly speaking for the director: 'Why are we made to suffer so! Why are there *geisha*? It's all wrong!' she cries.

Mizoguchi keeps Yamada in a medium shot because society had yet to grant women the power afforded by the close-up. A character's place in society determines technique. 'Close-ups cannot be avoided', Mizoguchi admitted (quoted in Takizawa 1952). But he kept them to a minimum.

Omocha attempts to manipulate the system and so survive. A *moga* (modern girl), she dons Western dress and declares that 'all men are our enemies'. Her traditional sister Umekichi, also forced to sell her body, remains unliberated and behaves as if she is honored to sacrifice her happiness to the needs of a man. Both sisters end up penniless and alone, as does O-Haru who descends from being attached to the Court of the Emperor to begging as an itinerant nun.

Mizoguchi: The artist in history

Mizoguchi's feminism finds no easy correlative in his biography. He observed firsthand the degradation of women in a family where his father abused his mother and older sister, while he could only stand by helplessly. When his mother died, his father sold his older sister to a *geisha* house, as O-Haru's father sells her to the Shimabara.

Yet Mizoguchi became known as a man who had 'suffered at the hands of women', and even one who came to 'hate women'. He chose the bohemian life of the artist, not without its dangers. In 1925 a *geisha* named Ichijō Yuriko fell in love with him and tried to move in with him as a means of pressuring him to marry her. Out of jealousy one day she attacked him with a long razor, slashing his back open in an incident which made national headlines (Asaka 1956).

Ichijō was delivered over to the police by Mizoguchi's assistant director Asaka Kōji, who had been present at the scene. Mizoguchi did not press charges. Rather, he continued to live with her, supported by her wages as a maid. Years later, Mizoguchi, exhibiting on his back ugly knife scars, remarked that 'woman is a dangerous thing', which has been translated also as 'women are terrifying' (Yoda n.d.).[1]

Mizoguchi went on to marry a dance-hall girl; in 1941 he had her committed to an institution because she suffered from hereditary syphilis. He proposed to Tanaka Kinuyo, the actress who played O-Haru and also appeared in 11 of his films. After she refused him, he apparently blocked her from directing films.

He had had difficulties with a woman producer, the actress Irie Takako. 'I don't think a woman should establish a production studio', he said (quoted in Morris 1967: 34).

In his personal history Mizoguchi may have been, as Satō (n.d.) puts it, 'a weak and undependable young man, protected by an unfortunate woman full of love for him'. This was his *geisha* sister, who married a rich aristocrat. In his films he persistently proposed justice for women.

Mizoguchi's history as a filmmaker, and his confrontation with the historical exigencies of his time, reveal an artist beset by contradictions. Looking back on his career when he was 51, he admitted, 'I see only a long series of compromises and disputes with capitalists (who are called today, producers), in order to make films which please me' (quoted in Morris 1967: 9).

He acknowledged the truths of Marxism in his approach to history, but did not stop there. 'I've always felt that communism solves the problems of class, but overlooks the problems of man and woman which still remain afterwards', he told critic Kishi Matsuo (1952). Always he depicted 'men and women as part of the social system of the time' (quoted in Morris 1967: 42), rather than in the abstract.

In the 1920s, under the direct influence of Marxism, he made what were termed 'left wing tendency films' (*keikō eiga*) chronicling the misery of the poor. A tendency film, as Joseph L. Anderson and Donald Richie (1982: 64) explain in their history of Japanese cinema, suggests the need to fight against a given social tendency, implying a call to rebellion and protest.

Almost immediately, Mizoguchi faced the censors. 'All scenes showing the revolt of the peasants against their masters were cut' from his first film, *Resurrection of Love* (*Ai ni yomigaeru hi*, 1922), and Mizoguchi himself was 'put on the carpet by the Police Department' (quoted in Morris 1967: 42). *Chronicle of the May Rain* (*Samidare zōshi*, 1924) chronicled the forbidden love of a *geisha* and a Buddhist priest. *No Money, No Fight* (*Uchen puchan*, 1925), about a Chinese soldier who refused to go to war unless he was paid, a 'satire on war', was banned.

Just as, in his romantic life, Mizoguchi does not seem to have lived by the feminist beliefs of his films, so, despite his belief in freedom and class equality, at times he acquiesced to the demands of the increasingly militaristic Japanese government. From personal experience he discovered how people are caught in the snares of politics. In 1925 he agreed to make a film urging an improvement in rice production (*The Song of Hometown* [*Furusato no uta*]) and in 1927 another glorifying the Russo-Japanese War (*The Imperial Grace* [*Kō-on*]). Still, censors cut a scene where a wounded soldier plays the accordion, and described it as 'anti-militaristic'.

Undaunted, in 1929 Mizoguchi went on to make *Metropolitan Sympathy* (*Tōkai kōkyōgaku*). This film, based on a left-wing source, was about a woman seduced by a rich man. Forsaking him, she allies herself with an idealist; the two determine to avenge class inequities. Cutting between the daily lives of rich and poor, Mizoguchi enlisted the montage method he was later to reject. The crew went on location in a proletarian neighborhood, disguising themselves as workers and concealing their equipment. The police soon arrived. Mizoguchi was ordered to portray the poor as more cheerful (Bock 1978: 39). The police returned as Mizoguchi was making the 1931 *And Yet They Go On* (*Shikamo karera wa yuku*) about a mother and daughter who must both become prostitutes to survive.

That he made a propaganda film the following year (*Dawn in Manchuria* [*Manmō kenkoku no reimei*], 1932) meant not that Mizoguchi lacked 'any usual acceptance of political affiliation', as Anderson and Richie (1982: 70) suppose reductively, but that the director was gaining himself breathing room. In 1937 the Home Ministry had set forth a code, demanding that films 'eliminate tendencies toward individualism as expressed in American and European pictures' (Ibid.: 128). Mizoguchi was incapable of glorifying 'the beauty of the peculiarly indigenous family system' (Ibid.) as mandated by this code; the appalling situation of the Japanese woman alone precluded such a perspective. Slice of life films describing 'individual happiness' were prohibited, even as the best of Mizoguchi's films cry out for just such happiness, in particular for his female characters.

In the conflict between *giri* (duty of obligation) and *ninjō* (human compassion and inclination), all the emphasis was now on duty and obedience, not least to the political authority. Forced in 1938 to make a film called *The Song of the Camp* (*Roei no uta*), Mizoguchi complied, then resigned from the Shinkō Kinema company in disgust. He moved on to other studios. The military government was again at Mizoguchi's door attacking *Osaka Elegy* (banned completely after 1940) and *The Sisters of Gion* for 'decadent tendencies'.

During the war, Mizoguchi made films about actors, 'my way of resisting' (quoted in Morris 1967: 37). When the government demanded a film showing 'true devotion to the cause', he filmed a version of an old chestnut, the story of the loyal 47 *rōnin* (*The Loyal 47 Ronin* [*Genroku chūshingura*], 1941) 'so I wouldn't have to make anything else'. Nor would he fight. 'Everybody was mobilized', he admitted in 1945. 'Me, I hid'. (Ibid.)

The post-war US Occupation (1945–52) presented its own set of edicts to Japanese filmmakers, among them that films be made about the struggle of women for equality. Mizoguchi, whose *Osaka Elegy*, as Satō (n.d.) says, offers the 'recognition of a woman's right to resistance against men', should have granted Mizoguchi safe harbor from the censors. Instead, SCAP (Supreme Commander of the Allied Powers) refused to approve Mizoguchi's *Utamaro and His Five Women* (*Utamaro o meguru gonin no onna*, 1946) merely because it was a period film, and so by definition 'favoring or approving feudal loyalty', never a Mizoguchi perspective.

Mizoguchi appeared in person at General Headquarters to argue that Utamaro was 'a popular democratic painter' (quoted in *Kinema Junpō*, January 1954). Promising to make a film set in the present about injustices toward women, he was permitted to proceed. These new strictures, he complained, made it 'absolutely impossible to make a period film'. At every step he was compelled to consult with Occupation authorities.

The Life of O-Haru: Feminism in its historical context

By 1950, Mizoguchi had been considering for five or six years making a film based on the satirical short stories and novels of Saikaku Ihara (1641–93), an author whose works were censored by the Army during World War Two. When Shōchiku refused this project, he resigned from yet another studio. *The Life of O-Haru* appeared in 1952 under the Shin Tōhō banner. Product of a split in the Tōhō employees' union and a series of strikes, Shin Tōhō financed its own films with everyone working 'on a general profit-sharing basis' (Anderson and Richie 1982: 171).

In *The Life of O-Haru*, Mizoguchi's meticulous depiction of the art of the Genroku era is treated ironically. The mise-en-scène shows the flowering of the arts during the period directly resulting from the great prosperity of the ascendant merchant class whose democratic energy is depicted in several Mizoguchi films, in particular *A Story from Chikamatsu* (*Chikamatsu monogatari*, 1954). 'Urban society in Japan had reached a peak of material prosperity' in the Genroku era, historian George Samson (1963: 151) notes, even as the *samurai* class, still at the top of the social hierarchy, faced bankruptcy.

As *samurai* were increasingly impoverished, the middle class grew rich. It at once supported a wide variety of art forms. Among these were the *ukiyo-e* (woodblock print) and *ukiyo zōshi* (illustrated tale) set in the floating world of the entertainment quarters. Textile art, the production of elaborate, richly textured textiles, reached considerable heights pictured to perfection in the mise-en-scène of *The Life of O-Haru*. Theatre saw the ascendancy of the great playwright Chikamatsu Monzemon, son of a *samurai* who wrote for the middle class, which alone could afford to frequent the theatres.

Against this backdrop of burgeoning wealth, Mizoguchi excoriates the continuing and brutal oppression of women. O-Haru's name means 'spring', another irony. Mizoguchi reveals that the Japanese woman, even at a moment of prosperity of this society, remained a sacrifice to Japan's advancement. Her misery is set in the mise-en-scène against a background of democratic and artistic energy.

The year is 1686, publication date of Saikaku's (1963 [1686]) *The Life of an Amorous Woman* (*Kōshoku ichidai onna*), Mizoguchi's source. Episodic in structure, *The Life of O-Haru* chronicles in descending order O-Haru's social decline. At the beginning she is attached to the Imperial Court. Next she becomes a concubine to a *daimyō* (feudal leader), Lord Matsudaira, bearing his child. Banished because Matsudaira grows too fond of her, O-Haru is sold by her father as a courtesan to the Shimabara. Too spirited for this role, she is reduced to becoming a maid at the establishment of a merchant. Briefly, happily, she is a wife to a fan-maker. Widowed, she seeks refuge as a nun. Banished, unjustly, from the temple, she is reduced to street prostitution.

Each episode begins in long shot, reflecting that O-Haru must be seen as a sacrifice to history, enslaved by an environment inhospitable to women. These opening establishing shots are held beyond their natural time in long takes, the better for Mizoguchi to reveal how his character is trapped in a hostile social landscape. Each episode is punctuated by a fade, a statement of the historical inexorability of women's fate. From each defeat, there is no return, only a downward descent.

Mizoguchi's camera gently tracks behind O-Haru in the long takes, as if to protect her. His structure sympathizes with her plight too: the film opens with O-Haru at the age of 50, a penniless streetwalker, taking refuge at a temple of the *rakan* (Buddhist saints). A statue dissolves, first slowly and then in full clarity to the young Imperial Court page Katsunosuke. O-Haru's travail is then revealed in flashback, the oppression of woman the foregone conclusion of history.

In a single take sequence at the restaurant where Katsunosuke has tricked O-Haru into meeting him, he speaks the credo of the film. He is 'loyal and sincere', Katsunosuke says. She might despise his low rank (O-Haru is a loyal citizen of Genroku Japan, a young woman schooled in the feudal hierarchies), but not his devotion. 'You can't understand the taste of nobility', O-Haru replies. Who at the Court really loves you or would marry you, Katsunosuke rejoins. 'Social prestige isn't happiness. Please accept my love'.

Passive, as women were required to be, whatever their personal desires, O-Haru sinks to the ground, allowing Katsunosuke to carry her out of the frame. Granting them privacy, and homage, Mizoguchi and his camera remain outside in the garden. Love does not triumph over centuries of feudal submission. When the police arrive, O-Haru reveals her identity with misplaced pride: 'I'm a daughter of Okui Shinzaemon, a *samurai* serving Choin-in [temple]'.

The social order is fate. O-Haru and her parents are exiled from Kyōto. She is 'guilty of misconduct with a person of inferior rank', the parents reproved for 'lack of parental supervision'. Ignoring the 180 degree line of continuity, even as his characters are not free to ignore the rules binding them in feudal Japan, Mizoguchi cuts to a shot behind the three defendants: the parents bow at once to the verdict. O-Haru hesitates, her head remaining up. Then she bows, but only slightly. No one but Mizoguchi sympathizes, or is free. The camera pans from under the bridge for a last glimpse of the three small defeated figures, trudging toward the horizon in extreme long shot.

Facing execution, Katsunosuke shouts, 'I hope the time will come when there is no social rank! And men can love!' These words are inflammatory in their historical context; there is no such plea for justice in Saikaku. Mizoguchi has the scribe walk away, so that Katsunosuke's last words remain unrecorded. In the last shot of the sequence the tip of the sword used to behead him is wet with Katsunosuke's blood.

The feudal order is supported by the patriarchy. O-Haru's father abuses her physically and verbally. The parents were to be seen as 'inhumane from our modern viewpoint', Mizoguchi wrote to his screenwriter Yoda Yoshikata, with 'the warped morality of feudalism'. The father was to be 'a real cheapskate, exactly like the typical misers in most Saikaku stories' (quoted in Yoda n.d.).

Heroic in her powerlessness, O-Haru demands to know how love can be immoral, a demand that is at once a feminist *cri de coeur*. In Saikaku's story, the O-Haru at the Imperial Court was 12 years old. Mizoguchi's O-Haru is old enough to speak her mind: 'What if our ranks do differ if we truly love each other?' An impoverished *samurai*, the father soon uses her as a chattel to fill empty coffers. When she objects to becoming a concubine, arguing that such a fate violates the wishes of Katsunosuke, her father pushes her and knocks her to the ground.

In such a historical context, women are not afforded the luxury of solidarity with each other, a diminished existence that in no way undermines Mizoguchi's pervading feminism. O-Haru's mother has been conditioned to serve the needs of the social order, not the wishes of her daughter, or herself. 'You'll be given a high rank!' she tells O-Haru, urging her to accept Lord Matsudaira's offer. In the household of the *daimyō*, Lady Matsudaira is persuaded to comply for the sake of the clan; rich women are equally pressured to sacrifice their desires. Later, out of jealousy, O-Haru is attacked by the merchant's wife when she learns that O-Haru had been a Shimabara courtesan.

In one shot O-Haru shows kindness to an abandoned courtesan playing her *samisen* (Japanese three-stringed musical instrument) in the sun. Only the aging prostitutes, people like herself who have long since given up hope that their survival is of interest to anyone, show her kindness. Saikaku's nameless first person narrator becomes a lusty seductress, a procuress and a schemer, 'prey to wanton feelings', one who masturbates, 'now with my heel, now with the middle finger of my hand'. Veteran of eight abortions, never bearing a child, she has slept with 'more than ten thousand men'. Passing through all the professions open to a single woman in the Genroku era, she opens a calligraphy and etiquette school for young girls, then works as a seamstress, then as a procuress.

Mizoguchi creates in O-Haru a woman seeking only to be loved for herself, not a wanton. If she pleases men sexually, she wants first to be loved and respected. She bears a son to Lord Matsudaira, only to be forced to say she was 'caused to bear' a child. Then she is separated from her son forever.

Through his signature deep focus shot Mizoguchi chronicles the ironic artistic abundance of the Genroku era. Fabulous textured *kimono* serve as concealing curtains at O-Haru's dance class. At the mansion of Lord Matsudaira, the *bunraku* puppet theater performs, enacting the story of O-Haru, the Lord and Lady, as if to reconcile Lady Matsudaira to the unkind fate of her husband's taking a concubine.

O-Haru's destiny is determined by the clan in a many-layered shot redolent of the power of the clan system, and includes, amid scrolls, calligraphy and art objects, at least ten planes of contrasting visuals within the single shot. Against a crowded mise-en-scène of objects no less than men, Mizoguchi expresses the power of the forces against which any individual woman is powerless. 'She's of no further use to us here', the clan leaders decide.

At Shimabara, O-Haru entertains a counterfeiter, who appears to be a 'wealthy country gentleman', in Mizoguchi's words (quoted in Yoda n.d.). They meet in a room adorned by a painted screen with elaborate wall-textiles. Their beauty is apparent in the black and white shot where Mizoguchi can contrast O-Haru's motionlessness with the frantic rush of *geisha* and servants as the counterfeiter flings his coins into the air. 'I can buy you with money!' the counterfeiter cries. O-Haru stands impervious to the clamor in her elaborately patterned *kimono* standing before a richly painted screen.

At Jihei's merchant establishment, against a background of exquisite textiles and *kimono*, his wife grabs O-Haru and cuts off her long glossy black hair to render her unattractive. About to rape O-Haru, the merchant prays before an elaborately decorated altar. Amid beauty, the newly rich merchants, patrons of the arts, exact their cruelty. The social revolution which displaced the *samurai* aristocracy does not bring women equality or respect.

So during a brief sojourn into happiness, when O-Haru marries a fan-maker, Mizoguchi also chronicles a historical moment when the world seems bursting with art and beauty. It is never out of aestheticism, but always with irony that Mizoguchi expresses his theme: in the midst of all this art, women suffered unrelentingly. The fan-maker is murdered, carrying an *obi* (belt for a *kimono*) meant as a gift to his wife, even as he has left no will and made no provision for her.

Saikaku and Mizoguchi share a contempt for religious hypocrisy. Saikaku had his heroine take up with a bonze (Buddhist priest) who keeps her a prisoner, hidden away in a temple as his wife. O-Haru is aided by a nun, who turns on her after catching her with the merchant, Jihei. Mizoguchi then adds an unacknowledged motivation for the nun's cruelty: 'Did you provide me with a visual demonstration in which you are hoping I'd join you?' For Mizoguchi, the long take, the 'most precise and specific expression for intense psychological moments' (quoted in Morris 1967: 10), best creates emotional response and most fully disturbs the spectator; thus, the nun here remains within the shot long after the viewer wishes her gone. All the temple scenes in this film, Mizoguchi wrote in his notes to Yoda (n.d.) for the second draft of his script, were to be similarly 'ironic'.

Forbidden to serve Buddha, O-Haru is banished yet again, this time to the sound of loud, almost screeching church bells. For the nun, religion has not been accompanied by compassion. Her implacable self-righteousness, a form of hubris, prevails even as O-Haru is filmed from a low angle, granting her moral superiority.

The ending of O-Haru: The social order as personal fate

On occasion Mizoguchi would tell Yoda (n.d.), 'I demand more socio-philosophical substance'. The ending of O-Haru reveals Mizoguchi's persistent attempt to satirize a particular social order. Indeed, he told Hazumi Tsuneo during his 1950 NHK radio interview that what he liked about Saikaku was that he was 'a critic of civilization'.

O-Haru's now grown son, the new Lord, has requested that she return to reside at the Matsudaira palace. The clan decides otherwise. Mizoguchi suggests that the feudal order diminished the power of even the highest figures of the *samurai* class. In this rigid unfeeling system, O-Haru's 'degenerate behavior' is termed by its elders to be shaming the clan. Demanding her 'deep repentance', they cast her out, and the highest placed *samurai* are enlisted in the effort to hunt her down when O-Haru escapes temporarily from their clutches.

The final sequence reveals O-Haru as a begging nun. In long shot, she moves from house to house, singing sutras, begging bowl in hand. A woman holding a child in her arms opens a door and offers O-Haru alms. Gender loyalty exists only when it is accompanied by class sympathy. Poor women remain the only people who come to O-Haru's assistance. A man at the next house waves O-Haru away.

O-Haru then turns to face the camera. Even medium shots are rare in Mizoguchi, but at the close of this film, as he did in *The Sisters of Gion*, he offers a startling close-up, demanding that the spectator look into O-Haru's ravaged face. O-Haru then turns and moves on. The camera tracks with her, her companion to the last. If O-Haru has been abandoned by those closest to her, the director will see her through.

At Mizoguchi's 'certain distance', the camera watches as O-Haru stops when the temple comes into view. She offers a prayer. When this time she trudges out of the frame, Mizoguchi does not choose to follow her. Hope is gone; her tale has been told.

Instead, he remains in an unexpected long take, in a shot devoid of human beings. He focuses on the temple in the distance so long that it becomes not merely itself, but a symbol of the entire social order he has indicted. He had always been interested, Mizoguchi told Takizawa Hajime (1952) in the year the film appeared, 'in the Church's past relationship with the Imperial Court'. In this film both institutions are prominent among O-Haru's oppressors.

Yoda has said that Mizoguchi stopped at the question of 'what then?' – what is to be done? – out of his deep commitment to Buddhism (quoted in Mellen 1976: 20). *The Life of O-Haru* does not bear him out. Mizoguchi all but glares at that temple, as if to chastise, not just religion, but all those feudal institutions which have oppressed the Japanese woman for centuries and for which the temple becomes emblematic. On the soundtrack is a loud choral lament. Isolating the causes, the sources of oppression, Mizoguchi has also clearly predicted a remedy.

Acknowledgement

The author would like to thank Leonard Schrader for his kind assistance with research materials for this chapter.

Note

1 For a good description of Mizoguchi's personal relationships with women, see Bock 1978: 38–41.

References

Anderson, Joseph L., and Richie, Donald (1982) *The Japanese Film: Art and Industry*, Princeton: Princeton University Press. Expanded edition.

Asaka, Kōji (1956) 'The Silent Films', *Kinema Junpō*, October.

Bock, Audie (1978) *Japanese Film Directors*, Tokyo: Kōdansha International.

Iwasaki, Akira (1961) 'Mizoguchi and Realism', *Kinema Junpō*, September.

Kishi, Matsuo (1952) 'A Talk With Mizoguchi', *Kinema Junpō*, April.

Kurosawa, Akira (1972) Unpublished interview with Leonard Schrader and Nakamura Haruji. May.

Mellen, Joan (1976) *The Waves at Genji's Door: Japan through Its Cinema*, New York: Pantheon.

Morris, Peter (1967) *Mizoguchi Kenji*, Ottawa: Canadian Film Institute, November.

Richie, Donald (1973) 'A Birthday Tribute to Kenji Mizoguchi'. Paper presented at the Museum of Modern Art Department of Film, May 17.

Saikaku, Ihara (1963 [1686]) *The Life of an Amorous Woman and Other Writings*. Edited and translated by Ivan Morris. New York: New Directions.

Samson, George (1963) *A History of Japan, 1615–1867*, Tokyo: Kōdansha International.

Satō, Tadao (n.d.) 'The Feminist Tradition in Japanese Film'. Unpublished manuscript.

—— (1982) *Currents in Japanese Cinema*, Tokyo: Kōdansha International.

Shindō, Kaneto (n.d.) Unpublished correspondence.

Shinoda Masahiro (1969a) 'Mizoguchi kara toku hanarete', *Kikan Film* 3: 154.

—— (1969b) 'Far from Mizoguchi'. Unpublished manuscript.

Takizawa, Hajime (1952) 'Interview with Mizoguchi Kenji', *Eiga Hyōron*, December.

Yoda, Yoshikata (n.d.) Interview with Leonard Schrader and Nakamura Haruji.

Mizoguchi Kenji Filmography

See Chapter 2, on *Osaka Elegy*, for a full filmography.

7

THE MENACE FROM THE SOUTH SEAS

Honda Ishirō's *Godzilla* (1954)

Yomota Inuhiko

In 1954, two years after Japan regained its independence following the San Francisco Peace Treaty, Tōhō managed to resume production following a protracted struggle with its trade union. This is also the year when the studio made two films that would long be remembered in film history: *Seven Samurai* (*Shichinin no samurai*, Kurosawa Akira) and *Godzilla* (*Gojira*, Honda Ishirō). Both films were remarkably successful both in Japan and abroad, and ever since that time '*samurai* film' and 'monster movie' have become mythologised as perhaps the two most representative genres of Japanese cinema.

Godzilla's producer, Tanaka Tomoyuki, initially had the idea of making a film about a gigantic monster that emerges from 20,000 fathoms below the sea. In light of this, it is significant that in March 1954 the US tested a 15-megaton hydrogen bomb in the South Pacific, which exposed numerous Japanese fishermen to lethal doses of radiation in the process. The news of this incident shocked the whole nation, for after Hiroshima and Nagasaki this was the third time that Japanese citizens had been killed and maimed from nuclear exposure. It is against this historical context of a keenly felt sense of emergency that Kayama Shigeru – who had already established his reputation before World War Two as the author of detective thriller novels and lurid adventure stories reminiscent of the work of H. Rider Haggard – wrote the original story of *Godzilla*. Tanaka modified Kamaya's original story into a more realistic plot, and assigned Honda Ishirō as the film's director and Tsuburaya Eiji as special effects artist. The titular monster's name – 'Godzilla' – was derived as a result of synthesising the words 'gorilla' and *kujira* (whale). It was kept strictly confidential during all stages of the film's pre-production.

Honda Ishirō (1910–1993) joined PCL (the company which later became Tōhō) in 1933. He spent his apprenticeship as assistant director to such established filmmakers as Yamamoto Kajirō and Naruse Mikio. Honda was also born in the same year as Kurosawa Akira, and the two of them worked as assistant directors for Yamamoto in the same period and remained lifelong friends. Tōhō was the production company most closely affiliated with the military and thus producer of the greatest number of propaganda films during World War Two. Due to these wartime commitments, however, it was not until 1949 that Honda had the opportunity to make his belated debut as a director. Honda's early documentary film, *Ise Island* (*Ise shima*, 1950), betrays the influence of Robert Flaherty, for whom he had a great respect and whose *Nanook of the North* (US, 1922) he especially admired. However, while Kurosawa actively expressed his individual style and progressed as an *auteur*, Honda was by contrast regarded as an artisan filmmaker capable of making various types of movies ranging from highbrow films to 'teen pics' within the restrictions of the Japanese studio system. In fact, during the 1950s he was one of the country's most prolific directors, making an average of three to four films per year.

Tsuburaya Eiji (1901–1970) was an art director immensely influenced by the aesthetics of German Expressionism. In 1926, he worked on Kinugasa Teinosuke's legendary *A Page of Madness* (*Kurutta ippeiji*) as an assistant cinematographer. Tsuburaya favoured visual images that conveyed an austere, shadowy atmosphere often through the use of low-key lighting. Tsuburaya's remarkable talent for directing special effects led to his involvement in a film produced in collaboration with Nazi Germany, *Atarashiki tsuchi/Die Tochter des Samurai* (*New Earth/Daughter of the Samurai*, 1937), in which he employed such techniques as matte shots and superimposition for the first time in Japan. During the Second World War, Tsuburaya made the most of his skills in the area of special effects when shooting war films. A film that drew particular praise was *The War at Sea from Hawaii to Malay* (*Hawai marē oki kaisen*, 1942) in which Tsuburaya vividly staged the infamous Japanese attack on Pearl Harbor using a carefully constructed studio set. His reproduction of the South Seas in the studio established his reputation and led to his participation in the shooting in Japan of Joseph Von Sternberg's *The Saga of Anatahan* (*Anatahan*, 1953).

Among other key personnel involved in the production of *Godzilla* – including the director of photography, art director, and lighting technician, among others – were a group of highly skilled veterans who had worked with established *auteur* Naruse Mikio. They included the musical composer, Ifukube Akira, who was strongly influenced by the folkloric music of the ethnic minorities from northern Japan such as the Ainus and Nivkhi. The style of his music for Naruse was known for its combination of an archaic rusticity and lyricism that was grounded in simple and straightforward rhythms. Ifukube created Godzilla's legendary scream by employing a double bass. Given the impressive group of artists and technicians involved in *Godzilla*'s production, it is obvious that Tōhō considered this monster film a serious piece of work for discerning audiences, rather than a hack job designed merely to entice children.

The plot of *Godzilla* is as follows. A Japanese fishing boat, making its way across the Pacific Ocean, is suddenly attacked by a mysterious monster and consequently sinks. At around the same time, an unspecified disaster occurs on Ōto Island, situated in a remote part of the Pacific. Ogata (Takarada Akira), a young employee on a ship, and a palaeontologist, Professor Yamane (Shimura Takashi), visit the island on a research exhibition. They witness the rituals and dances performed by the islanders for the purpose of pacifying the soul of a huge sea dragon that is said to emerge from the depths. It is revealed that the islanders have long worshipped this entity and have named it 'Gojira'. The gigantic footprints left on the island convince Professor Yamane that the mysterious monster is the cause of the series of recent disastrous incidents. Godzilla, a surviving dinosaur from the Jurassic period, had been resting under the sea for millennia, but a series of hydrogen bomb experiments have now disturbed and provoked the monster. It is soon revealed that this monster is making its way towards Tokyo. While the public inevitably panics, the government in Tokyo calls an emergency meeting where it is agreed that Godzilla must be destroyed. Professor Yamane is the only person to question this decision openly and to think past the hysteria. He proposes instead a rescue mission to save the monster, noting that Godzilla is in fact a victim of man-made nuclear technology. Yamane also suggests that examining the monster might lead to discoveries that could help human beings survive nuclear war. However, being extremely frightened and thus unusually aggressive, neither the government nor the public expresses any interest in the professor's proposal. In the meantime, Godzilla emerges from Tokyo Bay to lay waste the capital. Indifferent to the volleys of fire emanating from the Self Defence Forces, Godzilla goes on the rampage, destroying every building in sight and spewing radioactive rays from his mouth. Having exhausted himself demolishing much of Tokyo, Godzilla disappears back into the bay to recuperate.

The Japanese discover that the only way to confront and extinguish Godzilla is to use a secret weapon called the Oxygen Destroyer – an intensely hazardous substance requiring immense caution to avoid resulting in an even greater calamity. Interestingly, it is at this point in the narrative that a somewhat unexpectedly melodramatic element begins to surface. The only person capable of handling this dangerous material is one Professor Serizawa, an oxygen expert who in fact invented this substance. It so happens that Serizawa is also engaged to marry Yamane's daughter, but to make matters even more complicated, she is actually in love with Ogata. The young woman is tormented, unable to choose between her two admirers. Before long – and having been convinced by Ogata's sound reasoning – Serizawa agrees to permit use of the mysterious weapon. In the presence of a large crowd of anxious well-wishers, including Yamane and his daughter, Ogata and Serizawa thus go to sea in order to find Godzilla. While Ogata eventually returns to the patrol boat, Serizawa crashes into Godzilla with the Oxygen Destroyer, hence sacrificing his own life for his country and its people. The scene then changes abruptly upon the sight of Godzilla's silhouette appearing suddenly against the night sky and the unlit outline of the city. He emits powerful beams from his mouth while his dorsal fin flickers like neon signs. This sequence beautifully and effectively employs chiaroscuro, suggesting the aesthetic influence of German Expressionism. The miniature stage set of Tokyo, designed by Tsuburaya, is impeccably precise, and this and other scenes of destruction are packed with special effects that blend with the scenes of ordinary day-to-day life without any sense of awkwardness. Honda's talent undoubtedly shines through in his ability to deftly juxtapose three quite different cinematographic components: shots taken on life-size studio sets, the

Figure 11 The catastrophic power of *Godzilla* (1954). Tōhō/The Kobal Collection.

miniature shots, and superimpositions. Despite being openly dismissed by more sombre critics, *Godzilla* nevertheless gained worldwide approval. The beast's reputation travelled across the Pacific, leading the then young Susan Sontag (1966) to write her famous article entitled 'The Imagination of Disaster'.

The abrupt emergence from the south of this monstrous, unspeakable threat reminded Japanese audiences of the US military bombers that had reduced their cities to flaming ruins only a few years earlier. Indeed, these associations are explicitly drawn at various points in the film, such as the moment when people mourn 'yet another air raid' and the scene where city residents are forcefully relocated to the countryside. (This practice occurred during the air raids of the Second World War, although the former scene was removed from prints of *Godzilla* struck for US distribution.) The film also depicts television reporting of the monster's rampage that is particularly unsettling, and again evocative of war trauma. Images of Tokyo's casualties – devastated and strewn across a city reduced to rubble – flicker across the screen while a requiem sung by a girls' choir plays on the soundtrack.

However, despite the powerful wartime memories symbolically recalled through such scenes, the most commonly evoked reading of the concept of Godzilla remains the monster's powerful appropriateness as a metaphor for the nuclear bomb. The shipwreck depicted at the beginning of the film clearly recalls the 1954 exposure to radiation of the Japanese tuna fishing boat mentioned above. One of the survivors of Godzilla's first attack in the film actually decries his own misfortune by asking himself: 'What did I survive Nagasaki for?' (The scene containing this remark was also edited out from the US version of the film.) Like the nuclear bombs and the American military bombers that delivered them, the monster appears invulnerable as it ignores the immense firepower of Japan's conventional weapons such as artillery, tanks and aeroplanes. Moreover, when it emits lethal radioactive rays from its mouth, the monster itself appears to resemble a nuclear bomb. As if to reinforce this impression, Ogata comments at one point that 'Godzilla is indeed the hydrogen bomb itself overshadowing us Japanese'. Similarly, the fact that Serizawa (Ogata's competitor) decides, after prolonged meditation on the matter, to resort to a suicide mission in order to save the country brings to mind the *kamikaze* (divine wind) suicide pilots who were, by the end of the war, virtually Japan's only means of counterattack against the military might of the US. The significance of this drastic action taken by the character Serizawa is further complicated by his having lost an eye during the Second World War. Against the backdrop of a seemingly cheerful and prosperous post-war Japan, he is thus portrayed as an enigmatic critic of society.

In fact, matters are actually even more complicated. Godzilla is as much a threat menacing Japan as another victim of nuclear attack itself. That is, he is defined as a metaphor of post-war Japanese society that has survived the catastrophe caused by the bombings of Hiroshima and Nagasaki. *Godzilla* has a precedent in the Hollywood film, *The Beast from 20,000 Fathoms* (Eugene Lourie, US, 1953). This Warner Brothers B-film also features a nuclear bomb experiment and a monster; in this case, a nuclear blast at the North Pole awakens a dinosaur. Although the dinosaur attempts to raid Manhattan, a nuclear warhead attached to a US army missile finally destroys it. The film's characters do not hesitate to use nuclear arms. Instead, what the film communicates is the vehement message that nuclear weapons are indispensable when it comes to the repelling of the enemies of civilisation. By contrast, what is distinctive about *Godzilla* is that its characters actively engage in earnest discussions about the best way to deal with the monster. On being informed of Godzilla's likely attack trajectory, Yamane locks himself in his study and frets over the monster's survival. Given Godzilla's uniqueness, he also regards the monster as a singularly valuable specimen for study. In his view, analysis of the creature may result in discoveries that could ensure Japan's survival in the nuclear age.

A closer examination of the film also reveals yet another layer of meaning in that Godzilla may also be identified with numerous former Imperial soldiers who died in battle in the South Seas. A consideration of the places that Godzilla destroys after emerging from Tokyo Bay is thus insightful. Godzilla comes onto land from Shinagawa before continuing on to Shinbashi and Ginza. After turning Japan's busiest commercial district into a blazing inferno, he stomps upon the nation's political and communications hubs – the Diet Building and the Television Broadcasting Tower. What appears strange here, though, is that communication (of information) suddenly gets disrupted at this very point. By the time the national defence forces manage to re-identify the location of the monster, Godzilla has already moved to Shitamachi, the traditional shopping, entertainment and residential districts surrounding Sumida River. Having passed Ueno and Asakusa, he enters the river and then withdraws into Tokyo Bay. For those possessing even the slightest knowledge of Tokyo's spatial layout it must be noticeable that there is one important monument, the Imperial Palace, that is never depicted or referred to – despite the fact that geographical logic decrees that Godzilla would have certainly walked past it on this route. The question therefore remains: why did this monster, having travelled all the way from the South Seas to Japan, return into the sea at the very point where it should have reached the Imperial Palace?

It is helpful in this respect to recall that in the popular and mythical imagination of Japan, the South Seas had always been considered an ambivalent space which possesses both utopian charm and sacred qualities. After Japan experienced West European-style modernisation in the mid-nineteenth century, such popular sentiments concerning the region were actively promoted by the government because they provided a legitimate justification for the nation's colonial policies. Numerous colonisers left Japan for South Seas destinations such as Saipan and Palau and this was followed by military expansion. As a consequence of its defeat by the Allies in 1945, however, Japan lost all its pre-war colonies and a longing for the South Pacific in general was forbidden. Many Japanese soldiers died after being confronted with the overwhelming force of the US military and, significantly, only a relative handful survived the war. Yanagita Kunio, a renowned Japanese folklorist active during the Second World War, subsequently developed an anti-war theory based upon this phenomenon. In Yanagita's view, Japanese people have to meet their death in their homeland – the only place where the souls of the dead are considered able to rest peacefully. According to this doctrine, however, when soldiers die in battle abroad, the final destination of their souls remains undetermined and their souls therefore remain in limbo. Assuming Yanagita's view, Japan's numerous Pacific war-dead would therefore have been left in the South Seas, abandoned forever, and unable ever to return to their distant home.

The contemporary folklorist, Akasaka Norio, has thus provided an interpretation of Godzilla's journey towards the Imperial Palace in which the monster is identified as the embodiment of the unquiet ghosts of the soldiers who met with violent deaths far from home. As indirect evidence supporting this view, Akasaka points to the fact that Godzilla evoked Mishima Yukio's profound sympathy (cf. Yomota 1992: 13–18). So why then did the souls of fallen warriors assume the terrifying form of a monster? The Freudian concept of the 'return of the repressed' provides a crucial point of reference here. Godzilla was horrifying precisely because he embodied the souls of those who died during the war. That is to say that the mental image of the casualties of the war was placed in an abject relation to those Japanese who had survived the atrocities and who now enjoyed the prosperity and democracy of post-war life. This psychological process is also profoundly caught up with the issue of collective 'historical oblivion' felt by many Japanese people when it came to public discussion of the war. For instance, in the very year when Godzilla is imagined to have visited Tokyo on film, the Japanese Emperor Hirohito, then 54 years old but still the figurehead of the country, would have been uniquely absorbed in his marine biology studies.

This monster, saddled with such a burden of complex metaphors and covert meanings, is finally defeated by means of Serizawa's noble self-sacrifice. Nevertheless, it was only six months after the production of *Godzilla* in 1954 that the monster struck back in a sequel entitled *Godzilla's Counter Attack* (*Gojira no gyakushū*, Oda Motoyoshi, 1955). Ever since then, 24 more films (including a big-budget version of the Godzilla story made in the US in 1998) have been shot and this series of films is now regarded as a well-established genre in its own right. Indeed, the tally of Godzilla films only increases further if we also include specially edited versions (often featuring additional scenes) that have been released in territories such as the Philippines and the US. While Godzilla appeared as a sinister and menacing entity during the 1950s, he was transformed into a straightforward embodiment of Japanese nationalism for the 1962 *King Kong versus Godzilla* (*Kingukongu tai Gojira*, Honda Ishirō) in which he fights against foreign enemies in the foothills of Mount Fuji. Godzilla, alongside two other 'friendly monsters', also defended Japan from the invader from outer space, King Ghidora, in *The Greatest Battle on Earth* (*San daikaijū: chikyū saidai no kessen*, Honda Ishirō, 1964). In this way, Godzilla has been transformed from foreign menace into Japan's raging guardian deity while in the process he has lost his historically ambivalent meaning and has simultaneously learnt to give off a certain air of 'cuteness'. Godzilla and other post-war Japanese movie monsters can thus be divided into good and bad guys as if they are professional wrestlers fighting against one other. Certainly, within a fairly short space of time, monsters such as Godzilla no longer seem able to possess or communicate any overwhelming or awe-inspiring qualities. They even occasionally use joking gestures more familiar from print and television cartoons. This degradation of the 'Godzilla dynasty' parallels the decline of the Japanese studio system.

The year 1984 saw the emergence of a movement that aimed to restore the Godzilla film to the status of serious cinema. Evident in the Godzilla films of the 1990s is a certain critical tendency that attempts to transcribe the ambivalent notions of nationalism and anti-nuclear ideology inscribed in the original *Godzilla* to a contemporary context. For example, one of the more contemporary films opens with a prologue set on a remote island in the Pacific Ocean. Godzilla, in this rendition of the island's guardian spirit, saves a group of desperate Japanese soldiers from the Americans. Among the survivors is a soldier destined to become a major figure in Japanese financial circles. Years later, this character, who now owns a vast international information network, yearns to see his saviour, Godzilla, just one more time. Another film is set in a futuristic society after Japan's powerful economy has conquered the entire world. A group of evil Caucasians goes back into the past in a time-travel machine in an attempt to destroy Japan's utopian future through the malicious use of a robot dinosaur they have created, but Godzilla defeats this rival to ensure Japan's promised world-historical destiny. Moreover, in yet another of the films from the 1990s, a secret weapon made half a century ago in order to destroy Godzilla, ends up disrupting the ecosystem thus resulting in the emergence of a second monster that wrecks Tokyo. The narrative has Godzilla enact a rather melodramatic self-sacrifice and constitutes a critically acclaimed remake of the first film in the series. By contrast, the later Hollywood version of *Godzilla* (Ronald Emmerich, US, 1998) cites a French nuclear experiment (an actual contemporary event) as the cause of the disturbances that awaken the monster from his aeons of slumber. The narrative of this film principally revolves around the activities of a shadowy French security agency, and therefore eliminates from its storyline the idea of America as a nuclear threat. This concept of America has long been an essential core of the 'Godzilla genre'. As a result, this particular version of the Godzilla story received a negative critical response in Japan.

Half a century has now passed since *Godzilla* was produced, and the fact that both it and *Seven Samurai* were made at Tōhō in 1954 appears ever more intriguing. Although nobody paid attention to the association at the time, both films recount the protection of a vulnerable community against a foreign threat. Furthermore, Shimura Takashi, who played Professor Yamane in *Godzilla*, was assigned a similar role in *Seven Samurai* as a *samurai* leader. The mayor of Ōto Island in *Godzilla* is also played by the same actor who appears in *Seven Samurai* as the mayor of the village to which the titular *samurai* travel. Meanwhile, in real life, Honda Ishirō and Kurosawa Akira, as already noted, remained firm friends. Kurosawa asked his old friend for assistance in directing most of his later films, and Honda's influence can indeed be detected in such Kurosawa titles as *Kagemusha* (1980), *Ran* (1985), and *Dreams* (*Yume*, 1990).

Critics have frequently dismissed Honda as unworthy of serious consideration, regarding him merely as the director of entertainment films aimed at children. By contrast, they have elevated Kurosawa to the status of national treasure. As for the men themselves, by all accounts Honda and Kurosawa had nothing but respect for one another's work. Prospective studies of the history of Japanese cinema should therefore treat Honda's direction of monster movies and Kurosawa's interpretation of prestigious sources such as Shakespeare as equally deserving of serious discussion.

Translated by Sachiko Shikoda

References and Selected Bibliography

Broderick, Mick (ed.) (1996) *Hibakusha Cinema: Hiroshima, Nagasaki and the Nuclear Image in Japanese Film*, London and New York: Routledge.

Gojira no jidai [*The Era of Godzilla*] (2002) Kawasaki: Taro Okamoto Museum of Art.

Higuchi, Naofumi (1992) *Guddo mōningu, gojira: kantoku Honda Ishirō to satsueijo no jidai* [*Good Morning, Godzilla: Director Honda Ishiro and the Studio Era*], Tokyo: Chikuma.

Nagayama, Yasuo (2002) *Kaijū wa naze Nihon o osounoka?* [*Why Does the Monster Assault Japan?*], Tokyo: Chikuma.

Sontag, Susan (1966) *Against Interpretation*, New York: Farrar, Straus and Giroux.

Takarada, Akira (1999) *Nippon gojira ōgon densetsu* [*The Japanese Golden Legend of Godzilla*], Tokyo: Fusō.

Yomota, Inuhiko (1987) *Fūgiribi ga machidōshii* [*I Cannot Wait for the Release Date*], Tokyo: Seido-sha.

—— (1992) *Eiga takarajima: kaijūgaku nyūmon!* [*Film Treasure Island: An Introduction to Monster Studies!*], Washington, DC: Japan Information and Cultural Center.

Honda Ishirō Filmography

(Note: * indicates special effects supervision by Tsuburaya Eiji)

A Story of a Co-op (*Kyōdō kumiai no hanashi*, 1949)
Ise Island (*Ise shima*, 1950)
The Blue Pearl (*Aoi shinju*, 1951)
The Skin of the South (*Nangoku no hada*, 1952)
The Man Who Came to Port (*Minato e kita otoko*, 1952)
Adolescence Part II (*Zoku shishunki*, 1953)
Eagle of the Pacific (*Taiheiyō no washi*, 1953)*
Farewell Rabaul (*Saraba Rabauru*, 1954)*
Godzilla (*Gojira*, 1954)*
Love Make-up (*Koi-geshō*, 1955)
Cry-Baby (*Oen san*, 1955)
Beast Man Snow Man (*Jūjin yukiotoko*, 1955)*
Young Tree (*Wakai ki*, 1956)
Night School (*Yakan chūgaku*, 1956)
People of Tokyo, Goodbye (*Tōkyō no hito sayonara*, 1956)
Radon, Monster from the Sky (*Sora no daikaijū Radon*, 1956)*
Good Luck to These Two (*Kono futari ni sachi are*, 1957)
A Teapicker's Song of Goodbye (*Wakare no chatsumiuta*, 1957)
A Rainbow Plays in My Heart (*Wagamune ni niji wa kiezu: Dai ichibu, Dai nibu*, 1957)
A Farewell to the Woman Called My Sister (*Wakare no chatsumiuta: onēsan to yonda*, 1957)
Defence Force of the Earth (*Chikyū bōeigun*, 1957)*
Song for a Bride (*Hana yome sanjūsō*, 1958)
Beauty and the Liquidman (*Bijo to ekitai ningen*, 1958)*
The Great Monster Baran (*Daikaijū Baran*, 1958)
An Echo Calls You (*Kodama wa yondeiru*, 1959)
The Story of Iron-Arm Inao (*Tetsuwan tōshu Inao monogatari*, 1959)
Seniors, Juniors, Co-workers (*Uwayaku-shitayaku-godōyaku*, 1959)
The Great Space War (*Uchū daisensō*, 1959)*
The First Gas Human (*Gasu ningen dai ichigō*, 1960)*
The Scarlet Man (*Shinkoh no otoko*, 1961)
Mothra (*Mosura*, 1962)*
Suspicous Star Gorath (*Yōsei Gorasu*, 1962)*
King Kong vs. Godzilla (*Kingukongu tai Gojira*, 1962)*

Matango the Fungus of Terror (*Matango*, 1963)*
Undersea Battleship (*Kaitei gunkan*, 1963)*
Godzilla vs. Mothra (*Mosura tai Gojira*, 1964)*
Space Monster Dogora (*Uchū daikaijū Dogora*, 1964)*
The Greatest Battle on Earth (*Sandai kaijū: chijō saidai no kessen*, 1964)*
Frankenstein vs. the Subterranean Monster (*Furankenshutain tai chiteikaijū*, 1965)*
The Great Monster War (*Kaijū daisenso?*, 1965)*
Frankenstein's Monsters: Sanda vs. Gailah (*Furankenshutain no kaijū: Sanda tai Gaira*, 1966)*
Come Marry Me (*Oyome ni oide*, 1966)
King Kong's Counterattack (*Kingukongu no gyakushū*, 1967)*
Attack of the Marching Monsters (*Kaijū sōshingeki*, 1968)*
Atragon II/Latitude Zero (*Ido zero daisakusen*, 1969)*
All Monsters Attack (*Gojira-Minira-Gabara: ōru kaiju daishingeki*, 1969)*
The Space Amoeba (*Gezora-Ganime-Kameba: kessen! Nankai no daikaijū*, 1970)*
Mirrorman (*Mirāman*, 1972)
The Escape of Mechagodzilla (*Mekagojira no gyakushū*, 1975)

Appendix: *Godzilla* Filmography

Godzilla (*Gojira*, Honda Ishirō, 1954)
Godzilla's Counter Attack (*Gojira no gyakushū*, Oda Motoyoshi, 1955)
King Kong vs. Godzilla (*Kingukongu tai gojira*, Honda Ishirō, 1962)
Godzilla vs. Mothra (*Mosura tai gojira*, Honda Ishirō, 1964)
The Greatest Battle on Earth (*San daikaijū: chikyū saidai no kessen*, Honda Ishirō, 1964)
The Great Monster War (*Kaijū daisenso?*, Honda Ishirō, 1965)
The Great South Seas Duel (*Gojira-ebira-mosura: nannkai no daikettō*, Fukuda Jun, 1966)
Monster Island's Decisive Battle: Godzilla's Son (*Kaijūtō no kessen: gojira no musuko*, Fukuda Jun, 1967)
Attack of the Marching Monsters (*Kaijū sōshingeki*, Honda Ishirō, 1968)
All Monster's Attack (*Gojira-minira-gabara: ōru kaijū daishingeki*, Honda Ishirō, 1969)
Godzilla vs. Hedora (*Gojira tai Hedora*, Sakano Yoshimitsu, 1971)
Earth Assault Order: Godzilla vs. Gigan (*Chikyū kōgeki meirei: Gojira tai gaigan*, Fukuda Jun, 1972)
Godzilla vs. Megalon (*Gojira tai Megaro*, Fukuda Jun, 1973)
Godzilla vs. Mechagodzilla (*Gojira tai Mekagojira*, Fukuda Jun, 1974)
Revenge of Mechagodzilla (*Mekagojira no gyakushū*, Nakano Akiyoshi, 1975)
The Return of Godzilla (*Gojira*, Hashimoto Kōji, 1984)
Godzilla vs. Biollante (*Gojira tai Biorante*, Ōmori Kazuki, 1989)
Godzilla vs. King Ghidorah (*Gojira vs Kingugidora*, Ōmori Kazuki, 1989)
Godzilla vs. Mothra (*Gojira tai Mosura*, Ōkawara Takao, 1992)
Godzilla vs. Super-Mechagodzilla (*Gojira tai Mekagojira*, Okawara Takao, 1993)
Godzilla vs. Space Godzilla (*Gojira vs Supēsugojira*, Yamashita Kenshō, 1994)
Godzilla vs. Destroyer (*Gojira vs Desutoroia*, Okawara Takao, 1995)
Godzilla (Roland Emmerich, US, 1998)
Godzilla 2000: Millennium (*Gojira 2000: mireniamu*, Okawara Takao, 1999)
Godzilla vs. Megaguirus: The G Annihilation Strategy (*Gojira tai Mekagirasu: Jī shometsu sakusen*, Tezuka Masaki, 2000)
Godzilla, Mothra and King Ghidorah: Giant Monsters All-Out Attack (*Gojira-Mosura-Kingugidora: Daikaijū sōshingeki*, Kaneko Shūsuke, 2001)

8

SEVEN *SAMURAI* AND SIX WOMEN

Kurosawa Akira's *Seven Samurai* (1954)

D. P. Martinez

Seven Samurai (*Sichinin no samurai*, 1954) could be counted among the most analysed of films, in a league with *Citizen Kane* (US, Orson Welles, 1941), *Star Wars* (US, George Lucas, 1977), *Blade Runner* (US, Ridley Scott, 1982), and, up and coming, *The Matrix* (US, the Wachowski Brothers, 1999), but the mark of a great film is that it can always bear more scrutiny. This is true of Kurosawa's classic which has, in the main, been looked at through its 1950s subtitled version. It has been praised for its humanistic outlook (Richie 1996); for its critique of Japan's militaristic rulers; for revitalising the *samurai* film (*jidai-geki*) which had suffered under the censorship of both the Japanese government and US Occupation Forces (1945–52) (Desser 1992); and it has been understood as a plea for the establishment of the Self Defence Forces; as a glorification of traditional *samurai* Japanese values (Prince 1991; Davis 1996); and as a paean to the land and nature itself.[1] In fact, this new analysis of the role of women in the film will argue that the film encompasses all of these themes and more.

In his autobiography, Kurosawa plays down his interest in or ability to understand women. He presents even his marriage as somewhat accidental, arranged by his friends rather than being an outcome of his own romantic interests.[2] In this he appears to be a man's man; a director who, if he was interested in gender at all, was only interested in masculinity, in what 'real' men do in difficult situations. When Kurosawa does mention women in some detail, the story that stands out is that of his mother and how she kept the house from burning down by carrying a flaming pot outside (Kurosawa 1983: 21–2). He recalls her sitting soundlessly for weeks afterwards, burnt hands bandaged, in great pain. This, he notes, made her a 'typical woman of the Meiji era', and he adds: 'Years later when I read the historical novelist Yamamoto Shūgorō's *Nihon fudōki* [*Japanese Women*] . . . I recognized my mother in these impossibly heroic creatures' (Ibid.: 21). As Orbaugh (1996) notes, the strong silent wife is a key figure in the modern representation of Japanese women; and Kurosawa's work is full of such women. Yet he was also interested in women who were not so 'impossibly heroic'. A close look at the films reveals that they are peopled with fascinating, complex women who might occupy little screen time but whose personalities and motivations are essential to their plots.[3]

The core of this chapter's argument is that in making women's motivations central to many of his plots, Kurosawa often used them to set in motion the very events of his stories. On one hand, it is true that this is an old-fashioned Japanese view of women: they are of the inside, at the core of families, representing all that is best – and sometimes worst – of Japan, but they are also the true 'bosses' of the family – they control, calmly, subtly, everything. On the other hand, given the way in which Kurosawa's films were accessible to non-Japanese, it could be argued that the paradox of women's marginality (in terms of screen time) and centrality (in terms of plot) is a common situation and can be found almost everywhere. In fact, *Seven Samurai* could be compared with *The Iliad* (Homer 1986 edition), that most male-centred of epics, in which all the events are set into motion by the 'kidnapping' of one woman. In the Japanese film, a woman's ambiguous response to her 'capture' leaves viewers with a mystery equivalent to the unresolved problem that Helen of Troy poses for Western audiences: why do women do what they do? Women, as many men would claim, are a mystery. However, it is through men's *relationships* with women, whether they understand their motivations or not, that much is revealed. In the case of *Seven Samurai*, the role of women is linked to an issue left over from defeat in the Second World War, one which revisionist writers such as Smith (1998) argue has never been satisfactorily resolved for modern Japanese: when would it be right for them to take up arms again? In other words, what constitutes a just cause in which it would be right to resort to might?

Kurosawa and his generation

Kurosawa, born in 1910, was of *samurai* stock. He was also a man of his era educated both in Japanese traditions and in Western knowledge. Through his radical older brother he appears to have drifted towards a sort of socialism that later in his films appeared as a generalised humanism. Ōshima (1992) refers to this episode in Kurosawa's life as typical of his generation of filmmakers, and, pre-war, the Japanese film industry was a haven for leftist thinkers. The government's increasing censorship of the film industry in Japan becomes interesting in this light – equivalent, perhaps, to the McCarthy era in the US. Suddenly the liberal, often leftist, certainly bohemian world of Japan's fledgling new cinema was under threat and, in fear of imprisonment, or of not being able to make films, many filmmakers treaded carefully. Kurosawa himself was proud of not having made a typical war film at all during this time; directing only *The Most Beautiful* (*Ichiban utsukushiku*, 1944) about the stoic women who work in an optics factory.[4] That the Allied Forces also practised censorship was less a surprise to Kurosawa than the more pleasant fact that, in contrast to the war era, his films were now censored by people who knew something about cinema.[5]

Kurosawa was able to pass censorship with *Rashomon* (1950), winner of the first prize at the 1951 Venice Film Festival. The film's depiction of the impossibility of ascertaining the truth, or of giving a single meaning to any particular event, seems to reflect his own personal experience with the censors as well as the more general Japanese post-war experience, when much of what they had been taught to believe before was overturned by the new US-backed government. In challenging the fixed nature of reality *Rashomon* must stand as one of the first examples of post-modern art in the twentieth century. *Seven Samurai*, in contrast, appears to be a clear post-censorship attempt to come to terms with both the good and the bad of Japan's *samurai* heritage, without any of the ambiguity of *Rashomon*. Or is it?

The plot

In one version or another, the plot of *Seven Samurai* is well known. (Edited, cut to much shorter lengths in the US, Europe and the UK; later restored to its more than three hours; it has been remade, and used as the core for many films since 1954 when it was first shown in Venice.) A poor village is at the mercy of bandits, who raid it periodically, leaving its people with little to survive on. What is saved from the bandits goes to the government in taxes. These civil war era (fifteenth–sixteenth centuries) peasants are represented as crushed, squeezed at both ends by the machinery of war: the supplies needed by lords for their armies and their exposure to the violence of war as it rages across the land. War's aftermath is also dangerous: who are the bandits if not dispossessed farmers or unemployed mercenaries forced to survive by robbing others?

From a Confucian point of view, the farmers have the right to take action on their own. Their paternalistic leaders have failed in their duty, and one reading of the film would be to follow Moeran's (1989) point that *samurai* dramas always end by supporting Confucian ideology: chaos must be addressed, order restored and the society's leaders should do this; individual action is possible when the leaders are corrupt, but the old order must be restored, not a new one established. However, the farmers do not know how to fight, so how can they resist the bandits? The idea of hiring professionals is aired and the fact that many hungry *rōnin* (masterless *samurai*) are roaming the land raises the possibility of finding men who will fight in exchange for room and board. Seven *samurai* are found who are willing to take on the task of training the villagers to fight against a band of 40 and, ultimately, emerge victorious.

The suffering of ordinary people in times of war is the theme which connects *Seven Samurai* to other Kurosawa films (cf. Goodwin 1994); and in this film the *samurai*, who were often idealised in *jidai-geki*, are also more realistically depicted. It is not only the government that is represented as being corrupt, but finding a *samurai* willing to fight for a good cause without pay is problematic also, the code of the *bushidō* (warrior) notwithstanding. As Yoshimoto (2000: 242–4) notes, Kurosawa himself was aware that the film was realistic and yet not a 'true' history: in a more accurate tale, the love affair between the young *samurai*, Katsuhiro (Kimura Kō), and the farmer's daughter, Shino (Tsushima Keiko), would have resulted in concubinage for her; and the roaming *samurai* leader, Kanbei (Shimura Takashi), would have taken over the village and become its ruler. Moreover, there is an historical inaccuracy at the heart of the tale that is interesting. During the civil war era, farmers were allowed to use weapons: their armed headmen were the ancestors of the Tokugawa era (1600–1867) *samurai* elite. It was not until the Tokugawa era that farmers were, under pain of death, forbidden not only to carry weapons, but to resort to violence in order to solve their own problems (cf. Ikegami 1995). Thus there is a mystery at the heart of the story. Why have these farmers not fought back against their oppressors? One answer is that their spirits have been crushed – they see only the possibility of failure and fear that fighting will make things worse. This explanation might serve as an apologia for the political dissidents and ordinary citizens of the pre-war era: a downtrodden population could offer little resistance to the increasing militarisation of Japan.

However, there is another cause for the farmers' inaction, and this presents us with a more complex picture of the farmers' (and the Japanese) stasis: as will be seen below, the farmers are also guilty, guilty of collusion with the bandits – for this they must suffer. The film allows no one the prized possession of innocence, or at least not for long, if Katsushiro and Shino start out as its two young innocents. Luminous and lyrically beautiful as the film is in parts, it is ultimately a dark story that ends poised between a finely balanced pessimism and optimism: the farmers will go on, but have they learned anything? The noble warriors will continue to wander, perhaps doing more good deeds, but will they ever have a home, or descendants to care for them in death, or are they doomed to wander even as hungry ghosts in the afterlife? To read the film in this way, we need to pay close attention to the women in the story.

The mothers

Women punctuate and spur the action at all points in *Seven Samurai*, and if there is a dominant trope in relation to women, it is their link with nature and motherhood as established in almost every scene that involves a woman. For example, the film opens in this way: horsemen thunder through a dark landscape, they stop, look at a bucolic village and discuss whether or not to raid the place. 'Wait, wait, we took their rice just last autumn',[6] declares one of the bandits. 'Let's return when this barley has ripened', says the other. After they leave, a bird chirps, and part of the hedge over which the bandits were looking moves, a frightened man appears, a bundle of sticks on his back having hidden him from the bandits. He runs away as the birdsong calmly continues, and the scene shifts to the village where the birdsong merges with the cries and tears of a woman: 'There are neither gods nor bodhisattvas!'

We do not see the face of this wailing woman as, head bowed, children clutching her kimono, she continues her litany of woe: they have been devastated by drought, famine and taxes as well as the bandits' raids. 'We might as well kill ourselves!' she says.

Various men initially respond to her by concurring: the government is corrupt and won't help; they wish they were dead, etc. She stands up finally, enraged by this male passivity, screaming that the government might notice them if they all kill themselves, and manages to get a more aggressive reaction.

One intense young man, Rikichi (Tsuchiya Yoshio), defies the general mood: 'Let's kill them all' (*Mina o tsukkurosu* – literally, let's run them all through.)

The same naysayers who spoke earlier, speak again. It is impossible, they don't know how to do it, they would all die if they fought, why not just beg the bandits to leave them enough to live on? Rikichi silences them with: 'Have you forgotten what we've done for the rice we're eating now . . .?' (*Wasuretanoka oretachi no kutteru kome wa donna koto shite . . .*) At this all the men's heads, which have been hanging, lift and people look away in shame. 'Let's talk to headman Gosaku', shouts someone, and off the whole community goes.

The meeting in the headman's mill is shot to include Gosaku's daughter-in-law: framed behind the headman, she holds her child, patting his back as the men discuss hiring *samurai* to protect the village. This is the same woman who will come staggering out of the burning mill towards the end of the film, carrying her baby to safety despite having been speared by a bandit. Dying and without a word, she will hand him over to the would-be *samurai* Kikuchiyo – allowing the actor Mifune Toshirō one of his great screen moments as he wails: 'I was like this baby! This happened to me!'

The scene, perhaps unconsciously, echoes Kurosawa's story about his calm mother carrying a flaming pot to safety. This young woman, a minor character who appears only a few times in the film and speaks only one or two lines, embodies what the director considered the best of Japanese womanhood. Yet the wailing woman from the beginning of the film should not be forgotten: would the men have been moved to action if not prompted by her public outcry? Given the nature of Japanese village society, where everyone knew everyone else's business, the public discussion of people's grievances tended to be fairly calm. (I write as an anthropologist who lived in such a village for over a year.) Behind the scenes people might wail and shout, but to do so in public was a sign that the normal paths to dealing with a problem had all led nowhere. In this light, the men's commentary on the woman's soliloquy is similar to that of a Greek chorus rather than an argument with her: yes, you're right, the gods have failed us; the government has failed us; the inspectors have turned a blind eye; the bandits are a problem that has not been solved. The public outburst by the woman acts both as the sounding board for what all villagers are privately saying, and as a way of opening up a new avenue of discussion; literally: what do we do now? Without this public display of private mutterings, the men might well have taken no action. In short, the scene is that of a woman berating her men. Her lament implies: why do you not do what men should do?

This is an important question that the audience cannot, on a first viewing, appreciate. It seems the exaggeration of a desperate woman, but as the film continues it becomes apparent that her cry 'there are neither gods nor bodhisattvas' is not hyperbole; for a reason not yet understood, the villagers feel themselves to be abandoned by the gods, a loss which they have borne for some time, but which must finally be faced. If fighting the bandits is the only way to redress what they have done, they must resist – but can they do it? The response of Gosaku the headman is no, they need the help of trained men. But what sort of *samurai* do they get?

The answer to this comes through another mother, the only woman we see in any of the scenes set in the town where four village men go to find *samurai*. In town, in contrast to the village, there is no birdsong just the rather strident music that accompanies parading *samurai* as they saunter, giant-like in comparison to the weedy farmers, down the high street. They are terrifying and arrogant, not interested in helping anyone at all. It is only when the villagers are on the verge of giving up their search and have descended to fighting among themselves – two men wanting to return home, Rikichi leading the argument for staying – that something finally happens. The fight, both verbal and physical, is an interesting one: Manzō (Fujiwara Kamatari) wants to bargain with the bandits and Rikichi asks him, pointedly: 'What shall we use to bargain with? Shall we give them your daughter?' (*Omēntoko no musume dasu tsumorika.*)

Silenced by this, the four men become aware of a crowd, not helping but watching the spectacle of a kidnapped child being rescued by a *samurai*, and it is then that another woman appears: the mother of the child. Silent, on screen for about nine seconds initially, she moves as if blown by the wind, desperately torn between running to her weeping child and bringing some rice balls to the *samurai* to use as part of his disguise – a Buddhist priest, bringing food to the child and thief – but the close-up when she hands over the rice speaks volumes. It can be assumed that, previously, her pleas attracted the crowd and the *samurai*, but for the moment she is wordless. When the *samurai* kills the bandit, we see only the latter's almost-beautiful collapse in slow motion, but the pathos of his dying moment is undercut by the mother's weeping as she hugs her child. Men's nobility means nothing, it would seem, against the need to protect women and children.

The villagers have found themselves a kind and noble *rōnin* willing to take on their cause, just as he was willing to shave his head and pretend to be a Buddhist priest to save the child. Kanbei's shorn head has been much analysed, but another point must be made about his willingness to sacrifice the topknot, the symbol of the *samurai*'s masculinity: it is significant that the villagers who feel that the gods have abandoned them have now found themselves a defender who resembles a priest. In fact, given his age, willingness to take on their cause, and lack of interest in material rewards or in women (in contrast to his new apprentice Katsushiro and wild man Kikuchiyo), Kanbei seems to be very much on the path to priesthood.

One final mother should be considered: the old grandmother who appears in occasional shots of the villagers: she is virtually toothless, and bent with age. Yet, there is a moment when she holds the camera, swaying the hearts of the *samurai*, perhaps against their better judgement. The moment comes with the first capture of a bandit. The *samurai* have brought him to be questioned, but the villagers form a mob, baying – literally – to kill one of their oppressors. The *samurai* try to save him, citing the 'rules of combat', but are stopped by the sight of the old woman, staggering under the weight of the hoe she carries. 'Let her avenge the death of her son!' comes the cry, and the *samurai*, confronted with the depth of despair and hatred the villagers feel towards the armed men who so threaten their existence – a hatred that even a woman, old and tottering, can feel – allow the mob to close around the captive. It is a sobering moment and, combined with an earlier speech made by Kikuchiyo about how the farmers have been 'made' into sly weaklings who prey on lone *samurai* and bandits alike, it serves to teach the *samurai* a lesson: violence breeds violence and they are not guiltless when it comes to the villagers' suffering. Their glory has its price, not just in the solitary nature of their profession, but in repercussions for the farmers who provide the rice that is the mainstay of the feudal economy. This realisation has been carefully choreographed: beginning with the fear of what the *samurai* will do to their women, the villagers have seemed as afraid of their liberators as of their oppressors. And it is through the depiction of this concern with the sexuality of both the *samurai* and the women that Kurosawa reveals the secret at the heart of the village.

Daughters and lovers

The character of Shino, Manzō's daughter, provides the audience with a study in female complexity. She is pretty enough that Rikichi's threat to 'use' Shino to bargain with the bandits strikes fear deep into her father's heart. Manzō returns home to tell the headman how the search for *samurai* is progressing and follows this by cutting his daughter's hair. He wants to disguise her as a boy so that she will not 'chase after *samurai*', but she resists and ends by having him beat her while he hacks off her hair. There is an incredible, almost sexual, violence to this scene in which Manzō berates his daughter for being too attractive. His fear infects the other villagers who, despite remonstrating with Manzō for being overly fond of his daughter, decide to hide all their young women. His actions also spark a rebelliousness in Shino, who takes to wandering the village woods in her disguise, eventually meeting the young 'child' of the seven *samurai*, Katsushiro. In the wood's fairy tale-like setting of large trees, some marked with sacred rope (*shimenawa*) as if to let us know that this is a truly special space, timeless with its spring flowers, the couple have their first encounter. He chases after her, shouting that she should be drilling with the other men and, to bolero-like music, discovers she is a girl. Their 'wrestling' from the first is both fearful and aggressive on Shino's part: almost as if she wants the young man to rape her. This sort of passive aggression is a feature of their every encounter, with Shino fully aware that they could never marry ('I wish I had been born a *samurai*'s daughter', she cries at one encounter) and somehow keen to consummate their relationship. Yet both youngsters pull back, suddenly shy at crucial moments.

If Shino is complex – full of love, angry at her father, attracted to the very *samurai* she is not supposed to chase, aware of her place in the social hierarchy – Rikichi's missing wife (Shimazaki Yukiko) is a mystery. We get hints of her in various scenes: Kikuchiyo discovering a lovely kimono in the farmer's house; Rikichi's rage at being told he should marry; and various points in the dialogue that only make sense in retrospect. This very beautiful woman appears only when three *samurai* and Rikichi volunteer to attack the bandits in their lair in the hope of killing a few in order to lower the odds against them.

Figure 12 Passive aggression amid a fairy tale-like setting: Shino and Katsushiro in *Seven Samurai* (1954). Tōhō/The Kobal Collection.

Arriving after a night's journey, the *samurai* decide to set fire to the lodge where the bandits and a collection of half-naked women lie drunkenly sleeping. As the smoke curls through the lodge, there follows a scene that Richie (1996: 107) notes is 'utterly mysterious (and completely right)': a woman awakes, sits up, looks around her indifferently at the riotous display of her companions, and becomes aware of the fire. She is startled, for a moment, and then relaxes, with a smile, and does nothing to rouse the sleepers. All this to the shrill sound of a *noh* flute, sharp and staccato – as if to indicate the broken state of her mind. Later, after the finally awakened bandits have rushed out and a few are killed, she saunters out of the burning building, her body language languid, almost as if saying 'what a nice morning'. Rikichi sees her and runs to her; she pulls back in horror and returns to the building. 'She's my wife!' the farmer tells the *samurai* who have kept him from rushing into the furiously burning lodge. Like Kurosawa's mother and the young woman who, a few scenes later, will die saving her son, Rikichi's wife makes not a single sound.

 Why does she resist being rescued? For a long time I thought, as perhaps many viewers do, that she is too shamed by the degradation of her captivity to be able to return to her husband and former life. But this is not the case, as careful attention to the Japanese dialogue reveals. The key scene occurs later, when Shino has completed her seduction of Katsushiro, and Manzō, furious, has beaten her again. As she lies sobbing, he wails about the *samurai* who 'took her' and refuses to be comforted: 'It was a young person's thing, have sympathy', says the kindly, pragmatic *samurai* Shichirōji (Katō Daisuke), but Manzō disowns her. In response Rikichi shouts at him: 'Isn't it a good thing that they both like each other? It's not as if she had been *given* to bandits!' (*Suki de isshon natta mono guzu guzu yū kotā nē. Nobushi-zei ni kurete yattanoto wakega chigau zo.*)

This silences Manzō, his expression softens, but it is a revelatory moment that because of the existing subtitle – 'At least she was taken by a *samurai*, not a bandit!' – generally is not understood by English-speaking audiences.[7] Shino was not given to bandits, but Rikichi's wife was. She was a bargain the villagers tried to make, a bargain gone wrong because it did not stop the bandits from returning. It is the reason the woman at the beginning of the film is berating the men; it is why the women of the village arranged a public display of outrage: their fear that they might be given away. It is why the village needs a priest as well as a warrior to lead them. It is why the villagers are overprotective of their women, having failed Rikichi's wife in all respects. It is why, ultimately, the beautiful young woman, mad and broken, is willing to let her 'captors' die in the fire, but is also willing to run back into the fire: she does not want to return to the husband and the villagers who have used her so. She is all that is beautiful and noble about Japan betrayed. Her suicide is not caused by shame, but it is revenge. Similarly, headman Gosaku's stubborn refusal to leave his mill once the bandits come back to raid might be read as self-immolation. He had to atone for the decision he no doubt made or approved: the betrayal of a young woman, the betrayal of all that the farmers are meant to represent – the family, hearth, home, the land itself.

Rather than resist, the men of the village have colluded and this becomes a form of self-betrayal that renders them impotent in the face of the bandits; only when confronted by their women do they dare act. Through their resistance, the men learn to fight for what really matters and their resistance underscores that it is wrong to take to banditry instead of working, wrong to kidnap women, to orphan children, to rape and pillage – and this applies to the *samurai* as well as the bandits. In fact, it applies to *all* professional fighting men (even, it would seem, the US military) – their asocial nature a theme not just of Kurosawa's films, but of many westerns, war and detective films made by both North Americans and Europeans.

The film ends on this note, the three remaining *samurai* aware that they have 'lost': what have they in that village or anywhere else? No families, no land, no masters, only their honour providing a sort of nobility to who they are and what they do. And what is that compared with what the farmers have? Shino rejects Katsushiro; she has become a strong woman, with no desire to be the concubine of an apprentice warrior who hung his head in embarrassment rather than protect her from her father's blows. She is last seen planting rice – the powerful, modern symbol for all good and great things Japanese (Ohnuki-Tierney 1993). The associations between fertility, continuity and Japan's natural cycle are made clear by Shino giving voice to a song as she bends to work. Meanwhile Rikichi beats a drum to help the women keep time: the old rhythms of life are restored.

If there is a single message to this complex film, it is this: that only for one's land, for one's family, should men be moved to take up arms. All else is mere corruption. And when men's moral judgement fails, they would do well to listen to their women. In the end, *Seven Samurai* is not a film analogous to *The Iliad*, but to *The Trojan Women* (Euripides 1986 edition), the play that laments the horrors that men's violence brings to the very people they should be protecting. Kurosawa might not have understood women, but he certainly admired and respected them. Many of his films seem to make a similar point: in war the only heroes are the mothers, daughters and lovers who must endure the worst that men can do.

Notes

1 See Yoshimoto (2000: 206) for an overview of the various ways in which this film has been analysed.
2 Galbraith (2001: 56) neatly punctuates this story, revealing that Kurosawa had already been involved with his proposed bride-to-be.
3 It is not possible here to unpack all the intertextual relationships between the women in Kurosawa's films. To mention just a few, we might compare the women discussed below with the would-be-raped wife in *Rashomon* (*Rashōmon*, 1950), the kidnapped wife in *Yojimbo* (*Yōjinbō*, 1961), the seemingly dim *samurai*'s wife in *Sanjuro* (*Tsubaki Sanjūrō*, 1962), and especially the wilful princess who is forced to act the part of a mute in *The Hidden Fortress* (*Kakushi toride no san akunin*, 1958).
4 Galbraith (2001: 37) does note that Kurosawa wrote many 'typical' war film scripts during this time.
5 It remained a favourite irony of Kurosawa (1983) that his film *They Who Step on the Tiger's Tail* (*Tora no o o fumu otokotachi*, 1945) was banned by both governments for different reasons: once for its irreverence towards *samurai* traditions and later for its reverence towards *samurai* values.
6 Where I use quotation marks, I have translated from the Japanese, a process I worked on with the help of Yuka Kodama-Pomfret; in other parts I paraphrase longer dialogue from the film. My re-translations of this film are, in the main, no more, and no less, accurate than those of others since there is no one-to-one correlation between languages, especially not between English and Japanese. However, I have added the Japanese in key places where I think understanding the meaning is most important, and there is one point, discussed below, where my re-translation does matter in its difference from the restored British Film Institute 190-minute subtitled version. This chapter is not meant to be a critique of this translation: having done subtitling for television, I know full well the constraints of time, as well as the set ideas about what the audience can read, need to read or need to know, and what your producer will let you put in. Moreover, in its very edited version, the *Seven Samurai* subtitles had to make sense of a much-truncated story. The key difference between my translation below and that found in the film is probably caused by all of the above factors.
7 This scene was cut out of the 1950s European version, and the restored dialogue is so fast and furious that I had to check with native Japanese speakers to be sure I had understood it. I must thank both Matsunaga Hidetake and Yuka Kodama-Pomfret for taking time out of their busy schedules to look at this crucial scene with me.

References

Davis, Darrell William (1996) *Picturing Japaneseness: Monumental Style, National Identity, Japanese Film*, New York: Columbia University Press.
Desser, David (1992) 'Toward a Structural Analysis of the Postwar Samurai Film', in

Arthur Nolletti Jr. and David Desser (eds), *Reframing Japanese Cinema: Authorship, Genre, History*, Bloomington: Indiana University Press: 145–64.

Euripides (1986 edition) *The Trojan Women*. Translated by Shirley A. Barber. Warminster: Aris and Philips.

Galbraith, Stuart IV (2001) *The Emperor and the Wolf: The Lives and Films of Akira Kurosawa and Toshiro Mifune*, London: Faber and Faber.

Goodwin, James (1994) *Akira Kurosawa and Intertextual Cinema*, Baltimore: Johns Hopkins University Press.

Homer (1986 edition) *The Iliad*. Translated by Robert Fitzgerald. London: Collins.

Ikegami, Eiko (1995) *The Taming of the Samurai: Honorific Individualism and the Making of Modern Japan*, Cambridge, MA: Harvard University Press.

Kurosawa, Akira (1983) *Something Like an Autobiography*. Translated by Audie Bock. New York: Alfred A. Knopf.

Moeran, Brian (1989) *Language and Popular Culture in Japan*, Manchester: Manchester University Press.

Ohnuki-Tierney, Emiko (1993) *Rice as Self: Japanese Identities Through Time*, Princeton: Princeton University Press.

Orbaugh, Sharalyn (1996) 'General Nogi's Wife: Representations of Women in Narratives of Japanese Modernization', in Stephen Snyder and Xiaobing Tang (eds), *In Pursuit of Contemporary East Asian Culture*, Boulder, Co: Westview Press: 7–31.

Ōshima, Nagisa (1992) *Cinema, Censorship and the State: The Writings of Nagisa Oshima, 1956–1978*. Translated by Dawn Lawson. Cambridge, MA: MIT Press.

Prince, Stephen (1991) *The Warrior's Camera: The Cinema of Akira Kurosawa*, Princeton: Princeton University Press.

Richie, Donald (1996) *The Films of Akira Kurosawa*, Berkeley: University of California Press. Third edition.

Smith, Patrick (1998) *Japan: A Reinterpretation*, New York: Vintage Books.

Yoshimoto, Mitsuhiro (2000) *Kurosawa: Film Studies and Japanese Cinema*, Durham, NC: Duke University Press.

Kurosawa Akira Filmography

Sanshiro Sugata (*Sugata Sanshirō*, 1943)
The Most Beautiful (*Ichiban utsukushiku*, 1944)
Sanshiro Sugata, Part 2 (*Zoku Sugata Sanshirō*, 1945)
They Who Step on the Tiger's Tail (*Tora no o o fumu otokotachi*, 1945)
No Regrets for Our Youth (*Waga seishun ni kuinashi*, 1946)
One Wonderful Sunday (*Subarashiki nichiyōbi*, 1947)
Drunken Angel (*Yoidore tenshi*, 1948)
The Quiet Duel (*Shizukanaru ketto*, 1949)
Stray Dog (*Nora inu*, 1949)
Scandal (*Shubun*, 1950)
Rashomon (*Rashōmon*, 1950)
The Idiot (*Hakuchi*, 1951)
Ikiru (*Ikiru*, 1952)
Seven Samurai (*Shichinin no samurai*, 1954)
Record of a Living Being (*Ikimono no kiroku*, 1955)
Throne of Blood (*Kumonosu-jō*, 1957)
The Lower Depths (*Donzoko*, 1957)

The Hidden Fortress (*Kakushi toride no san akunin*, 1958)
The Bad Sleep Well (*Warui yatsu hodo yoku nemuru*, 1960)
Yojimbo (*Yōjinbō*, 1961)
Sanjuro (*Tsubaki Sanjūrō*, 1962)
High and Low (*Tengoku to jigoku*, 1963)
Red Beard (*Akahige*, 1965)
Dodeskaden (*Dodesukaden*, 1970)
Dersu Uzala (*Derusu Uzara*, 1975)
Kagemusha (*Kagemusha*, 1980)
Ran (*Ran*, 1985)
Dreams (*Yume*, 1990)
Rhapsody in August (*Hachigatsu no kyōshikyoku*, 1991)
Madadayo (*Mādadayo*, 1993)

9

WOMEN'S STORIES IN POST-WAR JAPAN

Naruse Mikio's *Late Chrysanthemums* (1954)

Catherine Russell

Ah, I'd like to smoke a good cigarette.

'Hey!' I shout,

But you see the wind swept it away.
> – Hayashi Fumiko, 'Diary of a Vagabond' (1997b)

The title of Naruse Mikio's 1954 film *Late Chrysanthemums* (*Bangiku*) evokes a familiar trope of Japanese poetics: the equation of women with flowers, whose beauty peaks and fades. There is beauty – to be sure – in the fading, as the flower and the woman become symbolic of the mortality of all things. And yet this iconography seems inadequate, if not inappropriate, to the representation of women in 1950s Tokyo. Indeed, Naruse's film challenges the paradigm of the title by situating his fading flowers – four middle-aged women who were *geisha* together before the war – in the midst of the complex social and economic landscape of post-war Tokyo. Their struggle for survival and self-esteem cannot be aestheticized in nature imagery; they are not objects for the poet's gaze, but subjects with their own stories to tell about modern Tokyo.

Like many of Naruse's films from this period – for example, *Repast* (*Meshi*, 1951), *Okāsan* (*Mother*, 1952), *Lightning* (*Inazuma*, 1952), *Sound of the Mountain* (*Yama no oto*, 1954), and *Flowing* (*Nagareru*, 1956) – *Late Chrysanthemums* offers an unusual perspective on the unequal opportunities available to women in Japanese modernity. Even if these films stop short of outright or explicit social criticism, there is an unmistakable, and often clearly articulated, sense that despite the democratic reforms of post-war Japan, women's social roles remain limited by traditional gender norms. Based on three short stories by the woman writer Hayashi Fumiko, *Late Chrysanthemums* deals with the everyday lives of women living outside the Family System of mainstream Japanese society.[1] And yet Naruse could not be thought of as a feminist director, as neither the language nor the ideology of contemporary feminism is applicable to his practice. His method is more one of passive observation, as he maps out his

124

Figure 13 The struggle for survival and self-esteem in post-war Tokyo: *Late Chrysanthemums*. BFI Stills, Posters and Designs.

characters' stories against a backdrop that is at once extremely modern, but also, aesthetically, very 'traditional' in its maintenance of a formal sense of architectural harmony. The film's mise-en-scène and its rhythmic pacing maintain an integral classicism within a film that, on other levels, depicts the harsh drama of cultural transformation.

Sometimes referred to as the 'number four' director of studio-era Japanese cinema (following Kurosawa Akira, Ozu Yasujirō, and Mizoguchi Kenji), Naruse has been marginalized by critics looking for stylistic traits of Japaneseness in Japanese cinema. As Philip Lopate has noted, Naruse 'seems to lack an immediately identifiable "arty" trademark' (1986: 168). His style may be more conventional than some of his more famous contemporaries, but it is nevertheless a very finely crafted mode of practice. One of the most succinct descriptions of Naruse's style is Kurosawa Akira's (1998: 13) observation that his films flow like a 'deep river with a quiet surface disguising a fast-raging current underneath', a metaphor that captures both the effect of Naruse's seamless montage and the emotional effects of his dramaturgy. This is a cinema of missed opportunities, averted eyes, failed marriages and broken families; and yet, as melodrama, it is also a cinema about 'ordinary people' with ordinary problems. Hasumi Shigehiko (1998: 61–87) has written most eloquently about what he describes as Naruse's 'double signature', the means by which he inscribes a taste for very simple things into the rhetoric of film language.

Audie Bock has written most substantially on Naruse's realist aesthetic, suggesting that his narrative may be 'too dark' for mainstream Japanese film criticism (Bock 1978: 102). She points out that his characters evoke neither pity nor contempt, and his heroines are women who complain about their plights (1983: 29). Bock also discusses the profound influence of Hayashi Fumiko's particular brand of realist cynicism and proto-feminist tenacity on Naruse's films of the 1950s. *Late Chrysanthemums* is based on three Hayashi short stories written in the late 1940s, two of them among her best-known works. *Bangiku* won the women's literary prize *Joryū bungakusha shō* in 1949 (Ericson 1997: 75) and *Suisen* ('Narcissus') was acclaimed by such literature authorities as Edward Seidensticker and Mishima Yukio (Ibid.: 87).[2] Screenwriters Tanaka Sumie and Ide Toshirō linked these two stories with a third, *Shirasagi* ('White Heron'), for the script of *Late Chrysanthemums*.

Naruse's use of first-person voice-over narration is an important element of his depiction of female subjectivity. It is a technique that he uses very sporadically and selectively, and it often includes words taken directly from the Hayashi source novels and stories.[3] Although Takamine Hideko is the actress most closely associated with Naruse (she appears in 17 of his films), Sugimura Haruko plays the lead in *Late Chrysanthemums*. A stage-trained actress, Sugimura was usually cast in supporting roles, perhaps the best known of which is as Shige, the older sister, in *Tokyo Story* (*Tōkyō monogatari*, Ozu Yasujirō, 1953). Her starring role in *Late Chrysanthemums* is one of the rare occasions that she was given to develop a complex character on the screen, and she is very much responsible for the success of this subtle film.[4]

Four days in the life of a city

Before examining the cultural and historical context of the film's production, an overview of the film's structure is in order, or at least a mapping of its complex weave of narrative lines. The stories that are told in the film are deeply embedded in a flow of itinerant street performers, vendors, beggars, deliverymen and anonymous passers-by, people who circulate among and between the characters and the city they live in. One cannot in fact separate the film from its context, because it overflows its own narrative to become a film about its spatial and historical setting, as much as it is about a constellation of characters. *Late Chrysanthemums* might be considered a *shōshimin eiga* (a home drama, or film about 'ordinary' or 'common' people), except that unlike most examples of this genre, there is no conventional family in the film. (Other examples of the *shōshimin eiga* include *Tokyo Story*, *A Brother and His Younger Sister* [*Ani to sono imōto*], Shimazu Yasujirō, 1939), and many other films by both Ozu and Naruse, including the latter's *Lightning* and *Mother*.)

The narrative of *Late Chrysanthemums* comprises four days, over which period several storylines unfold around the character of Kin (Sugimura Haruko), who exchanges visits with three of her old *geisha* colleagues. The film begins and ends at 11:25 am, indicated by a shot of a clock on Kin's wall, and the narrative closely observes the rhythms and cycles of everyday life in the city, such as meals, sunlight and shadows, newspaper and milk deliveries. The first day introduces most of the main characters. While Kin lives in a well-appointed home with a small garden, a maid, and a small dog, her friends have fallen on harder times. Her occupation as a money-lender and real-estate speculator is frowned on by her friends, who are nevertheless dependent on her resources. Kin has helped finance a small bar that Nobu (Sawamura Sadako) runs with the assistance of her husband. When Kin tries to find another friend, Tamae, at the hotel she works at, a woman throws a bucket of water after her as she leaves, a gesture of distaste directed at the money-lender.

Kin's third friend, Tomi (Mochizuki Yūko), works as a janitor in an office building where she also deals in black-market cigarettes. Tomi's character is as intriguing as Kin's; a typical Hayashi woman, she is hard-drinking and very practical. She won't pay Kin anything, but comes home to Tamae, her house-mate, with pork cutlets procured with *pachinko* (pinball game) winnings. Tamae (Hosokawa Chikako) is the most classically beautiful of the four women, and being rather sickly, comes closest to embodying the fading flower of the film's title. If there is a narrative trajectory to this film, it is Tamae's emergence from her dark home into the sunlight of metropolitan Tokyo where, in the last scene, she affects a certain gesture, a casual flip of the hand practiced by both Kin and Tomi, that indicates nothing and everything. It suggests an ability to be ironic, an ability to see oneself as a modern subject, in step with a world that is changing so quickly that one has to live in the moment to survive.

If there is a moral trajectory to the film it is, however, oblique. This is a narrative in which nothing happens beyond the day-to-day banalities of life in the city. Over the course of the film, Tamae and Tomi both see their grown children up and leave them; Kin receives disappointing visits from two former lovers, but the women all survive these setbacks and emerge renewed and ready to face whatever the city should throw up against them next. The first day ends with Seki, Kin's former lover, drinking alone at Nobu's bar. At home, Kin locks up her house, prays in front of her small shrine, and sleeps. Her deaf maid sleeps in the adjoining room.

The second day consists of six short scenes, each one involving one or more of the characters introduced in the first day. They are linked by brief shots of the streets outside the various locations. Even though we no longer follow Kin through the city, these shots are suggestive of a passage through the urban space. Less than 'establishing shots', they indicate the links between the various locales. They are not busy streets, but quiet pedestrian passages more evocative of the old pre-war *shitamachi* (the low city) than the industrialized post-war metropolis. Some transitions between scenes are, however, exceedingly abrupt, offering no indication of the new locale. From a scene in Nobu's bar where Tomi and Seki drink separately, alone, Naruse cuts to a close-up of a letter Kin is reading at her home. It is from Tabe, another former lover. She shows some old photographs of the two of them to her maid, and then she stares blankly at the mirror before a fade-out indicates the end of the day.

The third day begins with a visit from Seki, last seen drinking at Nobu's bar. Through a scattering of gossip dropped over the course of the film, we know that after a failed suicide attempt before the war, Kin had Seki arrested for attempted murder, and he was jailed and then sent to Manchuria. When he comes to see her, Kin is extremely rude and refuses to loan him money. In the transition from the night of the second day to the morning of Seki's visit, a musical theme of clacking sticks is resumed, a gentle rhythmic motif that suggests an off-screen source of an itinerant musician that is never revealed. This musical motif is first introduced during Kin's passage through the city collecting money in the first day of the narrative. As she turns into her own street, she glimpses Seki at the far end of the road. With the rhythmic tapping of the sticks, the two play hide-and-seek within the labyrinth of small passages, hidden stairways and shadowed lanes. Kin finally manages to get home without him seeing her. This short sequence, occurring early in the film, is at once ominous – as Seki has not yet been introduced as a character – and strangely peaceful, as the quiet city with deep shadows absorbs a lingering sense of unease.

The fluidity of the montage as the film cuts between various spaces and characters is enhanced by various visual motifs. For example, after Seki's visit on day three, the scene closes with Kin drinking tea alone in her pristine *tatami* room, while her maid sweeps, and the soft rhythmic clacking resumes. Cut to Tamae sweeping in a very similar composition, picking up the rhythm of the maid's broom. Kin arrives at Tamae's home to collect money. The graphic matching of domestic activity has effectively covered an ellipsis in which Kin has traveled from her home to her friend's. Through these techniques of sound effects and montage, Naruse's film is embedded in the rhythms and patterns of everyday life of women in the city.

This third day includes two short scenes involving Tomi's daughter Sachiko and Tamae's son Kiyoshi. It is at this point in the narrative, more than an hour into the one hundred minute film, that Tabe (Uehara Ken) arrives. The scenes that follow constitute the film's emotional climax, as Kin flirts with this returned lover, prepares herself behind closed doors, and they settle in for an evening of drinking, music and talk. However, after a few moments, Kin reveals in voice-over her disappointment with the man who, it turns out, has come to see her for the same reason as everyone else: to borrow money. As he gets drunker and drunker, Tabe makes a futile pass at Kin's deaf maid, while Kin goes to the other room and burns his photograph. It starts to rain, and Kin opens the doors to the garden, allowing the sensual softness of the night air into the room that is drained of passion.

This long scene is interrupted three times with another scene played out at Tomi and Tamae's home, which is much more darkly lit. The two women get drunk together, reciting classical poetry about wayward children and unreliable men.[5] Finally, they fall into a *futon* together but are too worried about their children to fall asleep. Tomi does Tamae's hair and flatters her about her former elegance. The cross-cutting between these two locales concludes with shots of Tamae sleeping and Tomi stumbling around drunkenly, Tabe sleeping alone, and Kin sleeping beside the maid, with the sound of rain linking the three spaces. While the scene with Kin and Tabe reveals the vulnerability of Kin's character beneath her hard-hearted appearance, the other scene offers a vision of women's camaraderie and spirited resistance to the cruelties of everyday life. The careful intercutting of the two scenes thus produces a contrast and, at the same time, a pattern of emotional tension and release, integrated in the end into the rhythms of everyday life: drinking, sleep, and rain.

The last day begins with the soft clacking of sticks. Kin says goodbye to Tabe, and at 11:25, she is with her real estate partner Itaya (Katō Daisuke), counting money, at exactly the same time they met on the first day of the film. Nobu arrives to tell Kin that Seki has been arrested, but Kin refuses to bail him out. She says, coldly, ' "Eat or be eaten" isn't just for men'. Meanwhile, Tamae and Tomi are seeing Tamae's son Kiyoshi off at the train station, where he is leaving for a coal-mining job in northern Hokkaidō. At the station they see two *geisha* in full regalia. They may look like dolls, out of place in the bustle of the station, but Tomi stares at them enviously, recalling past pleasures that are no longer available to her. She guesses they are off to a hot-springs resort. But then, on a bridge overlooking the railway tracks and the sprawl of the city, a young woman in a tight skirt and heels passes Tomi and Tamae with a swaying step. Tomi exclaims that she is 'imitating that [Marilyn] Monroe person', and promptly does her own imitation, which is what finally makes Tamae laugh and gesture with a bent wrist.

This concluding scene is followed by a last glimpse of Kin and Itaya out in the city on their way to see a property. Kin briefly searches for her ticket to exit a subway station, finds it in her purse, and proceeds down a long flight of steps with Itaya beside her. As the music rises, they move into extreme long shot, descending down to an unremarkable urban square. As an ending, this shot strongly suggests continuity and, like the women's laughter in the previous scene, a sense of change and transformation. The iconography of trains, bridges and stairs is not only symbolic, but locates the fiction within the documentary frame of location shooting. Significantly, both these final scenes are set in metropolitan Tokyo, outside the narrow streets and nostalgic space of the studio-created *shitamachi* labyrinth where the women's homes are located. Despite the suffering they have endured, they are ready and willing to make their way in the modern world in which they have come to know themselves.

Women and post-war democracy

When Naruse adapted Hayashi Fumiko's story *Meshi* in 1951, his career quickly bounced back from a war-time slump that was experienced by almost every Japanese director during the successive censorship policies of the Fifteen Years' War (1931–45) and the Allied Occupation (1945–52). His adaptations of Hayashi were produced within a political climate in which the role of women in the New Japan was a contested topic. Along with the democratic reforms of the post-war period came a recognition of women's rights and a nascent women's movement, as well as economic development that created more room for women in the workforce. The reforms included in the constitutional revisions of the Occupation were arguably among the most progressive legislations of women's rights that the world had ever seen (Pharr 1987). Women's rights and the reform of the Family System of Japanese society were seen by SCAP (Supreme Commander of Allied Powers – the designation of the American-led Occupation authority) as key elements of democratization, and they were strongly supported by Japanese women's organizations in their efforts to this end. Susan Pharr (1987: 245) argues that the experiment was a huge success, and obstacles such as an entrenched history of discrimination were overcome through the humanist agenda of the SCAP policy makers.

Others would disagree. While women achieved suffrage in 1945, many forms of discrimination remain deeply entrenched in social life, language, career expectations and public policy. The women's movement of the 1950s was split between those who advocated women's labor rights, and those who wanted the values of motherhood and homemaking protected (Buckley 1994: 153). As Miyoshi Masao has pointed out, many Japanese perceived democratic reforms such as women's rights as punishment for losing the war, and the ideology of male supremacy remained for many a cornerstone of the 'mythological "Japanese race"' (1991: 196). Women's social roles were at the crux of the contradictions implicit in Japanese modernity, and even today there are a diversity of women's movements and feminist positions in Japan (Buckley 1994). In Naruse's films we also find a mixed response to the opportunities afforded by a democratic society, as his female characters are not all prepared to abandon their roles as homemakers and mothers or the attendant 'good wife and wise mother' ideology. And yet they often find themselves, as in *Late Chrysanthemums*, unable to sustain these roles within the new terms of everyday life in modern Japan.

Naruse's films were very popular among female audiences and he was closely identified with women's subjects by his contemporary critics. In post-war Japan, half the cinema-going public was female, most of them 'office ladies' (OL) or unmarried women who went to the movies in groups. Twelve women's magazines were published in the 1950s, many of them containing film reviews and stories about actors and actresses (Aubrey 1953). *Late Chrysanthemums* was described by a *Kinema Junpō* critic as a *josei eiga*, or woman's film. This critic, Sugimoto Heiichi, appreciated the characterizations of women that went 'beyond the stereotypes', and noted how different these mothers were from the more typical depictions of motherhood in the *haha-mono* (mother film), including Naruse's own *Mother* (Sugimoto 1954: 51). And yet, despite his ultimate endorsement of the film as a 'tour de force', Sugimoto is critical of a perceived lack of psychological depth in *Late Chrysanthemums*.

A similar critique was articulated by Iida Shinbi in the film journal *Eiga Hyōron*. This critic praises Naruse's choice of subject matter in *Late Chrysathemums*, as well as his 'unparalleled skills in mise-en-scène'. However, he is critical of Naruse's adaptation of the Hayashi stories because of the way that the characters' different backgrounds are elided. He notes that in the original stories, the 'drifting sex life' of each of the women is provoked by some incident such as a rape or an abandonment (Iida 1954: 72). For Iida, Naruse's depiction of the four women lacks not only the depth of Hayashi's writing, but also her strong authorial point of view. Both Iida and Sugimoto describe *Late Chrysanthemums* as a *seitai eiga*, or 'ecological film', recognizing its sociological view of characters deeply immersed in their urban setting of post-war Tokyo. However, Naruse's lack of moral assessment of his characters clearly challenged the norms of humanist criticism of the period. Iida indicates how the dispersed, multi-focal narrative of *Late Chrysanthemums* is linked to an authorial modesty, as if Naruse were surrendering himself, in a sense, to his subject matter. Although Sugimoto acknowledges the strong performances of the principal actors, he is distressed by the cold-heartedness of the Sugimura character who is 'not hurt' (1954: 51). The attitude of 'eat or be eaten' (a phrase that Naruse takes directly from Hayashi) seems not to be appreciated by these critics. The perceived 'weakness' of Naruse is a theme that runs through the criticism of this director, both because of his attraction to women's stories and his refusal to offer clear 'messages' or morals regarding modern life.

In fact, what Naruse has done with the Hayashi material is more anthropological than psychological. Despite the characters' romantic longings and memories of the war and pre-war times, their activities and their movements through the city are governed mainly by the circulation of money. The itinerant beggars and salespeople who periodically interrupt the narrative, or are glimpsed in the street, or heard hawking their wares, further sustain the rhythms and patterns of commerce as the substance of everyday life in the city. They also inscribe a current of desperation and poverty within the cycles of everyday life, a tension that appears to be eased only by excessive drinking. As former *geisha*, Nobu and Tamae work in peripheral 'water-trade' establishments – the hotel and the bar – and Tomi is a regular at Nobu's watering hole, where she reminisces about her alcoholic adventures in Manchuria before the war.

Among the beggars who appear in the film is a nun who knocks at Tomi's door asking for alms, and there are other 'traditional' ritualistic practices represented in the film, including Naruse's signature brand of street musicians promoting a theatrical performance. Kin is observed praying to a small shrine in her home, and while these may be small details with no direct relevance to the narrative, they are indicative of the ways in which Japanese modernity has absorbed and incorporated elements of an older way of life. Naruse's use of domestic architecture in his framing and cutting of interior scenes is itself emblematic of the balance and harmony of traditional Japanese aesthetics, and it conveys the sense that the four main characters are rooted in the past. However, given the references to Manchuria and the war, it is a complicated past, profoundly implicated in the failures of the nation. The photograph of Tabe that Kin burns in disgust is a picture of him in uniform; her hopes for a rekindled love affair are dashed along with the pride that she – and he – once had in their country.

The co-existence of different values and practices is most clearly underlined by the late encounter with the 'Monroe person', but it is also implied in the two narrative lines concerning Tomi's daughter Sachiko (Arima Ineko) and Tamae's son Kiyoshi (Koizumi Hiroshi). Sachiko, who works in a restaurant, is a practical girl, much better equipped than her mother for the modern world. When Tomi comes looking for a loan, Sachiko tells her mother that she is getting married, tomorrow. Tomi sacrifices her *kimono* to pay for the wedding, but appears to drink most of the proceeds. Sachiko boldly asks Kin for a wedding gift of cash, meeting the money-lender on her own terms. She and her fiancé are moving to a rented room that they will have to share with other tenants in Tokyo's real-estate crunch – precisely the development that Kin seeks to get a piece of with her partner Itaya.

Kiyoshi is not quite as practical or hard-nosed as Sachiko, although he confesses to his mother that he is seeing a woman who is another man's mistress. Tamae raised him alone, telling people he was her brother, but when he gives her money from this woman, they argue about who has subjected whom to a life of hardship and ill-gotten gains. Kiyoshi's mistress wears *kimono*, as do the older women, whereas Sachiko wears the sensible skirt and blouse of the young modern woman. These fashion indices suggest that Kiyoshi is being drawn into his mother's anachronistic way of life. Kiyoshi eventually leaves his mistress and his mother for a paying job in the mines of Hokkaidō, a familiar theme of 1950s *shōshimin eiga* – the relocation of men and women around the country by corporate culture. The question of children and the ostensible rewards of motherhood is a key theme of the film. Visiting Kin, Tomi says, 'Money is everything. You must be happy in your nice house'. Kin replies: 'But you have a child. You are more fortunate than I'. Then she adds, 'Money moves around me, but nothing is really mine'. Later, when Tomi and Tamae are drunkenly assessing their losses in life, they decide that 'a woman's happiness shouldn't lie in her children'.

Naruse's films are littered with these homilies, none of which are ever convincing, or particularly conclusive. But they clearly register the characters' ongoing attempts to locate themselves and their happiness within the changing landscape of post-war Japan. The 20-year-old children in *Late Chrysanthemums* seem to know their places, or at least are able to find their way within the new demands of 'democratic' Japan. If the older women are left in mid-stride, they are nevertheless on their way to finding their own paths. It should be noted that their survival in the modern world is to some extent at the expense of others. Both Kin and Nobu are able to run their small businesses on the basis of small domestic hierarchies: Kin's deaf maid, who can't eavesdrop on her financial conversations, is a childlike companion to the money-lender; Nobu's husband, of Asian descent, but clearly not Japanese, takes orders from his wife in a way no Japanese man would do. Nobu asks Kin for a loan so she can have a baby, and it is Nobu who runs the bar, indicating an inverted social hierarchy of her family and family business. And yet neither of these women are depicted as authoritarian employers or household tyrants, so Naruse cannot be accused of any matriarchal fantasies of feminist social inversion. Instead, these relationships are symptomatic alternatives to the dominant model of the Japanese Family System in which women's place is tightly circumscribed.

While *Late Chrysanthemums* cannot be described as a feminist film, it should be recognized as engaging with questions of female subjectivity in the metropolitan culture of post-war Tokyo. The promises of democracy may have rewarded Kin's character, but at the expense of her sexuality, along with any conventional form of 'femininity', as the critical discourse on the film indicates. These promises have clearly failed the other characters, including the men, who are all deeply in debt. Because Japanese modernity includes the recognition of women's rights, the question of female subjectivity is a particularly crucial, if neglected, discourse of this period. As Rey Chow has argued in the context of Chinese cinema, the questions of woman's sexuality and social function are central to the cultural productions of modernity, precisely because they systematically challenge the norms of the pre-modern social formation (2000: 410). In the Japanese context, female sexuality remained 'contained' in the burlesque and striptease shows that began appearing in post-war Japanese film (Izbicki 1996); for the contours of female subjectivity we must look to the home drama and the *shōshimin eiga*. In Ozu's many films about arranged marriages and love marriages, and in Naruse's films about unhappy marriages, questions about women's role in the family and the effects of women's self-determination are explored in the realm of popular culture. These are the questions posed by *Late Chrysanthemums*, but this time the home drama is set in the homes of single women, outside the Japanese Family System.

In Miriam Hansen's discussion of the Hollywood cinema as a vernacular modernism, she points to the way that the international distribution of classical cinema might have 'advanced new possibilities of social identity and cultural styles' (2000: 341). One could certainly identify new male subjectivities in post-war Japanese cinema, exemplified perhaps by actor Mifune Toshirō's arrival on the scene in 1947, and a range of new female character types emerged after the war as well, including the determined young women represented by Sachiko/Arima Ineko in *Late Chrysanthemums*. The final encounter with that 'Monroe person' is emblematic of the iconography of a vernacular modernism that the older women in the film learn to read and to understand. Naruse's cinema is a site where a discourse of female subjectivity can be located within a filmic language that is neither strictly Japanese nor strictly Hollywood, but is that of Japanese modernity, understood as an urban, industrialized, mass media-saturated society.

Acknowledgements

Research for this chapter was partially supported by the Social Sciences and Humanities Research Council of Canada. Many thanks to Chika Kinoshita for research and translation assistance.

Notes

1 The Family System or *ie* system was adopted in the Meiji era (1868–1912) as a dominant model of patriarchal inheritance patterns, enshrining a national polity of 'nation-as-family'. In this system, women's rights were sublimated to the smooth functioning of a system devoted to the 'national good', including industrial development and imperialism. Aoki Yayoi (1997: 28) argues that this system still casts a shadow over contemporary Japan; certainly in the 1950s this system was only beginning to be dismantled.

2 Both *Bangiku* and *Suisen* are available in English translation (Hayashi 1986; 1997a).

3 For a more detailed discussion of Naruse's adaptation of Hayashi Fumiko's writing, see Russell 2001.

4 For a more detailed discussion of Sugimura, see Russell 2003.
5 Tamae quotes from the Islamic classic, *The Rubiyat*; Tomi from haiku by the poet Ikkyū (1394–1481). Sugimoto notes that while the latter is an appropriate reference for a 'simple' person such as Tomi, the former suggests more education than Tamae appears to have (1954: 51).

References

Aoki Yayoi (1997) 'Feminism and Imperialism', trans. Sandra Buckley, in Sandra Buckley (ed.), *Broken Silence: Voices of Japanese Feminism*, Berkeley: University of California Press: 17–31.

Aubrey, Suzanne (1953) 'Les Femmes et le Cinéma au Japon', *Cahiers du cinéma*, December: 42–7.

Bock, Audie (1978) *Japanese Film Directors*, Tokyo: Kōdansha.

—— (1983) *Mikio Naruse*, trans. Roland Cosandey and André Kaenel, Locarno: Editions du Festival International du Film de Locarno.

Buckley, Sandra (1994) 'A Short History of the Women's Movement in Japan', in J. Gelb and M. Lief Palley (eds), *Women of Japan and Korea: Continuity and Change*, Philadelphia: Temple University Press: 150–86.

Chow, Rey (2000) 'Digging an Old Well: The Labour of Social Fantasy in a Contemporary Chinese Film', in Gledhill and Williams 2000: 402–18.

Ericson, Joan (1997) *Be a Woman: Hayashi Fumiko and Modern Japanese Women's Literature*, Honolulu: University of Hawaii Press.

Gledhill, Christine and Williams, Linda (eds) (2000) *Reinventing Film Studies*, London: Arnold.

Hansen, Miriam (2000) 'The Mass Production of the Senses: Classical Cinema as Vernacular Modernism', in Gledhill and Williams 2000: 332–50.

Hasumi, Shigehiko (1998) 'Mikio Naruse or Double Signature', in Hasumi and Yamane 1998: 61–87.

Hasumi, Shigehiko and Sadao, Yamane (eds) (1998) *Mikio Naruse*, San Sebastian and Madrid: Festival Internacional de Cine de San Sebastian.

Hayashi, Fumiko (1986) 'A Late Chrysanthemum', in *A Late Chrysanthemum: Twenty-One Stories from the Japanese*, trans. Lane Dunlop, San Francisco: North Point Press: 95–112.

—— (1997a) 'Narcissus', trans. Joan Ericson, in Ericson 1997: 221–35.

—— (1997b) 'Diary of a Vagabond', trans. Joan Ericson, in Ericson 1997: 123–220.

Iida Shinbi (1954) *'Bangiku', Eiga Hyōron*, August: 71–3.

Izbicki, Joanne (1996) 'The Shape of Freedom: The Female Body in Post-Surrender Japanese Cinema', *US-Japan Women's Journal English Supplement*, 12: 109–53.

Kurosawa Akira (1998) 'Preface', in Hasumi and Sadao 1998: 13–14.

Lopate, Philip (1986) *Totally Tenderly Tragically: Films and Filmmakers*, New York: Anchor Books.

Miyoshi, Masao (1991) *Off Centre: Power and Culture Relations Between Japan and the United States*, Cambridge, MA: Harvard University Press.

Pharr, Susan J. (1987) 'The Politics of Women's Rights', in Robert El Ward and Sakamoto Yoshikazu (eds) *Democratizing Japan: The Allied Occupation*, Honolulu: University of Hawaii Press: 221–52.

Russell, Catherine (2001) 'From Women's Writing to Women's Films in 1950s Japan: Hayashi Fumiko and Naruse Mikio', *Asian Journal of Communications*, 11, 2: 101–20.

—— (2003) 'Three Japanese Actresses of the 1950s: Modernity, Femininity and the Performance of Everyday Life', *Cineaction* 60: 34–44.

Sugimoto Heiichi (1954) *'Bangiku'*, *Kinema Junpō* 96 (July 15): 51.

Naruse Mikio Filmography

Mr and Mrs Swordplay (Chanbara fūfu, 1930)
Pure Love (Junjō, 1930)
A Record of Shameless Newlyweds (Oshikiri shinkonki, 1930)
Hard Times (Fukeiki jidai, 1930)
Love is Strength (Ai wa chikara da, 1930)
Now Don't Get Excited (Nē kōfun shicha iya yo, 1931)
Screams from the Second Floor (Nikai no himei, 1931)
Little Man Do Your Best (Koshiben ganbare, 1931)
Fickleness Gets on the Train (Uwaki wa kisha ni notte, 1931)
The Strength of a Mustache (Hige no chikara, 1931)
Under the Neighbour's Roof (Tonari no yane no shita, 1931)
Ladies, Be Careful of Your Sleeves (Onna wa tamoto o goyōjin, 1932)
Crying to the Blue Sky (Aozora ni naku, 1932)
Be Great! (Eraku nare, 1932)
Moth-Eaten Spring (Mushibameru haru, 1932)
Chocolate Girl (Chokorēto gāru, 1932)
Not Blood Relations/The Stepchild (Nasanu naka, 1932)
Tokyo's Candy-Coated Landscape (Kashi no aru Tōkyō fūkei, 1933)
Apart from You (Kimi to wakarete, 1933)
Every Night Dreams (Yogoto no yume, 1933)
My Bride's Coiffure (Boku no marumage, 1933)
Two Eyes (Sōbō, 1933)
Happy New Year (Kinga shin nen, 1934)
Street without End (Kagiri naki hodō, 1934)
Three Sisters with Maiden Hearts (Otome-gokoro sannin kyōdai, 1935)
The Actress and the Poet (Joyū to shijin, 1935)
Wife, Be Like a Rose! (Tsuma yo bara no yō ni, 1935)
Five Men in the Circus (Sākasu gonin-gumi, 1935)
The Girl on Everyone's Lips (Uwasa no musume, 1935)
Kumoemon Tochuken (Tōchūken Kumoemon, 1936)
The Road I Travel with You (Kimi to yuku michi, 1936)
Morning's Tree-Lined Street (Ashita no namiki michi, 1936)
Feminine Melancholy (Nyonin aishū, 1937)
Avalanche (Nadare, 1937)
Learn from Experience, Parts I and II (Kafuku I, II, 1937)
Tsuruhachi and Tsurujiro (Tsuruhachi Tsurujirō, 1938)
The Whole Family Works (Hataraku ikka, 1939)
Sincerity (Magokoro, 1939)
Travelling Actors (Tabi yakusha, 1940)
A Fond Face from the Past (Natsukashi no kao, 1941)
Shanghai Moon (Shanhai no tsuki, 1941)
Hideko the Bus Conductor (Hideko no shashō-san, 1941)
Mother Never Dies (Haha wa shinazu, 1942)

The Song Lantern (*Uta andon*, 1943)

This Happy Life (*Tanoshiki kana jinsei*, 1944)

The Way of Drama (*Shibaidō*, 1944)

Until Victory Day (*Shōri no hi made*, 1945)

A Tale of Archers at the Sanjusangendo (*Sanjūsangendō tōshiya monogatari*, 1945)

A Descendant of Taro Urashima (*Urashima Tarō no kōei*, 1946)

Both You and I (*Ore mo omae mo*, 1946)

Four Love Stories, Part II: Even Parting is Enjoyable (*Yottsu no koi no monogatari, II: wakare mo tanoshi*, 1947. (Omnibus production with Toyoda Shirō, Yamamoto Kajirō and Kinugasa Teinosuke)

Spring Awakens (*Haru no mezame*, 1947)

Delinquent Girl (*Furyō shōjo*, 1949)

Conduct Report on Professor Ishinaka (*Ishinaka sensei gyōjōki*, 1950)

The Angry Street (*Ikari no machi*, 1950)

White Beast (*Shiroi yajū*, 1950)

The Battle of the Roses (*Bara gassen*, 1950)

Ginza Cosmetics (*Ginza geshō*, 1951)

Dancing Girl (*Maihime*, 1951)

A Married Life [also known as *Repast*] (*Meshi*, 1951)

Okuni and Gohei (*Okuni to Gohei*, 1952)

Mother (*Okāsan*, 1952)

Lightning (*Inazuma*, 1952)

Husband and Wife (*Fūfu*, 1953)

Wife (*Tsuma*, 1953)

Older Brother Younger Sister (*Ani imōto* [also known as *Ino And Mon*], 1953)

The Echo [also known as *The Sound of the Mountain*] (*Yama to oto*, 1954)

Late Chrysanthemums (*Bangiku*, 1954)

Floating Clouds [also known as *Drifting Clouds*] (*Ukigumo*, 1955)

The Kiss, Part III: Women's Ways (*Kuchizuke, III: Onna dōshi*, 1955)

Sudden Rain (*Shū-u*, 1956)

A Wife's Heart (*Tsuma no kokoro*, 1956)

Flowing (*Nagareru*, 1956)

Untamed (*Arakure*, 1957)

Anzukko (*Anzukko*, 1958)

Summer Clouds [also known as *Herringbone Clouds*] (*Iwashigumo*, 1958)

Whistling in Kotan [also known as *A Whistle in My Heart*] (*Kotan no kuchibue*, 1959)

When a Woman Ascends the Stairs (*Onna ga kaidan o agaru toki*, 1960)

Daughters, Wives and a Mother (*Musume, tsuma, haha*, 1960)

The Flow of Evening (*Yoru no nagare*, 1960)

The Approach of Autumn (*Aki tachinu*, 1960)

As Wife, As a Woman [also known as *The Other Woman*] (*Tsuma to shite, onna to shite*, 1961)

Women's Status (*Onna no za*, 1962)

Her Lonely Lane [also known as *A Wanderer's Notebook*] (*Hōrōki*, 1962)

A Woman's Story (*Onna no rekishi*, 1963)

Yearning (*Midareru*, 1964)

The Stranger Within a Woman [also known as *The Thin Line*] (*Onna no naka ni iru tanin*, 1966)

Hit and Run (*Hikinige*, 1966)

Scattered Clouds [also known as *Two in the Shadow*] (*Midaregumo*, 1967)

10

A CINEMATIC CREATION

Ichikawa Kon's *Conflagration* (1958)

Keiko I. McDonald

Ichikawa Kon (1915–) may well be the most prolific and versatile Japanese director active today. He has made some 70 films since his first in 1947. In matter and manner they range from musicals to sports documentaries and from light-hearted comedy to challenging adaptations of heavyweight literature. Though he tends to do well whatever he does, Ichikawa's reputation at home and abroad is closely linked to the *bungei eiga* (cinematic adaptation of a work of serious fiction).

Bungei eiga prospered alongside other popular genre cinema in the 1950s during the 'Golden Age' of post-war Japanese film. Modern literary works provided a wealth of source material for filmmakers anxious to explore themes consonant with the rapid social and cultural transformations under way in Japan. There has always been a huge interest among the Japanese filmgoing public in cinematic adaptations of literary works. The proliferation of *bungei eiga* was heralded by Mizoguchi Kenji's *A Picture of Madame Yuki* (*Yuki fujin ezu*, 1950), based on the best-selling novel by Funahashi Seiichi. A great deal has been written about that other notable instance, Kurosawa Akira's *Rashomon* (1950), adapted from Akutagawa Ryūnosuke's two short stories *Yabu no naka* (*In the Grove*) and *Rashōmon*.

An impressive line-up of films from the 1950s speaks for Ichikawa's affinity for this genre. His first was *Kokoro* (1955), based on the psychological novel by the Meiji writer Natsume Sōseki. Five more novel adaptations followed in quick succession: *The Harp of Burma* (*Biruma no tategoto*, 1956) was based on the didactic novel by Takeyama Michio; *Punishment Room* (*Shokei no heya*, 1956) was adapted from the novel by the then popular writer Ishihara Shintarō; *Conflagration* (*Enjō*, 1958) was based on Mishima Yukio's *Kinkakuji* (*The Temple of the Golden Pavilion*); *Fires on the Plain* (*Nobi*, 1959) was adapted from Ōoka Shōhei's novel about World War Two; and *Odd Obsession* (*Kagi*, 1958) drew on Tanizaki Jun'ichirō's fiction in diary form.[1]

Conflagration was Ichikawa's breakthrough film, the one that defined him as a director fit 'to join the ranks of master filmmakers of Japan' (Ichikawa and Mori 1994: 189). *Conflagration* stood out – and still does – for a number of reasons. To begin with, it offers a wonderful example of Ichikawa's gift for eliciting out-standing performances from his actors. In this case, he took his veteran leading man, Ichikawa Raizō (1931–69), in a surprising new direction. Since his 1954 debut in *Young Shogunate Partisans* (*Hana no Byakkotai*), this *kabuki* performer turned *jidai-geki* (period film) swashbuckling action film star had been every Japanese female film fan's heart-throb. He had also begun to receive great critical acclaim for his role as Lord Asano in *Forty-Seven Loyal Retainers* (*Chūshingura*, Watanabe Kunio, 1958). *Conflagration* marked Ichikawa Raizō's first appearance in a *gendai-geki* (contemporary drama film) and he won the year's Best Actor Award for his portrayal of the film's anguished, introverted stammering youth. Three years later, Ichikawa cast him in a similar type of heroic role – as an outcast this time – in *Broken Commandment* (*Hakai*, 1962).

Even more importantly, *Conflagration* exhibits Ichikawa's mastery of film style and narrative. He and his lifelong collaborator (and wife) Wada Natto made brilliant use of screen and screenplay in their powerful transformation of the rich and dense psychological concerns of the original novel.[2] The resulting work is a true 'cinematic creation' notable for its clearly skewed focus on the tortured mind of a disadvantaged, marginalized and disturbed young man and his relationship with his parents and the outside world. Ichikawa is a superbly versatile craftsman who knows exactly how to make the best use of timely flashbacks, pictorial compositions and economical editing. These work together in the film to create a seamless drama whose powerful sense of urgency is further enhanced by painterly use of the innovative widescreen process known as Daiei Scope that had been introduced earlier in the decade. This Japanese version of CinemaScope took its name from the film's production company, Daiei, one of the country's five major studios.

This brief introductory study of *Conflagration* will thus concentrate on questions related to narrative and film style. Ichikawa parts company with Mishima's narrative in a number of important ways. How so? Why? And to what effect? To answer these points is to understand the important difference between the notion of 'text' on page and 'text' on screen. Similarly, we need to investigate Ichikawa's use of the familiar adaptation principle of addition/deletion/alteration (Bluestone 1957: 21). Why are such changes necessary? How do certain scenes reveal Ichikawa's innovative incorporation of cinematic devices into the context of the film? Here too some credit must be given to his cinematographer Miyagawa Kazuo, a master craftsman best known for his work on Kurosawa's *Rashōmon* and Mizoguchi's *Ugetsu* (*Ugetsu monogatari* 1953).

It goes without saying that Ichikawa's first order of business was to assess the cinematic potential of Mishima's story. *The Temple of the Golden Pavilion* is a psychological novel which provides a troubling look into a troubled mind.[3] The plot winds tighter and tighter as Mizoguchi confronts the classic choices open to the alienated individual: keep talking to the outside world in the language that the world understands; or give up and talk only to yourself in the manic, tortured, self-referring language of delusion.

Rejected by society, Mizoguchi opts for anti-social isolation. The novel details the course of his regression, using his shifting relationship with the

Golden Pavilion in Kyōto as a reference point.[4] The novelist also seeks to engage our interest in abstract philosophical problems such as the nature of 'absolute beauty'. Mishima was himself a brilliant stylist. His book is a virtuoso balancing act. He chooses to tell his story in highly embellished language which at the same time speaks for his protagonist's limited vision and diminishing ability to express himself. To Mizoguchi's mind, the temple is more than merely symbolic; it is the stuff of eternity itself, the divine infliction that 'descended from heaven, sticking to our cheeks, our hands, our stomachs, and finally burying us' (Mishima 1959: 83). On a number of occasions, that conviction is expressed in abstract language clearly beyond the reach of this untutored acolyte:

> What ornamental objects could one put on such shelves? Nothing would fit their measurements but something like a fantastically large incense burner, or an absolutely colossal nihility. But the Golden Temple had lost such things; it had suddenly washed away its essence and now displayed a strangely empty form. The most peculiar thing was that of all the various times when the Golden Temple had shown me its beauty, this time was the most beautiful of all . . . a beauty that transcended the entire world of reality, a beauty that bore no relation to any form of evanescence. (84)

Passages like this explain why the initial process of scriptwriting *Conflagration* came to grief. Fortunately, an enterprising member of Ichikawa's team discovered some notes on material Mishima had collected in preparation for the writing of his novel. Ichikawa later acknowledged the peculiar importance of this find which, in effect, sidelined the book since it provided a source of major narrative incident for the notably different structure of the screenplay.

The film's thematic focus came to rest on a more vernacular account. Using Mizoguchi's relationship with his parents, classmates and the temple superior, Ichikawa focuses on 'the life of an unprivileged youth raised on the Japan Sea Coast, his suffering, and separation from his parents against the background of the Golden Pavilion' (Ichikawa and Mori 1994: 190). This was a reasonable approach, given studio policy in the mid-1950s. Ichikawa was famously good at literary adaptations which balanced his own high artistic standards with industry demands for greater 'communicability' and contemporary appeal. *Conflagration* does that and more. Ichikawa makes the social and cultural milieu of post-war Japan an integral part of his hero's struggle. Increasing opportunism and secularism wins out over moral integrity and devotion to community. Even priests are not exempt. This unsettled young man was not alone in feeling that the world around him was changing out of all recognition. As Dennis Washburn points out (2001: 172), *Conflagration* echoes the same 'dislocations' experienced by the post-war younger generation that can be found in many other Japanese novels and films of the 1950s.

Interestingly enough, Rokuonji Temple (commonly known as Kinkakuji) itself staged a year-long protest against the filming of a book whose temple superior falls far short of Zen ideals. Daiei negotiated a compromise, agreeing not to name the temple. In the film, therefore, it became Sōenji Temple and Kinkaku (Golden Pavilion) became Shūkaku. The film title too was adapted to the more discrete *Conflagration*.

The novel's account of Mizoguchi's experience follows the order of real events with time out now and then for reflecting on the past. The motif of alienation is well and quickly served by a glance back at a childhood characterized by squalid poverty, poor health and the affliction of stammering. The boy's endurance of shame is fixed once and for all in his mind by a single look of scornful, cold contempt from the pretty Uiko. He feels 'turned to stone' by it. That incident becomes the touchstone for his growing sense of isolation. And no wonder. The boy's relationship with his father takes a cruelly paradoxical turn in relation to the traumatic accident of witnessing his mother's infidelity. Mishima makes much of the role the father's hands play in attempting to shield his son from a later, very real insight into the 'hell' of his mother's sin. The father's death can only compound the damage already done by childhood experience of the world.

The rest of the novel explores Mizoguchi's inner conflict during and after the war through his shifting, precarious relationship with the pavilion. After the outer world loses touch with his inner world, the conflict unfolds in three stages. The first concerns the pavilion, a medieval masterpiece and symbol of the unattainable, of pure and 'outwardly beauty'. Mizoguchi is drawn to worship and surrenders himself to what appears to be the very antithesis of all that he is, and all that he derives from.

In the second post-war stage of his conflict, Mizoguchi actually *becomes* the temple. He projects his alter ego into it, as Arthur Kimball (1973: 70) rightly observes. That done, he can hope to control this artifact of eternity by using it to negotiate with the external world on his own terms. Thus, the golden pavilion serves as a touchstone for all his actions. Moments of emotional and moral crisis relate to it. One prime example includes his attempt to consummate his passion with a prostitute. The Golden Pavilion prevents it. Temple and conscience have become one. In this part, Mishima enriches his main narrative tapestry with Mizoguchi's relationships with the temple superior and two classmates, Tsurukawa and Kashiwagi. The former is Mizoguchi's opposite in every aspect. The latter, a Mephistophelian figure, is also physically handicapped, more like the youth he might have become had he been more eager to take vengeance on the world that rejected him.

The third stage shows Mizoguchi attempting to liberate himself. Mishima cites a Zen *kōan* to this effect: 'When ye meet the Buddha, kill the Buddha! When ye meet your ancestor, kill your ancestor! Only thus will ye attain deliverance' (Mishima 1959: 258). Before he realizes that elimination of one's attachment or obsession – the Pavilion – is the way of freedom, he must undergo several preparatory stages. Among them is his rebellion against the authoritative superior, an attitude expressive of his endeavor to free himself from bondage to this surrogate father. His return to his birthplace on the coast of the Sea of Japan signifies a lapse into a kind of pre-natal existence. Return to his mother's womb is made possible through his first successful sexual encounter with a prostitute.

Mizoguchi's refusal to accept Father Genkai's fatherly influence seals his fate, leading to the climactic moment of arson. Destruction becomes creation as Mishima lets us see how the new life demanded by Mizoguchi creates a new order, almost a heightened liveliness. The image of flames that pervades this dramatic highlight takes on another form at the end of the novel:

> Then I noticed the pack of cigarettes in my other pocket. I took one out and started smoking. I felt like a man who settles down for a smoke after finishing a job of work. I wanted to live. (258)

Many critics think this last paragraph speaks for Mizoguchi's perception of an inner world 'which is ventilated with breeze' (Asai and Satō et al. 1980: 184). Yet this ending also serves an ironic purpose in Mishima's narrative strategy. It emerges from the perspective of an author whose presence has made itself felt throughout, especially in Mizoguchi's pronouncements on beauty. Mishima had this to say: 'If a man wants to live, only a "prison" is open to him. This is what I wanted to suggest at the end' (quoted in Saitō 1980: 110).

Ichikawa's screenplay takes up matters left unspecified in the novel. First and last, the film provides greater narrative legibility. The arsonist is questioned by the police in the opening sequence. The final sequence shows him leaping from the moving train. His suicide is Ichikawa's invention. Unlike Mishima, he offers 'definitive' closure to the protagonist's causal line. In between those two events we hear Mizoguchi tell his story. It unfolds in two sections as he looks back on his life before and after the war. His account is punctuated by flashbacks connecting his psychological state with childhood events.

Though novel and film explore the same central problem of Mizoguchi's alienation, Ichikawa's approach is more simple and direct. Mishima's torturous philosophizing gives way to the facts of the matter. These remain the same: a troubled, stammering, underclass boy loses the protective father who stood between him and a mother whose behavior is anything but supportive. In Mishima's account, Mizoguchi's tortured mind deals with his conflict by elaborating upon a complex metaphorical structure with the Golden Pavilion at its center. Ichikawa dispenses with this complexity. He offers a straightforward presentation of the pavilion as a time-honored icon of eternal beauty. The film reveals its importance gradually, showing how instead of eliciting an ambivalent reaction from Mizoguchi, the temple evokes powerful associations with a rich cultural inheritance that Japanese people can be proud to call their own. The enemy Ichikawa studies is therefore not the madness within, but the vulgarity and corruption without.

The range of choices revolving around his central problem is simplified as well. Should he try to become a model son and temple acolyte or should he rebel? The film dwells on the consequential aspects of his case. Here we have a socially disadvantaged, troubled youth ill-equipped to choose wisely, even as his paramount need is to find some image he can identify with. First, he tries the path of least resistance: being the model son and acolyte. As such, he must attempt to communicate with the outside world. When Mishima's hero fails in this, he projects his alter ego onto the pavilion. Ichikawa's hero turns inward. He retreats into a self-referring world all his own. He feels ever more alienated and alone in a changing world which is both hostile and tantalizing by turns. The film follows the various stages of rebellion against the Father Superior and the world at large leading up to Mizoguchi's final fiery attempt to set things right. His motives for this climactic act are considerably simplified in the film. He wants to protect the pavilion's sempiternal purity from the contagion of the new debased, materialistic and secular society of post-war Japan.

Ichikawa makes frequent use of the principle of deletion. Uiko, the girl who humiliates Mizoguchi in the novel, is dropped, as is Mishima's focus on the boy's troubling sexual encounters. Mizoguchi's quest for normalcy in the arms of a prostitute is also treated differently. In the novel, he manages at least a physical consummation. In the film, he decides not to. One especially shocking episode in the novel is tamed out of all recognition in the film. Mishima has Mizoguchi and his friend Tsurukawa witnessing a tea ceremony in which a woman milks herself into a cup which an army officer drains of 'every drop of that mysterious tea' (Mishima 1959: 70). Ichikawa's young boys are discreetly titivated peeping toms in a scene that could offend no one. They admire the doll-like figure of a lovely solitary woman arranging flowers. In both these instances of deletion we see internal and external motives at work: a director anxious to communicate profound meaning finds ways to do so without falling foul of ever-vigilant censorship.

Ichikawa's narrative is tightly structured and narrowly focused, so it is interesting to see how he uses his cinematic rubric to keep it moving. The opening credits flash across a background view of pavilion blueprints. Mayuzumi Toshirō's disconcerting electronic soundtrack mixes suggestions of drums and strings. At one point a chorus breaks in with a sutra-like chant. These unsettling acoustic cues alert us that something is amiss, but what?

The music stops. Its entrancing, otherworldly atmosphere gives way to an abrupt transition to the gritty everyday world of police interrogation. Three officers are seen questioning Mizoguchi. His back is to the camera. Brief as it is, this scene fills us in quickly, coldly and efficiently. A young man's details are jotted down in a police report and along with his name, age, and place of birth, we learn about Mizoguchi's crime of arson, his father's death and his foiled attempt to poison himself. Ichikawa uses a standard reverse-field set-up though the camera also gives us a full view of Mizoguchi's face, with an emphasis on his blank expression. The slightly high-angle view points plainly to the socio-political forces brought to bear on this felon of just 21.

Mizoguchi sits silent. The music returns. Its eerie persuasiveness prepares us for a shift back in time to 1944, the last year of the war in the Pacific. A long shot shows Mizoguchi in a school uniform entering the temple gate. His pre-war schooling is given short shrift in cinematic time, yet our attention is focused on three important aspects of the young acolyte's struggle.

The first has to do with his stammer. The first scenes of this section show Mizoguchi's initial encounter with the temple superior, his assistant and fellow student Tsurukawa. Here, Ichikawa uses the technique of withheld information to dramatize Mizoguchi's affliction. The boy is seen being conspicuously silent throughout. Just as his silence is stretching our patience to the limit, a worker in the kitchen spills some rice, a precious commodity in wartime Japan. Mizoguchi's shout of dismay trails off into helpless, broken stammering. This is the first we know of this aspect of his torment. The temple superior's assistant laughs at Mizoguchi whose face in close-up, bathed in perspiration, dissolves into a schoolyard scene at home. A cadet is surrounded by admiring classmates. Mizoguchi is the odd one out, sitting alone on a bench. This glimpse of his alienated misery comes from the novel. Here, as in the temple, the misfit boy is mocked and bullied. Like his counterpart in the novel, he takes his revenge. The camera studies the beautifully carved scabbard of a classmate's sword, slashed by Mizoguchi's knife. This symbolic approach to his torment clearly anticipates the destruction of the pavilion.

Mizoguchi's fixation on the pavilion is gradually revealed in this section. Our first glimpse of the building itself comes immediately after his interview with the temple superior. We see it from the young man's line of vision. Only the roof is visible through the trees in the distance, yet his face in close-up speaks for the uncommon intensity of his gaze. The pavilion's second appearance is invested with Ichikawa's hallmark irony. Needless to say, this trait is most strongly presented in the surprisingly shocking twist at the end of *Odd Obsession* where the elderly housemaid serves as executioner as well as judge in a situation involving gross moral turpitude.[5] Here, the temple superior encourages his young charge to work hard in service of the temple, adding that he should think of it as belonging to his deceased father. Mizoguchi looks up at the venerable old man, his face aglow with admiration and respect. Another cut to the pavilion in the distance follows Mizoguchi's line of vision. It too is a focus of his youthful admiration though thanks to our privileged spectatorial perspective we are aware of an ironic discrepancy. Even as Mizoguchi sets to work in the courtyard, a beggar comes looking for a handout. The superior ignores him pointedly, turning his back to go inside, only to change his mind, come back out and give the man a pittance. We see that this is no holy man atoning for a fault, but a practiced hypocrite. We see him refuse the beggar but Mizoguchi does not. Now we see the pious old fraud making sure that his new acolyte sees his benefaction. And sure enough, Mizoguchi is taken in, his face transformed by a happy smile. How could he fail to aspire to be such a saintly priest? Who better to make good the loss of his own father?

The pavilion also commands attention in a third sequence which explains its role as a transcendent symbol of eternity, a point of reference and safe haven that Mizoguchi needs more desperately than most. The opening long shot gazes across the pond at the pavilion rising tier on tier into the summer sky. The silence is profound. The trilling of cicadas deepens our sense of reverential hush. Then suddenly a siren wails an air raid warning. A cut shows Mizoguchi cleaning the floor inside. His every gesture is devout, calling to mind Tsurukawa's earlier praise of him as a good and pure young man for lavishing care on a structure that could go up in flames any time now. The confident serenity of temple and garden certainly argue for a steadfast contrast to the world of everyday life, especially during wartime. We have already seen that contrast in a shot of a Kyōto street where houses are being pulled down to help control air raid fire storms. Mizoguchi's need for devotion to the pavilion is explained in the way that the carefully crafted narrative inter-relates past and present. His mother has just paid a visit to the temple superior. We see her approach her son who refuses to let her enter the pavilion. A retrospective flashback explains. Mother and son are seen in an air raid shelter. She says that the temple is no longer theirs. She clearly has no idea how disturbing the idea of that particular loss could be to her son. The soundtrack speaks for his state of mind with a mix of discordant strings and wooden clappers. The camera plays an innovative trick. The background light shifts from the shadows of the bunker to the white of a *shōji* screen. Mizoguchi's gaze is fixed – on what? An eyeline match shows a couple having sex behind the partition. Mizoguchi's painful memory of his mother's adultery is resurfacing. This is how past blurs into present in his troubled mind; how that connection serves the motif of betrayal will be explored later on. Novel and film share the image of the father's hand attempting to shield the eyes of his son from that disturbing carnal knowledge. The film condenses Mizoguchi's alienation and hatred for his mother in this short scene. It also connects with his father's observation that the pavilion, the most beautiful thing in the world, can rise above all the ugliness that surrounds it.

A fourth presentation of the pavilion links the father's remarks to Mizoguchi's fixation on it. He runs outside, telling his mother that he would gladly die with the pavilion in an air raid. He stops near the pond. The same cinematic trick is used to redouble our sense of this troubled mind in conflict with itself and the world. A close-up of Mizoguchi's surprised expression is identical to the one he wears in a second shot of him in black school uniform, rather than the makeshift uniform of wartime. A cut to the source of his surprise reveals his father in close-up. The camera shifts to gaze at the pavilion on the far shore of the pond. Mizoguchi looks up at the kindly fatherly face that speaks of the temple's transcendent, everlasting beauty. Yet suddenly, harsh reality asserts itself. His gaze is fixed on the object in his hands: the mortuary tablet bearing witness to his loss. Again, we understand his need to become the model acolyte in service of the temple, under the guidance of the idealized father substitute.

The second, far longer section of the film concerns Mizoguchi's coming to terms with the post-war transformation of Japan, even as his search for identity shifts ground. Here, Ichikawa's concern is to show how various forces outside and within himself contribute to Mizoguchi's state of rebellious confusion. We see the needy, idealistic youth become increasingly disillusioned with the changing world around him. With disillusion come alienation and increasingly reckless defiance of authority, both that of his father figure and that of society at large. A sense of betrayal and the loss of integrity, self-worth and filial piety become thematic currents as Mizoguchi tries and fails to relate to the changes in values and attitudes in occupied Japan. Ichikawa represents this in a number of ways.

The transition from pre-war to post-war is abrupt. The pre-war section ends with a shot of Mizoguchi in the pavilion, his face wet with tears. The sound of his weeping blends with strings on the soundtrack to give voice to the grief of a boy who has lost his father. The shocking suddenness of post-war change is conveyed by very different sights and sounds. A shot in newsreel style shows two busloads of GIs approaching the temple. The diegetic sound of brakes screeching to a halt is both irritating and disconcerting. Rowdy soldiers spill out and hurry into the temple gardens whose spirit of peace and quiet they clearly do not understand. A later parallel shot of students crowding the temple courtyard speaks for an equally insensitive tourist industry now growing by leaps and bounds. A close-up of brochures in English drives the point home, as does the order for another 5000 copies we hear being placed. Snippets of dialogue in passing let us know that the monks themselves are going with the cash flow. The superior gives various bank officials their fair share of his time. During the war his assistant opposed Mizoguchi's appointment as an acolyte, protesting that his own son should be selected. Now he is only too happy that his son had to look beyond a temple sinecure since the young man's coffee shop is clearly prospering.

The post-war prosperity of touristic temples has even less edifying con-sequences. We learn from kitchen chit-chat that the newly rich heads of temples frequent *geisha* houses and even have mistresses. And sure enough, the temple superior gets a call from the hospital announcing the birth of a son he has fathered on his mistress. Ichikawa's commitment to contemporaneity finds plenty of other examples of the divine betrayed by the vulgar profane. One such instance of commonplace human weakness is given a savagely ironic twist. It involves a visit to the pavilion by a GI and his Japanese girlfriend. To them, it is just another tourist attraction also handy for some heavy petting. Mizoguchi, alive to the possibility of the defilement he has reason to hate above all else, tries to prevent her from going inside. In the ensuing struggle she suffers a painful fall. The GI, far from being outraged, gives him two cartons of cigarettes – thanks for being the probable cause of a miscarriage. Ichikawa omits the sensual interest this scene has in the novel, though Mizoguchi's behavior on screen is nothing like as demonic as in Mishima's account where he actually stamps on the girl's stomach on the GI's orders. Director and novelist have one thing in common, though. Both present the motif of betrayal with each episode in the film and book ending with the superior having no qualms about accepting the cigarettes. Mizoguchi's distrust of him dates from this episode. It also marks the beginning of his break with reality and his fall into the hell of sociopathic righteousness.

Tsurukawa's untimely death helps speed that unhappy progress. He was Mizoguchi's only friend, the person who might have shown him the way to the goal his parents had in mind for him: priesthood at the Sōenji Temple. In the latter part of this second section, Mizoguchi's delusion presents him with a range of non-choices. Among them is his plan to break free of temple life, exposing the superior as a sinner and a fraud before returning to his birthplace. Here, Ichikawa borrows freely from the novel, though his approach to some shared events is refreshingly innovative. Single shots offer arrestingly impressive visual moments, as when Mizoguchi happens on a rendezvous between the superior and his mistress. He ducks into an alley so as not to be seen. There, he finds and follows a stray dog as if he is being led along the length of the shadowy passageway by the animal. Ichikawa uses deep space to take full advantage of the long, narrow alleys Kyōto is famous for. As they reach the main street at the far end, the dog disappears. A jolt leads to a close-up of the superior and his *geisha*. A cut to Mizoguchi shows his consternation. The superior scolds him for spying. The scene ends with a shot of the old man and his mistress taking a taxi. Its metallic getaway screech speaks for the furious hypocrite's rejection of his protégé. It is impossible not to smile at the bitter irony here, an affect of black humor that is Ichikawa's hallmark.

The film turns on the consequences of that chance encounter. Mizoguchi does all he can to make amends, but the old man ignores him. The loss of this second father is clearly more than Mizoguchi can bear. So what will he do? Close-ups of knife and sleeping pills suggest suicide. But will he? Ichikawa deliberately prolongs disclosure. As in the novel, Mizoguchi's return to his birthplace leads to his final destructive act. This journey sequence shows Ichikawa's cinematic mastery. The long shot of Mizoguchi standing alone on a promontory overlooking the Sea of Japan is aesthetically breathtaking. The overall effect is that of a monochromatic painting with the varied blacks of landscape and figure offering a dramatic contrast to the ghostly grays and whites of the sea. This shot is unmistakably reminiscent of an earlier happier image of Mizoguchi and his father facing the sea in this very same spot. The implications of this return bind us in powerful sympathy with the young man's sense of helplessness, loss and loneliness.

A similar mood prevails in the next scene. Mizoguchi arrives at the family temple that no longer belongs to them. He sees the head priest and a woman coming out the gate. A close-up of Mizoguchi quickly yields to an identical shot of the gate. This time a funeral procession is passing through, accompanied by the beating of a drum. A closer view shows Mizoguchi among the mourners. This scene is taken from an earlier part of the novel. Thanks to Ichikawa's sense of stylistic economy the ancient ritual serves to express Mizoguchi's agony of alienation. Taking advantage of the wide screen, the dolly moves with the procession along the beach. A close-up shows the father's face half buried in early summer flowers. It is matched by a close-up of the boy's vacant stare. A following shot shows the burning coffin. Its lid pops up with an unnerving sound matched by eerie electronic music. The camera closes in on the boy gazing intently into the flames, a telling detail we see now in retrospect.

Mizoguchi tries one last time to reconnect with the superior but is firmly rebuffed. The motif of betrayal has come full circle. The stage is set for the fiery climax. His motives are mixed, but clear to us. Earlier he declared to his friend Togari that the 'pavilion does not belong to anybody. Everybody is using it to make money. It does not change. I won't let it change!' Challenging the changing world and the temple superior, the rebellious youth tries to destroy the eternal along with himself. Here, Ichikawa uses the expressive power of the camera to let us 'see' the process of disintegration. Again here too, he makes the

Figure 14 The burning pavilion in *Conflagration* (1958): a medieval masterpiece and symbol of an unattainable, pure beauty. BFI Stills, Posters and Designs.

most of low-key lighting in order to achieve dramatic effect from black and white textures.

Mizoguchi enters the dark pavilion. A medium shot shows him striking a match and setting fire to a pile of straw. The screen lights up with leaping flames and billowing white smoke. The camera looks here and there as flames lick up to the rafters and along the floor. A close-up glance at the statue of temple founder Yoshimitsu shows fire reflected in his eyes. A cut to the outside shows the pavilion eaten alive by flames. Ichikawa makes dramatic use of the high contrast between black and white as the ghostly flames illuminate the very building they consume against the background of the pitch dark night. A cut to inside the monastery shows the monks apprised of the danger. A cut back to the pavilion shows Mizoguchi hurrying to escape the suffocating smoke. All through this sequence various shots are used to represent the burning building. At one point, it occupies the background, the superior (back to the camera) the

147

foreground. Another shot gives the temple foreground magnitude. Towards the end, the de-centered pavilion appears to melt away, collapsing out of frame, leaving only crackling fire to dominate the night sky.[6]

The effect is entirely convincing. We join the monks as spectators of this dread event. We are also privy to the superior's awareness that the burning pavilion reflects on his moral state. We hear him murmur 'It's Buddha's punishment', even as his friend Zenkai (out of focus) approaches from behind, chanting a sutra.

A cut to Togari's boarding house. There is a striking contrast between the rueful melody he plays on a flute and the fiery crackling still ringing in our ears. This sequence concludes with Mizoguchi's flight along a mountain path. Two dazzling pictorial shots follow a close-up of Mizoguchi's smiling face. They suggest a final backward look at how his strongest point of attachment in life is now reduced to just a series of countless sparks shooting sky high. A siren sounds in the distance. Drumbeats and disembodied electronic music join in as the scene shifts to the police station. Past and present are legibly interfused again in the initial close-up of Mizoguchi. Together with the lingering acoustics, the white smoke drifting around his face speaks for the burden his past has laid upon him.

A brief four-scene coda brings definite closure to the major causal lines left loose in the novel. We return to the police interrogation. A close-up of a knife and empty box of sleeping pills gives evidence of the failed suicide attempt. A cut to the temple precincts shows the suspect surrounded by policemen. Mizoguchi looks out across the pond. The camera catches a subtle change in his expression, a faint suggestion of a smile. A cut to the pond itself is typical of Ichikawa's cinematic style. The pavilion in all its glory temporarily appears to be reflected among the floating charred debris, but this visionary glimpse soon dissolves into the sad reality of just the murky pond and blackened ruins.

A cut back to the interrogation repeats the newsreel footage view of Mizoguchi as the apprehended suspect. Now we hear from the crowd that his mother has killed herself. A bystander adds that the temple superior has gone on a pilgrimage and that he has appealed to the Supreme Court on the defendant's behalf. Mizoguchi and several policemen board the train. He jumps. We cut to a shot which surveys the length of his corpse. It is covered with a rough straw mat, his naked feet sticking out. This image is as good as any epitaph.

In sum, therefore, though it shares the central problem of Mishima's original, Ichikawa's *Conflagration* is his own 'cinematic creation'. Rather than being a slavish filming of the novel, it is cinematically ambitious, but it never loses sight of the need to communicate with the viewer. No wonder audiences East and West continue to respond so deeply to Ichikawa's powerful portrayal of the plight of the film's anti-hero who is just, according to the logic of the film, 'an unprivileged youth'.

Notes

1 For further information on Ichikawa's career, see Allyn (1985) and Quandt (2001).
2 For a study of Wada Natto as a scriptwriter, see McDonald (1994).
3 For studies of Mishima's book, see Nakamura (1975), Muramatsu (1990), and Saitō (1980).
4 For a psychological approach to the novel, see Kimball (1973: 65–93). For a Nietzschean approach, see Starrs (1994: 43–6).
5 For a study of *Odd Obsession*, see McDonald (1979).
6 Most of these scenes used a replica of the pavilion built near the pond of Daikakuji Temple. The blaze itself used a half-size replica built on a riverbank.

References

Allyn, John (1985) *Kon Ichikawa: A Guide to References and Resources*, Boston: G.K. Hall.

Asai, Kiyoshi, and Satō, Masaru et al. (eds) (1980) *Kenkyū shiryō gendai nihon bungaku* [*Reference Guide to Modern Japanese Literature*], Tokyo: Meiji Shoin.

Bluestone, George (1957) *Novel into Film*, Berkeley: University of California Press.

Ichikawa, Kon and Mori, Yuki (1994) *Ichikawa Kon no eiga-tachi* [*The Films of Kon Ichikawa*], Tokyo: Waizu Shuppan.

Kimball, Arthur O. (1973) *Crisis in Identity and Contemporary Japanese Novels*, Tokyo: Tuttle.

McDonald, Keiko (1979) 'Symbolism of *Odd Obsession* by Ichikawa', *Literature/Film Quarterly* 7 (1): 60–6.

—— (1994) 'Wada Natto', in Chieko Mulhurn (ed.), *Japanese Women Writers*, Westport, CN: Greenwood Press: 448–56.

Mishima, Yukio (1959) *The Temple of the Golden Pavilion*, trans. Ivan Morris, New York: Berkeley Publishing Corporation.

Muramatsu, Takeshi (1990) *Mishima Yukio no sekai* [*The World of Yukio Mishima*], Tokyo: Shinchō-sha.

Nakamura, Mitsuo (1975) '*Kinkakuji* ni tsuite' [On *The Temple of the Golden Pavilion*], in Kawade Shobō (ed.), *Bungei tokuhon: Mishima Yukio* [*Book on Literature: Yukio Mishima*], Tokyo: Kawade Shobō: 28–35.

Quandt, James (ed.) (2001) *Kon Ichikawa*, Toronto: Cinemathèque Ontario.

Saitō, Junji (1980) *Mishima Yukio to sono shūhen* [*Yukio Mishima: His Art, Works and Other Writers*], Tokyo: Kyōiku Shuppan Sentā.

Starrs, Roy (1994) *Deadly Dialectics: Sex, Violence and Nihilism in the World of Yukio Mishima*, Honolulu: University of Hawai'i Press.

Washburn, Dennis (2001) 'A Story of Cruel Youth: Kon Ichikawa's *Enjo* and the Art of Adapting in 1950s Japan', in Quandt 2001: 155–74.

Ichikawa Kon Filmography

The Girl at Dojo Temple (*Musume Dōjōji*, 1945)
1001 Nights with Toho (*Tōhō sen'ichiya*, 1947)
A Flower Blooms (*Hana hiraku*, 1948)
365 Nights (*Sanbyaku-rokujūgoya*, 1948)
Human Patterns (*Ningen moyō*, 1949)
Endless Passion (*Hateshinaki jōnetsu*, 1949)
Sanshiro of Ginza (*Ginza Sanshirō*, 1950)

Heat and Mud [also known as *Money and Three Bad Men*] (*Netsudeichi*, 1950)
Pursuit at Dawn (*Akatsuki no tsuiseki*, 1950)
Nightshade Flower (*Ieraishan*, 1951)
The Sweetheart [also known as *The Lover*] (*Koibito*, 1951)
The Man without a Nationality (*Mukokuseki-sha*, 1951)
Stolen Love (*Nusumareta koi*, 1951)
Bunwawan Solo (1951)
Wedding March (*Kekkon kōshinkyoku*, 1951)
Mr. Lucky (*Rakkī-san*, 1952)
Young People (*Wakai hito*, 1952)
The Woman Who Touched Legs (*Ashi ni sawatta onna*, 1952)
This Way, That Way (*Ano te kono te*, 1952)
Mr Pu (*Pū-san*, 1953)
The Blue Revolution (*Aoiro kakumei*, 1953)
The Youth of Heiji Zenigata (*Seishun Zenigata Heiji*, 1953)
The Lover (*Aijin*, 1953)
All of Myself [also known as *All about Me*] (*Watashi no subete*, 1954)
A Billionaire (*Okuman chōja*, 1954)
Twelve Chapters on Women (*Josei ni kansuru jūnishō*, 1954)
Ghost Story of Youth (*Seishun kaidan*, 1955)
The Heart (*Kokoro*, 1955)
The Harp of Burma (*Biruma no tategoto*, 1956)
Punishment Room (*Shokei no heya*, 1956)
Nihonbashi (1957)
The Crowded Street Car (*Man'in densha*, 1957)
The Men of Tohoku (*Tōhoku no zunmutachi*, 1957)
The Pit (*Ana*, 1957)
Conflagration (*Enjō*, 1958)
Goodbye, Hello (*Sayonara, konnichiwa*, 1959)
The Key [also known as *Odd Obsession*] (*Kagi*, 1959)
Fires on the Plain (*Nobi*, 1959)
A Woman's Testament, Part Two: Women (*Jokyō II: Mono o takaku uritsukeru onna*, 1960)
Bonchi (1960)
Her Brother [also known as *Younger Brother*] (*Otōto*, 1960)
Ten Dark Women (*Kuroi jūnin no onna*, 1961)
The Broken Commandment [also known as *The Outcast*] (*Hakai*, 1962)
I am Two [also known as *Being Two Isn't Easy*] (*Watashi wa nisai*, 1962)
An Actor's Revenge (*Yukinojō henge*, 1963)
Alone on the Pacific [also known as *Alone Across the Pacific* or *My Enemy the Sea*] (*Taiheiyō hitoribotchi*, 1963)
Money Talks [also known as *The Money Dance*] (*Zeni no odori*, 1964)
Tokyo Olympiad (*Tōkyō orinpikku*, 1966)
Topo Gigio and the Missile War (*Toppo Jījo no botan sensō*, 1967)
Youth (*Seishun*, 1968)
Kyoto (1969)
Japan and the Japanese [also known as *Mt. Fuji*] (*Nihon to Nihonjin*, 1970)
To Love Again (*Ai futatabi*, 1972)
The Wanderers (*Matatabi*, 1973)
I Am a Cat (*Wagahai wa neko de aru*, 1976)
Between Women and Wives (*Tsuma to onna no aida*, 1976)

The Inugami Family (Inugami-ke no ichizoku, 1976)

The Devil's Bouncing Ball Song [also known as *Rhyme of Vengeance*] (*Akuma no temari-uta*, 1977)

Island of Horrors (Gokumontō, 1977)

Queen Bee (Joōbachi, 1978)

The Phoenix (Hinotori, 1978)

The House of Hanging (Byōinzaka no kubi kukuri no ie, 1979)

Ancient City (Koto, 1980)

Lonely Heart [also known as *Happiness*] (*Kōfuku*, 1981)

The Makioka Sisters (Sasameyuki, 1983)

Ohan (1984)

The Harp of Burma [also known as *The Burmese Harp*] (*Biruma no tategoto*, 1985)

The Hal of the Crying Deer [also known as *High Society of Meiji*] (*Rokumeikan*, 1986)

Actress (Eiga joyū, 1987)

Princess from the Moon (Taketori monogatari, 1987)

Crane (Tsuru, 1988)

Noh Mask Murders (Tenkawa densetsu satsujin jiken, 1991)

47 Ronin (Shijūshichinin no shikaku, 1994)

The Eight-Tomb Village (Yatsuhaka-mura, 1996)

Shinsengumi (Shinsen Group, 2000)

Dora-Heita (2000)

Kā-chan (2001)

11

MODERNIZATION WITHOUT MODERNITY

Masumura Yasuzō's *Giants and Toys* (1958)

Michael Raine

In 1955, Satō Tadao (1955: 29) wrote that Japanese films were fundamentally 'slower' than Western films. They interrupted the plot development essential to American cinema with an extraneous lyricism, which went beyond the expression of character subjectivity in European art films to contrast human drama with an unchanging and indifferent Nature. Satō detected a tragic view of life in traditional forms such as *haiku* and *naniwabushi* (popular narrative song) that lived on in the emotional life of the masses (*taishū*), claiming that the Japanese films then winning prizes at European film festivals constituted a form of '*kabuki* realism' (32). As Japan recovered from its post-war Occupation (1945–52), and critics came to terms with the sudden international success of Japanese cinema, such broad cultural explanations became widely accepted.

Against that orthodoxy, new director Masumura Yasuzō demanded a cinema of shocks that would blast spectators out of their comfortable orbit around a naturalist cinema of everyday life (*shizenshugi-teki fūzoku eiga*), typified by what he saw as Ozu Yasujirō's idealized middle-class passivity (Masumura 1958a: 24), and the abstract 'so-called realism' of Imai Tadashi's social concern (Masumura 1958b: 19).[1] In his first four films, Masumura emphasized the experience of conflict over transcendence and melodramatic reconciliation, rejecting communal emotion and atmosphere for the struggle between the individual and an oppressive mass society. Masumura's fifth film, *Giants and Toys* (*Kyojin to gangu*, 1958), also propagandized the importance of 'speed' in shaking off the 'pre-modern' trappings of mainstream cinema and society (Masumura 1958a: 24), but, at the same time, it recognized that individuality (*kosei*) in mass culture is also a commodity.[2] The film's absurdly rapid dialogue and formally overt techniques shocked contemporary audiences and recalled, for some recent viewers, the reflexive pyrotechnics of US director Frank Tashlin. Masumura's early films certainly lend themselves to such an interpretation, but a closer look at *Giants and Toys* also reveals a broader set of concerns. This parody of a recrudescent post-war celebrity culture developed an intensity of film style, specifically mise-en-scène, that challenged prevailing modes of

Figure 15 Giants and Toys (1958) parodies post-war celebrity culture by challenging prevailing modes of Japanese filmmaking. BFI Stills, Posters and Designs.

filmmaking and pointed toward the social and stylistic concerns of Japan's 'new wave' cinema that emerged around 1960. At the same time, as a gleefully mass-mediated critique of mass culture, the film also ventured a 'vernacular modernist' reflexivity distinct from the critical realism of 1950s' 'independent production' and the critical distance claimed by the even more disjunctive 'political modernist' films of the following decade.[3]

Giants and Toys

Daiei bought the rights to *Giants and Toys* because author Kaikō Takeshi had just won the prestigious Akutagawa Prize for new novelists. As with Ishihara Shintarō and the *taiyōzoku* (sun tribe) boom of two years earlier, prize-winning novelists were celebrities in the 1950s and the studio knew that the title alone would guarantee an audience. Masumura and his scriptwriter Shirasaka Yoshio expanded Kaikō's story, part of a developing literary genre of the 'business novel', into a pessimistic allegory of Japan's incipient high growth economy. The film follows the travails of Nishi, a new employee in the advertising department of a caramel company. Yokoyama, Nishi's college chum and now 'friendly rival' at another caramel company, introduces him to Kurahashi, a young executive at a third rival company, who becomes his girlfriend. Nishi helps his boss (Gōda) promote Kyōko, a broken-toothed proletarian girl, as a celebrity in order to sell the company's candy. Kyōko is shown to have no particular talents – Gōda likes her because her eyes move around and she has a long tongue! – but in Japan's already saturated image culture it is precisely her peculiar ordinariness that is most appealing. Gōda first creates Kyōko as a media figure through carefully placed magazine photo-spreads and appearances at fashion shows. That empty celebrity is then attached to the company's product in newspaper advertisements and television commercials with a topical 'outer space' theme. However, the plan fails when Kurahashi designs a superior campaign and Yokoyama entices Kyōko away to pursue a singing career. After a climactic showdown, Nishi realizes that he has no option but to don the spacesuit himself and carry the company flag through the streets of Tokyo.

Giants and Toys' broadening of Kaikō's already satirical story into an allegorical critique of Japanese capitalism was hardly original. Earlier films such as *Ten'ya wan'ya* (Shibuya Minoru, 1950) and *I'll Buy You* (*Anata kaimasu*, Kobayashi Masaki, 1957) had mocked the pusillanimity of company workers and the corruption of sports and celebrity culture. Beyond those *auteur* films, comic 'salaryman' series such as the *Boss* (*Ōban*, 1957–8) and the *Company President* (*Shachō*, 1956–71), as well as the *Black* (*Kuro*) series of industrial espionage films directed by Masumura himself in the early 1960s, were part of a popular genre cinema that sustained the Japanese studio system. Although the prestige productions of Mizoguchi and Ozu were widely seen, the 1950s was an industrial as well as an aesthetic 'Golden Age' for Japanese cinema. The postwar economic recovery and a cinema building boom brought in ever-larger audiences for a popular cinema that controlled up to 80 percent of the domestic market. Competition between the major studios (Shōchiku, Tōei, Tōhō, Daiei, Shin-Tōhō, later Nikkatsu) led to double and even triple bill programs so that by the end of the decade, Japan was producing over 500 films per year. This increased demand was one reason for the sudden appearance of new filmmakers in the late 1950s, but the results were not entirely positive. As *Giants and Toys* makes clear, cinema was also being challenged by television and by a growing culture of personal consumption. Although 1958 marked the peak of Japanese film attendance, production costs for that growing number of films had increased with the growing use of color and widescreen. New directors made on average four films per year, working within existing genres and adapting literary properties in a high-volume low-budget production system.

Once the economic miracle was underway, opinion magazines and even film journals in the late 1950s were inundated with articles on the coming 'age of mass communications'. Cornell-trained social psychologist Minami Hiroshi wrote a series of articles on the cinema and its audience while opinion journals translated American anxieties about modern alienation. The repeated subordination of Japan to the US in *Giants and Toys* – with its fads, advertising methods, and ideal body types all flowing from West to East – echoed common anxieties about political, economic, and cultural domination. Although that intellectual context supported an alternative to the studios in the leftist independent production (*dokuritsu puro*) movement, Masumura's film does not seem particularly successful as a straightforward political critique of post-war 'organization man'.

Nishi's absurd predicament is both comic and eventually disturbing but, lacking the naturalist density of the more socially conscious cinema, characters in *Giants and Toys* become ciphers that cannot sustain a class- or systems-based interpretation. So why did critics list the film as one of the ten best of 1958, and what significance does it hold for the history of Japanese cinema? In both cases, the answer has less to do with economics than with Masumura's controversial arguments about post-war subjectivity and the film's experiments in film style.

Masumura and *shutaisei*

According to Masumura's autobiographical eye, his upbringing in the transitional period from the relatively democratic Taishō era (1912–1925) to the increasingly militarist Shōwa era (1925–1989) underpinned his interest in individual consciousness and an awareness of the overwhelming power of the state over the weak subject. A self-declared 'philosophy kid', Masumura preferred the liberal philosophy of Locke and Hume to the idealism of Hegel and Heidegger, though he could not avoid the idealists' deep influence on wartime nativism (Masumura 1999: 59). Masumura was a contemporary of Mishima Yukio at the Law Division of the University of Tokyo, and moved to the Literature Division after graduation in 1948 to take a second degree in philosophy while working part-time as an assistant director for Daiei. Given this background, it is not surprising that Masumura's films and articles echoed debates among the intelligentsia, especially the debate over subjectivity (the *shutaisei ronsō*) most active in the late 1940s, when Masumura was a university student.

The *shutaisei* debate resulted from a rapprochement between the Japanese Communist Party (JCP) and other left-leaning groups that worked for social reform under the Occupation. Philosophers and literary critics such as Umemoto Katsumi and Ara Masato argued that a socialist revolution must be preceded by a subjective transformation, which would establish the political agency (*shutaisei*) through which revolutionary change could be achieved. However, Comintern policy shifted in 1948 and the JCP broke with the dissident leftists, condemning them as 'modernists' (*kindaishugi-sha*).[4] Like the later 'New Wave' directors, Masumura's intellectual matrix was broader than the party politics of the 'independent production' movement. He combined the materialism and existentialism of the New Left of the 1960s with a skeptical humanism that stemmed from his pre-war readings in liberal philosophy, his experiences in the war, and the post-war vicissitudes of the popular front.

The struggle over *shutaisei* established a vocabulary for thinking through the problem of structure and agency in post-war Japan. Even in film criticism, discussion of filmmakers who came of age after World War Two often turned on their representation of the subject (*shutai*, but also other rough analogues for 'self' such as *shukan, jiga, jiko, pāsonaritī*, etc.). The first films to be closely linked to this putatively novel, assertive subjectivity were the *taiyōzoku* films of 1956, most of them adapted from stories by the celebrated new novelist, Ishihara Shintarō, who had scandalized official Japan with his explicit tales of youth, violence, and sexuality.[5] Masumura worked as an assistant director on Daiei's *taiyōzoku* film, *Punishment Room* (*Shokei no heya*, Ichikawa Kon, 1956), and in his first directorial efforts continued the earlier film's investigation of post-war subjectivity, adding to it a loose comic sensibility that stemmed from his two years of study in Italy.

After graduating for a second time, Masumura applied for an Italian government scholarship to study for two years at the Centro Sperimentale della Cinematografia in Rome. For the rest of his life, Masumura remembered fondly the Centro's film history class and the Rome film circles that brought together people inside and outside the industry to discuss films from historical and aesthetic perspectives. He would castigate impressionist Japanese critics for not living up to the serious, historically informed, aesthetically sensitive, and practically engaged criticism that he experienced there. A new film culture, not simply new films, would be necessary if cinema was to play a role in creating post-war Japanese subjectivity. Masumura worked as a film journalist while living in Italy, writing for Japanese film journals and publishing the first extended history of Japanese cinema in a Western language, a 60-page article in *Bianco e nero* in 1954. The article concludes with a measure of impatience toward the preference in Europe for refined historical films from Japan. What Japanese cinema needed, he wrote, was a biting and lively take on modern Japan, a satirical form that was not possible under the militarist state and the Allied Occupation since filmmakers were not free to make fun of power (Masumura 1954: 66).

Masumura sought to fill that prescription after returning from Europe. His first four films (made in less than eight months) were program pictures, entertainment films churned out by each studio to fill their weekly double bills. Despite their commodity form, the films appealed to critics and cinephiles, partly because their generic outlines were overwhelmed by an astonishing semantic excess, and partly because they were accompanied by strongly worded manifestos calling for a new kind of cinema in Japan. The films are always conscious of their generic framework: the youth romance *Kisses* (*Kuchizuke*, 1957) ends with a kiss but it happens on a building site; *The Bright Girl's* (*Aozora musume*, 1957) abrupt shifts of tone make a mockery of the family melodrama; and when the doctor's girlfriend in the remake of *Warm Current* (*Danryū*, 1957) calls out 'Being your lover or your mistress is fine by me! I'll be waiting!', she shocks not only the commuters at the station, but also the audience that remembered the suppressed emotion of the original, directed by Yoshimura Kōzaburō in 1939. Masumura responded to attacks on his films by extending his critique of repression to Japanese film style itself, contrasting the 'Apollonian' use of close-ups and theatrical acting to create a sense of intimacy with his 'Dionysian' interest in exaggeration (Masumura 1958c: 31). Masumura's resistance inspired a new generation of university-educated assistant directors: Ōshima Nagisa, then a Shōchiku assistant director and part-time critic, enthused, 'When Masumura Yasuzō used a freely moving camera to depict a pair of young motorcycle riding lovers [in *Kisses*], this new generation had assumed a place in Japanese cinema as an intense, unstoppable force that could no longer be ignored' (Ōshima 1993: 26–7).

Masumura's touchstones were usually Italian; not so much neo-realism as more humorous and technically polished films such as Renato Castellani's *E primavera* (Italy, 1948), Luchino Visconti's *Bellissima* (Italy, 1951) and Federico Fellini's *I Vitteloni* (Italy, 1953). He claimed to find in Europe a space for a free subjectivity that had been lost in Japan:

> Breathing the air of Europe, I felt for the first time that I knew the meaning of the word 'human' [*ningen*]. In Japan, lacking a tradition of humanism, even if the value and beauty of the human being is accepted in the abstract, it cannot be truly achieved. A Japanese, trapped in a complex social structure and weak economy is a shabby, poor, and weak human being. Once I set foot on European soil, I could feel the raw truth of that 'beautiful, powerful humanity'.
>
> (Masumura 1958b: 18–19)

In the interests of liberating that human subject, Masumura wanted his characters to reject social constraints and act in an excessive fashion that 'even foreigners would think was crazy' (Masumura 1958c: 31). Where mainstream critics looked for beautiful renunciation, Masumura saw the corruption of an alternative Japanese history. He agreed with Satō's observation on the tempo of Japanese cinema, but insisted that renunciation was not a 'traditional mode of Japanese thought' (Satō 1955: 28). Rather, it was a political consequence of the Meiji government's repressive response to modernity:

> It's not true that there was no democracy before the war: at the very least, people in the Meiji period [1868–1912] had freedom. But as pressure from the Meiji state grew, they began to lose that freedom by not exercising it. They grew used to abandoning the self through the Taishō and Shōwa periods until freedom, love, and other precious emotions, even life itself, were calmly – no, eagerly – thrown away under the Emperor system.
>
> (Masumura 1958b: 17)

Masumura leveraged the cultural capital of his European education to make these 'eurocentric' pronouncements, attacking a state policy of technological development coupled with culture-based ideologies of social control that continued through pre-war, wartime, and post-war Japan.[6] In short, (economic) modernization without (political) modernity. For Masumura, as for the 'modernists' of the *shutaisei* debate, the liberation of the individual psyche was as important, aesthetically as well as politically, as the historical-materialist critique of social relations.

Masumura's fifth film, *Giants and Toys*, has much in common with his earlier works, but this first project over which he had full script approval leads to a more pessimistic conclusion. Unlike the earlier films that confront melodrama with a startling negation of the genre's controlling environment, in *Giants and Toys* Nishi is forced to recognize that he cannot desert his mentor and must instead subjugate himself to the company's demands. In a concluding sequence added to Shirasaka's script, a high-angle crane shot shows Nishi in the spacesuit walking through a crowd, which parts and mocks him as he passes. Although other 'salaryman' genre films tended to ameliorate the conflict between pleasure and duty by making them miraculously coincide, in this final image of self-alienation *Giants and Toys* searches for a more direct representation of the conflicted subject of high economic growth Japan. Only the sudden appearance of Nishi's erstwhile rival Kurahashi, who whispers encouragement, lends hope to this bleak ending. Nothing she says in this final scene can alter Nishi's grim future, but Kurahashi's cryptic direction – she has been Masumura's stand-in throughout the film – to 'smile, brightly' reminds us that *Giants and Toys* is less concerned with narrative than with its representation.

Masumura and film style

Before he left for Italy, Masumura's essay on Kurosawa Akira had won a prize in *Kinema Junpō*. He had praised Kurosawa for his ability to create tightly edited compositions – like modern architecture – that avoided the idealized, piteous beauty of resignation in the dominant tradition. Japanese cinema was still waiting, he claimed, for a director who could combine Kurosawa's strong compositional sense with a deep analytical intelligence (Masumura 1999: 19). Despite his later repudiation of 'the shot' in favor of 'the story', Masumura explored the expressive function of film style in his early writing. Sounding like the French New Wave critics-turned-filmmakers that he admired, he championed cinema in its specificity, contrasting the abstractions of literature with the detailed clarity of film (Masumura 1999: 130). In the 1950s at least, Masumura was more committed to a cinephilic embrace of film style (specifically, the mise-en-scène of setting, décor, and acting, coupled with the mobile deep space cinematography and disjunctive cutting that made those elements stand out) than populist ideologues or self-identified 'theme oriented' (*tēma shugi*) newspaper critics. He aligned himself with a global post-war cohort of young filmmakers and claimed in a 1959 manifesto that abstract concepts are secondary to lived experience: in true cinema the concrete image is primary and 'technique is thought turned into sensibility' (Masumura 1999: 124). That desire to make films do more than retell stories links *Giants and Toys* to a large-scale shift in the ambitions of young Japanese filmmakers. Unlike previous generations who were inculcated with the studio style, assistant directors such as Ōshima Nagisa and Yoshida Kijū wanted the image to take on a semiotic density made difficult by the constrained resources and generic requirements of the program picture.[7]

Daiei hoped that Masumura's medium-conscious direction could modernize the studio's reputation, so from the beginning *Giants and Toys* was no ordinary program picture (Ozaki 1958: 43). But the budget was far less than Mizoguchi Kenji had enjoyed, or guest directors such as Ozu could expect. Masumura's young team was working with B-list actors on a B-movie budget. Although the set and cast are impressively large, the company offices are no more than barely disguised sound stages and the lighting at times leaves faces in deep shadow.

158

There was not enough film and not enough time to perfect the dubbing (Ogi et al. 1958: 38), but Masumura compensated for these production limitations with a pop sensibility and rough aesthetic of artificiality and excess that runs throughout *Giants and Toys*. That iconoclastic aggression is evident from the first frames of the film. The Daiei studio logo is superimposed on a bright red background, the same intense Agfacolor red used in Kyōko's wardrobe and the caramel advertising campaign that she is invented to promote. As a raucous jazz song plays in the background, we see the back of a female form. When she turns, the shiny face and chipped teeth of Nozoe Hitomi do violence to the typical image of this 'doll-like' (*ningyō-kei*) actress, a type popularized in Japan by Audrey Hepburn. The shot is almost immediately transformed into a black and white photograph, which is then doubled and redoubled in time to a heavy drum beat. The titles follow, inscribed on rectilinear color blocks familiar, like the photographs, from the designs of the weekly magazines so important in this film and to Japan's culture of celebrity.

The introduction to the advertising department demonstrates *Giants and Toys'* at once excessive and expressive style. Four salesmen, including Nishi, inhabit a room full of toys – men are often infantilized in this film – but their conversation is both breakneck and cynical. Reverse cuts and deep staging open up new complexities, as when a cut reveals Gōda in the background while a worker complains about his nepotistic rise. As Gōda sweeps past the camera, we cut again, not to a continuity shot of his back, but to his desk, covered with toys, before the camera tilts up before he arrives in the shot. The four company men enter the frame and crowd around Gōda, but for all their importuning he takes the new boy Nishi to lunch, departing toward the back of the set as the other three show their disappointment in the foreground. The construction of this sequence typifies the film as a whole: camera movement is fluid and unceasing; cuts are dominated by spatially confusing reverse shots; yet the seeming chaos is made coherent by a punctuating composition, bringing a scene that began in the confused middle of things to an expressive close.[8] Here, the final shot models the significance of the scene: the junior employees struggle for attention, but Gōda chooses Nishi as his protégé.

Masumura encouraged the diagrammatic (*zushiki-teki*) quality of Shirasaka's script, inspired by Ito Sei's 1953 article, *Soshiki to ningen* ['Organizations and Human Beings'], a description of how Japanese social systems dominate the ant-like humans who service them (Masumura 1999: 320). Cinematography and the disposition of objects in *Giants and Toys* shift from being realistically motivated to having a similarly diagrammatic, commentary function. Ubiquitous charts illustrate the sales decline that structures the narrative, or are used as props for diegetically improbable lectures on Japan's peculiarly ill-fated climatic and social conditions. Masumura's frequent references to overpopulation anxiety find expression in the 'human flood' that begins and ends the film, while the romantic scene at the beach between Nishi and Kurahashi gives an ironic visual demonstration of the omnipresence of advertising and the impossibility of autonomous subjectivity in what Gōda calls the 'era of mass communications' (*masukomi jidai*). The cutaway to a large billboard advertising Nishi's World

Candy company and the tilt back down to the couple kissing create an overt cinematographic link between sex and salesmanship that is then made literal as Kurahashi expertly reverses Nishi's blatant attempt to press her for information.

Allegories of cinema and nation

The final destination of such symbolic mise-en-scène is allegory. In the first dialogue scene of the film, a lighter that fails to catch becomes the over-emphatic focus of all the characters' gazes, leading to a montage of fast dissolves illustrating the caramel business, all overlaid by the glinting reflection of the lighter. At various points in the film a similar sequence recurs, showing the mass production of candy at the World Candy factory or the mass reproduction of Kyōko's image in magazines and on television. It takes only a small interpretive step from this coupling of production and reproduction to see the regular clicking of the lighter flint as a metaphor for the motion of the film through camera and projector that is the condition of our seeing it. In the narrative, too, these three companies struggling to sell caramels in the face of declining demand are like the six film studios, using color, widescreen, and double or triple bills to compete as cinema's long post-war expansion came to an end. The emphasis in *Giants and Toys* on the technical reproducibility of radio, television, and photographic magazines serves as indication of the ways in which the many channels of trans-media exploitation in Japan's post-war celebrity culture were overwhelming the cinema. It is not difficult to see Shirasaka in the harried scriptwriter at the television station, given five minutes to write dialogue, and Masumura in Goda, ordered to attract customers with no budget and no dependable talent. Even Nishi's alienated despair matches the frustration of the new directors working in the program picture system. Masumura makes a comic point of this intertextuality: the tadpoles that Kyōko neglects when she becomes famous are named after Ishihara Yūjiro and Nakamura Kinnosuke, the biggest young stars of the modern day and period film genres.

The strain and insincerity of the advertising business echoes the film industry in particular, but *Giants and Toys* also makes general reference to the 'vernacular modernity' of high economic growth Japan. From the beginning, Nishi's predicament is framed in specifically national terms: the frenetic pace of the advertising world is explained by Japan's domination by consumerist trends from the United States. Characters constantly remind each other that they live in Japan and have no choice but to struggle. In the climactic showdown, Gōda tells Nishi that he is Japanese and cannot escape to the far-off countries where the 'blue eyed dolls' live.[9] Then, when Nishi dons the spacesuit costume in order to advertise the company's product, the older man congratulates him by declaring 'You're Japanese after all!' If Nishi is weighed down by his nationality, Kyōko seems light enough to float. Gender in *Giants and Toys* divides subjects that struggle under the demands of high economic growth Japan from subjects that thrive (at least temporarily) on the changes. After her grotesque image multiplies and blows away in the opening credits, we next see Kyōko from Nishi's point-of-view, refracted through the candy display case so that she is ambivalently an image and an object, an overtly desiring subject and something to be consumed. Repeated set-ups emphasize that her appearance changes to match the objects that accompany her: dowdy at first when she rides in a taxi, and as shiny as her red Austin with her new teeth and hairpiece later on.

All the old values mean nothing in this new world of image and affect. When the company records Kyōko's idealized proletarian biography for radio broadcast, she stumbles insouciantly through a script full of cultural platitudes at odds with her avaricious and slovenly family. Kyōko is usually the agent of the film's most egregious affronts: to the war wounded ex-soldiers she ignores or to the insultingly termed 'natives' (*dojin*) in blackface who lift her during her 'jazz' number. Nozoe Hitomi's performance becomes increasingly abstract until in her final scene Kyōko's kaleidoscopic display of emotions is as stylized as the paper streamers at the stage show. Even after she has deserted the two men, Kyōko is ambiguously present in the mise-en-scène of their climactic showdown. As Nishi retreats before Gōda's accusations, the panning camera reveals dozens of images of Kyōko in the background. Gōda even points to one as if she were there in person when he tells Nishi to make her wear the spacesuit. These confusions of object and image in *Giants and Toys* suggest that Kyōko's distinctive 'individuality' is no more than the effect of a system that flattens subjects into mechanically reproducible images: following the Marxian description of modernity, it seems that as Kyōko rises from ingénue to idol 'all that is solid melts into air' (Marx and Engels 1998 [1848]: 54).

Metaphorical layering is common to many films but national allegory was a particularly powerful reading formation in post-war Japan. Cold War politics affected every aspect of social life and fostered a widespread awareness of Japan's precarious geopolitical position. Masumura's own commentary recognized a similarity, but also a distinction between *Giants and Toys'* allegory of modern Japan and the vernacular representation of the 'madness of modern civilization' in Charlie Chaplin's comedies. At the end of those films, he wrote, Chaplin 'escapes the automation machines and disappears over the border with the girl he loves', but in Japan escape is impossible: one can only 'work like a madman till he dies' (Masumura 1999: 407). Even so, the sheer vitality of the female characters in *Giants and Toys* put another side to the story. Itō Sei wrote on the power of institutions and the weakness of the human subject, but he also argued that human freedom could not exist outside, but only inside and against those institutions. The demands of the system could not be ignored: one must 'feed the beast to avoid being eaten' (Itō 1973: 138). *Giants and Toys* shows a similar ambivalence: unlike contemporary social theorists such as Theodor Adorno, Dwight McDonald, or Richard Hoggart, the film sees no alternative to the middlebrow culture industry in either high modernist art or working-class culture. No simple cheerleader for neo-liberal economics, *Giants and Toys* also rejects the popular archeological model of culture that posited an unchanging stratum of Japaneseness barely covered by a disposable Americanization. Some of the female characters learn to thrive in that impasse. Unlike Nishi, for whom even romance has a profit motive, Kurahashi maintains a distinction between her self and her work: 'It's madness . . . but that's modern times (*gendai*) . . . If we stop to think, we'll be crushed'. Japan seems like the end point of Marx and Engels' dystopian logic: old ways of life, like the old advertising chief, disappear and the commodity form is revealed as 'brutal exploitation'. And yet the result is not a 'cosmopolitan' and undifferentiated 'world literature' (Marx and Engels 1998 [1848]: 55), but a specific historical consciousness – for the audience more than for the characters – of a Japan that is not the US, but also, at the same time, no longer 'Japan'.

'Thought turned into sensibility'

When *Giants and Toys* played at the Venice Film Festival in 1958, Italian critics dismissed it as 'Coca-Cola cinema' without distinguishing between the film's subject matter and its rhetoric. Readings of Masumura's film as national allegory risk a similar reduction: despite Masumura's erudition, in this film sensibility (style) takes precedence over abstract thought. The problem of subjectivity under post-war image capitalism is approached from the inside, through a somatic experience that the cinema is particularly well suited to provide. The narrative possibilities of Kyōko's deliquescent insubstantiality extend into Masumura's 'Dionysian' style that foregrounds volatile spaces – the dissolve montage of neon signs, or the advertising office dominated by transparent surfaces – and multiplies Kyōko's image on posters and magazine covers. Even meaning seems to evaporate in the barrage of sharp sound edits and incredibly gaudy props. These objects take on a visual prominence that cannot be explained by their narrative import: in an early scene Gōda and the company president are separated by a distractingly yellow vase of daffodils, while at the film's climax Gōda and Nishi face each other over a purple plastic dog. Characters in *Giants and Toys* are distributed in separate planes and look at the camera as often as they look at each other. Indeed, it is hard to see these figures as characters at all: the look is less a window onto interiority than an overt formal articulation.[10]

Sound also does more than tell stories in *Giants and Toys*. Shirasaka remembers that he had to write almost twice as much material for this film as for a typical film of the same length (Masumura 1999: 320), but the 'machine gun-like' dialogue serves a rhythmic and declamatory function rather than building a sense of character. Words become artificially repeated blocks of language, like the taxi driver who always moans about recession, or the candy company director who turns to the camera three times in a row to say 'What on earth?' with escalating vehemence. The sudden intimacy with the apparatus afforded by these reflexive moments hardly counts as 'critical distance' – the choreography of mise-en-scène in *Giants and Toys* is a style, not simply an alienating device. Nor can these caricatures bear the same historical-materialist claim to authenticity as the idealist teachers and villainous autocrats of the 'independent production' films.[11] *Giants and Toys* searches for a mode of representation appropriate to the experience of 'modernization without modernity' in 1950s Japan *within* the modes of representation made available by that specific historical situation. The film gambles that its staccato abstractions and the plastic

162

sheen of its garish images can themselves constitute a form of knowledge, to an audience attuned to film style as 'thought turned into sensibility'.

Most, however, were perplexed. Since the *taiyōzoku* boom, few films had featured unsympathetic protagonists and most rendered their moral calculus excessively clear. Although *Giants and Toys* was included in *Kinema Junpō*'s top ten for 1958 (one of only two directed by young filmmakers), Shirasaka remembers audiences muttering 'What the hell is this?' and some critics blamed Masumura for wasting his budget on the Agfacolor film stock and ignoring the unnaturalness of the performances. Others claimed the film itself was derivative, and accused him of caricature.[12] Even Ōshima Nagisa, who had praised Masumura for dispelling the 'victim consciousness' (*higaisha ishiki*) that infected most postwar melodrama, criticized him for failing to achieve critical distance (Ōshima 1993: 16). Ōshima turned *Giants and Toys*' critique of reproduction against itself, arguing that Masumura failed to achieve a fully autonomous subjectivity that could politically engage with post-war Japan. As a 'modernist', Masumura was complicit with the same social machinery that he condemned in *Giants and Toys*: his was only a 'false subjectivity' (*giji shutaisei*) that could not 'radically re-imagine the situation' since it was operating with 'one eye open and one eye closed' (quoted in Yamane 1992: 101–2). Although these claims might seem suspect in light of Ōshima's own adventures in celebrity, it is easy to find ammunition for his critique. Masumura was fêted in late 1950s media as a 'new director' (*shinjin kantoku*), and appeared regularly in magazines such as *Nihon* and *Shūkan Yomiuri* to argue his modernist position. Actress Nozoe Hitomi also appeared, like Kyōko, in the photographic front section of film journals and the weekly magazines that Masumura satirized in the film.[13] Despite his critique of advertising and the politics of manufactured personality, the beret-wearing Masumura became the very image of modern Japanese cinema in mainstream journalism, a position he lost only with the arrival of the Shōchiku 'New Wave'.

Caught between a resurgent nativism that regarded his cosmopolitan films with suspicion and a historical-materialist critique of the commodity form that could not forgive his complicity, Masumura came to seem politically naïve. Although he faded from discussions of the future of Japanese cinema, his 'technique as thought turned into sensibility' pointed toward the 1960s 'popular baroque' cinema of Suzuki Seijun's nihilistic action films, Misumi Kenji's florid period dramas, and the Tōhō musical comedies that exposed the absurdities of Japan's economic growth while paying lip service to the ideology of economic success. Early 'New Wave' films directed by Imamura Shōhei, Yoshida Kijū, and Shinoda Masahiro also borrowed their parodies of pop culture and interest in the ironies of a mediated society from *Giants and Toys*. Masumura's acceleration of sensory impression and interest in the somatic intimacy of thinking through film form, even in films made within the studio system, supposed that this too might be a form of knowledge to put alongside historical-materialist analysis. What Ōshima criticized as lack of critical distance in Masumura's films might now seem more familiar as immanent critique, a kind of 'vernacular modernism'. Unlike the 'New Wave' filmmakers who followed an 'ideology of critical distance' to a cinema without an audience in the 1960s, Masumura stayed at Daiei, emphasizing performance alongside mise-en-scène in a series of melodramas with powerful female actors such as Wakao Ayako. More comfortable with genre than *Giants and Toys*, studio films such as *A Wife Confesses* (*Tsuma wa kokuhaku suru*, 1961) and *Blind Beast* (*Mōjū*, 1969) continued to bridge the divide between art cinema (*geijutsu eiga*) and entertainment film (*goraku eiga*), representing to domestic mass audiences the very experience of ontological instability so characteristic of the 'modernization without modernity' of post-war Japan.

Acknowledgements

I would like to thank Alastair Phillips, Julian Stringer and Miriam Hansen for their advice on earlier drafts of this chapter.

Notes

1 Masumura was thinking of Ozu's family melodramas such as *Tokyo Twilight* (*Tōkyō boshoku*, 1957) and Imai films such as *Rice* (*Kome*) and *Story of Pure Love* (*Junai monogatari*), both made at Tōei in 1957.

2 Masumura emphasized that 'speed' meant something more than simply fast cutting and contemporary subject matter by claiming that even foreigners were bored by films such as *The Moderns* (*Gendaijin*, Shibuya Minoru, 1952) because the central character was too passive and psychologically opaque. The pacing of Masumura's own films depends far more on unpredictability and an excess of information than on average shot length. For Masumura's critique of European interest in exotic Japan, see Iwasaki and Masumura (1958: 28).

3 See Rodowick (1995) for a discussion of 'political modernism' in the cinema. Miriam Hansen has recently linked 'vernacular' and 'modern' to argue for a form of 'vernacular modernism' in popular cinema from the 1920s to the 1940s that combines the everydayness of this mass cultural form with the specifically modern aesthetic of a machine-based, accelerated mode of perception (Hansen 2000a: 332). Those films, while not attaining the interrogative abstraction of high modernism, undermined naturalized forms of social life and developed an alternative public sphere in which audiences came to terms with the changing conditions of their existence. Cinema in this argument constitutes a 'sensory-reflexive horizon for the experience of modernization and modernity' (Hansen 2000b: 10) similar to Walter Benjamin's attention to the possibilities of 'play' in activating a critical response to the world (Hansen 2004: 3–45).

4 See Koschmann (1993; 1996) for the changing strategies of the 'lovable communist party' and its dissident intellectuals. Umemoto's best-known book from this period was *Yuibutsu shikan to dōtoku* [*The Historical Materialist Perspective and Morality*], first published in 1949.

5 See Raine (2002) for a commentary on the Nikkatsu and Daiei *taiyōzoku* films. The most notorious of these films, Nakahiro Kō's *Crazed Fruit* (*Kuratta kajitsu*, 1956), was released on DVD by Criterion in June 2005.

6 See Garon (1997) for an extended argument to this effect.

7 See Ōshima (1993: 21–5) for the argument that critics must create a film culture supportive of ambitious films, and Yoshida's article 'Eiga no kabe: sutōrī-shugi hihan' [The Film Wall: A Critique of Storyism] for the argument that filmmakers must abandon the 'god-like' position of the nineteenth-century novelists to engage their own subjectivity (*shutaisei*) in a dialectical relation with the world beyond the walls of established cinema (Yoshida 1970: 32–8).

8 Cinematographer Murai Hiroshi recalls that Masumura never locked the head of the tripod, but carefully arranged the initial composition and then instructed him to follow the actors. Also, according to Murai, Masumura would shoot in all four directions so it was necessary to build a four-sided set. (See Masumura 1999: 351–2.)

9 Perhaps Gōda means only to point out that Nishi is fantasizing, but 'blue-eyed' was a common epithet for (Western) foreigners, for example in the many articles on Japanese cinema referring to 'blue eyed critics'.

10 Reflexivity in *Giants and Toys* is not always so overt. In the conference room, camera movement is generally aligned with the long axis of the room. Sometimes, as when Gōda introduces the space toys on which he will base his advertising campaign, the fast track of the camera emphasizes Gōda's strategy to overwhelm the directors and win their acceptance, while the framing of the director holding a ray gun provides a commentary on these infantile (albeit potty-mouthed) men with toys. But on other occasions, there is no ready explanation of the slow crane shot above and along the length of the table, or the timing of the 180-degree reverses from one end of the room to the other. Like the seemingly Cubist painting on the far wall, the articulation of these shots points to another layer of abstraction in which space is a property of the camera, not of the diegetic world.

11 See, for example, the (to Masumura's eyes equally caricatural) dominant protagonists of Imai Tadashi's *Here is a Spring* (*Koko ni izumi ari*, 1955) and Ieki Miyoji's *Stepbrothers* (*Ibo kyōdai*, 1957).

12 For Shirasaka's anecdote see the NHK documentary *Masumura Yasuzō no sekai*. Masumura embraced the charges, acknowledging the film's clear relation to *A Face in the Crowd* (US, Elia Kazan, 1957) and accepting that he was indeed a caricaturist – like his teacher, Mizoguchi! (See Masumura et al. 1958: 92–3.)

13 In other publicity material she visited a television production line and was also selected 'silver week' star in December 1958 by the *Shūkan Yomiuri*. 'Silver week' itself was another commercial invention. In 1955, Nagata Masaichi, head of Daiei, persuaded the other studios to promote the first week in November as a counterpart to the already established 'golden week' (a period at the end of April with three national holidays, during which people often went to the cinema). Along with the long-established holiday periods at New Year and *o-bon* (a time in August for memorializing one's ancestors), these periods marked the release of the biggest films of the year. A star's contract would typically require six starring vehicles per year, as well as cameos in all-star films for each of these periods.

References

Garon, Sheldon (1997) *Molding Japanese Minds: The State in Everyday Life*, Princeton: Princeton University Press.

Gledhill, Christine and Williams, Linda (eds) (2000) *Reinventing Film Studies*, London: Arnold.

Hansen, Miriam (2000a) 'The Mass Production of the Senses: Classical Cinema as Vernacular Modernism', in Gledhill and Williams 2000: 332–50.

—— (2000b) 'Fallen Women, Rising Stars, New Horizons: Shanghai Silent Film as Vernacular Modernism', *Film Quarterly* 54 (1): 10–22.

—— (2004) 'Room for Play: Benjamin's Gamble with the Cinema', *October*, 109: 3–45.

Itō, Sei (1973) *Itō Sei zenshū 17* [*Collected Works of Ito Sei* Vol. 17], Tokyo: Shinchō-sha.

Iwasaki, Akira and Masumura, Yasuzō (1958) 'Kigeki to Nihon no fūshi' [Comedy and Japanese Satire], *Eiga Hyōron* 15 (4): 23–31.

Koschmann, J. Victor (1993) 'Intellectuals and Politics', in Andrew Gordon (ed.), *Postwar Japan as History*, Berkeley: University of California Press: 395–423.

—— (1996) *Revolution in Subjectivity in Postwar Japan*, Chicago: Chicago University Press.

Marx, Karl and Engels, Freidrich (1998 [1848]) *The Communist Manifesto*, New York: Signet Classics.

Masumura, Yasuzō (1954) 'Profilio Storico del Cinema Giapponese' [Narrative History of Japanese Cinema], *Bianco e nero* 15 (12): 3–66.

—— (1958a) 'Eiga no supīdo ni tsuite' [On Speed in the Cinema], *Shinario* 14 (2): 20–4.

—— (1958b) 'Aru benmei: jōcho to shinjitsu to fun'iki ni se o mukete' [A Justification: Turning My Back on Emotion, Truth, and Atmosphere], *Eiga Hyōron* 15 (3): 16–19.

—— (1958c) 'Watashi no shuchō suru engi: kōei aru gyakkō' [My Assertive Performance Style: Glorious Resistance], *Eiga Hyōron* 15 (7): 28–31.

—— (1999) *Eiga kantoku Masumura Yasuzō no sekai* [*The World of Film Director Masumura Yasuzō*], Tokyo: Waizu Shuppan.

Masumura, Yasuzō et al. (1958) 'Eiga ni natta masukomi: "Kyojin to gangu" o meguru kantoku shinjin kyōkai zadankai' [Mass Communication on Film: The New Directors Group Round Table on *Giants and Toys*], *Kinema Junpō* 208: 91–3.

Ogi, Masahiro, Masumura, Yasuzō, Nakahira, Kō and Imamura, Shōhei (1958) 'Eiga wa zenshin suru!' [Cinema Marches On!], *Eiga geijustu* 6 (8): 33–44.

Ōshima, Nagisa (1993) *Cinema, Censorship, and the State, The Writings of Nagisa Oshima*, Cambridge, MA: MIT Press.

Ozaki, Hirotsugu (1958) 'Daiei satsueijo-ron' [On the Daiei Studio], *Kinema Junpō* 205: 40–3.

Raine, Michael (2002) 'Youth, Body, and Subjectivity in the Japanese Cinema, 1955–1960'. Unpublished PhD dissertation, University of Iowa.

Rodowick, David (1995) *The Crisis of Political Modernism: Criticism and Ideology in Contemporary Film Criticism*, Berkeley: University of California Press.

Satô, Tadao (1955) 'Nihon eiga no tenpo' [The Tempo of Japanese Cinema], *Eiga Hyōron* 12 (5): 27–33.

Yamane, Sadao (1992) *Masumura Yasuzō: ishi to shite no erosu* [*Masumura Yasuzō: Eros as Will*], Tokyo: Chikuma Shobō.

Yoshida Kijū (1970) *Jiko hitei no ronri* [*The Ethics of Self-Negation*], Tokyo: San'ichi Shobō.

Masumura Yasuzō Filmography

Kisses (*Kuchizuke*, 1957)
The Bright Girl (*Aozora musume*, 1957)
Warm Current (*Danryū*, 1957)
Precipice (*Hyōheki*, 1958)
Giants and Toys (*Kyojin to gangu*, 1958)
A Daring Man (*Futeki na otoko*, 1958)
Undutiful Street (*Oya fukō dōri*, 1958)
The Most Valuable Wife (*Saikō shukun fujin*, 1959)
Flood (*Hanran*, 1959)
Beauty is Guilty (*Bibō ni tsumi ari*, 1959)
Across Darkness (*Yami o yokogire*, 1959)
A Woman's Testament (Part One) (*Jokyō, dai ichiwa: mimi o kamitagaru onna*, 1960)
Afraid to Die (*Karakkaze yarō*, 1960)
The Woman Who Touched the Legs (*Ashi ni sawatta onna*, 1960)
A False Student (*Nise daigakusei*, 1960)

Desperate to Love (Ai ni inochi o, 1961)
A Lustful Man (Kōshoku ichidai otoko, 1961)
A Wife Confesses (Tsuma wa kokuhaku suru, 1961)
The Troublesome Sisters (Urusai musume-tachi, 1961)
Indulgence (Tadare, 1962)
The Black Test Car (Kuro no tesuto kā, 1962)
Life of a Woman (Onna no isshō, 1962)
The Black Report (Kuro no hōkokusho, 1963)
Lies, Part One: Playgirl (Uso, dai ichiwa: pureigāru, 1963)
Hooligans, Pure Thoughts (Gurentai junjōha, 1963)
Modern Fraudulent Story: Cheat (Gendai inchiki monogatari: damashiya, 1964)
What the Husband Saw ('Onna no kobako' yori: otto ga mita, 1964)
Manji (1964)
Black Express (Kuro no chōtokkyū, 1964)
Hoodlum Soldier (Heitai yakuza, 1965)
Seisaku's Wife (Seisaku no tsuma, 1965)
Tattoo (Irezumi, 1966)
Nakano Spy School (Rikugun Nakano gakkō, 1966)
Red Angel (Akai tenshi, 1966)
Two Wives (Tsuma futari, 1967)
Naomi (Chijin no ai, 1967)
The Wife of Seishu Hanaoka (Hanaoka Seishū no tsuma, 1967)
The Most Corrupted (Dai akutō, 1968)
Sex Check (Sekkusu chekku: dai ni no sei, 1968)
A Building Block's Box (Tsumiki no hako, 1968)
The Made Love (Nureta futari, 1968)
Blind Beast (Mōjū, 1969)
Thousand Cranes (Senbazuru, 1969)
Vixen (Jotai, 1969)
Play It Cool (Denkikurage, 1970)
Song of the Yakuza (Yakuza zesshō, 1970)
The Hot Little Girl (Shibirekurage, 1970)
Play (Asobi, 1971)
New Hoodlum Soldier: Front Line (Shin heitai yakuza: kasen, 1972)
Music (Ongaku, 1972)
Razor 2: The Snare (Goyō kiba: kamisori Hanzō jigoku zeme, 1973)
Akumyo: Notorious Dragon (Akumyō: shima arashi, 1974)
Arteries of the Archipelago (Dōmyaku rettō, 1975)
Lullaby of the Earth (Daichi no komoriuta, 1976)
Double Suicide of Sonezaki (Sonezaki shinjū, 1978)
Giardino dell'Eden (Eden no sono, 1980)
On This Child's Seventh Birthday . . . (Kono ko no nanatsu no oiwai ni, 1982)

12

QUESTIONS OF THE NEW

Ōshima Nagisa's *Cruel Story of Youth* (1960)

Mitsuhiro Yoshimoto

Ōshima Nagisa is usually regarded as the leading figure in the 'Japanese New Wave' of the 1960s. Born in 1932 as a son of a fishery specialist working for the Ministry of Agriculture and Forestry, Ōshima grew up in the Inner Sea area of western Japan. When he was seven, his father passed away, and the family moved to Kyōto, his mother's hometown. From 1950 to 1953, Ōshima studied at the Faculty of Law in the University of Kyōto, specializing in government. He was active in student theater and participated in the student movement, eventually serving as the chair of the Kyōto prefectural organization of student activists. After graduating from university, Ōshima started working as an assistant director at Shōchiku's Ōfuna Studios in 1954. He was promoted to the rank of director in 1959, and soon became a central figure in the 'Shōchiku New Wave'. According to the standard view of Japanese film history, Ōshima introduced a significant break in post-war Japanese cinema by making radically new types of political films. The purpose of this chapter is to re-examine this common perception and Ōshima's alleged newness coming from his handling of political issues directly related to the history of post-war Japan and the contemporary social situation. The following discussion will specifically focus on Ōshima's second film, *Cruel Story of Youth* (*Seishun zankoku monogatari*, 1960 – hereafter *Cruel Story*) and his critical writings of the late 1950s and early 1960s.

Youth film and social contestation

Ōshima made his first film, *A Town of Love and Hope* (*Ai to kibō no machi*), in 1959, but it was mostly unnoticed by critics and audiences. The film was controversial in its treatment of an irreconcilable class conflict, so that for a while Shōchiku refused to give him a chance to direct another film. It was with his second film that Ōshima made his sensational debut as a director of the new. Made and released in 1960 at the height of political turmoil and massive protests against the renewal of the US–Japan Security Treaty, *Cruel Story* established Ōshima as a leading figure in the generation of young filmmakers who rebelled against Japanese cinema's status quo.

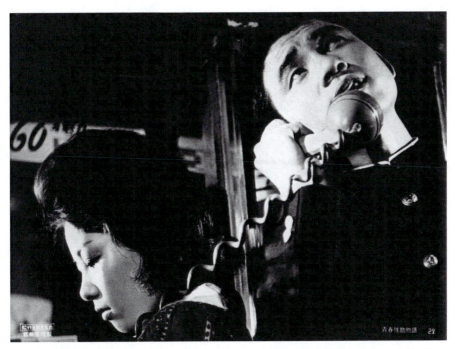

Figure 16 A jarring and unpredictable Japanese youth film: *Cruel Story of Youth* (1960).
BFI Stills, Posters and Designs.

The story and general setting of *Cruel Story* are fairly simple and conventional. The protagonists Kiyoshi (Kawazu Yūsuke), a delinquent university student, and Makoto (Kuwano Miyuki), a high school girl, are a restless young couple tormented by their inexplicable inner anger and a sense of powerlessness. In the film's first scene, a middle-aged businessman tries to take advantage of Makoto sexually, and when she refuses his advances, violently slaps her on the cheek. Kiyoshi, a total stranger, rescues Makoto from the man by beating him up, and unintentionally ends up extorting money from him. Throughout the film, both Kiyoshi and Makoto never hide their disdain for adults and members of the older generation who are content with the state of society where money is everything. Despite his alienation from money-driven society, Kiyoshi is equally suspicious of his activist friend and political protest against the government. Without being able to commit themselves to any ideal or goal, Kiyoshi and Makoto keep playing the game of a sexual scam where Kiyoshi extorts money from 'respectable' businessmen who think Makoto has agreed to an illicit sexual relationship with them. The young couple's initial feelings of thrill and exhilaration soon dissipate, however, with their realization that they are not only punishing seemingly upright businessmen for the latter's hypocrisy, but also losing their self-respect by commodifying their own bodies and minds. Eventually, it becomes impossible for Makoto and Kiyoshi to express their feelings of affection and love without at the same time hurting each

169

other, and in the film's final sequence they meet their own tragic deaths separately.

In many ways, *Cruel Story* is a typical example of the youth film. After World War Two, the presence of youth as such emerged as a distinct theme in Japanese cinema. Some of the most popular and critically acclaimed films of the post-war period dealt centrally with this subject. New images of Japanese youth presented in such films as *No Regrets for Our Youth* (*Waga seishun ni kui nashi*, Kurosawa Akira, 1946) and *Blue Mountains* (*Aoi sanmyaku*, Imai Tadashi, 1949) were closely linked to a dominant fiction which regarded Japan's defeat in World War Two as a liberation from the yoke of militarism, and as the beginning of a new democratic era. The idea of youth as a popular image came to stand for a new Japan, which was supposed to be born on August 15, 1945 with Emperor Hirohito's radio speech and the arrival of Douglas MacArthur a few weeks later. A decisively different image of youth began to appear in the mid-1950s when the so-called *taiyōzoku* or 'sun tribe films' attracted the attention of the media and critics. The phrase 'sun tribe' referred to the title of the novella *Season of the Sun* by a young university student writer, Ishihara Shintarō, which received the prestigious Akutagawa literary prize in 1956 and became an overnight sensation for its depiction of contemporary youth, sex, and violence. Ishihara's novella was immediately made into a film, thus inaugurating the new sub-genre of the 'sun tribe film'. *Season of the Sun* (*Taiyō no kisetsu*, Furukawa Takumi, 1956) itself was rather a forgettable film, and its primary significance lay in the sensational debut of Ishihara Shintarō's younger brother Yūjirō, a university student who was said to be a model for the novella's principal character. Because of his natural mannerism and 'Western' body (i.e. long straight legs), Yūjirō quickly rose to stardom, and became a new cultural icon of the post-war generation. Although only five 'sun tribe films' were made in the end – in addition to *Season of the Sun*, *Backlight* (*Gyakkōsen*, Furukawa Takumi, 1956), *Crazed Fruit* (*Kurtta kajitsu*, Nakahira Kō, 1956), *Summer in Eclipse* (*Nisshoku no natsu*, Horikawa Hiromichi, 1956), and *Punishment Room* (*Shokei no heya*, Ichikawa Kon, 1956) – Ōshima argued that they marked a permanent change through the introduction of more explicit sex and violence which tested the limits of representation imposed by the Japanese film industry's censorship board. However, the 'sun tribe film' was a short-lived phenomenon because of an enormous social pressure put on the film industry by various interest groups and the mass media. Despite the quick disappearance of the 'sun tribe film' from the scene, the representation of youth remained a dominant theme; so much so that one film company, Nikkatsu, decided to specialize in the genre of the youth film by capitalizing on the mega-star value of Ishihara Yūjirō and producing other youth stars such as Kobayashi Akira and Akagi Keiichirō, 'the Japanese James Dean'.

Many familiar visual and thematic motifs of the 'sun tribe film' can be found in *Cruel Story*, which is in fact a virtual catalogue of the new youth film's generic conventions. Like its predecessors, Ōshima's film features a delinquent university student and a young girl as protagonists, and focuses on their rebellion against society and adults. A generational difference is emphasized throughout, and patriarchal authority is markedly absent. Kiyoshi and Makoto ride in a motorboat on their first date in Tokyo Bay (cf. *Crazed Fruit*); later on in the film, they ride a motorcycle into the beach (cf. *Kisses* [*Kuchizuke*], Masumura Yasuzō, 1957). While both the motorboat and the motorcycle are symbols of speed, power, and free spirits, the beach and waterfront function as a privileged space for rebellious youth. Aloha shirts and sunglasses, the icons of the sun tribe, signify an escape from dull, everyday life. As a counterpart to the brightness of the sun and the ocean, alcohol, cigarettes, and jazz constitute the darkness of an enclosed space in the city. The signs of affluence (e.g. foreign cars including Mercedes, Packard, Ford) and poverty (e.g. Kiyoshi's cheap apartment) are juxtaposed in order to emphasize the protagonists' feelings of entrapment. The male protagonist's emotional blockage and frustration, caused by his inability to articulate why he is angry, is expressed through the depiction of violent fights and rapes (cf. *Punishment Room*).

Despite all these shared thematic and iconographic motifs, *Cruel Story* is not, after all, a typical youth film. Stylistically, it is far more jarring and unpredictable than the films mentioned above. For example, a percussive jazz strain is used from time to time as film music, yet its sudden appearance is not always justified either diegetically or thematically. Instead of creating an appearance of stylishness or producing symbolic meanings, the frequent use of a hand-held camera, long takes and swish-pans all refuse to satisfy the spectator's desire to translate audio-visual images into their putative discursive equivalents. The most famous image in the film that resists interpretation is the extreme long take of Kiyoshi eating an apple at an abortion clinic. After Makoto has had an abortion, Kiyoshi sits next to her bed and keeps biting an apple in a famous four minute, 45 second long take. The close-up of his face is accompanied by the sound of his biting the apple and the conversation between the clinic's doctor Akimoto and Makoto's elder sister Yuki. Akimoto and Yuki talk about their youthful idealism as student activists in the early 1950s and the eventual failure of their dreams. Yuki has left activism and Akimoto for an older man of wealth, and Akimoto has begun to perform abortions illegally in order to supplement his meager income. While listening to their conversation, Kiyoshi defiantly refuses Akimoto's prediction that he and Makoto will follow a similar path of failure. This is one of the most memorable scenes of the film, yet it is not easy to determine the meaning of the long take, either in diegetic or symbolic terms. The montage of the pregnant Makoto thrown to the ground by Kiyoshi and a concrete mixer is another example of unsettling images which do not yield any predictable meaning, yet still exert a powerful effect on the spectator. All these stylistic features contribute to the film's dark depiction of the young protagonists' misery, frustration, and desperation. Rather than merely being seen as part of the social landscape or as a new transitory phenomenon, these feelings are treated as the lived experience of young Japanese who have grown up in the specific historical context of post-war Japanese society.

Another distinct feature of *Cruel Story* is its systematic exclusion of environment as a represented image; that is, instead of depicting the situation in detail, the film almost exclusively focuses on characters and the thematic and stylistic representation of their inner turmoil and struggle. The combination of the use of Cinemascope and a telephoto lens in cramped interior scenes isolates the characters physically from their surroundings. This claustrophobic feeling is further accentuated by the collapse of distance between foreground and background, the frequent absence of establishing shots, and Ōshima's apparent lack of interest in constructing a coherent cinematic space or environment which would give a historical depth to fictional characters on screen. We learn nothing about Kiyoshi's family background such as details of his birthplace, parents, and upbringing. His elder brother appears briefly in a jail scene, but this does not lead to any new revelation about Kiyoshi. The same thing can be said about the circumstances surrounding other important characters, including Makoto's elder sister Yuki and her former boyfriend Akimoto. They belong to an earlier generation of student activists who fought against the post-war government's abandonment of a democratization policy and turn to the right in the early 1950s, but who eventually failed to achieve their goal because of tactical errors and psychological weakness. Neither Akimoto nor Yuki are conventionally rounded characters; instead, they stand as representative types belonging to the socio-political history of post-war Japan. These figurations of characters as distillations of political ideas and subjective positions can be best understood within the framework of what Ōshima tried to achieve in one of his early film scripts, *Deep-Sea Fishes* (*Shinkai gyogun*, 1957), which is about the student movement of the early 1950s and its inner struggle and betrayal involving different generations of characters such as high school teachers, college students and high school students. Because the sunlight does not reach beyond a certain depth in the sea, some kinds of deep-sea fishes emit light from their own bodies, thus enabling them to survive without being completely dependent on the surrounding environment of complete darkness. The deep-sea fish characters of the script's title therefore refer to human agents of action who refuse to be controlled by the environment and grope for a way to social change, and ultimately a revolution, by acting of their own free will. Although the narrative of the script most closely resembles that of Ōshima's fourth film, *Night and Fog in Japan* (*Nihon no yoru to kiri*, 1960), the figuration of characters as 'deep-sea fishes' also resonates well with the protagonists of *Cruel Story*: Kiyoshi and Makoto, and their counterparts from the earlier generation, Akimoto and Yuki.

In *Cruel Story*, the rebellious young people are not depicted as a mere social phenomenon to be observed or criticized. Instead, they appear as active agents of action situated in the specific context of post-war Japanese society. Although he sees a significant new development in the 'sun tribe films', particularly in their depictions of sex and violence permeated by the sense of a stifling situation, Ōshima insists that the impatience with the social status quo in these films remains quite superficial and abstract. Ishihara Shintarō, the author of the novella *Season of the Sun*, was a bourgeois youth who had no clear understanding of the concrete socio-political causes that lay underneath the stifling feelings shared by many young people. Moreover, the filmmakers who made the 'sun tribe films' observed the notion of impatient youth merely as a social phenomenon from the position of the distant observer. As a result, the 'sun tribe films' and their descendants, the Nikkatsu action movies, are surprisingly conservative in their treatment of youthful rebellion. The young heroes of these movies may appear to be a radically new type of Japanese person who has severed all ties with pre-war Japan, yet their defiant behavior still comes from rather old-fashioned problems concerning parent–child relationships or sibling rivalry. Because of the melodramatic sentiments underlying many popular youth films, it is not too difficult to convert a rebellious hero to a dutiful son as in the case of the quintessential sun tribe star, Ishihara Yūjirō. In contrast, the possibility of such co-optation is completely absent in *Cruel Story*. Ōshima consciously avoids images of family and familial links as a constitutive element in the formation of characters. As pointed out above, Kiyoshi is a lone hero without any family ties. The brief appearance of his elder brother at the jail does not draw him back into the sphere of his family. Instead, the utterly forgettable character of his brother reinforces how alone Kiyoshi is. The only family appearing in the film, that of Makoto, plays a similar role of negating the significance of this social institution. What the dysfunctional unit of the father and his two daughters shows is that the family in *Cruel Story* is not a foundational social unit giving its members a clearly defined sense of belonging and identity, but a mere reflection of the current state of society. Father says he cannot reprimand Makoto because there is no democratic social ideal or moral standard in society ('Times were tough after the war, but we had a way of life. I could have lectured you [Yuki] that we were reborn a democratic nation; that responsibility went hand-in-hand with freedom. But today what can we say to this child [Makoto]? Nothing. I don't want to tell her not to do something'.) Again, Makoto's family is represented to show precisely the insignificance of family as a site of social struggle and subject formation. Without family to fall back on in the last resort, the protagonists Kiyoshi and Makoto are forced to confront their problems as absolute individuals.

The utter loneliness of the protagonists can be discussed in terms of the film's thematic focus on the question of money. Almost every human relationship in the film revolves around money. The relationship of Kiyoshi and Makoto starts when the former saves the latter from a middle-aged businessman's sexual advances in front of a hotel. When Kiyoshi threatens to call the police, the man begs him not to do it and gives him 5,000 yen. Kiyoshi and Makoto meet again to have fun by spending this hush money. The subsequent development of their relationship is directly correlated to the circulation of money, through which their minds and bodies are increasingly objectified. When they try to get out of this cycle, unlike in a traditional lovers' double suicide drama, Kiyoshi and Makoto are forced to face their own deaths individually. Yuki and Akimoto, who see for a moment a glimpse of hope in the aimless rebellion of Makoto and Kiyoshi, were platonically in love with each other when they were students, but their relationship ended when Yuki started dating a richer man. Akimoto, who seems to remain faithful to his idealistic belief in helping the poor, turns out to be illegally performing abortions for money. Kiyoshi's friend, Itō, is a student activist who first appears in the film as a participant in the street demonstration against the US–Japan Security Treaty. Itō's enthusiasm for leftist politics is soon eclipsed by his concern for his own future prospects and economic stability. He abandons his activist girlfriend and switches to Makoto's friend Yōko, who is from a well-to-do family and can pay her would-be fiancé's college tuition. Kiyoshi, who is disgusted with Itō's opportunism, is also trapped by his affair with a middle-aged woman, Mrs Sakaguchi. Despite his contempt for this woman of leisure and what she represents, Kiyoshi cannot live without her financial support. For example, when Kiyoshi orders Makoto to have an abortion and gives her money, he gives her funds he has received from Mrs Sakaguchi after sleeping with her. A more comical depiction of his financial dependency occurs right after he is released from jail on bail through her effort. Kiyoshi and Makoto get into a taxi and try to throw off Mrs Sakaguchi who follows them in her immaculate Pontiac. For a moment, their plan seems to have succeeded. However, when it turns out that neither Kiyoshi nor Makoto has any money, Mrs Sakaguchi catches up with them and pays for a taxi fare herself.

Is it a political film?

Cruel Story distinguishes itself from the typical youth film through its many political references. The socio-political context in which the film's story unfolds is emphasized by the opening credit title sequence which uses newspaper headlines as a graphic background. Incorporation of a newsreel showing a violent clash between student demonstrators and the police in South Korea stands out as a key element early on in the film. In the same scene, immediately following the newsreel, a student demonstration against the renewal of the US–Japan Security Treaty is shown, and this further reinforces the importance of the contemporary geopolitical situation in East Asia as a general context for the film's narrative. The presence of Makoto's elder sister Yuki and her former boyfriend Akimoto introduces the topic of post-war Japan's earlier political struggles and puts the situation of 1960s Japan into historical perspective.

Upon closer examination, however, the significance and meanings of these political references and contextual cues turn out to be surprisingly oblique and indirect. For example, during the opening credits, the names of staff and actors appear in bold red against a background collage of numerous newspaper articles and advertisements. Together with jarring music, these newspaper fragments arranged in mosaic form cue the spectator into thinking that the film is going to be about current social issues and problems. At the very beginning of the film, in addition to its documentary aspects, spectators are thus seemingly alerted to the significance of contemporary socio-political events as a relevant interpretive context. Yet, significantly, the sequence does not show any headlines or texts in a clearly legible manner and so the newspaper articles fail to signify anything specific. What is important, therefore, is not some concrete message contained in a particular newspaper fragment, but the general evocation of a medium of mass communication which reports current political issues and social problems. In this sense, the credit sequence mostly serves to create a certain atmosphere, the effect of which is to put *Cruel Story* in the genre of the social problem film without making any openly political statement.

Similarly, the newsreel of the April Revolution in South Korea is not as unequivocally political as it may at first appear. The fall of the Syngman Rhee regime had great consequences for the geopolitical dynamics of the East Asian region and Japan's foreign policy, and in that sense there is nothing unusual about the quotation of the newsreel footage. Yet given the political turbulence and unrest inside Japan around that time, probably the more politically urgent image would be people's demonstration against the Japanese Prime Minister Kishi Nobusuke rather than the demonstration of young Koreans against the Korean president Syngman Rhee. Kishi's determination to renew the US–Japan Security Treaty and his heavy-handed treatment of mounting oppositional voices led to a political turmoil involving millions of ordinary Japanese taking part in demonstrations. The newsreel footage of Korean students protesting against the Syngman Rhee regime does not have any direct relation to the rest of the film; instead, it can be understood as a metonymic displacement of the absent image of Kishi Nobusuke and the military alliance between Japan and the United States.

The political impact of the newsreel is further attenuated by the syntax of the narrative; that is, the 'shock effect' of the newsreel is displaced from the level of content to that of form. The appearance of the monochrome depiction of a demonstration and its suppression is rather abrupt, and at first it is not clear why this footage is inserted in the film. But the perplexed reaction of the spectators at the time would not have lasted long because the newsreel images are immediately followed by the shot of Kiyoshi and Makoto talking to each other in front of a movie theater. Apparently they were supposed to go to the movies together, but Kiyoshi decided to go inside the theater without waiting for Makoto and watch the newsreel showing the violent clash between young Koreans and the armed forces. Thus, the sudden appearance of the images of protest and violence is retroactively justified as a diegetic detail and, as a result, the political implications of those images are to some extent subtly replaced with the aesthetic implications of narrative defamiliarization.

As these examples show, *Cruel Story* simultaneously foregrounds and conceals contemporary socio-political issues. Such ambivalence may be construed as an implicit critique of the kind of post-war Japanese leftist cinema exemplified by the works of directors such as Yamamoto Satsuo and Imai Tadashi. The 'politically progressive' films of these directors are typically organized around the Manichaean opposition of progressive leftist intellectuals and workers to the oppressive state and capitalists. The heroes often indulge themselves with victim consciousness and/or self-righteously condemn a social injustice inflicted upon them by corrupt officials, authoritative patriarchs, or wicked factory owners. Such a schematic moral view of society is markedly absent in *Cruel Story*. Even though Ōshima was clearly a sympathizer of the political left, *Cruel Story* is not a straightforward leftist film. In fact, the film's politics are highly ambiguous. It may be critical of the early 1950s generation of student activists and Communist Party members whose utopian enthusiasm quickly turned into disillusionment, compromise, and corruption of ideals, but as seen in Kiyoshi's dissociation from the student movement and the film's critical representation of his friend Itō, it does not necessarily endorse the 1960s new left and its political tactics. Despite the use of a newsreel showing an anti-government demonstration in South Korea and the incorporation of an actual May Day demonstration with the Red Flag in an early sequence, for the most part *Cruel Story* deals allegorically with the contemporary political situation. It does this by focusing on two apolitical protagonists, Kiyoshi and Makoto, whose nihilism, violence, and longing for pure innocence capture a certain strain of sentiment existing among both politically active and inactive young people of the time.

Victim consciousness and the politics of subjectivity

'We can live only by becoming a cog in the machine or an article for sale'. This is one of Kiyoshi's last remarks before he finally decides not to see Makoto any more. There is nothing unique or noteworthy about this remark; it is a rather conventional observation easily found in films dealing with modern social problems. There is, however, nothing predictable about *Cruel Story*, which, unlike popular melodramas and sentimental films, absolutely refuses to give any redemptive messages to the spectator. Kiyoshi dies like a dog, and Makoto's cruel death is almost like a suicide. In each case, death is simply presented as a material fact, which in itself does not signify anything The film's extremely cool and bleak view of modern society, where money irreversibly destroys the fabric of human relationships, is unique in post-war Japanese cinema. One of the few comparable films in its depiction of post-war Japan is *A Japanese Tragedy* (*Nihon no higeki*, 1953), directed by Kinoshita Keisuke at Shōchiku. It is perhaps not a coincidence that another Shōchiku master, Ozu Yasujirō, intensely disliked both films for what he considered to be their indecency. Yet the similarity between the two is in the end superficial; to be more precise, *Cruel Story* and *A Japanese Tragedy* are only similar to each other because the former is the exact opposite of the latter in terms of its construction of the protagonist's subjectivity. In Kinoshita's film, the mother sacrifices everything to support her son and daughter, yet in the end she finds herself abandoned by the egotistical children who are ashamed of her. In utter despair she kills herself by jumping in front of a train. In this tragic story, everybody appears as a victim: the mother is presented as a victim of circumstances and dehumanized social relations, and the children also think of themselves not as victimizers, but as victims of their mother and social injustice. It is such victim consciousness that the protagonists of Ōshima's film, particularly Kiyoshi, are determined not to succumb to. When Akimoto tries to lure Kiyoshi into the mindset of victim consciousness at his clinic, Kiyoshi absolutely refuses to commiserate with this former student activist over the failure of post-war ideals. As an act of defiance, Kiyoshi keeps biting an apple in the long take. Although he is certainly not represented as a responsible youth, one thing Kiyoshi is unwilling to do is to blame others or society for his personal misery from the perspective of an innocent victim.

One of the primary motivations behind Ōshima's cinematic practice in the early days of his career was to transform Japanese cinema into an intellectually powerful force comparable to the art, literature, and critical discourse that had had enormous influence on Japanese post-war public opinion. This means that *Cruel Story* and his other early films must be understood as part of a self-consciously intellectual project, which rejected both studio productions as commodified entertainment and socially conscious films from independent production collectives as mere illustrations of leftist political ideas. More specifically, the central issue in Ōshima's intellectual engagement with film practice was the question of how to overcome the victim consciousness so prevalent in both mainstream melodrama and leftist independent film in order to create images of an authentic subjectivity.

Cruel Story is exemplary in its negation of a victim consciousness which makes it impossible to create a truly democratic society. The film's protagonist Kiyoshi never succumbs to the temptation to condemn society from the position of an innocent victim. As is clear in the portrayals of his relationship with Makoto, Mrs Sakaguchi, and even lascivious businessmen, Kiyoshi is a victimizer as much as a victim. He exposes the moral hypocrisy of the establishment and the organized left, and at the same time acts as an economic and sexual predator. He is a new type of youth character who simultaneously arouses feelings of both sympathy and repulsion. In Ōshima's categorization, Kiyoshi is not yet a genuine subject, but only a virtual subject (*giji shutai*) because he does not know what he should do to change society. In contrast, Ōshima as a creator of the film must first establish himself as a genuine subject in order to articulate the political potential in the form of Kiyoshi's virtual subjectivity. Ōshima argues that a genuine subject cannot be a protagonist of his film because to the extent that in reality a genuine subject exists only as an ideal type, any representation of such a character would make the film too unrealistic and schematic. How then does Ōshima reconcile this argument with the earlier one about the necessity for establishing his own subjectivity as genuine and authentic in order to go beyond the dominant fiction of victim consciousness? Is it not the case that by considering his own subjectivity as authentic, Ōshima situates himself at the teleological end of a historical process whereby Japan is said to be transformed from a feudal to democratic society? Does Ōshima as an authentic subject therefore transcend history and the concrete situations of contemporary Japan where he claims such a subject can only exist as an ideal? Is it possible for Ōshima to become an authentic subject not by providing some concrete plan for a revolution, but by going outside of time and examining the present from the end of the linear evolution of social system and human consciousness? It is to solve these fundamental dilemmas of subjectivity that Ōshima insists on the necessity of 'endless self-negation':

> Once a filmmaker has created a work, the method expressive of his active involvement must be thought of as part of his external reality. To re-use a method that has become part of his reality signifies the loss of an involved attitude and a surrender to reality.

Instead, only the maintenance of a state of tension with reality and the discovery of a new method of perpetual active involvement will enable him to make works that are a true expression of himself.

(Ōshima 1992: 66)

According to Ōshima, the authentic subject can exist only in perpetual movement. Once it ceases to move and attaches itself to a fixed identity, it becomes part of the status quo, the social reality to be overcome. This is why Ōshima significantly changed his style from film to film throughout the 1960s. Radical film practice from Ōshima's perspective cannot be regarded as beginning from the invention of a radical film style. Instead, it involves the filmmaker's perpetual search for new film styles as a means of intervening in the concrete socio-historical situations where he or she lives as a subject in motion.

Conclusion

The newness of *Cruel Story*, which still holds well even now, comes from its radical rejection of genre cinema as such. Ōshima did not create this film in a vacuum. In fact, despite his criticism of modernists and established filmmakers, Ōshima makes many inter-textual references to post-war Japanese cinema. Besides the opening credits discussed earlier, some of the most obvious allusions and citations include, for instance, Akimoto's remark 'For our vanished youth!' (the antithesis of the theme of Kurosawa's *No Regrets for Our Youth*); Kiyoshi and Makoto sitting on tetrapods on the seashore (echoing Shūkichi and Tomi who sit on a breakwater in Ozu's *Tokyo Story* [*Tōkyō monogatari*], 1953); Kiyoshi speeding down the street on a motorcycle with Makoto sitting on a back seat (as their counterparts do in Masumura's *Kisses*), and so on. These iconographic and narrative details are neither a self-indulgent display of knowledge by a narcissistic *auteur*, nor mere intertextual borrowings from relevant genres. Instead, Ōshima succeeds in creating a unique, literally inimitable film precisely by using the common vocabulary of the best of Japanese studio productions. He does not simply radicalize the youth film genre, but dismantles it altogether by constructing a critical collage of its conventions in order to create completely new meanings and effects. (The collage of newspaper articles in the credit title sequence discussed earlier can thus be understood as a figurative representation of this method.) Because Ōshima's will to the new is visible in almost every scene, *Cruel Story* will therefore never cease to excite, provoke, and disturb its audiences, even those who remain unfamiliar with the particular political references and historical contexts depicted in it.

Reference

Ōshima, Nagisa (1992) *Cinema, Censorship and the State: The Writings of Nagisa Oshima*, Cambridge, MA: MIT Press.

Ōshima Nagisa Filmography

A Town of Love and Hope (*Ai to kibō no machi*, 1959)
Cruel Story of Youth (*Seishun zankoku monogatari*, 1960)
The Sun's Burial (*Taiyō no hakaba*, 1960)
Night and Fog in Japan (*Nihon no yoru to kiri*, 1960)
The Catch (*Shiiku*, 1961)
Shiro Tokisada from Amakusa (*Amakusa Shirō Tokisada*, 1962)
Pleasures of the Flesh (*Etsuraku*, 1964)
Violence at Noon (*Hakuchū no tōrima*, 1966)
Band of Ninja (*Ninja bugeichō*, 1967)
A Treatise on Japanese Bawdy Song (*Nihon shunka kō*, 1967)
Japanese Summer: Double Suicide (*Muri shinjū Nihon no natsu*, 1967)
Death by Hanging (*Kōshikei*, 1968)
Three Resurrected Drunkards (*Kaette kita yopparai*, 1968)
Diary of a Shinjuku Thief (*Shinjuku dorobō nikki*, 1968)
Boy (*Shōnen*, 1969)
The Battle of Tokyo, or the Story of the Young Man Who Left His Will on Film (*Tōkyō sensō sengo hiwa: eiga de isho o nokoshita otoko no monogatari*, 1970)
Ceremonies (*Gishiki*, 1971)
Dear Summer Sister (*Natsu no imōto*, 1972)
In the Realm of the Senses (*Ai no korīda*, 1976)
Empire of Passions (*Ai no bōrei*, 1978)
Merry Christmas, Mr Lawrence (*Senjō no merī kurisumasu*, 1982)
Max, Mon Amour (*Makkusu mon amuru*, 1986)
Taboo (*Gohatto*, 1999)

13

ETHNICIZING THE BODY AND FILM

Teshigahara Hiroshi's *Woman in the Dunes*
(1964)

Mitsuyo Wada-Marciano

Director Teshigahara Hiroshi's *oeuvre* remains interesting not least because it resists the two long-standing paradigms of Japanese cinema studies. These are, on the one hand, *auteurist* approaches to filmmakers such as Kurosawa Akira, Mizoguchi Kenji, and Ozu Yasujirō: and on the other, formalist analyses that focus on the stylistic uniqueness of these *auteurs'* work and inevitably compare it with the filmic 'criteria' of classical Hollywood cinema. By contrast, Teshigahara's career as a filmmaker is arguably too brief to qualify for true *auteur* status, and his filmmaking style too polysemous, too deliberately modernist, to be pigeonholed as yet another example of a 'uniquely Japanese' aesthetic. This difficulty has been recognized by many domestic critics. For example, film scholar Yomota Inuhiko alludes to the problem in an interview with Teshigahara from the late 1980s: 'Your [Teshigahara's] work is difficult to discuss. In the case of analyzing other filmmakers' work, one can find a certain stylistic pattern, yet yours is not the case. You might be a stumbling block for film critics, and every one of them has had trouble in discussing your *oeuvre*' (Yomota 1989: 71).

Besides *Woman in the Dunes* ([also known as *Woman of the Dunes*] *Suna no onna*, 1964 – hereafter *Woman*), Teshigahara directed a total of 20 films in his career. After making a few documentaries and experimental films during the 1950s, he adapted four of Abe Kōbō's novels in the 1960s: *Pitfall* (*Otoshiana*, 1962), *Woman in the Dunes*, *The Face of Another* (*Tanin no kao*, 1966), and *The Man Without a Map* (*Moetsukita chizu*, 1968). It was with these films' acclaim as variously 'modern', 'atypically Japanese', and 'international' in outlook that Teshigahara established his status as a globally acknowledged Japanese filmmaker. However, with the exception of the production of a few more documentaries, he suspended his filmmaking career for the following two decades, and he only resumed filmmaking with two *jidai-geki* (period films), *Rikyu* (1989) and *The Princess Goh* (*Gō-hime*, 1992), both of which marked a complete departure from his stylistically modernist experiments of the 1960s. Teshigahara passed away in April 2001, and at the time of his death he was more renowned in Japan as the head of the Sōgetsu flower arrangement school than as an influential film director. It is possible to say, therefore, that the eclectic and sporadic quality of Teshigahara's output provides the most likely explanation for why – with the notable exception of *Woman*, his best-known film – so little has been written on his work by scholars both in Japan and abroad.

Much of the critical discussion of *Woman* to date has centered on reading its imagery symbolically as a material register of Abe's existential concerns. *Woman* concerns a male entomologist who escapes from the commotion of the city to search for insects in the desert. After missing the last bus home, he is put up for the night by a mysterious widow who lives in a shack at the bottom of a deep sand pit. He soon finds himself trapped in the hole with this woman, and he becomes a grudging participant in her Sisyphean work to dig out the always encroaching sand. After several unsuccessful attempts at escape, he begins to embark upon a strangely erotic relationship with her, and by the end of the film he has lost his desire to be free.

On the evidence of published accounts, what appears to have most captured the critics' attention is the film's visual presentation of a modernist parable concerning the body, the self, and the landscape of enveloping sand. Indeed, the film's imagery often makes these objects indistinguishable from one another – as in the case, for example, of the sand that rests in the 'dunes' of the naked body's folds and creases.

Among the most important critical discussions of the film are two by Max Tessier and Wimal Dissanayake that approach it as a meditation on modern subjectivity. While Tessier (1979–80) notes the seamless parallel between this theme and cinematic technique in the film's poetic dissolution of identity, Dissanayake emphasizes 'Japanese thought' as an essential component of its exploration of the relation between body, self, and culture (Dissanayake 1990).[1] The gap between these two approaches – universalist on the one hand, and culturally essentialist on the other, with ethnicity being either ignored or overdetermined respectively – speaks of the need to anchor the film more firmly within the specific context of 1960s Japanese cinema and culture. For unacknowledged within existing critical accounts is a discussion of the ways in which this modern ethnic body/self has been historically constructed, as well as an acknowledgement of how its meanings have changed across time and for different audiences. It is well worth noting, therefore, that in the period before *Woman* won the Special Jury Prize at the 1964 Cannes Film Festival, it had been widely perceived in Japan to be opportunistic because of its exploitation of then current trends in the genre of film pornography. Moreover, what subsequently emerged as the dominant critical interpretation of the film's meaning – i.e. the reading of its presentation of the naked body as an artistic expression of the modern subject – gained legitimacy only after its success at Cannes. Clearly, there is a need to unravel the body from this modernist parable in order to explore how the filmic body created meaning in particular locales for specific audiences, and how that body works as a signifier of ethnicity. We may begin by asking how such legitimizing events as the acceptance of *Woman* in both international and domestic markets are inscribed within the formation of a modern, vernacular sense of Japanese identity.

Woman occupies a place historically between the twin major currents of the declining 1960s' Japanese film industry: the emergence of new models of independent film production and the promotion of an 'international Japanese' cinema. Its resulting oxymoronic status – the film's 'minor' status came from being an independent production, but the 'major' status accrued through its critical validation on the global stage – is both its key characteristic and also one that has impacted upon the production of most successful Japanese films ever since. *Woman* was produced outside the Japanese studio system, it was an independent project financed through multiple sources, and it was launched through promotion at an overseas film festival prior to domestic release – in all these respects, *Woman* may in fact be viewed as an important forerunner of contemporary Japanese filmmaking.

Teshigahara's film managed as well to balance artistic aspects with ethnic references so as to produce a measured address to both domestic and foreign audience expectations. Such negotiations have become the norm in contemporary Japanese cinema, particularly in the internationally successful work of directors Ōshima Nagisa, Imamura Shōhei and more recently Kitano Takeshi and Kore-eda Hirokazu. In the context of the production and reception circumstances of 1964 described above, it might be argued that *Woman* modulated ethnicity at various levels in order to appeal to Japanese and other contemporary audiences. In this chapter, I will examine the issue of ethnicity as displayed in two paradigms of filmic discourse: the ethnicized filmic body and ethnicity in international film.

At this point it should be evident that my analysis of *Woman* is going to depart from previous scholarly accounts that emphasize critical interpretation of the film text itself as a primary activity. This is not meant to denigrate the value of such a critical approach. (After all, a perception of the way in which the film itself constitutes a seductive invitation to viewers to engage in modern literary interpretive practices underlies my discussion of the film's negotiation of ethnicity.) In contrast, my main interest revolves around the question of how relations among the film, its initial overseas reception in 1964, and the influence of domestic and overseas film criticism work to further notions of Japanese identity. By shifting between critical discourses that engage the film synchronically and diachronically, I seek to illuminate its problematic bind of ethnicity as it operates amid universalist sentiments of filmmaking in Japan and the cross-cultural concerns of Japanese cinema studies.

The film of the flesh

In his article on *Woman*, Wimal Dissanayake deploys recent body discourse analysis to uncover cultural meanings embedded in the film. He writes:

> In *Woman in the Dunes*, the human body is portrayed as a central fact of self; this somatic facticity that runs through the novel inflecting all

human emotions, perceptions and ratiocinations has a metaphysical dimension rooted in *Japanese thought*. It is interesting at this point to compare the attitudes to body and mind in the Western and Eastern traditions of thought. The Western traditions, by and large, subscribing to a Cartesian duality, posit a definite separation of mind and body whereas the Eastern traditions posit a unity ... As Yuasa Yasuo remarks, true knowledge [in Japanese tradition] cannot be obtained simply through theoretical thinking; it can be obtained only through 'bodily recognition as realization' (*tainin* or *taitoku*), that is, through the utilization of one's entire body and mind. The body and the somatic experiences associated with it play a central role in the novel bearing much of its existential meaning. *And one thing that cinema in the hands of gifted filmmakers can do extremely well, is to capture the nuanced experiences and complex responses of the human body.*

(Dissanayake 1990: 48. Emphasis added)

For Dissanayake, the success of the film lies in its presentation of the ethnicized body rooted in 'Japanese thought'. However, the main problem with this idea is that it views ethnicity as a self-defining quantity, a trans-historical given, rather than as a cultural practice constructed within particular cultural, historical, and social economies. As I argue throughout this chapter, interpreting ethnicity *vis-à-vis Woman* calls for a more historically rooted approach, one that accounts for underlying politics and the structuring forces of modernity. In the case of this film's ethnicized body, for example, two specific areas may be utilized so as to reveal this connection between the political and the filmic. These are the frames of star discourse and film genre.

As evidenced in the last sentence of the above quotation, the blind spot in Dissanayake's argument lies in the question of how the ethnicized body might change through the process of adaptation from novel to film. One can argue that the act of adaptation itself modulates the ethnicized body – a change that often enhances the cultural materiality of a film. For instance, the materiality of the film is inextricable from the signified meanings of stars within popular culture. Once filmed, a body ceases to be anonymous, but becomes instead the body of a particular star, carrying with it specific connotations and cultural values. Okada Eiji, the leading actor in *Woman*, thus appeared for Japanese audiences in 1964 already branded as an internationally recognized Japanese body infused with a confident, ethnic male desire, i.e. a post-colonial masculinity, after his previous successful role as the lover of a white French woman in *Hiroshima Mon Amour* (Alain Resnais, France, 1959).[2] For domestic viewers, the externalized specularity of Okada's body on the world stage serves to authenticate his Japanese ethnicity. In other words, the ethnicity of his body reproduces the fundamental political asymmetry of Japan–West relations in the 1960s as constructed in the process of Japanese modernity.

Star discourse as well as the realm of body discourse itself was central to discussions of *Woman* in Japan in 1964, further confirming that any elaboration of so-called 'Japanese thought' needs to be examined within the film's specific socio-cultural contexts. Dissanayake's conceptual framing of the body, self, and place rests largely on the role of Niki (Okada), the male protagonist of the film:

> When discussing the dialectic of self and place in *Woman in the Dunes*, it is very important that we pay attention to the concept of the body that is so central to the textual strategies of the novel and the film. Once Niki is imprisoned in the sand pit, the only reality is the ever present sand and his own body. Much of the communication, experience of diverse emotions, imaginings, ruminations are anchored in the body.
>
> (Dissanayake 1990: 46)

Intriguingly, however, Dissanayake's emphasis on the body of the male protagonist is in sharp contrast with the body discourse created within the vernacular culture of the period. For while many Japanese critics of the day also pinpointed the connection between the film and the body, the concept of the body occupied for them a more specific place within the discourse of a con-temporary film genre, *nikutai eiga* (film of the flesh), and its risqué displays of female nudity. The 'film of the flesh' grew out of the analogous literary genre that appeared immediately after World War Two with the appearance of writer Tamura Taijirō's novel *Gate of Flesh* (*Nikutai no mon*, 1947). Film director Suzuki Seijun adapted the novel into a film of the same title in 1964, and then became the ringleader of the genre with his subsequent collaboration with Tamura on *Story of a Prostitute* (*Shunpū-den*, 1965). Imamura Shōhei's *The Insect Woman* (*Nippon konchūki*, 1963) and *Intentions of Murder* (*Akai satsui*, 1964), and Takechi Tetsuji's *Day-Dream* (*Hakujitsumu*, 1964), among others, were also categorized within the genre. Later the 'film of the flesh' merged into the broad genre of 'erotic film' (*ero eiga*) or 'pink film' (*pinku eiga*), and soon afterwards Nikkatsu studios repackaged these genres in the 1970s under the name 'Nikkatsu romance porn' (*Nikkatsu roman poruno*).

In 1964, Japanese film critic Futaba Jūzaburō raised the question of whether *Woman* actually deserved its positive reputation by drawing the connection between the film and the already popular 'film of the flesh': 'It's a deplorable fact that the reason why the film succeeded so much was due to the advertisement for the film – it's nothing but eroticism. If the film was successful without that reinforcement, I would have no objection to the film, and I believe that that should be the way for so-called art cinema to be successful without such an opportunistic advertisement' (Futaba 1964: 34). Indeed, it was not only Futaba who pointed out the exploitive aspects of the film's promotion, its borrowing from the eroticism of the literary pop-genre. The majority of film critics in the period – for instance, Toita Michizō (1964: 19), Daikoku Toyōshi (1964: 34), Tsumura Hideo (1964: 46–51), and Izawa Jun (1965: 41–2) – chose to evaluate *Woman* within the local context of emerging erotic cultural forms. Furthermore, with representations of the body and sex becoming increasingly prevalent in the Japanese film industry since the mid-1950s, it was inevitable that contemporary Japanese audiences would view *Woman* in the context of the soft porn paradigm, regardless of whether Teshigahara himself intended his film to be so categorized.

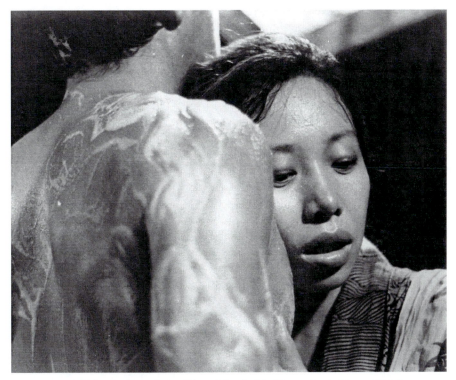

Figure 17 Kishida Kyōko and the 'film of the flesh': *Woman in the Dunes* (1964). Teshigahara/The Kobal Collection.

The ethnicized body and Japanese modernity

In post-war Japan this gendered, sexualized, and ethnicized body was often used for scaling the level of Japanese culture against the 'standard' of Western culture; i.e. probing the depths of Japanese modernity. Correspondingly, the re-inscription of a Western-styled female sexuality in the *nikutai* B-movies and novels of the period supports this pattern. The new risqué filmic expression had its source in adaptations of the earlier erotic *nikutai bungaku* (literature of the flesh) in the late 1940s. Writing of this period's literature, Igarashi Yoshikuni (2000: 48) observes that '[B]odies emerged in the immediate post-war period as ambivalent entities that represented both the liberation and the subjugation of Japan'. In Tamura's well-known novel *Gate of Flesh*, for example, the female body as sexual commodity expressed Japan's problematic relation toward the American occupier as both liberator and subjugator. Suzuki cast the voluptuous actress Nogami Yumiko in his subsequent adaptation, and other filmmakers used similar physical types; for example, Imamura drew upon actresses Hidari Sachiko and Harukawa Masumi for *The Insect Woman* and *Intentions of Murder* respectively. These actresses' well-endowed bodies represent an overt sexual desire more akin to Western pin-up images than the usual dainty Japanese stars

185

characterized by their 'innocent beauty'. (This was the typical image projected by pre-war stars such as Kurishima Sumiko, Tanaka Kinuyo, and Irie Takako.) The bombshell actresses were not simply inventions of the vernacular culture, but were affirmed by the preparatory influences of both French and Hollywood cinemas, as in the case of Brigitte Bardot's series of films starting with *And God Created Woman* (*Et Dieu . . . créa la femme*, France, Roger Vadim, 1956) and Marilyn Monroe's Hollywood movies of the 1950s such as *The Seven Year Itch* (US, Billy Wilder, 1955). The discursive claim that Japanese cinema had reached parity with Western cinemas was expressed in various domestic journals at the time, and the question was advanced – in rhetoric similar to Futaba's aforementioned criticism – of whether the 'films of the flesh' with their displays of 'Westernized' female bodies were sufficiently *geijutsu-teki* (artistic) when juxtaposed against Western cinemas.

The post-war literary trope of the Japanese female body's 'subjugation' by the US occupier was transformed by 1964 and reconfigured toward a more abstract and unreachable Western cultural value, reified in the name of *geijutsu-teki* as with *Woman*. This is a pattern which continued even into the 1970s. For example, in the case of Ōshima Nagisa's forced transfer of post-production of his film *In the Realm of the Senses* (*Ai no korīda*, 1976) to France, and in the face of Japanese censorship, the display of the eroticized body came to reiterate the inherent bind of modernity tied to the West, with the West once again cast in the role of liberator. Ōshima writes: 'In today's world, then, the film *In the Realm of the Senses* is accepted in what are called *the advanced nations – the free world*. . . . Why is something that is not considered "obscene" in a foreign country considered "obscene" here? Isn't Japan one of the advanced countries? Isn't Japan part of the free world?' (Ōshima 1992: 266. Emphasis added.) In other words, the film itself worked as evidence of a Japanese modernity revealed as incomplete in comparison with the liberalism of French culture and by extension 'the advanced nations' and 'the free world'. As the example of Ōshima's film indicates, the discourse of the body continues to reoccur in popular culture often hinging upon this sense of a somehow 'belated' or 'unfulfilled' condition of Japanese modernity.

It should be clear at this point that the ethnicized body evident in the star and genre discourses is embedded within the politics of Japanese modernity responding to an idealized West. *Woman*'s allegories of a modern, Westernized, urban male and a primitive sexualized female are directly related to the cultural use of sex and sexual expression as tropes of Japanese ambivalence in the post-war period. More than this, the image of the primitivized and sexualized female body allows for the opportunity to posit a type of 'Japanese thought' altogether different from Dissanayake's transcendent Eastern unity.

The uses of the female ethnicized body, in particular, carry a distinct post-colonial view, an expression of a reified, provisional modernity. As Rey Chow writes in her analysis of modern Chinese culture: '[T]he lesson . . . on the question of primitivism in East–West relations is not only the exploitation of the non-West by the West but how this dialectic between formal innovation and primitivism characterizes the hierarchical relations of cultural production *in* the "third world" as well ... [M]odern Chinese literature turns "modern" precisely by seizing upon the primitive that is the subaltern, the woman, and the child' (Chow 1995: 20–1. Emphasis in original). Similarly, *Woman*'s narrative arc of the man arriving from the city and encountering the woman living in the sandpit, and the two becoming a couple, fulfills the basic structure that Chow describes. Yet in the case of Teshigahara's film, the male body as a subjugated, trapped figure encompasses as well the universal aspect of an 'insufficient' modern subject (not necessarily a Japanese one) in the sense that modernity is always felt on the experiential level as a constantly changing and anxious present. The insufficiency of Niki's figure, his defining struggle to rationalize the irrational, highlights this problematic sense of modernity, one that allows for a broad audience identification. Thus, the film's images contain both the ethnic particularity of Japanese identity centering around the primitive female figure and that of the more universal predicament of the modern subject within the male figure. It is this balancing of the familiar with the exotic that helped make the film accessible to international audiences.

Ever since Kurosawa Akira's *Rashomon* (*Rashōmon*, 1950) won recognition at the 1951 Venice Film Festival, Japanese cinema's bid for international acceptance has been marked by the two-fold strategy of embracing literary modernism with often exotic images of traditional culture that are perceived to embody a historically transcendent Japanese uniqueness or identity. Dissanakaye's writing on the mysterious Eastern unity of mind and body appears to buy into this enterprise. Leaving aside for the moment such questions as whether this timeless 'Japanese thought' allows for change in the global fluidity of social life and culture, or whether all Japanese films deal with the body in the same manner as Dissanayake believes *Woman* does, my primary concern with such an interpretation is that it leaves intact and unexamined the terms by which the film constructs the ethnicized body, framing the body as a politically neutral, transparent literary trope – modern, yet with something to tell us about traditional culture. Yet the film's use of the ethnicized body forces us to address a more political question. What should we make of the essential paradox of Japanese national cinema, that in its bid for international recognition as a modern cinema, films such as *Woman* deploy images of an essential ethnicized other?

Ethnicity in 'international film'

The 'film of the flesh' appeared in a period during which the Japanese film industry made continuous efforts to send its films to international markets, often through exhibition and promotion at overseas film festivals. However, this project to create an international cinema was fraught with contradiction. The more Japanese filmmakers aimed to make an imaginary cinema for foreign audiences, the more they became trapped within a process of self-ethnicization. Indeed, one can view much of the exported Japanese cinema of the past 50 years as demonstrating some variation or other of this process. The film industry first sent *jidai-geki* such as *Rashomon, The Life of O-Haru* (*Saikaku ichidai onna*, Mizoguchi Kenji, 1952), and *Ugetsu* (*Ugetsu monogatari*, Mizoguchi Kenji, 1953) to festivals in the 1950s. Throughout the rest of that decade, the pervasive view in the industry was that only period films could be marketed to foreign audiences and that *gendai-geki* (contemporary film) were too lacking in both action and exotic iconography to be appreciated by Westerners.[3] This notion that certain films are unsuited, indeed are 'too Japanese' for the international market, was often cited as an explanation for why Shōchiku studios hesitated to send Ozu Yasujirō's 'home dramas' to international venues. The idea that only *jidai-geki* could translate the idiosyncrasy of Japanese national cinema to Western audiences was, in a sense, finally subverted by *Woman* – the first *gendai-geki* to receive a major award at a representative international festival. In addition, one may also say that the film's depictions of a new exoticism – including such elements as the tribal sandpit life, the loss of modern identity, and the naked Japanese female body – supplanted thereafter the position of the symbolic traditional image of the *kimono* in *jidai-geki*.

Woman was not simply the first *gendai-geki* accepted by the international festivals, however. In its combination of an ambivalent filmic identity – Western enough in its literary modernism yet sufficiently Japanese in its imagery – with the tactical promotion of independent film through international recognition (Satō 2001: 126–7), it also provided a prototype for later Japanese films. It was independently made by Teshigahara Productions (the director's own production company), with Tōhō providing support in the form of both financing and domestic distribution. In a similar fashion, the majority of commercial Japanese filmmaking now no longer follows the studio model of production, nor does it rely solely upon the targeting of the domestic audience, but instead reflects a similar configuration of independent filmmaking allied with studio distribution. Moreover, many of the recent internationally released Japanese films also deploy a modulated ethnicity. That is to say, they effectively manipulate elements of a mythic Japanese identity often mixing the exotic with the familiar in established genres such as the gangster film, horror, or melodrama. In horror films of the 1990s such as *Ring* (*Ringu*, Nakata Hideo, 1998), for example, the genre's reconstructed realities are used to retrieve traditional locales and time, giving a material sense of an ephemeral, numinous Japanese culture, while in melodramas such as *Maborosi* (*Maboroshi no hikari*, Kore-eda Hirokazu, 1995) a conscious link is made with the already established filmic aesthetics of Ozu and Mizoguchi through use of slow pacing and long takes. *Maborosi* also draws upon the austere black designer clothing of *comme des garçons* so as to invoke the designer's reinvention of Japaneseness for the international fashion scene.

As these examples indicate, the process of turning Japanese film into an international cinema is directly implicated in the cohesion of Japanese national cinema itself – in order to make it internationally accepted, the filmmaker modulates the cinema's ethnicity. The seemingly oxymoronic term *kokusai-teki na Nihon eiga* (Japanese-international film), which first gained prevalence among the mass media at the time of the post-war drive to internationalize the nation, starkly reveals this sense of how Japan's cinema becomes reified through international acceptance. Yet we should also not forget that international film festivals exhibit fundamental disparities between nations. As Julian Stringer writes: '[A]ll the major festivals established in the immediate post-war period (Berlin, Cannes, Edinburgh, Moscow, London, Venice) were closely aligned with the activities and aims of particular national governments . . . such events worked to promote official state narratives and hence perpetuate the continuation of the nation-state system itself' (Stringer 2001: 135–6). It should be obvious that no neutral criteria or values reside in the use of the term 'international'. Indeed, the term often signifies West-centered political, aesthetic, and especially economic regimes propagated under the guise of a general critical affirmation.

Once recognized by international film festivals, then, films are inscribed under the rubric of national cinema, thus constructing, in Stringer's terminology, an 'official' version of national culture. In this context, it is interesting to consider how *Woman* became generically separated from the discourse of the 'film of the flesh' after its 1964 Cannes award. In the months after the festival screening, *Woman* picked up all the major Japanese film awards offered by journals and newspapers, and along the way the reservations that had been exhibited by domestic critics towards its links with the 'film of the flesh' were disavowed. In contrast to this, prior to the success of *Woman* some 'films of the flesh' had been exported to international film festivals and markets in the 1960s but failed to achieve much recognition. For example, independent filmmaker Takechi Tetsuji's *Day-Dream* was one of the most successful 'soft porn' films at the domestic box-office; however, its scheduled release in Italy was canceled when it was confiscated on grounds of obscenity by the Italian authorities. In addition. Imamura's *The Insect Woman* and *Intentions of Murder* faced similar trouble in Italy and other European countries; although Imamura's two films were submitted to international film festivals (Berlin and Venice respectively), they were ultimately screened out of competition, with their international failure not only resonating at the domestic box-office but also serving to reinforce Japanese critics' negative assessments of them. In this regard, the reaction of the aforementioned critic Tsumura Hideo was typical. Tsumura criticized Imamura's films' sexual excess – a typical component of the 'film of the flesh' – as representing a lack of consideration of Japanese national honor:

> It's a business decision to export films such as *The Insect Woman* and *Intentions of Murder* abroad, yet we should consider Japan's honor and face when we send films to international film festivals, in other words, sending them to the center stage of the film world . . . The director of these films has a despicable attitude as an artist, and he lacks social morality.
>
> (Tsumura 1964: 51)

The contrasting critical reception of Imamura and Teshigahara's films, as well as the reinscription of *Woman*, post-Cannes, as an example of *avant-garde* and *auteur* cinema, provide ample evidence of how influential official critical affirmation has been (and remains) in Japan. In Imamura's case, the cycle of reception would ironically repeat itself in later years with the favorable recognition at Cannes of his *Ballad of Narayama* (*Narayama bushikō*, 1983), a film which once again highlighted ethnicity as a crucial part of its mythic national allegory. National cinema as configured in such international forums tends to construct ethnicity within an official narrative, erasing local experience and even revising national film history itself.

It would, however, be disingenuous to point to the political disparities of nations as the sole determining force for the creation of national cinema and its discourse. For the 1960s also brought a resurgence of Japanese nationalism, a consequence in part of economic growth. High economic growth began in Japan in the 1950s with annual average growth hitting almost 10 percent by the mid-1960s. Japan demonstrated its economic development by participating in the OECD (Organization for Economic Cooperation and Development) in 1963 – a fact clearly seen by the Japanese themselves as evidence that Japan was neither a developing nation nor still stuck in post-war financial straits. This recovery of national self-esteem was also symbolically reinforced in 1964 by the staging of the Tokyo Olympic Games. (During the preparations for the competition, areas of Tokyo ruined during World War Two were completely reconstructed.) Amid the period's great psychological and material transformations, a new unconscious nationalism became widespread and urged the establishment of an 'international Japan'. Viewed in this particular social context, Japanese cinema's continued bid for international acceptance may be seen as providing a way out of the impasse of Japanese modernity being tied to a strictly Western model.

Given the historical transformations of the period from domestic cultural production to global expansion, the status of *Woman* as one of the forerunners of Japanese 'international' cinema is no coincidence. Yet the shift toward a more fully international cinema brought other constraints on filmmaking to replace those previously imposed by the studios. The film's three *auteurs* – Abe Kōbō, Teshigahara Hiroshi, and composer Takemitsu Tōru – had a greater measure of artistic autonomy than they would have had under the old Japanese studio system. Viewed more broadly within the context of contemporary Japanese cinema, the 'independence' of this symptomatic independent film is not unqualified. From the beginning of the Japanese film industry's decline in the 1960s, many domestic filmmakers have remained dependent upon the universal values of the global market and the attendant commodification of ethnicity within this international structure. As I discussed at the beginning of this chapter, many film scholars have produced symbolic interpretations of *Women*, yet such methods of analysis do not simply signal limited critical approaches. *Woman* itself encourages the viewer to take that path, as if its comprehension depends on the viewer taking a universal perspective or a culturally essentialist view, interpreting the film within a background of tradition. This seduction is indeed characteristic of Japanese 'international' cinema, and we can read the ethnicized filmic body as one of the national cinema's singular deployments.

Notes

1 See also Ehrlich and Santos (2001). While mentioning the influence of Japanese traditional theater in the film's presentation, these two writers primarily stress the universal dimension of the film's symbolism.
2 Similarly, leading actress Kishida Kyōko's Western theatrical background carries an extra-diegetic value of intellectual, artistic brilliance, simultaneously detached from the cinema's conventions of glamorous beauty.
3 It is necessary to note here that some *gendai-geki* were indeed sent out to various international film festivals, and that a few of them received awards as well, such as *The Naked Island* (*Hadaka no shima*, Shindō Kaneto, 1960) at Moscow in 1960. The generalizations made in domestic Japanese film journals concerning which films were suitable for international festivals were specifically aimed at the more prestigious events, such as Berlin, Cannes, and Venice, as well as at the US Academy Awards.

References

Chow, Rey (1995) *Primitive Passions: Visuality, Sexuality, Ethnography, and Contemporary Chinese Cinema*, New York: Columbia University Press.

Daikoku, Toyōshi (1964) 'Kamihanki, Nihon eiga no jitsuryoku o tou' [The First Half of the Year: Interrogating the Power of Japanese Cinema], *Kinema Junpō*, 368: 34.

Dissanayake, Wimal (1990) 'Self, Place and Body in *Woman in the Dunes*: A Comparative Study of the Novel and the Film', in J. Toyama, J. and N. Ochner (eds) *Literary Studies East and West*, Honolulu College of Languages, Linguistics and Literature, University of Hawaii at Manoa and the East-West Center.

Ehrlich, Linda C. and Santos, Antonio (2001) 'The Taunt of the Gods: Reflections on *Woman in the Dunes*', in Dennis Washburn and Carole Cavanaugh (eds) *Word and Image in Japanese Cinema*, Cambridge: Cambridge University Press.

Futaba, Jūzaburō (1964) 'Kamihanki, Nihon eiga no jitsuryoku o tou' [The First Half of the Year: Interrogating the Power of Japanese Cinema], *Kinema Junpō*, 382: 34.

Igarashi, Yoshikuni (2000) *Bodies of Memory: Narratives of War in Post-War Japanese Culture, 1945–1970*, Princeton: Princeton University Press.

Izawa, Jun (1965) 'Nihon eiga no "donzoko" o tsuku' [How the Japanese Cinema Reached the Bottom], *Kinema Junpō*, 382: 41–2.

Ōshima, Nagisa (1992) *Cinema, Censorship, and the State: The Writings of Nagisa Oshima*. Trans. Dawn Lawson. Cambridge, MA: The MIT Press.

Satō, Tadao (2001) 'Nihon eiga no ayumi ni hitotsu no tenkanten o shimeshita eiga sakka' [A Filmmaker Who Marked a New Direction in the History of Japanese Cinema], *Kinema Junpō*, 1335: 126–7.

Stringer, Julian (2001) 'Global Cities and the International Film Festival Economy', in Mark Shiel and Tony Fitzmaurice (eds) *Cinema and the City: Film and Urban Societies in a Global Context*, Oxford: Blackwell: 134–44.

Tessier, Max (1979–80) 'Hiroshi Teshigahara: Images d'une crise de l'identité', *Cinema d'aujourd'hui: Le cinéma japonais au présent 1959–1979*, 15: 117–24.

Toita, Michizō (1964) 'Shōchō-teki ni shimesareta 'gendai' ['The Present' Indicated Symbolically], *Kinema Junpō*, 361: 19.

Tsumura, Hideo (1964) 'Nihon eiga no meiyo to shinjitsu o tou' [On Honor and Truth in the Japanese Cinema], *Kinema Junpō*: 375: 46–51.

Yomota, Inuhiko (1989) *Zen'ei chosho: Teshigahara Hiroshi to no taiwa* [*The Record of the Avant-Garde: Dialogues with Teshigahara Hiroshi*], Tokyo, Gakugei Shorin.

Teshigahara Hiroshi Filmography

Hokusai (1953)
The Twelve Photographers (*12-nin no shashinka*, 1955)
Flower Arrangement (*Ikebana*, 1956)
Tokyo 1958 (1958)
Jose Torres (1959)
The Pitfall (*Otoshiana*, 1962)
That Tender Age (*Shishunki*, 1964 – short)
Woman in the Dunes [also known as *Woman of the Dunes*] (*Suna no onna*, 1964)
White Lake (*Shiroi mizūmi*, 1965)
Jose Torres, Part II (1965)
The Face of Another (*Tanin no kao*, 1966)
Explosion Course (*Bakusō*, 1967)
The Man without a Map (*Moetsukita chizu*, 1968)
240 Hours a Day (*Ichinichi 240 jikan*, 1970)
Summer Soldiers (1972)
Out of Work for Years (1975 – short)
Moving Sculpture: Jean Tinguely (*Ugoku chōkoku: Jean Tinguely*, 1981)
Antonio Gaudí (1984)
Rikyu (1989)
The Princess Goh (*Gō-hime*, 1992)

14

DARK VISIONS OF JAPANESE FILM NOIR

Suzuki Seijun's *Branded to Kill* (1967)

Daisuke Miyao

> I think that motion pictures should create events by themselves
> . . . They should not restrict themselves to merely recreating what
> has actually happened . . . Once such events created on the screen
> occur in reality, motion pictures begin to have a relationship with
> the society for the first time.
>
> (Suzuki Seijun quoted in Ueno 1991: 114)

Suzuki Seijun's 1967 film *Branded to Kill* (*Koroshi no rakuin* – hereafter *Branded*)
– the story of a contract killer being dismissed by a gangster organization –
created a controversial real life incident when Nikkatsu, one of Japan's oldest
film studios, dismissed Suzuki, then one if its contract directors, ten months
after its release. On April 25, 1968, Suzuki was directing the television series
Aisai-kun konbanwa: aru kettō [*Good Evening, Mr Devoted Husband: A Duel*]. He
received a telephone call from the secretary of Hori Kyūsaku, the president of
Nikkatsu, and was told that the studio would not pay his salary for April. Just
like that, Suzuki Seijun was fired from Nikkatsu.

To be sure, *Branded* had not been a financial and critical success. The film
journal *Kinema Junpō* reported that the release of *Branded* on a double feature
with *A Bug That Eats Flowers* (*Hana wo kū mushi*, Nishimura Shōgorō, 1967)
'resulted in less than 2,000 viewers at Asakusa and Shinjuku and about 500 in
Yūrakuchō on the second day' (quoted in Ueno 1986: 336). Indeed, Yamatoya
Atsushi (1994: 38), one of *Branded's* screenwriters, recalls that the Nikkatsu
theater in Shinjuku where the film was originally screened was more or less
empty on its opening day.

More than this, some critics were less than positive about the film. For
example, Iijima Kōichi wrote in *Eiga Geijutsu* in August 1967: 'the
woman buys a mink coat and thinks only about having sex. The man
wants to kill and feels nostalgic about the smell of boiling rice. We
cannot help being confused. We do not go to theaters to be puzzled.'

(Quoted in Ueno 1986: 337)

Yet, however unsuccessful *Branded* may have been, Nikkatsu's dismissal of Suzuki was still a bolt from the blue. Mass demonstrations followed the filmmaker's lawsuit against the studio in June 1968 in accordance with the rebellious political climate of the time. Directors such as Ōshima Nagisa, Shinoda Masahiro, Wakamatsu Kōji, Adachi Masao, and Fujita Toshiya, together with cinematographers, screenwriters, journalists, and critics, as well as many ordinary filmgoers and students of various cinema clubs, all participated in the protest. Suzuki eventually won a lawsuit against Nikkatsu in 1971. Nevertheless, he was never again to be rehired by Nikkatsu or to work for any other studio, and no project involving Suzuki was to be released until 1977, when he was finally able to direct *The Story of Grief and Sorrow* (*Hishū monogatari*). This infamous incident became known as the 'Suzuki Seijun Problem'.

Why was Suzuki suddenly dismissed after *Branded*? None of Nikkatsu's other directors were fired during this period. When Suzuki's friend, Kobayashi Tetsuo, asked Hori about the reason for his decision on April 26, the latter answered:

> Suzuki makes incomprehensible films.
> Suzuki does not follow the company's orders.
> Suzuki's films are unprofitable and it costs 60 million yen to make one.
> Suzuki can no longer make films anywhere. He should quit.
> Suzuki should open a noodle shop or something instead.
>   (Quoted in Ueno 1986: 216)

Similarly, when Kawakita Kazuko, the leader of a cinema club that had already scheduled a Suzuki retrospective, asked Hori why Nikkatsu would prohibit the circulation of Suzuki's films after 1968, the studio's president replied:

> Suzuki Seijun is a director who makes incomprehensible films. Therefore, his films are not good. It is shameful for Nikkatsu to show his films. Nikkatsu cannot have an image of making incomprehensible films. Nikkatsu fired Suzuki Seijun on April 25. His films are prohibited from exhibition at any commercial theaters or at any theaters specializing in retrospective screenings.
>   (Quoted in Ueno 1986: 217; see also Kawarabata 1971: 466)

All of the films Suzuki had directed before *Branded* were studio products made by following their producers' requests; indeed, he was to claim in the 1990s that 'I have always made films for entertainment' (quoted in Yamane 1991: 94). After spending seven years since 1948 as an assistant director at the Shōchiku Ōfuna studio, Suzuki moved to Nikkatsu in 1956 and began his directing career with *Cheers at the Harbour: Triumph in my Hands* (*Minato no kanpai: shōri o waga te ni*). Under Nikkatsu's assembly line approach to filmmaking, Suzuki made various genre pieces, or 'program pictures', including *yakuza* (gangster) films, comic detective action films, romantic melodramas, war films, and teen films. These program pictures were released one after the other virtually on a weekly basis, and Suzuki was mostly assigned to direct *soemono eiga* (accompanying films) or *tsuide eiga* (B pictures) – that is to say, films accompanying 'A' category features on a double bill (Ueno 1991: 114). However, Suzuki was allowed neither to select his scripts and titles nor to make use of Ishihara Yūjirō, Nikkatsu's most famous star at the time. Instead, Suzuki's duty for the company was to bring his films in on low budgets (typically between one-third and two-thirds the cost of 'A' films) and within tight schedules (e.g. producing two to six films per year for more than a decade). In most cases, the release dates for his films had been set even before shooting began. According to leftist film critic Matsuda Masao (2001: 66), Suzuki was 'exploited by the capitalists at Nikkatsu'. For Suzuki, 'It was more of a job than getting any kind of enjoyment out of making a film' (quoted in Mes 2001). *Branded* was made as one such B-grade entertainment film.

During the lawsuit against Nikkatsu after his sudden dismissal, Suzuki talked about his experiences in making *Branded*:

> At that time, the planning division requested that I write a new scenario for a film that would accompany an erotic piece, *Hana o kū mushi*. They did not like one called *Dankon [Bullet Mark]* written by someone else. It was just another action flick. They told me that the release date was already set. When I gave them what I wrote, the studio head [Hori] said that he was finally able to understand it after he read it twice. I suggested that he stop this project, but he asked me to go ahead with it. Thus, I simply helped Nikkatsu to get through its crisis and it is unfair to criticize me retroactively.
>
> (Quoted in Ueno 1986: 226)

In other words, neither Hori nor general audiences expected *Branded* to be anything other than a B picture. Suzuki later confessed that '[Nikkatsu] did not care as long as the film was an action piece' and as long as it was made on time and within their budget (Yamane 1991: 96–7).

Moreover, *Branded* was released in the month of June. At that time, June was considered by film companies to be one of the worst months to release movies. Therefore, most companies chose this time of year to release low budget erotic films or hard-boiled films that were not expected to become a big box-office success. According to Takeda Ryūji (in Uedo 1986: 337), who worked at Nikkatsu at that time, Nikkatsu regarded *Branded* as one such trivial film that could be released in June.

If *Branded* was only a trivial B picture, then it should not have mattered very much whether it was comprehensible or not. The real issue regarding Suzuki's dismissal has to do with Nikkatsu's policy toward its contract directors in the late 1960s. What did Nikkatsu's dismissal of Suzuki, supposedly a mere director of B films, mean for the Japanese film industry at the time? This chapter closely examines *Branded* as an aesthetic text and locates it within the historical context of the Japanese film industry as well as the political and cultural conditions of Japanese society in the late 1960s. More specifically, it examines

Branded as a focal point for the convergence of Japanese film noir and the Japanese avant-garde.

Branded to Kill as film noir

The plot of *Branded* may be briefly summarized as follows: The hero, Hanada Gorō (Shishido Jō), is the No. 3 killer in the country, and he is turned on by the smell of boiling rice. He is asked to drive an important man in the gangster organization to an undisclosed location on a mountain in Nagano prefecture. On his way back home, Hanada's car breaks down in the heavy rain. There he meets a mysterious woman, Misako (Mari Annu). Misako offers him a job to kill an American investigator who is looking into a smuggling operation, but Hanada fails to shoot the target only because a butterfly lands on the muzzle of his rifle. The gangster organization now pursues Hanada. After killing many killers of the organization, he eventually comes up against No. 1 (Nanbara Kōji), who is actually the person who hired him in the first place. No. 1 adopts a curious strategy: he comes to Hanada's apartment to live with him. Finally, Hanada and No. 1 meet in a deserted boxing ring. Misako is accidentally killed during the duel. Hanada kills No. 1, but he is also fatally wounded and falls from the ring.

Film scholar Yomota Inuhiko (2001: 10) claims that the killers in *Branded* are 'references to American film noir'. An immediate problem with such an observation is that it is notoriously difficult to define 'film noir' as a specific genre. French film critics of the 1940s originally started using the term to describe American films of a 'dark' tendency, but at this point in history no such discursive category was used or recognized in the American film industry. Only after the term 'film noir' was imported back into the United States in the late 1960s did it become recognized as a commercial genre by Hollywood studios and hence adopted in the categorization and promotion of certain films. Since then, usage of the term has proliferated, and it now must be considered an overarching, and therefore inclusive, key concept in the study of the history of post-war US cinema (Naremore 1998).

Despite the difficulty of defining 'film noir' as a genre, though, there are certain textual manifestations of the noir style apparent in films made outside as well as inside the United States. Certainly, *Branded* is filled with narrative and visual motifs typical of films noirs. First, Suzuki's film uses chiaroscuro mono-chrome cinematography that emphasizes strong contrasts between light and shadow and is arguably derived from the work of German Expressionist directors. For example, in *Branded* an extreme long shot in which drunken Hanada wanders the street at night clearly recalls the visual atmosphere of German Expressionist films of the 1920s such as *Nosferatu* (*Nosferatu, eine Symphonie des Grauens*, Germany, F.W. Murnau, 1922).

The dark surfaces of film noir also came about as a result of the financial limitations imposed upon B pictures. In order to hide their cheap sets, lighting was used in such movies in a very sparse and economical manner. *Branded* – a B picture made in Japan – was eventually shot in black and white even though it was planned as a color film from the very beginning (Ueno 1986: 337). By 1967, most of the films made at major Japanese studios were produced in color and Suzuki himself was already famous for his unique use of color in films such as *Tokyo Drifter* (*Tōkyō nagare-mono*, 1966). The decision to shoot *Branded* in black and white must therefore be considered a conscious financial and strategic choice. Indeed, Suzuki later confessed that he liked the visual quality of *Branded* because it emphasizes the contrast between light and shadow (Motomura 2001: 55).

Second, noir films are usually tales of the big city, and *Branded* is no exception; it is set in Tokyo in the late 1960s. Suzuki insists that his films do not represent the actual social conditions existing at the time when they were made, yet *Branded* surely depicts the *zeitgeist* of Tokyo in 1967 (Yamane 1991: 90). More specifically, the film problematizes the distinction between the bright side and the dark side of the city following the preparations for the Tokyo Olympics of 1964. (It even reverses negative and positive in one scene – namely, the moment when Hanada looks for No. 1 hiding somewhere in tall buildings – so as to enhance the chiaroscuro atmosphere of the big city.)

In April 1964, Japan's Minister of Health and Welfare announced two new linked programs: the purification of the country together with health and physical education plans. Following this announcement, the sanitation of Tokyo's urban areas proceeded at a rapid pace, but only on a superficial level. Homeless people living in underpasses all over the city were displaced. The running schedule of 'vacuum cars' (tank trucks with a vacuum pump for collecting night soil) became restricted. Garbage cans became standardized. The publication of so-called *ero-guro* (erotic and grotesque) magazines became more tightly controlled (Sakurai 1993: 36–41). Many of Tokyo's dirty and smelly streams and canals were covered over. Laws controlling bars and nightclubs were revised and strengthened. In short, Tokyo's dirty, vulgar, and filthy things became hidden beneath an apparently clean surface. Moreover, the country's high rate of economic growth which began in the late 1960s fostered this distinction between the clean and developed surface and the hidden and isolated abject. As if indicating the film's status as a social critique of rapid urbanization and commercialization, Hanada delivers all his deadly shots in *Branded* from symbolical objects found in the modernized city. His first shot is fired from a huge advertising board depicting a cigarette lighter facing a train platform, and the second into a doctor's eyeball is fired by way of a water pipe when the man is washing up in the sink. After the third killing, Hanada jumps out of a window of a skyscraper and lands on top of a huge balloon used for the promotion of the lighter.

Third, such cinematic techniques as jump cuts, insertions of extreme close-ups, and dramatic camera movements result in the fractured narrative of *Branded* and enhance the film's nightmarish, film noir-inflected appearance. For example, one scene connects in a fragmentary way Hanada's first meeting with Misako and the first on-screen sex between Hanada and his newly-wed wife (Ogawa Mariko). This scene is constructed as a montage of close-ups of the emotionless face and eyes of Misako, the face and eyes of Hanada as he smells boiling rice, and a number of panning shots of Hanada's room.

Picking up on such distinctive aesthetic characteristics, critic Hasumi

Shigehiko (1991: 54–6) claims that *Branded* does not present its action in any 'specific time and space'. What Hasumi is implying here is that the film's narrative and style do not feature linear time progression or continuity of consistent spaces. The film's star, Shishido Jō, later claimed:

> [*Branded*] was a kind of a film that only real aficionados can understand after watching three times or so. There are scenes that ordinary movie fans cannot follow . . . A story [of No. 3 climbing up to the top killer] separately exists with another story of sex. It is caused by a bad script written by the Guru Hachirō group. [cf. Aside from Suzuki Seijun; this group also included Sone Chūsei and Yamatoya Atsushi.] They should have focused on one story and placed other details as subplots. Their ideas, such as the smell of boiling rice exciting the killer, were interesting but not convincing enough. That seemed to be the problem of the film. Also, Mari Annu, another ranked killer, collects butterflies. Wilder's [sic] *The Collector* [US, William Wyler, 1965] was released around that time, but this idea was not articulated very well . . . It seems that *Branded to Kill* was not convincingly realistic enough.
>
> (Shishido 1991: 66–7)

Shishido's retrospective claim about *Branded* highlights how the film's non-linear, fragmented narrative, as well as its core thematic ideas, spread in a disorderly fashion across the narrative. Suzuki's film is thus not composed around the linear psychological development of its protagonist, but instead its protagonist appears lost and dismayed in the midst of a nightmarish, fractured world created through use of specific cinematic techniques.

Fourth, *Branded* emphasizes the ambivalent characterization of its protagonist. Robert Sklar (1994: 253) claims that '[t]he hallmark of film noir is its sense of people trapped – trapped in webs of paranoia and fear, unable to tell guilt from innocence . . . The survival of good remains troubled and ambiguous'. In order to emphasize this feeling of entrapment, many films noirs adopt flashback and voiceover techniques. *Branded* does not overtly use voiceover and flashback, but Hanada often talks to himself in a paranoiac tone and he sometimes remembers the time he spent with Misako.

Hasumi (1991: 54) further points out that Hanada is a character 'trying hard to hang between his upward intention and his downward fear'. He seems to be afraid that he will become unable to resist his fate, or desire, of falling. As Hasumi suggests, *Branded* is – visually speaking – filled with motifs that emphasize the vertical axis. During the first mission, Hanada drives his car up to a mountain so as to escort an important figure to a cottage. On his way up there, he kills No. 2. As he physically drives up the mountain, he goes one up the killer ranking. He loves the smell of boiling rice that wafts up from a rice cooker. He is also obsessed with fire and with lighters that start fire. The most striking and comic example is the scene in which Hanada jumps up on to the advertising balloon – at this moment, he is literally hanging in the air.

When Hanada becomes obsessed with Misako, he begins to suffer from his upward intention and his downward fear/desire. Visually, Misako almost always appears with falling water (rain, shower, or a fountain), in opposition to Hanada's obsession with fire. She is fully connected to the images of pinned butterflies and dead birds that can no longer fly up into the air. In the climactic battle scene, Hanada has to go down under his car and crawl on the ground. Even after the final duel, Hanada has to stay suspended. His voice cries out that he has reached the top while his body falls down from the boxing ring. (The ring actually looks as if it is suspended in the air above the ground because of the extreme whiteness caused by strong lighting from above.) As Watanabe Takenobu (1981: 10) claims, '[H]eroes in Nikkatsu action films do not get along with the world around them until the end'. Hanada has to keep his ambiguous position in the world even after the closure of the narrative. Thus, *Branded* questions the protagonist's determined goal and standpoint right until the very end. This is the reason why film critic Ishigami Mitoshi wrote that 'the latter half of the film is disappointing because Hanada's characterization is confusing' (quoted in Ueno 1986: 337). Yet this confusing characterization itself seems to be the very point of *Branded*.

Branded to Kill as avant-garde

According to Charles O'Brien (1996: 8), the term 'film noir' originally suggested 'an essentially affective response to a group of [French] films that seemed to transgress the morality of the national culture'. In 1939, the film critic Georges Altman noted in *La Lumière* that:

> The public is embarrassed. The 'critics' are outraged in a fit of morality. Everyone who thinks the cinema is just a dubious form of entertainment or an abject form of pleasure simply cannot understand.
> (Quoted in Abel 1988: 266–7)

As sociologist Nakamura Hideyuki (2000: 148) argues, however, 'film noir' came to be appreciatively evaluated as a kind of 'avant-garde' culture in its subsequent American manifestation. Indeed, James Naremore (1998: 17–19) points out that film noir enjoyed a close relationship with versions of surrealism believed to embody subversive capabilities.

Since the mid-1950s, various groups in Japan – including surrealists Matsumoto Toshio and Terayama Shūji, student groups at Nihon University (Adachi Masao, Jōnouchi Motoharu), and 8mm filmmakers Iimura Takahiko and Ōbayashi Nobuhiko – had started to make experimental films. Many of these filmmakers were influenced by European avant-garde films of the 1920s and 1930s which playfully problematized modernized urban everyday life and emphasized the artificiality of linear narratives and conventional ideas of reality itself. More than anything else, what European avant-garde artists of the 1920s and 1930s and Japanese avant-garde artists of the 1960s tried to do was to astonish viewers with unexpected images that questioned daily and customary lives. By the mid-1960s, when the problems of urbanization and post-war modernization/Americanization had become widely recognized in Japan, avant-garde films had become popular there. In 1967, the First Sōgetsu Experimental Film Festival was successfully held, and Matsumoto made a commercial film, *Funeral Parade of Rose (Bara no sōretsu* – a gay version of the Oedipus story), in 1969. Even though the film was supposed to be a commercial feature, Matsumoto rejected a strictly linear presentation of the narrative and instead inserted such 'confusing' scenes as his interviewing the film's protagonist. *Funeral Parade of Roses* was distributed through the Japan Art Theater Guild (ATG), which was established in 1962 as an independent distributor of foreign art films as well as independent Japanese films. The ATG started to produce its own films in 1967, and went on to offer financial support and exhibition space to numerous experimental and independent filmmakers including Ōshima Nagisa, Shinoda Masahiro, Yoshida Yoshishige, and Shindō Kaneto.

Before his dismissal in 1968, Suzuki had not even thought of becoming an independent and so free to pursue his own projects, as directors such as Imamura Shōhei, Ōshima, and Yoshida already had. He regarded himself simply as a contract director, one who insisted that he could not make a film outside the studio system until the time he made *Zigeunerweisen* in 1980 (Itakura 2001). Indeed, Suzuki's films before 1968 were all collaborative works with cinematographers such as Nagatsuka Kazue and Mine Shigeyoshi, production designers including Kimura Takeo, and screenwriters, among others, from within the Nikkatsu studio stable. However, his filmmaking practice at Nikkatsu, as most typically projected in a noir-style film such as *Branded*, shared visual features and other aesthetic tendencies with the contemporary avant-garde and independent film movements. As if he were posing as an avant-garde artist, Suzuki often claims that he makes films simply to 'astonish' the viewer (Suzuki 1999), and of course he had a reputation at Nikkatsu for making unique and avant-garde films. For instance, Suzuki Akira (2000: 71), an editor who worked with Suzuki, claims: 'Mr. Suzuki Seijun shot films in an unusually elliptic manner so that other editors could not connect them consistently'. Suzuki later confessed: 'Why make a movie about something one understands completely? I make movies about things I do not understand, but wish to' (quoted in Teo 2000).

With its extensive use of jump cuts and elliptic editing, expressionistic lighting, quick panning, and extreme close-ups, *Branded* boasts a notably avant-garde aesthetic. One shot, in which a doctor pulls out his patient's artificial eye in close-up, refers directly to the surrealist classic *Un Chien Andalou* (France/Spain, Luis Bunuel and Salvador Dali, 1928). One scene superimposes Hanada's close-ups with painted white birds, butterflies, and rain. Yet the most striking example is an 8mm silent film, showing Misako being tortured by gangsters, which is projected as a film-within-the-film. This short silent film consists of seven shots:

1 Medium long shot of Misako naked and tied.
2 Medium shot of Misako in silhouette.
3 Low angle shot of Misako standing on a transparent floor.

4 Medium long shot of Misako and a large flame from an off-screen flame thrower.

5 Low angle shot of Misako and fire, shot from under the transparent floor. The camera pans to a window from which gangsters watch Misako.

6 Close-up of Misako tortured in fire.

7 Low angle shot of Misako falling down on the transparent floor.

Since it is a shot of torture by fire, the sixth shot appears to refer to the use of decentered close-ups against a black background in *The Passion of Joan of Arc* (*La Passion de Jeanne d'Arc*, France, Carl-Theodor Dreyer, 1927), a film that blends influences from the French, German, and Soviet avant-garde cinema movements. It is also worth noting that there is an interaction between the 8mm film and Hanada. After the second shot, Hanada pulls down a screen. When he sees the sixth shot, screened on a wall, Hanada touches the projected image of Misako and asks her where she is. He tries to read her lips saying merely, 'I love you'. This kind of interaction between on-screen images and people outside the screen was one of the practices of the avant-garde film movement. For example, Terayama Shūji attempted to blur the distinction between the inside and the outside of the screen in his films of the early 1970s such as *Death in the Country* (*Den'en ni shisu*, 1973) and *Laura* (*Rōra*, 1974).

In the late 1960s, at a time when many viewers of cinema aspired to interpret or use cinema ideologically and politically, Suzuki claimed that motion pictures did not contain any thoughts. He was opposed to including any principles or 'isms' (Hasumi 2001: 102). Suzuki wanted to say that motion pictures as media could be more chaotic and inconsistent than something that merely conveys linear and consistent messages and specific meanings. Suzuki's values therefore have much in common with independent avant-garde filmmakers of the period, no matter how seemingly apolitical his films appear to be. Critic Matsuda Masao (2001: 67) insisted that '[T]he films of Suzuki Seijun are the truly hard-working documentary that tried to capture the unreasonable world of a film studio ... where capitalists and labor are intensely fighting each other ... What does the killer's question, "Who is No. 1?" imply in *Branded to Kill?*' In this sense, whether consciously or not, *Branded* may be considered to be a self-referential modernist work made from within the Japanese studio system.

This kind of self-critical 'art cinema' was not what Nikkatsu wanted from its contract directors. By 1968, Nikkatsu was facing financial difficulties as the Japanese film industry declined rapidly throughout the 1960s and 1970s because of transformations in Japanese society such as the spread of television and other leisure industries.

Under these conditions, Hori requested in his New Year address of 1968 that all directors at Nikkatsu make comprehensible films that would appeal to broad audiences. According to Yamatoya, in the original script of *Branded*, Misako is burned to death by the gangster organization as shown in the 8mm film-within-a-film, yet a producer wanted her to come back in the finale as a melodramatic heroine (Yamatoya 1994: 56). As film critic Tahara Katsuhiro (1977: 66) insists, Nikkatsu had a concrete ' "project intention" in order to compete

Figure 18 An avant-garde film inconsistent with Nikkatsu's 'project intention': *Branded to Kill* (1967). BFI Stills, Posters and Designs.

with Tōei's popular *yakuza* melodrama' and required its contract directors 'to cooperate with the company's direction'. Nikkatsu wanted *Branded* to be an erotic melodrama, not an avant-garde film, and it felt that Suzuki had disobeyed the company's instructions. At the end of the 1960s, Suzuki's films were not regarded as consistent with Nikkatsu's 'project intention'.

Also in 1968, Hori made an announcement entitled 'About Reforming the Studio' in which he proposed industry rationalization by decreasing costs of all films and implementing drastic layoffs. In August 1971, Nikkatsu stopped producing films, and then three months after that it turned to the production of pornographic films. In retrospect, it is clear that the 'Suzuki Seijun Problem' was not only a mythical event that took place during the rebellious atmosphere of 1968 but also an incident that symbolizes the decline of Nikkatsu and with it the Japanese studio system and film industry as a whole. With *Branded*, Suzuki therefore became the scapegoat for Nikkatsu's financial difficulties and rationalization project. Nikkatsu pronounced Suzuki's career to be dead, at least for the next decade. The director had to wait until the critical and financial success of *Zigeunerweisen* in 1980 before regaining his status as a masterful filmmaker and obtaining well-deserved international recognition.

References

Abel, Richard (ed.) (1988) *French Film Theory and Criticism: A History/Anthology 1907–1939, vol. II 1929–1939*, Princeton: Princeton University Press.

Hasumi, Shigehiko (1991) 'Suzuki Seijun matawa kisetsu no fuzai' [Suzuki Seijun, or the Absence of Seasons], *Yuriika* 23(4): 38–57.

—— (2001) *Eiga kyojin, kataru [Cine-madman Speaks]*, Tokyo: Kawade Shobō Shin-sha.

Itakura, Kimie (2001) 'Film Maverick Finally Emerges', *asahi.com*. Online. http://www.asahi.cm/english/weekend/K2001110400118.html. Posted 4 November.

Kawarabata, Yasushi (1971) 'Shiki: Suzuki Seijun mondai no ichi saikuru' [A Personal Note: One Cycle of the Suzuki Seijun Problem], in Ogawa Tōru (ed.) *Gensō to seiji no aida: gendai Nihon eiga-ron taikei [Between Imagination and Politics: Anthology on Contemporary Japanese Film Criticism]*, Tokyo: Tōki-sha: 463–74.

Matsuda, Masao (2001) ' "Seijun kyotō" o megutte' [Regarding the 'Seijun Problem'], in Motomura 2001: 61–9.

Mes, Tom (2001) 'Japan Cult Cinema Interview: Seijun Suzuki', *Midnighteye*. Online. www.midnighteye.com/interviews/seijun_suzuki.shtml. Posted 11 October.

Motomura, Shūji (ed.) (2001) *Sō tokushū: Suzuki Seijun [Special Issue: Suzuki Seijun]*, Tokyo: Kawade Shobō Shin-sha.

Nakamura, Hideyuki (2000) 'Firumu nowāru/disukūru nowāru: kokumin eiga to geijutsu-sei 1938–1949 nen' [Film Noir/Discourse Noir: National Cinema and the Artistic, 1938–1949], in Yoshimi Shun'ya (ed.) *Media sutadīsu [Media Studies]*, Tokyo: Serica Shobō: 140–55.

Naremore, James (1998) *More Than Night: Film Noir in Its Contexts*, Berkeley: University of California Press.

O'Brien, Charles (1996) 'Film Noir in France: Before the Liberation', *Iris* 21: 7–20.

Sakurai, Tetsuo (1993) *Shisō to shiteno 60 nendai [The 1960s as Thoughts]*, Tokyo: Chikuma Shobō.

Shishido, Jō (1991) 'Akushon eiga wa korekara da' [Here Come Action Films], *Yuriika* 23(4): 58–67.

Sklar, Robert (1994) *Movie-Made America: A Cultural History of American Movies*, New York: Vintage. Revised edition.

Suzuki, Akira (2000) 'Jokantoku kara henshū-sha ni tenshin shita Nikkatsu jidai' [Nikkatsu Period When I Changed My Career from an Assistant Director to an Editor], in Nozawa Kazuma (ed.) *Nikkatsu 1954–1971: eizō o sōzō suru samurai-tachi [Nikkatsu 1954–1971: Samurai Warriors Creating Moving Images]*, Tokyo: Waizu Shuppan: 70–2.

Suzuki, Seijun (1999) *Branded to Kill*. The Criterion Collection DVD.

Tahara, Katsuhiro (1977) *Nihon eiga no ronri [Japanese Cinema's Logic]*, Tokyo: San'ichi Shobō.

Teo, Stephen (2000) 'Seijun Suzuki: Authority in Minority', *Senses of Cinema*, 8. Online. http://www.sensesofcinema.com/contents/00/8/miff/suzuki.html.

Ueno, Kōshi (ed.) (1986) *Suzuki Seijun zen eiga [All Films of Suzuki Seijun]*, Tokyo: Rippū Shobō.

—— (1991) 'Seijun ni yoru Seijun' [Seijun by Seijun], *Yuriika* 23(4): 103–18.

Watanabe, Takenobu (1981) *Nikkatsu akushon no kareina sekai [The Fascinating World of Nikkatsu Action]*, Tokyo: Mirai-sha.

Yamane, Sadao (1991) 'Seijun in Rotterdam', *Yuriika* 23(4): 87–102.

Yamatoya, Atsushi (1994) *Akuma ni yudaneyō [Leave it to the Devil]*, Tokyo: Waizu Shuppan.

Yomota, Inuhiko (2001) *Ajia no naka no Nihon eiga [Japanese Cinema in Asia]*, Tokyo: Iwanami Shoten.

Suzuki Seijun Filmography

Cheers at the Harbour: Triumph in my Hands [also known as Victory Is at Hand] (Minato no kanpai: shōri o wagate ni, 1956)
Pure Emotions of the Sea (Umi no junjō, 1956)
Town of Devils [also known as Satan's Town] (Akuma no machi, 1956)
Floating Hotel [also known as Inn of Floating Weeds] (Ukigusa no yado, 1957)
Eight Hours of Horror [also known as Eight Hours of Terror] (8 jikan no kyōfu, 1957)
Nude Girl with a Gun (Rajo to kenjū, 1957)
Beauty of the Underworld (Ankokugai no bijo, 1958)
Stepping out Spring (Fumihazushita haru, 1958)
Blue Breasts (Aoi chibusa, 1958)
Voice Without a Shadow (Kage naki koe, 1958)
Love Letter (Raburetā, 1959)
Passport of Darkness (Ankoku no ryoken, 1959)
Naked Age (Suppadaka no nenrei, 1959)
Take Aim at the Police Van (Sono gosōsha o nerae, 1960)
Beastly Sleep (Kemono no nemuri, 1960)
Undercover 0-line (Mikkō 0 rain, 1960)
Everything is Crazy (Subete ga kurutteru, 1960)
Go to Hell, Hoodlums (Kutabare gurentai, 1960)
Tokyo Knights (Tōkyō naito, 1961)
Reckless Boss (Muteppō taishō, 1961)
Man with the Hollow-tip Bullets (Shottogan no otoko, 1961)
New Wind over the Mountain (Tōge o wataru wakai kaze, 1961)
Bloody Channel (Kaikyō chi ni somete, 1961)
Million Dollar Match (Hyakuman doru o tatakidase, 1961)
Teen Yakuza (Haitīn yakuza, 1962)
Those Who Bet on Me (Ore ni kaketa yatsura, 1962)
Detective Bureau 23: Go to Hell, Bastard! (Tantei jimusho 23: kutabare akutō domo, 1963)
Youth of the Beast (Yajū no seishun, 1963)
The Bastard (Akutarō, 1963)
Kanto Wanderer (Kantō mushuku, 1963)
Flowers and the Angry Waves (Hana to dotō, 1964)
Gate of Flesh (Nikutai no mon, 1964)
Our Blood Doesn't Forgive (Oretachi no chi ga yurusanai, 1964)
Story of a Prostitute (Shunpū-den, 1965)
Story of the Bastard: Born under a Bad Star (Akutarō-den: warui hoshi no moto demo, 1965)
One Generation of Tattoos (Irezumi ichidai, 1965)
Carmen from Kawachi (Kawachi Karumen, 1966)
Tokyo Drifter (Tōkyō nagare-mono, 1966)
Elegy to Violence [also known as Fighting Elegy] (Kenka erejī, 1966)
Branded to Kill (Koroshi no rakuin, 1967)
The Story of Grief and Sorrow (Hishū monogatari, 1977)
Zigeunerweisen (1980)
Heat Shimmer Theater (Kagerōza, 1981)
Capone Cries Hard (Kapone ōi ni naku, 1985)
Yumeji (1991)
Pistol Opera (Shin koroshi no rakuin: pisutoru opera, 2001)
Princess Raccoon (Operetta tanuki goten, 2005)

15

EROTICISM IN TWO DIMENSIONS
Shinoda Masahiro's *Double Suicide* (1969)

Carole Cavanaugh

Shinoda Masahiro's 1969 film *Double Suicide* (*Shinjū ten no amijima*) heralded two emergent trends in Japanese media. One was its homeland eroticism, certainly not new, but new to the modern mainstream, offering a mild foretaste of the *pinku* (pink) movies of the 1970s. Another was its preoccupation with the two-dimensional image, a visual strategy unusual in the feature film. The absence of optical depth in a film of pre-modern passion released *Double Suicide* from the compulsion identified by André Bazin as inherent in the photographic medium: its urge to establish 'an integral realism, a recreation of the world in its own image' (Bazin 1967: 21). Shinoda produced a flat eroticism in an attenuated world, which, in its defiance of both the realism of the camera and the anti-realism of Hollywood sex, challenged the psychological boundaries of classical cinema more subversively than did his openly political Japanese New Wave contemporaries.

The visual flatness of *Double Suicide* was part of a cultural shift toward limiting the optical dimensions of storytelling, most noticeable in the developing medium of *manga* (comic books). In the late 1960s, comic books gained lasting appeal among disaffected young adults in Japan, who formed a readership at first nostalgically drawn to works for children by Tezuka Osamu but who soon demanded the plots that characterize *manga* today. Laborers and college students found common ground in the gritty stories of *gekiga*, graphic novels penned by artists such as Shirato Sampei and Saitō Takao. One of the most popular works among radical students was Chiba Tetsuya's and Takamori Asao's *Ashita no Jō* (*Tomorrow's Joe*), which ran from 1968 to 1973 in the popular magazine for young people *Shōnen*. The student movement embraced *manga* as a rejection of bourgeois society and its acquiescence to American political and cultural dominance.[1]

Manga are 'hand-held' movies that bypass the technological authority of the film apparatus, while at the same time invoking the reader's memory of cinematic techniques. Japanese comic books borrow the editing strategies of cinema, using multiple frames for long shots, close-ups, and reverse angles. Cinematic in its method, the form nonetheless rejects the defining elements of film: *manga* drawings typically forgo the illusion of depth and disobey the physical laws of real space. This rejection of depth and dimension favors the dynamics of graphic composition. Even when characters are molded with light and shadow, they are positioned frame to frame with regard for page design rather than for photographic and physical realism. Modern *manga* can be understood as surrealistic cinema in two dimensions, a design sequence that collapses both time and perspective.

Double Suicide, arriving in the same cultural moment as *manga*, participated in a similar experiment in surrealistic collapse. It may have been that the intentions of Shinoda's experiment were purely visual. But within the context of political protest against American hegemony of the 1960s, the striking graphics of *Double Suicide*, like the designs of *manga*, interrogate the imperatives of naturalism and realism – the twin values of Hollywood cinema. The aesthetics of *manga* are informative in mapping the visual boundaries of *Double Suicide*; Shinoda's native graphics allow him to retell a pre-modern story in active opposition to the camera that records it. The achievement of *Double Suicide* is its alienation, literally its 'making foreign', of the apparatus of its own production. Shinoda puts the camera 'in its place', as it were, outside the frame of Japanese storytelling.

Manga as a medium is anti-Western in that it does not rely on the *trompe l'oeil* effect of fixed-point perspective, the technique that creates the illusion of depth in post-Renaissance painting, photography, and film. The Japanese comic book is visually rich because, as many have observed, it reverts to the two-dimensional graphic possibilities of *ukiyo-e*, the woodblock prints of the Genroku (1688–1704) era. It was during this period, at the turn of the eighteenth century, that Chikamatsu Monzaemon wrote the *bunraku* puppet play *Shinjū ten no amijima*, the source of Shinoda's film. The ancient and modern graphic forms reinforce each other on Shinoda's self-consciously flat screen. Wide-eyed Koharu, the woman at the center of *Double Suicide*, seems to assume the attitude, posture, and black-and-white edge of a *manga* layout, while retaining the *ukiyo-e* stylistics the film adopts for so many of its images.

The association of *Double Suicide* with the two-dimensional aesthetics ascendant at the time of its source is complicated by the fact that it was also in this period that the lenses of the telescope and microscope arrived in Japan with their potential to recalibrate vision in terms of scientific observation. With the lens gradually came a set of cultural processes that go beyond mere looking to constitute not only a modern view of the world but a mindset that overemphasizes the value of 'the real' and 'the natural'. That optical adjustment would eventually subjugate the native arts to the imperatives of a style called realism, which purported to reflect the world objectively, in three dimensions, a promise that culminated in the arrival of the movie camera two centuries later.

The time of the story of *Double Suicide* marks the beginning of the end of native vision and its delight in the imagination of pure surface. It is photographic realism that Shinoda demotes in *Double Suicide* by situating the film in an era when popular aesthetics peaked in *ukiyo-e*, but also when indigenous vision was on the verge of its long descent toward modern collapse. The air of deflated tragedy in the film arises not only from the fate of the doomed lovers but also from the vulnerability of the pre-modern eye to the crushing power of realism.

Like both *manga* and *ukiyo-e*, *Double Suicide* is pre-photographic in every sense, especially in its denial of fixed-point perspective. To reject the illusion of depth – to insist instead on the two-dimensional actuality of the screen image – is to call into question the authority realism reserves for itself as the mainstay of modernity and its reproductions.

Double Suicide goes even further. The film plays with the concept of 'surface' by styling itself on the erotic optics of an art form associated with superficial pleasure, while at the same time questioning the potential of mainstream cinema for gratification in the erotic. Shinoda treats the subject of sexual possession – the paradox of both possessing the love object and being possessed by desire for it – not as pleasurable but as an existential problem. This problem appears in marked contrast to Hollywood's idea of the erotic, which in the 1950s and 1960s presented seductresses who brought uncomplicated enjoyment, such as Marilyn Monroe in *River of No Return* (US, Otto Preminger, 1954). Possession of the love object is the quest of the film and its achievement is offered as a guarantee of eternal freedom on a limitless natural landscape. In contrast, Shinoda's film trades on a double irony; it uses the camera to deny the three-dimensional privileges of film space and uses a formalization of eroticism to challenge the unrealistic promises of modern sex.

The *Double Suicide* story is simple and exactly follows the plot of its source. Jihei (Nakamura Kichiemon), a middle-class shop-owner, is married to his cousin Osan (Iwashita Shima). Because her family has set him up in the paper business, the usual obligations a man has to wife and family are even heavier. For about three years he has been involved with Koharu (Iwashita Shima in a double role), an elegant and popular prostitute under contract to a brothel. The relationship in itself does not transgress the mores of the time, but Jihei's excessive passion does. It is not infidelity that is the issue, it is his obsession, portrayed as a kind of illness that causes him to neglect his family and his business. He has promised to buy out Koharu's contract with money that he does not have. Tahei, his rich rival, plans to redeem her instead. Jihei's wife, aware that with no other recourse the two may kill themselves and leave her a widow with two children, has secretly sent Koharu a letter begging her to end the relationship. Koharu has vowed to abide by Osan's request, binding the women together in an unusual pact. Osan's family and Jihei's brother intervene, complicating the relationship. In the end, Osan's father forces a divorce. With no alternative left to them, Jihei and Koharu escape the city and end their lives.

The most striking feature of *Double Suicide* is the appearance of *kurogo*, traditional veiled puppeteers shrouded in black, whose presence is almost invisible to spectators of the *bunraku* puppet theater, but who become more intrusive as the film progresses. The insertion of mysterious figures to propel the action is a component of the film on which previous interpretations of *Double Suicide* have centered.[2] But more important than their symbolic meaning is the fact that with their inclusion Shinoda announces that while he may have adapted a traditional story he has not naturalized it. His stance against naturalism is in opposition to the directors Kurosawa Akira, Mizoguchi Kenji, and Kinugasa Teinosuke whose films recreated the 'look' of the historical period. Shinoda's project is not to familiarize the past, but to make it as strange as its pre-photographic mentality.

He appeals to native vision by opposing the imperatives of both naturalism (the way the story is presented) and realism (the way the film is photographed). In line with the Hollywood film, the naturalistic goals of pre-New Wave directors were dependent on hiding all evidence of the camera by masking its framing and editing in a narrative that appears to tell itself. Ōshima Nagisa in *Cruel Story of Youth* (*Seishun zankoku monogatari*, 1960) and *Night and Fog in Japan* (*Nihon no yoru to kiri*, 1960) jarred Japanese film with modern political critique; Shinoda transported the disruptions of the New Wave to the past, the rich setting of so many *samurai* movies that presented Japan as ahistorical and culturally continuous. Shinoda replaces the solidity of naturalistic mise-en-scène, typical of period films, with fragmentation and contingency in his use of fragile sets and the ironic inscription of *kurogo* puppeteers in the diegesis. How radical a step this fragmentation was becomes clear when we recall that, after modernization and until Japan gained international economic status in the 1980s, the imaginary of the ancient past as a dependable whole was the one constant for the Japanese amid shifting mid-century values. *Double Suicide* indicts the ideological complicity of award-winning films, such as *Rashomon* (*Rashōmon*, Kurosawa Akira, 1950) and *Gate of Hell* (*Jigokumon*, Kinugasa Teinosuke, 1953), which portrayed ancient Japan as a naturalized setting for modern liberalism, not only for international film festival audiences, but also for Japanese at home who welcomed the soothing continuity with the past that cinema conjured for them after the displacements of the Pacific War and American Occupation. Shinoda's film makes no pretense that the cinematic past is anything more than an artificial construction.

As the film opens, the complexity of its historical position is announced even before images appear on screen in the hypnotic tones of Takemitsu Tōru's score. Over the darkness, the ascent and descent of three metallic notes evoke the random harmonics of wind chimes or temple bells. The simple progression of tones is interrupted by a sforzando, a loud chord that unleashes a percussive layer of aggressive rhythms. The overture is brief, lasting less than 30 seconds, and resolves in the resonance of a single bell. The musical passage implies both the traditional and the contemporary, a conscious erasure of history that anticipates the ideological layering in the film about to unfold. The competing moods of the opening music – one simple and lilting, the other complex and insistent – capture the rival forces that will drive the lovers of Shinoda's erotic elegy to their deaths.

The film is never reluctant to display the artificiality of its internal and external structures. A faux-documentary opening signals Shinoda's project immediately with voice-overs of the director and writer, Tomioka Taeko, discussing on the telephone the construction of the unwritten ending of the film already underway. Do not expect the narrative perfection of classic cinema, the opening seems to warn; this film unfolds even before its own purposes have been realized. The backstage prelude, in which we see contemporary puppeteers prepare for a traditional performance, establishes the director as storyteller and the film itself as a fiction, reminiscent of the appearance on stage of the narrator in *bunraku*, a theatrical form that famously foregrounds its devices and techniques.[3] Just as the Buddhist *noh* theater shuns realism as an obstacle to aesthetic awareness and enlightenment, the secular puppet theater makes no attempt to hide the actions of the *kurogo* puppeteers and gives prominence to the chanter, who reads all the parts of the play from the text notably visible on the stage.

But the film is not modern mimicry of a foregone style. Lost is the cultural coherence of storytelling as performance, affirmed in the director's advice to the scriptwriter, as she considers the ending of the film, to abandon Chikamatsu's text and its literary constraints. His disavowal of his source in the first scene implies that an absolute return to pre-modern vision is impossible, whether through the naturalism of the pre-New Wave, or through the anti-naturalism Shinoda's own film is about to propose. *Double Suicide* may expose its own devices in a manner reminiscent of traditional performance, but it does so on a ground of dispersed meaning, a dispersal announced by the images of disembodied puppet heads beginning and ending the first scene. This synecdoche of decapitation reinforces the disconnection of the voices of the director and scenarist (the authors), who speak as displaced authorities over a film that will question the possibility of individual autonomy once the modern illusion of psychological wholeness is inoperable. Shinoda and Tomioka discuss the need to free the text from the 'prettiness' of the *michiyuki*, the literary ending of Chikamatsu's play, which culminates in the lovers' deaths. Locating their final lovemaking in a graveyard, Shinoda says, will capture, instead of romantic beauty, a 'fetishism for space' (*kūkan no fetishizumu*), meaning both the three dimensions of real space and the infinite abyss of the lovers' abjection.

A 'fetishism for space' also describes the movie camera's obsession with creating on a flat screen the illusion of three dimensions, a deception Shinoda will use his own camera to unveil. The director frustrates the photographic realism of the camera in two ways: by removing the optical vanishing point of every shot to a place outside the frame (obviating the photographic illusion of depth), and by shooting key scenes with a long focal-length lens, which has the effect of collapsing foreground and background.

The first four shots following the opening scene of the puppeteers and the credits – the beginning of the story of the two lovers – constitute a signature sequence for the film as a whole. The series of shots endorses the abandonment of quattrocento perspective in favor of a flat surface configured as a single-plane composition.

In the first shot, Jihei crosses a steeply curved bridge with his back to the camera. Before his figure can recede, a cut takes us to the other side of the arc of the bridge. In this second shot a band of Buddhist pilgrims dressed in white and traveling toward Jihei ascends the bridge. This shot is followed by two reverse shots in which Jihei, the individual on his way to sin, and the congregation on the road to salvation bypass each other near the apex of the bridge, which appears as a horizon high in the frame. Though Jihei and the pilgrims move directly toward and away from the camera in all four shots, a long focal-length lens collapses foreground and background to make it seem that the figures are moving up and down on the two-dimensional space of the screen, rather than receding and advancing. The focal length converts the three-dimensional space the lens photographs to appear as the two-dimensional sur-face it actually is when we see it on the screen. A long shot follows the sequence

[...] lge that Jihei and the pilgrims oppos-

[...] ensional space is so successful in the

[...] e might not possess the visual cues to

[...] he camera frames the shot so that the

[...] reen diagonally, obscuring the optical

[...] ny viewers the landscape aesthetics of

[...] n the renunciation of spatial depth.

[...] n at two dead bodies on the riverbank,

[...] e upward gaze initializes the course of

his obsession. The metaphorical and allegorical possibilities of this segment – with bridge, pilgrims, river, corpses, doomed man, and puppeteers – have been identified by Keiko McDonald (1983: 52–3) as the key to a system of symbols for *giri*, or duty, and *ninjō*, or desire, the conflicting values that drive the drama of Chikamatsu's play. Brett deBary (1993: 60–2) singles out the dualism in this interpretation, which produces the further dichotomies of feudal and modern, natural and social, controlled and free, in an endless succession of polarizing pairs – a reading that converges with the similarly dialectical interpretations of Bock (1978: 351–2) and Desser (1988: 174–8). DeBary rejects this dualism and goes on to position the film against Shinoda's relevant essays in a finely worked critique that addresses 'issues of nation and gender raised by a Japanese film text, Shinoda's *Shinjū ten no amijima*' (1993: 59). DeBary deliberately uses the Japanese title, which means 'love suicide at Amijima' to avoid dualistic misinterpretation of the English title *Double Suicide*.

The task at hand is more modest, a mapping of the optical structure of the film, but with respect for deBary's important encouragement that we sharpen 'our sense of the film as a historical product, counterbalancing tendencies to treat it as a purely aesthetic and autonomous cultural object' (1993: 62). An appeal to history must nonetheless include the aesthetics of modernization, which allied itself to the optical imperatives of photographic realism.

Violations of Hollywood transparency, the 'see-through' illusion that the story appears to photograph itself, are proposed as a system of visual puns, such as transparent backdrops in several scenes, or vertical bars through which we often view the movement of the actors. The film continually invites us to 'look through', that is, to see beyond its illusions. But 'seeing through' never implies depth. Figures move horizontally, never perpendicularly to the camera; or they move on a diagonal, never reaching the vanishing point or even their own destination. When the camera moves, it travels sideways across a flat horizontal plane. These camera strategies ensure that Shinoda's visual experimentation is not simply ornamental but is deeply embedded in cinematic structure.

Figure 19 Dimensional limitations: the final scene of *Double Suicide* (1969). BFI Stills, Posters and Designs.

The dimensional limitations of *Double Suicide* are charted in the first and final scenes, which are the only natural exteriors in the film. The interior scenes that make up the greater portion are stagy studio sets, meant to play up construct-edness and artificiality.[4] The interior shots also interrupt focal depth by stressing the decorated surface of backdrops, which are emblazoned with the calligraphic text of the play, with blow-ups of *ukiyo-e* prints, or with random splatters and heavy brushwork. The smeared surfaces of course connote blood, but they also recall abstract expressionist painting, a post-war art movement that abjured realist figuration and depth to explore instead the flatness of the canvas in resistance to the spatial illusions of photography and academic painting.

Accounting for flatness in *Double Suicide* becomes a commentary on every element of its construction and its pattern of curtailing the power of the camera. Scholar Audie Bock writes that Shinoda's adaptation was unlike other portrayals of Chikamatsu's on the screen because the director 'made a filmic analysis of the theatrical form of *bunraku*' (1978: 351). While we can agree with Bock's insightful observation thematically, structurally the process seems just the reverse: Shinoda made a dramatized analysis of the photographic form of cinema. This analysis could occur only if the capabilities of the camera (movement and perspective) were halted for examination. Shinoda deadens the camera, giving it little leeway within the film itself, much less the authority to analyze anything outside it. In the brief depictions of rushing crowds in the final scene, for example, the figures do not approach the camera so much as fill up the frame to overpower it. Their frenetic advance echoes the more formal address the *kurogo* earlier make to the lens, when one of them holds up for its examination the telltale letter Osan has sent to Koharu. Presenting something directly to the camera exposes its presence to the audience, diminishing its invisible omnipotence over the narrative.

DeBary's interpretation of this effect is perceptive, but it also reveals our mistaken expectations for photographic authority. '[T]heir exchange of letters is foregrounded visually and cinematographically, especially when Osan's letter to Koharu, in the hands of Magoemon [Jihei's brother], is made the subject of a zoom-in shot, which according to Shinoda's own theory of cinematic montage, produces it in an "other" temporality' (1993: 82). The 'other' temporality is produced not by a zoom-in shot, which does not occur and which would have asserted the command of the camera in its capacity to invade the space of the drama, but by the *kurogo* actor, who steps out of the space of the drama to present the letter to an immobilized camera. The temporal bounds are physically crossed when the *kurogo* takes the letter from Magoemon and holds it up to the lens, which then freezes the image. This action acknowledges the real-time presence of the camera and breaks the filmmaking taboo against violating naturalism. In a film about wrongdoing, the most serious sins *Double Suicide* depicts turn out to be its own transgressions against the sacred space of cinema.

As an added flourish to his anti-realist method, Shinoda negates the capacity of the film camera to reproduce movement by freezing the action at key intervals. Pictorial flatness is underscored by frozen images that anesthetize the camera and mark the three arcs of the plot. The first stilled image, noted above, is of the letter from the wife to the prostitute. The next is when Jihei throws his paper stock, his livelihood, in the air after his forced divorce from Osan. The final example is a series of four stills that depict Jihei stabbing Koharu through the throat.

Earlier in the film, frozen action, this time not by the camera but by the actors, tellingly surrounds Jihei's descent into passion, when he crosses the bridge to the entertainment quarter to visit Koharu once again. The musical passage that opened the film is repeated to become the theme of Jihei's erotic obsession. The bustle of the street is stilled in a tableau of townspeople turned manikins, and Jihei, isolated by his desire for Koharu, maneuvers through then and around then. Beautifully nude prostitutes, coldly posed, line Jihei's path. Lighted like marble statues, their bodies chill any impulse to see their perfect flesh as gratifying. Sex is depicted as subjugation to the female body, foregrounded in the figure of an exquisitely tattooed man, his back to the camera, squatting to make oral love to an indifferent nude. The graphic vibrancy of his tattoo is more voluptuous than his lovemaking, another stroke for the importance this film places on surface rather than substance. Jihei too will gratify Koharu orally in his worship of her body, his passion too emasculating for depiction as phallic conquest.

Desire is devoid of pleasure in *Double Suicide* in no less measure than it is empty of alien realism. The deflated eroticism of the film is integral to the flatness of its photographic structure. And as noted earlier, if cinematic realism is up for interrogation, then so is the modern ideology of gratification on which its circuitry of spectatorship is based. The film portrays passion as an addictive aberration. The confinement of sexual passion to the urban entertainment quarter in traditional Japan debilitates love; but just as debilitating is the modern limitation of sexual love to the definitions of commercial media. The challenge this film makes to the illusion of a world recreated in three dimensions is also a challenge to the illusion of sexual freedom offered by modernity. It is evident that by dying in violation of the law, Chikamatsu's characters submit to the very law they defy (deBary 1993: 81); but Shinoda implies more current relevance. The freedoms of the entertainment quarter, where the sex trade was confined, reinforced the structure of power that invented it no less than Hollywood sex reinforces the social codes it pretends to defy.

The subversion of codes returns us to *manga*, which, given its success since the early 1970s as a popular medium in multiple genres, has defied the authority of realism in designs *Double Suicide*, as a film, could only borrow inadvertently. Nonetheless, the closest resemblance to *manga* design occurs significantly at the turning point in the plot, when Osan, deciding to redeem Koharu for love of her husband, sees a vision of her. The prostitute's exquisite dress and coiffure in this image gently mock the domesticity of the woman who conjures her.[5] At this moment, *giri*, the social force at the heart of the conflict, is most strongly operative in the film. But it is not the law of patriarchy that morally binds these women; it is the promise of one human being to another in defiance of those laws.[6] One can imagine several ways this might have been portrayed, but Shinoda chose a double imagery that marks the screen as a two-dimensional design surface. Osan's profile and the standing figure of Koharu share the same plane in a way that only the *manga* page, with its contravention of physical space, dares duplicate in a popular modern medium.

Finally it is paper – the paper on which both *manga* and *ukiyo-e* are printed, the paper Jihei sells, the paper on which the source text is calligraphed, and the paper on which all the private promises and legal contracts binding the characters together are written – that draws together story, design, cinematic construction, and theme in *Double Suicide*. Shinoda could have chosen almost any *bunraku* play for this project, and there are many stories of love suicides, but he chose *Shinjū ten no amijima*, the one puppet play about people who are legally, romantically, and socially invested in 'putting it down on paper'. Koharu is bound by the paper contract that indentures her; Jihei is obligated by 29 written promises to redeem her; he is tethered to his wife's family by the business of paper; and lastly, Jihei is crushed by a paper document, a bill of divorcement.

Paper is the hallmark of the middle class and its mundane melodramas. In

Confucian thought, the merchant class is despised because of its reliance on legalistic paper agreements rather than on moral relationships. In an ideal Confucian world, rulers and ruled can exist without the artificial structures of the law; their interactions are mutually beneficial and based on moral character. The merchant class, whose existence is dependent solely on economic relations, is a necessary but unstable intervention in this hierarchy. This instability generates a system based on public contracts. For that reason the moral obligation sought and found in the private letter Osan writes to Koharu (so crucial it must be pushed at the camera) is fundamentally different from the legalistic agreements that surround it. Osan's written plea that Koharu not lead her husband to death and Koharu's determination to abide by it (even to the point of renouncing Jihei to a man she believes is a *samurai*) is the humanizing fulcrum of the film. Magoemon, Jihei's brother, notices that this one piece of paper is different from all the rest. He immediately recognizes it as a 'woman's letter' (*onna no fumi*), because it is written in *kana*, a woman's 'hand' or script. From ancient times a woman's hand (*onna-de*) has designated the category of the private, personal, poetic, and emotional, as opposed to the sinified writing of men, which categorizes the public, legal, and rational. The *onna-dōshi no giri* (the obligation of one woman to another), by which both Osan and Koharu feel they are bound, carries this same sense of *onna* (woman) as a designation for the private, non-legalistic realm. Koharu frantically insists to Magoemon, when he discovers the letter, that this one is her most important (*daiji na, daiji na*). It binds her to Osan in direct opposition to the legalisms of patriarchy by which the two women are forever separated by their oppositional roles in service to the male. In this single piece of paper and across its humble two dimensions the women map a private space on which they meet, if only briefly. No wonder Shinoda has a puppeteer hold *this* piece of paper up to the camera. If Osan and Koharu merely uphold the laws of patriarchy, Chikamatsu's play is pointless as drama.

Koharu's plea to Jihei that their bodies be found separately is her desperate attempt to fulfill her pledge to his wife. Jihei clumsily complies by brutally murdering her in a field before hanging himself some distance away. The ironic head-to-toe opposition of their corpses below the bridge in the final scene, unlike the side-by-side bodies Jihei earlier sees, reconstitutes them as graphic elements but also as precluded promise. The film ends with a reassertion of its images as pure two-dimensional design.

Double Suicide is about individuals trying to retrieve a private space, outside the realities of the law. Shinoda constructs the film as a similar retrieval – a recuperation of native vision in two dimensions, outside the foreign laws of realism.

Notes

1 For further reading on *manga*, see Schodt (1983) and Kinsella (2000).
2 Desser's (1988) interpretation, Bock's (1978), and McDonald's (1983) all converge powerfully on the black-hooded figure of the *kurogo* – the Japanese term referring to the manipulators of puppets and props, who are visible but clothed and hooded in

black, in the *bunraku* theater and in *kabuki*. The *kurogo* are linked by Bock and McDonald with 'fate', and by Desser with 'control' and 'insistence on assigned roles' (deBary 1993: 62).

3 For a discussion of *bunraku* aesthetics, the life of Chikamatsu, and a translation of the original play, see Keene (1964).

4 Awazu Kiyoshi designed the sets. 'In order to prevent the invasion of photographic reality, I had to make the *kurogo* omnipotent . . .' (Shinoda [1979: 19–20 – from 'The Cinematic Image Produces Space – Language'] – quoted in deBary (1993: 77)).

5 Every commentary on the film, including now this one, seems to note the fact that the director used his wife, Iwashita Shima, to play both Osan and Koharu, and many productive interpretations of the film have arisen from this observation. More importantly for our purposes, we should note that this inversion of the real (one woman playing two opposite parts) contributes to the subversion of cinematic naturalism. Many films use one actor to play multiple parts, but in this case the ploy is heuristic. We are not meant to admire the actor's skill as much as understand the existential embodiment of both passion and duty in a single person.

6 DeBary (1993: 82) sees this relationship as a reinforcement of patriarchy. 'Osan and Koharu repeatedly define their relationship as *onna-dōshi no giri* ("the duty of one woman toward another"), designating it as more than anything else a relationship produced and circumscribed through *giri* or the law'.

References

Bazin, André (1967) *What Is Cinema?*, vol. 1, trans. Hugh Gray, Berkeley: University of California Press.

Bock, Audie (1978) *Japanese Film Directors*, Tokyo and New York: Kōdansha International.

deBary, Brett (1993) 'Not Another Double Suicide: Gender, National Identity, and Repetition in Shinoda Masahiro's *Shinjūten no Amijima*', Iris, 16 (spring): 57–86.

Desser, David (1988) *Eros Plus Massacre: An Introduction to the Japanese New Wave Cinema*, Bloomington: Indiana University Press.

Keene, Donald (1964) *Four Major Plays of Chikamatsu*, New York: Columbia University Press.

Kinsella, Sharon (2000) *Adult Manga: Culture and Power in Contemporary Japanese Society*, Honolulu: University of Hawai'i Press.

McDonald, Keiko (1983) *Cinema East: A Critical Study of Major Japanese Films*, East Brunswick, NJ: Associated University Presses.

Schodt, Frederik, L. (1983) *Manga! Manga! The World of Japanese Comics*, Tokyo: Kōdansha International.

Shinoda Masahiro (1979) *Yami no naka no ansoku: Shinoda Masahiro hyōronshū* [*Repose in Darkness: Collected Critical Essays of Shinoda Masahiro*], Tokyo: Firumu Āto-sha.

Shinoda Masahiro Filmography

One-Way Ticket for Love (Koi no katamichi kippu, 1960)
Dry Lake [also known as *Youth in Fury*] *(Kawaita mizūmi, 1960)*
My Face Red in the Sunset (Yūhi ni akai ore no kao, 1961)
Shamisen and Motorcycle (Shamisen to ōtobai 1961)
Our Marriage (Waga koi no tabiji, 1961)
Glory on the Summit: Burning Youth (Yama no sanka: moyuru wakamono-tachi, 1962)
Tears on the Lion's Mane (Namida o shishi no tategami ni, 1962)

Pale Flower (*Kawaita hana*, 1963)

Assassination (*Ansatsu*, 1964)

With Beauty and Sorrow (*Utsukushisa to kanashimi to*, 1965)

Samurai Spy [also known as *Sarutobi*] (*Ibun Sarutobi Sasuke*, 1965)

Punishment Island [also known as *Captive's Island*] (*Shokei no shima*, 1966)

Clouds at Sunset (*Akanegumo*, 1967)

Double Suicide (*Shinjū ten no amijima*, 1969)

The Scandalous Adventures of Buraikan (*Buraikan*, 1970)

Silence (*Chinmoku*, 1971)

Sapporo Winter Olympic Games (*Sapporo orinpikku*, 1972)

The Petrified Forest (*Kaseki no mori*, 1973)

Himiko (*Himiko*, 1974)

Under the Cherry Blossoms (*Sakura no mori no mankai no shita*, 1975)

Ballad of Orin (*Hanare goze Orin*, 1977)

Demon Pond (*Yashagaike*, 1979)

Island of the Evil Spirit (*Akuryōtō*, 1981)

MacArthur's Children (*Setouchi shōnen yakyūdan*, 1984)

Allusion (*Tenshō-tan*, 1985)

Gonza the Spearman (*Yari no Gonza*, 1986)

The Dancer (*Maihime*, 1989)

Takeshi: Childhood Days (*Shōnen jidai*, 1990)

Sharaku (*Sharaku*, 1995)

Moonlight Serenade [also known as *Setouchi Moonlight Serenade*] (*Setouchi mūnraito serenāde*, 1997)

Owls' Castle (*Fukurō no shiro*, 1999)

Spy Sorge (2003)

16

TRANSGRESSION AND THE POLITICS OF PORN

Ōshima Nagisa's *In the Realm of the Senses* (1976)

Isolde Standish

The 28 May 1936 edition of the English language newspaper *The Japan Weekly Chronicle* reported the arrest of Abe Sada, who had been charged with the murder and 'mutilation' of Ishida Kichizō. The *Shūkan Asahi* elaborates: 'The arrest was made on Wednesday evening. In the morning the woman drank two bottles of *sake* and stayed in bed all day. She had with her the dagger she used to stab her victim' (*Shūkan Asahi Shōwa-shi* 1990: 152–3). No doubt protecting the sensibilities of its foreign readers, the *Japan Weekly Chronicle* failed to mention that Abe Sada also had in her possession the severed genitals of her former, now deceased, lover. During the course of the investigation leading up to her arrest, it was revealed that Sada and Kichi had spent a week of intense sexual activity ensconced in an upper room of a restaurant frequented by *geisha* and their clients. After killing Kichi and severing his genitals with a knife, Sada inscribed her name in blood on his limbs and the phrase 'Sada and Kichi together' (*Sada, Kichi futarikiri*) on his torso. The following morning, she left the room ordering a taxi. An hour later, she telephoned the restaurant explaining that Kichi had stomach cramps and was sleeping; he was to be woken at three that afternoon, at which time the body was discovered.

The 3 December 1936 edition of *The Japan Weekly Chronicle* returned to the story to report that, 'Only 150 tickets will be available to the public, and in addition 50 will be distributed among Government officials' (729). Such was the interest aroused by the court appearance of Abe Sada, the article continues, that:

> Applications for the latter have been pouring in and exceed by several times the number available . . . The news service makes the comment that interest in O-Sada's fate far exceeds that shown in the trials concerning the May 15 outbreak or the doings of the Blood Brotherhood. Rumours have been circulating that 'scalpers' are preparing to obtain tickets and offer them for sale at fancy prices. (729)

As a result of the reported orgiastic nature of her sexual relationship with her lover culminating in her act of murder and mutilation, Abe Sada achieved folk hero status within the popular imagination, a position she continued to hold well into the post-war period, her story forming the basis for at least three films including *A Woman Called Abe Sada* (*Jitsuroku Abe Sada*, Tanaka Noboru, 1975) and, more recently, *Sada* (Ōbayashi Nobuhiko, 1997) which won a prize at the 1998 Berlin Film Festival. However, the most famous is Ōshima Nagisa's 1976 version *In the Realm of the Senses* (*Ai no korīda* – hereafter *In the Realm*) which, filmed as 'hard-core', exploits the apparent excesses of desire through a series of fictional sexual encounters between the couple during the week of their confinement.

There are several reasons for the appeal to popular imagination of this crime story. First, as the article quoted above hints, it contrasts the private world of individual 'desire' with the political world of the military *coup d'état* prevalent throughout 1936, the week-long sexual 'orgy' representing the private counter-point to the public world of an intrusive hyper-militarist ideological position dominant at the time. This point is elaborated on in the 1975 Nikkatsu *romanporuno*[1] version, *A Woman Called Abe Sada* and the more recent, stylised *Sada*. Both versions purporting to be a 'true record' (*jitsuroku*) draw on imagery familiar to Japanese audiences of the failed military *coup d'état* of 26 February. This stylistic device not only gives the temporal setting a diegetic function, but also establishes the dichotomy between the 'private' and the 'public'; the 'public' providing a defining 'other' against which the 'pornotopia'[2] of the private world of Sada and Kichi is defined. In Ōshima's 1976 version, *In the Realm*, the temporal setting as an historical referent is only hinted at in a scene when Kichi passes a group of soldiers in the street and with the inclusion of motifs such as the 'rising sun' flag. However, the structuring opposition of 'private' and 'public', central to the Abe Sada narrative, is maintained through alternative narrative devices, such as the intrusion of maids and disapproving *geisha* into the private world of Sada and Kichi. These narrative devices, while marking the public/private thematic dichotomy, are more readily accessible to foreign audiences. The second, and perhaps more important, appeal to popular imagination of this incident lies in the fact that 'desire' is located in the female, in Abe Sada, the low ranking *geisha*/prostitute. The female, as active desiring subject, contrary to many Western pornography conventions, became a strong theme in the 1960s *pinku* (pink) soft-core genres.

In this chapter, I shall locate the Abe Sada narrative as recounted by Ōshima in *In the Realm* first from within the context of its production. I shall briefly trace the historical trajectory of the active female desiring subject from the post-war re-assertion of 'romance' in the 1950s through to the major studios' shift towards the *pinku* genres from the early 1960s, when the image of the 'prosti-tute' came to be equated with a sense of individual freedom achieved through her assumed sexual autonomy. Finally, I shall assess the impact of the film on Japanese debates on 'obscenity' (*waisetsu*). As Ōshima (1979) affirms in his writ-ing, *In the Realm* was from its first inception conceived as a transgressive film that, both through its production methods and through its content, would

Figure 20 The structuring opposition of private desire and the public gaze: *In the Realm of the Senses* (1976). Argos/Ōshima/The Kobal Collection.

challenge Japanese censorship laws and sensibilities. Through the controversy over the film in Japan and the trial that accompanied the publication, complete with illustrations of the screenplay, it made a major contribution to Japanese internal debates on what constituted 'obscenity' in the 1970s.

Transgression: A genealogy

Within early post-defeat Japanese films, 'romance', often set within the mise-en-scène of the Second World War, was used as a motif in which subjectivity was constructed out of heterosexual 'desire'. This was a point reinforced by SCAP (Supreme Commander, Allied Powers) directives to the film industry regarding the inclusion of kissing scenes in films (Hirano: 1992). Thus 'romance' became the vehicle which redressed the over-valuation, during the war period, of the sacrifice of the individual for the greater good of the group, the nation-state. This can be related back to such intellectuals as Sakaguchi Ango (1906–1955) who in his influential essay first published in April 1946, *Darakuron* [Discourse on Decadence], set out a philosophical dichotomy between the body (*nikutai*), representative of the individual, and the spirit (*seishin*). The 'spirit', during the latter stages of the war period, came to be equated with a hyper-militarist ideological position that was needed to maintain a situation of 'total-war'. In 'total-war', the individual was called upon to make great sacrifices – that is, to deny their own personal desires – for some abstract ideological entity defined as the innate spiritual essence of the

219

'family-state' (*kazoku kokka*). In the post-defeat period, the novelist Tamura Taijirō (1911–1983), elaborating on Sakaguchi Ango's philosophies, reasoned:

> All the established ideals have been deemed unworthy. The only things we can now place our trust in are our physical desires, our instincts; in short, we can only trust those things we have experienced ourselves through our own bodies. The only things that really exist are those desires that fill our bodies – the desire to eat when we feel hungry, to sleep when we are tired, the desire to be physically close to another.
>
> (Quoted in Slaymaker 2002: 92)

As I have argued elsewhere (Standish 2000), in 'national policy' films such as Tasaka Tomotaka's *Navy* (*Kaigun*, 1943) and Kinoshita Keisuke's *Army* (*Rikugun*, 1944), ideologies of the 'family-state' and the 'body-politic' (*kokutai*) were framed as a rite of passage, a 'spiritual' quest. The many remakes of *Miyamoto Musashi*[3] and Kurosawa Akira's 1943 film *Sugata Sanshirō* are also good examples of this tradition. The heroes must overcome their weaknesses, both physical and emotional, and attain some higher spiritual state. In both cases, the heroes' involvement with women and the temptations alluded to in the 'romance' sub-plots of the films are representative of the emotional weakness they must overcome. Women are thus the outward manifestation of the feminine side of the heroes' natures, which must be rejected as part of their 'rite of passage' to true manhood and success as warriors.

In the immediate aftermath of the war, as Sakaguchi Ango explains, these ideologies surrounding Japan's spiritual supremacy were exposed. The reality of Japan's defeat by American 'materialism' completely debunked them. This, combined with the public debates that grew out of the War Crimes Trials, and the introduction of concepts such as 'democracy' into Japanese life, led to a re-evaluation of the place of the individual in civil society. A quasi-concept of 'humanism' emerged as a derivative of Western philosophy. Transliterated in the *katakana* script to emphasise its sense of newness and foreignness, it became the 'buzzword' used to describe this human-centred world-view. In mainstream films heterosexual 'romance', as the expression of an individual's desire, became just one of the narrative manifestations of this world-view. As Foucault reminds us: 'If sex is repressed, that is, condemned to prohibition, non-existence, and silence, then the mere fact that one is speaking about it has the *appearance* of a deliberate transgression' (Foucault 1990: 6. My emphasis). One of the reasons for the popularity of the re-introduction of 'romance' in post-defeat films, such as Imai Tadashi's *Until the Day We Meet Again* (*Mata au hi made*, 1950) and the three-part *What is Your Name* (*Kimi no na wa*, Ōba Hideo, 1953–4) can be related to this sense of transgression through the assertion of individual 'desire'.

One of the important changes to come out of the post-war mainstream cinema's depiction of 'romance', and the more radical Tamura Taijirō-style novel, was the assertion of a female 'desiring' subject position, which had been totally denied in films produced in the post-1939 Film Law period. In the

1960s, Nikkatsu, in its attempts to lure back declining audiences, re-appropriated this female subject position in its soft-core pornographic genres. Two examples readily available in the West are Suzuki Seijun's films based on novels by Tamura Taijirō, *Gate of Flesh* (*Nikutai no mon*, 1964) and *Story of a Prostitute* (*Shunpū-den*, 1965). However, despite the centrality of female characters to these films, the new corporeal individuality expressed through carnal desire, just as with the 'romance' theme, was still framed within a political economy of masculine desire. Hence the recurrence of the same misogynistic themes and anxieties that were once played out in 'romance', in terms of the containment of women's sexuality within the institution of marriage and the constraints of child rearing. From the mid-1950s and the *taiyōzoku* ('sun-tribe') films, these same misogynistic themes and anxieties were allayed through physical violence, rape, coerced abortion and violent death.[4] Through these narrative devices, the authorial voice of masculine desire, channelled through heterosexual relations, remained dominant.

Some Japanese filmmakers, philosophers, intellectuals and artists, in the context of post-war re-industrialisation, sought to re-define individual subjectivity in terms of the primeval 'body' devoid of culture and, perhaps more importantly, the hyper-masculinist ideology that had been necessary to sustain 'total-war'. They sought the locus of the individual in desire expressed in the sexualised woman, the prostitute. However, despite this political use of the 'body' (*tai*) to counter the wartime over-determination of the 'spirit' (*seishin, yamato damashii*) in the ideologies of the 'body politic' (*kokutai*)[5], in these films the female body continued to be constructed as the emotional, the non-rational, and the hysterical; all aspects associated with the 'feminine'. Within this context, the sexualised female body sustains the very dichotomies that had underpinned the 'body politic' as the 'family state' (*kazoku kokka*) of the war period, and thus contributes to the ever-extending multifarious centres of power so central to Foucault's explications of the role of sexuality and the perverse in industrial society. In cinematic representations, these developments cannot be divorced from the changes taking place within the Japanese film industry in the 1960s. As box-office takings dwindled, studios sought ever-new sensational grounds to attract back audiences. Nikkatsu's forays into soft-core porn are clearly a factor that needs to be considered in the works of directors such as Suzuki Seijun. Also, as the television melodrama began to make inroads into Shōchiku's traditional female dominated audiences and as women found themselves increasingly isolated in the suburban apartment housing complexes (*danchi*), Shōchiku management was forced to reassess its policy. A result of which was the promotion of young assistant directors to full director status as a concerted attempt to cash in on the sensationalism that surrounded the *taiyōzoku* youth sub-culture. This new policy was instrumental in Ōshima's early rise to prominence as three of his 1960 productions – *Cruel Story of Youth* (*Seishun zankoku monogatari*), *The Sun's Burial* (*Taiyō no hakaba*), and *Night and Fog in Japan* (*Nihon no yoru to kiri*) – were constructed around the youth politics of the period.

The 1970s, Abe Sada and the politics of transgression

In the Realm should be considered on two levels; first, as a direct challenge to the censorship laws in Japan; and second, as a film in its own right. In the legal sense Ōshima challenged not only the infamous Japanese 'obscenity' law No. 175, but also, and perhaps more importantly, the symbolic structures of Japanese patriarchal authority. By depicting the male organ, Ōshima risked disrupting the correlation between the penis and its symbolic meaning as phallus. In terms of the film industry, Ōshima also saw the method of making *In the Realm* as ushering in a new system of filmmaking. By seeking foreign backing, importing film stock, shooting the film in Japan using Japanese actors and technicians and sending the undeveloped film abroad for processing and editing, Ōshima saw this as a potential revolutionary system of filmmaking that would free directors from the rigidities of the studio system and the constraints of censorship laws at one stroke. As Ōshima explains:

> In the world, restrictions on sexual expression in Japan are matchless. Excellent films by directors such as Wakamatsu Kōji and Kumashiro Tatsumi are not accepted sufficiently in the film world because of, for example, the need to hide pubic hair and the restrictions on sexual expression. I thought I would utilize a joint production to investigate to the limits the possibilities of sexual expression.
>
> (Ōshima 1979: 173)

The court case that began in Tokyo in 1977 surrounding the publication of the screenplay of *In the Realm*, complete with stills from the film, was one of several prominent cases of the 1970s relating to cinema and 'obscenity'. The defence in the earlier cases shifted internal Japanese debates on the question of 'obscenity' from the argument, 'because it is a work of art, it is not obscene' to 'why is obscene material bad?' The former position had been argued in two earlier landmark cases. The first ruling was in 1957 and based on the translation and publication of D.H. Lawrence's novel *Lady Chatterley's Lover*. This went against the defendants (the publisher and the translator) who were unanimously found guilty as charged. In the second ruling in 1969 on the de Sade case, the court acquitted the accused 'on grounds that the brutality and ugliness of de Sade's work militated against "wanton appeal to sexual passion", a requirement for a finding of obscenity' (Campbell and Noble 1993: 280). The ruling in June 1978 on the Nikkatsu *romanporuno* cases, upheld in the appeal ruling of 1980, as Matsushima points out, was a landmark change in the way 'obscenity' was viewed by the courts:

> The *romanporuno* case ruling, handed down at the Tokyo Court in June 1978, was a unanimous 'not guilty'. It stated that '[o]n the question of the permissibility of the depiction of suggestive images of genitalia and sexual acts, socially acceptable ideas change with the times'. With regard to the four films under indictment[6] '[t]he images are audacious

and open (*rokotsu*), but not to the extent that they give a feeling of indecency or a sense of sexual shame, when viewed from today's socially acceptable ideas, they do not constitute obscenity'.

(Matsushima 2000: 131)

Writing in the introduction to the complete Ōshima trial transcripts, Uchida argues that the Ōshima case, following on from the earlier Nikkatsu studio's *romanporuno* cases, broadened the debate to include:

[a]n investigation into the substance of 'obscenity' as a concept intro-duced into Japan from Europe during the period of Japan's moderniza-tion of the legal system under Meiji. When viewed historically from Japan's folk history, it is clear that, as a social more, it is incongruous and an unnatural type of crime.

(Uchida 1980: 2)

As such, it is a vestige from the Meiji Constitution which, as was argued, is in contravention to the clauses protecting freedom of expression under the post-war Constitution. Ōshima himself, locating the concept of 'obscenity' firmly within the cultural, argues in his preface to the screenplay that pornography exists in the imagination: '*In the Realm of the Senses* became the perfect porno-graphic film in Japan because it cannot be seen there. Its existence is porno-graphic – regardless of its content. Once it is seen, *In the Realm of the Senses* may no longer be a pornographic film . . .' (Ōshima 1992: 253). He continues: 'I daresay that internalized taboos make for the experience of "obscenity". Children, on the other hand, don't feel that anything they see is "obscene" ' (261). It was these culturally specific 'internalized taboos' that the film's con-tent, filmed as 'hard-core', attempted to challenge in order to bring Japanese censorship laws into line with international standards.

As Lehman (1993: 169–95) points out, *In the Realm* does not conform to conventions established in Western hard-core pornography as identified by Linda Williams in her seminal study *Hard Core* (1991). There are no 'money shots' in the conventional sense, the hero suffers a post-mortem castration and, perhaps most importantly, the flaccid penis is visible. As Lehman explains:

In one scene Oshima emphasizes a different view of the penis than that commonly found in hard-core. We see several close-up shots of the unerect penis of an old man who is first taunted in the street by women and a child after a child exposes him and who tries to have sex with one of the women [Sada] but, due to impotence, fails. In addition to being 'impressive', penises in hard-core are always erect or become so in moments . . . The close-up of the old man's flaccid penis after the woman has tried to arouse him is far removed from the spectacle of the phallicly powerful penis that dominates hard-core.

(Lehman 1993: 176–8)

However, despite its transgressive credentials, and this non-conformity with Western conventions, *In the Realm* is still a film supportive of a phallo-centric world view. Although Sada is clearly positioned as an active desiring subject, as with her counterparts in Western hard/soft-core pornography, her desire is structured to overvalue the penis as the sole source of her pleasure. In much the same way, Ibuki in *Gate of Flesh* and the adjutant in *Story of a Prostitute* metaphorically represent the phallus as the site of female desire/pleasure. In *In the Realm* this point is made even more obvious when, just before the scene with the old man described above, we are first introduced to Sada as she rejects the lesbian advances of a female colleague who then takes her to watch Kichi and his wife engaged in sex. As the structuring of this sequence of nine reverse-cut shots clearly locates Sada and her female companion as the active voyeurs who mediate the spectators' gaze, and Kichi as the object of their gaze, it is worth considering in some detail.

1   Medium close-up of the first *geisha*'s face partly obscured as she looks from the courtyard veranda through the small vertical opening of the dark wooden sliding door.

2   Cut to interior shot of Kichi's wife dressing him in his *fundoshi* (loincloth-style) underwear. He is standing impassively and she is positioned kneeling in front of him. The camera then cuts to a medium close-up low-angle shot of Kichi's upper naked torso and face, thus clearly identifying him and not his wife as the object of the woman's interest.

3   Cut back to a medium close-up shot of the first *geisha*'s face, her eyes tilted upward, thus linking the angle of the previous shot back to the direction of her gaze.

4   Cut to interior. Medium close-up of Kichi's wife still positioned screen left kneeling in front of Kichi, her face pressing in against his lower stomach as she attempts to tie his *fundoshi* at his back. As she adjusts the fabric around his upper left thigh, the camera pans down as she lowers her head to the level of his penis (which is not in view). She then, clearly aroused by her proximity to his penis, instigates sexual activity by slipping her hand under the still untied frontal flap of his *fundoshi*.

5   Cut back to the door, only now Sada is also positioned as viewing subject. She occupies the primary viewing position formerly occupied by her companion who is now positioned slightly above Sada, her head turned away from the camera as she explains, 'Each morning it is like this. Afterwards he goes to the market'. Following this dialogue she turns again to observe the interior action.

6   Cut to medium close-up of Kichi and his wife as Kichi stimulates her with his hand. She falls backwards to the floor, and as he bears down on her they both disappear out of the bottom of the frame.

7   Cut back to the two women's faces watching.

8   Cut to a medium close-up of the couple copulating on the floor. The camera pans quickly left along the line of their bodies, coming to rest on Kichi's buttocks as he thrusts, at which point his wife lowers her right leg to the

floor to allow the camera an unimpeded view of the movement of Kichi's penis in and out of the vagina. This shot both confirms the penis as the focus of the watching women's interest and establishes the 'hard-core' nature of the film.

9   Cut back to the two women. The camera is centred on a reaction shot of Sada as her head moves in small rhythmical movements in time with Kichi's thrusting motion. In this shot Sada is positioned in the centre left of the screen, her companion's face is partially obscured. Sada is thus defined as the central protagonist.

The camera then cuts to an exterior high-angle daytime shot of a group of *geisha* crossing a bridge and since Sada is among them this signifies a time ellipsis. This next sequence involving the old man again focuses the spectator's attention on Sada's interest in the penis through a reverse-cut shot sequence. As some children expose him, there follows a cut to a close-up of Sada's face actively looking; this is then followed by a medium close-up from Sada's point-of-view of his exposed flaccid penis. Her interested 'gaze' is given greater poignancy when contrasted with the reaction of the other women who recoil in mock horror. There then follows a series of shots built around Kichi's observations of, and his growing desire for Sada, beginning with his first encounter with her as she threatens a senior *geisha*/prostitute with a knife and culminating in a series of furtive attempts at consummation in the confines of his establishment. Within Japanese pornographic conventions, established in *pinku* films in the early 1960s and refined by Nikkatsu in the *romanporuno* genre of the early 1970s, Sada's behaviour and position as desiring subject, and Kichi's position as desired object, are not unusual. In fact, Ōshima's 1976 version is a close remake of *A Woman Called Abe Sada*, which also clearly locates the relationship between the two in terms of Sada desiring subject, and Kichi desired object.[7]

What is different between Western and Japanese pornography conventions of the 1970s is the locus of male pleasure. Ōshima clearly locates this pleasure in the woman's active desiring position within the film. If we take Ōshima at his word, men want women to desire them. As he explains, when he states that, with regard to the castration scene in *In the Realm*:

> I would like for that film and that incident not to be viewed in terms of a general kind of symbolism about castration, because the importance of it is that the incident actually took place and entered popular con-sciousness. *But once again, I think that is how men would want a woman to feel, and they don't think of that act in terms of pain or something like that.*
> (Quoted in Lehman 1980: 58. Emphasis in original)

When understood from within the context of a society that has traditionally favoured arranged marriages and placed the emphasis on the parent/child relationship over and above that of the husband/wife couple, this could also be taken as a plea for a greater emotional bonding between partners. Just as in Western pornography, the Japanese positioning of female desire is clearly from within a male-centric vision, it is just a different vision.[8] Williams' explication of the S/M theme of the film reinforces this:

> Sada's goal is to effect an impossible merger with/engulfment of her lover through mutually agreed upon strategies that cannot be reduced to fixed positions of domination or submission. This, I think, is the meaning of the final castration: it is not so much an emasculation (in the sense of what Kichi loses) as a fantastic and utterly perverse image of what the mythic sadomasochistic couple, 'Sada/Kichi together', gains. And this gain does not at all subvert the power of the phallus; rather, it moves it around, manipulating its dominance between the two poles of the couple.
>
> (Williams 1991: 222)

By the act of castration, Sada is acknowledging her 'lack' and fully accepting her deficiency and dependence on men. This is confirmed by the voice-over narration that concludes the film, stating the circumstances of Sada's arrest and adding that she had hidden in her clothing the severed genitals of her dead lover, and that she had a strange look of happiness on her face at the time of her arrest. It also explains why the actual Abe Sada received a relatively light prison sentence of six years and not the death penalty as so many of her 'feminist' compatriots did at this time (Hane 1993).

When taken from within the context both of Japanese 'obscenity' laws and of Japanese pornography conventions of the time, Sada's position as active desiring agent and Kichi's as desired object provide no conflict. What I would suggest did upset the censors' sensibilities was the display of Kichi's more than average size penis and the numerous shots of it in its flaccid state. These scenes become transgressive in that they open up fissures between the reality of the physical organ and its symbolic function within a patriarchal society. In this sense, if we elaborate on, and extend, Sakaguchi Ango's position, the ideology is exposed and some sort of 'humanity' is discovered in the naked carnal bodies of Sada and Kichi. Japanese censorship laws have constantly permitted the most grotesque caricatures of oversized penises to be displayed in everything from *manga* and *anime* to wood-block prints and *sake* cups decorated with copulating couples, but, until very recently, they have placed a total ban on the depiction of even pubic hair. In this sense the laws still uphold, not public decency as purported, but rather the symbolic phallus through prohibitions on the disclosure of the naked organ.

Notes

1 *Roman poruno* (romance pornographic) as a term had been coined by Japanese film reviewers and critics writing in the 1960s to make a distinction between *pinku* (pink) films deemed to have some artistic merit and those to be classified purely as low level 'soft-core' pornography. In the early 1970s when Nikkatsu decided to change their production policy towards the production of erotic films, they co-opted the term *roman poruno* to define their studio-based genre and, to distinguish this term from

earlier usage, they joined the two words together to form the one word *romanporuno* (Matsushima 2000).

2 'Pornotopia', a term used by Williams (1991: 160–4), refers to a 'separated utopia' in which escape from the 'real' world is offered as a temporary relief.

3 The novel *Miyamoto Musashi* written by Yoshikawa Eiji (1892–1962) was first published in serial form in 1935–9. It has been filmed many times. The two most famous examples are the two trilogies directed by Inagaki Hiroshi, the first in 1940 and the second version in 1954–6. The 1940 version was confiscated by the Occupation authorities, but the 1950s version is still available with English subtitles and was released on video with the titles *The Samurai Trilogy I: Miyamoto Musashi, The Samurai Trilogy II: Duel at Ichijoji Temple* and *The Samurai Trilogy III: Duel at Ganryu Island*.

4 The two main *taiyōzoku* films, both of which starred Ishihara Yūjirō, were *Season of the Sun* (*Taiyō no kisetsu*, Furukawa Takumi, 1956) and *Crazed Fruit* (*Kurutta kajitsu*, Nakahira Kō, 1956).

5 The Chinese character (*kanji*) *tai* used to refer to the physical 'body' is the same as that used in the compound *kokutai* referring to the 'body politic'.

6 The four films referred to, all released in 1972, were *High School Geisha* (*Jokōsei geisha*, Umezawa Kaoru), *The Porn Diary of an Office Lady: The Odour of a Female Cat* (*OL poruno nikki: mesuneko no nioi*, Fujii Katsuhiko), *Love Hunter* (*Rabuhantā: koi no karyūdo*, Yamaguchi Seiichirō) and *Loves Warmth* (*Ai no nukumori*, Kondō Yukihiko).

7 Another example, this time from the 1970s and also dealing with prostitutes, is the Nikkatsu production *Streets of Joy* (*Akasen Tamanoi nukeraremasu*, 1974), directed by the master of the *romanporuno* genre, Kumashiro Tatsumi.

8 Ussher defines the function of pornography for Western men in the following terms: 'Like other forms of representation constructed within the masculine gaze, pornography acts to deny or alleviate temporarily men's sexual anxiety through identification with phallic mastery. It counters man's underlying fear of woman – his fear of not being good enough, or hard enough, both literally and metaphorically. A fear of the devouring, consuming "woman", with her apparently insatiable sexuality; of being rejected, laughed at. In heterosexual pornography, where "man" is positioned as active subject and "woman" as responsive object, she becomes not a person, but a hole to be penetrated. The symbolic representation of "woman" in porn acts to denigrate her, to dismiss her and to annihilate her power. She is fetishised in the most obvious manner – split into part object (breast, vagina, mouth) rather than whole object – and the fears she provokes in man (castration, not being big enough, of not being "man") are contained' (Ussher 1997: 197).

References

Campbell Alan and Noble, David S. (eds) (1993) *Japan: An Illustrated Encyclopedia*, Tokyo: Kōdansha.

Foucault, Michel (1990) *The History of Sexuality: Volume 1 An Introduction*, London: Penguin Books.

Hane, Mikiso (1993) *Reflections on the Way to the Gallows: Rebel Women in Prewar Japan*, Berkeley and Los Angeles: University of California Press.

Hirano, Kyoko (1992) *Mr Smith Goes to Tokyo: Japanese Cinema under the American Occupation, 1945–1952*, Washington and London: Smithsonian Institution Press.

Lehman, Peter (1980) 'The Act of Making Films: An Interview with Oshima Nagisa', *Wide Angle* 4 (2): 56–61.

—— (1993) *Running Scared: Masculinity and the Representation of the Male Body*, Philadelphia: Temple University Press.

Matsushima, Toshiyuki (2000) *Nikkatsu romanporuno zenshi: meisaku, meiyū meikantokutachi*, Tokyo: Kōdansha.

Ōshima, Nagisa (1972) *Waga Nihon seishin kaizō keikaku*, Tokyo: Sanpō.

—— (1979) *Ai no korīda*, Tokyo: San'ichi Shobō.

—— (1992) *Cinema Censorship and the State: the Writings of Nagisa Oshima.* (Edited by Annette Michelson and translated by Dawn Lawson.) Cambridge, MA: The MIT Press.

Sakaguchi, Ango (1998 [1946]) '*Darakuron*' [Discourse on Decadence], in *Sakaguchi Ango zenshū* vol. 4, Tokyo: Chikuma Shobō. [Also translated in the *Review of Japanese Culture and Society* 1 (1): 1–5.]

Shūkan Asahi Shōwa-shi Vol I: jiken, jinbutsu, sesō shonen – 10-nendai (1990), Tokyo: Asahi Shinbun-sha.

Slaymaker, Doug (2002) 'When Sartre Was an Erotic Writer: Body, Nation and Existentialism in Japan after the Asia-Pacific War', *Japan Forum* 14 (1): 78–101.

Standish, Isolde (2000) *Myth and Masculinity in the Japanese Cinema: Towards a Political Reading of the Tragic Hero*, Richmond, Surrey: Routledge/Curzon.

Uchida, Takehiro (1980) *Ai no korīda saiban: zen kiroku*, vol. 1, Tokyo: Shakai Hyōron-sha.

—— (1981) *Ai no korīda saiban: zen kiroku*, vol. 2, Tokyo: Shakai Hyōron-sha.

Ussher, Jane M. (1997) *Fantasies of Femininity: Reframing the Boundaries of Sex*, London: Penguin Books.

Williams, Linda (1991) *Hard Core: Power, Pleasure, and the 'Frenzy of the Visible'*, London: Pandora.

Ōshima Nagisa Filmography

See Chapter 12, on *Cruel Story of Youth*, for a full filmography.

17

UNSETTLED VISIONS

Imamura Shōhei's *Vengeance is Mine* (1979)

Alastair Phillips

Imamura Shōhei once said to the poet Sugiyama Heiichi that he wanted to 'make messy, really human, Japanese, unsettling films' (quoted in Richie 1997: 31). His obsessive and visually intricate explorations of what he has termed 'the relationship of the lower part of the human body and the lower part of the social structure on which the reality of daily Japanese life supports itself' (17) certainly propose a provocative association between the unreliable nature of ordinary cinematic representation and the insecurities behind conventional Japanese social organisation. This chapter will argue that the distinctively interwoven relationship between the visual and the social in Imamura's cinema is especially evident in the case of one of his greatest commercial successes, *Vengeance is Mine* (*Fukushū suru wa ware ni ari*, 1979 – hereafter *Vengeance*).

Vengeance, which came at an important turning point in the director's career, may at first glance seem simply to be a retrospective investigative drama about a notorious Japanese serial killer during the 1960s, but the fluctuating geography of the film's narration, as well as its unsettling non-chronological structure, point to a particular concern with temporal and spatial fluidity. This interest in the instability of visual and social surfaces, characterised also by the constantly shifting identity of the murderous protagonist, may be seen as a central component of the wider disturbing claims about Japanese national history and culture that Imamura engages with so compellingly in this key film of the 1970s.

Imamura himself has played a leading role in the shifting fortunes of the Japanese film industry from the beginning of his career as an assistant director to Ozu Yasujirō on such films as *Tokyo Story* (*Tōkyō monogatari*, 1953) up to, most recently, his work on the Japanese related segment of the international compilation film, *11'09'01 – September 11* (UK/France/Egypt/Japan/Mexico/USA/Iran, 2002). After writing and directing several plays while at Waseda University in Tokyo, Imamura passed an examination to join Shōchiku studios as an assistant in 1951. There, along with Ozu, he also collaborated with the likes of Kobayashi Masaki and Nomura Yoshitarō. Imamura soon distanced himself from Ozu's rigid screen direction and precise framing of actors preferring to

Figure 21 The unreliable nature of cinematic representation and the insecurities behind Japanese social organization: *Vengeance is Mine* (1979). BFI Stills, Posters and Designs.

work with the satirical comic director Kawashima Yūzō with whom he moved to Nikkatsu in 1955. He later published a critical biography of his mentor, *Sayonara dake ga jinsei-da* [*Life is But Farewell*] (1969) – a title which resonates strikingly with the concerns of *Vengeance* (Imamura 1997b: 145–7).

What Imamura saw as Kawashima's deep aversion to authority and hypocrisy is certainly visible in his early work such as *Stolen Desire* (*Nusumareta yokujō*, 1958) – his debut film – and *Pigs and Battleships* (*Buta to gunkan*, 1961). With *The Insect Woman* (*Nippon konchūki*, 1963) the director also began to elaborate on his favoured depiction of the vital and tenacious 'Imamura woman' embodied in *Vengeance* by Kiyokawa Nijiko who plays the mother of the innkeeper, Asano Haru (Ogawa Mayumi). Imamura's interest in unearthing the more irrational elements repressed in conventional modern-day Japan has been a dominant theme in his subsequent filmography. It has also led to an ongoing investigation of the relationship between documentary and fictional film practice that is strongly visible in *Vengeance* along with a keen interest in the observational ethics underlying the ethnographic impulse. His radical investigative film, *A Man Vanishes* (*Ningen jōhatsu*, 1967), for example, explicitly drew attention to the artifice behind the conventions of Japanese social representation, and the revealing literal translation of his 1966 film, *Jinruigaku nyūmon*, known in English as *The Pornographers*, is 'An Introduction to Anthropology'. As Imamura himself says, 'In my work people take centre stage . . . There are no shots which do not contain human action . . . I want to capture the smallest action, the finest nuance, the most intimate psychological expression because filmmakers must concern themselves with more than facades' (Imamura 1997a: 125–6).

Vengeance represented Imamura's return to the dramatic form at a time when his own career was in flux. During much of the 1970s, Imamura had renounced fiction altogether, partly as a result of the financial losses suffered by Nikkatsu after *The Profound Desire of the Gods* (*Kamigami no fukai yokubō*, 1968) and partly from his professed frustration with working with actors, a turn towards television documentary production and his involvement in the foundation of the Yokohama Academy of Broadcasting and Film in 1975. (Now called the Japan Academy of Visual Arts and based in Kawasaki, the school's graduates include Miike Takashi.) Although other directors such as Fukasaku Kinji had originally wanted to tackle the property, *Vengeance* eventually led to the reunion between Imamura and Shōchiku. The studio was by now, of course, much changed in comparison to the more structured production regime of the 1950s.

The film was based on the best-selling prize-winning novel by Saki Ryūzō that fictionalised the real-life story of the serial killer Nishiguchi Akira which had gripped Japan during the latter part of 1963. Born, unusually, into a Catholic family in the hot spring resort of Beppu in Northern Kyūshū, Nishiguchi had killed an employee of Japan's nationalised tobacco company and his driver in October that year, then stolen money and travelled as far north as Hokkaidō in disguise while often swindling further funds. He subsequently killed a mother and daughter in an inn in Hamamatsu before murdering an elderly lawyer in Tokyo. The killer was finally apprehended, but only after his face had featured on more than half a million 'wanted posters' around the nation. He was hanged in 1970.

Saki had converted Nishiguchi's name to Enokizu Iwao. Although his book had been written after careful research using classified police files, Imamura went further and uncovered new documentary elements worthy of dramatic development. In a manner typical of much of his practice, he also worked in an intensive collaborative fashion during the gestation of the final shooting script. Ikehata Shunsaku was employed as an assistant to the main scriptwriter, Baba Masaru, and all three worked on an initial temporal structure before Baba and Ikehata wrote the first draft, followed by a second written only by Imamura, a third set of further revisions between Baba and Imamura and then a definitive fourth version devised solely by the director.

This high degree of preparation relates to the fact that Imamura rarely changes his scripts during rehearsals and shooting. By this stage, he prefers to concentrate instead on the visuals, especially in relation to the direction of actors and the construction of spatial relations within the screen frame. Individual scenes are therefore first closely plotted with his cast. This is usually an arduous process. Ken Ogata, who plays Enokizu in *Vengeance*, recalls, for instance, that 'in the course of producing a scene [in the film], and to further pursue the latent power required to make the scene all the more strongly appealing, every actor and staff [member was] required to be physically and mentally tough, stubborn and [perseverant]' ('Imamura Shōhei Home Page'). According to Imamura's long-standing colleague Kitamura Kazuo, who plays the former husband of Asano Haru (Ogawa Mayumi) in the film, the director also spends a lot of time getting the measure of the specific district in which he shoots. The acute sense of place in *Vengeance* is certainly vital to the film's distinctive emotional timbre as well as its obvious concern with the representation of regional and national identity. In another example of his collaborative method, Imamura then works closely on image construction with his Director of Photography – on *Vengeance* he devised the framings with his long-standing cinematographer Himeda Shinsaku – before filming using a high shooting ratio. This relates to the extended period usually required by Imamura for editing, something especially important in this film in particular given its intricate mosaic of different, but also inter-related, temporalities and locations.

Vengeance can thus, in fact, be seen as a carefully designed production despite Imamura's professed predilection for 'messy' cinema. It begins with a forlorn high-angle long shot of a police cavalcade driving through the mountains in the sleet. A sequence of yellow lights indicates the progression of the cars across the empty wintry terrain and the camera pans slowly to the right to keep them in view. This isolation of a single colour element – it is frequently yellow – is a recurring aspect of the overall design of the film's mise-en-scène. We cut dramatically to a low-angle close-up at a bend in the road which takes in just the headlights and radiator grilles of the passing vehicles before cutting again to a full-frame windscreen shot taken from outside the car which, we soon learn, contains Enokizu and the police officers who have arrested him. This is not yet obvious, however, and the fact that the camera gazes through the glass for some time heightens a sense of the scrutiny of a secondary visual surface within the texture of the film that is demonstrably resistant to clear explanation.

In just three stages, therefore, Imamura and his collaborators have established a particular regime of looking which will be emblematic of the film as a whole. Yann Lardeau has argued that the blurring of documentary and fictional film practice in Imamura's work can best be characterised 'not by the cinematographic material that is utilized, but by the quality of the look' (Lardeau 1982: 48). What does this look consist of here? First, there is a sense of detachment which is evoked by the issue of reduced vision. Second, there is a play between distance and proximity and then, finally, especially when we actually move inside the car, there is an inter-relationship of internal and external fields of observation. It is this shift between either *hikisoto* (from the outside) or *hikiuchi* (from the inside) that Imamura has suggested to Donald Richie is a key characteristic of his general cinematic principles. 'A lot of the decision depends upon the way the set is made, but a lot of it is psychological as well', he says. 'I always have to think of who is seeing this, who is doing the viewing. And putting the camera outside and letting it peer in gives a kind of intimacy that no other shot can' (quoted in Richie 1997: 40–1).

There is thus a particular kind of observational intimacy in *Vengeance*, but it is one that frequently leaves the spectator troubled by the lack of any core explanation for the guiding actions of the protagonist. Imamura has said that he wanted to make a film about a man with no *kokoro* (heart/self). Referring to the film's fictionalised portrayal of Nishiguchi Akira, he has argued that 'I think I can here see the lonely inner state of today's man' (quoted in Richie 1997: 19). It is certainly tempting to read this loneliness in terms of the circulation of the currencies of money and sexuality which permeate Enokizu's relationships with other characters, but as we have already begun to observe, there is perhaps a more fundamental aspect to the tensions hinted at within Imamura's existential position. Dennis Washburn has suggested that the film's 'aesthetic representation of violence as an expression of [Enokizu's] desire at once rejects the modern and inscribes its aims and desires'. In other words, 'it serves as a critique of modern culture and yet is deeply implicated in it' (Washburn 2001: 319). If we now consider the relationship between the unstable temporal and spatial visual surfaces in the film more closely, we may therefore see how Imamura's film seems to relate the investigation of Enokizu's actions and character to wider concerns about Japanese society and national identity.

The fragmented temporal structure of *Vengeance* offers one dimension of the ways in which the film opens up a discussion about the implications of the protagonist's trajectory. As Serge Daney (1998) has carefully observed, the narrative presents three distinctive temporalities. First, there is the re-presentation of the various criminal acts committed by Nishiguchi and then adapted as the basis of Saki's original novelisation. We may take this one stage further and observe another layering of intervention: that of Imamura and his collaborators. Second, there is the presentation of the police investigation as they close in on their object of scrutiny. This is a key aspect of the narration, for along with the recurring use of temporal markers indicated by the subtitles, it provides an anchor for the spectator from which to adjudicate the implications of the relationships between Enokizu's family past and recent present. Then third, and perhaps most devastatingly, Imamura also shows us the present itself with the fact of the murderer's capture and punishment removing any sense of the future. Instead, we are ordered to remain in the here and now as we watch, in the film's final frames, time itself being frozen in front of our eyes.

This reordering of the reliability of the film's temporal surface is frequently accompanied by two distinctive tropes. Sometimes Imamura cuts into the carefully woven structure of the film unexpectedly to suggest an alliance between the past and the present such as in the scenes which interlink the family home at Beppu and the Asano Inn. Elsewhere, the film moves dramatically from one time continuum to another with the dramatic intervention of explanatory titles serving to orientate the spectator. This can be observed in the sequence following the violent confrontation between Enokizu and his father (Mikuni Rentarō) after his release from prison. The film shifts to a close-up of the wheels of a train moving through a mountainscape and, along with a dramatic surge of music, we read from the tickertape-like titles that Enokizu appeared at a restaurant in Okayama on 26 October and then, without any shift in screen space, that he committed fraud in Hiroshima on 18 November. We cut into the carriage of the same train to see Enokizu himself looking carefully at a newspaper. It is now a different date. From the window we next see a townscape and on the soundtrack a guard announces the arrival of the train at Hamamatsu. This layering of four different temporalities onto three successive shots hints at more than just the complexities of unravelling the protagonist's individual journey. It also suggests, through its emphasis on travel and geography, a way of situating Enokizu in relation to the material fabric of Japan through cinematic means.

We may develop this notion by considering a further bi-focalisation of temporality not mentioned in Daney's original analysis. *Vengeance* is also a film about looking at the events of 1964 (and further back) from the different perspective of 1979. Imamura, like many of his colleagues in the Japanese film industry, would have experienced 1964 as a year of instability with the ongoing decline of several of the studios being marked by a decision no longer to employ mentored assistants, by studio salaried actors being increasingly in demand from the rival medium, television, and by studio technicians being increasingly subject to short-term contracts. It was also, of course, the year of the Tokyo Olympics – mentioned in the film – which alongside its organisational achievement was also recognised as being an emblematic symbol of Japan's successful economic recuperation after the Second World War. The decision to hold such a vast global event in post-war Japan was marked by huge, if vastly uneven, investment in the infrastructure of the nation with the opening of the *shinkansen* (new trunk line) between Tokyo and Ōsaka, as well as a new network of motorways, suggesting a transformation of the distances between previously separate regions of the Japanese archipelago. Imamura's film is set on the cusp of this period of rapid development and in its own journeying around the nation it seems to call into question the surface ideological rhetoric of national change and unity. *Vengeance* thus becomes a film about those unlikely to be rewarded with the promises of modernity from the perspective of someone looking back several years later.

According to national statistics, Japanese middle-class consciousness rose from 56 per cent in 1965 to 77 per cent in 1975 (Gordon 2003: 268) and its GDP was increasing at a rate of 10 per cent per annum between 1950 and 1973 (245–6), the year before the 'oil shock' of 1974. Knowing this outcome, and thus deliberately deciding to make a film set in milieux of the period which clearly obviate these optimistic scenarios, it is reasonable to assume that Imamura is indirectly calling into question the fruits of social change by asking for whom these benefits are available and thus, also, who is left behind. In the telling scene between Enokizu and Haru's mother set in a forlorn eel hatchery just after the couple have visited a lower-class urban race gathering, the watery landscape becomes a metaphor both for the unstable elements in their personal relationship (she fears he intends to kill her) and for the shifting currents of the social world that surrounds them. After gazing at a single eel trapped against a twig, Haru's mother comments, 'the outside world has changed', followed by Enokizu's remark that 'it sure has. It gets worse every day'. The shot of teeming constrained eels in a subsequent image suggests the same kind of unnatural entrapment hinted at by their unsettling conversation.

This sense of the dilution of the natural order relates to another means of uncovering the period between 1979 and 1964. As Marilyn Ivy has argued, the years between 1965 and 1975 were marked particularly by 'an accelerating destruction of both the environment and older lifeways [in Japan] as the increasing concentration of power, people and capital in the cities left many rural areas depopulated' (Ivy 1995: 100). One of the consequences of this, over the course of the temporal gap between the year in which *Vengeance* was set and the year in which it was made, was a rise in popular interest in the folkloric elements within traditional Japanese culture, especially concerning the construction of identity in relation to natural place. This was the period when, as Ivy has noted, 'new folklore societies and journals were formed throughout Japan as the ethno-documentary impulse merged with the touristic one' (59). Thus we see a revival of interest in the cultural anthropologist and folk literature scholar Yanagita Kunio (1875–1962) whose ethnographic portrait of a traditional Japanese community, *Tōno monogatari* [*Tales of Tono*], was much admired by Imamura. With its conjugation of unspoilt and developed landscapes, pure and impure waterways and visible traces of sacred rituals (such as the sight of pilgrims on the mountaintop at the end of the film), it is possible to view *Vengeance*'s representation of the natural world in the light of these concerns. Knowing the after-effects of Japan's rapid modernisation, such as the trail of pollution scandals during the late 1960s and 1970s and the continuing rise in the density of the nation's urban sprawl by the end of the decade, it is as if Imamura is looking back with hindsight in order to highlight the fissures and losses already coming into view within the main temporal framework of the film.

In Ivy's extensive analysis of popular concern with Japanese tradition and questions of estrangement from nature during the 1970s, she examines the mass publicity campaign launched by Japan National Railway exhorting an especially young female demographic constituency to 'Discover Japan'. In its recurring use of the representational trope of the journey, *Vengeance* can also be read as a spatial text in a number of ways. First, there is the obvious emphasis on the visual construction of nationhood visible in the film's treatment of landscape. Imamura's film provides a cognitive map of Japan since Enokizu's trajectory takes in so many distinctive aspects of Japan's geography from hot springs and coastal communities in the south to mountain landscapes and busy city streets in the north. The juxtaposition of two key scenes early in the film is typical of this pattern. We see the waves of the ocean at night from on board the ferry between Shikoku and Kyūshū, then the camera rises to reveal a standing figure – Enokizu – next to an older woman. Imamura cuts to a reverse-field shot of the killer and two women. Staring out at the landscape, Enokizu comments that the sea is very black where they are. The camera is unsettled as the framing lilts along with the motion of the water below. We then hear Enokizu's voice-over reading a suicide note to his family. This note provides the link to the next sequence set on board a fast-moving train as two police officers interrogate the Kyūshū stripper who had come across the murderer between January and August the previous year. In a high-angle shot through the windows of the train we see car headlights on a busy nighttime road. There is an announcement that the train is pulling into Matsue. As the officers leave, they hand another suicide note to the woman who reads the words 'I am on a journey to death. The terminus is my life'. The sense of movement and transition suggested by the camerawork and its description of place and transport is savagely undercut by the intuitive finality felt by Enokizu in relation to his journey through Japan and through life.

Vengeance also presents a highly mediated view of Japan which conveys an ironic aside to the apparently unconvincing claims about the resurgent sense of national pride and prosperity being made at the time. We see Enokizu purchase items at a local National Electronics store and there is close-up television footage of a national baseball match, but these sequences are explicitly pictured in relation to his murderous activities. Even the recurrent use of newspapers, radio and other print sources is seen only as part of a nationwide search for the killer. Japan's constituent parts are thus linked by a network of media sources that fail to cohere harmoniously, but instead form part of a disturbing but inconclusive investigation into the social fabric of the country.

The second revealing treatment of space in the film concerns its sense of unstable framing and mise-en-scène. Imamura and Himeda's camera is restless to the point that the film rarely stops moving. As Donald Richie has argued, many of Imamura's bravura kinetic moments relate to a distinctive use of space (and time) that creates the impression of 'an overflowing vitality . . . which bursts the confines of the frame' (Richie 2001: 191). In the case of *Vengeance*, it can also be suggested that the material textual qualities of the filmmaking seem to offer a direct correspondence with the flux and uncertainty contained within the diegetic structure of the film and its subsequent presentation of self and nationhood. As Mikuni Rentarō has observed in relation to Imamura's style in general, 'the camera's field of vision is infinite. It can be placed anywhere . . . It is never orientated in one precise direction' (Niogret 2002: 125). The pliability of looking operations in the film suits its tendency to act at times as also a form of documentary.

We can observe the implications of these decisions more fully in the sequence of the film concerning Enokizu's arrival at the Asano Inn. We see the previously mentioned train pulling into Hamamatsu station with the window frame of the carriage within the frame of the screen revealing the buildings and residents of the town. As Enokizu gets up from his seat, the camera concentrates on a rear-view medium close-up vision of the killer which is retained as the camera follows him onto the platform within the same shot. Because of the decision to shoot in natural light, his body is silhouetted as he makes his way through the ticket barrier, but when he emerges into the strong daylight of the busy townscape and the camera recedes a little now to present him in long shot, his features are revealed more fully even though the surface of the image is broken up by disruptive shafts of late afternoon sunshine. As the camera comes in closer again he turns, for the first time, to survey the townscape and also, fleetingly, us. In so doing, he thus seemingly confronts the spectator with a sense of awareness that the televisual-like reality of this particular long take is, in fact, a knowing grammatical element of a carefully constructed set of looking relations. When Enokizu then enters a waiting taxi, the camera reiterates this sense of self-awareness by framing him through the window of the static vehicle as he converses with the driver. The car pulls away, but instead of following it, the camera remains and tilts upwards slightly and to the right before the shot concludes with an image of how the taxi and Enokizu have disappeared into the complex social organisation of the urban built environment.

There is a similar pattern to the treatment of spatial relations in the subsequent arrival of Enokizu at the Asano Inn. We cut to a static shot of two women walking down a residential backstreet. As their figures recede, the taxi arrives from the same direction in which they are heading. The shallow colour field is broken only with the interruption of the car's yellow indicator flashing. As the car passes the camera, we pan leftwards so that by the time the vehicle comes to a halt, there is another version of the window frame within the screen frame motif, this time containing both the figure of Enokizu and the alley down which he will walk to find his accommodation. As the murderer walks down the narrow passage, the camera follows him in the same messy 'live' fashion we saw with the previous exit from the station. This time, the turn to the spectator is even more overt and disruptive as the furtive figure suddenly turns around as if to confront our gaze and upset the secrecy of the moment. With the narrowness of the composition being emphasised by concrete walls on either side, the spatial field is both fluid and compressed. The sense is of entering another world hidden within the ordinarily depicted world of Japanese social reality.

This feeling of uncovering a new kind of social energy is visible in the way the long take develops when Enokizu enters the *genkan* (hallway) of the inn. As he turns towards the source of the loud cheering inside, the camera turns with him and tracks his gaze as we see him looking through the frame of an opened *shōji* screen at the innkeeper, Asano Haru, ending a noisy game of Mah-jong. For a moment, Enokizu disappears from view as the camera moves closer to observe Haru peering through the portal up at the figure of the visitor. Instead of cutting, the camera simply pans rightwards as Haru gets up and opens the door to welcome her guest. The two converse before moving up the stairs and along with Enokizu we begin to engage in a detailed spatial apprehension of the contours of the inn and how its rooms and corridors inter-relate. This is narrative cinema as a kind of social ethnography.

The third way in which the film may be read in terms of its unsettling spatial configurations lies in its representation of that most typical trope of the Japanese journey narrative: the inn. It is possible to argue that the Asano Inn is the spatial core of *Vengeance* for it is certainly the site from which so many of the diegetic elements of the film radiate. Enokizu's sexual and emotional relationship with the innkeeper and her mother are the key means, for example, by which we begin to uncover the killer's distorted sense of self. The earthy and familial, if also shady and duplicitous, world of the inn is also explicitly contrasted with Enokizu's family relations back in Beppu where a sense of marginality is expressed more through religious background than through social class. The inhabitants of the Asano Inn are trapped in a lower position within Japan's regulated social order. Its owner – Haru's patron – wonders if the forthcoming Olympics will help his textile business. Haru herself expresses surprise that Japan is larger than she thought when she pores over a map with Enokizu upstairs in the bedroom. Baishō Mitsuko, who plays Kazuko (Enokizu's wife) in the film, has argued that Imamura's distinctiveness as a Japanese film director lies in his determination to portray 'what people attempt to camouflage. He wants to expose everything that exists in people, even the ugliness of dirty things' (Niogret 2002: 101). This is one of the ways in which the Asano Inn functions. It takes the themes identified by Marilyn Ivy as key oppositional ideological markers within Japanese literature – 'exile and exclusion, travel and return, visitation and withdrawal' (1995: 32) – to offer a chilling portrait of what was being left behind in the modern Japan of 1964.

This chapter has argued that *Vengeance* is a film in which the distinctively unstable and fluid nature of its treatment of cinematic space and time is constructed in such a way as to suggest an analogous relationship between form and subject, especially concerning the retrospective representation of Japanese social relations of the 1960s from the viewpoint of the late 1970s. In its depiction of the 'messiness' of life, it is, however, bounded by an intense awareness of the *limitations* of this endeavour. Yann Lardeau has posited that in diegetic terms there is an inherent sense of constraint for as we move across Japan, along with the killer, we see how he is increasingly forced to contain his movements, enter into disguise and cover his field of vision with darkened glasses (Lardeau 1982: 47–8). The spectator also becomes progressively distanced from the motivations of the protagonist as the implications of his actions and their true consequences are subverted in favour of the containing logic of his arrest, rather than the explanatory potential of his interrogation. We are thus left with a set of questions which the ending of the film explicitly refers to.

In a situation which curiously bears some similarity to the ending of Ozu's *Tokyo Story*, in which the daughter-in-law is also left alone with the father, we see Kazuko and Enokizu's father dispose of the killer's ashes on a mountain top. As they throw his bone parts into the sky, we cut to their direct field of vision and watch the fragment freeze in still-motion in front of their eyes. In one devastating shot, Imamura even inserts a reverse-field shot from somewhere in space, as if from Enokizu's point-of-view, which similarly freezes the perplexed couple in mid-action. Many critics have interpreted this sequence as a means of representing Enokizu's residual defiant primal energy. Smith (n.d.) argues that this 'act of supernatural power . . . is wholly in keeping with the Japanese belief in the power of the dead to linger on as vengeful ghosts. So the concluding scene emerges as a fierce confrontation between two polar conceptions of vengeance, that of the Judeo-Christian God of the father and the willful Japanese *kami* of the dead son, each struggling to declare that the final "vengeance is mine" ' ('Vengeance'). This may well be true, but as a coda to what has been said in this chapter, we must similarly acknowledge the implicit presence of an authorial agent powerfully evoking here not just the protean energy of the subject of this film, but also the inherent medium-specific limitations of cinema to tell us everything about the world that it seeks to register.

Acknowledgements

The author would like to thank Julian Stringer and Mark Kurzemnieks for their kind assistance in helping to provide research materials for this chapter.

References

Daney, Serge (1998) *Cinéjournal 1981–1986*, Paris: Editions des Cahiers du cinéma.

Gordon, Andrew (2003) *A Modern History of Japan*, New York and London: Oxford University Press.

Imamura Shōhei (1997a) 'My Approach to Filmmaking', in Quandt 1997: 125–8.

—— (1997b) 'My Teacher', in Quandt 1997: 145–7.

Imamura Shōhei Home Page. Online. http://www.issay.com/shohei-imamura/english/ e_message.html36mikuni

Ivy, Marilyn (1995) *Discourses of the Vanishing: Modernity, Phantasm, Japan*, Chicago: Chicago University Press.

Lardeau, Yann (1982) 'Je tue donc je suis', *Cahiers du cinéma* 342: 47–8.

Niogret, Hubert (ed.) (2002) *Shohei Imamura: Entretiens et Témoignages*, Paris: Dreamland éditeur.

Quandt, James (ed.) (1997) *Shohei Imamura*, Toronto: Toronto International Film Festival Group.

Richie, Donald (1997) 'Notes for a Study of Shohei Imamura', in Quandt 1997: 7–44.

—— (2001) *One Hundred Years of Japanese Cinema*, Tokyo: Kōdansha.

Smith, Henry (n.d.) *'Vengeance is Mine'*. Online. http://www.columbia.edu/cu/ealac/dkc/ chushingura/vengeance_is_mine_film_notes.html. Accessed 9 March 2005.

Washburn, Dennis (2001) 'The Arrest of Time: The Mythic Transgressions of *Vengeance is Mine*', in Washburn, Dennis and Cavanaugh, Carole (eds) *Word and Image in Japanese Cinema*, Cambridge: Cambridge University Press: 318–41.

Imamura Shōhei Filmography (feature films only)

Stolen Desire (Nusumareta yokujō, 1958)
Nishi Ginza Station (Nishi Ginza eki-mae, 1958)
Endless Desire (Hateshi naki yokubō, 1958)
My Second Brother (Nianchan, 1959)
Pigs and Battleships (Buta to gunkan, 1961)
The Insect Woman (Nippon konchūki, 1963)
Intentions of Murder (Akai satsui, 1964)
The Pornographers (Jinruigaku nyūmon, 1966)
A Man Vanishes (Ningen jōhatsu, 1967)
The Profound Desire of the Gods (Kamigami no fukaki yokubō, 1968)
History of Postwar Japan as Told by a Bar Hostess (Nippon sengo shi: madamu onboro no seikatsu, 1970)
Vengeance is Mine (Fukushū suru wa ware ni ari, 1979)
Eijanaika (1981)
The Ballad of Narayama (Narayama bushikō, 1983)
Zegen (1987)
Black Rain (Kuroi ame, 1989)
The Eel (Unagi, 1997)
Dr. Akagi (Kanzō sensei, 1998)
Warm Water Under a Red Bridge (Akai hashi no shita no nurui mizu, 2001)
11'09'01 – September 11 (UK/France/Egypt/Japan/Mexico/USA/Iran, 2002 – segment only)

18

PLAYING WITH POSTMODERNISM

Morita Yoshimitsu's *The Family Game* (1983)

Aaron Gerow

In most discourse on Morita Yoshimitsu's *The Family Game* (*Kazoku gēmu*, 1983), the title is emblematic, a metaphor for the family reduced to role playing in which individual worth becomes quantified in terms of class rankings. A seemingly average married couple, Mr and Mrs Numata (played by Itami Jūzō and Yuki Saori respectively), hires a tutor named Yoshimoto (Matsuda Yūsaku) to help their youngest son Shigeyuki (Miyagawa Ichirōta) with high school entrance examinations, as if all they care about is which school he can enter. The tutor, from a minor college himself, does succeed in getting the boy into a good school, but as if criticizing the family's, if not society's, hypocrisy, wreaks havoc upon the celebration party they put on. Communication ends in failure and relationships are rendered impersonal amid a strict social hierarchy, noisy consumerism, and a vacant industrial landscape. In this discourse, Morita becomes a biting social satirist, taking skilful jabs at contemporary Japan. There is, however, another discourse I would like to pursue that exists alongside this, one evident in these comments by the critic Ikui Eikō (1984: 38–9):

> *The Family Game* is introduced as depicting the contemporary face of the family through the examination war in an ironically humorous manner. Yet themes that can be explained in words are, to Morita Yoshimitsu, no different from the ordinary plates they sell at the supermarket. What is really important in his films is the strange spice that has been added, the world of wry humor.

What Ikui implies is that the game here is not simply confined to the world of the characters, or to words themselves, perhaps because it extends to the cinematic sign itself and a certain take on (spicing of) the social critique it propounds. Maybe, one can say, it is not just the Numata family playing a game here, but Morita himself, a game that necessarily involves the audience as well.

This second discourse does not necessarily negate the first (e.g. by arguing that Morita is not truly a satirist), rather, it takes one step back and attempts to relocate this satire, asking what contexts are involved in defining or not defining *The Family Game* as a critique. It is these contexts, I would contend, ones centered around 1980s Japan and a certain discursive engagement with postmodernism, that not only complicate interpretation of a text that itself questions interpretation, but also makes set contexts essential in its play of criticality. By combining an analysis of the often contradictory critical reception of the film, interviews by Morita, and other contexts brought to play in the film, with the text's own problematization of signification, we shall see that Morita's game, which extends far beyond *The Family Game*, plays with words and interpretations, framing the social critique just as that critique becomes the frame necessary for his game.

One of the central terms intersecting with the text and its game is 'postmodernism',[1] but observers differed over whether or not Morita was criticizing this state. Keiko McDonald (1989: 61), for instance, inserts the word in the title of her essay on the film, and focuses on the 'impersonal, competitive postmodern society' that she sees as criticized in the text. Citing Jean Baudrillard, Osabe Hideo (1984: 34) labels *The Family Game* the first film he has seen to 'specifically depict the structures of a society of sign consumption', in which reality is reduced to mere simulations. As with MacDonald, Osabe senses criticism in the film's stance: 'By inserting one strange invader or challenger into the family, the director depicts the dangers hidden beneath today's bright, white world with an eccentric style' (Osabe 1985: 20). Yet Osabe carefully refrains from asserting any intentionality – saying 'whether or not the author is conscious of it or not' – and claims as well, in a telling play of words, that if this is 'family as simulacrum', Morita's text itself is a 'simulation' (1984: 35).

The critic Kawamoto Saburō (1985), one of Morita's staunchest promoters, goes one step further to praise Morita less for his critique of postmodernity, than for his ability to (re)present it. Citing Morita's *oeuvre* in the context of Japanese cinema and culture, Kawamoto asserts that Morita stands out precisely because he presented a new cinema that represents a new age. If the celebrated Nikkatsu *roman poruno* (romance porn) of director Kumashiro Tatsumi (e.g. *Street of Joy* [*Akasen Tamanoi: nukeraremasu*], 1974; *The Woman with Red Hair* [*Akai kami no onna*], 1979) showed women tenaciously struggling at society's margins, Morita's *roman poruno* – *The Stripper of Rumor* (*Maruhon: uwasa no sutorippā*, 1982) and *Pink Cut: Love Hard, Love Deep* (*Pinku katto: futoku aishite fukaku aishite*, 1983) – presented classless sex workers who happily ply their trade with none of the sweaty, physical presence of Kumashiro's heroines. If youth films of the 1960s and 1970s focused on angry, frustrated teens burning with hunger and desire, the three contented heroes in *Boys and Girls* (*Shibugakitai: bōizu to gāruzu*, 1982) lightly play truant in a brightly empty landscape. Thus if Japanese cinema of the 1970s was always 'full', piling on detail to represent a heavy reality of emotion and sensuality, Morita's minimal aesthetics of 'less' is satisfied with a light, abstract world. To Kawamoto, this 'transparency' is new to Japanese cinema and reflects a 'new sensibility' concomitant with what in contemporary discourse was called 'the new human species' (*shinjinrui*).

In an interview with Morita, Kawamoto tries to delineate *The Family Game* through this difference. He aligns Morita with new playwrights of the 'fake' such as Noda Hideki and contrasts the film with the critically acclaimed 1970s television home dramas of Yamada Taichi: 'I think Yamada's world is a copy of reality whereas yours turns reality into a fiction' (Morita and Kawamoto 1983: 57). Kawamoto was not the only critic to make much of the Japanese title of Morita's 1981 35mm debut, *No yōna mono* (it means 'something like . . .'). An item in Morita's film is only 'like' what it is; not the actual thing, but only its simulacrum. To Kawamoto, everything in Morita's films from living spaces to the landscape seems designed, with the Numata house appearing like an unlived showroom dwelling.

Kawamoto does not fail to find criticality in the film, but asserts an approach fundamentally different from previous cinema. A teacher publicizing everyone's test scores and throwing the worst out the window would, in a 1970s social problem film, be condemned through shots of humiliated students, but here all the students enjoy this practice. It is Morita's 'theatrical space', Kawamoto argues, that 'is the best means of criticizing or nullifying today's examination system. Theatricalizing it in this way is better than treating it seriously' (Morita and Kawamoto 1983: 58). Nevertheless, Kawamoto (1985: 30–6) asserts that 'deep within Morita Yoshimitsu is a bright sense of emptiness, a sense that unified world principles have been lost'. Without values that are certain, 'Morita Yoshimitsu less delves into deep meaning than enjoys deforming, rearranging, mixing and mismatching a world that appears on the surface'. If this is the extent of his critique, then more than condemning postmodernity for 'decomposing human beings into "human beings" ', 'Morita Yoshimitsu bravely and brightly enjoys that' (Ibid.).

The year of *The Family Game*'s release, 1983, was the cusp of the first wave of discourse on postmodernism in Japan. It was thus not unusual to see the film being taken up as a marker of the age by commentators in fields other than film criticism. Yoshimoto Takaaki (1985), one of the most influential post-war intellectuals, found in the film 'the skill and the strength to self-assert clearly in images the sense, fashion, and lifestyle of the contemporary world, announcing the coming of a new age'. The sociologist Mita Munesuke (1995: 28) used *The Family Game* to illustrate his three broad divisions in post-war Japanese social history. If Japanese before and during the high growth economy defined their reality first through 'ideals' and then through 'dreams', attempting to change reality according to those visions, in the post-high growth era, from the mid-1970s on, they no longer try to shape reality, but just remain content with reality as 'fiction' (*kyokō*). To Mita, the Numatas' dining table, shaping a unidirectional gaze among family members, is not unrealistic, but rather 'accurately fixes the un-reality, the "un-naturalness" or fictionality of reality itself' in an age where families now watch television when eating. The sociologist Sakurai Tetsuo (1983: 206–13), in delineating a similar epochal shift, groups Morita with writer Murakami Haruki and musician Sakamoto Ryūichi in a generation that, disillusioned by the radical student movement of the 1960s, came to distrust 'earnestness' (*omoiire*), if not meaning itself. He thus connects them to a culture-wide rejection of meaning, a celebration of meaninglessness, but one that still critiques, rather than simply rejecting, signification. The problem to Sakurai, however, is that their audiences often mistake this critique for the utter rejection of meaning, thus giving corporate power or conservative ideology room to maneuver.

Not a few blamed Morita himself for commodifying characters and the body in the film. Many note the film's use of various signs to mark the characters: the father and his soy milk, the mother and her leatherwork, older brother Shin'ichi (Tsujita Jun'ichi) and his telescope. If Kawamoto cites this as an indication of people transformed into signs, Murakami Tomohiko (1984: 60–5) argues that these signs add little or nothing to the characters; they are mere information, a list of extras attached to a catalog of characters. Lining up these characters at the table is equivalent to the commodity catalogs central to 1980s consumer culture, turning, Murakami says, *The Family Game* into a counterpart of Japanese fashion magazines. This is possible because the signs of characters have become separated from their bodies. It is said that Morita's cinema empties the body of its physicality, so much so that Yamane Sadao (1993: 23–4) claims that *Kitchen* (1989) achieves the impossible of creating a 'plastic Ozu Yasujirō' in which the body itself has been expunged.

Whichever position one takes, it is clear that contemporary criticism, while celebrating *The Family Game* overall, was sometimes divided over whether the film was a critique of postmodernism, or rather embodied that condition. Morita's own statements on two primary images, the Numatas' table and the industrial landscape Shin'ichi sees from Mieko's window – both of which numerous critics have taken as critiques of contemporary society – only complicate matters. When Kawamoto remarks that the film depicts a young generation that, like Shin'ichi, can find beauty in such a landscape, Morita adds, 'I like it myself. I don't think it's empty at all' (Morita and Kawamoto 1983: 58) As for the table, the director admits, 'I like eating lined up side by side . . . I prefer it when there's no one facing me. I like it that way, and that's the only reason why [I used that table]' (Morita 1985: 61). While director's comments should always be viewed critically, especially with such a playful cineaste as Morita, they again complicate the process of fixing an interpretation of the text.

One of *The Family Game*'s fascinating aspects is that the issue of its own interpretation is anticipated or even doubled by its own thematic foregrounding of the problems of interpretation, if not of signification itself. Interpretation is frequently pursued by the characters and urged upon the spectator. The mother wants to know the meaning of everything, from Shigeyuki's silence while studying to his storming out of the apartment. The audience is also confronted with many conspicuous signs, such as the toy rollercoaster or the helicopter, which seem to demand elucidation. Yet just as these symbols are often hard to read, interpretation is shown to be a problem in the film. Yuriko (Kobayashi Asako), for instance, who has been shown in the film watching Shigeyuki in class, calls Shigeyuki stupid for interpreting her confession of love as a trick set up by Tsuchiya. On several instances, characters disagree on interpretations. For instance, after Shin'ichi expresses his envy of Mieko at being able to view the industrial landscape everyday, Mieko immediately follows with another interpretation: it's just 'ordinary' (*heibon*). These conflicting interpretations are further complicated by our spatial unease during the scene. The strangeness of Mieko's home (the entrance seems to be in a department store; the living room, with its window showing mere color, is spatially ambiguous; and her room is reachable only by elevator) warps our own interpretation of the landscape as Shin'ichi's point of view. Later appearances of the same landscape divorced from a subjective structure further detach it from his vision.

Shigeyuki's prank of writing 'twilight' (*yūgure*) in his notebook is another moment complicating interpretation. Some commentators have attempted to connect the word to Shigeyuki's situation – for instance, his immanent 'long drawn-out purgatory' of exam hell (McDonald 1989: 62) – but the play of interpretation in the scene also deserves analysis. Shigeyuki's writing is presented in a combination of extreme close-up, shots of various landscapes colored by the setting sun, and a loud collage of sounds (the pencil, the bus, etc.). The rhythmic montage between the word and the landscape shots is practically a montage of association, as if the images presented are the definition or referent of the word. That reading is problematic, however. Not only is it impossible to visualize an abstract, inherently relational temporal concept as 'twilight' through mostly still images of specific objects, the images do not even fit some of the dictionary definitions of the Japanese term (which, for instance, stipulate that twilight is a period of time *after* sunset). The barrage of sound, literally grainy as the graphite scratches across the paper, reminds us, in Barthesian terms, of the 'grain of the voice' or, perhaps, the grain of the photographic image that refuses the confines of meaning. The tutor Yoshimoto tops off this complication of meaning by responding to the mother's query as to whether '*yūgure*' must mean something with, 'No, it's not that. It's just a prank'. He effectively declares that the word or action means nothing other than playfulness.

A further analysis of the scene reveals it to include an investigation of the processes of signification itself, especially in relation to repetition. Shigeyuki's act is a rejection of the principle of rote learning: that, by repeating a word often enough, one can fully grasp its meaning. He does facetiously declare at the end that he now has complete comprehension of *yūgure*, but his repetition, if not also the repeated montage we see, is essentially meaningless, tearing the signified away from the signifier. In some ways, his act is an assertion, one echoing the novels of Shimizu Yoshinori, that entrance examinations are not about meaning but rather about grasping the structure (the game) of signifiers. What is interesting is that Yoshimoto's act of slapping him is less a rejection of that assertion and a restatement of the centrality of meaning, than an alternative form of repetition. Repetition is one of the central devices in *The Family Game*, especially in the way a character is repeatedly tied with an object or action. In some cases, this creates significant structures, such as when the association of the soy milk with the father renders Yoshimoto's request for soy milk, after the mother asks him to report Shigeyuki's change of school preference, an ironic declaration that he has been made father of this family. Yoshimoto's act of slapping is a more playful, if not less meaningful, form of repetition. Certainly it has various functions in the film, denoting the tutor's otherness, contrasting with the mother's coddling, and foreshadowing the violent dinner scene, but its

Figure 22 Breathing and slapping: Yoshimoto and Shigeyuki in *The Family Game* (1983). BFI Stills, Posters and Designs.

meaning has again been subject to conflicting interpretations, from McDonald's (1989) positive view of it as warm-hearted discipline to Marie Thorsten Morimoto (1994) locating it within the inherent violence of the knowledge system.

One must look more closely at how the slapping 'signifies' in the film. The slapping is unlike Shigeyuki's act of exact repetition, writing the same thing over and over again without variation. First, it is preceded by a curious action: Yoshimoto noisily breathing in through the nostrils. The breathing and the slapping become associated in the film, as if the breathing 'means' a slap is coming, but not through mere repetition. Shigeyuki is able to figure out this 'meaning' before the second act occurs, precisely because Yoshimoto's breathing was unusual; simply put, the extraordinariness of the act created a gap of meaning (the sense that it must mean something because it differs from the usual) which the slap then filled. This 'meaning' does not remain stable, however, precisely because Yoshimoto, and eventually Shigeyuki, do not exactly repeat it. They insert delays, feints, and other blows on subsequent occasions, playing with the meaning. The last act of slapping at the dinner table in fact takes place without Yoshimoto even breathing noisily. Seemingly these variations are not so much variations of meaning, as tricks to fool the opponent (which Yoshimoto uses to the full at the dinner table) and challenge their interpretation of the moment, if not the very act of trying to read meaning into actions themselves.

Significantly, *auteurist* readings of Morita have focused on a similar 'slippage (*zure*) from set formulae' (Murakami 1981: 62) as central to his playful film-making. Morita's humor, if not his filmmaking as a whole, is often termed 'off-beat'. He assumes or establishes a certain rhythm or structure, only to shift it slightly through twists and deformations. *The Family Game* abounds in such examples, from Shigeyuki gargling coffee to the parents having intimate talks in the car. The locus of these slippages is certainly the tutor, who can provide a catalog of eccentric actions and dialogue: touching the father's hand, blurting out 'I'm a tutor' when the subject of his dandruff comes up, eating an apple peel (rare among Japanese), and so on. Whether we consider the slippages in the film to be significant – functioning, for instance, as alienation devices that expose hidden norms – in part depends on how we read Yoshimoto's role in the film.

The tutor is without a doubt different, as discourse on the film has labeled him an 'alien', 'stranger', 'intruder', 'trickster', and 'challenger'. In directing his actors, Morita composed a precise 'resumé' for every central character except Yoshimoto; little is known about him or where he is from (only his girlfriend's apartment appears in the film). He is seemingly from another world, traveling to the Numatas' home by boat and insisting, in a *gesellschaft* society where people are defined by apartment numbers, on a *gemeinschaft* where everybody knows each other's name. One can argue that he is alien even to the society of signs. When asked by Shigeyuki to read the beginning of *Narrow Road to Oku*, a classical Japanese text, he does not get it wrong, but reads the old usage of *kana* letters as is (e.g. *kuwakaku* or *kwakaku*) instead of transforming them into modern pronunciation (*kakaku*). Several commentators have noted how, especially in his ambiguous sexual actions (assuming roles both maternal and paternal, both heterosexual and homosexual), he appears to cross borders and transgress social or sexual roles (see Osabe 1985; Knee 1991; Morimoto 1994).

One is still left with the question of his significance or criticality. Adam Knee's (1991: 45) reading is rather unequivocal, seeing in Yoshimoto the 'denial and defiance of the context and values of the Numatas' lives', but one can argue that that is truer of the original novel than of the film. In Honma Yōhei's work (1984), Yoshimoto is eccentric, but more serious and goal-oriented than in the film. His stated aim is to fashion the stuttering, drooling, and smirking Shigeyuki into an individual who expresses his own opinion, acts upon it, and defeats others in a competitive society. It is precisely because he has this clear goal that the tutor declares defeat at the end: there is no violent dinner scene, but rather the realization, after the necessity of reporting Shigeyuki's preference to the school, that his efforts have come to naught. His thoughts are much clearer in the novel because of his close relationship with Shin'ichi, who is the narrator in Honma's version. Shin'ichi shares Yoshimoto's critical perspective on the family, and in fact provides considerable analysis as to why the family is malfunctioning. He is the enlightening consciousness in the novel, albeit a tragic one, knowing full well why this family is defective, yet being unable to act against it.

In the novel, Shin'ichi is much like the camera of classical cinema, constantly using lenses to observe people with an analytical perspective that discerns their thoughts and emphasizes narratively important actions. Morita's film exchanges this camera for one that is more detached, playing up the ambiguities of figures such as Yoshimoto by downplaying questions concerning his goals and thoughts. Just as the tutor appears to take different sides, first helping Shigeyuki pass his examinations and then attacking the family, Morita's camera does not restrict itself to one perspective, but playfully varies it. Not a few observers have remarked on the flatness of the film's space, especially the frontality of the shots of the dining table. But the dinner table is in fact shown in a variety of ways: from the side, in a diagonal forward track, in a low-angle circular camera movement, using inner frames, and finally in a high-angle crane shot. This is the same kind of playful repetition that Yoshimoto teaches Shigeyuki. Thus to Aoki Makoto (1983: 64–5), if 'Morita Yoshimitsu neither condemns nor laments this "something like a family" ', it is in part because he 'sends in an unknown, invader-like tutor' who just 'exposes, disturbs, and then leaves'.

Aoki and others still perceive a critical function for Yoshimoto amid this ambiguity, but it is a criticality tempered by its function in the film and its context. Consider, for instance, the place of the critical in Morita's career. Frankly, Morita never lived up to expectations that he would become the new social satirist of Japanese cinema. While *Keiho* (*39: Keihō dai-sanjūkyū-jō*, 1999) is a social problem film and *Copycat Killer* (*Mohōhan*, 2002) and the 'You Idiot' (*Baka yarō!*) series parody society in their excess, most of his work consists of romances and commercial star vehicles that have received little critical praise. Morita himself strongly shunned such labels as satirist, proclaiming himself the 'robot of the Japanese film world' who not only does not have his 'own world', but who is also ' "nothing" – I myself don't exist' (Morita 1983: 120–1). In his own discourse, *The Family Game* was another in his 'catalog' of films, one aimed at awards and one that helped him make his infamous declaration, through advertisements he took out in film magazines in 1984, that he was a 'pop director' (*ryūkō kantoku*). From an *auteurist* perspective, Morita is best seen as a filmmaker carrying the formal experimentation of his 8mm days into commercial cinema. His camera or sound style can shift significantly from film to film, from the long takes of *And Then* (*Sorekara*, 1985) to the digital collages of *Copycat Killer*. If *The Black House* (*Kuroi ie*, 1999) explores the line between horror and comedy, *Haru* (1996) investigates the extent to which written words can compose a film. Perhaps Morita is like Yoshimoto himself, repeating his stylistic experiments, but in a cinematic game of feints that throws his viewers off balance.

This repetition, however, can be connected to what the philosopher Nibuya Takashi (1999), in referring to 1980s Japan, calls the 'age of repetition'. If the decade of the 1970s was the era of change, the 1980s was born of the growing realization that nothing was really different despite all the variation. Repetition was its own trap, but it also freed one of the need to change, and thus artists such as musician Matsutōya Yumi, Sakamoto Ryūichi – and perhaps Morita Yoshimitsu – succeeded by masterfully manipulating variation within a repetition of the same. *The Family Game* ends with nothing changed, a conclusion that can be read as pessimistic, but that also confirms that 'slippages' in the film depend upon an unchanging structure. The game of slaps provides excitement precisely because there is a basic form through which the variations can be read; even if Shigeyuki might be trying to change that form – by getting the last slap – Yoshimoto leaves before that happens, ensuring that the structure remains unchanged. One can also say that Yoshimoto rejects Shigeyuki's facetious test answers because that game goes beyond the limits, undermining the function of a test itself, rather than playing within its boundaries (which is what Yoshimoto seems to prefer). The question is whether any of Morita's slippages twist the structure enough to bring it down. Certainly writers such as Murakami do not think so, nor does Suzuki Hitoshi (1984), who astutely indicates one of the film's central contradictions. If it is satire, he says, it is so because it pokes fun at the 'weak circle' of the family. But the concept 'family', Suzuki argues, is inherently unrepresentable in cinema (even if one can manage to get actors with actual familial resemblance). The family Morita creates to criticize the family is then already a 'weak circle' itself; his satire is insufficient because it assumes or copies what it is out to condemn.

This assumption of a framing structure in satirical play reminds us of Asada Akira's (1989: 273–8) description of infantile capitalism. In criticizing post-modernism in 1980s Japan, Asada argues that the childlike play of Japan's capitalism of purely relative competition still necessitates an aegis protecting the children as they play. He suggests that this is the emperor system (echoing Karatani Kōjin's argument that Japanese postmodernism never deconstructed such structures as the emperor), but with *The Family Game* we can also call this the 'family' or even 'criticality'. These are some of the main structures that allow Morita (or Yoshimoto) to play his own games; they set the framework against and also within which variations can be made. This gets to the heart of one of the central ambivalent terms in the text: the game. To many critics, it is the game (as family) that is being criticized in the film, but this elides the status of the film's own games. Morita's game, I would argue, depends on the critical equation of the family with the game, both so that that assertion can be played with, and also so that games can be pursued amid the protection of a fixed structure. Both Morita and Kawamoto (1983; cf. Morita and Tsukushi 1984: 43–7) argued that *The Family Game* demanded new forms of film criticism, ones that went beyond the then prevalent demand for critical realism, but the film skillfully provides fodder for such a demand, while also engaging in the cinematic play that would enthrall the new generation of critics raised by Hasumi Shigehiko, Yamane Sadao, and others.

The Family Game deftly weaves between being called a socially critical text and an exercise in mere commodified play. Morita's game, one that extends into contexts of reception and criticism, encompasses both these discourses and encourages the audience to play with the tension between alternative interpretations. For despite the film's problematization of interpretation, it actively encourages spectator input in the text. This is evident in the use of sound. Although *The Family Game* features no music track, it is an extremely musical film, and not simply because of its rhythmicality: music is repeatedly cited in the text, from Doris Day's 'Teacher's Pet' to Togawa Jun (an eccentric rock singer who plays the neighbor), from Aki Yōko (a famous singer-songwriter who appears as Yoshimoto's girlfriend) to Oscar Peterson's rendition of *My Fair Lady*. When the mother and Shin'ichi listen to Peterson's album, and all we hear is silence, Morita is establishing both a model for spectator involvement (i.e. we supply the music) and an alternative to all the sounds that invade every space in the film.

This playful use of silence and music is in some ways the lesson Morita offers us in the film. Remember that Shigeyuki's act of rote repetition was, in his words, a way of 'making a boring time enjoyable'. This is his means of coping with the postmodern era, but Yoshimoto rejects it. His lesson – really the only thing he teaches Shigeyuki in the film – is the more enjoyable game of adding one's shifts and feints into the repetition. Nothing really changes, but this game is one of those 'certain kinds of know-how' that Morita mentions, a way of 'switching the tensions and rhythms of life' that he puts into his films as an offering for young people (Morita and Tsukushi 1984: 43–7). In these terms, Morita's game of variation and repetition is an attempt to provide the post-modern equivalent of Miriam Hansen's vernacular modernism (2000: 12), a 'horizon in which both the liberating impulses and the pathologies of [here post]modernity were reflected . . . transmuted or negotiated'. Neither a com-plete celebration nor a rejection of postmodernity, *The Family Game* posits a playfulness beyond its textuality that, for better or worse, may have been one possible way of coping with postmodern Japan.

Note

1 Defining the term 'postmodernism' is difficult, given not only the debates over its meaning in Europe and the US, especially over whether it represents the radical undermining of the Enlightenment's grand narratives and myths of subjectivity and meaning or instead consumer capitalism's ultimate rendering of reality into a simula-tion composed of pastiche without parody, but also the problems in applying the concept to a non-Western nation such as Japan which lacks an Enlightenment or a similar experience of modernity. The book *Postmodernism and Japan* (Miyoshi and Harootunian 1989) discusses these problems in detail. Critics who used the term in reference to *The Family Game* exhibited these same problems and rarely used the concept with precision. What is important here is that they generally used the term to denote a new attitude toward the filmic image, one different from the past and ambivalently related to the creation of political meaning and commodity culture.

References

Aoki, Makoto (1983) 'Mogibutsu no sekai ni ikiru gendaijin' [Contemporary People Living in an Age of Simulation], *Kinema Junpō*, 863: 64–5.

Asada, Akira (1989) 'Infantile Capitalism and Japan's Postmodernism: A Fairy Tale', in Miyoshi and Harootunian 1989: 273–8.

Hansen, Miriam (2000) 'Fallen Women, Rising Stars, New Horizons', *Film Quarterly*, 54 (1): 10–22.

Honma, Yōhei (1984) *Kazoku gēmu* [Family Game], Tokyo: Shūeisha.

Ikui, Eikō (1984) 'Tahahaha . . . no warai o sasou Morita Yoshimitsu no sekai' [The World of Morita Yoshimitsu, Inviting Laughter Ha Ha Ha], *Asahi Jānaru* [*Asahi Journal*], 26 (1): 38–9.

Kakeo, Yoshio (ed.) (1985) *Omoide no Morita Yoshimitsu* [*Remembering Morita Yoshimitsu*], Tokyo: Kinema Junpō.

Kawamoto, Saburō (1985) 'Dezainā toshite no Morita Yoshimitsu' [Morita Yoshimitsu as a Designer] in Kakeo 1985.

Knee, Adam (1991) 'The Family Game Is up', *Post Script*, 11 (1): 40–7.

McDonald, Keiko (1989) 'Family, Education, and Postmodern Society', *East-West Film Journal*, 4 (1): 53–67.

Mita, Munesuke (1995) *Gendai Nihon no kankaku to shisō* [*The Thought and Sensibility of Contemporary Japan*], Tokyo: Kōdansha.

Miyoshi, Masao and Harootunian, H. D. (eds) (1989) *Postmodernism and Japan*, Durham, NC: Duke University Press.

Morimoto, Marie Thorsten (1994) 'A Women's Place is in the Kitchen of Knowledge: Premodern and Postmodern Representations of Food (for Thought) in Japanese Film', in Nitaya Masavisut, George Simson, and Larry E. Smith (eds), *Gender and Culture in Literature and Film East and West*, Honolulu: University of Hawai'i Press.

Morita, Yoshimitsu (1983) 'Shinario wa sanryū, kantoku sureba . . .'. [The Scenario Is Third Grade, If You Direct It . . .], *Shinario* [*Scenario*], 39 (9): 120–3.

—— (1985) 'Rongu intabyū' [Long Interview] in Kakeo 1985.

Morita, Yoshimitsu, and Kawamoto, Saburō (1983) '*Kazoku gēmu* taidan' [Discussion on *Family Game*], *Kinema Junpō*, 863: 56–61.

Morita, Yoshimoto, and Tsukushi, Tetsuya (1984) 'Wakamono-tachi no kamigami: Morita Yoshimitsu' [The Gods of Young People: Morita Yoshimitsu], *Asahi Jānaru* [*Asahi Journal*], 25 (24): 43–7.

Murakami, Tomohiko (1984) 'Jōhō sōsa shisutemu toshite no Morita Yoshimitsu' [Morita Yoshimitsu as a System for Manipulating Information], *Imēji fōramu* [*Image Forum*], 49: 60–5.

Nibuya, Takashi (1999) *Tennō to tōsaku* [*The Emperor and Aberration*], Tokyo: Seidosha.

Osabe, Hideo (1984) 'Kazoku gēmu', *Imēji fōramu* [*Image Forum*], 42: 34–5.

—— (1985) 'Mittsu no Morita Yoshimitsu ron' [Three Thoughts on Morita Yoshimatsu] in Kakeo 1985.

Sakurai, Tetsuo (1983) ' "Omoiire" kara no dassō' [Escape from Earnestness], *Chūō Kōron* [*Central Review*], 98 (10): 206–13.

Suzuki, Hitoshi (1984) 'Kazoku' [Family] in Yamane Sadao (ed.), *Nihon eiga 1984* [*Japanese Film 1984*], Tokyo: Haga Shoten.

Yamane, Sadao (1993) *Eiga wa doko e iku ka* [*Where Is Film Going?*], Tokyo: Chikuma Shobō.

Yoshimoto, Takaaki (1985) *Jūsōtekina hikettei e* [*Towards a Multi-Layered Negation*], Tokyo: Yamato Shobō.

Morita Yoshimitsu Filmography

8mm films

POSI-? (1970, 20 min.)
Hex (1970, 3 min.)
Sky (1970, 3 min.)
Film (*Eiga*, 1971, 40 min.)
Seaside (1971, 3 min.)
Eating (1971, 3 min.)

Midnight (1971, 5 min.)
Light (1971, 15 min.)
Mother (1971, 3 min.)
Weather Report (*Tenki yohō*, 1971, 30 min.)
Nude (1971, 3 min.)
Film (1971, 3 min.)
Telephone (*Denwa*, 1971, 5 min.)
The Art of Perspective (*Enkinjutsu*, 1972, 90 min.)
Physical Check-up (*Kenkō shindan*, 1972, 20 min.)
Industrial Belt (*Kōjō chitai*, 1972, 35 min.)
Tokyo Suburban Belt (*Tōkyō kinkō chitai*, 1973, 35 min.)
Painting Class (*Kaiga kyōshitsu*, 1974, 30 min.)
Girl's Taste (*Shōjo shumi*, 1974)
The Steam Express (*Suijōki kyūkō*, 1976, 80 min.)
Live in Chigasaki (*Raibu in Chigasaki*, 1978, 85 min.)

35mm films

Something Like Yoshiwara (*No yōna mono*, 1981)
Boys and Girls (*Shibugakitai: bōizu to gāruzu*, 1982)
The Stripper of Rumor (*Maruhon: uwasa no sutorippā*, 1982)
Pink Cut: Love Hard, Love Deep (*Pinku katto: futoku aishite fukaku aishite*, 1983)
The Family Game (*Kazoku gēmu*, 1983)
The Third-Year Affair (*Sannenme no uwaki*, 1983)
Deaths in Tokimeki (*Tokimeki ni shisu*, 1984)
Main Theme (*Mein tēma*, 1984)
And Then (*Sorekara*, 1985)
All For Business' Sake (*Sorobanzuku*, 1986)
House of Wedlock (*Uhohho tankentai*, 1986)
You Idiot! I'm Mad (*Baka yarō! Watashi, okottemasu*, 1988)
Love and Action in Osaka (*Kanashii iro ya nen*, 1988)
Man of 24 Hours (*Ai to Heisei no iro-otoko*, 1989)
Kitchen (*Kitchin*, 1989)
You Idiot! 2: I Want to Be Happy (*Baka yarō! 2: Shiawase ni naritai*, 1989)
You Idiot! 3: Strange Guys (*Baka yarō! 3: Henna yatsura*, 1990)
Happy Wedding (*Oishii kekkon*, 1991)
You Idiot! 4: You! I'm Talking about You (*Baka yarō! 4: You! Omae no koto da yo*, 1991)
Last Christmas (*Mirai no omoide: Last Christmas*, 1992)
I've No License! (*Menkyo ga nai!*, 1994)
Haru (*Haru*, 1996)
Lost Paradise (*Shitsurakuen*, 1997)
You Alone Can't See (*Kiriko no fūkei*, 1998)
Keihmo (*39: Keihō dai-sanjūkyū-jō*, 1999)
The Black House (*Kuroi ie*, 1999)
Colorful (*Karafuru*, 2000)
Copycat Killer (*Mohōhan*, 2002)

Video movies

You Idiot! V: What's Bad About Sexy? (*Baka yarō! V: Etchi de warui ka*, 1994)
You Idiot! V 2: I'm a Problem (*Baka yarō! V 2: Watashi, mondai desu*, 1994)

As actor

Tokyo Biyori (*Tōkyō biyori*, 1997)
Sleepless Town (*Fuyajō: Sleepless Town*, 1998)

19

TRANSGRESSION AND RETRIBUTION

Yanagimachi Mitsuo's *Fire Festival* (1985)

Donald Richie

Fire Festival (*Himatsuri*, 1985) is a film about transgression and retribution, about nature revenging itself upon destructive modern man. At the same time, as its director Yanagimachi Mitsuo has often stated, the film is not about ecology. This is not a paradox. Yanagimachi is observing life as it is, not as it ought to be. Mankind and the natural world are opposed because man must live off it and hence despoil it. Ecological concerns are feeble in the face of this fact. Saving the earth is possible only through the eradication of an overweening mankind so therefore the central theme of Yanagimachi's film is the necessity of a personified nature killing the transgressive protagonist and his entire brood.[1]

Before making *Fire Festival*, Yanagimachi noted that his previous films were similarly about the opposition between person and environment. The unconstrained biker in *God Speed You, Black Emperor* (1976) pollutes wherever he is; the violent newspaper-boy in *A Nineteen Year Old's Map* (*Jūkyūsai no chizu*, 1979) plans enormous destruction; and the junkie trucker in *A Farewell to the Land* (*Saraba itoshiki daichi*, 1982) shoots up in the desert he has made of the countryside. Though none of them slaughters his family (the trucker merely murders his wife) they are all pictured as possessed. In the absence of any further evidence, these protagonists could be seen as possessed merely in the sense of being psychologically disturbed. But in *Fire Festival*, Yanagimachi supplies the required evidence – the possession is literal in that the protagonist is taken over. After we have witnessed the appearance of nature as a deity in the film, we can no longer believe in mere psychological disturbance.

Yanagimachi has also argued that there are similar 'irrational elements which now seem to have been something on the order of the divine' in his other films.[2] In *God Speed You, Black Emperor* there are supernatural scenes of the mother's new religion; in *A Nineteen Year Old's Map* there are long, preternatural sunrises and paranoid hallucinations; and in *A Farewell to the Land* there is the eclipse of the sun, the mysterious death of the little boys and their supposed resuscitation through the shaman. In making *Fire Festival*, however, Yanagimachi wanted to develop the relationship between nature and man further, and so he added

Figure 23 *Fire Festival* (1985): a film about transgression and retribution, nature revenging itself upon modern man. BFI Stills, Posters and Designs.

deities making what he has called 'a kind of triangle – man, nature, and the gods'.

Man's inadvertently thoughtless and transgressive way with nature is visible from the first sequence onwards. Trees are felled, birds are caught and animals are killed. The stillness of the mountains is invaded by the inane advertising jingles of an itinerant vending truck. This is presented without comment as an ordinary scene of industry, enterprise and development in contemporary Japan. While the lumbermen fail to question their activities, the protagonist himself remains aware. He and his fellow workers retain something of the fear their ancestors felt when tampering with the natural order. In the midst of their destruction they still perceive nature as a goddess and try superstitiously to placate her. When the young assistant profanes nature by using sacred laurel branches to make a bird trap, he is forced to face the mountain landscape, drop his trousers and expose himself to her because, as the protagonist tells him, 'she's a woman, she likes that kind of thing'. He knows this because he is, as he jokingly boasts, especially intimate with her himself. 'Only I', he says, 'can make the goddess feel like a woman'. For him a swim in her sacred lagoon must be performed naked. He jokes about his various rendezvous and his later feckless swim in her sanctuary may be seen as copulative.

If he knows her, however, she also knows him. He is no more transgressive than any other animal – the only threat is that there are now more humans than ever, and that they all have better power saws and more dynamite – but he is aware of his actions, and he boasts of them. It is hubris therefore that attracts jealous deities and in the horrific denouement of the film she chooses him. He has embraced, used and taunted nature and now she embraces and crushes him in turn. He becomes what the director has identified as an *ikenie* (scapegoat): he who takes on himself the sins of all the others. In Japanese mythology, as in Greek, he who is chosen by the gods is destroyed.

Fire Festival is set in Nigishima, a village of some 15,000 inhabitants located in Kumano on the Wakayama coast of southwest Japan. It is a place where the forested mountains descend directly to the sea. It is early autumn and the woodmen are at work, among them Tatsuo (Kitaōji Kin'ya), a man in his early forties, and his side-kick, the 19-year-old Ryōta (Nakamoto Ryōta). Relations between the woodmen and fishermen, always uneasy, are now strained even further when someone dumps 100 liters of fuel oil into the waters of the fish hatchery. The villagers believe that this is an act of opposition to a planned public marine park, a development that will bring money into the community. Tatsuo is regarded with suspicion because he alone has refused to sell his land to the development agency. There is no proof, however, and so with suspicion remaining, nothing is done.

When Tatsuo takes his fisherman friend Toshio (Yasuoka Rikiya) with him to shoot monkeys, there is local criticism since fishermen do not consort with lumberjacks. When Tatsuo borrows Toshio's boat, there are even louder complaints. The reason for borrowing the boat is that Tatsuo's former girlfriend, Kimiko (Taichi Kiwako), has returned to help run her sister's bar and to renew her affair with him. In the closed small town there is nowhere else they can meet without causing comment. Another reason, however, is that Tatsuo can also take Ryota along to keep watch.

Once more, someone fouls the hatchery and two empty oil barrels are found near Tatsuo's house. Disregarding the suspicion, he again borrows Toshio's boat and proceeds to the cove near the goddess's sanctuary and the hatchery. There, he disregards the taboo and takes a swim. In the meantime, the most active of the land speculators, Yamakawa (Miki Norihei), visits Tatsuo's home and hints that selling would be a good idea since the other villagers are beginning to suspect him of dumping the oil into the hatchery.

Still, no one takes any action. Lumbering goes on until, one day, there is a storm, and the woodcutters head for home, all except for Tatsuo. He remains and there he meets the deity, the mountain goddess. He has had moments of awareness before, but now the encounter changes him. During the annual *himatsuri* that follows shortly, he suddenly turns violent and has to be restrained after some young men light their torches before the arrival of the sacred flame from the deity's shrine. Tatsuo's outrage indicates that he is now her creature.

At home, he and his family – mother, sisters, wife and two children – are observing the 17th anniversary of his father's death. Tatsuo loads his rifle and, one by one, kills them all. He shows the bodies of his dead sons to the sea and then smears himself with their blood, just as he has done before with a captured dove. Finally, he props his rifle against his chest and for the last time presses the trigger. Shortly, there is yet another oil spill in the hatchery.

Yanagimachi has recognized that the film confuses people for some reason. He argues that audiences expect some cathartic moment after the murders, but that is not the kind of film he wanted to make. Instead, he has made an explicitly religious film that contains an enormous, even frightening, neutrality. As he has said: 'I think nature is like blotting paper. You, a human, put a mark on it and the mark spreads, sinks in and disappears. Our human feelings too, they are so small and nature is so enormous. We live only for seventy-some years, but nature goes on forever. To nature we mean nothing at all'. This is because nature – the third leg of the triangle – is god.

One of the reasons that *Fire Festival* may confuse is that, despite Yanagimachi's disclaimer, it really does seem at first to be about ecology. Trees are destroyed, the seacoast is 'developed', small birds are killed, monkeys are shot, boar are baited and fish are poisoned. These are all acts that mirror a concern for the world now that man is predominant. If this were all the film was about, however, it would remain an ineffectual plea for people to be more thoughtful. What transpires is that ecological concerns are merely a way of introducing the film's central theme. Writer and director go on to demonstrate why things are not otherwise; why lack of ecological concern is merely a symptom of something deeper. The disease itself, if that is what it is, resides in a complete, natural incompatibility between man and nature.

The viewer's confusion is partially created by the ecological scenario not being played out to its full conclusion. Instead, the goddess, nature invisibly personified, enters and takes over in a way our rational age does not permit. The appearance of a deity in an otherwise realistic film is confusing because our rational assumptions do not permit such an assumption. Indeed, modern audiences can accept such an appearance only in religious films where the emergence of such a figure as Jesus Christ is assumed, or in horror films which explicitly deal with the evil gods of the underworld. In either case, these appearances are standardized and expected, and are not in themselves presented realistically. When such a miracle exists within a realistic film there is bafflement. One remembers the critical consternation that greeted the return of the dead in Carl-Theodor Dreyer's *Ordet* (Denmark, 1954). After everything has been carefully presented as quotidian, the viewer is suddenly asked to believe the impossible.

Consider then the climax of *Fire Festival*: the meeting with the goddess. Deep in the once sacred forests of Kumano the foresters are felling trees again with their power saws, hurrying because a storm is coming. As the wind rises and the rain begins, they run for shelter with the exception of Tatsuo who stays behind, as if he knows what is coming. Drenched by the rain, torn by the wind and deserted by his young friend, he embraces one of the great trees. There is a sudden calm. The rain instantly stops, the wind abruptly ceases and the sun immediately appears. There is silence and the sense of a great presence. Tatsuo knows who it is. It is the goddess, nature herself. He had earlier claimed she could not resist him – he had swum in her forbidden lagoon – and now she chooses him. When he tries to run away, a tree falls in his path – a sign that the way is forbidden. He says only: 'I understand'. The wind resumes, turns into a gale and he makes his way to the stream where, as though knowing what is required, he drinks. At once the great wind stops. The goddess has received her promise, his libation. The combination of the rain machines, kleig lights, airplane motors, Nakagami Kenji's script, Tamura Masaki's photography, Takemitsu Tōru's score, actors and Yanagimachi Mitsuo's direction create a transcendent sequence – the goddess has appeared, invisible but indubitable. We are now prepared for her retribution.

If we think of Robert Bresson, Yanagimachi's favorite director and the one from whom he has learned the most, it becomes more apparent what he is doing. *God Speed You, Black Emperor*, with its opaque, empty shots, might be a continuation of Bresson's *Au hasard, Balthazar* (France, 1966). Watching the truck driver with his spoon and his needle in *A Farewell to the Land* is to remember Fontaine in *A Man Escaped* (*Un Condamné à mort s'est échappé*, France, 1956). When we witness the easy, meaningless drowning of the little boys in the same film we recall the equally casual death of the girl in *Mouchette* (France, 1967). In the blood-drenched climax of *Fire Festival* we see the equally 'meaningless' slaughter of the family at the end of *L'Argent* (France, 1983). With his wide-open, staring and unmoved lens, Yanagimachi is indeed close to the French director, but he also has stylistic debt to the Japanese director Mizoguchi Kenji. In interviews Yanagimachi has often acknowledged an admiration for Mizoguchi's detached, almost documentary eye and refusal to hardly ever use close-ups. Through his own sense of detachment Yanagimachi can lead us to perceive the gratuitous collusions and unremarked connections that make up life. Like both Bresson and Mizoguchi, he shows us that humans are part of something much larger than the society that they construct. In other words, he shows them as part of nature itself. The wandering mother and her children are part of the field of flowering weeds in Mizoguchi's *Sansho the Bailiff* (*Sanshō dayū*, 1954) and the enchanted potter and lovesick ghost are a part of the lawn and the lake in *Ugetsu* (*Ugetsu monogatari*, 1953). In Yanagimachi's films, man is still linked, but he is also baffled and alienated. The drugged truck-driver in *A Farewell to the Land* stares at the rice fields and we, in turn, look at them – rippling, alive, vibrant. 'In a way', Yanagimachi has said, 'he discovers the beauty of nature through drugs, a beauty he has not noticed before. He wants to become a part of nature, to melt into it as it were. This is a very Japanese concept, but I don't think it is possible to merge with nature. Society and nature are quite the opposite of each other'.

This is the opposition that Yanagimachi's opaque and disturbing neutrality is suggesting. It is an opposition not between the individual and society, but between society (and thus also the individual) and nature: the world as it is, the world we have not remade, the world as the gods made it. Traditionally Japan is supposed to have kept its closeness to this natural world. Even now, when Japan has leveled its mountains, cut down its forests, dammed its rivers and cemented its coastline, one still hears that there is a kind of symbiotic closeness between nature and the Japanese. Gardens and flower arranging are then mentioned, but people are unmindful of the fact that these too are intrusions into the natural order.[3]

The natural order is the only order in Yanagimachi's film. The gods are all *shintō* gods. *Shintō* is the original, pre-Buddhist, animistic religion of Japan where a large rock or tree or waterfall may be a deity. It was a pantheistic form of pure nature worship long before being perverted into the state religion during World War Two. Its myriad gods are still considered present and are respected in the many shrines throughout the country. With *Shintō* there is an ancient opposition between those who live by the produce of the forest and those who live by the produce of the sea. This duality is one of the aspects of the plot of the late Nakagami Kenji's story that Yanagimachi based the film upon. Indeed, the original title of the film was to have been *A Festival of Forests and the Sea* but the producers thought it made the feature sound too anthropological and changed it, despite leaving numerous indications of their original intent in the script: 'He's from the mountains, he doesn't know the sea'; 'Mountain folk don't know what the sea is like'; and Tatsuo's angry words when he rejects the developer's agent, saying that he will have 'no shitty marine park – as though anything good could come from the sea'.

By this near removal of a major theme, the film was made to misleadingly emphasize the role of the Wakayama *himatsuri* which had originally been seen as only a small part of the overall picture. Many films are compromised by their producers. It is after all their money and they feel it is their right, or even their duty, to suggest or insist on changes. The prevalence of such supervision is attested by the large number of 'director's-cut' re-releases once the continuing popularity of an older film is seen to justify such an expensive procedure. In Japan such interference is quite normal. Filmmaking is even more of a communal effort there that it is in the West and an urge to agree along with a reluctance to counter authority is customary. Historically, it was only those directors who had proved their box-office prowess, such as Mizoguchi, Ozu Yasujirō, Kinoshita Keisuke, and a few others, who were not interfered with and were allowed to make the films they wanted.

Yanagimachi had no such clout. Further, the making of *Fire Festival* was complicated by the fact that the film's debut producer Parco – an affiliate of the large department store chain Seibu – remained unsure of how to both produce and market its new product. The released film was not the version originally envisioned by writer and director. The original was going to be more frank and transgressive and situated on more than one level that included a sociological dimension. It was going to break a long-standing taboo and concern itself with the question of the perceived pariah group currently referred to under the euphemism of *burakumin*. For centuries these people (in no other way different from the majority of Japanese) have been set apart and discriminated against, even though there have been laws (the first over a century ago) passed against such prejudice.

Traditionally *burakumin* groups have been ostracized, forbidden to intermarry with the general population, and restricted to the lowest forms of labor. Among the reasons sometimes given for the creation of such a class has been the fact that members previously performed such despised duties as those of execu-tioners, torturers and handlers of the dead. It is now thought more likely, how-ever, that such occupations were all that was available to such an artificially created social group. That this group was considered necessary at all is considered to be caused by Japan's decision to isolate itself politically from the rest of the world so that there were no neighbors to demonize. In other words, the self-justifying 'other' had to come from within. Nowadays 'members' are encouraged to 'pass' so that the whole vexed question will not come up. The localities in which these are found have had their names changed so that *burakumin* origins cannot be traced. Nonetheless, even now directories are privately published with new names linked to old so that wary concerns may consult them and avoid hiring anyone from this stigmatized class. Though it has been officially announced that the caste does not exist, prejudice against it still continues.

Nakagami Kenji (who also wrote the script for *A Nineteen Year Old's Map*) was a famous member of this proscribed caste who fought against stigmatization to become one of Japan's finest and most serious writers. He naturally concerned himself with the experience of this stigma and the script for *Fire Festival* (based on a newspaper account of such a family murder) was to have been no different from his other works. Though any direct references were soon removed from the script, there is still enough evidence in the film, such as the presence of dog-training, social rivalries, village prejudice and the part of the Kumano coast known as the home to *burakumin* communities, to suggest that the character of Tatsuo is a member of Japan's pariah minority. He thus knows all about being a figure against whom the majority can maintain its own favorable image through contrast to his despised class. Tatsuo refuses to go along with village plans to make a profitable marine park, he will not sell his property, and he is the one who is accused of poisoning the fish. He is perceived as transgressive long before the goddess actually chooses him as her personal transgressor.

Nakagami and Yanagimachi also introduced another transgressive theme into their script by choosing to emphasize the homoeroticism of Tatsuo and the young Ryōta. The older man is very much the phallic male. He fingers himself, displays a pretended erection, and lives up to his name, Tatsuo. The word means 'son of the dragon', but *tatsu* almost means 'stand up', and is used to refer to erections. While the name is a common one, its use in these particular circum-stances is meaningful. The attraction between Tatsuo and Ryōta is kept on the homosocial level where most men keep it, but there are also indications of something deeper. Tatsuo takes Ryōta along when he takes Kimiko out to make love to her. He is to be a lookout – in more senses than one. He is to observe the older man in action. And both of them are aware of this.

There are several scenes where Ryōta stares at a half-naked Tatsuo and the older man is romanticized in slow motion as if from Ryōta's point of view. There is also much sexual reference: 'Ryōta's wiped his cock on the funny papers' and 'Tatsuo's built like a horse'. Later, during the storm in the forest, Tatsuo embraces Ryōta. This is explained by the youth complaining of being cold, but the implication is that Tatsuo wants his young companion there when the goddess 'makes love' to *him*. Throughout, there are many references to a common homosociality. There is much jocular affection, arms around shoulders and playful messing around. Women are routinely disparaged. Tatsuo believes it is manly to make a woman stand up while being taken, and later brags about it: 'Hey, Ryōta, just done it standing up'. All women are like the goddess. They like male members, love to look at them and this is interpreted as somehow disreputable. An even more explicit sequence was cut from the film before release. Tatsuo and Ryōta make a trip to the larger town of Shingū where Kimiko has opened up her own place – a 'snack bar' with available girls. The girls make the advances expected of their profession, but Tatsuo recoils and when Ryōta shows interest he is taken away.

Parco's new film branch was not going to confront two such taboo subjects as the *burakumin* on the one hand and homosexuality on the other. Even while the film was in the planning stage there were cautious attempts at interference. As the filming progressed (at one time it broke down for over a month) these attempts grew stronger and more frequent. Nakagami left the project before the film was finished, in anger it is said, and Yanagimachi had to patch the script together as best he could. He fought for as many of the forbidden references as possible but any systematic display was denied him. There is no doubt that the *Fire Festival* we now see is not the picture that the writer and director originally planned. Yet, in a way, the producer's interference actually strengthened the power the released film now displays. These themes – *burakumin* prejudice, homosexuality – are now unemphasized, but also unexplained. Their oblique appearance complicates and enriches the viewer's experience. By being there, but by often being invisible like the goddess herself, they heighten expectation and thus prepare the ground for retribution. As Yanagimachi says, they 'act as agents in the film, as x's in the equation'. This is true, and the equation says that violation equals chastisement. At the same time, the simplicity of such an equation is rendered less obvious by what is left out. By not allowing the director to explain, the producers gave him the power to suggest. The strength of *Fire Festival* lies in its ability to demand that we deduce, make conjectures and infer what it implies. This imprecision makes for mystery and its incomprehensibility suggests that such violation will always be with us.

The final sequence of the film shows that the sanctuary has again been polluted. But Tatsuo is dead. A hand releases the dogs. We see someone in the mountains looking down on the despoiled hatchery. His back is toward us but he has Tatsuo's dogs with him. The rising sun shimmers on the oily water. Critics have found this conclusion particularly impenetrable. Yet, as Yanagimachi argues: 'We never see Ryōta's face, we can only surmise that it is he who is taking the dead man's place. Yet, who else could it be? The sun is coming up (we shot that scene at five in the morning) and the dogs are praying (we tranquilized them) and there is someone with his back to the camera and he has again polluted the waters of the bay. For some reason, this confuses people. I suppose they expect some cathartic moment after the murders, but that is not the kind of film I was making'. The director was clearly making a film in which the need for a scapegoat, the *ikenie*, continues. It is a film in which the loved one becomes the beloved and all the problems it deals with are seen as permanent.

Did Tatsuo have a hand or was it Ryōta from the first? He is certainly not a very good boy. Early on in the film, we see him kick a wounded dog and he also knocks down an old man and takes Tatsuo's rifle and threatens him. Is the film a political allegory about Japan's own lost innocence? Such questions can be asked only if one believes that the film is, on the one hand, a kind of murder mystery and, on the other, a film with an agenda all of its own.

Presented with such a problematical feature film, Parco lost what courage it still maintained and released *Fire Festival* precipitously, doing nothing simultaneously to promote it. Yanagimachi would probably not subscribe to the idea that the tampering actually increased the film's mystery, and hence its power, but he did believe that given a chance an audience would have accepted what he and Nakagami had to say. There was, however, little publicity and no major critic in the Japanese press took the film up. Since the film itself contained no concessions to easy comprehension, it died at the box-office. Abroad, its worth was recognized to some extent as it won a prize at the 1985 Locarno Film Festival, but this did little to recoup Parco's losses.

After the failure of *Fire Festival*, Parco's production company folded. Nakagami subsequently took Ryōta with him to the United States. He had originally discovered the young man working on a road gang near Shinshū and introduced him to Yanagimachi who decided to cast him in the role under the same name. Ryōta's highly credible performance is the very promising work of a first-time amateur and Nakagami, it is said, had plans for him. In New York, the two men, neither of whom could speak English, approached the famous Actor's Theatre and attempted to enroll the young actor. Whatever then occurred, there was a quarrel and Nakagami, it is claimed, deserted the youngster and returned alone to Japan. At least this is the story that was told in Tokyo. Finally, already ill, Nakagami died.

Yanagimachi's film was accounted a failure and in Tokyo, as in Hollywood, a financial failure means no more work. The Locarno prize had, however, impressed Warner Brothers, and the director was shortly approached to direct *Shadow of China* (Japan/US, 1990).[4] Since this film also failed to make money, Yanagimachi's chances to continue directing became even fewer. Finding funding, he made one final feature film, *About Love, Tokyo* (*Ai ni tsuite, Tōkyō*, 1992). Again, it had a transgressive theme: the fate of a young Chinese who comes to Tokyo to find work. It was brilliantly realized but, unmarketed, it similarly failed to make a profit. Though shown at a foreign festival – Berlin – it also failed to win any prizes. Since then, with the exception of the television documentary, *The Wandering Pedlars* (*Tabisuru pao-jiang-hu*, 1995), shot in Taiwan, Yanagimachi directed nothing at all in the intervening ten years. (He finally returned to the international film scene in 2005 with *Who's Camus Anyway?* [*Kamyu nante shiranai*].) Among the principals of *Fire Festival*, Ryōta alone enjoyed a happy ending. Somehow finding his way back to Japan from New York, he is now a contented husband and a happy father working in the municipal office of a small community on the outskirts of Tokyo.

Despite all these travails, the power of *Fire Festival* has allowed the film to live on in the minds of those who have experienced it. It is occasionally revived in art cinemas abroad though it remains unseen in Japan. Its power is such that it is impossible to forget once seen. Not only does it reach beyond appearances to suggest a further reality, it also displays a seriousness of intent rare in any national cinema.

Notes

1 There have been other interpretations of this film. For example, the jacket of the KINO VHS edition of the film states: 'At once nature's mystic voice and its amorous despoiler, Tatsuo embodies the spiritual link to nature that the community must sacrifice in order to prosper'.
2 All quotations from Yanagimachi are taken from an undated private interview with the author.
3 It has been suggested by some critics that *Fire Festival* is therefore an allegory. Tatsuo is Japan, still aware of nature but no longer respectful. Nature has a way of dealing with such presumption. Usually it is earthquakes or typhoons, but here it is the somewhat novel method of spiritual possession. Such a reading is certainly possible but it limits the power of the film. Yanagimachi is not concerned with intellectual constructions but with structured emotions.
4 If the director had thought the department store intrusive, he found the Hollywood studio impossible. It also had its problems. Yanagimachi spoke no English, yet he was directing an English language film. The film's star, Chinese actress Gong Li, knew no English either and had to memorize what were to her meaningless lines. The director was constantly fighting consequent script changes and in addition, it is said, he found the lead actor, John Lone, difficult to work with.

Yanagimachi Mitsuo Filmography

God Speed You, Black Emperor (1976 – documentary)
A Nineteen Year-Old's Map (*Jūkyūsai no chizu*, 1979)
A Farewell to the Land (*Saraba itoshiki daichi*, 1982)
Fire Festival (*Himatsuri*, 1985)
Shadow of China (Japan/US, 1990)
About Love, Tokyo (*Ai ni tsuite, Tōkyō*, 1992)
The Wandering Peddlers (*Tabisuru pao-jiang-hu*, 1995 – documentary)
Who's Camus Anyway? (*Kamyu nante shiranai*, 2005)

20

COMMUNITY AND CONNECTION
Itami Jūzō's *Tampopo* (1985)

Linda C. Ehrlich

In *Tampopo* (1985), directed by Itami Jūzō (1933–1997), a celebration of connectedness and consumption joins a celebration of the cinema in a 'comedy of manners' about Japanese society. Through parody and imaginative linkages, Itami attempts to gently illuminate underlying absurdities in contemporary Japanese social rituals.[1] The result is a surprisingly open-ended story which both satisfies and leaves viewers hungry for something a little more substantial.

A wide range of cinematic genres are celebrated in this story which is ostensibly about the remodeling of a noodle shop and its owner. From the opening moments, Itami gracefully manages to include aspects of the Western with its veneration of the tough-but-tender hero, as well as nods to the martial arts film, spy film, woman's film, romantic melodrama, instructional documentary, whimsical slapstick, buddy film, road movie, and *chanbara* swordfight film. There is even an element of sophisticated self-reflexivity with the inclusion of direct address to the camera.

Tsuji Nobuo has posited the idea that 'playfulness' is as much an intrinsic quality of Japanese art as the two other qualities delineated by the art historian Sherman Lee, namely 'decorativeness' and 'realism' (Tsuji 1986: 9–13).[2] Tsuji describes the Japanese sense of playfulness as childlike and free of ideology – a simple, and life-affirming optimism (14).[3] *Tampopo* is firmly rooted in this sense of playfulness, and it is the very 'glue' that holds the diverse fragments together.

Itami often compared the plot of *Tampopo* to that of *Rio Bravo* (US, Howard Hawks, 1959), citing the John Wayne character as the prototype for Gorō (Yamazaki Tsutomu) (Glaessner 1988: 102).[4] The framing stories in both films can be easily sketched out. In *Rio Bravo*, an honest sheriff tries to bring an impulsive murderer and his scheming, wealthy brother to justice while at the same time helping a host of secondary characters to improve themselves. In *Tampopo*, a resolute widow (Miyamoto Nobuko), who owns a failing roadside restaurant, conquers the highly competitive world of the small noodle shop with the help of a cadre of male *sensei* (teachers).[5] These *sensei* arrive intermittently throughout the film but, in the end, they help form a supportive group

Figure 24 Tampopo (1985) gently illuminates absurdities in contemporary social rituals through parody and imaginative linkages. Itami/The Kobal Collection.

that transforms both the mediocre noodle shop and the somewhat dowdy Tampopo herself. A cross-section of contemporary Japanese society passes through Tampopo's world from the overworked salaryman and post-war entrepreneur to the dropout and proper young lady of a marriageable age.

Rio Bravo

If, as Itami has indicated, *Tampopo* is, in part, a parody of films like *Rio Bravo*, we can start to draw new insights into it from a consideration of Hawks' film. *Rio Bravo* starred John Wayne (Sheriff John T. Chance), Dean Martin (Dude/ nicknamed Borachón, a deputy sheriff coming off a two-year drinking spree), Walter Brennan (Stumpy, a crippled old man with a fiery spirit), and Ricky Nelson (Colorado Ryan, a young gunman out to prove himself), with Angie Dickinson (Feathers) as the feisty love interest. Like *Tampopo*, *Rio Bravo* is also a genre hybrid (of the Western and police film, in particular), and a showcase for a host of well-known performers (a singer and a teenage idol as well as the star figure of Wayne). In the background of *Rio Bravo*, as in Itami's film, lie several central themes: the theme of transformation (Dude's transformation from drunk to respected deputy sheriff); the theme of romance between a tough, relatively inarticulate man and a woman; the theme of the group working together to reach a goal (in Hawks' film this involved bringing the evil Burdette family to justice); and the theme of how the 'little guy' must persevere, especially when pitted against the mercenary outside world (in *Rio Bravo*, three men are pitted against a group of contract killers).

According to Hawks, *Rio Bravo* was made in response to *High Noon* (US, Fred Zinnemann, 1952), a film whose premise he found patently ridiculous: 'Gary Cooper ran around trying to get help and no one would give him any . . . at the end of the picture he is able to do the job by himself', he argued (quoted in Bogdanovich 1996: 65). Yet as Robin Wood (1996: 100) perceptively points out, without the secondary characters the seemingly infallible Sheriff Chance would have been defeated. Calling the preservation of self-respect the central theme of *Rio Bravo*, Wood notes that it is precisely this sense of the self that makes up the foreground and core of this unconventional Western.

Strong women, weak men

In her article on 'The Hawksian Woman', Naomi Wise (1996: 115) notes the principle of feminine superiority in many of Hawks' action films by describing his female characters as having a combination of the decisiveness and courage of the male protagonists with an added sense of warmth and humor. Wood defines the Hawks woman as 'sturdy and independent yet sensitive and vulnerable, the equal of any man yet not in the least masculine' (1996: 89). Those exact descriptors could also be written for the character of Tampopo in Itami's film. Feathers differs in that she occupies an intriguing position on the cusp between virtue and deceit – she seems at first to be a dishonest gambler traveling from town to town, but later reveals herself to be loyal and steadfast, albeit prone to emotional outbursts. Like Tampopo, however, Feathers is the kind of woman who refuses to give in and take the easy solution.

But who exactly is this Tampopo herself? On one level, she is a shrinking violet turned successful entrepreneur. As Inouye (2001: 134) comments wryly: 'In the end, Tampopo realizes the capitalist dream of establishing a profitable business'. On another related level, she is also a highly motivated woman, full of initiative, yet also warm-hearted and somewhat hesitant. One wonders, however, if she is the true center of the story, or merely an excuse for a plethora of diverging narratives? Is she as uncomplicated as a dandelion (the literal translation of the word *tampopo*) or as artificial as a name no one would ever be given except in jest? Undoubtedly, she is not as strong as the protagonist of Itami's *Taxing Woman* (*Marusa no onna*, 1987) who aggressively hunts for tax evaders and manages to foil their clever schemes. Tony Rayns (1988: 102) offers a lukewarm opinion of *Tampopo* in this regard, writing that 'the film often loses sight of Tampopo's supposedly steady progress in her art'. What has happened then to the 'sense of self' noted by Robin Wood when it is transformed into the Japanese version?

Itami Jūzō: Writer, actor, director

Clues to Itami's construction of the Tampopo character can be found by looking at the arc of his career in the performing arts. Alan Stanbrook (1988: 9) has compared Itami to a *rōnin* (masterless samurai) in that he was 'his own man'. Yet, as the son of distinguished classical director Itami Mansaku (who died in 1946 when his son was just 12), Itami Jūzō grew up under a large shadow.[6] Mark Schilling (1999: 253, 257) has pointed out that Itami Jūzō's films are marked by didactic moments tempered with a concern for public appeal. Like Kurosawa Akira before him, Itami served as a point of entry into Japanese cinema for many non-Japanese filmgoers and he worked hard to reach both his domestic and his foreign public. He was the author of over 20 books, including *Listen Women, Nippon sekenbanashi taikei* [*A Panorama of Japanese Gossip*] and *Osōshiki nikki* [*The Funeral Diary*], this last being about the making of his debut film. He also served as a talk show host and was the author of a website which chronicled the progress of his filmmaking. As a fledgling director, Itami tackled the incongruities of contemporary Japanese society with a marksmanship that grew increasingly less precise with each subsequent film. At times this offered unwanted results: in 1992, following the release of *Anti-Extortion Woman* (*Minbō no onna*), he was attacked by the *yakuza* who slashed his face and neck.

An actor since the 1960s, Itami served as an apprentice under some of Japan's finest directors, including Masumura Yasuzō (*A False Student* [*Nise daigakusei*], 1960), Ichikawa Kon (*I am a Cat* [*Wagahai wa neko de aru*], 1975), and Shinoda Masahiro (*McArthur's Children* [*Setouchi shōnen yakyūdan*], 1984). Itami also appeared in Nicholas Ray's *55 Days at Peking* (US, 1963) and in the cinematic adaptation of *Lord Jim* (UK/US, Richard Brooks, 1965). In Ichikawa's *The Makioka Sisters* (*Sasameyuki*, 1983), based on the novel by Tanizaki Jun'ichirō, Itami gave an impeccable performance as a mid-level manager, hemmed in by his role as *muko-yōshi* (a husband 'adopted' into a family where there are no sons). This patriarchal, but basically powerless, male role type was satirized again by Itami in the part he played in Morita Yoshimitsu's *The Family Game* (*Kazoku gēmu*, 1983). In addition, Itami acted in the theater in such plays as *The Strange Mandarin* by the avant-garde director Terayama Shūji.

Itami's directorial debut came when he was already 52 years old. 'Your father's profession is like a huge mountain in front of you. It took me fifty years to convince myself I could climb the mountain, too', he told Alan Stanbrook (1988: 9). A look at the titles of Itami's ten films reveals his concern with the institutions underlying superficial layers of Japanese society: *The Funeral* (*Osōshiki*, 1985), *A Taxing Woman* and its sequel in 1988, *Tales of a Golden Geisha* (*Ageman*, 1990), *Anti-Extortion Woman* (*Minbō no onna*, 1992), *The Last Dance* (*Daibyōnin*, 1993), *A Quiet Life* (*Shizuka na seikatsu*, 1995 – based on the book by Ōe Kenzaburō), *Supermarket Woman* (*Sūpā no onna*, 1996), and his final film *Woman of the Police Protection Program* (*Marutai no onna*, 1997). Itami once identified a common thread throughout his films: 'the concern with ritual, with the correct way of doing things . . . Rules are to do with the alignment of the self and the world, an alignment that often results in a sense of isolation' (quoted in Glaessner 1988: 102). His response to these rules was a form of satire that veered from the subtle to the exaggerated, but always with an eye to the human qualities of both extremes.

In 1997, following an indication that an article on an alleged affair would be published in *Flash*, a Japanese tabloid magazine, Itami Jūzō jumped to his death. As a Japanese artist who chose suicide, he followed a long line of contemporary writers from his country who include Akutagawa Ryūnosuke, Kawabata Yasunari, Dazai Osamu and Mishima Yukio. Now, as we view and re-view films like *Tampopo*, we cannot help but ask ourselves how the comedy in them is affected, in retrospect, by the vicissitudes in the life of the writer and director. Can we return to *Tampopo*, after its author's suicide, with the same sense of delight?

Links

Beyond the turmoil in its director's life, one aspect of *Tampopo* that *can* continue to delight is the structural underpinning of the film. *Tampopo* is clearly structured around a series of interwoven episodes and anecdotes. Characters in the different vignettes are linked by similar sympathies, as well as by similar cravings and appetites. A seemingly endless assortment of stories and diversions ricochet from the narrative framing device of the resuscitation of the failing noodle shop which call to mind the classical literary form of *renga* (linked verse). Tampopo herself can be seen as just one more link in this chain.

A brief digression to examine the 'game' of verse-writing in *renga* will provide an insight into the way Itami plays with linkages in *Tampopo*. *Renga* rose to prominence in the fifteenth and sixteenth centuries and is still practiced, to some extent, today. Nijō Yoshimoto (1320–88), the compiler in 1356 of *Tsukuba-shū* [*The Tsukuba Anthology*], the first anthology of *renga* in Japanese literary history, describes the three primary modes of linking in *renga* as: through word, through mood of nature, and through contrast and unusual associations (Ueda 1991: 46, 48). Ueda Makoto summarizes that the purpose of *renga* is to have 'the rhythm of actual human life, with its swiftly changing pace, its totally unpredictable turn, and its apparently chaotic arrangement of events' (Ibid.: 53).

In *renga*, poetic verses need not connect in some direct, obvious way, but may do so in a more oblique fashion to produce a sense of 'unity in variety/variety within unity' (Ueda 1991: 39, 46). The first stanza traditionally sets the tone – the season, the time of day, and so on – and the verses that follow may provide an indirect commentary on or extension of the one before. Like the initial stanza in *renga*, the first scene in *Tampopo* sets the stage. We are in a movie theater; we are an audience watching another audience gather. Or, more exactly, we are the screen, and the audience in the film is watching us. This playful sleight-of-hand reminds us that, right from the outset, we are part of the game.

A chain-like, amoeba-like structure ties together the loosely linked sequences of *Tampopo* as well. The food motif is an obvious one, but what other unifying associative links are there? Is *Tampopo* just a random 'mix and match' or do scenes inter-relate and comment on each other, thus revealing a hidden complexity beneath the comic buffoonery? Serper (2003: 70–95) finds principles of juxtaposition (adult/young, reserved/outspoken, yin/yang) and symbolism (of clothing and objects) in *Tampopo* that serve as a means of creating an 'aesthetic tension' as well as a sense of eroticism. Inouye (2001: 136) points out that additional scenes surround the framing story 'like charms added to a bracelet, like moments of play and festivity that punctuate the routine of economic production'. What helps tie together these 'charms'?

Food links

Food has provided the impetus for films from a host of cultures such as *The Scent of Green Papaya* (France, Anh Hung Tran, 1993), which lovingly recreated a Vietnamese courtyard kitchen, and *The Dead* (UK/Ireland/US, John Huston, 1987) which centered around an Irish banquet. In the world of Japanese cinema, Ozu Yasujirō's characters enjoyed *The Flavor of Green Tea over Rice* (*Ochazuke no aji*, 1952) or (literally) *The Taste of Mackerel* (*An Autumn Afternoon* [*Sanma no aji*], 1962). The final link in *Tampopo*, as credits roll, is the primal eating scene of a child breast-feeding. As Itami Jūzō indicated in his interview with Tony Rayns (1988: 101–2), a '*ramen* [*rāmen*] Western' such as *Tampopo* occupies an interim state where 'sex and eating are not yet clearly separated'. Itami also noted how food is tied into a series of rules and taboos, and how it holds out the possibility of ways to break the taboos (Glaessner 1988: 102). Serper (2003: 84–92) describes how Itami draws on associations from the traditional *shunga* (erotic woodblock print) and from popular *manga* (comic books) to remind the viewer that certain foods – the lobster, peach, oyster and conch, ice-cream cone and carrot – mimic the shape of human sexual organs.

Train links

The train is ubiquitous in Japanese cinema (and society). It runs through a wide range of films from Ozu's *Tokyo Story* (*Tōkyō monogatari*, 1953), where a train carries family members toward and away from reunions, and Toyoda Shirō's *Snow Country* (*Yukiguni*, 1957), with its famous train tunnel scene taken from Kawabata Yasunari's novel, to Kurosawa's *High and Low* (*Tengoku to jigoku*, 1963), where a train is used as a means of capturing the kidnappers. In *Tampopo*, trains travel through cinematic space, linking characters and vignettes. When trains appear, we are aware that some characters are moving on, and that new characters are appearing. High-angle shots of Tokyo are punctuated by the raised form of train platforms. Customers get off the train to enter *en masse* into a small *tachigui* (noodle stand) where steaming bowls of noodles are consumed by people standing at the counter. A panicky husband runs by the passing train from the previous vignette as he hurries to his wife who is dying of overwork in their tiny, child-filled apartment.[7] Trains pass by the amorous gangster and his moll while they are immersed in their culinary lovemaking. During Gorō and Tampopo's 'date', trains can be seen at a distance. The two potential lovers stare away from each other, out of the window, like trains passing in the night.

Teaching links

As one scene in *Tampopo* elides into another, knowledge is passed down. David Stratton (1986: 20) exclaimed in *Variety* that 'the viewer learns how to make noodle soup in three minutes flat, and how to make the best turtle soup. This is a film that's as informative as it is funny'. Gorō's young sidekick, the wide-eyed Gun (Watanabe Ken), is instructed by an imposing elderly *sensei* in the delicate ritual of eating *rāmen* (the lowliest of noodles and hardly worthy of such cere- mony). Gorō and Pisuken (Yasuoka Rikiya), another of Tampopo's suitors, instruct Tampopo's timid son Ryūta how to stand up for himself in the face of bullies. A proper middle-aged Japanese lady tries to instruct her *ojōsan* (proper young girl) pupils how to eat spaghetti Western-style without making a sound, only to have her lesson subverted by the loud slurping of the Western man at another end of the restaurant. In the case of Tampopo herself, it becomes appar- ent that one teacher is never enough: a group is needed in order for the heroine to survive. In addition to the main actors, *Tampopo* offers a rich look at familiar faces, including Igawa Hisashi (the dying woman's husband), Okada Mariko (the spaghetti *sensei*), Hara Izumi (the crazy old woman) and Ōtaki Hideji (the rich old man).

Tied in with the theme of transmission of knowledge in *Tampopo* is the theme of the trickster – not only the con man, but also the noble trickster who knows how to work the system to his or her own advantage. In Japanese mythology, tricksters such as the *kitsune* (Fox), *Susano-o* (the Storm God) or *Momotarō* (the Peach Boy) are able to use their special powers to create open spaces where others only see restrictions.[8] *Tampopo* is full of such fluid, liminal characters who expose hypocrisies underlying the surface level of society while simultaneously celebrating the reversals and triumphs of the underdog. Within an ever- expanding frame, the pompous are cut down to size and those without confidence are elevated to a more secure status.

Remaining links

Andrew Horton (1991: 9) has argued that comedy is 'plural, unfinalized, dis- seminative, dependent on context and the intertexuality of creator, text and contemplation'. How much context must one have then in order to interpret Itami's satire? A particularly difficult vignette for an audience unfamiliar with Japanese culture is the scene in which the men in suits order dinner. Why is it funny that the gaggle of older businessmen all order the same thing, and that the *kaban mochi* (the youngest employee) orders French delicacies with great aplomb? Also difficult for the novice audience seem to be the vignettes of the hobos singing goodbye to their teacher, and the one in which the elderly woman squeezes the soft (and expensive) peaches in the gourmet store, not to mention the 'Spaghetti etiquette' scene in the *manā kyōshitsu* ('Miss Manners' classroom'). Every episode in *Tampopo* is not equally transparent, and a good balance must be found between setting the scene and over-explaining.

An even more important concern is the question of why there is no strong female voice in *Tampopo*. In contrast to this, we have the relatively inarticulate gangster's moll, the dying wife, the elderly 'food fetishist' and the seductive 'gold-digging' young wife. Tampopo's own initiative and drive cannot be over-looked, yet we always see her through the perspective of others. Had the prot-agonist in this film been male, and the horde of 'trainers' and mentors female, it would have been a very different kind of parody indeed. Why, as Serper (2003: 81) points out, are the men's bodies covered in the erotic scenes while the women's bodies are exposed? In a similar fashion, Robin Wood (1996: 101) notes the relative lack of female friendships in Howard Hawks' films and the way the Hollywood director tended to focus on the glories of male camaraderie.

With the protagonist Tampopo's dependence on a cadre of male *sensei*, *Tampopo* appears to be a reversal of Itami's subsequent tendency to portray strong women and weak men in his 'woman films': *A Taxing Woman*, *A Taxing Woman's Return*, *Anti-Extortion Woman* and *Supermarket Woman*. While Gorō evokes the archetype of the 'chaste warrior' that conjures up an image of Miyamoto Musashi,[9] Itami described the character of Tampopo in the following way: 'a very jolly sort of person who dedicates herself to the perfecting of a particular task. The image I had in mind was the sort of woman who works in McDonald's. I tried to make her not too Japanese but more dry and less emotional' (quoted in Glaessner 1988: 102).

Concluding notes

Inouye eloquently sums up the mixed fare that makes up *Tampopo* by suggesting that

> Seen at its best, the world of *Tanpopo* [sic] represents an inclusion of the homeless and the wealthy, the female and the male. It is about cooper-ation, accomplishing good deeds, and the softening of hearts. Seen at its worst, it is about a fiercely competitive world of success at all costs, disrupted by occasional fits of irrelevant, excessive behavior that decor-ate the chain of work as it rules within one of the most productive societies on earth.
>
> (Inouye 2001: 144)

In *Tampopo* – at its best – lessons of transmission and transformation fill the screen, as do lessons of reversals. There are hobos who are more elegant than well-padded businessmen in fancy suits, and tough men who are softer inside than noodle dough. Community is constructed on screen and craft is celebrated. A host of teachers – a truck driver, a failed physician who ministers to the homeless, a chauffeur-cum-chef – all appear at intervals to move the process of rejuvenation forward and – task completed – fade off into the sunset in the hallowed tradition of the Western. *Tampopo* presents a chain which is robust, yet with weak links. As we allow ourselves to be led along this chain, we sharpen our gaze outwards, in an irreverent look at the flipside of Japanese daily rituals. Skillfully, Itami also turns the camera on us, so we too might look inwards at how we too could form some variant of this parodic chain. Theoretically, the chain could continue even beyond the last image on the screen. One of the weakest links in the chain, however, is the figure of Tampopo herself. Like the plant from which the film takes its name, the lowly dandelion, *Tampopo* is far from the elegant *sakura* (cherry blossom) of Japanese cinema, but it nonetheless has its own appeal.

Notes

1 Parody (in Japanese, the loanword *parodī*) calls to mind Edo-period works of art such as Shibata Zeshin's scrolls of badgers dressed up as priests or Itō Jakuchū's *Vegetable parinirvana* with a *daikon* radish taking the place of the deceased Shakyamuni Buddha surrounded by turnips, squash and eggplants as mourners.
2 The Chinese character for play includes the image of a child and of movement in an indirect, unhurried fashion.
3 For further reading on the Japanese sense of play, see Dalby (1986) and Hendry and Raveri (2002).
4 Yamazaki Tsutomu's early performance as an embittered young man in Kurosawa's *High and Low* (*Tengoku to jigoku*, 1963) was followed by his roles in Kurosawa's *Red Beard* (*Akahige*, 1965) and *Kagemusha* (1980), and his leading role as Hideyoshi in Teshigahara Hiroshi's *Rikyu* (1989). In addition, he has appeared in Shinoda Masahiro's *Demon Pond* (*Yashagaike*, 1979), a version of the *It's Hard to Be a Man* series (*Zoku otoko wa tsurai yo*, 1969), as well as Itami's *Shizuka na seikatsu* (*A Quiet Life*, 1995).
5 In 1969, Itami married the actress Miyamoto Nobuko. She starred in all of his subsequent films. For additional biographical information on the director, see Stone 1997: 441–4.
6 Itami Mansaku is best known as the director of *Capricious Young Man* (*Akanishi Kakita*, 1936), one of the most whimsical of the *chanbara* films. Only two of his films now survive. Anderson and Richie (1982: 91) described the hero of *Akanishi Kakita* in the following manner: 'not a hero in any conventional sense of the word, being instead a very ordinary man, weak in body if strong in spirit'.
7 Serper (2003: 72) compares this form of connecting scenes with the traditional word game of *shiri-tori* in which 'one takes turns saying a word beginning with the last syllable of the word given by one's opponent'.
8 These kinds of unexpected juxtapositions combined with a sense of playful transformation can be seen in Japanese folklore, with its tales of foxes that assume the form of bewitching women, or in prints such as Utagawa Kuniyoshi's *Composite Head* in which a fierce-looking man's head is actually made up of a series of male bodies. See Linhart and Früstück 1998.
9 Miyamoto Musashi (1584?–1645) was known as a great warrior and the author of *Gorin no sho* [*The Book of Five Rings*]. He is usually portrayed as a celibate fighter who turns his back on women for fear of their possible weakening influence (Barrett 1989: 43–57).

References

Anderson, Joseph L. and Richie, Donald (1982) *The Japanese Film: Art and Industry*, Princeton: Princeton University Press. Expanded edition.
Barrett, Gregory (1989) *Archetypes in Japanese Film: The Sociopolitical and Religious Significance of the Principal Heroes and Heroines*, Selinsgrove: Susquehanna University Press.

Bogdanovich, Peter (1996) 'Interview with Howard Hawks', in Hillier and Wollen 1996: 50–67.

Dalby, Liza (1986) 'The Parameters of Play', in Mildred Friedman (ed.), *Tokyo: Form and Spirit*, New York: Abrams: 201–15.

Glaessner, Verina (1988) 'Eat! Eat! It is Mother's Last Meal', *Monthly Film Bulletin*, 651: 102.

Hendry, Joy and Raveri, Massimo (eds) (2002) *Japan at Play: The Ludic and the Logic of Power*, London and New York: Routledge.

Hillier, Jim and Wollen, Peter (eds) (1996) *Howard Hawks: American Artist*, London: British Film Institute.

Horton, Andrew S. (ed.) (1991) *Comedy/Cinema/Theory*, Berkeley: University of California Press.

Inouye, Charles Shiro (2001) 'In the Show House of Modernity: Exhaustive Listing in Itami Juzo's *Tanpopo*', in Dennis Washburn and Carole Cavanaugh (eds), *Word and Image in Japanese Cinema*, Cambridge: Cambridge University Press: 126–46.

Linhart, Sepp and Früstück, Sabine (eds) (1998) *The Culture of Japan as Seen through Its Leisure*, Albany: State University of New York Press.

Rayns, Tony (1988) '*Tampopo*', *Monthly Film Bulletin*, 651: 101–2.

Schilling, Mark (1999) *Contemporary Japanese Film*, New York: Weatherhill.

Serper, Zvika (2003) 'Eroticism in Itami's *The Funeral* and *Tampopo*: Juxtaposition and Symbolism', *Cinema Journal* 42 (3): 70–95.

Stanbrook, Alan (1988) 'Ronin with a roguish grin', *Films and Filming*, 403: 9–10.

Stone, Judy (ed.) (1997) *Eye on the World: Conversations with International Filmmakers*, Los Angeles: Silman-James Press.

Stratton, David (1986) '*Tampopo (Dandelion)*', *Variety*, 324 (6): 20, 22.

Tsuji Nobuo (1986) *Playfulness in Japanese Art*, Lawrence, KS: The Spencer Museum of Art, University of Kansas.

Ueda Makoto (1991) *Literary and Art Theories in Japan*, Ann Arbor, MI: Center for Japanese Studies, The University of Michigan.

Wise, Naomi (1996) 'The Hawksian Woman', in Hillier and Wollen 1996: 111–19.

Wood, Robin (1996) '*Rio Bravo*', in Hillier and Wollen 1996: 87–102.

Itami Jūzō Filmography

The Funeral (*Osōshiki*, 1984)
Tampopo (1985)
A Taxing Woman (*Marusa no onna*, 1987)
A Taxing Woman's Return (*Marusa no onna II*, 1988)
Tales of a Golden Geisha (*Ageman*, 1990)
Anti-Extortion Woman (*Minbō no onna*, 1992)
The Last Dance (*Daibyōnin*, 1993)
A Quiet Life (*Shizuka na seikatsu*, 1995)
Supermarket Woman (*Sūpā no onna*, 1996)
Woman of the Police Protection Program (*Marutai no onna*, 1997)

21

THE IMAGINATION OF THE TRANSCENDENT

Kore-eda Hirokazu's *Maborosi* (1995)

David Desser

Between text and context, any understanding and appreciation of Kore-eda Hirokazu's internationally acclaimed theatrical debut *Maborosi* (*Maboroshi no hikari*, 1995) must also take into account a particular intertext: the films of Ozu Yasujirō. Though *Maborosi* both continues and anticipates the young director's thematic interests – loss, trauma, memory – and reproduces certain stylistic procedures of post-1990s Asian art cinema – long takes, de-dramatized narratives – the film work of Ozu provides Kore-eda with a model he can appropriate for his own ends. Ozu's status in the West as an archetypally 'Japanese' director may be controversial and full of misunderstandings, but his stature as a world-class director with a demonstrable sensibility that includes recognizable signature elements means that Kore-eda can confidently assert the Ozu intertext and know that it will be recognized. By the same token, Ozu's status in Japan, where his stylistic elements and peculiar consistency have their own standing, similarly enables Kore-eda to be confident that his intertextual allusions will be acknowledged. Kore-eda's intertextual dialogue with Ozu's cinema represents the younger director's efforts to highlight the themes of loss, trauma, and memory through the stylistic and narrative structures that enabled Ozu similarly to deal with timeless and transcendental issues. That there have been almost universal invocations of Ozu in reviews of *Maborosi* should not dissuade us from fully appreciating the manner in which Ozu's cinema works to enrich the considerable depths of this film.

Kore-eda Hirokazu was born in Tokyo in 1962. He graduated from the Department of Literature at Waseda University. He started his career in television where he became a highly successful documentarist. *Maborosi* was his first feature film. It received its North American premiere in 1995 at the Toronto International Film Festival and it went on to play at the Vancouver International Film Festival thereafter. The film was nominated for the Golden Lion at the 1995 Venice International Film Festival where it won the prize for Best Director. Worldwide theatrical distribution of the film followed and its subsequent release through mainstream distribution sources on DVD attests to

Figure 25 A young woman withdraws from the world after the untimely death of her husband: *Maborosi* (1995). TV Man Union/The Kobal Collection.

the success of the film, making it something of a rarity among contemporary Japanese feature films. Outside the works of Kitano Takeshi, very few non-animated Japanese films merit theatrical release and wide distribution. As we will see, film festivals have been receptive to a certain strand of Japanese 'art' film, into which category *Maborosi* may be said to fit, but few receive wide acclaim, theatrical distribution and easy access on home video. Kore-eda's theatrical follow-up to *Maborosi, After Life* (*Wandafuru raifu*, 1998), was similarly well received, but his third feature film, *Distance* (2001), fell into the more typical obscurity of current Japanese cinema worldwide, showing at film festivals (including prestigious ones), but receiving no theatrical distribution. *Nobody Knows* (*Dare mo shiranai*, 2004) was more successful. It was distributed internationally after Yagira Yūya won Best Actor and Kore-eda was nominated for the Golden Palm Award at Cannes.

The universal invocations of Ozu's cinema in reviews of *Maborosi* should not repress the other directors often highlighted by way of comparison. In particular, Krzysztof Kieslowski and his *Three Colours: Blue* (France/Poland/Switzerland/UK, 1993) is frequently called into play. It is perhaps a thematic link between the two films that such critics have in mind, where a young woman withdraws from the world after the untimely death of her husband, or the symbolic and poetic feel to both films which strongly rely on imagery and silences. There is even, perhaps coincidentally, an eerie similarity to the cover art used on the home video versions of both films – a medium close-up of the starring actress against a blue background (obviously appropriate to

274

Kieslowski's film) gazing enigmatically a bit off-screen. Here, however, newspaper and Internet reviews can only take us so far, as we note that virtually no review is able to invoke a contemporary Japanese film or filmmaker by way of comparison. Yet *Maborosi* is very much a part of a challenging group of works in the Japanese art cinema – a group linked by stylistic and thematic concerns very much worth exploring.

Consider the following. Early in *Maborosi*, Yumiko dreams of her grandmother, perhaps afflicted with Alzheimers, telling her that she must return to Shikoku to die. Indeed, when Yumiko was a young girl, her grandmother disappeared. Plagued into adulthood by this loss, Yumiko mourns that she could not stop her grandmother from leaving. How much greater is Yumiko's loss later when her husband, Ikuo, commits suicide, leaving her with a three-month-old child? In *Okaeri* (Shinozaki Makoto, 1996) Kitazawa Takashi is perplexed by his wife's irrational actions, only to learn that she has schizophrenia. He is in danger of losing her to a debilitating and difficult disease. But what has brought this on? Could it be Yuriko's separation from her parents, who live in far-away Hokkaidō? Perhaps it is the loss of her youthful dreams of being a concert pianist? Perhaps it is the sense of betrayal by her husband? In *The Eel* (*Unagi*, Imamura Shōhei, 1997), Yamashita Takurō has lost his wife's affections to another man. In a shocking moment of violence, he stabs her to death. Imprisoned for eight years, he loses all sense of connection to other people and when he is paroled he is in danger of missing out on a chance for redemption when he meets Hattori Keiko, a young woman who has recently tried to commit suicide. In *Tokyo Lullaby* (*Tōkyō yakyoku*, Ichikawa Jun, 1997), Hamanaka Kōichi returns to the wife and family he abandoned some years earlier. Just why he left is vague and what he hopes to achieve on his return is only gradually revealed. Missed opportunities and a lack of communication keep the characters essentially where they start. In *Tokyo Fair Weather* (*Tōkyō biyori*, Takenaka Naoto, 1997), Shimazu Mikio mourns the loss of his wife, Yōko, who died of cancer at age 34 after 11 years of marriage. Just before her death, Yōko was diagnosed with myodesopsia, a persistent buzzing in the ear, and thus seems, in consonance with her treatment of a neighbor-boy, quite as schizophrenic as the sad Yuriko in *Okaeri*. Schizophrenia, too, afflicts Keiko's mother in *The Eel*. In *Suzaku* (*Moe no Suzaku*, Sentō Naomi, 1997), Eisuke, abandoned by his mother, lives with his aunt and uncle in the country. His grandmother, early in the film, mourns the loss of her husband some years back. Later and more importantly, Eisuke, his cousin, and his aunt cannot recover from the disappearance of his uncle, Kōzō, who seems either, like Ikuo of *Maborosi*, to have committed suicide, or, like Kōichi of *Tokyo Lullaby*, simply to have disappeared, this time never to return. In *Village of Dreams* (*E no naka no boku no mura*, Higashi Yōichi, 1995) identical twins Tashima Seizō and Tashima Yukihiko publish a book of their drawings about their childhood village in 1948 – a village, like their youth, long gone.

In these films, all made between 1995 and 1997, the preponderance of disappearances, suicides, and murder which lead to a sense of profound loss, alienation, and hopelessness is obvious. One may reasonably add Kitano's

Hana-Bi (*Fireworks*, 1997), with its focus on Miyuki's terminal illness and Nishi's profound sense of alienation, to this list of films that deal with what Kore-eda himself called 'a feeling of lack of certainty about anything – a universal undefined feeling of loss' (*Maborosi* New Yorker Films DVD 'Special Features' section). This thematic link is but one commonality among all these films. No less obvious are the stylistic similarities primarily revolving around the long take. It is the primary style of *Maborosi*, *Suzaku*, *Okaeri*, and *The Eel*. An often static camera is used, combined with a propensity for long shots. It is likely that the immediate stylistic influence on these films derives from the Taiwanese New Wave of Hou Hsiao-hsien, Edward Yang, and Tsai Ming-liang. The success of these films in Japan and at international film festivals may very well have been the inspiration for Japanese filmmakers to try a re-entry onto the world scene. Although, as we will see, there has been some tendency to see the marks of Ozu on these filmmakers, especially Hou, it is similarly true that the works of now all-but-ignored European filmmakers such as Jacques Tati, Robert Bresson, and Michelangelo Antonioni are equally likely as cinematic predecessors. This tendency toward the long take is, in fact, not attributable to Ozu, but more clearly to Hou and Tsai. It continues to manifest itself in more recent Japanese films, across ostensible genres. Such films include *M/Other* (Suwa Nobuhiro, 1999), an otherwise engaging melodrama of a young woman simply not certain she wants to take on the responsibilities of motherhood to her boyfriend's child, or a sort of horror film such as *Charisma* (*Karisuma*, Kurosawa Kiyoshi, 1999) where the camera's distance defeats expectations of engagement with the characters and the relative lack of editing mitigates against a sense of tension. Clearly it works for *Eureka* (Aoyama Shinji, 2000), the most challenging Japanese film of recent years, another story of murder, alienation, and a chance for redemption, all told in a crisp 217 minutes! Certainly, traditional Japanese cinema, associated, say, with the films of Mizoguchi Kenji, was lauded in the West for this style. Yet camera movement, especially the tracking camera, was a typical component of Mizoguchi's long takes, whereas the style as it has devolved from the work of Hou and Tsai is quite resolutely static.

In addition to thematic convergences on loss and alienation and the stylistic tendency toward long takes, these films also rely on visualizations of remarkable similarity. The use of rural landscapes in contemporary films is striking for the sense of loss such landscapes already cause in their audience, given the overwhelmingly urban nature of contemporary Japanese society. *Village of Dreams* easily captures this sense of loss, especially by focusing the film on children. *Suzaku* utilizes its rural landscape ironically. The film was shot in the mountains south of Nara, and concerns a small village steadily declining in population precisely because of its isolated nature. Hopes for the development of a rail line to revitalize the town are dashed when the project is canceled. *Maborosi* revels in the majesty of its seaside location and dares the audience to object to the long takes, especially in the climactic scene where the 'mysterious lights' of the title (*Maboroshi no hikari*) reach out to grab Yumiko. Both *Suzaku* and *Maborosi* find it impossible to resist a shot taken through a cave, from within the darkness toward the light, and the play of darkness and light across the cityscapes of *Maborosi*, *Okaeri*, and *Tokyo Lullaby* is similarly prevalent. The landscape – rural or urban – exerts a hold on the filmmakers in the way Taipei does for Tsai or Yang or Paris did for the French *nouvelle vague*. The cinephilia of these directors is too clear to ignore and thus we may claim that the turn to Ozu on the part of Kore-eda is a deliberate strategy, which will now be considered.

A sort of prayer

Aoyama Shinji had this to say about his thrillingly minimalist magnum opus *Eureka*: 'This film is a sort of prayer for modern man, who is searching for the courage to go on living' ('*Eureka*'). This aptly describes *Maborosi*, whose primary, if not sole, theme is how its protagonist, Yumiko (Esumi Makiko), manages to overcome, to transcend, her overwhelming grief in the face of her first husband's inexplicable suicide. Already plagued throughout her young life by her grandmother's disappearance some years earlier, Yumiko is plunged into a profound lethargy bordering on total withdrawal when her childhood love, Ikuo, kills himself some few months after the birth of their son, Yūichi. This occurs about 20 minutes into the story and the rest of the 110 minutes of the film's running time does not so much examine as observe Yumiko's gradual turn to an acceptance of life. From the puzzlement expressed by Yumiko's mother shortly after the young man's suicide, 'Why did Ikuo die? It's a riddle', to Yumiko's own anguished cry over one hour later in the film, 'I just don't understand!', Kore-eda provides no easy answers. Ikuo's motivation remains always a mystery. There is a certain ambiguity here: did he deliberately commit suicide or did the mysterious 'phantom light' of the film's title lure him? And, as Roger Ebert observes, 'What is the reason for the light?' (Ebert 1997). More to the point, how Yumiko overcomes her awesome grief to attain a level of contentment and happiness is not, and cannot be, shown. Instead, Kore-eda relies on the film's implicit connections to Ozu and the stylistic devices he used to engulf the character and the audience in a vision of the transcendent.

To accomplish this, Kore-eda deliberately restricts his film's drama: 'When I was making *Maborosi*, I deliberately eliminated a lot of things. If you heard only the story – a woman loses her husband to suicide, takes the child . . . and remarries, moving to a harbor town on the Noto Peninsula – you'd expect to hear *enka* [old-fashioned emotional songs] on the soundtrack. Like something Shōchiku would make' ('Documentarists of Japan'). The reference to Shōchiku is to the studio's vaunted melodramas of the 1950s, a mode Kore-eda deliberately avoids. Yet it was precisely at Shōchiku that Ozu made his anti-melodramas, his de-dramatized, understated versions of the *shomin-geki* (films about the lower-middle classes) that were the studio's bread and butter. In this respect, he has made something Shōchiku would, and did, create: Ozu's films. By the same token, Kore-eda uses a strategy similar to Ozu's in terms of character expression and insight: 'I thought I'd try to limit the expression of emotion, to create a different kind of emotional expression that didn't depend on close-ups . . . to communicate the character's feelings' (Ibid.).

It is tempting to see the Ozu intertext in *Maborosi* through the lens of Paul

Schrader's influential, yet often criticized *Transcendental Style in Film: Ozu, Bresson, Dreyer*. Schrader's 1972 book was the first sustained attempt in English to come to terms with the seemingly unique sensibilities on view in Ozu's post-war films. (Schrader does not deal with the pre-war and wartime films, probably because they were not available to him. That he could deal so closely and carefully with Ozu's cinema at all in 1972 is testimony to his prescience and powers of observation. As scholars of Japanese cinema, we do ourselves a great disservice in too easily dismissing his book as reductive and essentialist.) Schrader's book was translated into Japanese in 1981 as *Seinaru eiga: Ozu, Bresson, Dreyer* by a pioneering Japanese film scholar, the late Yamamoto Kikuo, a professor at that time at Waseda University. It is likely that Schrader's own reputation as an important screenwriter (e.g. *Taxi Driver*, US, 1976; *Raging Bull*, US, 1980) and director (e.g. *American Gigolo*, US, 1980) accounts for the translation into Japanese. But it was also the first sustained look at Ozu by a Western critic in book form (Donald Richie had published two essays on Ozu in *Film Quarterly*, one in 1959, the other in 1963/4) and, further, it linked Ozu to acclaimed, if specialized, Western directors Robert Bresson and Carl-Theodor Dreyer. Given the major theme of *Maborosi* – overcoming loss and grief – the 'religious' interpretation of Ozu's films put forward by Schrader seems all too appropriate. While this chapter by no means accepts the syllogism that Ozu equals transcendental style/*Maborosi* equals Ozu/therefore *Maborosi* equals transcendental style, the apparent recollections of some of Schrader's primary concepts should nevertheless be pointed out. Ultimately, this accepts only the middle portion of the equation, *Maborosi* equals Ozu, although as we will see Kore-eda's film has some stylistic variations.

Schrader defines trascendental style as 'a general representative filmic form which expresses the Transcendent' (Schrader 1972: 8–9). 'Transcendental style seeks to maximize the mystery of existence; it eschews all conventional interpretations of reality: realism, naturalism, psychologism, romanticism, expressionism, impressionism, and, finally, rationalism . . . To the transcendental artist these conventional interpretations of reality are emotional and rational constructs devised by man to dilute and explain away the transcendental' (10–11). In order to construct the appropriate film style, filmmakers are obliged to focus on: '1. The everyday: a meticulous representation of the full, banal commonplaces of everyday living, or what Ayfre quotes Jean Bazaine as calling "le quotidien" ' (39). '2. Disparity: an actual potential disunity between man and his environment which culminates in a decisive action; what Jean Semolue calls "un moment decisif" when writing of Bresson's films' (42). '3. Stasis: a frozen view of life which does not resolve the disparity but transcends it' (49). Thus, in looking at *Maborosi* we note a fierce determination to focus on 'le quotidien'. Yumiko and Ikuo drink coffee together at a neighborhood restaurant; they paint a bicycle sitting in an alleyway. They ride together on the bike through the quiet night-time streets. Kore-eda emphasizes these commonplace activities through the sheer duration of these shots. They paint the bike and later ride it in single-take shots each lasting slightly over one minute. Other commonplace activities include two scenes of Yūichi being bathed; a shot of the old man napping in a boat; Yūichi playing ball on the slope outside the seaside house; the two children walking through the rural landscape until they finally hitch a ride home; Yumiko and Tamio sitting together underneath their bedroom window after making love – again, shown in a single-take of more than one minute in length. These long takes are, precisely, that 'meticulous representation' of everyday living without the hyper-realism or implicit critique, say, of a film such as Chantal Akerman's famously 'banal' *Jeanne Dielman, 23 Quai du Commerce, 1080 Bruxelles* (France/Belgium, 1976). Instead, the focus is on 'dailiness' as highlighted previously in Ozu's films and extended further here.

Schrader's notion of disparity comes in the form of Yumiko's inability to reconcile her inner turmoil, her unspoken grief and anger over Ikuo's suicide, with the monumental environment in which she finds herself living. Kore-eda is fascinated by the endless ocean outside the bedroom window, the rugged coastline of the Sea of Japan on which a village has been precariously constructed, and a fierce winter storm which rattles the windows and walls of a traditional Japanese rural home. Amid this backdrop, Yumiko cannot control her torment. Obsessively playing with or looking at a last reminder of Ikuo – a bicycle bell whose sound is a leitmotif of Ikuo's loss – fearful of another loss (the old lady who goes out fishing as the storm comes in), she finally takes her decisive action: leaving home to wait for a bus that, surprisingly, she does not board when it arrives. It is as if her decision not to board the bus came as she waited, unseen by the distant camera, inside the small bus shelter. As the bus pulls away, we are surprised to see Yumiko emerge from the shelter. Perhaps a victim of phantom light herself, she follows a funeral procession to the seashore. Will she herself succumb? Or is this phantasmal funeral Ikuo's last rites? His funeral, like a good deal of the film's 'dramatic' moments, is elided. Perhaps Yumiko's long-repressed plaintive cry, 'I just don't understand!', is her final acceptance of this fact, an acceptance that enables her to go on with her life.

Thus the film may conclude with stasis, a frozen view of life which does not resolve the disparity but transcends it. Yumiko never voices her resolution. After the very long take that culminates with Yumiko's plaintive cry, Kore-eda offers only one more scene. In six shots over the course of almost four minutes, he brings his film to a peaceful, leisurely close. We first see a distant shot taken from across the harbor into which Tamio and the children enter. Tamio is teaching Yūichi to ride a bike – Kore-eda is too subtle to remind us of the centrality of the bicycle as a symbol of transcience and loss. Instead, the bike is transformed into an image of dailiness, of the quotidien – a father teaching his son to ride. Then we see Yumiko coming downstairs and she sees her father-in-law sitting on the veranda of the house. She walks over to him and sits down, offering the observation, 'It's getting warm, isn't it?' The old man replies, 'It certainly is'. The camera cuts to the two of them side by side, gazing off-screen. Only two more shots remain, the first a high-angle, long shot across the roofs of the village, the sea in the background, the sounds of bike riding and laughter only dimly heard. And then a still-life, a classic coda, a shot from within

Yumiko and Tamio's bedroom, the room a little untidy, lived-in, the sea visible through the open window in the background as the curtains sway gently in the summer breeze. For Schrader such a final shot indicates 'Complete stasis, or frozen motion, [which] is the trademark of religious art in every culture . . . a still-life which connotes Oneness' (1972: 49). Clearly these two final shots are something like still-lifes, motion barely detectable in shot lengths of 1:05 minutes and twenty-one seconds respectively, and a sense of peace and contentment is palpable.

'It's getting warm, isn't it?'

To anyone even vaguely familiar with Ozu's cinema, the invocation of the weather in the film's last bit of clearly audible dialogue and the still-life 'coda' clearly recall films such as *Late Spring (Banshun*, 1949), *Early Summer (Bakushū*, 1951) and *Tokyo Story (Tōkyō monogatari*, 1953). Roger Ebert notes the following about *Maborosi*: 'The camera, for example, is often placed at the eye level of someone kneeling on a *tatami* mat. Shots begin or end on empty rooms. Characters speak while seated side by side, not looking at one another. There are many long shots and few close ups; the camera does not move, but regards' (Ebert 1997). We should not, on the one hand, make too much of any one of these things. The *tatami*-eye view is a frequent one for shooting interiors of the Japanese home, especially those with *tatami* rooms. The eye-level view is the most frequent in all cinemas everywhere. In Japan, this level is a bit lower than in the West, but hardly a definitive structure. (In fact, Ozu's camera is lower than the eye-level of someone seated on *tatami*, but that may not be worth pursuing here.) Japanese cinema for generations has eschewed the close-up; in fact, Ozu has many more close-ups or medium-close shots than many of his contemporaries. Mizoguchi Kenji made films in which he used only one or two close-ups. There is a myth about Ozu's lack of camera movements, though it is true that later in his career he used fewer such movements. Still, pans and dollies are frequent in his films until the mid-1950s and his pre-war films are positively giddy with camera tracks, pans, tilts, and dollies. By the same token, there are a number of tracking shots in *Maborosi* – the nighttime bicycle ride of Ikuo and Yumiko, or the youngsters exploring the winterscape of Sosogi. Nevertheless, that combination of *tatami*-level shots, (relative) lack of camera movement, the focus on rooms recently emptied of their subjects, does indeed typify the rarefied world of Ozu. Ebert also notes the 'characteristic tea kettle in the foreground of a shot and a scene in which the engine of a canal boat makes a sound . . . uncannily similar to the boat at the beginning of Ozu's *Floating Weeds* ([*Ukigusa*] 1959)' (Ibid.). In fact, if we look at *Maborosi* from a systematic perspective, we find that most of the major narrational principles favored by Ozu are reproduced in Kore-eda's film.

The universal invocations of Ozu in reviews in the West of *Maborosi* indicate both the status of Ozu and Kore-eda's confidence about the acknowledgement of his intertextual references. As Nornes and Yeh note in their interesting hypertext study of Hou's *City of Sadness* (Taiwan, 1989):

By the late 1980s, Ozu's position as an 'international auteur' and one of history's great film directors had been established through lengthy debates in film journals, books by Richie and Bordwell [both translated into Japanese] [etc.]. In Japan, Ozu was the New Wave filmmakers' emblem for everything wrong with Japanese cinema. However, in the 1980s his reputation was resurrected, and he swiftly became canonized as one of their greatest directors. This was largely due to the articles, lectures, speeches and books of Hasumi Shigehiko.

(Nornes and Yeh 1994)

Hasumi's insistence that Ozu was *not* 'the most Japanese of Japanese directors' represented a certain rebellion against Western standards, a deliberate swipe at essentialist and reductive readings of Ozu in the West. This sort of rebellion was continued by Hasumi when he helped introduce the films of Hou Hsiao-hsien into Japan, all the while claiming that Hou was not influenced by Ozu. 'Hasumi was also one of the first writers to promote Taiwanese film in the early days of the Taiwan New Cinema. Hasumi was careful to avoid comparisons of Hou and Ozu, but other critics and audiences were certainly not'. (Ibid.) Yet in a symposium, 'Yasujiro Ozu in the World', organized by Hasumi in Tokyo on December 11, 1998, participants included Hou Hsiao-hsien and his screen-writer Chu Tien-wen (Rosenbaum 2000). This kind of playfulness is typical of Hasumi. Kore-eda seems less playful, but also no less ambivalent about links to Hou. He directed a television documentary about Hou in 1993, *Eiga ga jidai o utsusu toki: Hou Hsiao Hsien (Hou Hsiao Hsien: When Film Represents an Age)*, and the music for *Maborosi* was composed by Chen Ming Chan, who did the scores for Hou's *Dust in the Wind* (Taiwan, 1986) and *The Puppetmaster* (Taiwan, 1993). Similarly, the long take-long shot method in *Maborosi* is far closer to Hou than to Ozu, who rarely utilized especially long takes. The average shot length of Ozu's late films is around seven seconds whereas Kore-eda's here is well over twenty-one seconds. And Kore-eda has a large number of shots that last over one minute, one shot that lasts over two minutes, and the climactic take is over three minutes in duration. Combined with the low-key lighting and shot scale, this is obviously closer to Hou than to Ozu and more in keeping with the Japanese and Taiwanese art cinemas mentioned above.

The two most important structures Kore-eda derives from Ozu are de-dramatization and narrative ellipsis. The first is a consequence of the second. As Ozu tends to elide certain dramatic moments in a film – refuses, that is, to move his narration by a series of climaxes – so, too, Kore-eda skips over those moments that structure mainstream films. Yumiko returns to Ōsaka to attend her brother's wedding, but that ceremony is elided, as is the return trip to Sosogi. There is, as noted, never a funeral or other remembrance of Ikuo's death. Quite surprising is the major ellipsis following Ikuo's death. Here I have in mind the transition from the time that Yūichi, Yumiko's child, ages from 3 months to 5 years old. A scene in Yumiko's apartment finds her mother bathing 3-month-old Yūichi as Yumiko essentially sits and mopes. The scene lasts a somewhat lengthy 2:20 minutes, one of the longer takes in the movie. Near the end of the scene, the mother says, 'Why did Ikuo die? It's a riddle'. From there the film cuts to the exterior alley where we last saw Ikuo, then it cuts back to Yumiko. Somewhat uncharacteristically, Kore-eda uses an insert shot, of the bicycle bell, certainly to emphasize how significant it is as a leitmotif. Then we see four exterior shots devoid of Yumiko or any character that we know, followed by two shots of Yumiko walking the bike – the bike associated, of course, with Ikuo. It is easy to imagine Yumiko's unvoiced thoughts and feelings. Then there is a fade-out. Fade-outs typically mean that time passes. How much time in this case? We fade in on the bike, which may deceive our sense of time passing through the fade-out. But as we cut to the alley in front of Mrs Ōno's shop, where Yumiko and her mother thank Mrs Ōno for arranging a new father and sister for Yūichi, which is to say a new husband for Yumiko, we discover that five years have passed since the fade-out. Yumiko and Yūichi soon leave the Kansai area for a new home by the sea.

What is interesting about this is the question of when, where, and how Mrs Ōno arranged for Yumiko to meet and marry a new man. There would be drama in such a meeting, pathos in Yumiko's acceptance of a proposal of marriage, sad reminders of her loss of her true love. Instead, it all takes place off-screen. This is typical, of course, of Ozu, where in a number of his 'marriage' films we never even see the groom, the man who will, and does, take the daughter away from the aging, single parent. That pathos is not what Ozu is after. Whatever motivates Yumiko to accept a marriage, and how she lived and struggled in the almost five years since Ikuo's death, are all unimportant to Kore-eda. What is important to the filmmaker is Yumiko's ultimate ability to overcome that loss, live with that loss, live again.

While a fade-out is a typical transitional structure to indicate the passage of time and a narrative ellipsis, Kore-eda utilizes some favored Ozu devices to elide the other major dramatic moment in the film: Ikuo's death. There is a certain subtle foreshadowing the last time Yumiko, and we, see Ikuo. The scene begins with Yumiko hanging clothes outside on their small balcony when she sees Ikuo walking down the alley. He has come home to bring the bike back and get an umbrella in case it rains. The two go downstairs. Then there is a long shot down the alley from Yumiko's point of view, Ikuo trailing off down the lane twirling the umbrella in an almost Chaplin-esque fashion. Perhaps I am reading too much into that. Nevertheless, this long shot may portend Ikuo's fate in the way it recalls the opening scene of Yumiko's grandmother similarly walking away from the camera toward an empty urban horizon. We watch Ikuo for eighteen seconds, a long time simply to see someone walk away. Next there is a direct cut; it is raining and the camera focuses on the now-empty clothesline, holding on it for eleven seconds – again a long time to watch nothing happen. Except that the clothesline is a typical Ozu 'pillow-shot' – a transitional space empty of human characters, but which suggests their presence in their absence. The empty clothesline may again portend Ikuo's fate precisely by the absence of clothes. A direct cut follows to Yumiko bathing her son in the background of the frame, while in the mid-ground screen left there is a teapot, steam emanating from its spout. We cannot help but notice this teapot as the shot is held for 35 seconds. Another direct cut takes us to the exterior of her apartment where we see Yumiko open the window and look out. A final cut in this scene reveals Yumiko asleep on the floor, only to be awakened by a knock on the door from a policeman.

Obviously, we sense something is wrong by the time Yumiko looks out the window, but do we sense Ikuo's shocking suicide across the series of cuts from his walk, to the night-time rain, the empty clothesline, to Yumiko's bathing the child? I think we do, precisely by the length of the takes and the use of the rain, the clothesline, and the tea kettle. Ikuo's off-screen suicide not only spares us the violence of his death (the policeman at the station says there is not enough of the body left to identity; a whistle Yumiko earlier gave Ikuo is essentially all that remains), but leaves an emptiness in the heart of the narrative. Why did he do it? We never know. But we do not need to know. What we need to know is that Yumiko can overcome, transcend, this enigma, this mystery, and that she can do so precisely by investing herself in the dailiness of life. She lives not for the highs and lows, but for the moments in between, the only moments we see.

Acknowledgements

The author would like to thank Aaron Gerow for his help in the research for this chapter.

References

'Documentarists of Japan 36 12: Koreeda Hirokazu' (1999) *Documentary Box* 13, 10 August. Online. http://www.city.yamagata.yamagata.jp/yidff/docbox/13/box13-1-e.html

Ebert, Roger (1997) '*Maborosi*', *Chicago Sun Times*, 21 March. Online. http://www.suntimes.com/ebert/ebert_reviews/1997/03/032105.html

'*Eureka*'. Online. http://www.rottentomatoes.com/m/Eureka-1107897/about.php

Nornes, Abé Mark and Yeh, Yueh-yu (1994) '*City of Sadness*'. Online. http://cinemaspace.berkeley.edu/Papers/CityOfSadness/onation.html

Rosenbaum, Jonathan (2000) 'Is Ozu Slow?' *Senses of Cinema* 4. Online. http://www.sensesofcinema.com/contents/00/4/ozu.html

Schrader, Paul (1972) *Transcendental Style in Film: Ozu, Bresson, Dreyer*, Berkeley: University of California Press.

—— (1981) *Seinaru eiga: Ozu, Bresson, Dreyer*. Trans. Yamamoto Kikuo. Tokyo: Firumu Āto-sha.

Kore-eda Hirokazu Filmography (feature films only)

Maboroshi (*Maboroshi no hikari*, 1995).
After Life (*Wandafuru raifu*, 1998)
Distance (2001)
Nobody Knows (*Dare mo shiranai*, 2004)

22

THERAPY FOR HIM AND HER

Kitano Takeshi's *Hana-Bi* (1997)

Darrell William Davis

Hana-Bi stands out for its use of Japanese contextual elements. Compared to Kitano 'Beat' Takeshi's earlier films, it organizes a series of everyday moments into a tragi-romantic patchwork. Its deft use of ordinary practices stimulates extraordinary aesthetic effects. The most casual of situations – playing catch, a guessing game, family snapshots – are rendered portentous and fateful because they are placed within sequences of distracted reverie. Occasionally, viewers must work to sort out the temporal and causal relations between scenes, but this is not necessarily disorienting. 'Everydayness' is a vehicle to transport characters and plot back and forth, here and there. In *Hana-Bi*, the more innocuous the situation, the likelier it will be used as a portal to memory, premonition, or daydreams. Quotidian details are given a special status and function and they are prone to flights of abstraction. Mundane chores of exposition are usually left to minor characters.

This means the film is simultaneously modest and grandiose, like its title. The meaning of *hanabi* ('flower fire') may range from a humble, hand-held sparkler to an awesome, night-blooming burst of color and flame. What the references have in common are connotations of beauty, evanescence, and surprise. 'If you don't expect it, a little firecracker can scare you', says Kitano (Milestone Releasing Press Kit 1998 – hereafter MPK).

The film is unusual in its mixture of genre, contemplation, and combinatory stylistic patterns. In another essay I have called these patterns 'pointillist', after the technique used by the painter in the film, Horibe (Davis 2001).[1] Kitano also departs from his usual concerns through the functions ascribed to national iconography. Typical images of the national, whether they appear in scenery, graphic style or scenes of everyday life, work to soothe the anxieties of trauma-tized protagonists. This is pronounced in the experience of Horibe, the artist, and offers the option that he, rather than Nishi, the man of action, is the primary narrative agency. Here Kitano seems to approach a more orthodox figuration of Japanese national cinema, without sacrificing the elements that first got him noticed as a director. These familiar elements include gangster milieux, male bonding, appalling violence, and savage, black humor. Ambiguity, subtle

Figure 26 Both modest and grandiose: *Hana-Bi* (1997). Bandai Visual/The Kobal Collection.

psychological states, memory, and romance are the relatively unusual ingredients, as well as explicit references to traditional Japanese motifs. *Hana-Bi*, then, is a key film, a cross-over to new territory in the Kitano portfolio. Its status is as a work that reconciles the violent anarchy of a Kitano gangster picture with the contemplative aesthetic of a prestigious international art film. The film could be seen then as a Trojan Horse, two films in one.

The aesthetic effects discussed in this chapter are organized in three main constellations: uniforms, puzzles, and sights. *Hana-Bi* is at once a satisfying gangster film, a Kitano Takeshi vehicle, and a prize-winning entry at the 1997 Venice International Film Festival. These three aspects are complementary thematically, narratively, and especially via characters' interlocking points of view.

Uniforms

After the credits sequence, *Hana-Bi* immediately announces itself as a gangster picture. Correction: the scowling, slightly ridiculous *chapatsu*-blonde punk actually interrupts what begins as an art film, literally, with the lyrical music and paintings of the credits. The abrupt point-of-view introduction presents intimidation and violence as facts of life. They are troublesome, like mosquitoes or traffic, but they can be endured or swatted away, at least to a character with enough *sang froid*. That character is Nishi (Kitano), the hero of the film. Nishi has more important things on his mind than two-bit punks. This conveys the film's overall aims, a gangster film that will satisfy genre fans, but also is something more than that.

The two punks wear uniforms, which are a visible and important part of Japanese social life and play a significant role in *Hana-Bi*. The hood's dirty-blonde *chapatsu* hair flags an affiliation: a mild statement of juvenile defiance and would-be gangsterism. The hair signifies no less clearly than does a uniform. *Chapatsu* plus blue jump suit work together. Nishi's conservative navy suit and car clearly sets off the punks' ineffectual intimidation. Uniforms work as specific social *kata*, or forms, and are functionally equivalent to how films affiliate with generic forms. So does their conspicuous refusal by individuals, who use them as 'anti-uniforming' (McVeigh 2000) or 'swerving' to a different, usually opposing purpose (*detournement* – Debord 1956).

In Japan, uniforms carry a certain nostalgic quality deriving from their introduction in the educational reforms of the Meiji period (1868–1912) and because they continue to be worn by all students, through high school. They represent residues of early modernization and organizational culture, but continue to signal group or occupational identity. They are material markers of institutional life cycles (McVeigh 2000). The salaryman's uniform, dark suit, tie, and briefcase, indicate a rapidly disappearing era of lifetime employment and loyalty to the firm. Salarymen, at least in popular imagination, also perversely consume schoolgirl uniforms and other fetishes (baggy socks, used underpants) which are for display and sale in the abusive exchanges of *enjo kōsai* (compensated dating with minors).

As for gangsters, they too are members of a traditional guild and so attire is appropriate to their rank: tracksuits for errand boys and drivers (*chinpira*/punk); casual street clothes, such as aloha or silk shirts for soldiers (*aniki*/brother); Giorgio Armani, Yamamoto Yohji or Yves St Laurent suits for the executive level (*oyabun*/elder). Note the brief – and only – scene in the police station: Nakamura viciously scolds a punk who tries to extort money for the soiling of his Armani. The hapless punk receives the third degree, less because of the attempted extortion than because an Armani is beyond his proper rank. Equally improbable, he also demands the taxi fare to Kyūshū, at the far end of the archipelago. At the very top, at least in popular culture, the *yakuza* godfather wears Japanese-style *kimono* or *yukata*. Recently there has arisen public discourse in Japan about *kimono* as male fashion statement, an affectation so old-fashioned that it is mutating, 'swerving' into radical chic, with a hint of neo-nationalism (Joyce 2003; Dalby 1993).[2]

Set in Los Angeles, Kitano's film *Brother* (2000) takes great care in the display of splendid Yamamoto Yohji suits worn by the star and his African-American gang. The film is something of an extreme in its exteriority. Like scarecrows, suits prevail over characters and iconic, pseudo-American settings over story. *Brother* repeatedly depicts men sizing each other up on the basis of external details. Clothes, sunglasses, race, and language: all these are employed as hermeneutics of intimidation in a tale of a Japanese gangster who successfully challenges the mafia with his newly found black brothers. Their gold chains and baggy hip-hop wear are soon exchanged for tailor-made Yamamoto Yohji. This is less a signal of Japanese ascendancy over American or Italian than a more conventional notion of would-be legitimacy, the highly sought-after status of businessman over gangster (Hollander 1994; Lurie 2000). Yamamoto was also the costume designer for Kitano's *Dolls* (2002). *Dolls* is more stylized, with explicit referral to classical motifs: the seasons, fate and forms such as the *bunraku* doll theater. The wooden performances, particularly in the faces of the leads, recall the flat artifice of dolls but also the life endowed in them through the hands, voices, and instruments of the masters.

In *Hana-Bi* there are many uniforms worn by the working class, ranging along a continuum. Razor-sharp types come alive through costume and casting. These types may be sympathetic, like the white jumpsuit and rubber boots of a junkman, Tetsu, and his glue-sniffing helper, who also wears sports *chapatsu* hair. Tetsu is introduced through a characteristic confrontation with a little workman wearing cheap gloves and baseball cap (see Appendix – Scene 12). Off-screen sound tells us there has been a collision, then we see two men facing-off in front of a stricken pick-up truck. The shot is framed in profile, only their heads are cut off, so the uniforms and size difference of the two figures are the most salient things in the shot.

Several narrative moments privilege uniforms and associated ideas of work and subservience. Minor characters are placed in two scenes to help Nishi kill time, and they all wear uniforms, which clearly indicate their 'manual' status. Sushi apprentices sheepishly play catch in the street near the stakeout; perhaps they are on a break because business is bad, or the boss is away. Identifiable by their white frocks, headband, and wooden clogs, they are playfully scolded by Horibe. Nishi also pretends to play with them. On the way to the bank, there is a laborer at the curb, pretending to be shot by Nishi (Scene 24). This worker is especially interesting because of the two-toed *tabi* he wears on his feet as protection from stray nails. He is a litmus test of Nishi's disguise as a uniformed traffic cop, betraying alarm as Nishi pulls up in his faux-police car. (Could he be a foreign, possibly illegal, guestworker?) When Nishi points his gun, the laborer laughs and pretends to clutch his wound, grimacing. He plays along with Nishi-Kitano's game of masquerade, a game no less deadly for its simplicity.

Beneath the obvious displays of class and job description, Kitano undermines the uniformity of Japanese uniforms. When social expectations follow the gear too closely, they beg to be exploited. There is a sly critique articulated about uniformity and presumptions of homogenization via masquerade and role reversals. If Japanese society is one that automatically follows external markers of job and authority, then this is a society easily hoodwinked. Although the film has many scenes of youngsters trying to pull scams such as the extortionist punk or the kid who tries to sell Tetsu a hot taxi, this is also how Nishi the pretend-cop pulls off a discreet bank robbery.

Preparation for the robbery is as meticulous as the kid's sales attempt is sloppy. Tetsu easily calls his bluff and drives him away. Moments later, Nishi himself turns the tables and correctly spots the car as stolen. He then gets it for a fraction of the initial price. Next, the methodical precision of the taxi's alteration into a black-and-white police car recalls a child's play with paints or crayons. When Nishi obtains a crisp police uniform, transformation of the vehicle, and himself, is nearly complete. Tetsu throws in a child's hand-cranked siren and the disguise is ready. The beauty of Nishi's quick-change act is that he reverses into a role that he already occupies, a cop with an outside agenda. When he robs the bank, he blends in with the office's bland surroundings, dominated by meek blue-suited office ladies (OL).

Nishi is not alone in this game of role-playing. His charade as uniformed officer parallels Horibe's impersonation of an artist, or artiste, complete with elegant French beret. Both are imposters, but only partially. Both men pose as something they are not, the better to become someone else (cop-as-robber; ex-cop-as-painter) and thereby distract themselves from thoughts of death. For both men their play is serious therapy. Insistent cross-cutting between the two scenes of creative transformation (Scenes 18–20) drives home the point. Improvisation, recycling, and *bricolage* are the principles in common, as well as re-functionalizing children's toys and found objects.

In general, uniforms signal parallels and rhymes between the hierarchical worlds of gangsters and cops. The dress, behavior, and speech of both realms show a distinct pecking order. Apprentice cops are novices and bumblers, subject to hazing at any moment. So are the *chinpira*, low-ranking gangster lackeys. When order is not strictly observed, tragedy can strike. Because he has a hot date, Nakamura wears a suit on plainclothes duty, and he cannot stay over on a stakeout. Horibe fills in and is shot. Similarly, a foolish *chinpira* makes a joke and is bashed with a Chinese vase. When a customer calls the assassin Tōjō 'boy' (*kozō*), his head is blown off.

An inversion of rank and gender takes place at the junkyard, which is a kind of serendipitous playground in *Hana-Bi*. The glue-sniffing helper bangs Uncle Tetsu's head as he reads and tells him to get back to work, a feeble bit of payback for his earlier abuse. Other than that, women's uniforms serve mostly to stabilize and confirm prevailing social norms. Examples are nurses at the hospital, as well as Mrs Tanaka's post at a lunch counter, when her uniform vaguely recalls a nurse's cap.

Nonetheless there is a key experiment in 'abnormal' composition that involves a nurse, a figure of righteous, yet intimate compassion (Scene 2). In the hospital, Nishi sits at a table facing right, graphically matched with his wife from the previous shot. As he and the doctor talk, a nurse walks through the shot, stops to serve tea, then moves right out of the shot, only to sit at her station with her head back in the foreground, blocking the main characters. Her out-of-focus presence, together with the rustling leaves in the far background, creates a perceptual puzzle with no thematic motivation. It was a 'weird shot', admitted Kitano, 'but I figured I could get away with it. Film theory is always evolving and the audience is evolving with it. I think we can afford to turn things around a little, and the audience will follow' (MPK).[3] For director and cinematographer Yamamoto Hideo, it was a case of 'let's try it this way' and the result was accepted.

Puzzles

All kinds of games, benign and manipulative, are played in this film, as in 'head games'. Nishi and Miyuki spend time playing guessing games, puzzles, magic tricks, and sleights of hand. These are privileged moments. In the funny guessing game, Nishi confounds Miyuki by using the rear-view mirror to correctly guess each card, with a final switch to a candy bar. This is subtly echoed at the end of the film.[4] At the beach, the end of the line, a point-of-view shot shows Nishi watching the side mirror for his colleagues' arrival. What approaches from behind is dreaded and inevitable; the interval measures out the final precious minutes in their lives.

The suspense here contrasts with the surprise use of jump-cuts to an action's effects, Kitano's jack-in-the-box trademark: from the sudden cut to a punk wiping the windshield to more shocking matches-on-action that ambush us. Cutting from the flick of a lighter to a gunshot; from 'suicide' character to a sudden splash of red, these are clear instances. Another interruptive construction is a pleasant one, as seen in the sudden cut to a beaming, angelic florist (Scene 19). The interruptions and shifts in tone are unsettling, but they also make up the signature of a famous *auteur*.

Crucially, Kitano plays games with time, juggling various temporalities to mix sequences of memory, fantasy, and everyday life. The film was re-edited fourteen times (MPK). This play with time is unusual in Kitano's films, but *Hana-Bi* is also typical of the director's work in abrupt shifts of tone: from humor to extreme violence and back. This depends on skipping ahead, jumping forward to the punch line. Recall 'Beat' Takeshi's background as a stand-up comedian, one-half of a duo called 'Two Beats'. Examples can be seen at the lake, not only with the unlucky clerk but also in the sick joke played on the novice *yakuza*. After having kicked him in the face at the bar, Kitano humiliates him again, and then makes him eat his own bullets. This reprises the sadistic trick played by the scary gangster in the white suit, Tōjō, who pulls the trigger point blank in Nishi's face. Click.

Looking at the film's overall segmentation, there are two major flashbacks in the first part of the film: Scenes 1–2 and 13. The shooting in Scene 13 is clearly marked as subjective past through slow motion and sound, and glimpses of this event have been briefly inserted (Scenes 4, 5 and 10). This is the central causal event of the film. But Scenes 1 and 2 are not signaled as clearly. The order of these events – whether they are causes or effects and where they belong in relation to the credits sequence – is in doubt, and because they come at the beginning we see them as a temporal anchor for subsequent events (what cognitive psychologists call the 'primacy effect').

This temporal ambiguity has repercussions down the line. The dissolve from the blue sky into the first scene does not specifically punctuate a move backward in time. Only the brief inserts of Nishi standing by his car, lost in thought, suggest temporal play, that is, the surrounding events may belong in the past, to his memories (Scenes 1, 3). It is initially hard to place the Nishi+car insert. Is it a flashback-within-a-flashback? We struggle to put this into the order established at the beginning of the scene when it is actually the reverse, a flashforward. The establishing actions belong to an earlier time, as indicated by the inserts of Nishi, who mulls over these events. Only in Scenes 8–9 is the location of the Nishi+car inserts confirmed, somewhere near Horibe's place by the water.

Similarly, in Scene 2 Horibe is shot, but it is matched so tightly with Nishi's action at the hospital that it could be one of his thoughts. Is Nishi foreseeing, imagining or remembering this? Even wishing for Horibe's death? None of the above. The lighter:pistol match-on-action encourages us to infer Nishi's projection, when in fact it is a parallel action happening at the same time. The shooting itself occurs in a strange subjective space (whose?) in slow motion – but for one crucial detail, the azaleas next to Horibe as he falls. These purple spring flowers connect the shooting with the everyday temporality of the stakeout van, emphasized by Horibe's chat with his daughter only moments before. But the flowers must also be the catalyst for Horibe's subsequent epiphanies. Only then do we see Nakamura at the hospital informing Nishi of the shooting.

Later, when we are informed of Horibe's suicide (Scenes 8–9) the pattern is similar: car park punks, a trip to hospital, then at home, a sad reminder (tricycle) and finally a phone call with bad news. Horibe has tried to kill himself, we are told in voice-over, but has not been successful. We expect to hear of his near-drowning because of an earlier close-up of his feet in the sand, not feeling the pull of cold waves. Again, late in the film there are strong (too strong!) suggestions of Horibe's suicide by *seppuku* (ritual disembowelment) which remain unfulfilled.

The almost ritual repetition of Horibe's torment – shooting, drowning, sleeping pills, stabbing – shows a path toward a revenge story for a friend's emasculation, but this is a path not taken. We have instead a potent series of fantasies that are transferred to Nishi and acted out in real life.

The suggestion I make here involves a version of the repressive hypothesis, the infectious productivity of Horibe's inner vision. Insight is incitement. Thanks to his shooting and near-death, Horibe is the seer and real narrator in *Hana-Bi*, while Nishi is the actor-puppet. If painting is Horibe's therapy for his loss, painting also determines Nishi's crime spree and his transformation into a romantic outlaw. Each step on the couple's journey is a *projection* of Horibe's imagery, matched by the evolution of his visual style. As Nishi and Miyuki travel, Horibe's work becomes more insistent and abstract, from simple cartoons and pointillism to woodcut imagery to the use of pictorial ideograms dissolved with landscape photography. It also becomes more traditionally 'Japanese', as it approaches the theme of suicide as an artistic statement. Gradually the road trip and the paintings start to merge; paintings assert a prescriptive norm, rather than remaining just a parallel mirroring device. The story is inverted, but also unified, making it the result of Horibe's feverish thoughts, and the entire narrative configuration is reframed within his mind's eye.

The basic economy in this puzzle is one of compensation and substitution. The catalyst for seeing afresh is loss, anguish. Insight requires suffering, apparently. But if Nishi acts out fantasies of freedom and Horibe paints his, they are both reacting to intense personal tragedies, the loss of kin. Though it appears to be Nishi who encourages Horibe and others, it is Horibe's sensuous thinking that uses Nishi as mouthpiece/actor. Both have lost family and perhaps this is why Nishi's wife seems unstable, only half there. Like an autistic child, Miyuki is mute and behaves like a sexless, sometimes mischievous, dependent. When she makes a gesture of adult intimacy at the temple, Nishi rebuffs her. Since the death of her own child she has regressed mentally, in addition to the toll taken by her disease. As for children, they appear obliquely, through props and walk-on vignettes, like the child asking grandpa about the temple bell. The girl at the beach (Kitano's own daughter) is similarly a foil for suffering, witnessing the harsh culmination that we can only hear. Children and women, therefore, are the loss in the inner lives of both Nishi and Horibe, haunting them until they are compelled to create distractions to fill the darkness and rage.

Sights

On the set, Kitano is known for playing what he calls the 'survival game', rewriting the script to follow only the most interesting performances of his cast. Those who cannot deliver are eliminated from the story:

> Kayoko Kishimoto was really excited when I first told her I wanted to work with her on this film. When I told her she had no lines, she thought I was joking. When she came to the set and she found out she really had no lines, she thought her character was going to be killed off immediately. She was a little disturbed throughout the movie because she wanted to act, but felt like she couldn't without any lines. But I think that disturbance worked well for her terminally ill character. I was afraid that it might be the death of the film to have her completely silent throughout the movie. I had to somehow mask this fact and not let the audience notice that she doesn't say a word during the movie. Only when she utters her last line, do they realize that it's her first. (MPK)

When the doctor suggests that Nishi take her away, he says 'talk to her as much as possible'. But rather than speak, Nishi and Miyuki silently act out their intimacy. Sexual expression too is conspicuous in its absence. Instead, they enjoy seeing the sights. Restorative tourism, with stops for occasional beatings and shootings. A key element of their journey is the various landmarks they visit: Mt Fuji, *kare-sansui* rock gardens, a famous temple, cherry blossoms, snowdrifts, a traditional Japanese inn (*ryokan*). Given the nature of their trip, these places are highly romanticized. The landscapes and traditional icon-ography are a retail(or)ing of Japanese aesthetics to suit Kitano's movement into the international art cinema (Davis 2001). Kitano handles this much like an 'outsider' or foreigner discovering these sights for the first time. This may explain why *Hana-Bi* is well-liked internationally. Furthermore, her illness and his robbery/killings entail a fatality to the trip, which suggests in turn *michiyuki*, from the standard *kabuki* and *bunraku* doll theater repertoire. *Michiyuki* is the trope of lovers eloping to commit suicide together (*shinjū*).

The *michiyuki* motif is as much an interior journey of the artist, Horibe, as it is Nishi and Miyuki's road trip. It is possible to trace the relations between Nishi's story and the presence of paintings in the mise-en-scène. As with paintings, so with flowers, landscape, and women. The film progresses and

Horibe's paintings become more insistent, not content to remain in the background. They intrude into the narrative and threaten to take it over. In this sense the paintings are sights to the same extent as the specific locations visited by the doomed couple.

Paintings are visible from the start, from the angel composition in the credits to the hospital (angels, again), the bar (a mythological picture of sea-gods), and the office of the *yakuza* (a large, hallucinatory dragon). This dragon is the sort of iconography typical in gangster tattoos and another bit of Orientalist kitsch, a Sharaku print of a *kabuki* actor, appears in the background. Note how this print later becomes demonized: the *kabuki* actor becomes a hideous skull holding what was the actor's head. At first, the paintings remain in the background, much like the flowers that just happen to be in the shot. But with the floral epiphany of Horibe, the paintings take flight and start to insinuate themselves into the diegetic substance of the story.

Examples include cross-cutting between Horibe painting and Nishi remaking a stolen taxi into a police car, which is a fairly direct transposition of Horibe's animal-floral hybrids. The juxtaposition of cherry blossoms with a painting of the same subject is another shuttle between setting and mental state, and later we see the insertion of a brightly colored painting of fireworks into an extra-diegetic shot of real *hanabi* at Nishi and Miyuki's campsite. A rainy day follows, for Horibe and for his pointillist composition.

As the film continues, more time is taken with vignettes of play that go off the narrative rails but have sensuous, emotional impact. The key scene here is the remarkable floral epiphany experienced by Horibe which, in a gangster picture, is an audacious moment. The epiphany is doubly striking because, true to form, it is presented as a surprise, abruptly, in four snapshots sandwiched between two oblique views of Horibe in his wheelchair (Scene 18). Only later do we get a point-of-view construction motivating the paintings. (Of course the sequence is a reference to Kitano's own conversion to painting following his serious motorcycle accident in 1994.)

More subtle are shifts in Horibe's visual style, which can be mapped onto the various places where Nishi and Miyuki stop. In addition to a segmentation based on setting and action, we could also trace the journey of Horibe's stylistic phases: floral *bricolage* (Scenes 18–20), then pointillist (27), and finally ideogrammatic (33). The shifts from cartoon to mosaic to symbolism are clearly marked. An illustrated story of a journey is accompanied by transformations in the travelers' outlook, mediated by the illustrator's style. The parallel between physical travel and metaphysical travail also shifts as the story moves along. A parallel between movement and reflection gives way to projection of movement; the details of Nishi's story conform to and are pushed forward by progress in Horibe's visual thinking.

At the most general level, Kitano's juggling of time is like a solvable riddle in the first dozen scenes, but this gives way to simpler, more interiorized structures of event+desire. Compare Horibe's shooting, a false match-on-action with Nishi's flick of a lighter, with the match-cut of Nishi's last shot at the *ryokan* (click) with a splash of red on canvas. This is a more fabulous, composite narration freely weaving between diegetic levels, reflexivity and historical allusion.

Hana-Bi is in the end a story of elimination, gradually stripping away the non-essentials. But it is also recursive, returning to familiar haunts. Once the protagonists go on the road the plot slows and smells the proverbial flowers. From time to time the needling violence of the city intrudes, but it is a distraction and cannot derail the inevitable. The artist, Horibe, drives this momentum, relentlessly seeking new subjects and ways to represent them. In this sense too it is a survival game, but the survivors are not the protagonists, but the narrator. When Horibe splashes a can of paint at the suicide painting, he looks unhappy with his new composition, as if he is at his wits' end. But how else to end it? Horibe's therapy, despite repeated proximity to death, is a repetition-compulsion. He reproduces, revisits, and re-mediates his own trauma, and Nishi's, to complete his own therapy, and hers, his closest accomplice in crime and creativity. Her therapy, her immolation. This places Nishi-Kitano, the intractable fighter and violent cop, in the truly novel position of feminine sacrifice.

Appendix: Segmentation of *Hana-Bi*

Credit sequence (music over): scrapbook Vol. 7 and paintings. 'Kitano blue sky', fight with punks (musical theme continues, then suddenly truncated). CU (close-up) of punk attendant cleaning windshield, then kicked off car. Cityscape with bridge; title credit (musical theme resumes). CU of red graffiti on car space: *Shi-ne* (Drop Dead). Car on seaside road. Tilt up to blue sky. Dissolve . . .

1 Preparing stakeout: Horibe, Nishi, driver in car. Stop for beancakes, Horibe suggests a stop at hospital (insert: Nishi in front of car); a game of catch with sushi boys. CU of azaleas in bloom – May. In stakeout van, backstory of Nishi's loss. Nakamura has a date, so he leaves with Nishi. From van, Horibe talks to his family by mobile.

2 Hospital (angel painting in stairway); insert of Nakamura and driver. Nishi with Miyuki, his wife and cigarette lighter. Match-on-action to Horibe shot twice next to azalea bush. Crosscut Nishi, Horibe. Nishi with Doctor (nurse in foreground). Bad news of Horibe.

3 (Insert CU of Nishi. cf. 1). Weeks later, Horibe and Nishi at seaside. Horibe considers painting. Seaside road; Horibe in wheelchair on beach. Feet get wet.

4 Café: Nishi visits Tanaka's widow (Tanaka shot – brief inserted flashback, slow motion).

5 Bar (mythological painting in background). Nishi with Nakamura, Kudō (Nakamura shot – brief inserted flashback, slow motion); CU of painting; later, with *yakuza* thugs. Chopsticks in gangster's eye.

6 Reprise of credit sequence. Horibe watching family on beach. Nishi in car park and a second run-in with punks, this time with knife. Nishi injured.

7 Hospital (CU of angel painting): Nishi's knife wound; prognosis for Miyuki, proposal to travel. New shirt.

8 Nishi's home: tricycle; Miyuki asleep; phone call.

9 Voiceover (Nakamura) of phone call: suicide attempt. Car: Kudō asks Nishi a question. Horibe (insert). In car, Nakamura's report. Fish jumping (Horibe's POV [point-of-view]?). Cityscape at night (musical theme).

10 Dragon painting in gangsters' office (*kabuki* print in background). Nishi is threatened. Cross-cut with brief inserted flashback of killer: shooting in subway. In car, Nakamura's backstory.

11 Horibe opens paint box.

12 Café: Tanaka's widow; junkman and helper introduced.

13 Pursuit of gunman in subway, as in 4, 5, and 10; slow motion, point-blank shooting.

14 Junkman interrupts, gives Nishi police lamp.

15 Home: game with cakes, puzzles. Horibe tries on beret.

16 Junkman with punk; Nishi buys taxi (overhead shot).

17 Station: detectives interrogating punk (Armani suit extortion).

18 Insert of Horibe (CU of paintings); Nishi spray-paints taxi.

19 Horibe's epiphany at florist (POV, with azaleas in background). Floral-animal watercolors.

20 Cross-cutting Nishi and Horibe at work: spray paint vs. watercolors.

21 Gangsters' office: an insolent customer is shot point blank, as in 10.

22 Match cut to Nishi in target practice. Nishi's new uniform.

23 Insert of Miyuki packing; junkyard haggle; Nishi on his way (siren).

24 Bank robbery (surveillance video); play with laborer.

25 Hit and run victim; Horibe's painting; car abandoned. Junkman reads of robbery in paper, scolded by helper.

26 Landscape, Mt Fuji. Fun on the road; guessing game with cards. Joke 1.

27 Horibe's new 'pointillist' style using ink markers.

28 In town: Mrs Tanaka's package; Nakamura phones, empty house. Gangsters' office: *Kabuki* print now changed into a skull. Horibe's package.

29 Dud fireworks, followed by real fireworks (Miyuki). Joke 2.

30 Horibe vs. Nishi. Horibe paints, lies to Nakamura. Nishi plays slapstick games: mistimed snapshot 3; falling into rock garden 4; temple bell 5; unlucky clerk at lake 6. Jokes 3–6.

31 Lakeside: *yakuza* come after Nishi; detectives talk to monks, as in 30 (Joke 5).

32 Fun on the road: bullets, grilled minnows in campfire 7; Miyuki stuck in snow 8. Jokes 7–8.

33 Window, ice, dissolve to . . . 'snow', 'light', 'suicide' characters in red: 'ideogrammatic' painting style.

34 *Ryokan: yakuza*, again. Nishi kills three. Match-on-action cut to Horibe's painting, as in 33. Joke 9.

35 Nakamura arrives, sees carnage. Nishi asks him to wait. On the beach, a final game with girl and kite. Joke 10. Wife thanks Nishi, two shots. End credits.

Acknowledgements

Thanks to Milestone Releasing's Dennis Doros and Amy Heller for permission to use their materials.

Notes

1 Kitano refers to his own early paintings as pointillist, and by this he means incrementally filling up space, considering his early efforts manual labor rather than artistic creation (see MPK). As a result, he says, they have for him a kind of religious or penitential meaning.
2 See Joyce (2003), which includes a photograph of famously fashionable Prime Minister Koizumi clad in *kimono*, holding a ceramic tea bowl.
3 From an interview with Shinozaki Makoto, *Studio Voice* (November 1997). Shinozaki has made a documentary on the making of Kitano's *Kikujiro* (1999), as well as a made-for-television movie based on the time Kitano spent in Asakusa (*Asakusa Kid*, 2002).
4 It is also foreshadowed by numerous scenes in the car, with front-to-back conversations mediated by the driver's rear-view mirror. Such moments also signify status, as a driver is conventionally in a subservient position to the passenger in the back seat.

References

Dalby, Lisa (1993) *Kimono: Fashioning Culture*, New Haven: Yale University Press.

Davis, Darrell William (2001) 'Re-igniting Japanese Tradition with *Hana-Bi*', *Cinema Journal* 40 (4): 55–80.

DeBord, Guy (1956) 'Methods of Detournement', *Les Levres Nues* 8 (May). Online. The Situationist International Text Library. http://library.nothingness.org/articles/SI/en/display. Accessed 26 April 2003.

Hollander, Anne (1994) *Sex and Suits: the Evolution of Modern Dress*, New York: Knopf.

Joyce, Colin (2003) 'Kimono Comeback as Japanese Men Let it All Hang Loose', *Sydney Morning Herald*, 22–23 February. Reprinted from *The Telegraph* (London).

Lurie, Allison (2000) *The Language of Clothes*, New York: Henry Holt.

McVeigh, Brian (2000) *Wearing Ideology: State, Schooling and Self-Presentation in Japan*, London: Berg.

Milestone Releasing (1998) Press Kit for *Fireworks*, New York: Milestone Releasing.

Kitano Takeshi Filmography

Violent Cop (*Sono otoko kyōbō ni tsuki*, 1989)
Boiling Point (*3–4 × 10 gatsu*, 1990)
A Scene at the Sea (*Ano natsu ichiban shizukana umi*, 1991)
Sonatine (1993)
Getting Any? (*Minna yatteru ka?*, 1995)
Kids Return (1996)
Hana-Bi (1997, released in the US as *Fireworks*, 1998)
Kikujiro (*Kikujirō no natsu*, 1999)
Brother (2000)
Dolls (2002)
Zatoichi (2003)
Takeshis' (2005)

23

THE ORIGINAL AND THE COPY

Nakata Hideo's *Ring* (1998)

Julian Stringer

James Naremore (2000a: 1–16) has recently called upon cinema scholars to pay renewed attention to the much maligned topic of film adaptation. As he puts it:

> The study of adaptation needs to be joined with the study of recycling, remaking, and every other form of retelling in the age of mechanical reproduction and electronic communication. By this means, adaptation will become part of a general theory of repetition, and adaptation study will move from the margins to the center of contemporary media studies. (15)

Studies on Japanese cinema adaptation may similarly benefit from the kind of critical makeover advocated by Naremore. After all, much work on the topic, however interesting and illuminating, has tended to reproduce one or other of two fairly limiting approaches. On the one hand, writers in the field sometimes too readily accept the commonplace assumption that the adaptation process consists primarily of the act of translating texts from one particular sign system (the novel) into another (film).[1] On the other hand, attention has usually been focused upon texts which may be said to be highbrow or otherwise prestigious, either because modelled upon canonical literary works or else made by '*auteur*' filmmakers possessing unique individual 'vision'.[2] As a result of the combined force of these two assumptions, Japanese adaptation studies usually conform to long-established notions of authorial integrity and reproduce the view that only intellectually 'superior' cultural forms are suitable for analysis. In other words, they appear to suggest that the investigation of film adaptation is most properly explored as an addendum to the study of *something else* (e.g. the study of a great film director or Japan's long-established and roundly celebrated literary traditions).

Given the widespread prevalence of such deeply entrenched attitudes, relatively little attention has consequently been paid to adaptations of popular literature[3] or of other mass media such as radio and television. More than this, recycled, remade and retold media phenomena – for example, remakes and sequels – have been largely cast aside from consideration. Such a studious maintenance of the

distinctions between 'high' and 'low' cultural texts within Japanese adaptation studies has ensured that while scholars have subjected *Throne of Blood*
(*Kumonosu-jō*, Kurosawa Akira, 1957) to ongoing in-depth critical investigation,
the animated sequel *Ghost in the Shell 2: Innocence* (*Inosensu: Kōkaku Kidotai*, Oshii
Manoru, 2004) has yet to receive anything like an equivalent level of attention.

There is also little evidence to date to suggest that adaptation studies of
Japanese cinema have sought to move, in Robert Stam's (2000: 54–76) words,
'beyond fidelity' – which is to say, beyond the fetishisation of notions of textual
originality. As Constantine Verevis (2004: 87) points out in the context of a
recent discussion of film remakes:

> As in the case of film genre, a fundamental problem for film remaking
> has arisen from 'the ever-present desire for a stable and easily identifi-
> able set of objects for analysis', and a related attempt to reduce film
> remaking to a '*corpus* of texts' or set of 'textual *structures*'. In addition to
> problems of canonicity, these textual accounts of remaking risk
> essentialism, in many instances privileging the 'original' over the
> remake or measuring the success of the remake according to its ability
> to realise what are taken to be the essential elements of a source text –
> the property – from which both the original and its remake are derived.[4]

It is important to point out that questions concerning how antecedent texts
such as novels, short stories, and plays are aesthetically transformed into audio-
visual media are perfectly necessary, legitimate, and interesting in their own
right. However, a critical approach overwhelmingly invested in the study of
high literature, *auteur* directors, and literature–film interactions cannot help but
reassert Japanese film's subservient relationship to prior literary 'originals' at
every turn. To the extent that these continue to be virtually the *only* matters
dealt with by critical writing, then, Japanese film adaptation scholarship is
currently labouring away under the weight of a slew of disarranged ideas. When
a novel is turned into a film, what has to be cut out? What is gained or lost in
the transference from page to screen? Which is 'better' – the book or the film?
Yes, these are all compelling intellectual concerns. However, posing such questions to the exclusion of all else immediately forecloses upon the development of
other important and illuminating critical perspectives.

Following Naremore and Verevis, it is therefore worth pursuing the topic of
media remaking and recycling so as to discover what may be learned concerning
historical attitudes towards the production, circulation, and reception of popular Japanese movies. International remakes of Japanese film provide a particularly valuable source of information in this regard, raising questions not just of
other cinemas' cannibalisation of Japanese source material but also Japan's own
appropriation of non-Japanese products.[5]

The recent global ascendancy of Japanese horror cinema, or 'J-horror', provides a particularly vivid example of these processes in operation. Among
numerous other titles that have contributed towards the establishment of the
'J-horror' and linked 'Asian horror' cultural brands (Lim 2007), the *Ring* series

of media texts – exemplified by, but certainly not restricted, to Nakata Hideo's famous chiller *Ring* (*Ringu*, 1999) – has so far attracted by far the lion's share of attention. By focusing on the *Ring* franchise, it becomes possible to engage with some of the complex inter-media and cross-cultural relations forged in recent years, both inside and outside Japan, among remade, recycled and re-circulated, and popular as well as highbrow, cultural artefacts. At stake in the present analysis, in other words, is the question of the extent to which theories of repetition may help to advance understanding of the workings of media institutions as well as specific texts in sophisticated contemporary media cultures such as Japan's.

A first observation to make here concerns the sheer popularity of horror in Japan, across East Asia, and now in many other parts of the world as well. However, while Mark Jancovich's statement that '[i]n recent years, it could be argued, the horror film has taken over from the western as the genre that is most written about by genre critics' (Jancovich 2002: 1) may or may not apply to the case of US cinema, it certainly does not hold true for Japanese cinema studies. Despite a long and varied history of horror film production – a history that the recent success of 'J-horror' is helping to bring to light – relatively little critical work currently exists on the subject.[6] As a result of this, a first and welcome consequence of the recent international popularity of Japanese horror films such as *Ring* is the opportunity it affords to open up, revisit and re-evaluate an otherwise under-analysed object of attention. Beyond this, however, critical perceptions of Hollywood remakes of contemporary Japanese horror provide a particularly valuable source of information concerning attitudes towards the international circulation, translation, and cross-cultural reception of popular Japanese media (Hills 2005).

Certainly, the *Ring* phenomenon constitutes one of the cross-cultural, cross-media sensations of contemporary global pop culture. In terms of content, its various narrative components are complex and multi-faceted, but the bare bones of its story are well known. *Ring* concerns a videotape virus which infects anyone who watches it, condemning them to die within a week. The video curse originates from the unquiet mind of a vengeful young woman who died a brutal death and now possesses the ability to transfer – or translate or adapt – her thoughts and memories on to videotape. In Japanese manifestations of the story, such as the 1998 theatrical film version, *Ring*, this girl is called Yamamura Sadako and she exists in a lonely place – the damp, dank bottom of a deep, dark well that doubles as both her mortal burial site and spectral hidey-hole.

In the UK and other reception contexts, *Ring* comes with connotations of 'extreme' Asian cinema, and it is frequently lumped in indiscriminately with other well-known examples of contemporary Japanese horror, such as *Battle Royale* (*Batoru Rowaiaru*, Fukasaku Kinji, 2000) and *Audition* (Miike Takashi, 2000), thus downplaying its specific *kaidan* (ghost story) connotations. However, the *Ring* series also trails in its wake a long and shadowy history entirely of its own.

Author Suzuki Koji's novel *Ringu* was first published in Japan in 1991. It was adapted into a tele-fantasy series, *Ringu: Kanzenban* (*Ring: Complete Edition*), for Fuji Television Network in 1996, and then transformed into a theatrical feature film released in Japan in 1998 on a double bill with *The Spiral* (*Rasen*, Iida Joji, 1998 – adapted from Suzuki's second novel published in 1995). In East Asia, these versions of *Ring* then spawned the theatrically released sequels *Ring 2* (*Ringu 2*, Nakata Hideo, 1999) and *Ring 0: Birthday* (*Ringu 0: Bāsude*, Tsuruta Norio, 2000) as well as a South Korean movie adaptation, *The Ring Virus* (Kim Dong-bin, 2002). In Japan, further Suzuki novels (securing tie-in movie deals) followed, including another circularly inspired title, *Loop* (first printed in Japan in 1998). All of this publishing activity augmented the release of a veritable throng of *Ring*-related *manga* (comic books) including *Ring, Ring: Volume 2, Spiral, Birthday*, and *The Curse of Yamamura Sadako*. In turn, a mini-torrent of cultural allusions, pop culture references, and parodies soon began to emerge from various international quarters, including a US gay male porno-graphic version entitled *The Hole* (US, Wash West, 2003 – tagline: 'In seven days you will be gay, if you aren't already').[7]

As is widely known, remake rights to *Ringu* were very soon optioned in Hollywood and a US version, *The Ring* (dir. Gore Verbinski), was subsequently released around the world in 2002. One year later, Suzuki's 1991 novel *Ringu* was published for the first time in an English translation in the United States. (Other Suzuki translations have since also appeared.) At the same time, other Japanese horror films, such as *Dark Water* (*Honogurai Mizu no Soko kara*, Nakata Hideo, 2002) and *Pulse* (*Kairo*, Kurosawa Kiyoshi, 2000) were also optioned by Hollywood studios and before long released as US remakes. Hollywood's sequel to its own initial adaptation of the 1998 Japanese *Ringu, Ring 2*, was directed in the United States by Nakata himself and given a high-profile international release in 2005.

Two observations are worth making about all of this *Ring*-related activity. To begin with, the *Ring* phenomenon is cross-cultural and multi-media. It touches the film, television, and publishing industries of (most obviously) Japan, South Korea, and the United States. It therefore comprises multiple texts – or more properly, a series of mutually penetrating inter-texts – that encompass a range of both print and electronic semiotic systems.

Second, while it is reasonable to claim that the *Ring* phenomenon has an identifiable initial source – namely, the publication in Japan in 1991 of Suzuki's novel *Ringu* – it is hard to take this novel as in any simple sense an 'original' aesthetic artefact that is then 'adapted' in numerous different versions. Consider in this regard the fact that the 1998 *Ring* film arguably constitutes more of a transposition of the 1996 television series than the 1991 novel, while the 2002 US remake appears to be more an adaptation of the 1998 film than a translation of the 1991 novel. (To repeat, at the time the 2002 US film was made, Suzuki's novel was not yet available in an English-language edition.) In short, we are confronted in the case of the *Ring* phenomenon with an extreme confusion over what is the 'original' and what is the 'copy'. Japanese cinema studies' customary investment in the discourse of fidelity – that is to say, in notions of film's subservience in the face of a prior and privileged literary source – is on this particular occasion revealed to be a fatally flawed critical methodology.

Another way of putting this is to say that the focus of adaptation studies might at times shift to incorporate analysis of Japanese cinema's inter-media, cross-cultural, and inter-semiotic complexities. For example, examining the process by which *Ringu* became *The Ring* allows for the unravelling of varied perspectives, both in Japan and elsewhere, on how, why, and to what effect/ affect the Hollywood studio DreamWorks remade this particular Japanese ghost story. Such knowledge promises to reveal much about cross-cultural attitudes towards transnational Japanese media adaptations as well as the specific conditions of the marketplace that govern the deep-seated desire for textual fidelity.

To get straight to the heart of the matter, therefore: when filmmakers, commentators, and audiences talk about the 'original' *Ring*, what precisely do they think they are talking about? In the absence of an English-language translation of Suzuki's 1991 novel, for example, Hollywood folklore advanced the claim that cult value circulated around subterranean bootleg copies of the 1998 theatrically released Japanese feature film – it is this 'version' of the *Ring* tale that is thus said to inform the thinking of those people invested with the job of making the subsequent Hollywood adaptation(s). Some of these accounts recall – no doubt intentionally, and sometimes to the point of parody – the kind of urban legend embodied in the story of Sadako's own secret deadly videotape. Thus, for example, *The Ring*'s director, Gore Verbinski, recalls a private viewing of Nakata's 1998 film: 'It was the worst quality videotape I had ever seen – the dub of a dub of a dub. I couldn't even read the subtitles' (Arnold 2002: 16D). Similarly, when DreamWorks distributed *The Ring* on video and DVD in 2003 it re-circulated the 1998 *Ringu* at the same time. *Variety* noted that the studio ended up 'using novel packaging for *Ringu*, making it look like one of the bootlegs snapped up by U.S. fans obsessed with the original' (Bloom 2003: 6) – thereby reproducing in the process the assumption that it is the 1998 film that is the 'original' text subsequently translated and adapted.

Confusion over the 'original' *Ring* versus its 'copy' manifests itself in other ways as well. In marketing discourse, the Tartan Asia Extreme UK DVD release of Nakata's 1999 *Ring 2* carried a quotation from critic Alexander Walker of the *Evening Standard* that speaks of 'More disturbing episodes for fans of the original'. Meanwhile, in their entry on '*The Ring*' (*sic* – they are referring to Nakata's 1998 *Ringu*) in *The Midnight Eye Guide to New Japanese Film*, Tom Mes and Jasper Sharp (2005: 261) assert that the 1999 Japan-produced *Ring 2* 'branched off from the original concept in a well-constructed but uncalled-for sequel that continued right where the original left off, before Nakata stepped out of the franchise'. However, whereas use of the word 'original' in this particular context aligns that specific value with the work of director Nakata on the 1998 film, a further quotation on the very next page aligns the values of originality with literary author Suzuki instead: '. . . Nakata's creepy handling of the flickering found footage of Sadako's video (the contents of which were never described in the original novel), full of grainy, drenched-out colours periodically interrupted by bursts of static' (Ibid: 262).[8]

Further consideration of the varied cultural reception of *Ring*-related inter-texts in terms of perceptions of originality reveals yet more ambiguity and unanticipated complexity. In addition, the forging of cultural distinctions around the specific values ascribed either to precursor text or to 'copy' is of particular significance. For instance, on the occasion of the theatrical release of the US remake in 2002, the *Daily Yomiuri* put the question in the starkest possible terms when writer Naomi Tajitsu (2002: 27) asked the key question: 'What is the purpose of a remake? . . . To pay homage to an original? To top the original? Or to create something entirely independent of the original?' (In answering her own question, Tajitsu argues that Hollywood's *The Ring* does the first – i.e. it pays homage to the original. However, she also fails to clarify exactly which text is the 'original' in this specific context.)

The question, 'What is the purpose of a remake?', is an extremely provocative one. Why, indeed, go to all the fuss and bother of remaking a prior text? Clearly, in the eyes of many, the *raison d'être* of a Hollywood remake of an Asian horror film is not so much to provide homage as to make money. In recent years, East Asia has become simply the latest region of the world to have its soul-chilling ghost, horror, and thriller tales swallowed whole by Hollywood capital and know-how. Before the days of *Ring, Dark Water*, and *Pulse*, Europe was in the ascendancy: for example, *The Vanishing* (Netherlands, George Sluizer, 1988) was remade as *The Vanishing* (US, George Sluizer, 1993); *La Jetée* (France, Chris Marker, 1962) was remade as *12 Monkeys* (US/UK, Terry Gilliam, 1995); *Insomnia* (Norway, Erik Skoldbjaers, 1997) was remade as *Insomnia* (US/UK, Christopher Nolan, 1999); *Purple Noon* (France, René Clement, 1960) was remade as *The Talented Mr Ripley* (US/UK/Italy, Anthony Mingella, 1999); and *Open Your Eyes* (Spain, Alexandro Anemaba, 1997) was remade as *Vanilla Sky* (US, Cameron Crowe, 2001). With *The Ring*, therefore, it is possible to claim that Hollywood continues to do what Hollywood has always done – namely, absorb world culture and sell it back to the rest of the world in a more expensive version. To their credit, perhaps, Hollywood executives hardly hide their intentions in this regard, stating plainly that their aim is not just to sell Sadako (now called Samara in the US film versions) back to Japan, but to reach the rest of the Asian market as well, including Hong Kong, South Korea, and Thailand. They want to establish and maintain control over what very speedily revealed its ability to become a global media franchise. They want to swallow the *Ring* phenomenon whole so as to be able to sell and tell a story that goes on and on, with no commercial end in sight.

To explain and justify this particular aspect of the cultural politics of film adaptation, studio executives, filmmakers, publicists, and commentators alike sometimes invest in notions of universal value. For example, director Nakata Hideo himself explains his films' appeal to international audiences along these kinds of lines: 'I think the fear of the unknown is universal' (quoted in Chia 2002: 34).

At the same time, however, culturally specific values are also attached to *Ring* and its remakes, and these are sometimes read back retrospectively on to the phenomenon so as to make sense of prior and antecedent inter-texts. Yet in reports and reviews published, both inside and outside Asia, upon the release of the 2002 US remake, it is noticeable that consensus has not been reached concerning the meaning of such values. For example, and not unexpectedly, some Asian commentators attack the process whereby the US cannibalises – or in academic *lingua franca* 'deracinates' (Lim 2007) – Asian movies. For example, Daniel Yun, chief executive officer of Raintree Pictures (who co-produced the Hong Kong/Thailand horror film *The Eye* [Oxide Pang Chun and Danny Pang, 2002]) states flatly that: '[T]he West is good for certain things – big budgets and special effects', and Kenneth Tan of the Singapore Film Society complains that some of the 'mystique' and the 'unease' of Nakata's 1998 *Ring* had 'been erased in Hollywood's storytelling style', which is 'more direct and overt' and has 'neat endings' (Oon 2003). *Yomiuri Shimbun* similarly proclaimed (December 26, 2002) that 'the creepiness and fear factor of *Ringu* were more or less thrown out the window in its remake', while in the US the *New York Times* (June 8, 2003) stated that 'The ghosts in *Ringu* are far too elusive to be busted in the time-honored can-do manner of the American action-horror film'. It continued: 'The unnerving distinction of Asian genre pictures like *Ring* is that they're willing to admit the possibility that spirits are simply with us, day in and day out, and there's not much we can do to make them go away'. In all of these instances, culturally specific values are perceived to be lost in translation once a Japanese *kaidan* is remade in Hollywood.

This does not constitute the whole story, however. The 2002 US remake has its fair share of admirers, many of whom feel no need to defend the antecedent Japanese film(s) just because it is a prior text or was made in Asia. For instance, *The Japan Times* (October 30, 2002) claims that '[I]n what must be a first, the Hollywood remake is actually better than the original' [*sic* – this presumably refers to Nakata's 1998 film], claiming that big budgets and special effects actually enhance the sensual horror of this particular Hollywood product. In Hong Kong, the *South China Morning Post* (November 14, 2002) also believed that DreamWorks 'seems to have got it right' – although, ironically, the primary explanation for this is the belief that the US studio possessed the wisdom to approach Nakata's 1998 'original' in a spirit of reverent fidelity; 'the main reason is that DreamWorks had the common sense not to mess with things too much'. Elsewhere, director Verbinski attempts to explain the specific character-istics of his own 2002 US remake by hedging his bets: 'The original (*sic*) is so elusive, and it's also tricky because American audiences have a desire for resolution' (Arnold 2002: 16D) – this despite the fact that the narrative ending of his film is simultaneously 'closed' and (perfectly befitting its status as one component of a global franchise) also cannily 'open'.

Significantly, in all of the accounts quoted above, both detractors and defend-ers of the 1998 *Ring* and 2002 *The Ring* alike are conspicuously silent on the question of Suzuki's 1991 novel. This is to say that – unusually and ironically – the discourse of 'novel into film' has to date been all but absent from English-language accounts of the *Ring* phenomenon. In this sense, then, the release of the 2002 US film has done the English-language publishing industry a service in motivating the translation of Suzuki's literary achievements, and in turn this may over time lead to the belated publication of scholarly adaptation studies investigating how and why 'the *Ring* film' (but which one?) differs from 'the novel'. These possible future studies could reframe perceptions of the

Figure 27 Ring (1998): an ever-increasing spiral of malevolence. Omega/Kadokawa/The Kobal Collection.

'originality' of various *Ring*-related inter-texts and hence revisit the intriguing question of what the purpose of a remake actually is.[9]

There would certainly be much to contemplate in this regard. For example, consider the fact that a central question which future work might need to engage with is the matter of why the novel's central investigating male char- acter, Asakawa, has been transformed in all subsequent film versions (Japanese, South Korean, US) into a woman (Reiko [Matsushima Nanako] in Nakata's 1998 *Ring*). In Japan and elsewhere, what conditions of the marketplace decree that a female protagonist is deemed more suitable to appear at this particular historical juncture in a popular teen-oriented horror franchise?[10]

To summarise, the cross-media, cross-cultural success of *Ring*, alongside the existence of its numerous and equally visible international inter-texts, reverses one of the most widespread yet limiting assumptions concerning studies on Japanese film adaptation. In this particular case, there does not appear to be a clear-cut and hence obvious 'original' source text that is then adapted, copied, or otherwise 'messed with' in subsequent transformations. Instead, no end is in sight for the very many different versions of this story: in a very literal sense, the medium that carries the *Ring* tale really is the message. Let us recall for a moment the solution to the mystery of Sadako's videotape; in order to save your own life, you have to make a copy of the tape and then show it to someone else, thus allowing the virus successfully to pursue its mission of adapting and leaking out into the world in an ever-increasing spiral of malevolence. In other terms, the *Ring* virus itself resembles the very processes of textual translation it so gleefully spawns. *Ring*, *The Ring*, and all the rest, provide a paradigmatic example of the kinds of cultural 'retellings' which Naremore suggests have by now completely infiltrated contemporary media culture.

Notions of media recycling and remaking also point to the very many narratives of repetition, circularity, and endless return that, as Aaron Gerow (2002) perceptively notes, are a hallmark of modern Japanese cinema. Aside from *Ring*, these films include the equally chilling *Pulse*, *Uzumaki* (also known as *Whirlpool*, Higuchinsky, 2000), and *Tomie* (Oikawa Ataru, 1999 – a teen-oriented female revenge saga), as well as ostensibly non-horror titles such as *Turn* (Hirayama Hideyuki, 2001 – a loose remake of *Groundhog Day* (US, Harold Ramis, 1993)). As a selection of individual cultural artefacts, these films starkly demonstrate the horror genre's centrality to processes of media recycling in what Gerow terms 'postmodern' Japan. The cumulative effect of the production of such a strong series of movies is much more forceful, however, leaving the indelible impression that a nightmare is spiralling endlessly, without resolution. This is one of the reasons why it is becoming easier and easier to begin to argue that the horror film – for long periods of time one of the most perennially overlooked genres in English-language Japanese cinema studies – may yet prove to be one of its most fascinating as well as its most instructive cultural forms. Horror adapts; like a virus, it goes on and on.

Finally, while this chapter has sought to draw attention to inter-media and cross-cultural processes rather than pursue the more traditional concerns of the 'novel-into film' paradigm, it is also true that the latter still has much to teach us. In the case of *Ring*, one reason for this is that Suzuki's 1991 novel is quite self-aware of its own status as a horror narrative, and it also demonstrates keen awareness of the complex relations among print media (journalism) and electronic media (film, television, and video).

To given an example, one theme explored in the book concerns the nature of the publishing industry and the perceived market conditions for horror fiction. While Suzuki – who is himself often (and usefully) compared with famed US author Stephen King[11] – takes pains in interviews to stress that he does not label himself a horror author, and moreover never deigns to read the stuff, horror cultural reference points abound in his work. Specifically, the 1991 novel refers to a number of Japanese inter-texts (e.g. *Godzilla*) concerned with the destructive and violent capabilities of the sea, thus demonstrating once again the importance of water to the horror imagination of a nation prone to typhoon, *tsunami*, and other destructive natural phenomena. In addition, it draws upon references to particular US horror inter-texts, including the *Friday the 13th* slasher film series and the demonic child narratives of both *The Exorcist* and *The Omen* publishing and movie franchises. Perhaps more surprisingly, one of the horror videos available for rent in the log cabin housing Sadako's cursed videotape is *The Legend of Hell House* (UK, John Gough, 1973), an adaptation of celebrated US author Richard Matheson's 1972 novel *Hell House* and a point of reference that connects *Ring* to older traditions of classic American horror fiction.[12] Such generic referencing links the film and publishing industries at the same time as it introduces transnational connections between popular regional horror fictions.

In this chapter, I have not sought to offer an interpretative analysis of the content or style of Nakata's 1998 *Ring*. Neither have I attempted to explicate its 'meaning' within the context of its initial assembly and circulation – a focus which might entail looking at such topics as the relation between film and television production in Japan in the mid-1990s, the rise of Suzuki and Nakata as media 'stars', and the culturally and historically specific nature of Japan's teen-oriented popular culture.[13] Instead, I have tried to suggest that Japanese cinema studies may be usefully revisited through the prism of film's relationship to other media, including but not exclusively restricted to the novel. In the contemporary period, for example, such an approach may be extended in several intriguing directions, taking into account not just the importance of television, radio, and popular fiction, but also the ever-growing number of significant cinematic adaptation of *manga* (cf. *Nowhere Man* [*Munō no Hito*, Takenaka Naoto], 1991), *Ping Pong* [Masuri Fumihiko], 2002).

Notes

1 The 'novel into film' paradigm has understandably reigned supreme in the case of articles on Japanese cinema published over the years in the influential US journal *Literature/Film Quarterly*, as well as in the specialist publication *Asian Cinema*. In terms of book publishing, Keiko McDonald (2000) is the scholar most widely associated with the rigorous study of literature–film transformations. McDonald is also the author of a singular study of relations between Japanese theatre and film (McDonald 1994).

2 Much writing on the films of director Kurosawa Akira may be said to conflate these two perspectives. For example, they both underpin James Goodwin's 1994 study *Akira Kurosawa and Intertexual Cinema* – a book that otherwise advances a relatively sophisticated understanding of how inter-textual meaning is forged through inter-cultural processes.

3 An exception to this critical norm is provided by Bernstein (2000) who considers issues of adaptation around *High and Low* (*Tengoku to Jigoku*, Kurosawa Akira, 1963), which was adapted from US pulp novelist Ed McBain's (Evan Hunter) 1959 book *King's Ransom*.

4 Italics in original. Verevis' quotations here are from Altman 1999.

5 For example, the Korean film *The Quiet Family* (Kim Ji-woon, South Korea, 1998) was remade as *The Happiness of the Katakuris* (*Katakuris no Kōfuku*, Miike Takashi, 2004), and *Shall We Dansu?* (Suō Masayuki, 1996) was remade in the US as *Shall We Dance?* (Peter Chelsom, 2004).

6 The most obvious manifestation of this recent critical fascination is McRoy (2005). The appearance of this new volume of critical essays augments widespread coverage of contemporary Japanese horror in the specialised print media (e.g. Lu 2002) as well as in a plethora of 'cult' publications (e.g. Weisser and Weisser 1997; Hunter 1998). Prior to these developments, only a very few isolated examples of scholarly studies of aspects of Japanese horror had been published in English, covering *Godzilla* (*Gojira*, Honda Ishirō, 1958 – discussed in Chapter 7 of this volume by Yomota Inuhiko) and other topics (cf. Gill 1998; Napier 1998; Noriega 1987).

7 Thanks to Gary Needham for this reference.

8 It is not true that the contents of Sadako's videotape were never described in Suzuki's novel. It is a vital structuring sequence, described at length (Suzuki 2004 [1991]: 73–80).

9 In this possible future scenario, other missing terms include: the 1991 novel's relationship to the 1996 television series; the television series' relationships to the first and subsequent films; and the novel's possible relationship to prior antecedent 'versions' of Suzuki's writing in the form of short stories, and so on.

10 It is also worth asking why it is that in the 1991 novel Sadako is *ryōsei* (literally 'both sexes' – i.e. a hermaphrodite), whereas in subsequent film versions she has been transformed into an unambiguous (if hideous) young woman.

11 Only a few months after Suzuki's *Ring* was published in Japan, King's *Dolores Claiborne* (1992) was published in English in the US. Both novels concern domestic and familial violence; both place a vengeful female at the centre of narrative agency; and both adopt the narrative device of having a central character fall down a deep, dark well as a means of presenting and exploring themes of violence and morality.

12 In its review of the 2002 US remake, *The Ring*, the *Washington Times* (October 23, 2002) claims that the film conversely 'poaches on the plot of Matheson's 1958 novel, *A Stir of Echoes*'. (A Hollywood adaptation of the book had been released under the same title in 1999, directed by David Koepp.)

13 Were I to pursue this latter topic, I might point to the fact that there is an interesting correspondence between *Ring* and a contemporaneous incident widely reported in the Japanese media at the time – '*Pokemon* panic'.

Shortly after the broadcast of the 1996 *Ring* television series, 'Computer Warrior Polygon' (*Dennou Senshi Porigon*) – or episode 38 of the popular television show *Pokemon* – was aired on national television. The December 16, 1997, screening of this episode resulted in what was widely believed to be an example of 'mass hysteria'. In the show, character Pikachu and his friends use special electrical powers to stop a 'virus bomb'. As the alleged result of being exposed to the show's use of subliminal televisual aesthetics, such as strobe lights and flash effects, 618 children and teens were reportedly rushed to hospitals with convulsions, headaches and vision problems. Within two days, newspapers and other media had reported that the *Pokemon* attacks were now the talk of the schoolyards, and that in a spiralling avalanche of psychosomatic or real contagion, 13,000 others evidencing 'at least minor symptoms' of seizure had been taken to hospital (see *Asahi Shimbun*, December 17, 1997; *Yomiuri Shimbun*, December 17, 1997; *Yomiuri Shimbun*, December 18, 1997).

References

Altman, Rick (1999) *Film/Genre*, London: British Film Institute.

Arnold, Thomas K. (2002) 'Asian Remakes Sell U.S. Videos', *USA Today*, 25 October: Life section, 16D.

Bernstein, Matthew (2000) '*High and Low*: Art Cinema and Pulp Fiction in Yokohama', in Naremore 2000b: 172–89.

Bloom, David (2003) 'Tale of the Tape', *Variety*, 3 March: 6.

Chia, Adeline (2002) 'Playing on People's Fears', *The Business Times*, Singapore, 17 May: 34.

Gerow, Aaron (2002) 'The Empty Return: Circularity and Repetition in Recent Japanese Horror Films', *Minikomi: Informationen des Akademischen Arbeitkreis Japan N.*, 64: 19–24.

Gill, Tom (1998) 'Transformational Magic: Some Japanese Superheroes and Monsters', in Martinez 1998: 35–55.

Goodwin, James (1994) *Akira Kurosawa and Intertextual Cinema*, Baltimore and London: Johns Hopkins Univesity Press.

Hills, Matt (2005) 'Ringing the Changes: Cult Distinctions and Cultural Differences in US Fans' Readings of Japanese Horror Cinema', in McRoy 2005: 161–74.

Hunter, Jack (1998) *Eros in Hell: Sex, Blood and Madness in Japanese Cinema*, London: Creation.

Jancovich, Mark (2002) 'General Introduction', in Mark Jancovich (ed.), *Horror: The Film Reader*, London and New York: Routledge: 1–19.

Lim, Bliss Cua (2007) 'Generic Ghosts: Remaking the New "Asian Horror Film" ', in Gina Marchetti and Tan See Kam (eds), *Hong Kong Film, Hollywood and the New Global Cinema*, London and New York: Routledge: 109–25.

Lu, Alvin (2002) 'Horror: Japanese-Style', *Film Comment*, January/February.

Martinez, D. P. (ed.) (1998) *The Worlds of Japanese Popular Culture: Gender, Shifting Boundaries and Global Cultures*, Cambridge: Cambridge University Press.

McDonald, Keiko (1994) *Japanese Classical Theater in Films*, London and Toronto: Associated University Presses.

—— (2000) *From Book to Screen: Modern Japanese Literature in Film*, London: M.E. Sharpe.

McRoy, Jay (ed.) (2005) *Japanese Horror Cinema*, Edinburgh: Edinburgh University Press.

Mes, Tom and Sharp, Jason (2005) *The Midnight Eye Guide to New Japanese Film*, Berkeley, CA: Stone Bridge Press.

Napier, Susan J. (1998) 'Vampires, Psychic Girls, Flying Women and Sailor Scouts: Four Faces of the Young Female in Japanese Popular Culture', in Martinez 1998: 91–109.

Naremore, James (2000a) 'Introduction: Film and the Reign of Adaptation', in Naremore 2000b: 1–16.

—— (ed.) (2000b) *Film Adaptation*, London: The Athlone Press.

Noriega, Chon (1987) 'Godzilla and the Japanese Nightmare: When *THEM!* Is U.S'., *Cinema Journal*, 27 (1): 63–77.

Oon, Clarissa (2003) 'A Different Ring To It?', *The Straits Times*, Singapore, 8 January.

Stam, Robert (2000) 'Beyond Fidelity: The Dialogics of Adaptation', in Naremore 20000b: 54–76.

Suzuki, Koji (2004 [1991]) *Ring*, London: HarperCollins. (First published in Japan as *Ringu*, Tokyo: Kadokawa Shoten, 1991.)

Tajitsu, Naomi (2002) 'Ring Doesn't Quite Come Full Circle', *Daily Yomiuri*, October 31: 27

Verevis, Constantine (2004) 'Remaking Film', *Film Studies* 4 (summer): 87–103.

Weisser, Thomas, and Mihara Weisser, Yuko (1997) *Japanese Cinema Encyclopedia: Horror, Fantasy and Science Fiction Films*, Miami: Vital Books.

Nakata Hideo Filmography

Ghost Actress (*Joyūrei*, 1996)
Ring (*Ringu*, 1998)
Joseph Losey: The Man With Four Names (*Joseph Losey: yottsu no na o motsu otoko*, 1998)
Ring 2 (*Ringu 2*, 1999)
The Sleeping Bride (*Garasu no Nō*, 2000)
Chaos (*Kaosu*, 2000)
Sadistic and Masochistic (2001)
Dark Water (*Honogurai Mizu no Soko kara*, 2002)
Last Scene (2003)
Ring 2 (US, 2005)

24

THE GLOBAL MARKETS FOR *ANIME*

Miyazaki Hayao's *Spirited Away* (2001)

Rayna Denison

Anime (animated film and television) have been a part of global screen culture since the 1960s (Drazen 2003). From that time these animated Japanese series and films became part of American children's television, before a second wave of *anime* films in the 1980s brought a new dystopic future vision to the world. Miyazaki Hayao's films span these two extremes – from child-friendly narratives featuring cuddly creatures to films that deal with death, war and adult responsibility. Alongside Tezuka Osamu, renowned as the grandfather of Japanese *anime* (Drazen 2003: 4–12; Napier 2001a: 16), Miyazaki is probably the best-known and best-regarded Japanese animator in the world. Thanks to a 1996 distribution deal struck between Miyazaki's film company and Disney, his *anime* films are now also among the most widely available in the world.

Despite *anime*'s significant presence in many of the world's larger markets for film and television, little academic work has been undertaken to investigate its global impact. Where studies of *anime* as a global phenomenon do exist, they tend to understand the globalisation of *anime* as its Americanisation (Napier 2001a: 23). This chapter intends rather to think of *anime* as global in the sense that John Tomlinson proposes, that globalisation in culture relates to 'how our sense of cultural belonging – of being "at home" – may be subtly transfigured by the penetration of globalizing media into our everyday lives'. (Tomlinson 1999: 10) Many authors, especially those working on *anime* fandom, have claimed that it is *anime*'s 'otherness' and difference from 'mainstream' culture that inspires its fans (Cubbison 2005; Napier 2001b). Such claims, although valid, obscure the increasing niche that *anime* occupies in film and television culture inside and beyond Japan. In the UK, for instance, recent years have seen an explosion in the availability of *anime* on the high street, on cable television and in cinemas. *Anime*'s increasing familiarity and consistent presence therefore suggests that it is slowly becoming absorbed into the 'mainstream', rather than being straightforwardly alternative to it. This chapter will consequently seek to redress some of the imbalance in scholarship about *anime*'s 'difference' by examining three markets in which *anime* have traditionally thrived: Japan, *anime*'s birthplace and most significant market; France, where Miyazaki's films in

Figure 28 *Anime* in the world: *Spirited Away* (2001). Touhoku Shinsha/The Kobal Collection.

particular have thrived; and America, which has a long history of presenting *anime* to audiences (albeit surreptitiously) often in re-edited and dubbed forms.

The theme of identity through language is central to Miyazaki's *Sen to Chihiro no kamikakushi* (originally released in Japan in 2001.) A similar theme played out at the level of the film's release in its various global and linguistically distinct markets as gradually *Sen to Chihiro no kamikakushi* became *Le Voyage de Chihiro* which in turn was reinscribed with the title *Spirited Away*.[1] As these titles suggest, the further Miyazaki's film moved west, towards its American release in September 2002, the more negotiation and change took place. More-over, the further the film travelled, the more it moved away from its initial 'blockbuster' roots. In Japan the film was a popular hit, breaking all box-office records, whereas by the time *Spirited Away* was released in the United States it was being positioned as art worthy of Academy Award-winning status. The changes were wrought at the level of *Sen to Chihiro*'s text, through linguistic translations and in its marketing, as Japanese elements were progressively siphoned off or altered in attempts to market the film to the maximum of potential global audiences.

The term 'global markets' is an apt one because, although *Sen to Chihiro* may have changed to suit its circumstances, it never became the exclusive cultural property of any nation other than Japan. Instead, Japaneseness will be shown to have been essential to *Sen to Chihiro* in its movement through cultures, however much the notion of the national was conflicted and contested. First, as the nature of *Sen to Chihiro*'s multiple translations may suggest, every major 'global' film released is in fact significantly altered so that it can be sold to linguistically and culturally distinct markets (Hewitt 2003: 73). Second, due to the success of American film abroad, other geo-cultural film products and markets remain under-scrutinised (Hesmondhalgh 2002: 178–81). As the film under consider-ation here is Japanese in origin, discussions of 'globalisation' will be inverted, as they do not, and cannot in their American conceptualisation, account for the shifting power relations that manipulated *Sen to Chihiro* after it left its domestic market. Nor do America-centric discussions of the blockbuster account for *Sen to Chihiro*'s domestic success (e.g. Neale and Smith 1998; Sandler and Studlar 1999). Instead, the idea of global markets helps to shift the focus away from reliance on nationally based markets for film to focus rather on linguistic and cultural markets that explain more fully how *Sen to Chihiro* was able to synthesise the needs of various markets through its imagery and multiple language tracks.[2]

Remembering Japan: National identity and domestic negotiation in *Sen to Chihiro*

Within Japan, *Sen to Chihiro*'s aesthetic look and imagery had a vital role to play in its success. The film was not sold through an essentialist or pure image of national identity, but rather evinced a broad spectrum of hybridised identities: with mixed Japanese and Western styles of architecture, décor and costuming; in its characterisation and even in its marketing. For this reason, even in its domestic market, *Sen to Chihiro* was reliant on a more supra-national identity to attract audiences, its preliminary contemporary setting reflecting the broader hybrid nature of Japanese culture itself.

Before examining *Sen to Chihiro*'s marketing in Japan, however, it is imperative to understand how the film appealed to national, domestic audiences at a textual level. Doing so will help to explain why particular elements and characters later featured heavily in *Sen to Chihiro*'s advertising. The narrative of *Sen to Chihiro* has been related to that of *Alice in Wonderland*, particularly the 1951 US Disney version (*The Economist* 2002: 122). In the film, Chihiro, a young lethargic Japanese girl, wanders through a tunnel into a mysterious spa resort where gods go to unwind. In the process Chihiro's parents are transformed into pigs by the sorceress Yubāba, the leader of the resort, which is set in a traditional Japanese-style bath house. In order to survive in this enchanted realm Chihiro has to work, and to save her parents and the boy who befriends her, she undertakes a quest. This, while a rather drastic reduction of the film's narrative, reflects the transition from the real to the enchanted undertaken in *Sen to Chihiro* as well as the narrative impetus to repair Chihiro's ruptured 'normal' life and to escape the enchanted one she enters.

What is perhaps most significant is that in *Sen to Chihiro* it is fantasy elements which are most obviously Japanese. Modern Japan appears for only a very limited time as the framing story for *Sen to Chihiro*'s narrative. Chihiro and her parents travel to their new home in their European car (clearly marked by a rear badge as a German-made Audi) with Chihiro surrounded in the back seat by the trappings of modern Japanese society (a Kinokuniya bookstore bag, a Miffy-character carrier bag, and a wilting bunch of non-domestic sweet-pea flowers that disintegrate during the film's opening scenes). This framing story and the normality it represents are indicative of Miyazaki's negative reading of contemporary Japan, filled as it is with signs of consumerism and personal lethargy.

Chihiro's clothing also becomes symbolic of her character's (national) identity throughout the film. At first she wears an oversized white T-shirt with a green stripe, a pair of orange shorts, and yellow trainers that look disproportionately large on her skinny frame. By contrast, Chihiro's 'Sen' costume, her uniform at the bath house, is 'Oriental' and traditionally Japanese, consisting of shorts and a top with kimono sleeves in a co-ordinated terracotta orange, white and dark blue colour scheme (see Minear 2001 on Orientalism and Japan). Her appearance in this uniform coincides with her renaming by Yubāba as 'Sen', an act which steals Chihiro's memory of her real name and identity. It is only when Haku, Chihiro's friend and potential romantic interest, returns her original clothing that she regains her identity by reading the farewell card from the framing story. On regaining her name, Chihiro re-adopts her original clothing but wears a hair band made for her by her friends in this enchanted land. Thus it is that her identity crisis can be mapped at the level of her costuming, with, in the end, her original Westernised identity reasserted, but with some small alterations that will help her to recall her 'Japanese' adventure.

As well as clothing reflecting the 'real' and 'fantastic', *Sen to Chihiro* could also be interpreted as playing European and Japanese architectural styles off against one another. The ostentatious Japanese bath house acts as a site of untrustworthy fantasy and magic whereas Zenība's (Yubāba's twin) European-style house represents a site of the 'authentic' or trustworthy. It is at Zenība's simple, thatched, rural home that Chihiro's quest comes to a close. Surrounded by old-fashioned spinning machinery and a range-stove, Chihiro is given the advice that will enable her to return home and help her to free her parents and Haku.

By comparison, the gaudy bath house run by Yubāba is reminiscent of the most traditional but outlandish of Japanese architectural styles. It has a formal Japanese garden complete with sliding paper doors through which Chihiro wanders near the beginning of her adventure. Other aspects of the bath house also reflect the opulence inherent in certain forms of Japanese architecture and traditional art, such as Yubāba's enormous Satsuma-ware style vases, and the theatrically painted walls and sliding doors of the bath house itself. The positioning of this opulent traditionalism as fantastic has two levels of significance. First, it connotes the traditional identity lost to Chihiro's modern Japanese character, but also and somewhat contradictorily, its juxtaposition with both the 'real' world and Zenība's home creates the bath house as an unstable and treacherous environment, but one with valuable lessons for modern (Japanese) society.

Compounding this interpretation, the characters most closely associated with an 'Oriental' or Japanese identity are presented as conflicted in *Sen to Chihiro*. Haku's dual identity as boy and dragon, as love interest and Yubāba's henchman, provides one good example of this trend. Several more of the most transparently Japanese characters in this film also have their identities immediately obfuscated through the donning of actual masks. Kaonashi (literally translated as 'No Face'), a mysterious figure cloaked in black, has as his face a decorated mask and has the ability to vanish from sight entirely. Furthermore, the river god that Chihiro helps to clean enters the bath house as an *Okusare-sama* or 'Stink Spirit' and is also revealed from under his layer of filth as having a face reminiscent of a Japanese theatre mask. Hence there is evidence of identity crises in many of *Sen to Chihiro*'s traditional Japanese characters: Haku's inability to remember himself, Kaonashi's search for a place to belong and the Stink Spirit's need for transformation. The plurality within these characters, specifically those characters linked visually to Japanese culture, points to a crisis of identity at the heart of *Sen to Chihiro*'s narrative, caused at least in part by the film's need to succeed beyond as well as within its national boundaries. Thus there is little sense of a straightforward Japanese identity in *Sen to Chihiro*'s narrative and imagery; uncertainty and transformation are the rule rather than the exception in Miyazaki's most psychologically complex animated world to date.

Selling a fantasy of Japan: *Sen to Chihiro*'s domestic marketing

Transformation also became the mainstay of *Sen to Chihiro*'s domestic advertising. The print campaign alone for the film included over thirty images and there were nine additional theatrical trailers and ten television advertisements produced just for the Japanese market, making it far more diversified than the advertising for previous Miyazaki films (*Sen to Chihiro* DVD 2001; Denison

2005). These latter trailers and television advertising 'spots' provide evidence of two main phases of Studio Ghibli's push to make *Sen to Chihiro* a success: trailers introducing the aesthetic look of the film and a secondary phase that aimed to introduce its narrative and characters to potential audiences. However, there are interesting differences between *Sen to Chihiro*'s cinema and television trailers, not just in content but also caused by the different demands of the media in which they were employed. For example, towards the end of *Sen to Chihiro*'s campaign the advertisments made for television began to comment upon its record-breaking status, with three calling the film a *dai-hitto* or 'big hit', Japan's rough equivalent to 'blockbuster' status.

In a similar vein, one print advertisement took time to thank Japanese audiences for *Sen to Chihiro*'s success while showing scenes of celebration drawn directly from the film's bath house character imagery. It went as far as to imply a link between the film's bath house god-clients and the film's Japanese audiences, saying, 'Our clients, they are gods!' (Studio Ghibli 2002: 80–3). These appeals to a sense of national community among audiences in the advertising for *Sen to Chihiro* may well have been one of the reasons for its phenomenal success at the Japanese box-office, but it remains a fact that this success was engineered and managed.

Though the idea of transformation was central to the concept of marketing *Sen to Chihiro*, so too was the selling of it through reference to its Japanese aspects. Among the thirty or more images from the campaign, most stress some aspect of what might be termed the film's Japaneseness either through imagery – settings and characters, for example – or through the written copy that accompanied images from the film. A variety of these references are visible in one advertisement which appeared in the *Yomiuri Shinbun* newspaper advertising both the film and some of its ancillary goods (*Yomiuri Shinbun*, August 3, 2001, section 12: 23). The advertisement focuses on two sets of images: Chihiro riding Haku in dragon form on the left-hand side, and in the centre of the advertisement, a group image of the film's bath house characters celebrating. The aim of the advertisement appears to have been two-fold: on one hand to sell merchandising artefacts such as books and magazines related to the film; on the other to thank audiences again for making the film a popular hit in Japan (cf. Austin 2002: 39, n.80; Klinger 1991: 119). To the latter end, Yubāba is presented saying thank you in the copy while holding a pair of fans decorated with the flag of Japan and in the foreground the word 'Japan!' (*Nihon–!*) has been added to re-emphasise the image. The appearance of this image in a national newspaper less than a month after *Sen to Chihiro*'s release in cinemas in Japan indicates how vital the domestic market was in terms of the film's success. This fact was compounded by the appearance of this same image of Yubāba, albeit with changeable text, in four publications (*Supōtsu Nippon*, July 27, 2001, pullout section: 19; *Asahi Shinbun*, August 10, 2001, section 5: 25; *Yomiuri Shinbun*, August 10, 2001, section 5: 26; *Chihōgami*, August 11, 2001, section 6: 27).

This is not to suggest, however, that the marketing of *Sen to Chihiro*'s Japanese facets in Japan was any more straightforward than the film's presentation of its Japanese characters. The efficacy of the marketing was wholly dependent upon the ability of potential audiences to recognise references to particular aspects of

Japanese culture. To enhance such recognition, *Sen to Chihiro*'s epiphenomenal magazines tended to contain explanations to educate audiences on the origins of Miyazaki's imagery. For example, the *Roman Album* magazine for the film contained a six-page article entitled 'Searching for "Chihiro" ', tracing the roots of the film back to Japanese festivals such as *Shimotsuki* in which priests invite spirits to enter their bodies (Mizutami 2001: 128–9). Further, the article contains a variety of references to the film's architectural styles – the bath house's interior as borrowed from the Meguro Gajoen wedding venue in Tokyo with other buildings inspired by the *Edo Tōkyō Tatemonoen* (Edo Tokyo Buildings Park). Also supplied with the articles were pictures of the kinds of masks that informed many of *Sen to Chihiro*'s supernatural characters (Ibid.: 128–33). These detailed explanations reinforced the authenticity of Miyazaki's imagery in its Japanese context while also explaining that imagery for those unaware of its Japanese origins.

What emerges from *Sen to Chihiro*'s Japanese incarnation and promotion is therefore a complex tapestry of appeals to domestic audiences through the national as real and fantastic. Audiences with a range of competencies were targeted, including those knowledgeable about traditional Japanese culture, as well as about modern Japanese history and cultural trends. Moreover, the appeals to patriotic audiences in Japan were made blatant for *Sen to Chihiro* – with graphics and language directed to the heart of Japanese national identity. These competencies were not, however, significant only in the film's domestic market. As will be shown below, *Sen to Chihiro*'s translation into French and English changed the film's cultural points of reference, with some references to Japan emphasised while others were masked or elided.

En Français: Le Voyage de Chihiro

The exhibition of *Sen to Chihiro* in France illustrates neatly the beginning of this process of transformation. The transformation took place on a variety of fronts from those concerning exhibition to others relating to the alteration of the film text itself. *Le Voyage de Chihiro* therefore reveals movement away from the film's popular 'blockbuster' roots towards a conception of it more concerned with the film as a work of art.

The first location in which this shift of markets from the popular to what might be termed niche or elitist for *Sen to Chihiro* takes place is the film's introduction to Europe through inclusion in film festivals (Harbord 2002).[3] Perhaps the most significant of these to the film's global life was its inclusion at the 2002 Berlin Film Festival where it was entered in the main competition, under its Japanese title but with English and French titles appended to the programme (see: http://www.berlinale.de/external/de/filmarchiv/doku_pdf/20023223.pdf). As Julian Stringer (2003: 82) states: 'festivals can make or break new films. Certainly, many of the larger events act as launching pads for foreign (i.e. non-US), marginal or "difficult" movies, and as such constitute an alternative distribution network for contemporary world cinema'. In the case of *Le Voyage de Chihiro*, the Berlin Film Festival acted rather more like the 'launching pad' from Stringer's argument, as an extravagant premiere, as the film already had distribution via the Disney–Ghibli deal. However, the free publicity and high profile market entry that this premiere for *Le Voyage de Chihiro* provided must be understood as part of its marketing to Europe.

Perhaps the single most important aspect of the film's French release, however, and the reason that *Le Voyage de Chihiro* might be thought of as transitional, was that it was released in not one but two versions shown side-by-side in French cinemas. Though not unusual exhibition practice *per se*, in the French context both films were advertised roughly equally, while in the United States it was the dubbed version that was emphasised most. The two new versions consisted of a re-dubbing of the film by French actors (including Florinne Orphelin as Chihiro and Anne Ludovik as Yubāba) and another version of the film in which French-language subtitles were provided for the Japanese language track. It is at this juncture more than perhaps anywhere else that the conception of *Sen to Chihiro* as Japanese becomes problematic. Leigh Dale and Helen Gilbert (2001: 190) make the assertion about the Japanese language that it provides a point of 'constant and strict division between notions of inside and outside, which also functions to strengthen a sense of cultural exclusivity', suggesting how much of the film's national identity would have been encoded through its language track. Thus *Sen to Chihiro*'s alteration would have, to an extent, altered its national make-up. Further, it suggests that the French language was not as dominant in its domestic market as American English is thought to be in the US.

Therefore, *Le Voyage de Chihiro* differs at the level of text from *Sen to Chihiro*. The dubbing of the film into French, while retaining the original image track, begins a process of cultural explication and misapprehension not found in the Japanese version of the film. For example, the French version contains a scene in which Yubāba tells Chihiro that eight million gods come to the bath house when tired. This is a slightly disingenuous literal translation from the Japanese where reference to 'eight million' gods is a shorthand way of describing the pantheon of deities worshipped in Japan. Further, in a film with a central theme of identity and the power of names, it is somewhat surprising that Haku's real name – Nigihayami Kohaku Nushi – is altered to the descriptive '*l'espirit de la rivière Kohaku*' (spirit of the Kohaku River) when spoken, even though the subtitled French kept the longer and more complicated Japanese name.

Significant, too, as regards names in *Le Voyage de Chihiro*, is the way in which French and Japanese pronunciations of character names were changed to accommodate the French accent. Thus Chihiro's relatively crisp, clipped Japanese consonants and short vowel sounds become transformed in French so that the protagonist's name is enunciated as 'Shi-iro' instead. For these reasons, linguistic naturalisation such as this should be given due consideration. What is heard in this instance both authenticates *Le Voyage de Chihiro* for general French audiences, and reduces its Japanese authenticity for invested, fan audiences. Releasing subbed and dubbed versions simultaneously allows both sets of potential French audio-viewers to engage with it in their preferred manners, maximising *Le Voyage de Chihiro*'s profit-making potential.

The reasoning behind the provision of two versions of the film in France is reflected in the promotional campaign for it. In France, reviews of the film appeared in both popular and specialist print media, providing evidence for a thriving popular and additionally a more elitist market for the film in this French context. It was ostensibly to attract both 'art house' and popular audiences that *Le Voyage de Chihiro* was produced in two formats simultaneously. For example, film journals *Cahiers du Cinema*, *Positif* and *Cinéastes* all ran articles on *Le Voyage de Chihiro* and its creators around the time of its release (*Cahiers du Cinema* 567:14–22; *Cinéastes* 6, 2002: 12–24; *Positif* 494: 6–16). These journal-style publications all serve a relatively knowledgeable cinephile clientele in France, and articles in magazines such as *Mad Movies*, *Studio* and *Le Cinéma S.F.X.*, which also carried in-depth articles and reviews of *Le Voyage de Chihiro*, served a more popular audience for Miyazaki's work (*Le Cinéma S.F.X.* 96: 42–5; *Mad Movies* 141: 40–7; *Studio* 177: 112–17).

This body of response to, and promotion of, *Le Voyage de Chihiro* was the largest the film received outside Japan and interesting currents of debate run through it. The film's national and generic identities, for example, are condensed into a single set of discussions centring on what is alternately termed '*l'animation japonaise*' and '*anime japonaise*'. The distinction made between these two terms is a deliberate one. '*L'animation japonaise*' appears in *Cahiers du Cinema* and acts as part of a movement designed to 'rescue' *Le Voyage de Chihiro* from discussion as '*anime*'. The journal shows its low opinion of this Japanese medium of filmmaking, calling it both vulgar and violent in comparison with Miyazaki's filmmaking style (Chauvin and Higuinen 2002: 14–15). Also germane to this argument, however, is the emphasis both of the phrases mentioned above put on the national specificity of the '*japonaise*'. Elsewhere, Betrand Rouger (2002: 40) refers to *Le Voyage de Chihiro* as '*produit de la culture nippone*', or as the product of Japanese culture. Clearly, then, there is a thread that runs through discussion of *Le Voyage de Chihiro* which works to promote the film as belonging to Japanese culture, even as some such as the *Cahiers* critics work to disassociate it from its Japanese filmmaking tradition.

In these various ways, *Le Voyage de Chihiro*'s exhibition in France therefore reflects a similar plurality of meaning to that displayed in Japan. Certainly, its promotion in this context was very different: a slow platform release from its Berlin premiere through to a lower-key promotional campaign that relied on review coverage much more than was the case in its domestic release. *Le Voyage de Chihiro*'s exhibition context also changed, however, and the two versions of it shown in French cinemas illustrate the ways in which the 'original' text's meanings began to be filtered for easier consumption both in linguistic and in cultural terms. However, the film's French exhibition context was to have more in common with *Sen to Chihiro* than was to be the case in its eventual release in the United States some five months later.

Spirited away to America

The most obvious difference between *Spirited Away* and the versions of the film it succeeded was that this was the first time a director other than Miyazaki became associated with it. A promotional focus was found for America in the person of director John Lasseter, who became the central promotional personality driving Miyazaki's film into the country. On the strength of his performance as a director for Disney's corporate partner, Pixar, Lasseter was chosen as the executive producer for the dubbing of *Sen to Chihiro* into English. Something of a star director in his own right, Lasseter's involvement with the project helped to give the animated film a focal point, which is to say an American voice, from the beginning of its re-production (Klinger 1991: 127). Lasseter's importance to the project continued even as far as its DVD release, for which he provided an interview about the making of *Spirited Away*. One comment he made bears particular scrutiny in order to understand how Disney, and Lasseter specifically, understood the process of re-dubbing:

> We added a few words here and there just to inform someone of what they're looking at, but tried to weave it in in a way that was very natural. And the goal was to have these characters be good – good acting, great casting, but also to have them be speaking American. So when you listen to it, it is just natural. Natural American English coming out. And we're so proud of the English version of this movie.
>
> (Lasseter commentary for US *Spirited Away* DVD, 2003)

This comment illustrates a series of hierarchies at work in Lasseter's efforts to re-dub *Sen to Chihiro*. The first is a linguistic hierarchy which infers the primacy of what the producer calls 'American', as might be expected from his role in the reproduction of *Spirited Away*. This slippage is probably deliberate, as the accents reproduced in the film are exclusively American in origin. Thus Americanised English takes precedence over any other accented version of the language and English itself is presented as preferable to any alternative linguistic predecessor the film might have, helping to naturalise *Spirited Away* for potential US audiences.[4] This hierarchy of languages reproduces John Rennie Short's analysis of English as a global language in which he posits that 'English is required to be competitive in global markets' (Short 2001: 130). It would appear that this was the case in America for *Spirited Away*, as in the US the film was released theatrically primarily in its (re)dubbed format.

Lasseter further builds linguistic hierarchy through omission, when he makes reference to his pride in the 'English version of this movie'. Refuting notions of the primacy of the image, Lasseter (as might be expected from his relationship with *Spirited Away*) prefers vocal acting over the image. For Lasseter what is important in his version is the English language and 'good acting', not the beauty inherent in the film's imagery. This short speech carefully positions the film in its American market: it focuses on the 'American' aspects of the re-dubbing in an attempt to naturalise and explain the 'foreign' and 'Oriental' aspects it contains, in order to make it more accessible. Therefore, the use of Lasseter in the promotion for *Spirited Away* acted to authenticate the American version of this Japanese film.

However, at the level of the image track, which remained unchanged in both

Spirited Away and *Le Voyage de Chihiro*, the film was reliant on essentially Japanese images and source materials. As in the French translation of the film, the American dialogue is occasionally used to explain the unusual countenances of characters. One good example can be found in the film's Radish Spirit – a white god who resembles somewhat a Japanese *daikon* radish and who wears a red lacquered Japanese dish lid on his head – whose appearance goes completely unexplained in *Sen to Chihiro*. In the film's promotional materials in Japan, the god's name is given as *Oshira-sama*, or the White Spirit, whereas in America the god is given the more descriptive name of Radish Spirit (Akimoto 2001: 21).

This explanation of relatively minor characters is somewhat incongruous when considering the facets of the image track that remain lost, or become mystified, in its American and French incarnations. Foremost among these are the many occasions in which written Japanese is used in *Sen to Chihiro* to add context or subtle shades of meaning to its narrative. The link between the mysterious town and Japanese New Year festivals, for example, is made on the side of the first building that Chihiro's family approaches. It has the characters for *shōgatsu* (New Year) written on its side. A further example can be found in the scene previously mentioned where the White or Radish Spirit shares an elevator with Chihiro. In the film the bath house's elevators are clearly labelled 'Up' and 'Down' in large gold Japanese characters, and the floor where the Spirit departs reads '*niten*', literally, Second Heaven. In the French and American versions of *Sen to Chihiro*, these nuances and jokes become transcribed into little more than further evidence of the film's Oriental origins. This is not to suggest that the film's translations were poor, nor to imply that viewing it in its 'original' form provides some extra cache of cultural capital for those who understand Japanese. Rather, it is intended to suggest that, just as '*America exported does not equal America at home*: the discourses are predicated on misrepresentations and partialities' (McKay 1997: 13 – italics in original), so too is reception of Japanese film outside Japan often based around partial recognitions and uneven cultural awareness that can foster *different* interpretations of the film.

Sen to Chihiro's 'voyage' from its domestic setting across various global film markets was marked by high levels of critical praise while it concurrently underwent various processes designed to make it an easily appreciable international cultural object. Nowhere is this more obvious than in the presentation of *Spirited Away* (and not *Sen to Chihiro*) with the American Academy Award for Best Animated Feature. In practical terms this award had the effect of re-opening the US film market to *Spirited Away* after it had achieved only modest previous success at the American box office (listed at http://us.imdb.com/Business?0245429). However, it also re-enforced the linguistic hierarchies set up by Lasseter and the film's American distributors, by ignoring its Japanese language incarnation. As an Oscar-winning film, therefore, *Spirited Away* took on a further layer of identity, this time one which compounded its relationship with the US film industry and market.

Plurality and hybridity were therefore the essence of *Sen to Chihiro* in all its incarnations. Considered as a whole, it belongs at least in part to every national market for which it was translated, be it in dubbed or subtitled form. Simultaneously its images provided not a vision but visions of a Japan that were never themselves 'pure'. In its 'mythical' aspect *Sen to Chihiro* harks back to a vision of Japan largely lost from that nation's modern social experience. That small glimpse of Miyazaki's impression of modern Japan seen in the framing story is itself influenced both by European and by American culture. However, Miyazaki's presentation of this lost national identity is anything but straightforward, as reflected in his juxtaposition within *Sen to Chihiro* of magical but treacherous traditional Japanese landscapes and idyllic old-fashioned European settings. Additionally, the film transforms for its audiences dependent on their experience of it (what version in what language for instance). The less that is known of the film's origins, the greater the likelihood of audiences' finding in Miyazaki's imaginings of Japanese society a generalised sense of modernity opposed against a traditional or mythical Orient.

It should be understood then that *Sen to Chihiro*, *Le Voyage de Chihiro* and especially perhaps *Spirited Away* negotiated markets across the globe that were not wholly distinct but which bled into one another. When the film won at Berlin, for example, adverts appeared in Japanese newspapers proclaiming a triumph: the same information also appeared in the film's press kit in the US (http://www.nausicaa.net/miyazaki/sen/presskit.html). While its presentations in these markets were as different as its different phases of promotion (as blockbuster, as niche film, as art house film), several key elements remained constant, perhaps most importantly its director, Miyazaki, and its imagery.

Sen to Chihiro therefore cannot be considered as a 'stateless' object, to paraphrase Napier's and others' claims for *anime* (Napier 2001a: 24–7); but it might well qualify as global. The differing versions of the film illustrate the mutable nature of the 'global' *anime* text; as circulation over increasingly broad geo-cultural and geo-linguistic audiences help to redefine global film culture boundaries in ever more porous terms. The negotiations discussed here suggest that *anime*, particularly of the family-oriented kind that Miyazaki tends to produce, might be better placed than many live action films to endure the vagaries of dubbing and translation. By using Tomlinson's formulation of global culture it becomes possible to read *Sen to Chihiro*'s insistent Japaneseness, however vaguely recognisable abroad, as an inherent part of its global identity. As a member of what might termed a third wave of *anime*, a wave defined by cable television and the advent of the Internet and DVD technologies that have made *anime* more globally accessible, *Sen to Chihiro*'s acceptance into important global markets for film and television illustrates just how deeply *anime* have penetrated into, and become a part of, culture the world over. In its journey from *Sen to Chihiro*, to *Le Voyage de Chihiro*, to *Spirited Away*, this film suggests the need for us to reappraise Japanese cinema, to consider how and why *anime* and other kinds of film are becoming entrenched parts of global cinema culture.

Notes

1 There were various other titles applied to *Sen to Chihiro*. These include *Henkien Kätemä* in Finland, *La Città Incantata* in Italy, and *El Viaje de Chihiro* in Spain.

2 Significantly, the image track for the film remained unchanged for the whole of *Sen to Chihiro*'s release while its language track was entirely altered on a regular basis. This suggests that the consistency in film of the primacy of the image may in a global sense have some relevance, but also that language is a vital part of how film speaks to its audiences.

3 *Sen to Chihiro* received many European premieres and award nominations, particularly towards the end of its theatrical life in late 2002. For example, it was nominated for the Screen International Award (for a non-European film) 2002 at the European Film Academy Awards, announced on 7 December in Rome. *Sen to Chihiro* was also included as part of the programme at the Sitges Film Festival in October 2002 in Spain. Information from http://www.imdb.com and http://www.nausicaa.net (Accessed April 29, 2003).

4 Significantly, reviews of the American dub for *Spirited Away* make frequent reference to its stars whereas this was only infrequently the case with the French dub. Importantly, Kirk Wise, the director of the dub and of Disney films such as *Beauty and the Beast* (US, 1991) is mentioned on several occasions, again to emphasise the quality of those attached to this relatively unknown project (Ebert 2002; Horwitz 2002: C05; Mitchell 2002: E11; Turan 2002).

References

Akimoto, I. (ed.) (2001). *Roman arubamu: Sen to Chihiro no kamikakushi* [Roman Album: Spirited Away], Tokyo: Tokuma Shoten Publishing.

Austin, Thomas (2002) *Hollywood, Hype and Audiences: Selling and Watching Popular Film in the 1990s*, Manchester: Manchester University Press.

Chauvin, J.-S. and E. Higuinen (2002) 'Le Triangle D'or de la "Japanimation"', *Cahiers du Cinema*, 567: 16–20. April.

Cubbison, L. (2005) 'Anime Fans, DVDs, and the Authentic Text', *Velvet Light Trap*, 56 (Fall): 45–57.

Dale, Leigh and Gilbert, Helen (2001) 'Looking the Same? A Preliminary (Postcolonial) Discussion of Orientalism and Occidentalism in Australia and Japan', in Paul Williams (ed.) *Sage Masters of Modern Social Thought*, London: Sage: 177–95.

Denison, Rayna (2005) 'Cultural Traffic in *Japanese Anime*: The Meanings of Promotion, Reception and Exhibition Circuits in *Princess Mononoke*', University of Nottingham. Unpublished PhD thesis.

Drazen, P. (2003) *Anime Explosion! The What? Why? & Wow! of Japanese Animation*, Berkeley, CA: Stone Bridge Press.

Ebert, Roger (2002). 'Miyazaki's *Spirited Away*'. *Chicago Sun-Times*. Online. http://www.suntimes.com/ebert/ebert_reviews/2002/09/092007.html (Accessed May 3, 2003).

Harbord, Janet (2002) *Film Cultures*, London: Sage.

Hesmondhalgh, David (2002) *The Cultural Industries*, London: Sage.

Hewitt, C. (2003) 'The X Factor', *Empire*, May: 71–89.

Horwitz, J. (2002) 'An Animation Sensation: "*Spirited Away*" into Wonderland', *The Washington Post*, September 20: C05.

Klinger, Barbara (1991) 'Digressions at the Cinema: Commodification and Reception in Mass Culture, in James Naremore and Patrick Bratlinger (eds) *Modernity and Mass Culture*, Bloomington: Indiana University Press: 117–34.

McKay, George (ed.) (1997) *Yankee Go Home (& Take Me With U): Americanization and Popular Culture*, Sheffield: Sheffield Academic Press.

Minear, R. H. (2001) 'Orientalism and the Study of Japan', in Paul Williams (ed.) *Sage Masters of Modern Social Thought*, London: Sage: 337–49.

Mitchell, E. (2002) 'Film Review; Conjuring up Atmosphere Only Anime Can Deliver', *The New York Times*, September 20, Section E: 11.

Mizutami, G. (2001) ' *"Chihiro" o sagashite*' (Searching for 'Chihiro') in Akimoto 2001: 128–33.

Napier, Susan (2001a) *Anime from Akira to Princess Mononoke: Experiencing Contemporary Japanese Animation*, New York: Palgrave.

—— (2001b) 'Peek-A-Boo Pikachu: Exporting and Asian Subculture', *Harvard Asia Pacific Review*, Fall: 13–17.

Neale, Steve, and Smith, Murray (eds) (1998) *Contemporary Hollywood Cinema*, London: Routledge.

Rouger, Betrand (2002) '*Le Meilleur des Mondes*', *Mad Movies*, April: 40–1.

Sandler, Kevin S. and Studlar, Gaylyn (eds) (1999) *Titanic: Anatomy of a Blockbuster*, New Brunswick, NJ: Rutgers University Press.

Short, J. R. (2001) *Global Dimensions: Space, Place and the Contemporary World*, London: Reaktion Books.

Stringer, Julian (2003) 'Raiding the Archive: Film Festivals and the Revival of Classic Hollywood', in Paul Grainge (ed.) *Memory and Popular Film*, Manchester: Manchester University Press: 81–96.

Studio Ghibli (2002). *Naushika no "Shinbun kōkoku"tte mita koto arimasuka* [Have you Seen the 'Newspaper Advertising' for *Nausicaa*?], Tokyo: Tokuma Shoten and Studio Ghibli.

Tomlinson, John (1999) *Globalization and Culture*, Cambridge: Polity.

Turan, Kenneth (2002) 'Under the Spell of *Spirited Away*', *Los Angeles Times*.

Miyazaki Hayao Filmography

Lupin III (*Rupan Sansei*, October 24, 1971–March 26, 1972 [Episodes 7–23]). (Dir. Takahata Isao and Miyazaki Hayao). Tokyo Mūbī Shinsha (TV Series)

The New Lupin III (*Rupan Sansei (shin)*, October 2, 1977–October 6, 1980 [Episodes 145 and 155]). Tokyo Mūbī Shinsha (TV Series)

Future Boy Conan (*Mirai shōnen Konan*, 1978). Nippon Animation NHK (TV Series)

Lupin III: The Castle of Cagliostro (*Rupan Sansei Kariosutoro no shiro*, 1979). Tokyo Mūbī Shinsha

Sherlock Hound (*Meitantei Hōmuzu*, 1982 [six episodes]). Tokyo Mūbī Shinsha and RAI (Italian TV station)

Nausicaa of the Valley of the Wind (*Kaze no tani no Naushika*, 1984)

Castle in the Sky (*Tenkū no shiro Rapyuta*, 1986)

My Neighbor Totoro (*Tonari no Totoro*, 1988)

Kiki's Delivery Service (*Majo no takkyūbin*, 1989)

Porco Rosso/The Crimson Pig (*Kurenai no buta*, 1992)

The Sky-Coloured Seed (*Sora-iro no tane*, 1992)

What Is It? (*Nandarō*, 1992 – five short advertisements for Nihon Terebi). TV Spots.

On Your Mark (1995 – music video)

Princess Mononoke (*Mononoke hime*, 1997)

Spirited Away (*Sen to Chihiro no kamikakushi*, 2001)

Howl's Moving Castle (*Hauru no ugoku shiro*, 2004)

FILM AVAILABILITY

The films discussed in the book's chapters are available on DVD and/or VHS with English-language subtitles from the following companies in the US and UK:

I Was Born, But . . . (US: New Yorker Films)
Osaka Elegy (US: Home Vision Entertainment)
Humanity and Paper Balloons (UK: Eureka)
Ornamental Hairpin (currently unavailable in the US and UK)
Late Spring (US: Criterion; UK: Tartan)
Life of O-Haru (UK: Artificial Eye)
Godzilla (US: Simitar Video; UK: British Film Institute)
Seven Samurai (US: Criterion; UK: British Film Institute)
Late Chrysanthemums (US: World Artists Home Video)
Conflagration (US: New Yorker Films)
Giants and Toys (US: Wea Corporation)
Cruel Story of Youth (US: New Yorker Films)
Woman in the Dunes (US: Image Entertainment; UK: British Film Institute)
Branded to Kill (US: Criterion; UK: Second Sight Films)
Double Suicide (US: Criterion)
In the Realm of the Senses (US: Fox Lorber; UK: Nouveau Pictures)
Vengeance is Mine (US: Home Vision Entertainment; UK: Eureka)
The Family Game (not currently available on a commercial basis in the US or UK, but available in a number of university collections)
Fire Festival (US: Warner Home Video)
Tampopo (US: Fox Lorber)
Maborosi (US: New Yorker Films; UK: ICA Projects)
Hana-bi (US: New Yorker Films; UK: Momentum Pictures Home Entertainment)
Ring (US: Universal Studios; UK: Tartan)
Spirited Away (US: Walt Disney Home Video; UK: Optimum)

GLOSSARY

aniki   brother

anime   animated film and television

benshi   figure in Japanese early film who stood to one side of the cinema screen and explained the contents of the film to the audience

bungei eiga   cinematic adaptation of a work of serious fiction

bunka seikatsu   cultural living

bunraku   traditional form of puppet drama

burakumin   ostracized social group within Japan that has conventionally been forbidden to inter-marry with the general population and restricted to the lowest forms of labour

bushidō   warrior; *bushidō* code

chambara   swordplay films

chapatsu   blonde

chinpira   punk

Chūshingura   Literally refers to the 'Loyal League', but is better known as the 'Forty-Seven *rōnin*'. The story tells of a group of *samurai* who became *rōnin* after their master was forced to commit *seppuku* for assaulting a court official who had insulted him. They avenged him by killing the court official after patiently waiting and planning for over a year. In turn, the soldiers were themselves forced to commit *seppuku*, but died knowing that they had ful-filled their honourable obligations. Made into a puppet play in 1748, the narrative soon became a *kabuki* favourite and it remains one of Japan's most enduring national tales to this day

dai-hitto   'big hit'; Japanese equivalent of a 'movie blockbuster'

daimyō   feudal leader

danchi   suburban apartment housing complex

dojin   pejorative term for 'native'

dokuritsu puro   independent production

Edo   pre-modern Tokyo

engawa   long corridor

enjo kōsai   compensated dating with minors

enka   old-fashioned emotional song

ero eiga   erotic film; *pinku eia*

ero guro nansensu   'erotic, grotesque, nonsense': form of aesthetic modernism which flourished during the inter-war period and influenced various media such as photography, graphic design, painting, poetry, soft-core pornographic literature and detective fiction

fundoshi   loincloth

futon   Japanese-style quilt for sleeping

geijutsu eiga   art cinema

geijutsu-teki   artistic

geisha   hostess

gekiga   graphic novels of a gritty tendency

gendai   modern times

gendai-geki   contemporary drama film

genkan   hallway

giji shutaisei   false subjectivity

giri   a debt, duty of obligation

go   strategic Japanese board game played on a chequered board with black and white stones

goraku eiga   entertainment film

hade   colourful

haha-mono   mother film

haiku   traditional 17 syllable verse form comprising three metrical units of five, seven and five units

hanabi   flower fire

heibon   ordinary

hibachi   charcoal brazier

higaisha ishiki   victim consciousness

hikisoto   from the outside

hikiuchi   from the inside

himatsuri   fire festival

hiragana   indigenous Japanese writing system; one of the three components of the written Japanese language, alongside *kanji* and *katakana*

hyūmanisumu   humanism

ie   Family System; adopted in the Meiji era (1868–1912) as a dominant model of patriarchal inheritance patterns, enriching a national polity of 'nation-as-family'

ikenie   scapegoat

jidai-geki   period drama film

jitsuroku   true record

josei eiga   woman's film

juneiga undo   'pure film movement': cultural discourse which challenged the popularity of mainstream commercial *shinpa* film and *jidai-geki* and advocated a modernized system of film production and spectatorship allied to the status of cinema being based on the intrinsic qualities of the recorded moving image

kaban mochi   youngest employee in a company

kabuki   highly stylized traditional popular drama

kaidan   ghost story

324

kakoware-mono   mistress, literally 'confined woman'

kamikaze   divine wind; suicide pilots in the Second World War

kana   a 'woman's hand' or script; *onna-de*

kanji   Chinese characters; one of the three components of the written Japanese language, alongside *katakana* and *hiragana*

Kansaiben   Ōsaka dialect

kantoku   director

kata   social forms

katakana   notation system for writing words borrowed from a foreign language; one of the three components of the written Japanese language, alongside *kanji* and *hiragana*

kazoku   family

kazoku kokka   the family state

keikō eiga   'tendency' films; films with a tendency to represent proletarian culture from a leftist point-of-view

kengeki eiga   *chanbara*; swordfighting film

kimono   long loose robe with wide short sleeves

kindaishugi-sha   'modernist'; modernism/modern thought

kitsune   fox

kizewa-mono   late flowering genre of *kabuki* plays set in Edo which portrayed the lives of common people rather than legendary heroes

kokoro   heart/self

kokugakushu   scholarly movement which flourished during the Edo period [1603–1868] concerned with the innate character of Japanese culture

kokumin eiga   People's Cinema

kokusai-teki na Nihon eiga   Japanese-international film; a term signalling Japanese cinema's overseas acceptance that first became prevalent in the post-war period

kokusaku eiga   'national policy film' during the Second World War

kokutai   the body politic

kosei   individuality

kozō   boy

kūkan no fetishizumu   'fetishism for space'

kurogo   veiled *bunraku* puppeteers shrouded in black whose presence is almost invisible to theatre spectators

kyokō   fiction

kyūha   'old school' drama

manā kyōshitsu   'Miss Manners classroom'

manga   comic book

marumage   traditional hairstyle appropriate only for married women or *kakoware-mono*

masukomi jidai   era of mass communications

michiyuki   the trope of lovers eloping to commit suicide together (*shinjū*) in *kabuki* and *bunraku*

modanisumu   'modernism'; contemporary manners and customs in modernity

moga   modern girl/flapper

Momotarō   the Peach Boy

mono-no-aware   notion of a gentle sensitivity to the fleeting nature of things. Originally defined by the *kokugakushu* literary scholar Norinaga Motori [1730–1801]

mu   'nothing'

muko-yōshi   a husband 'adopted' into a family where there are no sons

Naikaku Johokyoku   Cabinet Propaganda Office during the Second World War

naniwabushi   popular narrative song form during the Edo period

nigiyaka   lively

nikutai   the body

nikutai bungaku   literature of the flesh

nikutai eiga   film of the flesh

ningen   human

ningyō-kei   doll-like

ninjō   human compassion

ninkyō yakuza eiga   chivalrous gangster film

Noh   traditional drama with dance and song evolved from *Shintō* rites

obi   a belt for a *kimono*

o-bon   a time in August for memorializing one's ancestors

oiran   high-ranking courtesan

ojōsan   proper young girl

OL   (office lady; female professional worker

omoire   earnestness

onna   woman

onna-de   a woman's hand; *kana*

onna-dōshi no giri   the duty or obligation of one woman to another

onna no fumi   woman's letter

oshōgatsu   Japanese New Year. Although Japan adapted the solar calendar in 1873, the term refers to the lunar New Year and is marked by a series of festivities and ceremonies which begin on New Year's Eve, shortly before midnight when Buddhist temples ring bells 108 times to remember the nation's hardships

oyabun   elder; *yakuza* boss

oyama   female impersonator

parodi   'parody'

pachinko   pinball game

pinku eiga   'pink film'; erotic film

rakan   Buddhist saints

rāmen   thin wheat noodles originally imported from China

renga   literary verse form in which a series of independent short verses are linked into one long poem

rensageki   'chain drama' involving a combination of live drama and projected film

roman poruno   'romantic pornographic'; soft-core erotic film genre

rōnin unemployed/leaderless *samurai*

ryokan Japanese-style inn

ryōsei 'both sexes'; hermaphrodite

ryosai kenbo ideology of 'good wife, wise mother' dating back to the Meiji era

ryūkō kantoku pop director

sake fermented liquor made from rice

sakura cherry blossom

sarariman/salaryman Japanese white-collar office-worker

samisen three-stringed musical instrument

samurai feudal army officer; member of military caste

SCAP Supreme Commander of Allied Powers: General Douglas MacArthur; responsible for the implementation of the Allied Occupation of Japan 1945–1952

seikatsu kaizen undo daily life reform movement

seishin the spirit

seitai eiga ecological film

sensei teacher

seppuku ritual suicide; disembowelment

shitamachi the low city

shimenawa sacred rope

Shi-ne drop dead

shinjin kantoku new director

shinjinrui 'the new human species'

shinjū double suicide

shinkansen 'new trunk' railway line

Shinko-Shashin New Photography

Shinko Shashin Kenkyukai New Photography Association

shinpa 'the new school': form of contemporary urban theatrical melodrama which was popular during the late Meiji period [1868–1912]and characterized by a more naturalistic performance style than traditional *kabuki*

shinpura raifu undo simple life movement

Shintō pre-Buddhist animistic religion revering ancestors and nature-spirits

shiri tori traditional word game in which one takes turns by saying a word beginning with the last syllable of the word provided by one's opponent

shizenshugi-teki fūzoku eiga naturalist cinema of everyday life

shōgatsu New Year

shōji wood or paper screen

shokugyō fujin professional modern woman

shomin eiga/shomin-geki home drama of everyday folk

shōshimin eiga home drama of lower-middle-class people

shukanshi weekly magazines

shunga erotic image, literally 'spring picture', usually made in woodblock print form, which flourished between the mid-seventeenth century and the early nineteenth century

shutaisei political agency/subjectivity

shutaisei ronsō   debate over subjectivity

soemono eiga   accompanying film; *tsuide eiga* or b picture

Susano-o   the Storm God

Tabi   light footwear

tachigui   noodle stand

taishu   the masses

taiyōzoku eiga   'sun tribe' film

tampopo   dandelion

tatami   straw matting

tēma shugi   theme-oriented

tsuide eiga   b film

ukiyo-e   woodblock print of the Genroku (1688–1704) era

ukiyo-zōshi   illustrated tale of the Genroku era

urusai   noisy

wabi-sabi   aesthetic conception of the impermanent and imperfect nature of things characterized in material terms by earthy, unpretentious and plain qualities

waisetsu   obscenity

yakuza   gangster

yūgure   twilight

zure   slippage

zushiki-teki   diagrammatic

BIBLIOGRAPHY OF WORKS ON JAPANESE CINEMA

Compiled by Rayna Denison, Alexander Jacoby, Yuna de Lannoy, Mori Toshie, Alastair Phillips, and Julian Stringer.

I: Reference

Asahi Graph Henshū-kyoku (ed.) (1925–1930) *Nihon eiga nenkan* [*Japan Film Yearbook*], Tokyo: Tōkyō Asahi Shinbun Hakkō-sho.

Bock, Audie (1978) *Japanese Film Directors*, Tokyo, New York and Oxford: Kōdansha International for the Japan Society and Phaidon.

Buehrer, Beverley Bare (1990) *Japanese Films: A Filmography and Commentary, 1921–1989*, London: St James Press.

Galbraith, Stuart IV (1990) *The Japanese Filmography: A Complete Reference Guide to 200 Filmmakers and over 1,250 Films Released in the United States, 1900 through 1994*, Jefferson, NC: McFarland.

Jiji Tsūshin-sha (ed.) (1961–1970) *Eiga nenkan* [*Film Year Book*], Tokyo: Jiji Tsūshin-sha.

Jiji Eiga Tsūshin-sha (ed.) (1973–) *Eiga nenkan* [*Film Year Book*] Tokyo: Jiji Eiga Tsūshin-sha.

Kinema Junpō-sha (ed.) (1973) *Nihon eiga sakuhin zenshū* [*Encyclopedia of Japanese Film*], Tokyo: Kinema Junpō-sha.

—— (ed.) (1976) *Nihon eiga kantoku zenshū* [*Encyclopedia of Japanese Film Directors*], Tokyo: Kinema Junpō-sha.

—— (ed.) (1988) *Nihon eiga to terebi kantoku zenshū* [*Encyclopedia of Japanese Film and Television Directors*], Tokyo: Kinema Junpō-sha.

—— (ed.) (1995) *Nihon eiga jinmei jiten joyū-hen* [*Biographical Dictionary of Japanese Film Actresses*], Tokyo: Kinema Junpō-sha.

—— (ed.) (1996) *Nihon eiga jinmei jiten dan'yū-hen* [*Biographical Dictionary of Japanese Film Actors*], Tokyo: Kinema Junpō-sha.

—— (ed.) (1997) *Nihon eiga jinmei jiten kantoku-hen* [*Biographical Dictionary of Japanese Film Directors*], Tokyo: Kinema Junpō-sha.

Kondō, Keiichi (ed.) (1929) *Eiga sutā zenshū* [*The Complete Guide to Film Stars*] vols. 1–6, Tokyo: Heibon-sha.

—— (ed.) (1930) *Eiga sutā zenshū* [*The Complete Guide to Film Stars*] vols. 7–10, Tokyo: Heibon-sha.

Macias, Patrick (2001) *Tokyoscope: The Japanese Cult Film Companion*, San Francisco: Cadence Books.

Makino, Mamoru (ed.) (1989a) *Senzen eizō riron zasshi shūsei* [*An Anthology of Pre-war Film Theory Journals vols. 1–3*]: *Engeki eiga* [*Theatre Film*], Tokyo: Yumani Shobō.

—— (ed.) (1989b) *Senzen eizō riron zasshi shūsei* [*An Anthology of Pre-war Film Theory Journals vols. 4–7*]: *Gekijō-gai* [*Theatre District*], Tokyo: Yumani Shobō.

—— (ed.) (1989c) *Senzen eizō riron zasshi shūsei* [*An Anthology of Pre-war Film Theory Journals vol. 8*]: *Eiga chishiki* [*Film Knowledge*], Tokyo: Yumani Shobō.

—— (ed.) (1989d) *Senzen eizō riron zasshi shūsei* [*An Anthology of Pre-war Film Theory Journals vols. 9–11*]: *Eiga shūdan* [*Film Group*], Tokyo: Yumani Shobō.

—— (ed.) (1989e) *Senzen eizō riron zasshi shūsei* [*An Anthology of Pre-war Film Theory Journals vols. 12–14*]: *Eiga-kai* [*Film World*] Tokyo: Yumani Shobō.

—— (ed.) (1989f) *Senzen eizō riron zasshi shūsei* [*An Anthology of Pre-war Film Theory Journals vols. 15–21*]: Eiga to ongaku [*Film and Music*], Tokyo: Yumani Shobō.

—— (ed.) (1990) *Nihon eiga shoki shiryō shūsei* [*An Anthology of Early Japanese Film Documents vols. 1–5*]: *Katsudō shashin zasshi* [*Journal of the Moving Picture*] and *Katsudō no sekai* [*The World of the Moving Picture*], Tokyo: San'ichi Shobō.

—— (ed.) (1991) *Nihon eiga shoki shiryō shūsei* [*An Anthology of Early Japanese Film Documents vols. 6–9*], Tokyo: San'ichi Shobō.

—— (ed.) (1992) *Nihon eiga shoki shiryō shūsei* [*An Anthology of Early Japanese Film Documents vols. 10–14*], Tokyo: San'ichi Shobō.

McCarthy, Helen (1993) *Anime!: A Beginner's Guide to Japanese Animation*, London: Titan.

Mes, Tom and Sharp, Jasper (2005) *The Midnight Eye Guide to New Japanese Film*, Berkeley: Stone Bridge Press.

Nihon Eiga-shi Kenkyū-kai (ed.) (1996) *Nihon eiga sakuhin jiten* [*A Complete Dictionary of Japanese Films from 1896 to August 1945*], Tokyo: Kagaku Shoin.

—— (ed.) (1998) *Nihon eiga sakuhin jiten* [*A Complete Dictionary of Japanese Films from August 1945 to December 1988*], Tokyo: Kagaku Shoin.

Sekai Eiga-shi Kenkyū-kai (ed.) (1997) *Hakurai kinema sakuhin jiten: Nihon de senzen ni jōei sareta gaikoku eiga ichiran* [*Encyclopedia of Foreign Film: A Catalogue of Foreign Films Exhibited in Pre-war Japan*], Tokyo: Kagaku Shoin.

—— (ed.) (2004) *Hakurai kinema sakuhin jiten: Nihon de sengo (1945–1988) ni jōei sareta gaikoku eiga ichiran* [*Encyclopedia of Foreign Film: A Catalogue of Foreign Films Exhibited in Post-War Japan 1945–1988*], Tokyo: Kagaku Shoin.

Sengo Nihon Eiga Kenkyū-kai (ed.) (1978) *Nihon eiga sengo ōgon jidai* [*The Golden Age of Post-War Japanese Films*], Tokyo: Nihon Bukku Raiburarī.

Tsuji, Kyōhei (1989) *Jiten eiga no tosho* [*Encyclopedia of Film Books*], Tokyo: Gaifū-sha.

Tsukada, Yoshinobu (ed.) (1965a) *Eiga zasshi sōkangō mokuroku Taishō-hen* [*A Catalogue of Film Journals in the Taisho Era*], Tokyo: Tsukada Yoshinobu.

—— (ed.) (1965b) *Eiga zasshi sōkangō mokuroku Shōwa-hen* [*A Catalogue of Film Journals in the Showa Era*], Tokyo: Tsukada Yoshinobu.

Yamaguchi, Takemi (1937) *Nihon eiga shōshi* [*The Japanese Film Book Catalogue*], Tokyo: Eiga Hyōron-sha.

II: History, theory and criticism

Abe, Yoshiaki (2000) *Nihon eiga ga sonzai suru* [*Japanese Films Exist*], Tokyo: Seido-sha.

Akiyama, Miho and Katsura, Chiho (1994) *Sukuriputā: onna-tachi no eiga-shi* [*Script-writers: Women in Film History*], Tokyo: Nihon Terebi Hōsōmō.

Anderson, Joseph, and Richie, Donald (1982) *The Japanese Film: Art and Industry*, Princeton: Princeton University Press. Revised edition.

Barrett, Gregory (1989) *Archetypes in Japanese Film: The Sociopolitical and Religious Signifiers of the Principal Heroes and Heroines*, Selinsgrove: Susquehanna University Press/London: Associated University Presses.

Bernardi, Joanne (2001) *Writing in Light: The Silent Scenario and the Japanese Pure Film Movement*, Detroit: Wayne State University Press.

Bock, Audie (1978) *Japanese Film Directors*, Tokyo: Kōdansha International.

Bowyer, Justin (ed.) (2004) *The Cinema of Japan and Korea*, London: Wallflower Press.

Broderick, Mick (ed.) (1996) *Hibakusha Cinema: Hiroshima, Nagasaki, and the Nuclear Image in Japanese Film*, London: Routledge and Kegan Paul.

Brophy, Philip (2005) *100 Anime*, London: British Film Institute.

Burch, Noël (1979) *To the Distant Observer: Form and Meaning in the Japanese Cinema*, London: Scolar Press.

Buruma, Ian (1984) *A Japanese Mirror: Heroes and Villains of Japanese Culture*, London: Jonathan Cape.

Cazdyn, Eric (2002) *The Flash of Capital: Film and Geopolitics in Japan*, Durham, NC: Duke University Press.

Davis, Darrell William (1996) *Picturing Japaneseness: Monumental Style, National Identity, Japanese Film*, New York: Columbia University Press.

Denshigakuen Sōgō Kenkyū-sho (ed.) (1998) *Anime no mirai o shiru* [*Knowing the Future of Animation*], Tokyo: Ten Bukkusu.

Desjardins, Chris (2005) *Outlaw Masters of Japanese Film*, London and New York: I.B. Tauris.

Desser, David (1988) *Eros Plus Massacre: An Introduction to the Japanese New Wave Cinema*, Bloomington: Indiana University Press.

Dissanayake, Wimal (ed.) (1988) *Cinema and Cultural Identity: Reflections on Films from Japan, India, and China*, Lanham, MD: University Presses of America.

—— (ed.) (1993) *Melodrama and Asian Cinema*, Cambridge: Cambridge University Press.

Dym, Jeffrey (2003) *Benshi, Japanese Silent Film Narrators, and Their Forgotten Narrative Art of Setsumei: A History of Japanese Silent Film Narration*, Lewiston NY: Edwin Mellen Press.

Ehrlich, Linda, and Desser, David (eds.) (1994) *Cinematic Landscapes: Observations on the Visual Arts and Cinema of Japan and China*, Austin: University of Texas Press.

Eiga Shobō (ed.) (1980) *Nippon no kigeki eiga 1* [*Japanese Comedy Films vol.1*], Tokyo: Eiga Shobō.

—— (1984) *Nippon no kigeki eiga 2* [*Japanese Comedy Films vol.2*], Tokyo: Eiga Shobō.

Eleftheriotis, Dimitris, and Needham, Gary (eds.) (2006) *Asian Cinemas: a Reader and Guide*, Edinburgh: Edinburgh University Press.

Endō Tatsuo (1973) *Eirin rekishi to jiken* [*The Motion Picture Code of Ethics Committee: History and Incidents*], Tokyo: Perikan-sha.

Funabashi, Kazuo (1996) *Kaisō no Nihon eiga ōgonki* [*A Retrospective of the Golden Age of Japanese Film*], Tokyo: Shimizu Shoin.

Furukawa, Takahisa (2003) *Senji-ka no Nihon eiga* [*Wartime Japanese Film*], Tokyo: Yoshikawa Kōbunkan.

Galbraith, Stuart IV (1994) *Japanese Science Fiction, Fantasy and Horror Films: A Critical Analysis of 103 Features Released in the United States, 1950–1992*, Jefferson, NC: McFarland.

Gerow, Aaron (1996) *Writing a Pure Cinema: Articulations of Early Japanese Film*, Ann Arbor, MI: UMI.

—— (2001) *The Word Before the Image: Criticism, the Screenplay, and the Regulation of Meaning in Prewar Japanese Film Culture*, Cambridge: Cambridge University Press.

Gerow, Aaron, and Nornes, Abé Mark (2001) *In Praise of Film Studies: Essays in Honor of Makino Mamoru*, Victoria: Trafford/Kinema Club.

Gosho, Heinosuke (1978) *Waga seishun* [*My Youth*], Tokyo: Nagata Shobō.

Grossman, Andrew (2001) (ed.) *Queer Asian Cinema. Shadows in the Shade*, Binghampton: Harrington Park Press.

Haraguchi, Tomo (ed.) (2000) *Nihon kyōfu (horā) eiga e no shōtai [An Invitation to Japanese Horror Film]*, Tokyo: Heibon-sha.

Hasegawa, Nyozekan (1943) *Nihon eiga-ron [Theory of Japanese Film]*, Tokyo: Dainihon Eiga Kyōkai.

High, Peter B. (2003) *The Imperial Screen: Japanese Film Culture in the Fifteen Years' War, 1931–1945*, Madison: University of Wisconsin Press.

Hirai, Teruaki (1993) *Jitsuroku Nihon eiga no tanjō [Documentary: The Birth of Japanese Film]*, Tokyo: Firumu Āto-sha.

Hirano, Kyoko (1992) *Mr. Smith Goes to Tokyo: The Japanese Cinema under the American Occupation, 1945–1952*, Washington, DC: Smithsonian Institution.

Iijima, Tadashi (1955) *Nihon eiga-shi jōkan gekan [Japanese Film History vols. 1–2]*, Tokyo: Hakusui-sha.

—— (1984) *Senchū eiga-shi: shiki [Wartime Film History: A Personal Note]*, Tokyo: MG Shuppan.

Imaizumi, Yōko (2004) *Eiga no bunpō: Nihon eiga no shotto bunseki [The Grammar of Film: An Analysis of Shots in Japanese Films]*, Tokyo: Sairyū-sha.

Imamura, Miyo (1967) *Nihon eiga bunken-shi [A History of Japanese Film Literature]*, Tokyo: Kagamiura Shobō.

Imamura, Shōhei (ed.) (1969) *Sayonara dake ga jinsei da: eiga kantoku Kawashima Yūzō no shōgai [Life is But Farewell: The Life of a Film Director Kawashima Yuzo]*, Tokyo: Nōberu Shobō.

Imamura, Shōhei et al. (eds) (1985) *Kōza Nihon eiga [A Course in Japanese Film]: Nihon eiga no tanjō [vol. 1: The Birth of Japanese Film]*, Tokyo: Iwanami Shoten.

—— (1986) *Kōza Nihon eiga [A Course in Japanese Film]: Musei eiga no kansei [vol. 2: The Completion of the Silent Film]; Tōkī no jidai [vol. 3: The Age of the Talkie]; Sensō to Nihon eiga [vol. 4: The War and Japanese Film]*, Tokyo: Iwanami Shoten.

—— (1987) *Kōza Nihon eiga [A Course in Japanese Film]: Sengo eiga no tenkai [vol. 5: The Development of Post-War Film]; Nihon eiga no mosaku [vol. 6: The Expansion of Japanese Film]*, Tokyo: Iwanami Shoten.

—— (1988) *Kōza Nihon eiga [A Course in Japanese Film]: Nihon eiga no genzai [vol. 7: The Present State of Japanese Film]; Nihon eiga no tenbō [vol. 8: The Prospects for Japanese Film]*, Tokyo: Iwanami Shoten.

Imamura, Taihei (1943) *Nihon eiga no honshitsu [The Real Nature of Japanese Film]*, Tokyo: Shin Taiyō-sha.

—— (ed.) (1991a) *Nihon geijutsu to eiga [Japanese Art and Film]*, Tokyo: Yumani Shobō.

—— (ed.) (1991b) *Nihon eiga no honshitsu [The Real Nature of Japanese Cinema]*, Tokyo: Yumani Shobō.

Inomata, Katsuhito (1974) *Nihon eiga meisaku zenshi senzen-hen sengo-hen [A Comprehensive History of Classic Japanese Film of the Pre-war and Post-War Period]*, Tokyo: Shakai Shisō-sha.

—— (1975) *Nihon eiga meisaku zenshi gendai-hen [A Comprehensive History of Classic Japanese Film: The Modern Age]*, Tokyo: Shakai Shisō-sha.

Itami, Mansaku (1961) *Itami Mansaku zenshū 1–3 [The Complete Works of Itami Mansaku vols. 1–3]*, Tokyo: Chikuma Shobō.

Itō, Daisuke (1976) *Jidai-geki eiga no shi to shinjitsu [The Poetry and Truth of Period Films]*, Tokyo: Kinema Junpō-sha.

Itō, Masaichi (1965) *Kiri to toride: Tōhō daisōgi no kiroku [Fog and Fortress: A Record of the Great Toho Strike]*, Tokyo: Rengō Tsūshin-sha.

Iwamoto, Kenji and Tomonori, Saiki (1988) *Kinema no seishun* [*Japanese Cinema in its Youth*], Tokyo: Riburopōto.

Iwamoto, Kenji (ed.) (1991) *Nihon eiga to modanizumu 1920–1930* [*Japanese Films and Modernism 1920–1930*], Tokyo: Riburopōto.

—— (ed.) (1998) *Nihon eiga no rekishi 1–3* [*The History of Japanese Film vols. 1–3*], Tokyo: Nihon Tosho Sentā.

—— (ed.) (2004) *Nihon eiga to nashonarizumu 1931–1945* [*Japanese Films and Nationalism 1931–1945*], Tokyo: Shinwa-sha.

Iwasaki, Akira (1973) *Eiga ni miru sengo sesō-shi* [*A History of the Social Conditions of the Post-War Period as They Appeared on Film*], Tokyo: Shin Nihon Shuppan-sha.

—— (1975) *Senryō sareta sukurīn: waga sengo-shi* [*The Occupied Screen: My Post-War History*], Tokyo: Shin Nihon Shuppan-sha.

Jam Films Project (ed.) (2002) *Shōto firumu kakumei: Featuring Jam Films* [*The Revolution of Short Film: Featuring Jam Films*], Tokyo: Pia.

Kakita, Kiyoji (1992) *Nihon eiga kantoku kyōkai no 50 nen* [*50 Years of the Directors' Guild of Japan*], Tokyo: Kyōdō-Kumiai Nihon Eiga-Kantoku Kyōkai.

Kamei, Fumio (1989) *Tatakau eiga: dokyumentarisuto no Shōwa-shi* [*Films at the Front: The History of a Showa Documentarist*], Tokyo: Iwanami Shinsho.

Katō, Atsuko (2003) *Sōdōin taisei to eiga* [*Film and the General Mobilization System*], Tokyo: Shin'yō-sha.

Kawamoto, Saburō (1986) *New Trends in Japanese Cinema*, Tokyo: Japan Foundation, Office for the Japanese Studies Center.

—— (1994) *Ima hitotabi no sengo Nihon eiga* [*Revisting Post-War Japanese Film*], Tokyo: Iwanami Shoten.

Kido, Shirō (1956) *Nihon eiga-den: eiga seisakusha no kiroku* [*The Story of Japanese Film: A Film Producer's Record*], Tokyo: Bungei Shunjū-sha.

Kinema Junpō-sha (ed.) (1976) *Sekai no eiga-sakka 31 Nihon eiga-shi* [*Filmmakers of The World 31: Japanese Film History*], Tokyo: Kinema Junpō-sha.

Kinugasa, Teinosuke (1977) *Waga eiga no seishun: Nihon eiga-shi no ichisokumen* [*My Youth in Film: A Perspective on Japanese Film History*], Tokyo: Chūō Kōron-sha.

Kirihara, Donald (1992) *Patterns of Time: Mizoguchi and the 1930s*, Madison: University of Wisconsin Press.

Kishi, Matsuo (1935) *Nihon eiga-ron* [*Theory of Japanese Film*], Tokyo: Shorin Juntendō.

—— (1937) *Nihon eiga yōshiki-kō* [*Theory of Japanese Film Form*], Tokyo: Kawade Shobō.

—— (1970) *Jinbutsu Nihon eiga-shi* [*Japanese Film History: Personalities*], Tokyo: Dabiddo-sha.

Kitagawa, Tetsuo (ed.) (1970) *Nippon no dokuritsu puro* [*Japanese Independent Productions*], Tokyo: Eiga Wakamono-tachi Zenkoku Jōen Iinkai.

Kitano, Taitsu (1998) *Nihon anime-shi-gaku kenkyū josetsu* [*An Introduction to the History of Japanese Animation*], Tokyo: Yahata Shoten.

Ko, Cho and Ko, Sen (1999) *Man'ei: kokusaku eiga no shosō* [*Aspects of National Film*], Tokyo: Pandora.

Kobayashi Nobuhiko (1995) *Ichi shōnen no mita seisen* [*The Sacred War: A Boy Observed*], Tokyo: Chikuma Shobō.

Komatsu, Hiroshi (1991) *Kigen no eiga* [*The Origins of Cinema*], Tokyo: Seido-sha.

Kumai, Kei (1996) *Eiga no fukai kawa* [*The Deep River of Film*], Tokyo: Kindai Bungei-sha.

Kuwabara, Ietoshi (1993) *Kirareta waisetsu: eirin katto-shi* [*Cut Eroticism: The History of the Japanese Motion Picture Code of Ethics Committee*], Tokyo: Yomiuri Shinbun-sha.

LaMarre, Thomas (2005) *Shadows on the Screen. Tanizaki Jun'ichirō on Cinema and 'Oriental' Aesthetics*, Ann Arbor, MI: University of Michigan Press.

Lent, John A. (ed.) (2001) *Animation in Asia and the Pacific*, Eastleigh: John Libbey.

Lippit, Akira (2005) *Atomic Light (Shadow Optics)*, Minneapolis: University of Minnesota Press.

Makino, Mamoru (ed.) (2003) *Nihon eiga-ron gensetsu taikei dai-ikki: senji-ka no eiga tōsei- ki [A Comprehensive Guide to Japanese Film Theory: The Period of Film Control During the War vols. 1–10]*, Tokyo: Yumani Shobō.

—— (ed.) (2004) *Nihon eiga-ron gensetsu taikei dai-niki: eiga no modanisumu-ki [A Comprehensive Guide to Japanese Film Theory: Modernism and Film vols. 11–20]*, Tokyo: Yumani Shobo.

Makino, Masahiro (1968) *Katsudōya ichidai [The Life of a Film Maker]*, Tokyo: Eikō Shuppan-sha.

Masumoto, Yoshitoshi (1987) *Jinbutsu Shōchiku eiga-shi: Kamata no jidai [Personalities in Shochiku Film History: The Age of Kamata]*, Tokyo: Heibon-sha.

McDonald, Keiko I. (1983) *Cinema East: A Critical Study of Major Japanese Films*, East Brunswick, NJ: Associated University Presses.

—— (1994) *Japanese Classical Theater in Film*, Rutherford: Fairleigh Dickinson University Press; London: Associated University Presses.

—— (2000) *From Book to Screen: Modern Japanese Literature in Films*, Armonk, NY and London: M.E. Sharpe.

—— (2006) *Reading a Japanese Film: Cinema in Context*, Honolulu: University of Hawai'i Press.

McRoy, Jay (ed.) (2005) *Japanese Horror Cinema*, Edinburgh: Edinburgh University Press.

Mellen, Joan (1975) *Voices from the Japanese Cinema*, New York: Limelight.

—— (1976) *The Waves at Genji's Door: Japan through Its Cinema*, New York: Pantheon.

Misono, Kyōhei (ed.) (1971) *Kaisō Makino eiga [A Retrospective of Makino Films]*, Kyōto: Makino Shōzō Sensei Kenshō-kai.

—— (ed.) (1974) *Jidai eiga shūtaisei Misono-korekushon [The Misono Collection of Period Films]*, Tokyo: Katsudo Shiryō Kenkyū-kai.

Murakami, Tadahisa (1936) *Nihon eiga sakka-ron [A Theory of Japanese Filmmaking]*, Tokyo: Ōrai-sha.

Murakami, Yoshiaki, and Ogawa, Norifumi (2000) *Nihon eiga sangyō saizensen [Japanese Movies Now]*, Tokyo: Kadokawa Shoten.

Nagata, Masaichi (1957) *Eiga jigakyō [A Personal Scroll of Film]*, Tokyo: Heibon Shuppan.

Namiki, Shinsaku (1986) *Nihon puroretaria eiga dōmei (Prokino) zenshi [A Comprehensive History of the Japanese Proletarian Film League]*, Tokyo: Gōdō Shuppan.

Nanbu, Kyōichirō, and Satō, Tadao (1973) *Nihon eiga hyakusen [One Hundred Selections from Japanese Cinema]*, Tokyo: Tabata Shoten.

Napier, Susan J. (2000) *Anime: From Akira to Princess Mononoke: Experiencing Contemporary Japanese Animation*, New York: Palgrave.

Nikkatsu Kabushiki Gaisha (ed.) (1962) *Nikkatsu 50 nen-shi [50 Years of Nikkatsu]*, Tokyo: Nikkatsu Kabushiki Gaisha.

Noda, Shinkichi (1984) *Nihon dokyumentarī eiga zenshi [A Comprehensive History of Japanese Documentary Film]*, Tokyo: Shakai Shisō-sha.

Nolletti, Arthur Jr., and Desser, David (eds) (1992) *Reframing Japanese Cinema: Authorship, Genre, History*, Bloomington: Indiana University Press.

—— (2005) *The Cinema of Gosho Heinosuke:Laughter Through Tears*, Bloomington: Indiana University Press.

Nornes, Abé Mark (2003) *Japanese Documentary Film: The Meiji Era through Hiroshima*, Minneapolis: University of Minnesota Press.

Nornes, Abé Mark, and Fukushima, Yukio (eds) (1994) *The Japan/America Film Wars: World War I Propaganda and Its Cultural Contexts*, London and New York: Routledge.

Nozawa, Kazuma (ed.) (2000) *Nikkatsu 1954–1971*, Tokyo: Waizu Shuppan.

Ogawa, Tōru et al. (eds) (1970) *Gendai Nihon eiga-ron taikei* [*A Survey of Japanese Film Theory*]: *Kojin to chikara no kaifuku* [*vol. 2: The Recovery of Individuality and Power*]; *Nihon Nūberubāgu* [*vol. 3: The Japanese New Wave*], Tokyo: Tōju-sha.

—— (1971) *Gendai Nihon eiga-ron taikei* [*A Survey of Japanese Film Theory*]: *Sengo eiga no shuppatsu* [*vol. 1: The Beginning of Post-War Film*]; *Dochaku to kindai no sōkoku* [*vol. 4: The Conflict Between the Indigenous and the Modern*]; *Gensō to seiji no aida* [*vol. 5: Between Fantasy and Politics*], Tokyo: Tōju-sha.

—— (1972) *Gendai Nihon eiga-ron taikei* [*A Survey of Japanese Film Theory*]: *Nihon ni ikita gaikoku eiga* [*vol. 6: Foreign Film in Japan*], Tokyo: Tōju-sha.

Okabe, Ryū (ed.) (1968) *Nihon eiga-shi sokō* [*A Sketch of Japanese Film History*]: *Nagai Shin'ichi shi* [*vol. 1: Mr. Nagai Shin'ichi*]; *Noda Kōgo shi no bu* [*vol. 2: The Role of Mr. Noda Kogo*]; *Uchida Tomu shi no maki* [*vol. 3: The Role of Uchida Tomu*], Tokyo: Firumu Raiburarī Kyōgi-kai.

—— (ed.) (1969) *Nihon eiga-shi sokō* [*A Sketch of Japanese Film History*]: *Tomonari Yōzō shi no maki* [*vol. 4: The Role of Tomonari Yozo*], Tokyo: Firumu Raiburarī Kyōgi-kai.

—— (ed.) (1970) *Nihon eiga-shi sokō* [*A Sketch of Japanese Film History*]: *Nakata Toshizō shi no maki* [*vol. 5: The Role of Nakata Toshizo*], Tokyo: Firumu Raiburarī Kyōgi-kai.

—— (ed.) (1971) *Nihon eiga-shi sokō* [*A Sketch of Japanese Film History*]: *Rengō eiga geijut-suka kyōkai shiryō* [*vol. 6: Rengo eiga Documents*], Tokyo: Firumu Raiburarī Kyōgi-kai.

—— (ed.) (1972) *Nihon eiga-shi sokō* [*A Sketch of Japanese Film History*]: *Shiryō Nippon no haiyū gakkō* [*vol. 7: Documents about Japanese Acting Schools*], Tokyo: Firumu Riaburarī Kyōgi-kai.

—— (ed.) (1973) *Nihon eiga-shi sokō* [*A Sketch of Japanese Film History*]: *Shiryō Kaeriyama Norimasa to Tōmasu Kurihara no gyōseki* [*vol. 8: The Records of Kaeriyama Norimasa and Thomas Kurihara*], Tokyo: Firumu Raiburarī Kyōgi-kai.

—— (ed.) (1974) *Nihon eiga-shi sokō* [*A Sketch of Japanese Film History*]: *Shiryō Takamatsu Toyojirō to Ogasawara Meihō no gyōseki* [*vol. 9: The Records of Takamatsu Toyojiro and Ogasawara Meiho*], Tokyo: Firumu Raiburarī Kyōgi-kai.

—— (ed.) (1975) *Nihon eiga-shi sokō* [*A Sketch of Japanese Film History*]: *Shiryō Nippon hassei eiga no sōsei-ki* [*vol. 10: Documents from the Dawn of Japanese Sound Films*], Tokyo: Firumu Raiburarī Kyōgi-kai.

—— (ed.) (1980) *Nihon eiga-shi sokō* [*A Sketch of Japanese Film History*]: *Jidaigeki shūsei* [*vol. 11: An Anthology of Historical Films*], Tokyo: Firumu Raiburarī Kyōgi-kai.

Ōshima, Nagisa, and Yoshimura, Kōzaburō et al. (eds) (1984) *Nihon eiga o yomu: paionia-tachi no isan* [*Reading Japanese Cinema: The Heritage of the Pioneers*], Tokyo: Dagereo Shuppan.

Poitras, Gilles (1999) *The Anime Companion: What's Japanese in Japanese Animation*, Berkeley: Stone Bridge Press.

Rayns, Tony (ed.) (1984) *Eiga: 25 Years of Japanese Cinema*, Edinburgh: Edinburgh International Film Festival.

Richie, Donald (1961) *Japanese Movies*, Tokyo: Japan Travel Bureau.

—— (1972) *Japanese Cinema: Film Style and National Character*, London: Secker and Warburg.

—— (1982) *The Japanese Movie*, Tokyo: Kōdansha.

—— (1990) *Japanese Cinema: An Introduction*, Hong Kong and Oxford: Oxford University Press.

—— (2001) *A Hundred Years of Japanese Film*, Tokyo: Kōdansha.

Saeki, Tomonori (ed.) (1996) *Eiga tokuhon: Itō Daisuke* [*A Film Reader: Ito Daisuke*], Tokyo: Firumu Āto-sha.

Sakuramoto, Tomio (1993) *Daitōa sensō to Nihon eiga* [*The Greater East Asia War and Japanese Film*], Tokyo: Aoki Shoten.

Sanga-sha (ed.) (1991) *Kimi no na wa to Shōwa 20 nendai* [*What Is Your Name? and the Showa Era*], Tokyo: Sanga-sha.

Satō Tadao (1970) *Nihon eiga shisō-shi* [*A History of Japanese Film Theory*], Tokyo: San'ichi Shobō.

—— (1979) *Nihon eiga no kyoshō-tachi* [*Master Filmmakers of Japan*], Tokyo: Gakuyō Shobō.

—— (1982) *Currents in Japanese Cinema: Essays*, Tokyo: Kōdansha.

—— (1995) *Nihon eiga-shi* [*Japanese Film History vols. 1–4*], Tokyo: Iwanami Shoten.

—— (1996) *Nihon eiga no kyoshō-tachi* [*The Great Film Directors of Japanese Film vols. 1–2*] Tokyo: Gakuyō Shobō.

—— (1997) *Nihon eiga no kyoshō-tachi* [*The Great Film Directors of Japanese Film vol. 3*], Tokyo: Gakuyō Shobō.

Satō, Tadao et al. (eds) (1993) *Shinkō Kinema senzen goraku eiga no ōkoku* [*Shinko Kinema: The Kingdom of Pre-war Films for Pleasure*], Tokyo: Yamaji Fumiko Bunka Zaidan.

Schilling, Mark (1999) *Contemporary Japanese Film*, New York: Weatherhill.

—— (2003) *The Yakuza Movie Book: A Guide to Japanese Gangster Films*, Berkeley: Stone Bridge Press.

Shiba, Tsukasa and Aoyama, Sakae (1998) *Yakuza eiga to sono jidai* [*Yakuza Films and Their Time*], Tokyo: Chikuma Shobō.

Shimizu, Akira (1994) *Sensō to eiga: senji-chū to senryō-ka no nihon eiga-shi* [*War and Film: The History of Japanese Cinema During the War and Under the Occupation*], Tokyo: Shakai Shisō-sha.

Shimizu, Akira et al. (eds) (1991) *Nichibei eiga-sen Pāru Hābā 50 shūnen* [*The Film War Between Japan and the USA: The 50th Anniversary of Pearl Harbor*], Tokyo: Seikyū-sha.

Shin Tōhō Honsha no Kai Kiroku Henshū Iinkai (ed.) (1991) *Soshite daremo inakunaru Shin Tōhō honsha 11 nen no kiseki* [*And No One Will Be There: Eleven Years of Shin Toho*], Koganei: Shin Tōhō Honsha no Kai Kiroku Henshū Iinkai.

Shioda, Nagakazu (1992) *Nihon eiga 50 nen-shi 1941–1991* [*50 Years of Japanese Film History*], Tokyo: Fujiwara Shoten.

Shōbayashi, Fumio (1994) *Kyōto eiga sangyō-ron* [*A Theory of the Kyoto Film Industry*], Kyōto: Keibun-sha.

Shōchiku (1996) *Shōchiku 100 nen-shi* [*100 Years of Shochiku*], Tokyo: Shōchiku.

Silver, Alain (1983) *The Samurai Film*, Overlook, NY: Woodstock.

Standish, Isolde (2000) *Myths and Masculinity in the Japanese Cinema: Towards a Political Reading of the 'Tragic Hero'*, Richmond: RoutledgeCurzon.

—— (2005) *A New History of Japanese Cinema: A Century of Narrative Film*, London and New York: Continuum.

Sugibayashi, Takashi (2003) *Shōwa senji-ki no Nihon eiga* [*Wartime Japanese Films of the Showa Era*], Suwa: Chōei-sha, Rogosu Kikaku-bu.

Takamine, Hideko (1976) *Watashi no tosei nikki jō, ge* [*My Professional Diary vols. I and II*], Tokyo: Asahi Shinbun-sha.

Takano, Etsuko (2000) *Josei ga eiga o tsukuru to iukoto* [*How Women Make Film*], Tokyo: Asahi Shinbun-sha.

Takenaka, Tsutomu (1974) *Nihon eiga jūdan 1: keikō eiga no jidai* [*A Cross-Section of Japanese Film vol. 1: The Age of Proletarian Film*], Kyōto: Shirakawa Shoin.

—— (1975) *Nihon eiga jūdan 2: itan no eizō* [*A Cross-Section of Japanese Film vol. 2: The Unorthodox Image*], Kyōto: Shirakawa Shoin.

—— (1976) *Nihon eiga jūdan 3: Yamagami Itarō no sekai* [*A Cross-Section of Japanese Film vol. 3: The World of Yamagami Itaro*], Kyōto: Shirakawa Shoin.

Tamura, Shizue (2000) *Hajimeni eiga ga atta: shokuminchi Taiwan to Nihon* [*At the Beginning There Was a Film: Colonial Taiwan and Japan*], Tokyo: Chūō Kōron Shin-sha.

Tanaka, Jun'ichiro (1980a) *Nihon eiga hattatsu-shi* [*The History of the Development of Japanese Film vols. 1–5*], Tokyo: Chūō Kōron-sha.

—— (1980b) *Nihon eiga-shi hakkutsu* [*The Discovery of Japanese Film History*], Tokyo: Tōju-sha.

Tanikawa Yoshio (ed.) (1993) *Nenpyō: eiga 100 nen-shi* [*A Chronological Table of 100 Years of Japanese Films*], Tokyo: Fūtō-sha.

Tōei Kabushiki Gaisha (ed.) (1992) *Kuronikuru Tōei 1947–1991* [*The Toei Story 1947–1991*], Tokyo: Tōei.

Tōhō Kabushiki Gaisha (ed.) (1982) *Tōhō 50 nen-shi* [*50 Years of Toho*], Tokyo: Tōhō Kabushiki Gaisha.

Toki, Akihiro (ed.) (1994) *Kyōto eiga zu-e: Nihon eiga wa Kyōto kara hajimatta* [*The Graphics of Kyoto: Japanese Cinema was Born in Kyoto*], Tokyo: Firumu Āto-sha.

Tsurumi, Shunshuke (1959) *Gokai suru kenri: Nihon eiga o miru* [*The Right of Misunderstanding: Looking at Japanese Cinema*], Tokyo: Chikuma Shobō.

Tsutsui, Kiyotada (2000a) *Jidai-geki eiga no shisō* [*Thoughts on Period Films*], Tokyo: PHP Kenkyū-sho.

—— (ed.) (2000b) *Ginmaku no Shōwa* [*The Showa Era on Screen*], Tokyo: Seiryū Shuppan.

Tsutsui, Kiyotada and Katō, Mikirō (eds) (1997) *Jidai-geki eiga towa nani ka* [*What Are Jidai-Geki Films?*], Kyōto: Jinbun Shoin.

Tsuzuki, Masaaki (1995) *Nihon eiga no ōgon jidai* [*The Golden Age of Japanese Film*], Tokyo: Shōgakukan.

Tucker, Richard N. (1973) *Japan, Film Image*, London: Studio Vista.

Uriu, Tadao (1947) *Eiga-teki seishin no keifu* [*The Development of the Spirit of Film*], Tokyo: Getsuyō Shobō.

—— (1981) *Sengo Nihon eiga shō-shi* [*A Short History of Post-War Japanese Cinema*], Tokyo: Hōsei Daigaku Shuppan-kyoku.

Various (1981) *Japanese Experimental Film, 1960–1980*, New York: American Federation of Arts.

Washburn, Dennis, and Cavanaugh, Carole (eds) (2001) *Word and Image in Japanese Cinema*, Cambridge: Cambridge University Press.

Yahiro, Fuji (1974) *Jidai eiga to 50 nen* [*Fifty Years of Period Films*], Tokyo: Gakugei Shorin.

Yamada, Kazuo (1970) *Nihon eiga no gendai-shi* [*A Modern History of Japanese Film*], Tokyo: Shin Nihon Shuppan-sha.

—— (1976) *Yameru eizō* [*Ailing Images*], Tokyo: Shin Nihon Shuppan-sha.

—— (2003) *Nihon eiga no rekishi to gendai* [*Japanese Cinema: Past and Present*], Tokyo: Shin Nihon Shuppan-sha.

Yamaguchi, Katsunori and Watanabe, Yasushi (1977) *Nihon animēshon eiga-shi* [*The History of Japanese Animation Film*], Ōsaka: Yūbun-sha.

Yamaguchi, Takeshi (2000) *Aishū no Manshū eiga* [*Sorrowful Manchu Films*], Tokyo: Santen Shobō.

Yamamoto, Kikuo (1983) *Nihon eiga ni okeru gaikoku eiga no eikyō* [*The Influence of Foreign Films on Japanese Cinema*], Tokyo: Waseda Daigaku Shuppan-bu.

Yamane, Sadao (1993) *Sekai no naka no Nihon eiga* [*Japanese Films in the World*], Nagoya: Kawai Bunka Kyōiku Kenkyū-sho.

Yamauchi, Shizuo (2003) *Shōchiku Ōfuna satsuei-sho oboegaki* [*Shochiku Ofuna Studio Memoranda*], Kamakura: Kamakura Shunjū-sha.

Yomota, Inuhiko (2000a) *Nihon no joyū* [*Japanese Actresses*], Tokyo: Iwanami Shoten.

—— (2000b) *Nihon eiga-shi 100 nen* [*100 Years of Japanese Film History*], Tokyo: Shūei-sha.

Yoshida, Chieo (1978) *Mō hitotsu no eiga-shi: katsuben no jidai* [*Another Film History: The Age of Katsuben*], Tokyo: Jiji Tsūshin-sha.

Yoshimura, Hideo (2000) *Shōchiku Ōfuna eiga* [*Shochiku Ofuna Films*], Tokyo: Sōdo-sha.

Yoshimura, Kōzaburō (1985) *Kinema no jidai* [*The Age of Kinema*], Tokyo: Kyōdō Tsūshin-sha.

Yūki, Ichirō (1985) *Jitsuroku: Kamata kōshinkyoku* [*Documents: The March of Kamata*], Tokyo: Besuto Bukku.

III: Selected reading on Japanese culture and society (in English)

Azuma, Eiichiro (2005) *Between Two Empires: Race, History, and Transnationalism in Japanese America*, New York: Oxford University Press.

Befu, Harumi, and Guichard-Auguis, Sylvie (eds) (2003) *Globalizing Japan: Ethnography of the Japanese Presence in Asia, Europe and America*, London: Routledge.

Benedict, Ruth (1947) *The Chrysanthemum and the Sword: Patterns of Japanese Culture*, London: Secker and Warburg.

Bernstein, Gail. L. (ed.) (1991) *Recreating Japanese Women, 1600–1945*, Berkeley: University of California Press.

Bornoff, Nicholas (1991) *Pink Samurai: The Pursuit and Politics of Sex in Japan*, London: Grafton.

Bowring, Richard John, and Kornicki, Peter (eds) (1993) *The Cambridge Encyclopedia of Japan*, Cambridge: Cambridge University Press.

Buruma, Ian (1985) *A Japanese Mirror: Heroes and Villains of Japanese Culture*, Harmondsworth: Penguin.

Calichman, Richard F. (ed.) (2005) *Contemporary Japanese Thought*, New York: Columbia University Press.

Clements, Jonathan, and Tamamuro, Motoko (2003) *The Dorama Encyclopedia: A Guide to Japanese TV Drama Since 1953*, Berkeley: Stone Bridge Press.

Conte-Helm, Marie (1996) *The Japanese and Europe: Economic and Cultural Encounters*, London: Athlone.

Cooper-Chen, Anne (1997) *Mass Communication in Japan*, Ames: Iowa State University Press.

Craig, Timothy (2000) *Japan Pop!: Inside the World of Japanese Popular Culture*, Armonk, NY: M.E. Sharpe.

Dale, Peter N. (1987) *The Myth of Japanese Uniqueness*, London and New York: Routledge.

Derusha, Will, Acereda, Alberto, and Tobin, Joseph J. (2004) *Pikachu's Global Adventure: The Rise and Fall of Pokemon*, Durham, NC: Duke University Press.

Gluck, Carol (1985) *Japan's Modern Myths: Ideology in the Late Meiji Period*, Princeton: Princeton University Press.

Gordon, Andrew (ed.) (1993) *Post-War Japan as History*, Berkeley: University of California Press.

—— (2003) *A Modern History of Japan*, New York: Oxford University Press.

Hardacre, Helen (1989) *Shinto and the State, 1868–1988*, Princeton: Princeton University Press.

Harootunian, H.D., and Miyoshi, Masao (eds) (1989) *Postmodernism and Japan*, Durham, NC: Duke University Press.

—— (eds.) (1993) *Japan in the World*, Durham, NC: Duke University Press.

Hendry, Joy (2003) *Understanding Japanese Society*, London and New York: Routledge.

Hibbett, Howard (ed.) (1977) *Contemporary Japanese Literature: An Anthology of Fiction, Film, and other Writing Since 1945*, New York: Knopf.

Iwabuchi, Koichi (2003) *Recentering Globalization: Popular Culture and Japanese Transnationalism*, Durham, NC: Duke University Press

—— (ed.) 2004 *Feeling Asian Modernities: Transnational Consumption of Japanese Television Dramas*, Hong Kong: Hong Kong University Press.

Karatani, Kijin (1993) *Origins of Japanese Literature*, Durham, NC: Duke University Press.

Keene, Donald (1972) *Landscapes and Portraits: Appreciations of Japanese Culture*, London: Secker and Warburg.

Kikuchi, Yuko (2004) *Japanese Modernisation and Mingei Theory: Cultural Nationalism and Oriental Orientalism*, London: RoutledgeCurzon.

Kinsella, Sharon (2000) *Adult Manga: Culture and Power in Contemporary Japanese Society*, Richmond: Curzon.

Marra, Michele (ed.) (1999) *Modern Japanese Aesthetics: A Reader*, Honolulu: University of Hawaii Press.

Martinez, D.P. (ed.) (1998) *The Worlds of Japanese Popular Culture: Gender, Shifting Boundaries and Global Cultures*, Cambridge: Cambridge University Press.

Maruyama, Masao (1962) *Thought and Behaviour in Modern Japanese Politics*, Oxford: Oxford University Press.

Mitchell, Richard H. (1983) *Censorship in Imperial Japan*, Princeton: Princeton University Press.

Moeran, Brian (1989) *Language and Popular Culture in Japan*, Manchester: Manchester University Press.

Myers, Ramon H., and Peattie, Mark R. (eds) (1984) *The Japanese Colonial Empire 1895–1945*, Princeton: Princeton University Press.

Nakane, Chie (1972) *Japanese Society*, Berkeley: University of California Press.

Reischauer, Edward (1995) *The Japanese Today: Change and Continuity*, Cambridge, MA: Harvard University Press.

Ryang, Sonia (ed.) (2000) *Koreans in Japan: Critical Voices from the Margin*, London: Routledge.

Schilling, Mark (1997) *The Encyclopedia of Japanese Pop Culture*, New York: Weatherhill.

Slaymaker, Douglas (ed.) (2000) *A Century of Popular Culture in Japan*, Lewiston: The Edwin Mellen Press.

Storry, Richard (1991) *A History of Modern Japan*, Harmondsworth: Penguin.

Stronarch, Bruce (ed.) (1989) *Handbook of Japanese Popular Culture*, New York: Greenwood Press.

Tanaka, Stefan (1993) *Japan's Other: Rendering Past into History*, Berkeley: University of California Press.

Tanizaki, Junichiro (1977) *In Praise of Shadows*, Stony Creek, CT: Leete's Island Books.

Totman, Conrad (2005) *A History of Japan*, Oxford: Blackwell.

Treat, John Whittier (ed.) (1996) *Contemporary Japan and Popular Culture*, Richmond: Curzon.

Tucker, Anne (2003) *The History of Japanese Photography*, New Haven: Yale University Press.

Varley, Paul (1984) *Japanese Culture*, Honolulu: University of Hawaii Press.

Vlastos, Stephen (ed.) (1998) *Mirror of Modernity: Invented Traditions of Modern Japan*, Berkeley: University of California Press.

Waswo, Ann (1996) *Modern Japanese Society 1868–1994*, Oxford: Oxford University Press.

Whittier Treat, John (ed.) (1996) *Contemporary Japan and Popular Culture*, Honolulu: University of Hawaii Press.

Yoshino, Kosaku (1992) *Cultural Nationalism in Contemporary Japan: A Sociological Enquiry*, London: Routledge.

IV: Journal articles (in English)

Much excellent work on Japanese cinema has been published in specialist and sometimes quite hard to find journals, and many of these remain available only in this form. Here is a selection of some of the most substantial and important of these journal articles.

Abel, Jonathan E. (2001) 'Different from Difference: Revisiting *Kurutta Ichipeiji*', *Asian Cinema* 12 (Fall/Winter): 72–96.

Allison, Anne (2000) 'A Challenge to Hollywood?: Japanese Character Goods Hit the US', *Japanese Studies*, 20 (1): 67–88.

Anderson, J.L. (1955) 'Japanese Film Periodicals', *The Quarterly Review of Film, Radio, and Television* 9.4 (Summer): 410–23.

——— (1973) 'Japanese Swordfighters and American Gunfighters', *Cinema Journal* 12 (Spring): 1–21.

——— (1988) 'Spoken Silents in the Japanese Cinema', *Journal of Film and Video*, 40 (1): 13–33.

——— (1996/7) 'Tales from Peripheries: Why Write About Japanese Movies?', *Asian Cinema*, 8 (2): 9–43.

Baskett, Michael (2003) 'Dying for a Laugh: Post-1945 Japanese Service Comedies', *Historical Journal of Film, Radio and Television* 23 (4): 291–310.

Bordwell, David (1979) 'Our Dream Cinema: Western Historiography and the Japanese Film', *Film Reader* 4: 45–62.

——— (1995) 'Visual Style in Japanese Cinema, 1925–1945', *Film History* 7 (1): 5–31.

Branigan, Edward (1976) 'The Space of *Equinox Flower*', *Screen* 17 (2): 74–105.

Buruma, Ian (1987) 'Humor in Japanese Cinema', *East-West Film Journal* 2.1 (December): 26–31.

Casebier, Allan (1987) 'College Course File: Japanese Film and Culture', *Journal of Film and Video* 39.1 (Winter): 52–64.

Chang, Joseph (1989) '*Kagemusha* and the *Chushingura* Motif', *East-West Film Journal* 3.2 (June): 14–38.

Cohen, Robert (1981) 'Toward a Theory of Japanese Narrative', *Quarterly Review of Film Studies* 6 (2): 181–200.

Davis, William D. 'Back to Japan: Militarism and Monumentalism in Prewar Japanese Cinema', *Wide Angle* 11.3 (July 1989): 16–25.

Denison, Rayna (2005) 'Disembodied Stars and the Cultural Meanings of *Princess Mononoke*'s Soundscape', *Scope: An Online Journal of Film Studies*, 3. Online. http://www.scope.nottingham.ac.uk/article.php?issue=3&id=83

Desser, David (1983) 'Kurosawa's Eastern "Western": *Sanjuro* and the Influence of *Shane*', *Film Criticism* 8.1 (Fall): 54–65.

——— (2003) 'New Kids on the Street: The Pan-Asian Youth Film', *Scope: An Online Journal of Film Studies*, May. Online. www.scope.nottingham.ac.uk/reader/chapter.php?id=4

Dym, Jeffrey A. (2000) 'Benshi and the Introduction of Motion Pictures to Japan', *Monumenta Nipponica*, 55: 509–36.

Ehrlich, Linda C. (1992) 'Water Flowing Underground: The Films of Oguri Kohei', *Japan Forum* 4.1 (April): 145–62.

Freiberg, Freda (1992a) 'Tales of Kageyama', *East-West Film Journal* 6.1 (January): 94–110.

——— (1992b) 'Genre and Gender in World War II Japanese Feature Film: *China Night* (1940)', *Historical Journal of Film, Radio and Television* 12 (3): 245–52.

——— (2000) 'Comprehensive Connections: The Film Industry, the Theatre and the State in the Early Japanese Cinema'. *Screening the Past*. Online. http://www.latrobe.edu.au/screeningthepast/firstrelease/fr1100/fffr11c.htm

Fujiki, Hideaki (2006) '*Benshi* as Stars: The Irony of the Popularity and Respectability of Voice Performers in Japanese Cinema', *Cinema Journal* 45.2 (winter): 68–84.

Geist, Kathe (1986/7) 'Narrative Style in Ozu's Silent Films', *Film Quarterly* 40 (winter): 28–35.

Gerow, Aaron (1994) 'The *Benshi*'s New Face: Defining Cinema in Taishō Japan', *ICONICS*, 3: 69–86.

—— (1999) 'A Scene at the Threshold: Liminality in the Films of Kitano Takeshi', *Asian Cinema* 10 (spring/summer): 107–15.

—— (2006) 'Recent Film Policy and the Fate of Film Criticism in Japan'. *Midnight Eye*. Online. http://www.midnighteye.com/features/recent-film-policy.shtml

Hall, Jonathan M. (2000) 'Japan's Progressive Sex: Male Homosexuality, National Competition, and the Cinema', *Journal of Homosexuality*, 39 (3/4): 31–82.

High, Peter B. (1984) 'The Dawn of Cinema in Japan', *Journal of Contemporary History*, 19 (1): 23–57.

Hirano Kyoko (1988) 'The Japanese Tragedy: Film Censorship and the American Occupation', *Radical History Review* 41 (April): 67–92.

—— (1998) 'The New Generation of Japanese Producers', *Post Script* 18 (Fall): 78–88.

Hitchcock, Lori (2003) Third Culture Kids: A Bakhtinian Analysis of Language and Multiculturalism in *Swallowtail Butterfly*', *Scope: An Online Journal of Film Studies*. February. Online. www.nottingham.ac.uk/film/scopearchive/articles/third-culture-kids.htm

Imamura Taihei (1953) 'Japanese Art and the Animated Cartoon', trans. Tsuruoka Furuichi, *The Quarterly Review of Film, Radio and Television* 7.3 (September): 217–22.

Iwabutchi Masayoshi (1961) 'Japanese Cinema 1961', *Film Culture* 24 (Spring): 85–8.

Iwamoto, Kenji (1993) 'Japanese Cinema Until 1930: A Consideration of its Formal Aspects', *Iris* (16): 9–22.

Iwamura, Dean R. (1994) 'Letter from Japan: From Girls Who Dress up Like Boys to Trussed-up Porn Stars: Some Contemporary Heroines on the Japanese Screen', *Continuum*, 7 (2): 109–30.

Izbicki, Joanne (1996) 'The Shape of Freedom: The Female Body in Post-Surrender Japanese Cinema', *US–Japan Women's Journal English Supplement*: 109–53.

Kirihara, Donald (1985) 'A Reconsideration of the Institution of the Benshi', *Film Reader*, 6: 41–53.

—— (1987) 'Critical Polarities and the Study of Japanese Film Style', *Journal of Film and Video* 39 (1): 17–26.

Ko, Mika (2004) 'The Break-Up of the National Body: Cosmetic Multiculturalism and Films of Miike Takashi', *New Cinemas: Journal of Contemporary Film*, 2 (1): 29–39.

Komatsu Hiroshi (1992) 'Dream Pictures in the Far East: The Discovery of the Komiya Collection', *Griffithiana* 44–45: 1–5.

—— (1994) 'Questions Regarding the Genesis of Nonfiction Film', *Documentary Box* 5 (15 October): 1–5.

—— (1995) 'From Natural Color to the Pure Motion Picture Drama: The Meaning of Tenkatsu Company in the 1910s of Japanese Film History', *Film History*, 7: 69–86.

Komatsu, Hiroshi, and Musser, Charles (1987) 'Benshi Search', *Wide Angle*, 9 (2): 72–90.

Kuwahara, Yasue (1996) '*Inamura Jane*: Keisuke Kuwata and the Japanese Popular Consciousness', *Asian Cinema* 8 (spring): 109–20.

Lehman, Peter (1987a) 'The Mysterious Orient, the Crystal Clear Orient, the Non-existent Orient: Dilemmas of Western Scholars of Japanese Film', *Journal of Film and Video* 39: 5–15.

—— (1987b) 'Oshima: The Avant-Garde Artist without an Avant-Garde Style', *Wide Angle* 9 (2): 18–31.

Leyda, Jay (1954) 'Films of Kurosawa', *Sight and Sound* 24.2 (October/December): 74–8, 112.

Lopate, Philip (1986) 'A Taste for Naruse', *Film Quarterly* 39.4 (Summer): 11–21.

Malcomson, Scott (1985) 'The Pure Land Beyond the Seas: Barthes, Burch and the Uses of Japan', *Screen* 26 (3–4): 23–33.

Mason, Gregory (1989) 'Inspiring Images: The Influence of the Japanese Cinema on the Writings of Kazuo Ishiguro', *East-West Film Journal* 3.2 (June): 39–52.

Masters, Patricia Lee (1993) 'Warring Bodies: Most Nationalistic Selves', *East-West Film Journal* 7.1 (January): 137–48.

McDonald, Keiki (2003) 'A Woman Director's Rising Star: The First Two Films of Hisako Matsui (b. 1946)', *Asian Cinema*: 55–74.

McKnight, Anne (2005) 'Safety Last: Risk, Interactivity and Video Activism in Contemporary Tokyo', *New Cinemas: Journal of Contemporary Film*, 3 (3): 169–85.

Miner, Earl Roy (1956) 'Japanese Film Art in Modern Dress', *The Quarterly Review of Film, Radio, and Television* 10.4 (Summer): 354–423.

Murphy, Joseph A. (1993) 'Approaching Japanese Melodrama', *East-West Film Journal* 7.2 (July): 1–38.

Newitz, Annalee (1995) 'Magical Girls and Atomic Bomb Sperm: Japanese Animation in America', *Film Quarterly*, 49 (1): 2–15.

Nieuwenhof (1984) 'Japanese Film Propaganda in World War II: Indonesia and Australia', *Historical Journal of Film, Radio and Television*, 4 (2): 161–77.

Noriega, Chon (1987) 'Godzilla and the Japanese Nightmare: When *Them!* Is U.S.', *Cinema Journal*, 27 (1): 63–77.

Nornes, Abé Mark (1999a) '*Pōru Rūta*/Paul Rotha and the Politics of Translation', *Cinema Journal*, 38 (3): 91–108.

—— (1999b) 'For an Abusive Subtitling', *Film Quarterly*, 52 (3): 17–33.

Nygren, Scott (1987) 'The Pacific War: Reading, Contradiction, and Denial', *Wide Angle* 9 (2): 69–70.

—— (1989) 'Reconsidering Modernism: Japanese Film and the Postmodern Context', *Wide Angle* 11 (3): 6–15.

—— (1991) 'New Narrative Film in Japan: Stress Fractures in Cross-Cultural Postmodernism', *Post Script*, 11(1): 48–56.

Peterson, James (1989) 'A War of Utter Rebellion: Kinugasa's *Page of Madness* and the Japanese Avant-Garde of the 1920s', *Cinema Journal* 29.1 (Fall): 36–53.

Phillips, Alastair (2003) 'Pictures of the Past in the Present: Modernity, Femininity and Stardom in the Post-War Films of Ozu Yasujiro', *Screen*, 44(2): 154–66.

Prindle, Tamae K. (1998) 'A Cocooned Identity: Japanese Girl Films: Nobuhiko Oobayashi's *Chizuko's Younger Sister* and Jun Ichikawa's *Tsugumi*', *Post Script*, 18 (Fall): 24–37.

Rayns, Tony (1986) 'Nails That Stick out: A New Independent Cinema in Japan', *Sight and Sound*, 55: 98–104.

Richie, Donald (1986) 'Viewing Japanese Film: Some Considerations', *East-West Film Journal*, 1 (1): 23–35.

—— (1995) 'The Japanese Film: A Personal View, 1947–1995, *Asian Cinema*, 7 (2): 3–17.

Russell, Catherine (1995) 'Overcoming Modernity: Gender and the Pathos of History in Japanese Film Melodrama', *Camera Obscura* 35: 130–57.

—— (2003) 'Three Japanese Actresses of the 1950s: Modernity, Femininity and the Performance of Everyday Life', *Cineaction*, 60: 34–44.

Satō Tadao (1977) 'War as a Spiritual Exercise: Japan's "National Policy Films"', *Wide Angle* 1 (4): 22–4.

Schrader, Paul (1974) 'Yakuza Eiga: A Primer', *Film Comment* 10.1 (January): 9–17.

Shapiro, Jerome F. (2001) 'Growing Old with Kurosawa and the Bomb: Japanese Aesthetic Traditions and the American Desire for an Authentic Response', *Asian Cinema* 12 (Fall/Winter): 50–71.

Silverberg, Miriam (1993) 'Remembering Pearl Harbor, Forgetting Charlie Chaplin, and the Case of the Disappearing Western Woman: a Picture Story', *Positions* 1 (1) (Spring): 24–76.

Smith, Greg M. (2002) 'Critical Reception of *Rashomon* in the West', *Asian Cinema* 13 (2) (Fall/Winter): 115–28.

Stephens, Chuck (2002) 'High and Low: Japanese Cinema Now: A User's Guide', *Film Comment*, 38 (1): 35–46.

Stern, Leslie (1983a) 'Variations on Japanese Independence', *Framework* 22/23 (Autumn): 67–70.

—— (1983b) 'Image Forum: An Interview with Katsue Tomiyama', *Framework* 22/23 (Autumn): 71–73.

Stringer, Julian (2002a) 'Shall We F***?: Notes on Parody in the Pink', *Scope: An Online Journal of Film Studies*, December. Online. www.nottingham.ac.uk/film/scopearchive/articles/shall-we.htm

—— (2002b) 'Japan 1951–1970: National Cinema as Cultural Currency', *Tamkang Review*, 33 (2): 31–53.

Thompson, Kristin (1977) 'Notes on the Spatial System of Ozu's Early Films', *Wide Angle* 1: 8–17.

Thompson, Kristin and Bordwell, David (1976) 'Space and Narrative in the Films of Ozu', *Screen* 17 (2): 41–73.

Thornton, S. A. (1995) 'The Shinkokugeki and the Zenshinza: Western Representational Realism and the Japanese Period Film', *Asian Cinema*, 7 (2): 46–57.

Turim, Maureen (1991) 'Psyches, Ideologies, and Melodrama: The United States and Japan', *East-West Film Journal* 5.1 (January): 118–43.

Wada-Marciano, Mitsuyo (1998) 'The Production of Modernity in Japanese National Cinema: Shochiku Kamata Style in the 1920s and 1930s', *Asian Cinema*, 9 (2): 69–93.

Yoshimoto, Mitsuhiro (1989) 'The Postmodern and Mass Images in Japan', *Public Culture* 1/2 (1989): 8–25.

—— (1991) 'Melodrama, Postmodernism, and Japanese Cinema', *East-West Film Journal* 5 (1): 28–55.

V: Further reading on directors

Honda Ishirō (Chapter 7)

Honda, Ishirō (1994) *Gojira to waga eiga jinsei* [*Godzilla and My Life with Film*], Tokyo: Jitsugyō no Nihon-sha.

Honda, Ishirō and Inoue, Hideyuki (1994) *Kenshō Gojira tanjō: Shōwa 29 nen Tōhō satsuei-sho* [*The Birth of Godzilla at Toho Studios in the Twenty-Ninth Year of Showa*], Tokyo: Asahi Sonorama.

Tanaka, Fumio (1993) *Kami (Gojira) o hanatta otoko: eiga seisakusha Tanaka Tomoyuki to sono jidai* [*The Man who Let the God (Godzilla) Loose: The Life and Time of Film Producer Tanaka Tomoyuki*], Tokyo: Kinema Junpō-sha.

Ichikawa Kon (Chapter 10)

Breakwell, Ian (1995) *An Actor's Revenge*, London: British Film Institute.
Heibon-sha (ed.) (2000) *Kantoku Ichikawa Kon* [*A Film Director: Ichikawa Kon*], Tokyo: Heibon-sha.
Ichikawa, Kon (1998) *Ichikawa Kon* [*The Complete Films of Ichikawa Kon*], Kyōto: Kōrin-sha.
Ōba, Yōko (ed.) (1988) *Kon: The Complete Film Works of Kon Ichikawa*, Kyōto: Kōrin-sha.

Imamura Shōhei (Chapter 17)

Imamura, Shōhei (1996) *Harukanaru Nihonjin* [*My Memories of Japanese People*], Tokyo: Iwanami Shoten.
Kinema Junpō-sha (ed.) (1971) *Sekai no eiga-sakka 8: Imamura Shōhei, Urayama Kirio* [*Filmmakers of the World 8: Imamura Shohei and Urayama Kirio*], Tokyo: Kinema Junpō-sha.
Satō, Tadao (1980) *Imamura Shōhei no sekai* [*The World of Imamura Shohei*], Tokyo: Gakuyō Shobō.
Yokota, Tomiko (ed.) (1971) *Imamura Shōhei no eiga zen sagyō no kiroku* [*The Complete Works of Imamura Shohei*] Tokyo: Haga Shoten.

Kitano Takeshi (Chapter 22)

Abe, Yoshiaki (1994) *Kitano Takeshi vs. Bīto Takeshi* [*Kitano Takeshi vs. Beat Takeshi*], Tokyo: Chikuma Shobō.
Jacobs, Brian (ed.) (1999) *'Beat' Takeshi Kitano*, London: Tadao Press.
Kitano, Takeshi (2003) *Takeshi ga Takeshi o korosu riyū: zen eiga intabyū-shū* [*The Reason Why Takeshi Kills Takeshi: Interviews on His Complete Films*], Tokyo: Rokkingu On.

Kurosawa Akira (Chapter 8)

Abe, Yoshiaki (ed.) (1991) *Kurosawa Akira shūsei 2* [*A Kurosawa Akira Anthology no. 2*], Tokyo: Kinema Junpō-sha.
Davies, Anthony (1988) *Filming Shakespeare's Plays: The Adaptations of Laurence Olivier, Orson Welles, Peter Brook and Akira Kurosawa*, Cambridge: Cambridge University Press.
Desser, David (1983) *The Samurai Films of Akira Kurosawa*, Ann Arbor, MI: UMI Research.
Erens, Patricia (1979) *Akira Kurosawa: A Guide to References and Resources*, Boston: G.K. Hall.
Goodwin, James (ed.) (1994) *Perspectives on Akira Kurosawa*, New York: G.K. Hall.
Kinema Junpō Henshū-bu (ed.) (1989) *Kurosawa Akira shūsei* [*A Kurosawa Akira Anthology*], Tokyo: Kinema Junpō-sha.
Kinema Junpō-sha (ed.) (1970) *Sekai no eiga-sakka 3: Kurosawa Akira* [*Filmmakers of the World 3: Kurosawa Akira*], Tokyo: Kinema Junpō-sha.
—— (ed.) (1993) *Kurosawa Akira shūsei 3* [*A Kurosawa Akira Anthology no. 3*], Tokyo: Kinema Junpō-sha.
Kurosawa, Akira (1984) *Gama no abura: jiden no yō na mono* [*The Oil of the Toad: Something Like an Autobiography*], Tokyo: Iwanami Shoten.
Kurosawa, Akira, and Harada, Masato (1991) *Kurosawa Akira kataru* [*Kurosawa Akira Talks*], Tokyo: Fukutake Shoten.

Mellen, Joan (2002) *Seven Samurai*, London: British Film Institute.

Richie, Donald (ed.) (1990) *Rashomon*, New Brunswick, NJ: Rutgers University Press.

Satō, Tadao (1969) *Kurosawa Akira no sekai* [*The World of Kurosawa Akira*], Tokyo: San'ichi Shobō.

Tsuzuki, Masaaki (1976a) *Kurosawa Akira jō: sono ningen kenkyū* [*An Analysis of the Personality of Kurosawa Akira*], Tokyo: Intanaru Shuppan.

—— (1976b) *Kurosawa Akira ge: sono sakuhin kenkyū* [*An Analysis of the Films of Kurosawa Akira*], Tokyo: Intanaru Shuppan.

Uekusa, Keinosuke (1985) *Waga seishun no Kurosawa Akira* [*The Akira Kurosawa of My Youth*], Tokyo: Bungei Shunjū-sha.

Masumura Yasuzō (Chapter 11)

Masumura, Yasuzō (1999) *Eiga kantoku Masumura Yasuzō no sekai* [*The World of Film Director Masumura Yasuzo*], Tokyo: Waizu Shuppan.

Yamane, Sadao (1992) *Masumura Yasuzō: ishi toshite no erosu* [*Masumura Yasuzo: Eros as Will*], Tokyo: Chikuma Shobō.

Miyazaki Hayao (Chapter 24)

Kawakita, Yashio (1992) *Nichijōsei no yukue: Miyazaki anime o yomu* [*On the Trail of Ordinariness: Reading Miyazaki's Animation*], Tokyo: JICC Shuppan-kyoku.

Miyazaki, Hayao (1992) *Hikōtei jidai* [*The Age of the Flying Boat*], Tokyo: Dai Nihon Kaiga.

Shimizu, Masashi (2001) *Miyazaki Hayao o yomu: bosei to kaosu no fantajī* [*Reading Miyazaki Hayao: Fantasies of Maternity and Chaos*], Suwa: Chōei-sha.

Tadano, Tōshirō (1994) *Tonari no Totoro wa osu ka, mesu ka? Miyazaki Hayao no bokenteki sekai* [*Is Tonari no Totoro Male or Female? The Matriarchal World of Miyazaki Hayao*], Tokyo: Nihon Tosho Kankōkai.

Mizoguchi Kenji (Chapters 2 and 6)

Amaguchi, Takeshi (ed.) (1999) *Eiga kantoku Mizoguchi Kenji* [*Mizoguchi Kenji Film Director*], Tokyo: Heibon-sha.

Andrew, Dudley, and Andrew, Paul (1981) *Kenji Mizoguchi: A Guide to References and Resources*, Boston: G.K. Hall and Co.

Andrew, Dudley, and Cavanaugh, Carole (2000) *Sanshō Dayū*, London: British Film Institute.

Freiberg, Freda (1981) *Women in Mizoguchi Films*, Melbourne: Japanese Studies Centre.

Le Fanu, Mark (2005) *Mizoguchi and Japan*, London: British Film Institute.

McDonald, Keiko I. (1984) *Mizoguchi*, Boston: Twayne Publishers.

Nishida, Noriyoshi (ed.) (1991) *Mizoguchi Kenji tokushū* [*Anthology on Kenji Mizoguchi*], Tokyo: Kinema Junpō-sha.

O'Grady, Gerald (ed.) (1996), *Mizoguchi the Master*, Toronto: Cinemathèque Ontario.

Sasō, Tsutomu (2001) *Mizoguchi Kenji: Zen sakuhin kaisetsu 1: 1923-nen Nikkatsu Mukōjima jidai* [*Mizoguchi Kenji: A Complete Guide to Mizoguchi Films 1: 1923: The Period of Nikkatsu Mukojima*], Tokyo: Kindai Bungei-sha.

—— (2002) *Mizoguchi Kenji: Zen sakuhin kaisetsu 2: Nikkatsu Kyōto surampu jidai* [*Mizoguchi Kenji: A Complete Guide to Mizoguchi Films 2: The Slump Period in Nikkatsu Kyoto*], Tokyo: Kindai Bungei-sha.

—— (2003) *Mizoguchi Kenji: Zen sakuhin kaisetsu 3: ningen* [*Mizoguchi Kenji: A Complete Guide to Mizoguchi Films 3: 1925: Ningen*], Tokyo: Kindai Bungei-sha.

—— (2005) *Mizoguchi Kenji: Zen sakuhin kaisetsu 4: Kami ningyō haru no sasayaki, Kyōren no onna shishō* [*Mizoguchi Kenji: A Complete Guide to Mizoguchi Films 4: A Paper Doll's Whisper of Spring, The Passion of a Woman Teacher*], Tokyo: Kindai Bungei-sha.

Satō, Tadao (1982) *Mizoguchi Kenji no sekai* [*The World of Mizoguchi Kenji*], Tokyo: Chikuma Shobō.

Shindō, Kaneto (1975) *Aru eiga kantoku no shōgai: Mizoguchi Kenji no kiroku* [*A Life of a Director: The Record of Mizoguchi Kenji*], Tokyo: Eijin-sha.

Tsumura, Hideo (1977) *Mizoguchi Kenji to iu onoko* [*The Man Called Mizoguchi Kenji*], Tokyo: Sōbun-sha.

Yoda Yoshikata (1970) *Mizoguchi Kenji no hito to geijutsu* [*Kenji Mizoguchi: The Man and His Art*], Tokyo: Tabata Shoten.

Yomota, Inuhiko (ed.) (1999) *Eiga kantoku Mizoguchi Kenji* [*Mizoguchi Kenji Film Director*], Tokyo: Shin'yō-sha.

Naruse Mikio (Chapter 9)

Bock, Audie (1984) *Naruse: A Master of the Japanese Cinema*, Chicago: Art University of Chicago.

Chūko, Satoshi, and Hasumi, Shigehiko (1990) *Naruse Mikio no sekkei* [*The Design of Naruse Mikio*], Tokyo: Chikuma Shobō.

Murakawa, Hide (1997) *Naruse Mikio enshutsu-jutsu* [*The Directing Style of Naruse Mikio*], Tokyo: Waizu Shuppan.

Tanaka, Masasumi (ed.) (1995) *Eiga tokuhon: Naruse Mikio* [*A Naruse Mikio Film Reader*], Tokyo: Firumu Āto-sha.

Ōshima Nagisa (Chapters 12 and 16)

Kinema Junpō-sha (ed.) (1970) *Sekai no eiga-sakka 6* [*Filmmakers of the World 6: Oshima Nagisa*], Tokyo: Kinema Junpō-sha.

Mellen, Joan (2004) *In the Realm of the Senses*, London: British Film Institute.

Ōshima, Nagisa (1975) *Taikenteki sengo eizō-ron* [*A Theory of the Post-War Film Image Based on Personal Experience*], Tokyo: Asahi Shinbun-sha.

—— (1993) *Ōshima Nagisa 1960*, Tokyo: Seido-sha.

Satō, Tadao (1973) *Ōshima Nagisa no sekai* [*The World of Oshima Nagisa*], Tokyo: Chikuma Shobō.

Ozu Yasujirō (Chapters 1 and 5)

Atsuta, Yūharu, and Shigehiko, Hasumi (1989) *Ozu Yasujirō monogatari* [*The Story of Ozu Yasujiro*], Tokyo: Chikuma Shobō.

Cheuk-to, Li, and Li, H. C. (eds) (2003) *Ozu Yasujiro 100th Anniversary*, Hong Kong: Hong Kong International Film Festival.

Chiba, Nobuo (2003) *Ozu Yasujirō to 20 seiki* [*Ozu Yasujiro and the Twentieth Century*], Tokyo: Kokusho Kankōkai.

Desser, David (ed.) (1997) *Ozu's Tokyo Story*, Cambridge: Cambridge University Press.

Firumu Āto-sha (ed.) (1982) *Ozu Yasujirō o yomu* [*Reading Ozu Yasujiro*], Tokyo: Firumu Āto-sha.

Gillet, John, and Wilson, David (eds) (1976) *Ozu: A Critical Anthology*, London: British Film Institute.

Hamano, Yasuki (1993) *Ozu Yasujirō*, Tokyo: Iwanami Shoten.

Inoue, Kazuo (1993) *Hi no ataru ie: Ozu Yasujirō to tomoni* [*The Sunny House: With Ozu Yasujiro*], Tokyo: Firumu Āto-sha.

—— (ed.) (1994) *Ozu Yasujirō sakuhinshū* [*Works by Ozu Yasujiro*], Tokyo: Rippū Shobō.

Ishizaka, Shōzō (1995) *Ozu Yasujirō to Chigasakikan* [*Ozu Yasujiro and Chigasakikan*], Tokyo: Shinchō-sha.

Kida, Shō (2000) *Ozu Yasujirō no shokutaku* [*The Dining Table of Ozu Yasujiro*], Tokyo: Haga Shoten.

Kinema Junpō Henshū-bu (ed.) (1989) *Ozu Yasujirō shūsei* [*An Ozu Yasujiro Anthology*], Tokyo: Kinema Junpō-sha.

—— (ed.) (1993) *Ozu Yasujirō shūsei 2* [*An Ozu Yasujiro Anthology no. 2*], Tokyo: Kinema Junpō-sha.

Maeda, Hideki (1993) *Ozu Yasujirō no ie* [*The House of Ozu Yasujiro*], Tokyo: Shoritsu Yamada.

Nagai, Kenji (1990) *Ozu Yasujirō ni tsukareta otoko: bijutsu kantoku Shimogawara Tomo no sei to shi* [*A Man Charmed by Ozu Yasujiro: The Life and Death of the Art Director Shimogawara Tomo*], Tokyo: Firumu Āto-sha.

Nakamura, Hiro-o (2000) *Wakaki hi no Ozu Yasujirō* [*Ozu Yasujiro in His Youth*], Tokyo: Kinema Junpō-sha.

Nishimura, Yasuhiro (1993) *Yasujiro Ozu Retrospective Catalogue*, Tokyo: Matsutake Eizō Honbu Eizō Gaishitsu.

Sakamura, Ken, and Hasumi, Shigehiko (eds) (1998) *Digital Ozu Yasujirō: Camera Man Atsuta Yūharu no me* [*From Behind the Camera: A New Look at the World of Director Ozu Yasujiro*], Tokyo: Tōkyō Daigaku Sōgōkenkyū Hakubutsukan.

Satō, Tadao (2000) *Kanpon: Ozu Yasujirō no geijutsu* [*The Art of Ozu Yasujiro*], Tokyo: Asahi Shinbun-sha.

Shōchiku Kabushiki Gaisha (ed.) (1993) *Ozu Yasujirō shin hakken* [*Rediscovering Ozu Yasujiro*], Tokyo: Kōdansha.

Takahashi, Osamu (1982) *Kenrantaru kage: Ozu Yasujirō* [*Brilliant Shadow Painting: Yasujiro Ozu*], Tokyo: Bungei Shunjū-sha.

Tanaka, Masasumi (ed.) (1989) *Ozu Yasujirō sengo goroku shūsei 1946–1963* [*An Anthology of Ozu Yasujiro's Postwar Interviews: 1946–1963*], Tokyo: Firumu Āto-sha.

—— (ed.) (1993) *Zen nikki Ozu Yasujirō* [*The Complete Diaries of Ozu Yasujiro*], Tokyo: Firumu Āto-sha.

Tsuzuki, Masaaki (1993) *Ozu Yasujirō nikki: mujō to tawamureta kyoshō* [*Ozu Yasujiro Diary: A Giant Who Played With Mujo*], Tokyo: Kōdansha.

Shimizu Hiroshi (Chapter 4)

Tanaka, Masasumi et al. (eds) (2000) *Eiga tokuhon: Shimizu Hiroshi* [*A Shimizu Hiroshi Film Reader*], Tokyo: Firumu Āto-sha.

Shinoda Masahiro (Chapter 15)

Kinema Junpō-sha (ed.) (1971) *Sekai no eiga-sakka 10* [*Filmmakers of the World 10: Shinoda Masahiro and Yoshida Yoshishige*], Tokyo: Kinema Junpō-sha.

Shinoda, Masahiro (2003) *Watashi ga ikita futatsu no Nihon* [*Two Japans I Have Lived In*], Tokyo: Satsuki Shobō.

Yamanaka Sadao (Chapter 3)

Chiba, Nobuo (1998) *Kantoku Yamanaka Sadao* [*Director Yamanaka Sadao*], Tokyo: Jitugyō no Nihon-sha.

—— (1999) *Hyōden Yamanaka Sadao: wakaki eiga kantoku no shōzō* [*Yamanaka Sadao: A Biographical Portrait of the Young Film Director*], Tokyo: Heibon-sha.

Katō, Yasushi (1985) *Eiga kantoku Yamanaka Sadao* [*Yamanaka Sadao Film Director*], Tokyo: Kinema Junpō-sha.

VI: Electronic Resources

Asian Film Connections: Japan: online educational resource
http://www.usc.edu/libraries/archives/asianfilm/japan/

Bright Lights Film Journal: online film journal with database of articles on Japanese film
http://www.brightlightsfilm.com/japan.html

British Association for Japanese Studies: publisher of *Japan Forum*
http://www.bajs.org.uk/

CineMagaziNet!: bilingual Japanese/English online film journal
http://www.cmn.hs.h.kyoto-u.ac.jp/

Eirin: independent commission for classification of Japanese film
http://www.eirin.jp/

European Association for Japanese Studies
http://www.eajs.org/

Hoga Central: English language news and articles on Japanese film
http://www.hogacentral.com/index.html

Illuminated Lantern: online film journal on popular Asian cinema
http://illuminatedlantern.com/cinema/index.shtml

Internet Movie Database
http://www.imdb.com/

Japanese Embassy (UK)
http://www.uk.emb-japan.go.jp/en/embassy/jicc.html

Japanese Embassy (US)
http://www.embjapan.org/english/html/index.htm

Japanese Film Festivals: database in Japanese
http://www.jpnfilm.com/

Japanese Movie Database: Japanese language database
http://www.jmdb.ne.jp

Japanese Studies Network Forum: scholarly network based in US
http://www.jsnet.org/

Japan Foundation (London)
http://www.jpf.org.uk/

Japan Foundation (New York)
http://www.jfny.org/

Japan Foundation (Los Angeles)
http://www.jflalc.org/?act=

Japan Society (UK)
http://www.japansociety.org.uk/

Japan Society (New York)
http://www.japansociety.org/

Japan Society (California)
http://www.usajapan.org/

Japan Times: online edition of daily English language Japanese newspaper
http://www.japantimes.co.jp/

Kawakita Memorial Film Institute: private Tokyo-based library and research institute
http://www.kawakita-film.or.jp/index.html

Kinema Club: scholarly organization for the study of Japanese moving image media
http://pears.lib.ohio-state.edu/Markus/Welcome.html

Kurosawa Akira Digital Museum (CD-Rom)
http://alloe.jp:16080/alloe3/pro2/kudm_e/

Mark Shilling's Tokyo Ramen: film-related blog from film critic of *Japan Times*
http://japanesemovies.homestead.com/

Midnight Eye: Online international journal on Japanese cinema
http://www.midnighteye.com/index.php

National Film Center: Tokyo-based facility dedicated to the preservation of Japanese film
http://www.momat.go.jp/english/nfc/index.html

Nippon Connection: Annual film festival in Germany devoted to Japanese film
http://www.nipponconnection.de/

Ryuganji Japan Film News: English language news site on Japanese film
http://www.ryuganji.net/

Senses of Cinema: Online journal with extensive Japanese film-related archive
http://www.sensesofcinema.com/

Teaching and Learning about Japan: educational resource
http://www.csuohio.edu/history/japan/index.html

Udine Far East Film Festival: Annual festival in Italy for popular East Asian cinema
www.fareastfilm.com/

INDEX

Note: Page numbers in **bold** denote an illustration. An "n" following a number denotes a note.

351

Manufactured by Amazon.ca
Acheson, AB

11212111R00210